THE EXPERIMENTAL DARK

Contemporary Uses of Traditional Black & White Photographic Materials

The Experimental Darkroom is a book focused on traditional black & white photographic materials—darkroom chemistry and silver gelatin paper—now used in many non-traditional ways. The book starts with a comprehensive digital negatives chapter. Topics are divided into five sections: cameraless experimentation, camera experimentation, printing experimentation, finished print experimentation, and a section highlighting contemporary photographers who use these approaches today. Each process under discussion is accompanied by photographic examples and a step-by-step method written in a "Just the facts, ma'am" style. Topics included are:

- Photograms and clichés verre
- Lumen prints
- Chemigrams
- Pinhole and zoneplate
- Holgas
- Chromo
- Liquid emulsion and modern tintype
- Lith printing
- Sabattier
- Mordançage
- Bleaching and bleachout
- Toning, traditional to experimental
- Applied color and abrasion tone
- Encaustic, photomontage, and collage
- Bromoil

The Experimental Darkroom encourages taking risks and having fun. Over 400 images and 71 artists are included in its 276 pages. The outcome will be an expansion of creative options for the silver gelatin print. The options are engaging and now more accessible with digital negatives. Images are no longer solely captured in camera or on analog film. The darkroom is no longer always dark. The print is no longer a pristine and accurate rendition of what the camera sees. Photographers are pushing the boundaries of black & white photographic practice. It is an exciting time to get into the darkroom and play!

Christina Z. Anderson's work focuses on the contemporary *vanitas* printed in a variety of 19th century photographic processes. Anderson's work has shown nationally and internationally in 120 shows and 60 publications. Anderson has authored books which have sold in over 40 countries—*The Experimental Photography Workbook*, *Gum Printing and Other Amazing Contact Printing Processes*, *Gum Printing: A Step by Step Manual Highlighting Artists and Their Creative Practice*, *Salted Paper Printing: A Step-by-Step Manual Highlighting Contemporary Artists*, and *Cyanotype: The Blueprint in Contemporary Practice*; also *Digital Negatives with QuadToneRIP: Demystifying QTR for Photographers and Printmakers* co-authored with Ron Reeder, and *Handcrafted: The Art and Practice of the Handmade Print* co-authored with Wang, Jianming, and King. Anderson is Series Editor for Focal Press/Routledge's Contemporary Practices in Alternative Process Photography series and Professor of Photography at Montana State University. To see her work, visit christinaZanderson.com.

Contemporary Practices in Alternative Process Photography Series

The Contemporary Practices in Alternative Process Photography series focuses the lens on a variety of alternative, historical processes from the medium's 180-year history. Each book outlines a step-by-step approach to a particular medium, and features contemporary artists who use that particular process regularly in their practice. The richly illustrated books in this series serve as guidebooks for those new to alternative processes, refresher courses for professionals already familiar with each medium, and a source of inspiration for all.

Series titles in order of publication

Golaz, Annette. *Cyanotype Toning: Using Botanicals to Tone Blueprints Naturally* (2022)
Malde, Pradip and Mike Ware. *Platinotype: Making Photographs in Platinum and Palladium with the Contemporary Printing-out Process* (2021)
McPhee, Leanne. *Chrysotype: A Contemporary Guide to Photographic Printing in Gold* (2021)
Reeder, Ron and Christina Z. Anderson. *Digital Negatives with QuadToneRIP: Demystifying QTR for Photographers and Printmakers* (2021)
King, Sandy, Don Nelson and John Lockhart. *Carbon Transfer Printing: A Step-by-Step Manual Featuring Contemporary Carbon Printers and their Creative Practice* (2020)
Anderson, Christina Z. *Cyanotype: The Blueprint in Contemporary Practice* (2019)
Ross, Denise. *The Handmade Silver Gelatin Emulsion Print: Creating Your Own Liquid Emulsions for Black and White Paper* (2019)
Harmon, Clay. *Polymer Photogravure: A Step-by-Step Manual Highlighting Artists and their Creative Practice* (2019)
Anderson, Christina Z. *Salted Paper Printing: A Step-by-Step Manual Highlighting Contemporary Artists* (2018)
Anderson, Christina Z. *Gum Printing: A Step-by-Step Manual Highlighting Artists and Their Creative Practice* (2017)

THE EXPERIMENTAL DARKROOM

Contemporary Uses of Traditional Black & White Photographic Materials

CHRISTINA Z. ANDERSON

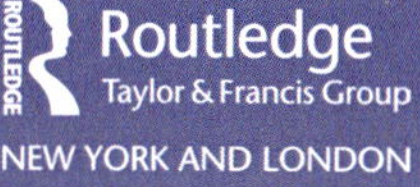
NEW YORK AND LONDON

First published 2023
by Routledge
605 Third Avenue, New York, NY 10158

and by Routledge
2 Park Square, Milton Park, Abingdon, Oxon, OX14 4RN

Routledge is an imprint of the Taylor & Francis Group, an informa business

Library of Congress Cataloging-in-Publication Data
A catalog record for this title has been requested

ISBN: 978-1-032-14957-8 (hbk)
ISBN: 978-1-032-13186-3 (pbk)
ISBN: 978-1-003-24194-2 (ebk)

DOI: 10.4324/9781003241942

Typeset in Adobe Caslon Pro and Century Gothic
by Christina Z. Anderson

Publisher's Note:
This book has been prepared from camera-ready copy provided by the author.

Cover image: *Carol's Roses*, eighty-four 7.5″ × 7.5″ unique lumen prints printed on eighty-four different black and white/silver gelatin papers © Christina Z. Anderson 2021

Exercise caution in the handling of all photographic chemicals. Use of any such chemicals constitutes some risk, and some are poisonous. The publisher and author accept no responsibility for injury or loss arising from the procedures or materials described in this book whether used properly or improperly. The workplace should be well ventilated. Chemicals should be mixed only in the manner described. Avoid contact between the chemicals and eyes, skin, clothing, and furniture. Do not eat or drink while using chemicals. Keep them away from pets and children. Wear protective eye wear and gloves if necessary. In short, be mindful of all safety procedures for yourself and others.

Table of Contents

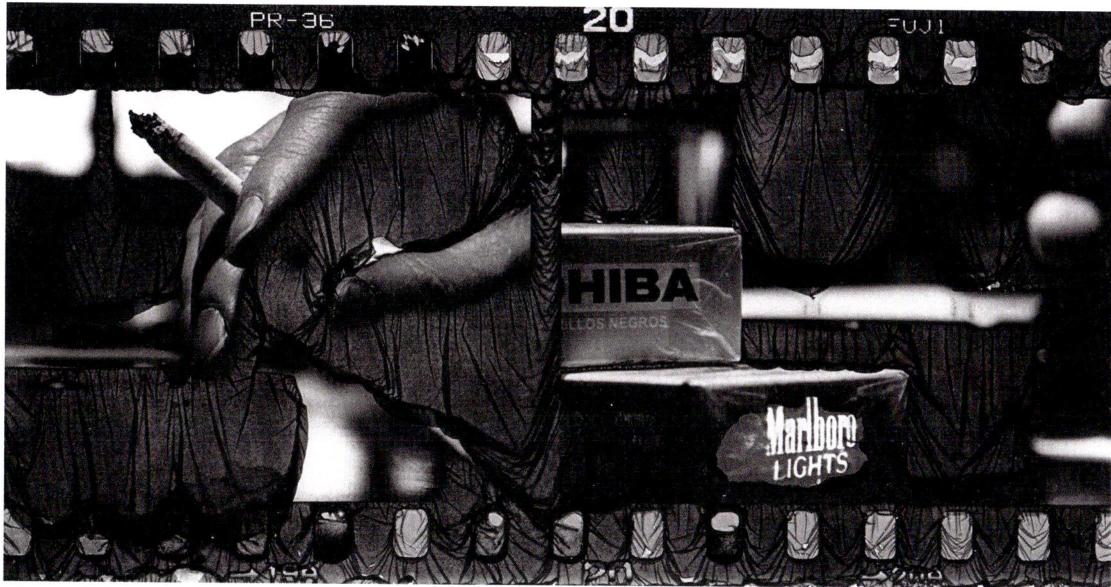

Figure P.1. *Marlboro Man*, silver gelatin mordançage, 13.5″ x 6.8″ © Christina Z. Anderson 2006

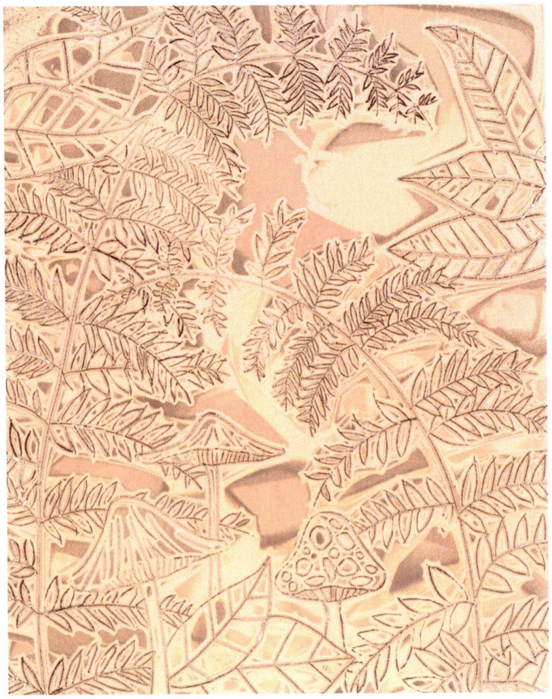

Figure P.2. *Mushroom*, hard resist chemigram © Fran Browne 2019. Fran Browne is a Montana State University School of Film and Photography alumna who uses analog, experimental, and alternative processes in her work. Browne's photographic focus is the beauty in the mundane and the decay and abandonment of small town America. To see more of Browne's work follow her @imagesbyfran.

Preface

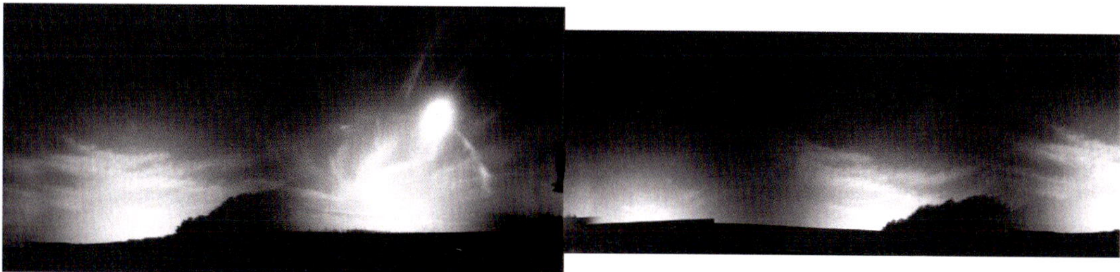

Figure P.3. *Up the River*, paper negative from a homemade cardboard pinhole camera, contact printed, 13″ x 5″ © Chris Byrnes 2022. To see more of Byrnes' work follow her on Instagram @lady_camera_obscura.

In 1995 I enrolled in a painting class at Montana State University. I was not planning on pursuing a degree since I already had a BA, but it was so enjoyable that I continued taking one class after another and then ended up with a degree. One of the requirements for my painting degree was a beginning black and white photography class. After the first few weeks in the class with Professor John Hooton I was hooked and there was no turning back. Along with my BFA in painting I finished a BA in photography, which became my medium of choice.

When I graduated in 2000 with no access to a darkroom, I asked Paul Monaco, the director of the School of Film and Photography at Montana State University, if he needed someone to teach, which would grant me access. Several weeks later Paul offered me a job teaching beginning black and white photography. I had no idea that teaching would become my profession.

In those first classes I taught students how to make pristine black and white prints. Spring 2001 I was offered a chance to teach Experimental Photography, much more my interest along with alternative processes. Whereas in the beginning black and white classes it was all about the perfect print, in the experimental class it was all about how to mess it up! Over the years my expertise grew in experimental and alternative process photography, which I continue to teach and practice today.

My first foray into authorship began with my rudimentary manual *The Experimental Photography Workbook* (2001). No one book included all the processes I wanted to teach and some processes were not even in the literature. That first labor-intensive semester I researched and compiled weekly handouts for every process. Then, to save time at the copy machine, I spiral-bound all the handouts together. It occurred to me that others might be interested in this manual. The *Workbook* took off. *The Experimental Darkroom* is the outcome of that book and two decades of teaching.

This book would not have happened without key people who paved the way. I thank Paul Monaco for giving me the chance to teach in 2000. I thank John Hooton, Charlotte Trolinger, and Rudi Dietrich for being my influential photography professors in the 1990s. It was Charlotte's Experimental Photography class that I took over Spring 2001 when she went on sabbatical. I thank Sam Wang for being my graduate professor while I pursued my MFA at Clemson University. I thank Mark Nelson, Sandy King, Ron Reeder, Clay Harmon, and Ike Eisenlord for teaching me most of what I know about digital negatives. I thank Malin Fabbri for selling that rudimentary *Experimental Photography Workbook* on her alternativephotography.com website. Because of Malin I have sold books in at least forty countries. We all stand on shoulders of giants, some who are unsung heroes.

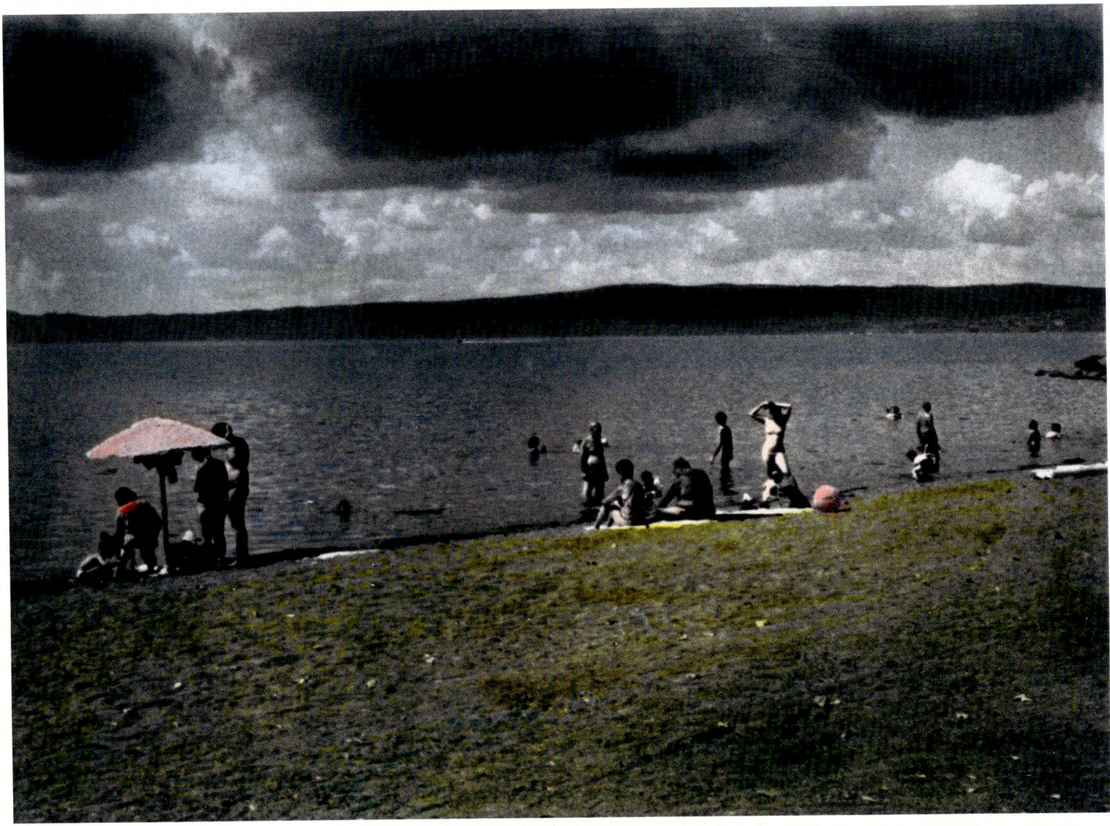

Figure I.1. *The Beach on the Lake*, selenium toned, hand colored silver gelatin print, 25.3 x 18 cm © Margrieta A. P. Jeltema 2021. "We fill our days and encounters with stories, old and new ones, that weave themselves in ever richer patterns, forever eluding us, forever beckoning us to discover new threads and to make sense of what we feel and see. Often I wonder what photography is about and why it is so important for me. Why is it important for me to still use film and even glass plates? My favorite camera is more than 100 years old, a turn of the century whole plate camera. Its magic lies in its extreme simplicity. I use all the formats between 35 mm and whole plate. There is the joy of expectation, the handling of the films, the smell of the chemicals, the errors and all the experimenting and learning that goes with it. My love for the material world of ancient cameras, with their glass plates and gelatin films, has extended naturally to the making of all kind of prints. Though I like to make archival ink-jet prints, the making of silver gelatin prints is a richer pleasure." Margrieta Jeltema was born in the Netherlands. She has lived and worked in the Netherlands, Italy, Algeria, the Caribbean, Chile, Portugal and Romania. During her biology studies with a major in philosophy at Wageningen (the Netherlands), Margrieta studied bronze casting, painting, etching and ceramics. Her work embraces poetry and sculpture, but her main creative outlet is photography. During the last few years she has received a number of awards, nominations and publications in the International Photographic Awards (IPA), Px3, Black and White Spider Awards, International Aperture Awards, WPGA awards, *Shotz Magazine*, *Seities*, *Gammelgaard Monochrome*, *Prix de la Découverte*, *Photoreview*, *Lensculture*, *Fotofilmic*, *Street and Fine Art Photography* and *Black & White Photography*. The series *My Heart of Glass*, *The Shaded Gardens of Bucharest*, and *A Chinese Mother in Italy* were published in *Dodho*. Jeltema exhibits internationally. To see more of Jeltema's work visit www.margrij.com.

Introduction

The Experimental Darkroom is a book on the changing landscape of the silver gelatin darkroom. The book's focus is on traditional black and white/silver gelatin paper and darkroom chemistry often now used in non-traditional ways. The book particularly focuses on processes that I have found to be the most engaging for students over the last twenty-two years of teaching.

The backdrop to the contemporary darkroom begins in the 1960s and even before. Around that time photographers had a desire to quit being beholden to large corporations like Kodak that controlled the photographic market. Photographers found *alternatives* to silver gelatin printing. Processes such as Vandyke brown, cyanotype, palladium, and salted paper were referred to as *alt*(ternative). Silver gelatin was not "alt" at that time but part of the "establishment."

Today "alternative process photography" (alt process, alt pro, alt) references hand-crafted printing as alternative to *digital* ink jet, though these boundaries are not so—forgive the pun—black and white. Silver gelatin has quietly slipped into the alt category sometime within the last decade, though some will still debate that; probably they are correct when it comes to the pristine silver gelatin print. What, in fact, constitutes a photograph is the subject of whole books today, with some arguing an ink jet print, since it is not "written with light," is not even a photograph. This book focuses on *experimental* silver gelatin practice as part of the alt pro movement and leaves the theorizing (and arguing) about what constitutes photography or alt to others.

The precursor to this book is the 2001 *Experimental Photography Workbook*. As I said in the Preface, it began as a spiral-bound compilation of all my class handouts that I used in my *Experimental Photography* class at Montana State University and ended up a full-color 6th edition book in 2012. The book was in need of a few changes, not least of which was a digital negatives chapter since so many incoming freshmen were no longer bringing their parent's film camera with them to college. I ended up rewriting much of the book, tightening it up, removing unnecessary sections, and expanding discussions on the more popular processes. There is now more systematic and exacting information, documentation of recent experimentation, a lengthy artist section, and all new photographs.

What has been the hallmark of today's silver gelatin darkroom is that artists are pushing the boundaries of chemistry and paper. There really isn't a need anymore to print pristine silver gelatin, because that is effectively done digitally., Nor is there a need anymore for the silver gelatin darkroom to document the world, because that is being done in digital color. The black and white darkroom has been liberated from its utilitarian roots. Chemistry-based black and white photography may no longer be a requirement in photographic curricula but it is still a popular elective, because it fulfills needs on a physical and emotional level. Physically, some processes are still better done chemically than digitally. Emotionally the need to create with one's hands has never been stronger. The black and white darkroom holds a magic that the digital dimroom cannot approximate: the magic of an image materializing in the developer, the magic of chance happenings. In the 20th century, the darkroom was work. Today it is a conscious choice.

How to use this book

This book assumes familiarity with the black and white darkroom at a beginning to intermediate level. Many experimental methods of image making are introduced. The book encourages trying new things, taking risks, and having fun, with the ultimate outcome an expansion of creative options and expression. To excel in any one of them takes time and commitment. Try the processes at first with play in mind, without seeking perfection. Perfection is a creative "wet blanket" when learning. Then choose one or two to take to a deeper level. It is truly an exciting time for silver gelatin paper!

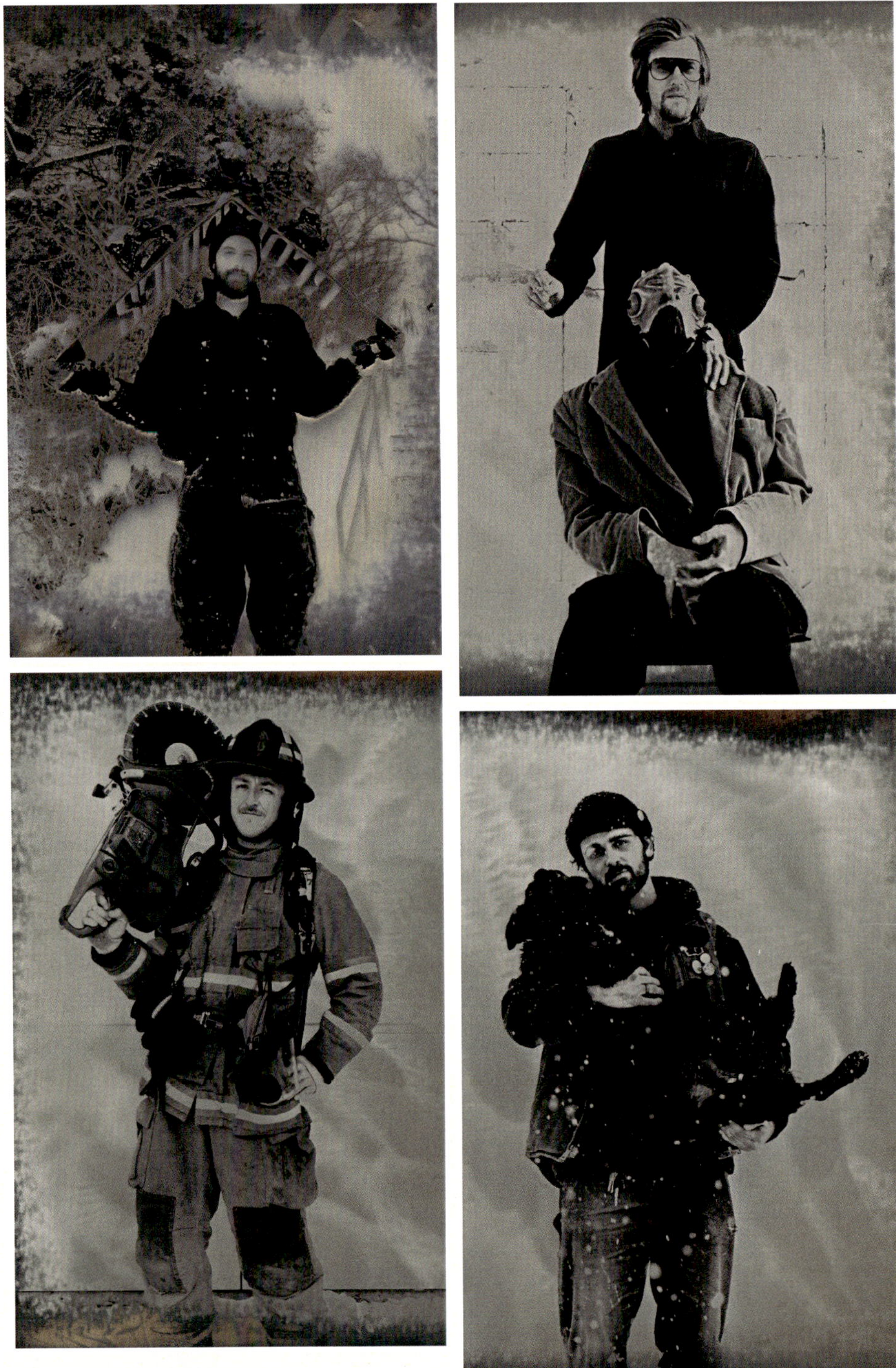

Figures 1.1–1.4. *Portraits* series, silver gelatin chromos, 6.5″ x 10″ © Eric R. Hinsperger 2017. "These portraits show each person's unique interest. I used digital negatives to print them in the traditional experimental darkroom. The chromo process creates 'iridized' borders with a smoky run-off on each end. The prints have a beautiful metallic, sensual finish that must be seen in person to experience the full spectrum, as they do not scan well." Eric R. Hinsperger is an American photographer and award winning Director of Photography currently living in Portland, Oregon. His work has been featured in multiple magazines, local store fronts, and recently 2021 Best Oregon Short Film (OSFF).

Setting Up the Contemporary Darkroom

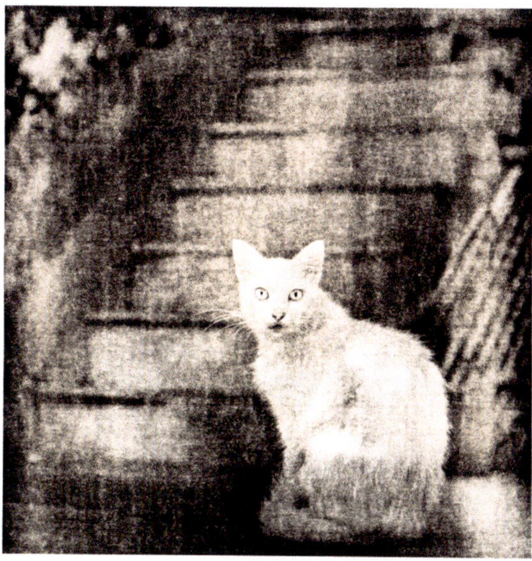

Figure 1.5. *Gato Blanco*, lith print, Slavich Unibrom 160, Fotospeed LD20 50/50 ml in 3 liters water © Douglas Ethridge 2022

All chemicals should be treated with utmost respect. Go to www.msds.com and download the SDSes (Safety Data Sheets) for every chemical used in the darkroom and store them in a readily available notebook in alphabetical order for easy access. Have the local poison control number handy and prominent! Label all chemistry. Have an eyewash kit in the darkroom in case splashes into the eye occur. Immediately clean up any spills that occur. Avoid contact between the chemicals and eyes, skin, clothing, and furniture. Minimize absorption of chemicals through breathing, ingestion, or skin contact. Do not eat or drink while using chemicals. Wear protective eye wear and gloves if necessary. Always keep hands clean. Dispose of hazardous materials according to state regulations. Always keep chemistry locked up and away from children and pets. The workplace should be well ventilated. Chemicals should be mixed only in the manner described.

Use of any chemicals constitutes some risk, and some are poisonous. The publisher and author accept no responsibility for injury or loss arising from the procedures or materials described in this book whether used properly or improperly. In short, be mindful of all safety procedures for yourself and others!

This book assumes the reader has a working black and white darkroom with the typical chemistry: paper developer, stop, fixer, hypoclear/fixer remover, and, of course, silver gelatin paper.

Three other necessary items are a contact printing frame, OHP transparency film, and a Stouffer step wedge. See **Digital Negatives for the Darkroom** for further clarification on digital needs (computer, software, printer).

Supplies and chemistry are listed in this chapter according to process. If a process is not listed, it doesn't need anything extra aside from the usual black and white chemistry and paper. These lists are comprehensive but not exhaustive as some processes have many potential choices and directions.

Where there are italics in a list, the italicized items are a substitute for the item directly above—for instance, under **Toning** you can purchase commercial brand toners or make them yourself using the chemistry in italics.

Photograms and clichés verre

- 4″×5″ pieces of glass or plastic for the enlarger
- Flat black spray paint, optional
- Direct positive paper if desired

Lumen prints

- Non-UV resistant plexi or glass larger than paper
- Ferric ammonium citrate and potassium ferricyanide for cyanolumens, if desired
- Sodium carbonate and ascorbic acid (Vitamin C) for phytograms, if desired

Chemigrams

- Hard (e.g. Golden MSA varnish) and soft resists
- Xacto knife and tweezers

Pinhole and zoneplate

- .003 brass shim stock or other metal
- Flat black spray paint
- Needles

- Black gaffer's tape
- 600 grit sandpaper
- Zone plate
- Camera body cap

Holga

- Holga camera from FreestylePhoto.biz
- Black gaffer's tape
- Film

Chromo

(See **Appendix** for chemistry for advanced formulas.)

- Arista Ultra or Ilford Warmtone paper
- Arista Chromo Stabilizer and Activator
- EcoPro developer

Liquid emulsion and modern tintype

- Liquid emulsion, variable contrast
- Krylon Crystal Clear acrylic glossy spray
- **Oil** (!) based clear varnish (tintype)
- Liquid emulsion hardener
- Trophy aluminum
- Methylated alcohol, gum sandarac, and oil of lavender for varnish, optional
- Rockland tintype bulk developer

or

- *Ammonium thiocyanate*
- *Sodium sulfate*
- *Sodium carbonate*
- *Dektol*

Lith printing

- Foma papers
- Potassium ferricyanide
- Lith developer

or

- *Hydroquinone*
- *Potassium metabisulfite*
- *Potassium bromide*
- *Potassium hydroxide*
- *Sodium sulfite*
- *Boric acid crystals*
- *Sodium bisulfite*
- *Paraformaldehyde*

Sabattier

- Sodium sulfite
- Catechol
- Sodium carbonate
- Phenidone
- Potassium bromide
- Sodium thiosulfate

Mordançage

(See **Appendix** for chemistry for advanced formulas.)

- Copper chloride
- Glacial acetic acid
- Drugstore or 10–20v hydrogen peroxide
- Copper sulfate
- Potassium bromide
- Krylon Crystal Clear acrylic glossy spray

Bleaching and bleachout

- Potassium bromide
- Potassium ferricyanide
- India ink, tech pens, or Sharpie markers

Toning

(See **Appendix** for chemistry for more formulas.)

- Potassium bromide
- Potassium ferricyanide
- Tea, loose or tea bags
- Walnut husks
- Liquid frisket/maskoid and/or frisket film
- Selenium toner, gold toner, iron-blue toner, copper toner, sepia toner, Halochrome™

and/or

- *1 g gold chloride*
- *Distilled water*
- *Ammonium thiocyanate*
- *Copper sulfate*
- *Ferric ammonium citrate*
- *Glacial acetic acid*
- *Potassium citrate*
- *Sodium bicarbonate*
- *Sodium carbonate*
- *Sodium chloride (salt)*
- *Sodium sulfide*
- *Sodium thiosulfate*
- *Sodium, ammonium or potassium hydroxide*
- *Tartaric acid*
- *Thiourea*

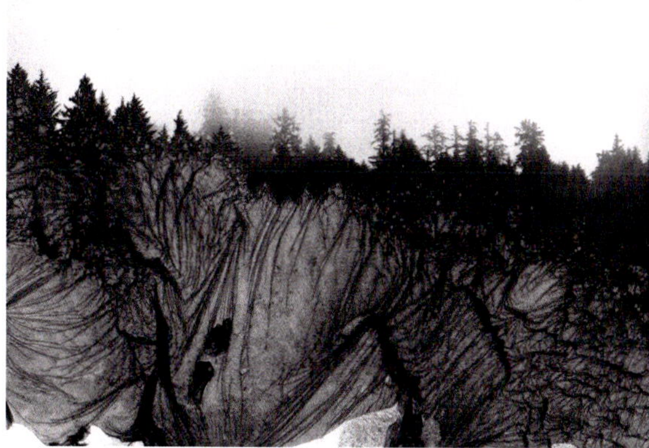
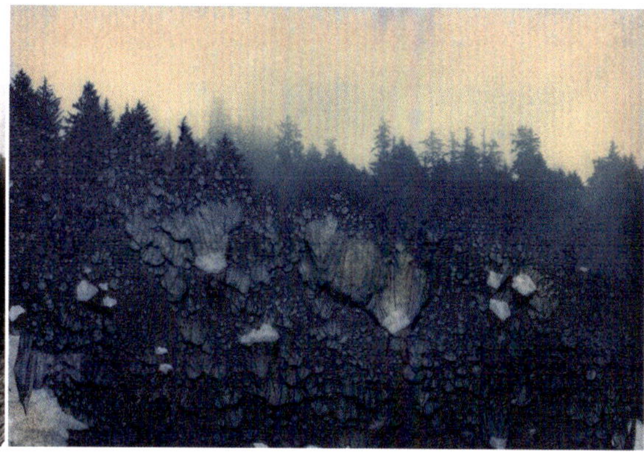

Figures 1.6–1.7. Left, *Coastal Treeline*; right, *Blue Costal Treeline*, untoned and blue/copper toned gelatin silver mordançages © Aubrey Irwin 2021. Aubrey Irwin is a Montana-based photographer with a focus on alternative processes. Irwin is pursuing a BA in Film and Photography and English Composition from Montana State University, Bozeman, graduation Spring 2022.

Applied color and abrasion tone

- Photo oils
- Frisket removable low-tack film
- 100% cotton balls
- Q-tips
- Toothpicks
- Marlene, naphtha, or Arista cleaner
- Krylon Crystal Clear acrylic glossy spray
- Ivory black and burnt sienna pastels

Encaustic, collage, photomontage

- Heat gun
- Brushes
- Cradled wood panels or other support
- Acrylic glossy medium and matte medium
- PVA glue
- Encaustic paints, purchased

or

- *Beeswax*
- *Dammar resin*
- *Pigments*

Bromoil

- Black or colored lithographic ink
- Naphtha, mineral spirits, or Simple Green
- 6″ ceramic tiles
- Palette knife
- 2″ brayer
- 4″ brayer
- Bromoil brush or men's shaving brush
- Cosmetic foam wedges or 1″ nylon flat brush
- Chamois cloth
- Blotter paper
- Large piece of glass
- Bromoil kit from Bostick and Sullivan

or

- *Copper sulfate*
- *Potassium bromide*
- *Potassium dichromate*

Sources for supplies

Artcraft Chemicals
ArtcraftChemicals.com
B&H Photo
BHphotovideo.com
Bostick and Sullivan
Bostick-Sullivan.com
Freestyle Photographic Supplies
FreestylePhoto.biz
Photographer's Formulary
PhotoFormulary.com
Stouffer Industries (step wedges)
http://www.stouffer.net

Figures 2.1.–2.3. Top, *The Kanga Cricket Wall* © Leanne McPhee 2021. 9″ x 6″ lumen print, fixed and alkaline-gold toned. Middle, *The Bubble Taps* © Leanne McPhee 2021. 9″ x 6″ lumen print, fixed. Bottom, *The Shelter Shed* © Leanne McPhee 2021. 9″ x 6″ lumen print fixed and alkaline-gold toned. All three images were from 4″x 5″ Ilford FP4 125 film negatives, scanned to create a digital negative with suitable contrast, contact printed onto Ilford MGFB Multigrade Warmtone Semi-Matte silver gelatin paper, and exposed under UV light for 9 minutes 50 seconds to 10 minutes 30 seconds.

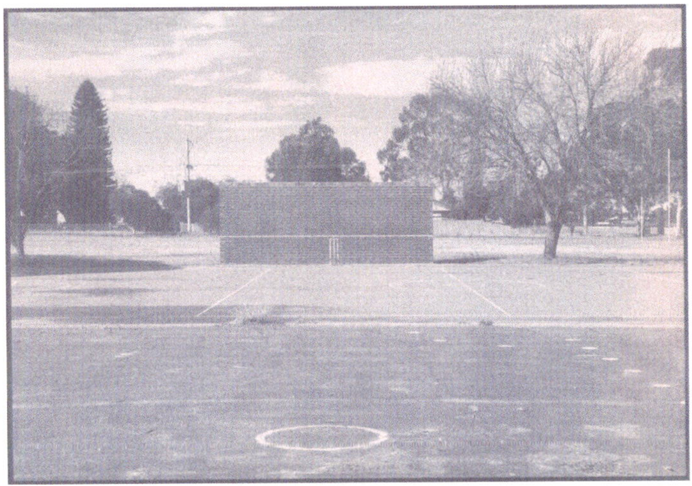

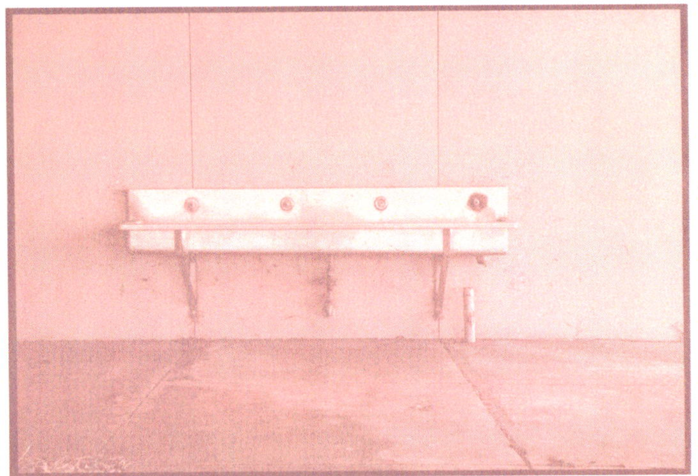

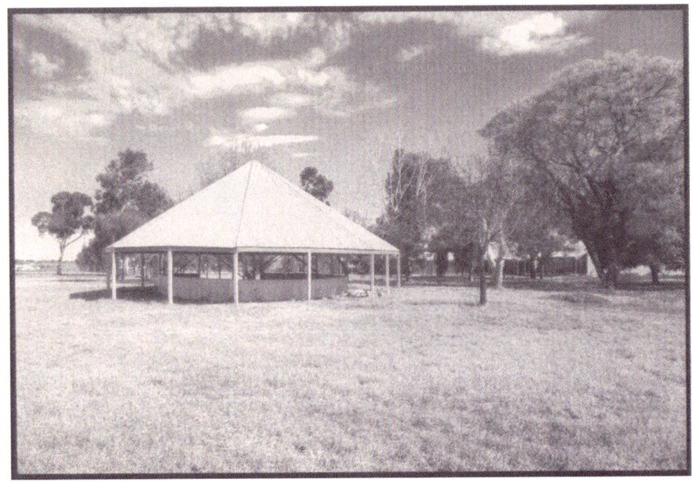

"At three points over fifteen years, I photographed my primary school. The images in this series were taken after the primary schools in the region were closed and one 'super school' created. The iconic shelter shed, Kanga cricket wall, and bubble taps are captured in their dismantled state amongst bleached grass and debris."

Leanne McPhee is an Australian fine art photographer with expertise in a variety of alternative photographic processes, particularly new chrysotype and salt printing. McPhee has work held in public and private collections in Australia, China, Italy, and the US, delivers hands-on workshops, and is the author of *Chrysotype: A Contemporary Guide to Printing in Gold*. To see more of McPhee's work visit leannemcphee.com.

Digital Negatives for the Darkroom

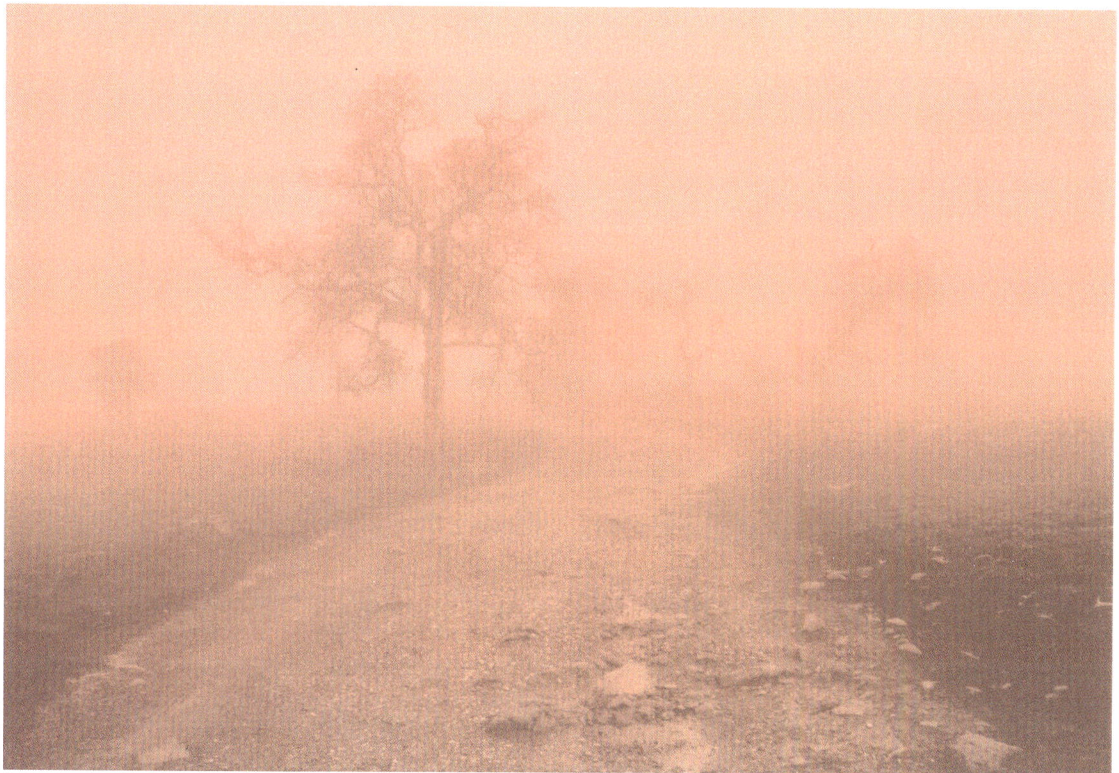

Figure 2.4. *2018 Campfire, Paradise, California*, lumen print on Oriental Warmtone paper, all day exposure, digital negative created using the Lumen QTR profile, © Christina Z. Anderson 2021

Let's be honest: there is no such thing as an "easy" digital negative. "Easy" would entail merely inverting an image in Photoshop and printing it out. Because digital inks have a density range from black to white (full ink to no ink) greater than many processes can handle, merely printing out an image "as is" can't be done. You would sacrifice tonal detail in the print on one or the other end. Either the highlights would be paper white and blown out with no detail in order to preserve detail in the shadows, or the shadows would be blocked up black in order to expose long enough to have detail in the highlights.

There are essentially two methods to make all the tones from white to black match the density range of the paper. One method is to create a curve and in Photoshop place it on top of the negative to compress the tones to fit. The other is to tell the printer driver to make the tones fit. Digital negative systems are usually variations of these two methods. Examples of these two systems are PDN and QTR respectively.

Precision Digital Negatives (PDN) Curve Calculator III (CCIII) software allows you to create *custom* curves in Photoshop. It is a proprietary (and patented) software created by Mark Nelson (precisiondigitalnegatives.com). CCIII software has a wonderful option to generate a family of contrast curve choices straight to Photoshop.

QuadToneRIP (QTR), developed by Roy Harrington, replaces the printer's proprietary driver software with its own and directs certain inks to print in certain places in certain amounts. See *Digital Negatives with QuadToneRIP, Demystifying QTR for Photographers and Printmakers* for an in-depth treatment of QTR. QTR can be used on both Windows and Mac computers. Instructions in this chapter are for the Mac.

This chapter will introduce these two methods—using a curve in Photoshop or adjusting inks within the printer driver. The first method will be similar to PDN, but the curve will be *generic*, not custom, and the negative will be an *all-ink* negative, not colorized. A generic curve will get you in the ballpark to a "pretty good" digital negative and with many of the experimental processes, pretty good is plenty fine.

The second method will be a crash course version of QTR. If this becomes your method of choice, I recommend the *Digital Negatives with QuadToneRIP* book previously mentioned to understand this system fully. I admit, QTR is dense, more on the expert level of digital negative making, and takes time to learn, but once you do you'll be amazed at its power.

Photoshop software

Photoshop is the premier image-editing software, and now with monthly subscription fees available for all Adobe software, it is much more affordable. This and an Epson printer are all that is necessary for the first method of applying curves in Photoshop.

Epson ink jet printer

Essentially any inkjet printer will produce a digital negative. However, to date, Epson printers have the densest inks, perhaps the only printer brand to have dense enough inks, to block light effectively. QTR can only be used with Epson printers. This book will refer to the P900, but the methods described can be applied readily to other Epson printers.

QTR and Print-Tool software

For the QTR method you will need to download and install two pieces of software. These are QuadToneRIP and Print-Tool, both available from the QuadToneRIP website. See further how to download and install.

Build QTR Curve software

Build QTR Curve is a Java script developed by David Eisenlord and available for a free download. It is an invaluable tool for automatically generating curves. It can be used with both methods. See further how to download and install.

Transparency material

Digital negatives for the silver gelatin darkroom are printed on one of two types of "paper," Pictorico High Gloss White Film (opaque white, not necessary for our purposes) or transparency material which is transparent in a milky sort of way. Both films have a coating which absorbs a considerable amount of ink without the printer dots merging together and puddling. Transparency film is often referred to with the acronym OHP for *overhead projection film*. In this chapter when we talk about film we are referring to this digital transparency substrate, not traditional analog film unless "analog" is specified.

I am a fan of Fixxons and its low cost. The negative film ($49/100 sheets) is adequate for all but the densest negatives. However, in humid climates thinner transparency film has a tendency to curl ever so slightly, and it will jam in the printer. It also seems to never dry, and is more prone to pizza wheel marks as the still-wet ink on the OHP is being transported through the printer. If this is the case, use Pictorico ($22/20 sheets).

Pictorico comes in Premium and Ultra Premium which has an even thicker ink-receiving layer. Premium is fine for the silver gelatin darkroom as is Fixxons, except lumen printing; purchase Pictorico Ultra Premium for lumen negatives because a lumen negative needs a heavier ink load.

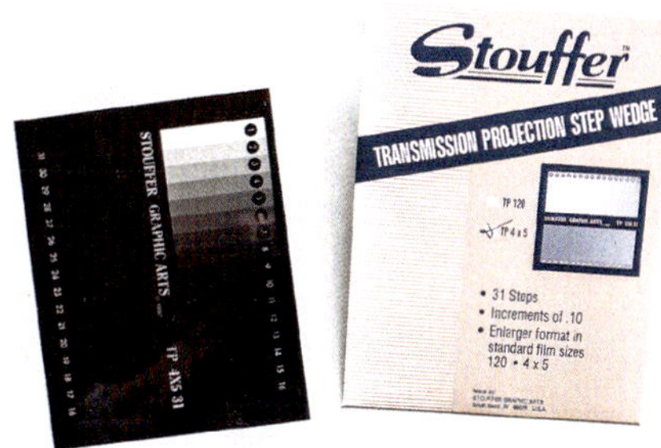

Figure 2.5. 4″ x 5″ 31-step wedge

Stouffer step wedge

With both of these systems, the first step is to find a correct exposure time to give the darkest black on the silver gelatin paper using as much exposure as necessary but not too much (overexposure). This can be done two ways, one less complex just using a piece of OHP and an opaque piece of something, and one more complex but also more accurate using a Stouffer analog film step wedge. It seems strange to use analog film to judge digital film exposure, but the Stouffer step wedge is calibrated in *accurate* ½ stop (21-step) or ⅓ stop (31-step) increments so exposure can be pinpointed with simple math. The 31-step wedge is best for fine-tuning your exposure time. There are inexpensive step wedges (around $20) and more expensive larger step wedges (around $75, pictured above). I cannot stress enough how useful a step wedge is in the darkroom. Buy them at Stouffer.net, Amazon.com, bhphotovideo.com.

Digital step wedges

Whereas the analog film step wedge is used to calculate correct exposure time, digital step wedges are used after the exposure time is determined to create your own curves if desired or the necessary QTR profile. A digital step wedge has tonal steps ranging from 0% (clear) to 100% (maximum black) in evenly inked steps of 5% density from clear/no ink to black. It is constructed so that the Photoshop eyedropper tool reads the same percent gray as is written on each step. By definition the digital step wedge is a perfectly linearized image. Our goal is to create a negative which will translate the tones written on the wedge into exactly the same tones in the final print. A digital step wedge is included in the QTR package—**Applications/QuadToneRIP/Curve Design/Images/21step.psd**. One is also included in Eisenlord's Build QTR download.

Contact printing frame

Digital negatives are generally printed out at the same size as the final print and the silver gelatin paper exposed in direct contact with the negative. There needs to be a way to keep the negative and paper in tight contact during exposure, and that is easily done with a contact print frame (see Bostick-Sullivan.com). You can make a homemade contact print frame thus: use cloth tape to hinge a sheet of ¼″ plate glass along one edge to a piece of 4-ply mat board. Place a sheet of some thin compressible material on the mat board, then the coated paper, then the negative, and lower the plate glass onto everything. The weight of the glass is usually sufficient to make good contact.

My students have found that printing out small negatives (4″ × 5″) and using them to *projection* print in the enlarger works! This would therefore require only the typical darkroom enlarging easel. The images are slightly grainy, but if grain does not bother you, there is much room for experimentation with this method. In fact, why not print 35 mm sized digital negatives for even more grain?

Determining exposure for all methods

Determining exposure with no step wedge

The aim is to determine the *minimum* exposure needed to obtain *maximum* black when printing through the OHP negative.

1. Set up the enlarger with a grade 2 filter, the enlarger head high enough (~2 feet) from the baseboard so its light path covers an 11″ × 14″ contact frame, a 35 mm negative carrier in the enlarger, a 50 mm lens wide open to F2.8, and the light path focused so its edges are sharp.

2. Take a piece of silver gelatin paper out of the pack under darkroom safelight and place a sheet of OHP over half of the paper.
3. Place a sheet of opaque material so it covers both halves and leaves a strip uncovered at the top.
4. Make a 5 second exposure and move the opaque material down half an inch to uncover another strip and make another 5-second exposure. Continue this process for 60 seconds until there is a series of twelve 5-second exposures (120 total seconds and 24 5-second exposures if there is no max black).
5. Develop the test sheet and dry it. Note the step where there is no difference between the OHP and non-OHP side. This is the minimum exposure capable of giving maximum black.

Once this printing time is determined for that paper, it doesn't change. This is the exposure that will be used for all further calibration. If a final print turns out to be too light or dark, it is often an indication of another problem in the workflow.

Determining exposure with a step wedge

Calculating an exposure time is easy with a Stouffer step wedge since a step wedge is measured in *stops* just like a camera, and photographers know stops. The correct exposure time—the amount of time it takes to get the paper as dark as it needs to be and no darker (overexposure)—is found by *overexposing* the step wedge to make sure at least two or more steps on the Stouffer's merge together with no differentiation. Once that is done the rest can be calculated mathematically—or merely consult Table 2.1 where the math is already done for you.

You can purchase a 21-step wedge (½ stop each step) or a 31-step wedge (⅓ stop each step). *Tip: Don't buy the more expensive* **calibrated** *ones; they are not necessary.*

1. Back the step wedge with your film of choice, Fixxons, Pictorico, etc. *Tip: tape the film and the step wedge together on either end with rubylith tape, an opaque red tape that blocks light, available from Uline or other places. This will provide a nice rectangle of paper white on either end for comparison purposes.*
2. Set up the enlarger with a grade 2 filter engaged, the enlarger head high enough (~2′) from the baseboard so its light path covers an 11″ × 14″ contact frame, a 35 mm negative carrier in the enlarger, a 50 mm lens wide open to F2.8, and the light path focused so its edges are sharp.
3. Expose the step wedge for 60 seconds, process and dry the step wedge print.
4. Note the first step number to match paper black (you must have at least two steps that are 100% black and if not, repeat the test with a 120 second exposure). Locate that step number in Table 2.1 and next to it will be the correct exposure time.

Each increment of the 31-step wedge corresponds to ⅓ stop and a mathematical number of 0.794 (.8 for ease) which is used to add time (by dividing the exposure time) or subtract time (by multiplying the exposure time) depending on how many maximum black steps are showing on the print. Each increment of the 21-step wedge corresponds to ½ stop and a mathematical number of 0.707 (.7 for ease). *Example: if Steps 1–4 are all*

	60 sec.	60 sec.	120 sec.	120 sec.
Max black :	21-step/ 1/2 stop	31-step/ 1/3 stop	21-step/ 1/2 stop	31-step/ 1/3 stop
Step 1:	60	60	120	120
Step 2:	42.4	47.6	84.8	95.3
Step 3:	30	37.8	60.0	75.7
Step 4:	21.2	30	42.4	60.1
Step 5:	15	23.8	30.0	47.7
Step 6:	10.6	18.9	21.2	37.9
Step 7:	7.5	15.0	15.0	30.1
Step 8:	5.3	11.9	10.6	23.9
Step 9:	3.7	9.5	7.5	19.0
Step 10:	2.6	7.5	5.3	15.1

Table 2.1. The table is based on enlarger exposure times of a Stouffer 21- or 31-step wedge backed with film. 1/3 stop is equal to .794, 1/2 stop is equal to .707. By multiplying (to subtract time) or dividing (to add time), the correct time can be found. Transparency film is included in these calculations but the Stouffer film's base+fog is not, because of its minimal (1/6 stop) effect. If desired, you can multiply the final exposure time x .89 to remove the Stouffer film's base+fog, too. Also note that transparency films can differ in density. Here the added density of 1/2 stop (.707) is computed into the calculations which is about what Pictorico Premium and Fixxons compute to be.

	To make steps darker multiply exposure by:	To make steps lighter multiply exposure by:
21-step		
1 step	1.4	.707
2 steps	2.0	.50
3 steps	2.8	.35
4 steps	4.0	.25
31-step		
1 step	1.26	.794
2 steps	1.59	.63
3 steps	2	.50
4 steps	2.5	.397

Table 2.2. This table is for quick calculations if you decide to vary exposure slightly. 1/3 stop is a slight difference; 1/2 stop is noticeable. If you vary a full stop, you might want to check your workflow.

maximum black, Step 4 needs to move 3 steps back to Step 1. The initial 60 second exposure time is multiplied 3x consecutively by .794 or .707. Then, optionally, the film density is subtracted *since you won't be printing through film (multiply by .89) and then ½ stop is* added *to account for Pictorico OHP density by dividing the final amount by .707. Tip: if you forget these numbers, use easy to remember numbers .7, .8, and .9.*

Once the exposure time is determined for *that* paper under *that* enlarger/lens/enlarger height combination, use that time for either digital negative system. If in a gang lab with multiple enlargers with different ages and strengths of light bulbs, it may be necessary to adjust the time when using a different enlarger. Suggested times are Arista FB 15 seconds, Ilford MGFB 19 seconds, Ilford Warmtone 38 seconds, Foma 131 Warmtone 48 seconds.

Creating the Photoshop curve

The curve creation process for all negatives is the same: plugging in a set of coordinates in the Photoshop curve dialogue panel. The only difference is in the actual coordinate numbers. Each of these curves will be created and then saved to your hard drive. They are then used for all future images and will not have to be created again. These curves are based on Epson printers that use Ultrachrome inks. Table 2.3 shows the input/output curve points. Since 0/0 and 100/100 are already in place, there are at most nine pairs of coordinates to enter into the curve panel.

All papers	Warmtone papers
0/0	0/0
X/10	2/10
X/20	4/20
2/30	5/30
4/40	8/40
7/50	12/50
11/60	16/60
18/70	23/70
29/80	38/80
64/90	70/90
100/100	100/100

Table 2.3. If there's an "x" Photoshop won't allow two points so close together so skip it and enter the next pair.

1. Open an image in Photoshop and convert it to Gray Gamma 2.2 (**Edit/Convert to Profile/Gray Gamma 2.2**).

2. Add a curve layer (**Layer>New Adjustment Layer>Curves**)(Figure 2.6).

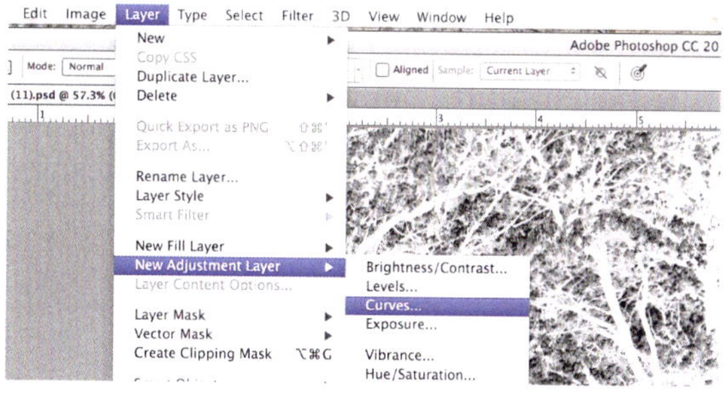

Figure 2.6.

3. Go to the dropdown menu in the Curves Panel located at the very top right corner and select **Curve Display Options** to make sure the Curves Panel is set to **Pigment/Ink %** (Figure 2.7).

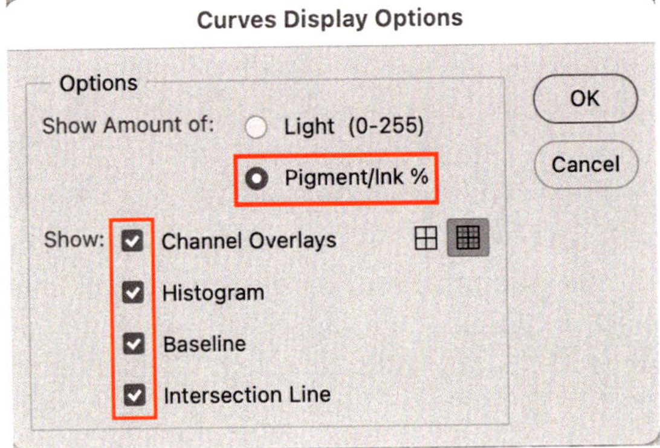

Figure 2.7.

4. Click on the diagonal line just above the bottom left to create a point on the curve. The **Input/ Output** numbers will appear in the Curves panel at the bottom (Figure 2.8). Each horizontal background line in the curves panel corresponds to 0, 10, 20, 30, 40, 50, 60, 70, 80, 90, 100% Output. The left/right arrow keys toggle Input. The up down arrow keys toggle Output. *Tip: if the curves panel background grid doesn't show all the gridlines, Option+Click within the grid to toggle it on.*

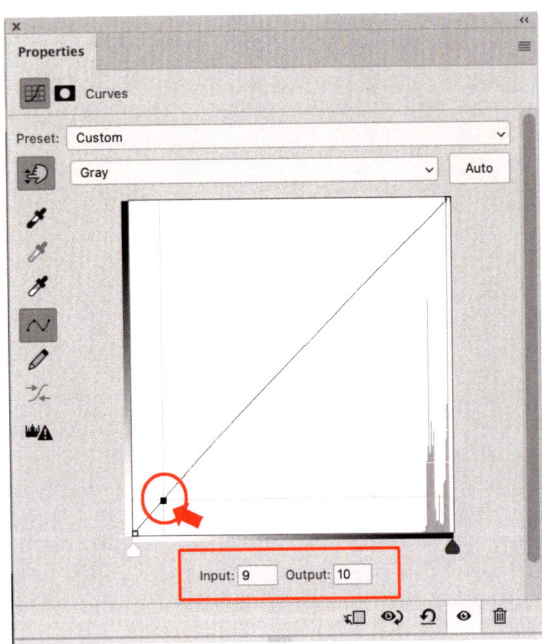

Figure 2.8.

5. Enter the Input/Output numbers, starting with the x/10 pair and continuing up the line with x/20, x/30, etc. Don't change 0/0 and 100/100. There are only 9 pairs of numbers to enter.

6. Select any point and with the +/- keys toggle up and down the curve from point to point to check that all Input/Output values are set accurately.

7. In the dropdown menu in the **Curves Panel** click **Save Curves Preset** and name it with the corresponding name like *Arista-15sec.acv* (Figure 2.9). Your curve work is done!

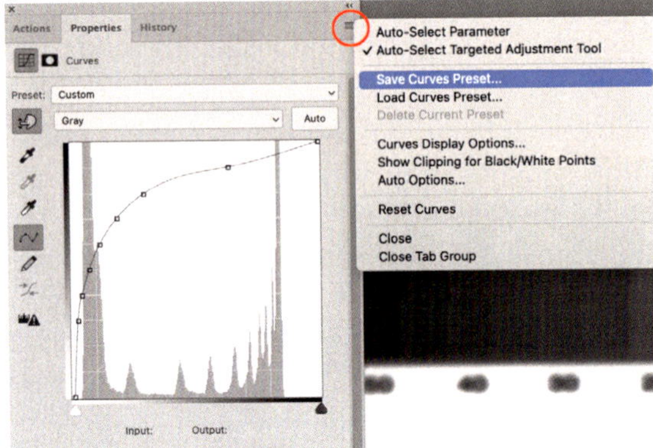

Figure 2.9.

Applying the curve to a negative

1. Open a digital image and convert it to 16 bit (**Image>Mode>16 bit**) and Gray Gamma 2.2 (**Edit>Convert to Profile>Gray Gamma 2.2**).

2. Size it to no larger than 300 ppi and 7.5″ × 9.5″ if you want ¼″ borders on 8″ × 10″ paper for 8.5″ × 11″ OHP film, and "save as" (**File>Save As>imagename_neg.tif**) to not write over the original.

3. Do any kind of image adjustments needed and for the final step do one or two sharpening steps if desired:

- **Filter>Sharpen>Unsharp Mask Amount 50–150%, Radius 0.5, Threshold 0** and/or
- **Layer>Duplicate Layer** then with that layer selected, **Filter>Other>High Pass Radius 10.** Set that layer at blend mode of **Soft Light** on the layer's panel drop down menu. View the

image at 50%, and with the duplicate layer active, play with the opacity slider at the top right of the Layers panel to see when it looks sharp enough but not too sharp. Flatten the two layers (**Layer>Flatten Layers** or **Command+E**). Save (**Command + S**).

4. Invert the image (**Command+I**).
5. Apply a curves adjustment layer to the image (**Layer>New Adjustment Layer>Curves**).
6. Click the dropdown menu in the curves panel, click **Load Preset** and load the curve (Figure 2.10).

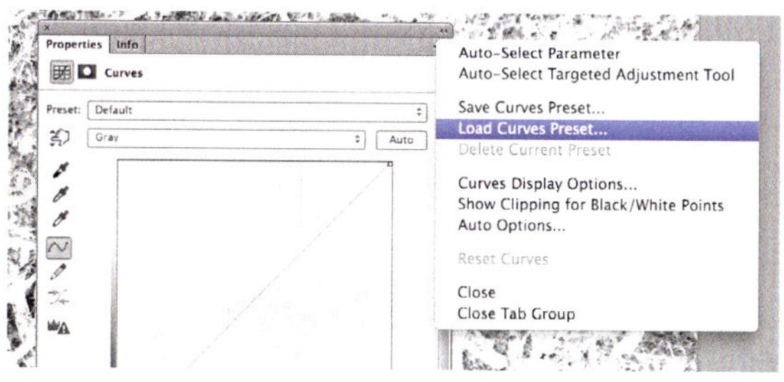

Figure 2.10.

7. Save the image (**Command+S**). Do not flatten these two layers but save the negative with the curve always separate. That way the image can be printed with a different curve, if desired.
8. Go to **File/Print**. Unfortunately printer drivers are different, but on the P900 look for the following choices if you have them. On the first print dialogue panel under Color Handling select:

- **Photoshop Manages Colors**
- **Epson Premium Glossy Photo Paper** (it doesn't matter in this dropdown menu here since Photoshop is managing colors, not the printer).
- Check **Send 16-bit data** if the image is in 16-bit.
- **Normal Printing**.
- **Rendering Intent**: Perceptual.
- **Black Point Compensation** unchecked.

Up at top of this panel click the dropdown Print Settings menu and choose **Printer Settings** and under Basic click:

- **Media Type**: Premium Photo Paper Glossy
- Under **Print Quality** select **Quality Options** and move slider almost to the far right so you can *uncheck* Black Enhance Overcoat, Gloss Smoothing, High Speed, Finest Detail, and Bottom Edge Print Quality Priority.

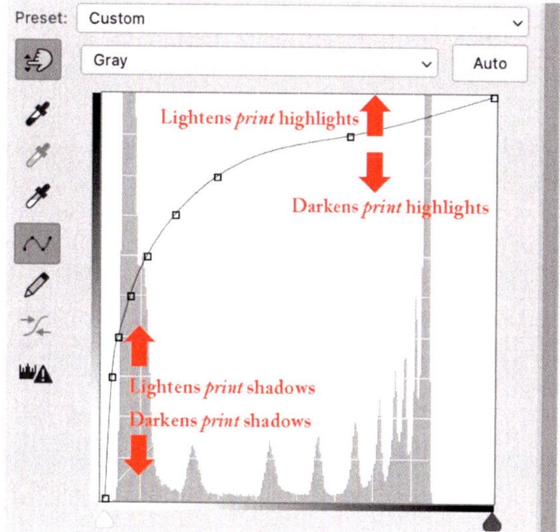

Figure 2.11. A curve is not cut in stone. Sometimes a perfectly linearized negative makes for a boring, predictable print. Points on the curve can be moved up or down to taste. Moving a point up lightens the **print** (not the negative in other words); moving a point down darkens the **print**. Easy to remember—sky (up) is lighter and earth (down) is darker. Small adjustments to curve points go a long way so be judicious.

- Up at the top of this panel click the dropdown Print Settings menu again and under **Layout** choose **Flip Horizontal** so print will ultimately be right-reading.
- If necessary only, under the dropdown Printer Settings menu select **Advanced Media Control** and move the **Color Density** slider towards +50 if you find your negatives aren't dense enough.
- Save and print. Be sure to print on the correct side of the OHP film. Tip: do the "lick and stick" test—lick a finger and see if it sticks to a corner of the OHP; if so, that is the side to print on. If the Pictorico cut-off corner is at the top right, that means the printable side is facing you.

9. Let a negative dry for at least an hour face up with nothing on top, or dry it with a blow dryer on warm. Then store it in a notebook sleeve.
10. Print an image and assess. If you want to make any changes in the way the tones look in the image, see Figure 2.11 and move points slightly, and smoothly, up or down. No curve is cut in stone!

This completes the generic curve in Photoshop method. The QTR method follows.

QuadToneRIP

QTR allows complete control over a printer's inks through the use of custom QTR **profiles**. A QTR profile—technically an **ink descriptor file**—is a set of commands or computer functions written in a .txt file. The .txt file which tells the printer what to do is stored in a specific folder. When the QuadToneRIP driver is used to print a negative, a particular profile for that process is selected from a dropdown menu, and the driver prints the negative as instructed in the .txt file.

Installing QTR and Print-Tool

Before you begin your QTR journey, install QTR and Print-Tool on your computer using the following steps.

1. Go to http://www.quadtonerip.com/html/QTRdownload.html and download the software:
   - **QTRIP2.8.0.dmg** or the latest QTR program. *QTR-CurveView.app allows you to see a visual of a .txt/.quad file, and comes within the QTR package.*
   - **Print-Tool-2.3.2.app.zip**, the printer driver
2. Double click on the QTR software icon. A folder called **QuadToneRIP** will be installed in your **Applications** folder. Another folder also installs in the library at **/Library/Printers/QTR/quadtone/QuadP900** (or P800, 3880, etc.). Folders containing software for all supported Epson printers will be installed in the same location at **/Library/Printers/QTR/quadtone/**. Note that the forward slash in front of Library needs to be included.
3. Plug your Epson P900 (or P800, 3880, etc.) printer into the computer and turn it on.

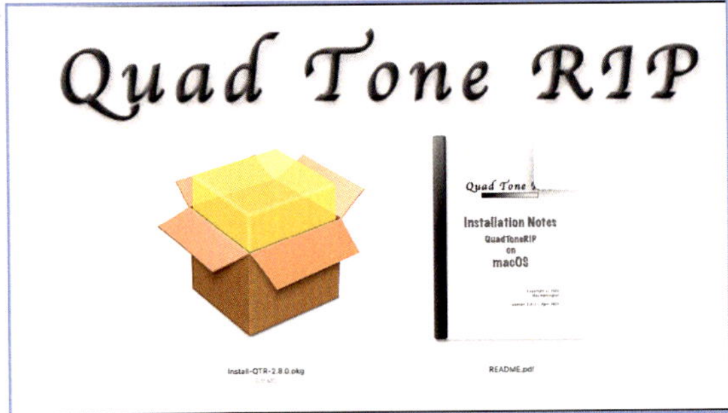

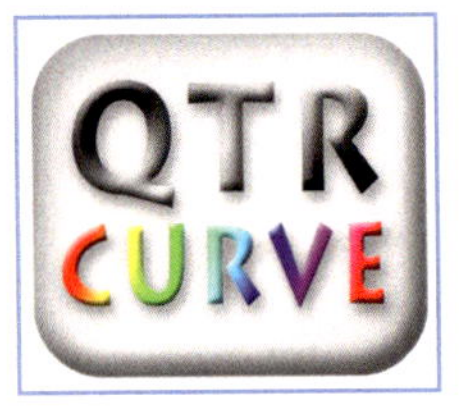

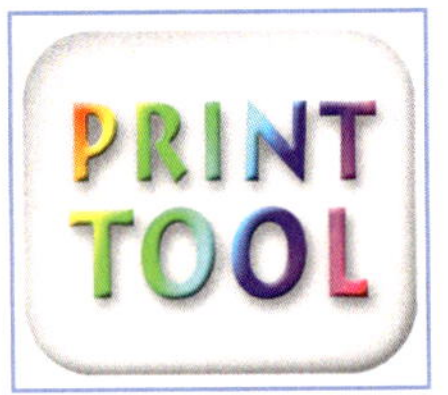

Figures 2.12–2.14. When downloading QTR the package will look like this, the Install icon along with a tutorial. After installation, you'll notice QTR comes with QTR-CurveView in the folder along with other things. Print-Tool is a separate download. Tip: keep Print-Tool and QTR-CurveView in your dock for easy access.

4. In **Applications/QuadToneRIP/Profiles/** double-click the **P700–900-UC** folder (or P800-UC, etc.) to open and double-click the **InstallP900.command** in that folder to install the printer.
5. Double-click on **Print-Tool** to open. *Tip: keep Print-Tool readily available by right-clicking on the Print-Tool icon and choosing Options/Keep in Dock.*
6. At the very top of the Print-Tool window see if your printer, now called *Quad*P900 (or *Quad*P800, etc.) appears in the dropdown menu after Printer. If so, both QuadToneRIP and Print-Tool have successfully installed.

Installing a profile

Once a profile is created, it has to be installed before it can be used.

1. Drag any profile into **Applications/Quad ToneRIP/Profiles/P700–900-UC** (or P800-UC, etc.) and double-click the **InstallP900.command** within that folder. As the profile is installing, a window pops up (Figure 2.15) that verifies installation. If there are problems with the profile's installation, it will say so in this window, so check for error messages. You can also verify installation by going to **/Library/Printers/QTR/quadtone/QuadP900** (case sensitive) and look for the profile after installation. Double-click on the .quad profile (or right-click and **Open With QTR-CurveView**) in that folder to see a visual of the profile.

2. Open an image file in Print-Tool, following the instructions on **Printing with the Print-Tool App** in this chapter. The newly installed profile should appear in the third panel's Curve 1 dropdown menu (you may have to quit and restart Print-Tool for it to appear, if Print-Tool was open during profile installation). *Tip: each profile is stored as a .txt file in Applications, and as a .quad file in the Library. It is best practice to keep a file folder with a copy of .txt profiles in your documents folder that is backed up regularly because with a computer crash the Applications folder and Library folder are not always included in a backup. Also, when deleting an installed profile, both the .txt file and the .quad file have to be deleted or the profile remains.*

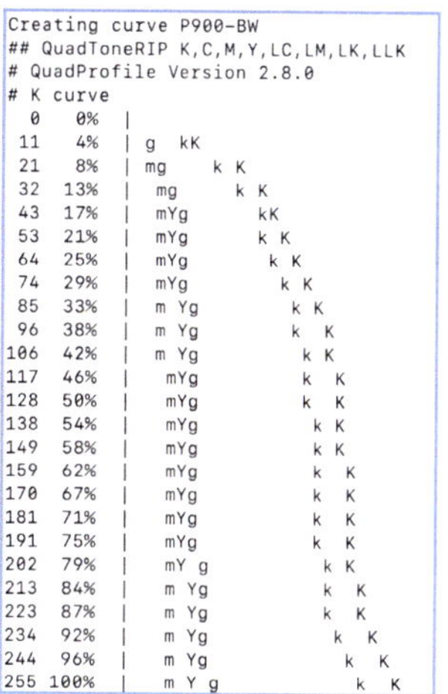

Figure 2.15. When a profile is being installed you will see a graphical representation of the ink distribution that the profile will deliver, as illustrated to the left, if you have "GRAPH_CURVE=YES" in your QTR profile.

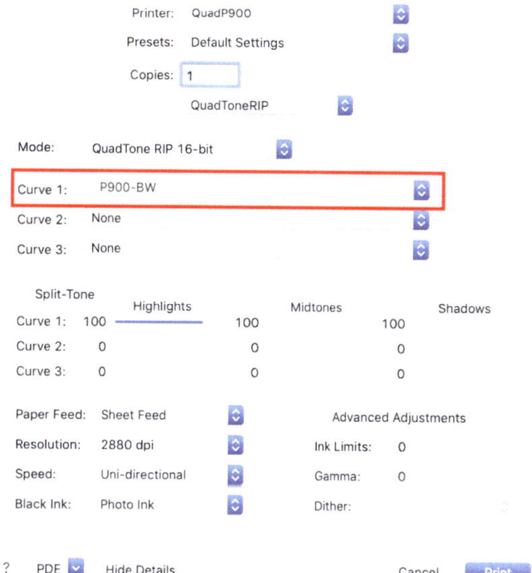

Figure 2.16. Profiles appear in Print-Tool's Curve 1 dropdown menu.

Installing the Build QTR Curve tool

Although this software is not necessary to use with QTR, this java script developed by David "Ike" Eisenlord automates the process of measuring a scanned step wedge with the press of a button.

1. Download David Eisenlord's Build QTR Curve (https://www.davideisenlord.com/?p=229).
2. In the download there are two items: a 21-step wedge and the Build QTR Curve java script. The step wedge is in Gray Gamma 2.2, necessary when using Build QTR Curve.
3. Drag the Build QTR Curve java script file into the Photoshop scripts directory (**Applications/Photoshop/Presets/Scripts**).
4. To check if you have successfully installed the file, open Photoshop and in the **File** dropdown menu scroll to **Scripts** and **Build QTR Curve** will appear as a choice in the Scripts dropdown menu.

Step 2

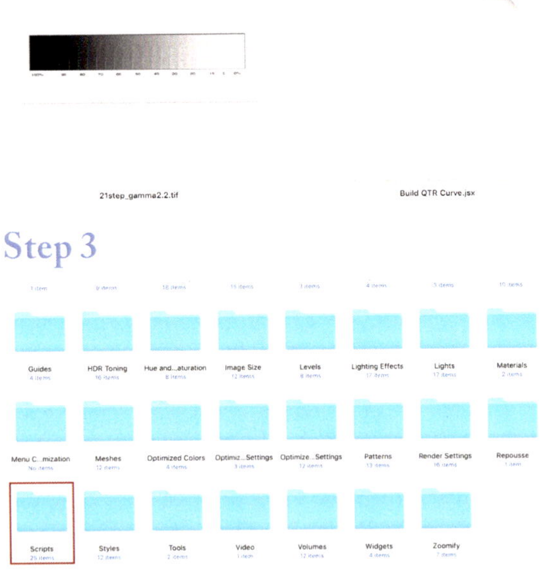

Step 4

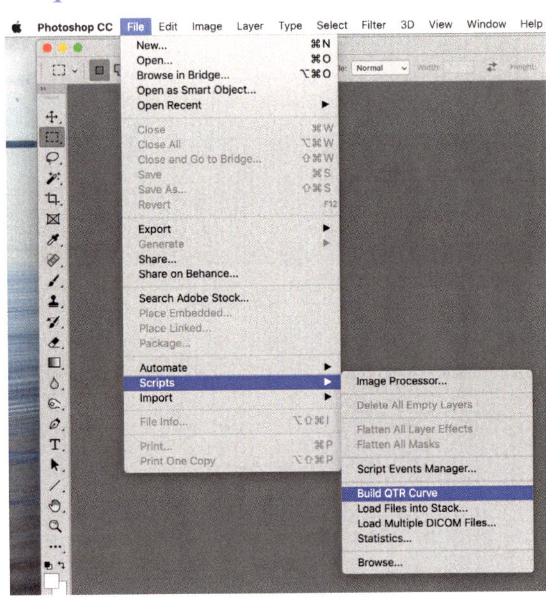

Step 1

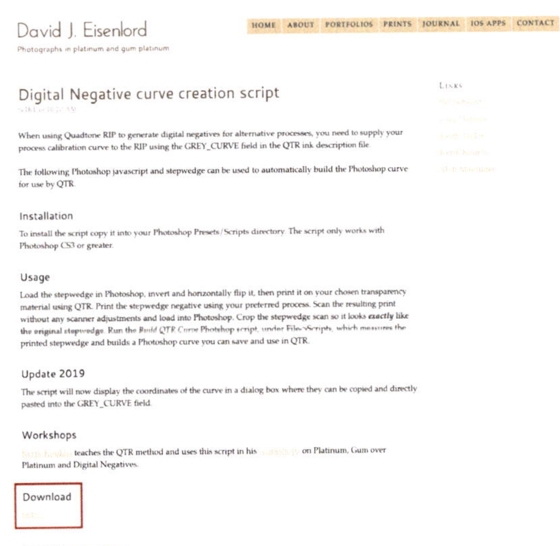

Figures 2.17-2.20

Understanding profile terminology

This is a crash course in QTR speak. Functions preceded by a # are turned off. Functions (**blue**) remain unaltered. Variables (peach) are the ones that are modified.

#CURVE_NAME= P900-BW

#PROCESS INFO Ilford MGIV 2 filter 19 sec. 50mm lens at F2.8, enlarger 25" high, 35 mm carrier

Above is merely informational for the user and preceded by a hashtag to turn off.

PRINTER=QuadP900

Make sure the correct printer name is here, but I have also deleted this line entirely and a profile if in the correct folder to begin with will install in the correct folder to end with.

CALIBRATION=no

Profile is not being used to color calibrate.

GRAPH_CURVE=YES

This allows a visual graph of the curve.

N_OF_INKS=8

This matches the number of inks in the printer. However, in the P700/P900 that has 9 inks (Matte Black and Photo Black are considered one), they can be treated as 8-ink printers and Violet is unused.

DEFAULT_INK_LIMIT=100

Leave default at 100 and adjust inks individually.

LIMIT_K= 45.5

Each ink is limited to a certain max amount.

BOOST_K=

Use if needing more contrast and lighter highlights.

LIMIT_C=10.4
LIMIT_M=10.4
LIMIT_Y=10.4
LIMIT_LC=6.5
LIMIT_LM=6.5
LIMIT_LK=39
LIMIT_LLK=13
N_OF_GRAY_PARTS=1

Profiles are 1–3 parts. In a one-part profile inks follow the black (K) curve; in a two-part profile inks follow black (K) and light black (LK); in a three part profile light light black (LLK) is usually the third part. The QTR silver gelatin profile used herein is a one-part profile. Note that LK refers to Gray and LLK refers to Light Gray in a P700/P900 printer; Violet is not used.

GRAY_INK_1=K
GRAY_VAL_1=100

Gray Ink 1 is usually K and set to a Value of 100.

GRAY_HIGHLIGHT=0

Increasing this value darkens shadows of the print and lightens print high tones, generally not useful in a digital negative.

GRAY_SHADOW=0

Greater than 0 darkens midtones to highlights of the print but also lowers contrast.

GRAY_GAMMA=1

Gamma less than 1 lightens the midtones/greater than 1 darkens the midtones of the print. A most useful function for a one-part profile.

GRAY_CURVE="0;0 4:20 7:30 15:40 27:50 41:60 56:70 73:80 90:90 100;100"

Either an .acv curve file can be directly dragged here or its Input/Output numbers are entered between straight quotes starting with the 0;0 coordinates.

COPY_CURVE_C=K
COPY_CURVE_M=K
COPY_CURVE_Y=K
COPY_CURVE_LC=K
COPY_CURVE_LM=K
COPY_CURVE_LK=K
COPY_CURVE_LLK=K

The Copy Curve lines direct which inks to follow which part and here, being a one-part profile, all inks follow black (K).

#GRAY_OVERLAP=0

Overlap up to 100 can be useful to smooth tonal transitions and grain in multi-part profiles; in a one part profile it is not necessary and is turned off.

#LINEARIZE="100:100...0:0"

Measurements from a densitometer or a spectrophotometer are entered here between straight, not curly quotes. This can be used alone or together with Gray Curve. LAB numbers ascend lowest to highest. Densitometer numbers highest to lowest. Here the Linearize function is turned off with a hash tag and the profile is linearized with Gray Curve but if you have a densitometer it is best to use Linearize first and then fine tune with Gray Curve second.

Making a one-part profile

Ink	90% Base	(P800) Base	110% Base	120% Base	(P900) 130% Base	140% Base	150% Base
K	31.5	35	38.5	42	45.5	49	52.5
C,M,Y	7.2	8	8.8	9.6	10.4	11.2	12
LC,LM	4.5	5	5.5	6	6.5	7	7.5
LK	27	30	33	36	39	42	45
LLK	9	10	11	12	13	14	15

```
PRINTER=QuadP800
N_OF_INKS=8
DEFAULT_INK_LIMIT=100
BOOST_K=
LIMIT_K=35
LIMIT_C=8
LIMIT_M=8
LIMIT_Y=8
LIMIT_LC=5
LIMIT_LM=5
LIMIT_LK=30
LIMIT_LLK=10
N_OF_GRAY_PARTS=1
GRAY_INK_1=K
GRAY_VAL_1=100
GRAY_HIGHLIGHT=0
GRAY_SHADOW=0
GRAY_GAMMA=1.2
GRAY_CURVE="0;0 5;10 9;20 14;30 21;40
34;50 49;60 67;70 83;80 95;90 100;100"
COPY_CURVE_C=K
COPY_CURVE_M=K
COPY_CURVE_Y=K
COPY_CURVE_LC=K
COPY_CURVE_LM=K
COPY_CURVE_LK=K
COPY_CURVE_LLK=K
```

```
PRINTER=QuadP900
N_OF_INKS=8
DEFAULT_INK_LIMIT=100
BOOST_K=
LIMIT_K=45.5
LIMIT_C=10.4
LIMIT_M=10.4
LIMIT_Y=10.4
LIMIT_LC=6.5
LIMIT_LM=6.5
LIMIT_LK=39
LIMIT_LLK=13
N_OF_GRAY_PARTS=1
GRAY_INK_1=K
GRAY_VAL_1=100
GRAY_HIGHLIGHT=0
GRAY_SHADOW=0
GRAY_GAMMA=1.0
GRAY_CURVE="0;0 4;20 7;30 15;40 27;50
41;60 56;70 73;80 90;90 100;100"
COPY_CURVE_C=K
COPY_CURVE_M=K
COPY_CURVE_Y=K
COPY_CURVE_LC=K
COPY_CURVE_LM=K
COPY_CURVE_LK=K
COPY_CURVE_LLK=K
```

Table 2.4 and Figure 2.21. A silver gelatin negative should be neutral in color to respond to variable contrast filters equally. Colored dark inks, C, M Y, are set to equal (low) amounts and colored light inks LC and LM, are also set to equal (low) amounts, with neutral black inks, K, LK and LLK doing the light blocking. The P800 has the densest inks so here that is the base profile. The P900 needs about 30% more ink to equate to a P800 negative. These are merely starting points to develop your own profiles. Top right are QTR profiles for those two printers.

Printing silver gelatin is somewhat different than printing other alt processes. The enlarger prints with incandescent, not UV light, and color filters from yellow to magenta can be utilized for contrast control over and above the contrast built into the digital negative. A neutrally colored negative that responds predictably to contrast filters is best.

Silver gelatin paper, mass-manufactured under strict parameters, also has a much more predictable response than individually hand-coated paper. The table above has a range of ink loads to test, but chances are that most silver gelatin papers will respond to an ink load between 90 and 130%.

Finally, silver gelatin has more exposure *latitude*, where exposure times can be decreased or increased up to ½ stop either way as a useful tool.

Most of the profile is determined with the correct minimum exposure time to get maximum black and the correct ink load to get paper white. The next two functions for profile adjustment are Gamma and Boost in that order. At the outset, Boost is inactive in these profiles.

Installing software

1. Download and install QuadToneRIP, Print-Tool, and Build QTR Curve as instructed in this chapter.

Finding the correct exposure time

2. Determine the exposure time with a Stouffer 21- or 31-step wedge as instructed in this chapter.

Creating a starting profile

3. In the **Applications/QuadToneRIP/Profiles** folder locate the P900-UC folder (or P800, etc.). In this folder you will see a number of profiles ending in .txt, and a command called **InstallP900.command**. Select an existing .txt profile in the P700–900-UC folder and select **File/Duplicate**. It doesn't matter which file because you will be typing over the existing profile. Relabel this new profile BW.txt with no spaces in the file name. *Tip: QTR is for printing positives as well as negatives. If you are using QTR for negatives only, make a folder in the profiles folder labeled "Others" and drag unused profiles into it so they aren't installed. Also, a profile is in two locations; to delete an installed profile, you will have to move both the .txt file and the .quad file to the trash.*

4. Double-click to open the profile and type in the following information in place of the existing profile. Remove any information in the old profile that is not in the new profile, e.g. toner information, etc. Don't use returns until at the end of a line of code. Quotation marks are straight, not curly quotes. A hashtag in front of a line inactivates it so

it won't direct the printer to do something.

```
#CURVE_NAME=P900 BW
PRINTER=QuadP900
CALIBRATION=no
GRAPH_CURVE=YES
N_OF_INKS=8
DEFAULT_INK_LIMIT=100
BOOST_K=
LIMIT_K=45.5
LIMIT_C=10.4
LIMIT_M=10.4
LIMIT_Y=10.4
LIMIT_LC=6.5
LIMIT_LM=6.5
LIMIT_LK=39
LIMIT_LLK=13
N_OF_GRAY_PARTS=1
GRAY_INK_1=K
GRAY_VAL_1=100
GRAY_HIGHLIGHT=0
GRAY_SHADOW=0
GRAY_GAMMA=1
GRAY_CURVE=0;0;100;100
COPY_CURVE_C=K
COPY_CURVE_M=K
COPY_CURVE_Y=K
COPY_CURVE_LC=K
COPY_CURVE_LM=K
COPY_CURVE_LK=K
COPY_CURVE_LLK=K
```

5. Double click **InstallP900.command**. A terminal window pops up that shows which profiles are being installed. If the profile has an error, the script will tell you. Verify installation by going to **/Library/Printers/QTR/quadtone/QuadP900** and look for the profile. *On newer computers, you may have to change read/write permissions. If so, right click on the folder and choose* ***Get Info****. At the bottom of the Get Info panel you will see* ***Sharing Permissions****. Click the password-protected lock open, presuming you have administrative access, change* ***Read Only*** *to* ***Read/Write****, and click the lock closed.*

Testing the profile

6. Go to the **Applications/QuadToneRIP/Curve Design/Images** folder and locate the **21step.psd** digital step wedge (or the 21-step-g2.2.tif step wedge in the Build QTR Curve folder). *Tip: the QTR step wedge is* **untagged***; the Build QTR Curve step wedge is Gray Gamma 2.2. As long as No Color Management is selected in Print-Tool, there is no need to tag the QTR step wedge with a profile. If you decide to do so, make sure to* **assign** ***(Edit/Assign Profile/ Gray Gamma 2.2)****, not* **convert***, because convert will change the step wedge's exact 5% increments.*

7. Drag the digital step wedge to the Print-Tool icon and print it on transparency according to **Printing with the Print-Tool App** (with **Negative** box checked!) using the profile you installed, which should now appear in the Curve 1 dropdown menu.

Evaluating and modifying the profile

8. Expose the digital step wedge on the silver gelatin paper of choice and evaluate. *Tip: tape the step wedge on one edge with Rubylith tape to ensure a strip of paper white for comparison purposes. First make sure there is only one step of paper white.*

- If the step wedge seems light overall and more than one step is paper white, lower the Total Ink load in the profile according to the chart, reinstall the profile and print another step wedge.
- If the step wedge seems dark overall and there is no paper white, raise the Total Ink load in the profile according to the chart, reinstall the profile and print another step wedge.

9. Assuming maximum black and paper white are now achieved but the tones in-between are blocked up, adjust Gray Gamma.

- If shadows are blocked up, lower Gray Gamma to somewhere between 0.3–1.0, starting with 0.7 (use a 0 before fractional amounts).
- If highlights are blocked up raise Gray Gamma to 1.0–1.4. A little goes a long way and it will affect all tones. You can use fractional amounts like 1.25.
- If both shadows and highlights do not have enough separation, a slight raise of both Total Ink to open up the blacks and Gamma to darken the whites might be in order.

10. Print another step wedge and evaluate the highlights.

- If highlights are still too light, put a number after Boost that is lower than the K ink amount.
- If highlights are still too dark, raise Boost to a number higher than the K ink amount.

11. Once you are able to print a step wedge with 21 discreet steps from Dmax (the darkest dark possible in a process) at Step 100% to paper white at Step 0%, and the steps in-between look not too dark, not too light, with nice separation, it is time

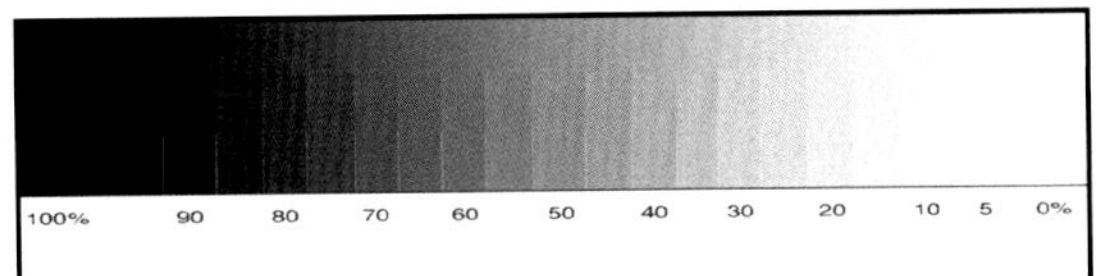

Figure 2.22. When a step wedge is scanned to run through Build QTR Curve it must be cropped exactly like this—with the ample white bottom area—or an error message may occur.

to linearize. Note that if prior adjustments have been good, this linearization step will be minimally invasive.

Linearizing the profile with Build QTR Curve

12. Scan in 16-bit grayscale with no adjustments. Open the scanned step wedge in Photoshop and convert it to Gray Gamma 2.2 if it is not already there (**Edit/Convert to Profile/Gray Gamma 2.2**). Crop it so it looks just like Figure 2.22 with the wide white bottom or else you may get an error message upon running the script.

13. Select **File/Scripts/Build QTR Curve**. The script will generate a curves layer along with a set of Gray Curve coordinates. Select the curve coordinates (**Cmd+A**), copy (**Cmd+C**), and paste (**Cmd+V**) the line of coordinates along with straight quotation marks after Gray Curve in place of the curve coordinates in the profile. Curve coordinates are entered in pairs between the straight quotes with a semicolon between each Input/Output number and a space between the pairs.

14. Double click on the curve layer to open up the Adjustment Curve panel. If you have chosen exposure time for maximum black, ink load for paper white, and Gamma for opening up the tones in-between, the curve generated by Build QTR Curve should be very close to the diagonal line and minimally invasive. See Figure 2.23. for the difference between a curve that does too much heavy lifting and one that is minimally invasive. If it is doing way too much heavy lifting go back to the drawing board with ink loads and Gray Gamma. If the curve looks good, but has a bump or so in it, select the point or points that need to be smoothed. Simply select the point you want to move, use the cursor key to tap it left or right until the curve is smoother. Make a note of the smoothed point's new coordinates and change them accordingly in the string of numbers that you just pasted after Gray Curve. Repeat as needed. Run **InstallP900. command** and the new profile is done.

Printing and evaluating the print

15. After editing an image in Photoshop, convert the image to Gray Gamma 2.2 (**Edit/Convert to Profile/Gray Gamma 2.2**), save the image as a .tif or .psd, and close.

16. Follow the instructions on the **Printing with the Print-Tool App** to make a few different negatives to print in your process of choice.

17. If you find prints to be consistently too light or too dark, adjust exposure by up to ½ stop either way. If the contrast is off, use a different filter.

Printing the monochrome negative

1. It is best practice to always start with an image that is raw, .tif or .psd (not .jpg), 16 bit, and in Adobe RGB 1998 or ProPhoto RGB colorspace. This produces an image with the greatest gamut of bits and color within which to edit and retain best detail from highlights to shadows.

2. Do any kind of adjustments to the image that it might need. It is not necessary to size an image before sending it to Print-Tool because you can size an image within Print-Tool itself.

3. For a final editing, suggested sharpening methods, if desired, are as follows. *Tip: An image destined for a negative can be sharpened much more than one destined to be a digital print.*

- Recovery sharpening (**Filter/Sharpen/Unsharp Mask Amount 50-150%, Radius 0.5, Threshold 0**).
- More global sharpening (**Layer/Duplicate Layer**) then with that layer selected choose **Filter/Other/High Pass/Radius 10**. Set that layer at blend mode of **Soft Light** on the layer's palette drop down menu. With the image at 50% view size, play with the opacity slider at the top right of the Layers Palette to see when it looks sharp enough but not too sharp. Flatten these two layers.

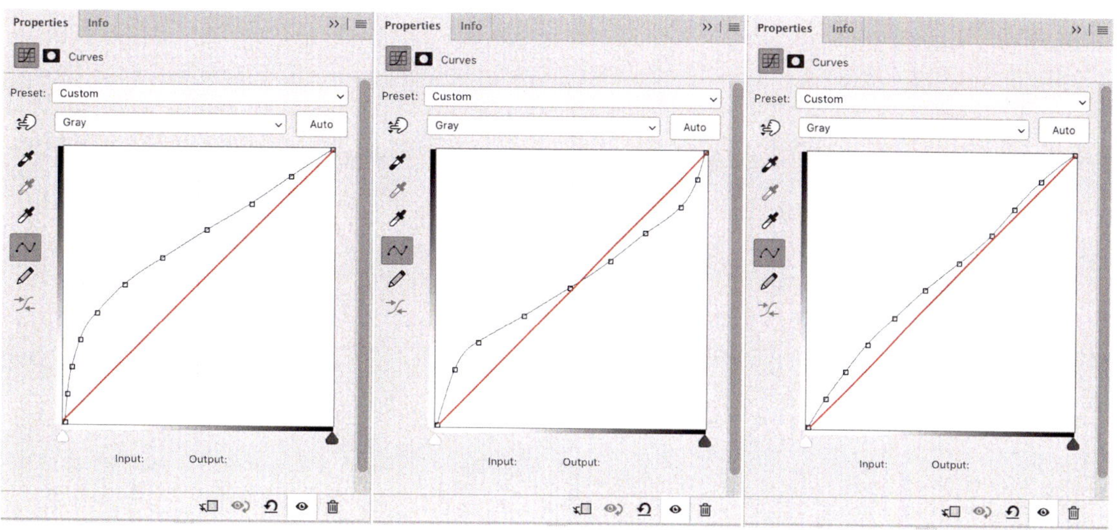

Figure 2.23. The curve on the left, derived from Build QTR Curve, indicates the chosen ink load is too low because through the entire profile, the curve wants to lighten the print. Points above the diagonal lighten, below the diagonal darken (think up/sky/light, down/earth/dark). The curve in the middle, though more appropriate with less heavy lifting required, indicates the highlights are too light, needing a lower ink load—perhaps. The curve on the right indicates the best profile of these three—little heavy lifting done by the curve to linearize the profile.

4. When all editing is done, save the edited RGB image (**Command + S**) in case you ever want to go back to it, convert the image to Gray Gamma 2.2 (**Edit/Convert to Profile/Gray Gamma 2.2**), and then save again, this time save *as* to not save over the RGB edited file (**Shift+Command + S**), and close.

5. Drag the image to Print-Tool and print with the appropriate profile as illustrated in **Printing with the Print-Tool App** further.

6. When ready to print the negative in the darkroom, always set up the enlarger the same way to achieve consistent results.

- The bottom of the enlarger head rests at the same height (about 25″ from lens to contact frame).
- The lens is set to the same f-stop each time, e.g. wide open or a stop or two down if necessary.
- The light path is focused to cover the entire contact printing frame.
- The filter pack is set at a 2 filter and the filter pack is engaged.

7. Determine the exposure time with a Stouffer 21- or 31-step wedge as outlined in this chapter. Generally warmtone papers will require 2–3× the exposure as coldtone papers. Example: with an enlarger raised to 25″ from lens to contact frame, a 50 mm lens wide open to f2.8, a 35 mm carrier in the enlarger head, Ilford MGIV will expose in 19 seconds and Ilford Warmtone in 38 seconds. With the same setup, but a 150 mm lens set to f5.6, and a 4″× 5″ negative carrier in the enlarger head, Ilford MGIV will expose in about half that time.

8. Place the negative on the paper, emulsion to emulsion, and put this sandwich in the contact printing frame so the negative is face down, visible through the glass, with the emulsion side of the silver gelatin paper facing up to the enlarger through the glass.

9. Expose and process as normal for a silver gelatin print. Evaluate the image just as you would with a normal print and make adjustments accordingly:

- If the overall image is *slightly* too light or too dark, add or subtract exposure respectively.
- If the whites are *slightly* gray/dull, move to a higher contrast filter.
- If the whites are *slightly* lacking detail, move to a lower contrast filter.
- If greater than slight adjustments are needed, revisit the profile.

QTR profile for lumen printing

A lumen print negative has to be very dense and contrasty. Certainly you could try and print a lumen print with a normal silver gelatin digital negative, but chances are the negative will be too thin and you'll want more contrast. Here is a lumen print QTR profile that works well for all day exposures in full sun. All parts of the profile below in blue remain the same; peach is what changes. If you want an even denser negative, raise K and Y higher in equal proportions. Note that the only inks utilized in this profile are K and Y because they are the only inks that hold back appreciable amounts of light. All other inks are dialed down as low as possible but still used so as not to clog the ink cartridge nozzles from disuse. This profile is perfect for a P800 and works well for a P900, but if you find you need a denser negative for the P900 raise K and Y to 65 and leave all others the same. Note: be sure to use **Pictorico Ultra** for your OHP because of the higher ink load necessary for this negative.

```
#Lumenprint
N_OF_INKS=8
DEFAULT_INK_LIMIT=100
BOOST_K=
LIMIT_K=50
LIMIT_C=5
LIMIT_M=5
LIMIT_Y=50
LIMIT_LC=5
LIMIT_LM=5
LIMIT_LK=5
LIMIT_LLK=5
N_OF_GRAY_PARTS=1
GRAY_INK_1=K
GRAY_VAL_1=100
GRAY_HIGHLIGHT=0
GRAY_SHADOW=0
GRAY_GAMMA=1.0
GRAY_CURVE="0;0 8;10 16;20 29;30 41;40 54;50 65;60 75;70
82;80 90;90 100;100"
COPY_CURVE_C=K
COPY_CURVE_M=K
COPY_CURVE_Y=K
COPY_CURVE_LC=K
COPY_CURVE_LM=K
COPY_CURVE_LK=K
COPY_CURVE_LLK=K
```

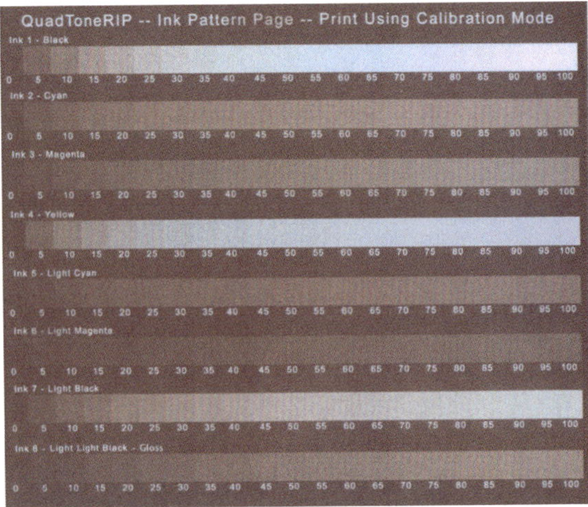

Figure 2.24. Ilford MGIV matte lumen print of the QTR ink pattern page. The QTR ink pattern page prints rows of each ink individually from 0% to 100% and is used to discover which inks hold back the most light in your process of choice. It shows that Black and Yellow inks are the suitable choices for the lumen print profile, and to a lesser extent, Light Black. To learn how to use the Ink Pattern Page, beyond the scope of this book, check out *Digital Negatives for QuadToneRIP*.

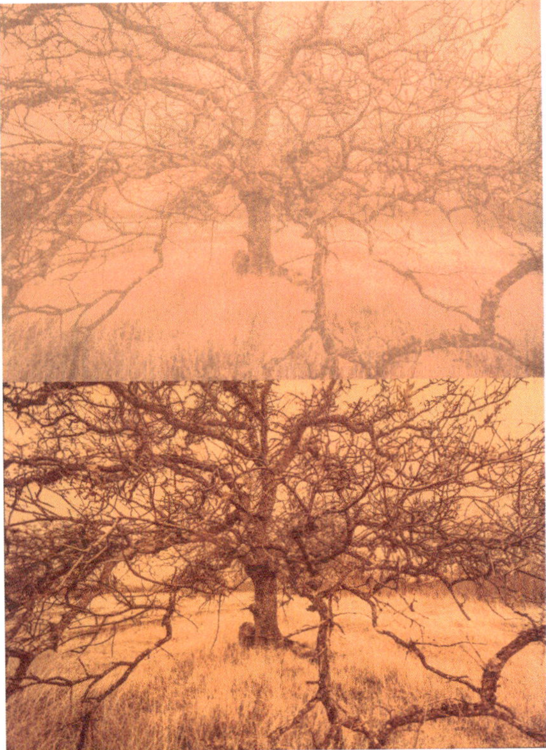

Figure 2.25. Here is the same image on Ilford Warmtone printed with a salted paper profiled negative (top) and a lumen print profiled negative (bottom) to illustrate how a suitably profiled negative does wonders for lumen prints.

Figure 2.26. The dreaded "pizza wheels" which always show up in highlight areas where there is more ink.

Troubleshooting the digital negative

Pizza wheels: When there are large areas of highlights in the negative (e.g. clouds, sky) sometimes microscopic pinprick dots where the teeth on the track wheels that advance the paper in the printer mar the ink. They can be seen by holding the negative obliquely against something dark and looking through a loupe. They end up printing microscopic black dots marching across the image.

- With an Epson printer, under **Advance Media Control** change the slider next to **Increase Drying Time per Pass** to +20 up to +50, the **Paper Thickness** to 15, and the **Platen Gap** to Wider.
- Use the front load feeder where pizza wheels are not used to transport the paper during printing.
- In the P800 and P900 in the window on the printer itself go under the Maintenance menu and select Thick Paper.
- In Print-Tool use unidirectional printing and 2880 super.
- Switch to a more ink-absorbent transparency film like Pictorico Ultra.
- Some photographers have devised a method of disengaging the pizza wheels entirely by tricking the printer into thinking the front load feeder is being used when it is not, and then using the top paper feeder with the pizza wheels disengaged. Search the web for this method because I would hate to recommend something I have not tried that has consequences for the operation of your printer.

Posterization: This is where instead of continuous tone there is a flattening of tone in some areas.

- In a curved negative the curve is too drastic, so slightly move curve points closer to the diagonal line in the curve dialogue panel.
- Always photograph in as lossless and uncompressed a capture system as you can (RAW for digital SLRS or at least TIFF, never JPEG).
- Don't over-edit an image; also, edit in 16-bit mode not 8-bit mode.

Troubleshooting the QTR negative

I don't see my profile listed in the Terminal window but I don't see any error message.

- Double-click the install command again.
- One of the folders or files in the chain **/Library/Printers/QTR/quadtone/QuadP900** folder is Read Only. Right click (or type **Command+i**) on each folder starting with the QuadP900 folder. At the very bottom under Sharing & Permissions verify that each folder is set to Read and Write. Change by clicking on the Lock and changing permissions as needed.

The installer shows an "illegal curve name" message.

- No spaces or symbols are allowed in a curve name, and it can't be over 40 characters. Only use hyphens and dashes.

I am using a numerical string after Gray Curve and get an "invalid curve" message in the installer.

- Quotation marks must be straight, not curly.
- Numbers start with 0;0 and end with 100;100.
- Numbers must be written with a semicolon between each number in a pair and a space between pairs, like this: "0;0 8;10 16;20..." etc.

I installed a new profile and it does not show up in the Print-Tool curves menu.

- Print-Tool may have been open while installing the profile. Quit Print-Tool and re-open it.

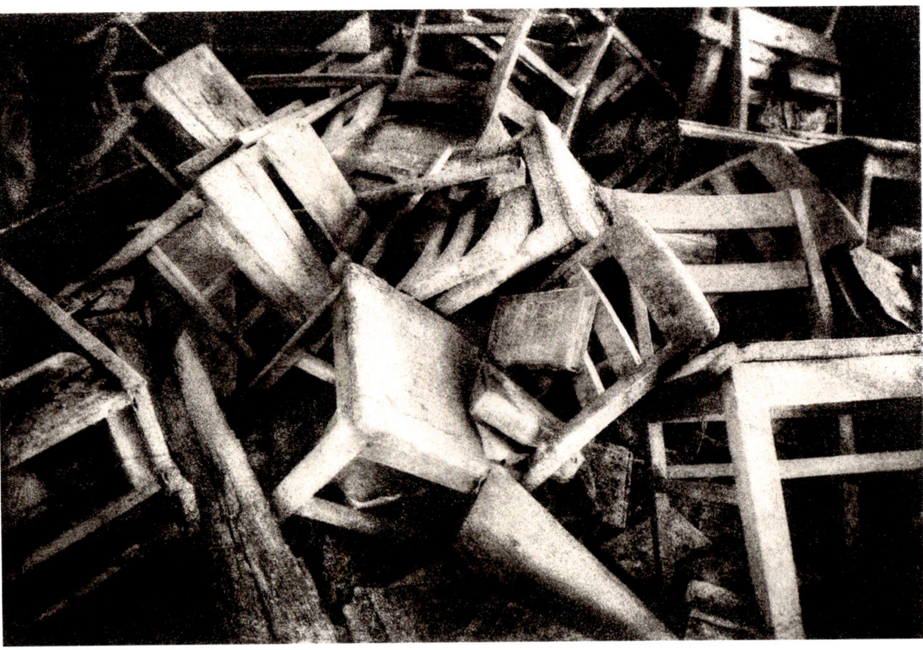

Figure 2.27. *Library Chairs, New Orleans*, from the series *Still Lives After Katrina*, bromoil print, 6″ x 8″ © Jill Skupin Burkholder 2006

I installed a new profile but the test print looks just like the previous print.

- Verify that the profile installed by going to the Library folder and see if it is there.
- Make sure that you did in fact select the new profile to print.
- Check the profile to make sure that there is no hashtag in front of Gray Curve, which would inactivate the curve line of code.

I printed my negative with a profile that was working but now it is quite dark (or light).

- Quit Print-Tool, run the installer again, verify that the proper .quad file is present, open Print-Tool and try again.

I deleted a .txt file but the profile is still in the QTR dropdown menu, how do I get rid of it?

- Go to the .quad folder and simply delete all of the .quad files. Quit Print-Tool if it is open. Run the installer again and this will generate new .quad files that are presently in the profiles folder.

I loaded a negative instead of a positive into Print-Tool, checked the "flip for emulsion" check box and the image did not print reversed.

- The **Prefs** button next to the **Negative** check box works *only* if you check the Negative check box.

My test strip looks good but my print is too light or too dark.

- Many QTR users find that additional fine tuning of the profile and/or exposure "to taste" is necessary. Recheck the exposure time and profile by printing a step wedge alongside the image. Silver gelatin printers can make exposure adjustments of about +/-15% whereas with other processes it may be safer to adjust the profile.
- Make sure the image is Gray Gamma 2.2 (**Edit/ Convert to Profile/Gray Gamma 2.2**) if all calibration process has been in Gray Gamma 2.2.
- If exposure is fine and Gray Gamma is set properly, adjust the .acv curve to taste by moving the data points on the curve up to lighten the print and down to darken the print (Figure 2.11).

Light and/or dark areas of my print have no detail.

- This is one area where it is very useful to have a step wedge as part of your negative. If a step wedge that previously printed fine shows a problem with the whites or blacks, the problem is most likely in exposure or development. If the step wedge looks good, then go back to the image on your computer and use the eyedropper tool to measure your highlights and shadows. Any areas which read 100% or 0% are going to print with no detail. Adjust the image and reprint the negative.

Printing with the Print-Tool app

The Print-Tool app will be used every time you print with the QTR system. Before using it, convert an image to Gray Gamma 2.2 (**Edit/Convert to Profile/Gray Gamma 2.2**), edit, size, sharpen, save as a .tif or .psd (**Shift+Command+S**), and close. Print-Tool has a check box for converting a positive to a negative and for flipping an image, so there is no need to invert or flip beforehand.

1. Drag the image to the Print-Tool app and position it as desired in the print area. Make sure on the first screen that the Printer is **Quadxxx** (QuadP900, etc.), the right size of paper is chosen (e.g. 8.5″ × 11″ or US letter), the Scale Factor is **100%**, the Embedded Profile is **Gray Gamma 2.2**, Print Color Management is **No Color Management**, and the **Negative** box is checked which will print the positive as a negative. *Tip: you can rotate the image with the Rotate tool and add text to the canvas with the Text button.*
2. Click on the **Prefs** button and in this panel check **Flip for Emulsion Side** so the negative prints flipped and the final print will be right-reading (Prefs will not work if negative box is not checked!). There are options in this panel to print a border of different sizes around the image if desired. Press **Done** and then **Run Print** to open up the next panel.
3. In this panel, Printer should still be *Quad*xxx. and in the **Layout** drop-down menu select **QuadToneRIP** which opens up the next panel.
4. In this panel choose Mode: **QuadToneRIP 16-bit**, and installed profiles appear in the Curve 1 drop-down menu. Choose Resolution **2880 dpi** (2880 dpi super if you have problems with pizza wheel marks on the negative), Speed **Unidirectional**, Black Ink **Photo Ink**, and click **Print**. Let the negative dry for an hour or more or blow dry with a hair dryer on high for a minute or two and then print in your process of choice. *Tip: Lick and stick! Lick a finger and touch a corner of the transparency film surface lightly. Your finger will stick to the printable side.*

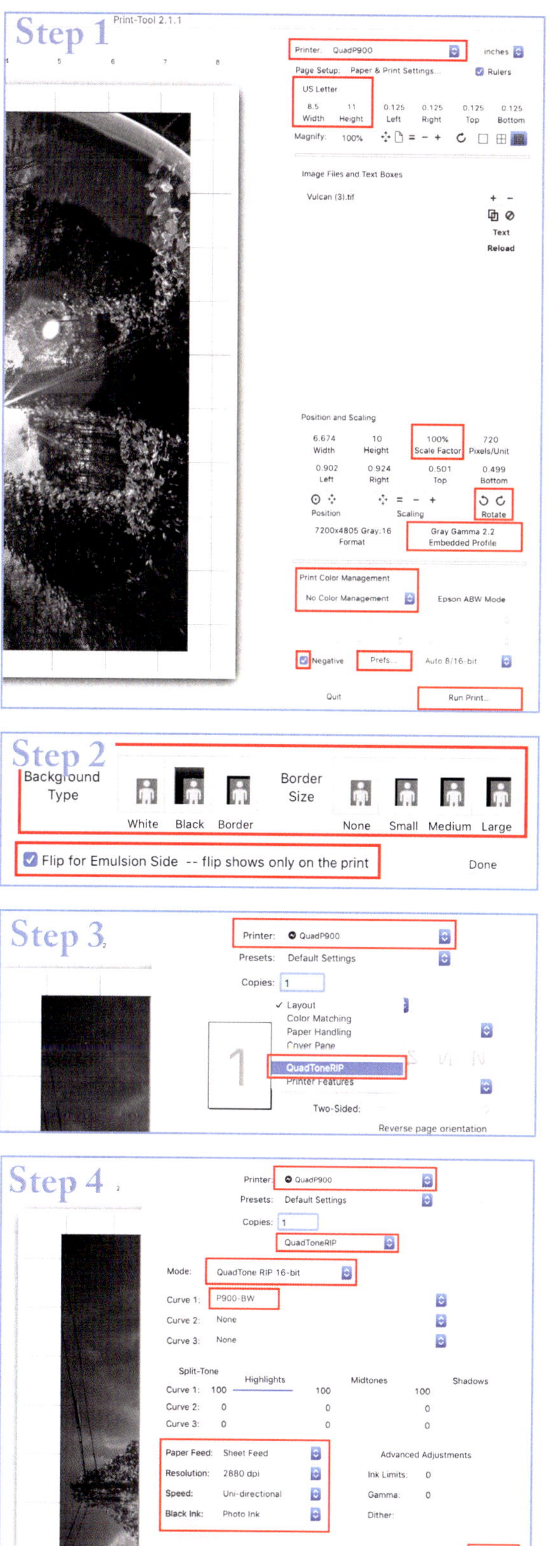

Figures 2.28–2.31. Don't forget to check the Negative box and Flip for Emulsion Side!

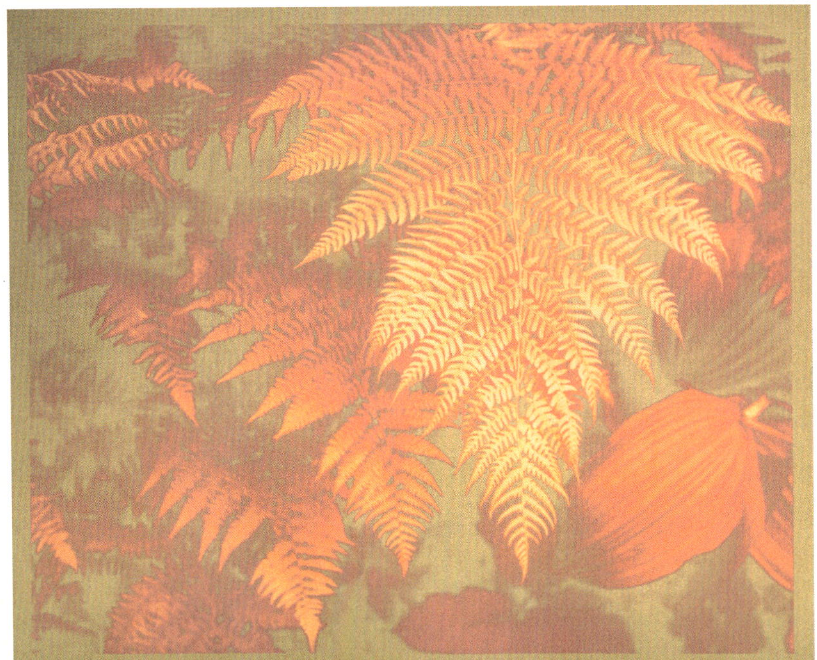

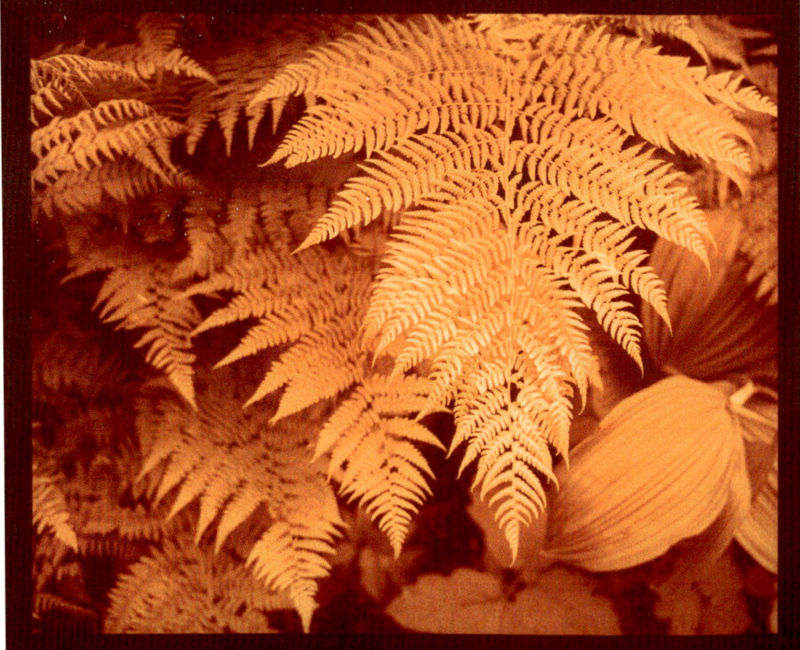

Figures P1.1–P1.2. Top, *Ferns 2*, Ilford Gallerie FB paper, two day exposure under cloudy conditions, 12″ x 9″; bottom, *Ferns 1*, Ilford Warmtone FB paper, ten hour exposure under full sun, 12″ x 9″ © Dani Hatfield 2021. "These two images of the ferns show the differences that exposure time and paper choice can make in an image. A shorter exposure on Ilford Warmtone paper resulted in an image with deep red and terracotta tones. The other image was made using a different paper, Ilford Gallerie FB, which produces different tones than that of Ilford Warmtone. The image was left out for twice the time to counteract cloudy weather, but this overexposure resulted in the greenish solarization of the shadows." Dani Hatfield is a graduate from the MSU School of Film and Photography. Growing up on the outskirts of Yellowstone National Park has made much of her work revolve around nature and the inherent beauty of the outdoors. She enjoys working in a wide variety of digital and alternative photographic processes. To see more of Hatfield's work follow her @danihatfield.photo or visit her website danihatfield.com.

PART ONE

Cameraless Experimentation

Process	Negative used	Resist used	Developer used	Fixer used	Activator/ Stabilizer used	Room or outside light exposure	Chemicals create colors	Light creates colors	Light & chemicals create colors
Photogram			Yes	Yes					
Chemigram		* *	Yes	Yes		Yes		Yes	
Lumenprint	*		* * *	Yes		Yes		Yes	Yes
Chromo	Yes		Yes	Yes	* * * *	Maybe	* * * * *	Maybe	Yes/maybe
Sabattier	Yes		Yes	Yes		Yes			
Duotone Sabattier	Yes		Yes	Yes		Yes	Yes-pot. bromide		

P1.2. The chart above will make sense as you explore this book more, though there are always exceptions to the rule. There are areas of commonality that processes share, but also differences. For example, all but the photogram use room light as part of the equation. All use fixer, but one (lumen prints) does not use developer, etc.

* Occasionally a negative is used outside in full sun
* * Only process to use a resist
* * * Only process to not use developer
* * * * Only process to use activator/stabilizer
* * * * * Only process that specifically uses chemicals to plate out silver

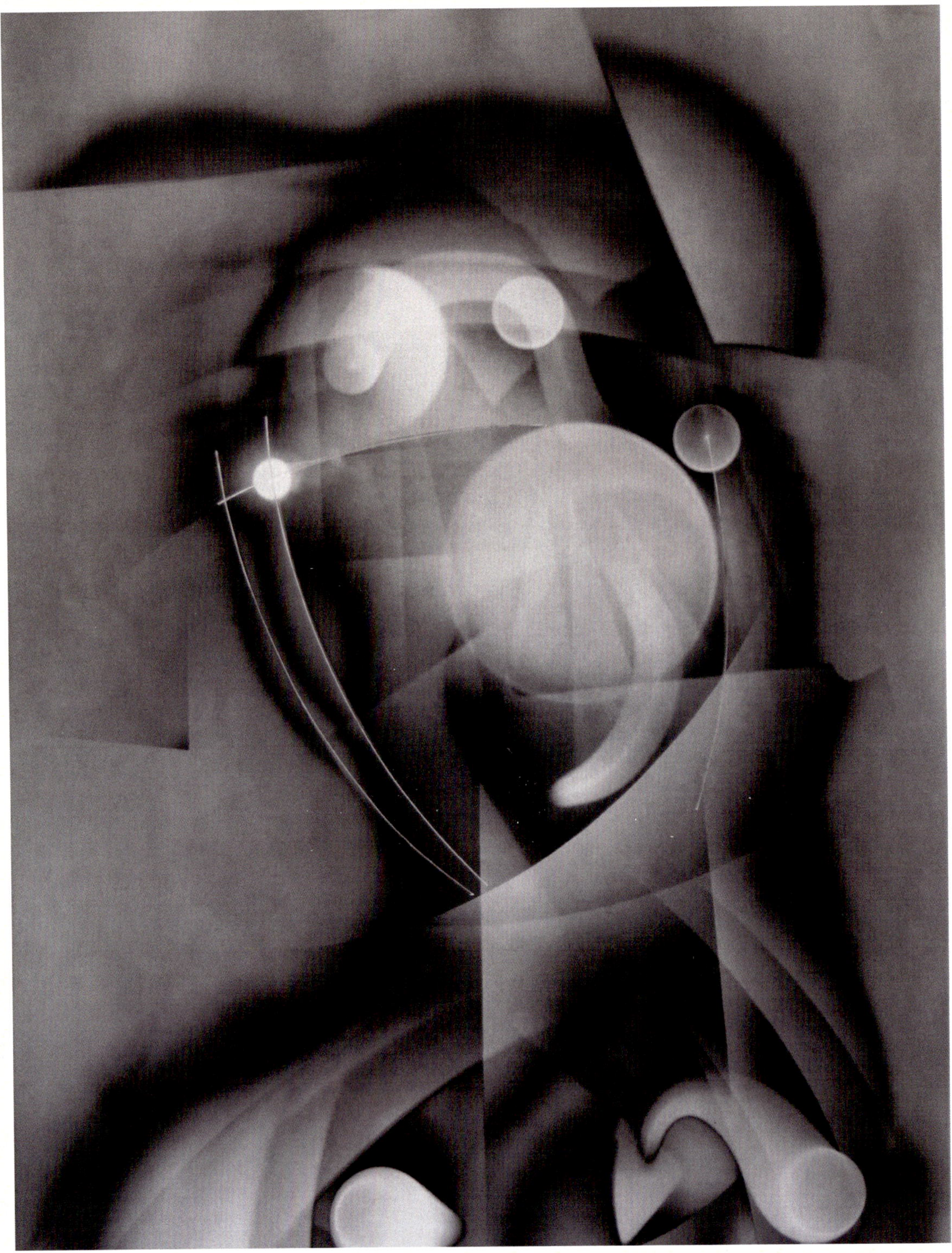

Figure 3.1. *Portrait Study*, unique luminogram photogram on silver gelatin paper, 20″ x 24″ © Mike Jackson 2019. See the **Contemporary Experimental Artists** chapter for more of Jackson's work.

Photograms and Clichés Verre

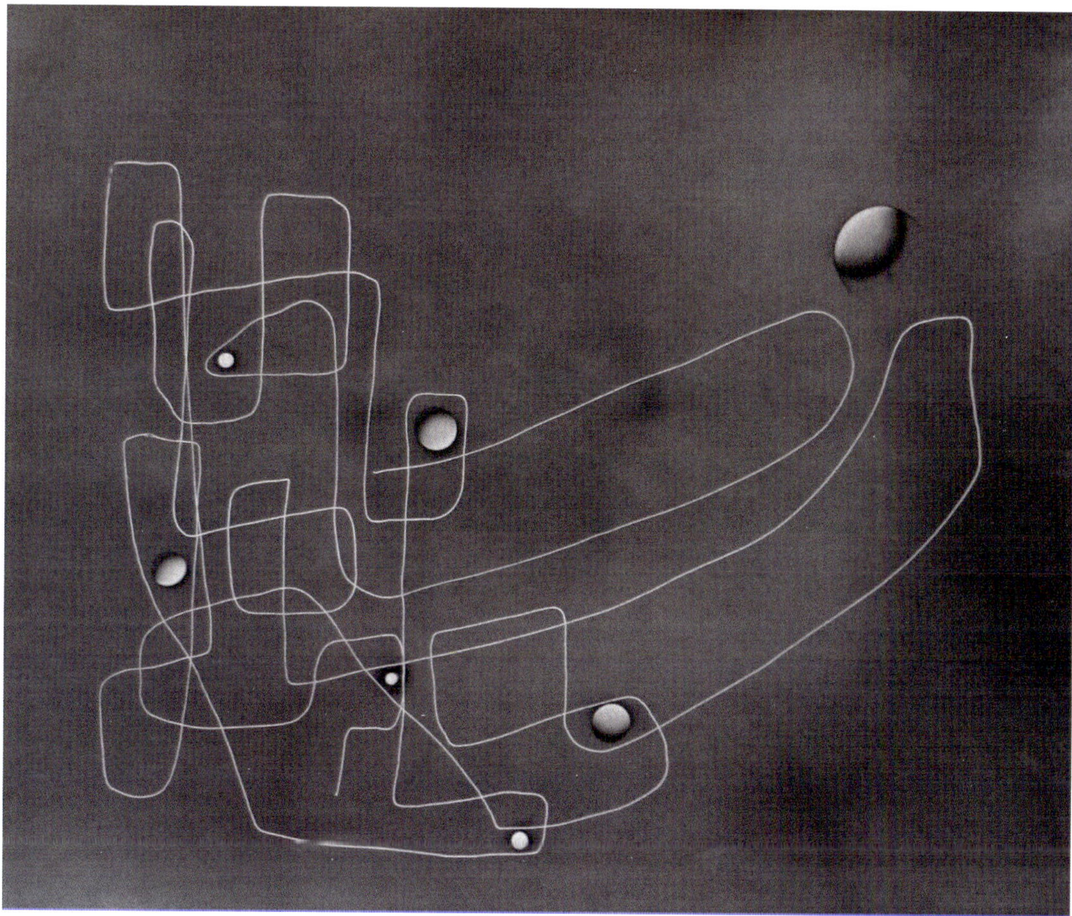

Figure 3.2. *The Land*, unique luminogram, pen on silver gelatin paper, 24˝ x 20˝ © Mike Jackson 2019

A photogram is a photographic image that is produced without a camera. Objects of varying opacities are placed on paper and then the paper is exposed under the enlarger. Where the objects rest, varying shades of white to gray will result, depending on the opacity of the objects. The more opaque, the whiter the paper underneath stays.

The first photogram was created by William Henry Fox Talbot, one of the founding fathers of photography. Around 1834 he put flower specimens on top of silver nitrate-sensitized leather and paper and exposed them to light.

Once cameras became the norm, photograms fell out of vogue, until the early 1900s when interest in them was renewed. Christian Schad made photograms starting around 1918, and called them "Schadographs." He used arrangements of objects and trash—torn tickets, receipts, rags—on film. Man Ray was doing the same in 1921. He discovered the process while working in his darkroom one day, when he accidentally put an unexposed piece of photographic paper into his developer. Waiting for an image to appear, which didn't, he decided not to waste the paper. He placed a funnel, graduate, and thermometer on the paper and turned on the

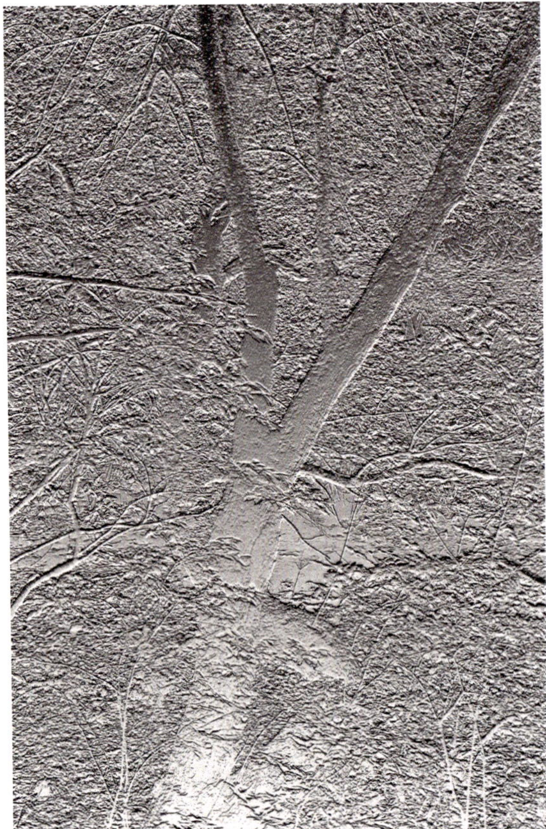

Figure 3.3. *Untitled*, silver gelatin bas relief, 5″ x 7″ © Mark L. Eshbaugh 2020. "This image started from a 35mm film negative, enlarged onto a 5″ x 7″ or larger sheet of ortho film and tray developed in Sprint chemistry. Ortho film is a high contrast film, and you can use either print developer or film developer (which is my preference for a slightly lower contrast negative) to process. The first printing creates a film positive. I then take that 5″ x 7″ positive and contact print it onto another sheet of ortho film which when processed is the enlarged negative. Once I have both a positive and negative of the same size, a bas relief can be created by putting the two slightly out of register and contact print the sandwich onto silver gelatin paper."

darkroom light. An image began to form, and the rest is photogram history.[1] He dubbed his creations "Rayographs." Man Ray continued to experiment, and when Lazlo Moholy-Nagy saw Man Ray's Rayographs in Paris, he brought the technique to the Bauhaus, an art design school in Germany that was started in 1919, shut down by Hitler prior to World War II, and was reborn in Chicago as the Institute of Design in 1937. Photograms are still alive and well today and often the first assignment in beginning black and white photography classes to introduce students to light, paper, and chemistry.

Today photograms have become much more sophisticated and no longer just for beginners. There are photographers who specialize in just photograms. A new form of photogram is the lumen print discussed in the next chapter, which differs from a photogram insofar as the paper is exposed to room or sunlight for very long amounts of time, the paper is never developed in paper developer, and the final image is merely fixed.

Photogram variables to consider

To make a successful photogram, there are many variables to try:

- Opacity of the object from translucent to opaque
- Height of the object from the paper
- Object 2D or 3D
- Object moving, still, or removed for part of the exposure time
- Paper exposed to light under the enlarger, or in the developer, or partially developed and re-exposed under the enlarger
- Film used instead of paper to make a negative
- Intensity and length of light under the enlarger
- Intensity and length of a light source other than an enlarger, e.g. flashlight or matches
- Light source moving or still
- Light direction(s) to achieve a sense of space

It is challenging to produce a balanced, interesting composition in a photogram. There should be enough space for shapes to "breathe," i.e. consider negative space as well as positive. The objects within the space should dialogue with each other conceptually and visually. All of these variables make for much trial and error and paper.

Exposure time

A trial exposure time to start with is F8 for 15 seconds for an 8″ × 10″ black and white print, depending on the particular paper used and its speed as well as the height of the enlarger and brightness of the enlarger bulb. You want the paper to achieve maximum black (see the **Digital Negatives** chapter) but a lot depends also on the opacity of the objects on top of the paper. The more opaque, the longer the exposure time can be.

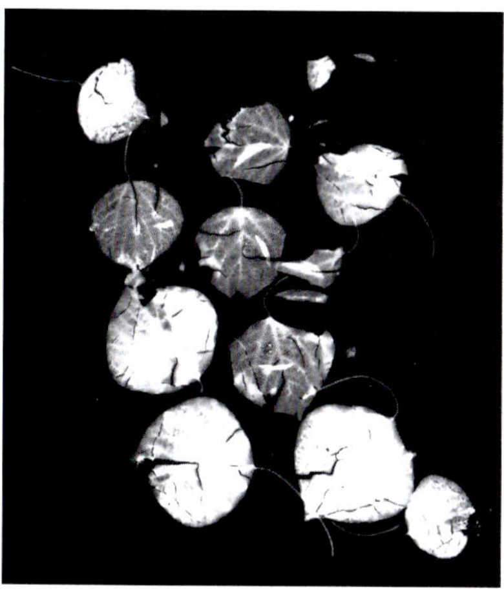
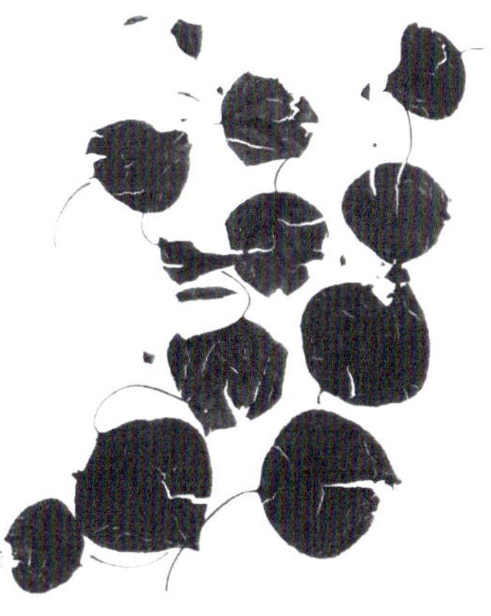
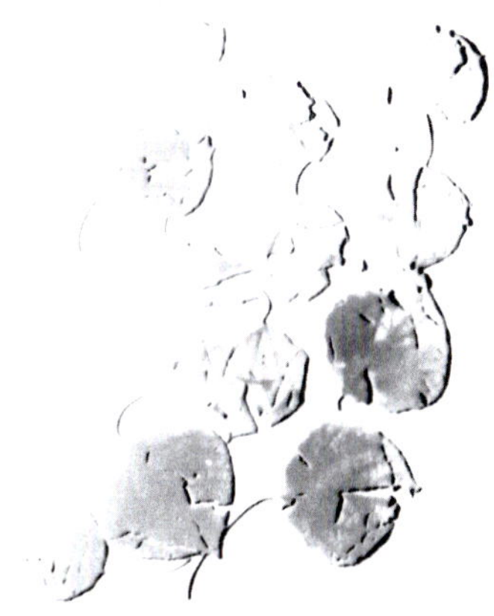

Figures 3.4–3.6. *The Sequence of Three*, from left to right, photogram, reverse photogram, and bas relief photogram © Cheyenne O'Donnell 2021. O'Donnell discovered that better bas relief photograms come with an initial image that is higher contrast, not a fully tonal image with lots of grays. O'Donnell is an alumna of Montana State University's Film and Photography program.

Direct projection photogram

With this method, use a 4″ × 5″ glass negative carrier, microscope specimen plate, or even a couple sheets of acetate to sandwich different substances on or between the glass/plastic. Think of the process this way: Whatever is placed on the glass/plastic becomes a "negative" through which light from the enlarger is projected onto the paper.

Reverse photogram

If a previously made photogram (white objects on a black background) is used as a *negative* and contact-printed to another piece of silver gelatin paper, a reverse photogram results: black objects on a white background. This takes a much longer exposure because the light has to travel through silver gelatin paper to expose the paper below, somewhere close to 3 stops more which is 8× the original exposure (time × 2 × 2 × 2 = 3 stops). A 15 second exposure now becomes perhaps 90–120 seconds. When doing reverse photograms and bas relief photograms use RC paper for the negatives because it lays flat. Fiber base paper buckles slightly and blur occurs.

Bas relief photogram

If both these photograms, the original photogram and the reverse photogram made as discussed above, are sandwiched together slightly off-register, this sandwich can be used as a negative to make a *bas relief* print. Now the light has to travel through two pieces of silver gelatin paper and therefore the exposure will be even longer. One of my students, Sam Norsworthy, found that an initial photogram exposure of 15 seconds became 4 minutes for a bas relief photogram. Note: there is no reason to stop down the lens aperture on the enlarger when making photograms. Use the widest open aperture your lens allows because the sharpness of the print has nothing to do with lens aperture when contact printing like this.

Direct positive paper

Harman has released a new direct positive RC paper that when used in the photogram process will produce black objects on a white background. It is a fixed grade, high contrast paper (similar to Ilford multigrade grade 3½–4). It comes in glossy and luster surfaces. Two caveats: the paper needs to be used under red safelight only, not amber. And, with direct positive paper you have to think backwards, in that less exposure is darker and more exposure is lighter.

Tips and ideas

- Layer multiple pieces of glass with objects sandwiched in-between. Objects further away from the paper will produce grayer, softer-edged effects.

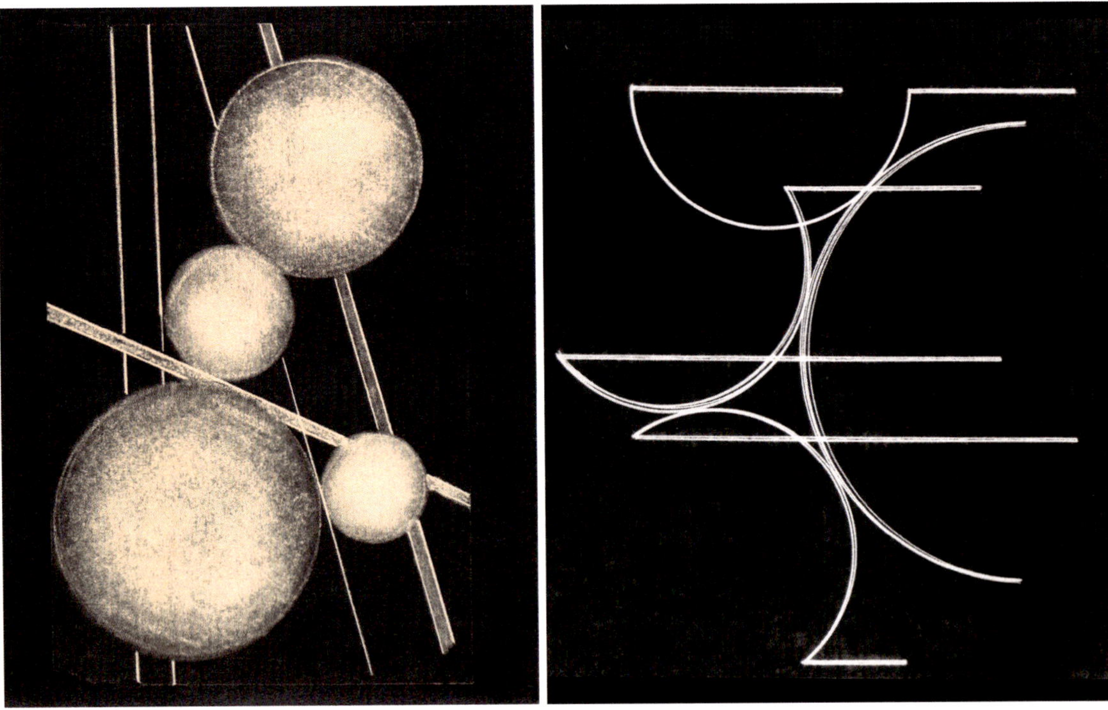

Figures 3.7–3.8. Left, *Geometry 201*, unique oxidized gelatin silver cliché verre print from graphite and charcoal drawing, 8″ x 10″; right, *Geometry 18*, unique oxidized gelatin silver cliché verre print from graphite drawing, 8″ x 10″ © Patricia A. Bender 2018. For more of Bender's work see the **Contemporary Experimental Artists** chapter.

- Translucent objects that bend light rays such as glass cups, pitchers, and crystal work great.
- Items with the printed word either found or printed digitally onto transparency work good singly or layered with other objects.
- Painted or smoked cellophane or saran wrap creates intriguing, malleable shapes.
- You can expose a negative in the enlarger (or in contact with the paper in a contact printing frame) along with objects to get a combination of photographic image and object.
- "Draw" with a penlight, lighter, or matches. If you are going to use flame, you must get permission to do so from the darkroom manager, have your instructor present, and be careful using flame around chemistry!
- Sabattier the photogram while in the developer by flashing light briefly right over the tray. See the **Sabattier** chapter.
- Tone or handcolor the finished photogram; see the **Toning** and **Applied Color** chapters.

Cliché verre

Cliché verre is French for "glass negative," that today refers to the negative, the product, and the process. It is an old process, dating almost from the beginnings of photography. A glass plate was covered with soot or dark varnish and allowed to dry, then etched with a needle. This glass plate negative was contact printed to silver gelatin paper and resulted in a photographic drawing on paper.

Where the varnish was scratched completely off with the needle it would print black, and where it was scratched off only slightly it would print in gray tones depending on how much varnish was removed with the scratching. All of a sudden you have the possibility of black, white, and a multitude of gray tones in between.

Today we don't need to use messy soot or smelly varnish. A can of black spray paint, or acrylic paint, India ink, fogged film, markers on plastic, acetate, paper, polyester, Mylar, even an exposed black piece of RC paper can all achieve similar effects.

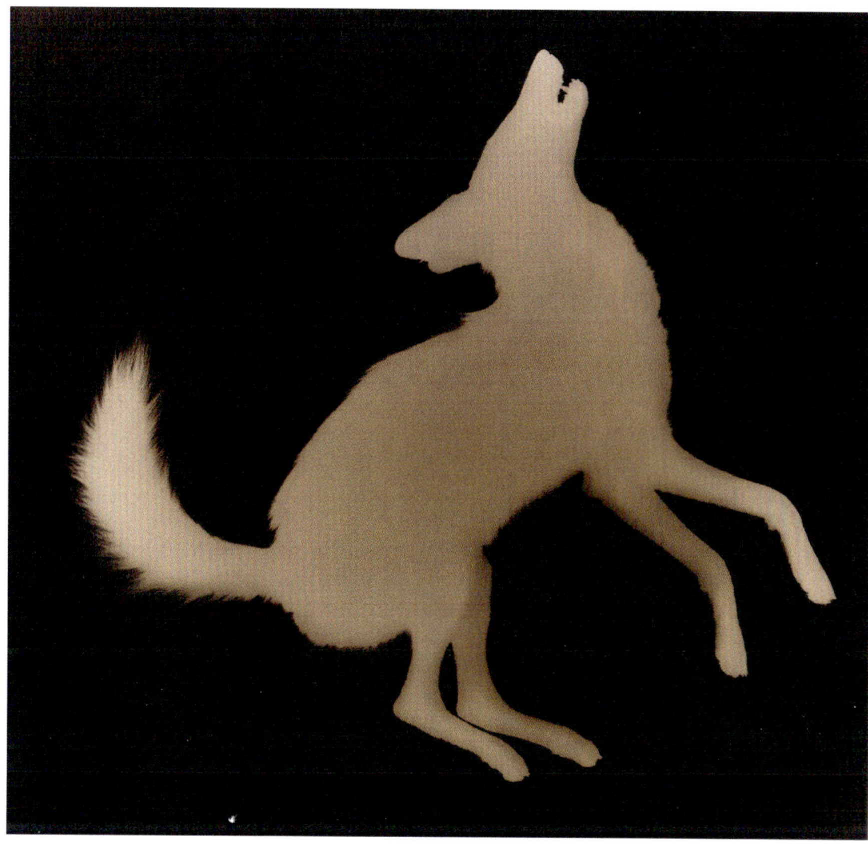

Figure 3.9. *Coyote*, from the series *Las Sombras/The Shadows*, 40″ x 40″ © Kate Breakey 2005. "The images in this series are 'contact prints' of living things—plants, insects and birds. Their imprint, a ghostly shadow, is burned directly onto paper with light to make a permanent record, the only document of their brief existence here on this earth. The series ranges from the tiniest of creatures—scorpions and beetles, bats and mice, to larger mammals, coyote and deer, a bald eagle and everything in between, snakes and birds, possum and rabbits—several hundred individual plants and creatures in all made over a 10 year period." To see more of Breakey's work visit www.katebreakey.com.

Making a cliché verre

1. Cover some form of plastic or glass base with various opacities of substances.
2. Use tools such as these to scratch into the opaque substance:
   - Engraving tools
   - Dentist tools
   - Toothpicks
   - Xacto knives
   - Needles
3. Scratch gently and evenly if the cliché verre is going to be used as a negative so the marks don't look ragged when enlarged.
4. Use these substances to vary the density in a more fluid manner:
   - Water
   - Lysol
   - Fantastic cleaner
   - Formula 409
   - Mr. Clean
5. Expose the cliché verre to the silver gelatin paper and process the print as normal.

Endnotes

1. Davenport, Alma. *The History of Photography: An Overview*. Albuquerque: The University of New Mexico Press, 2000, p. 167.

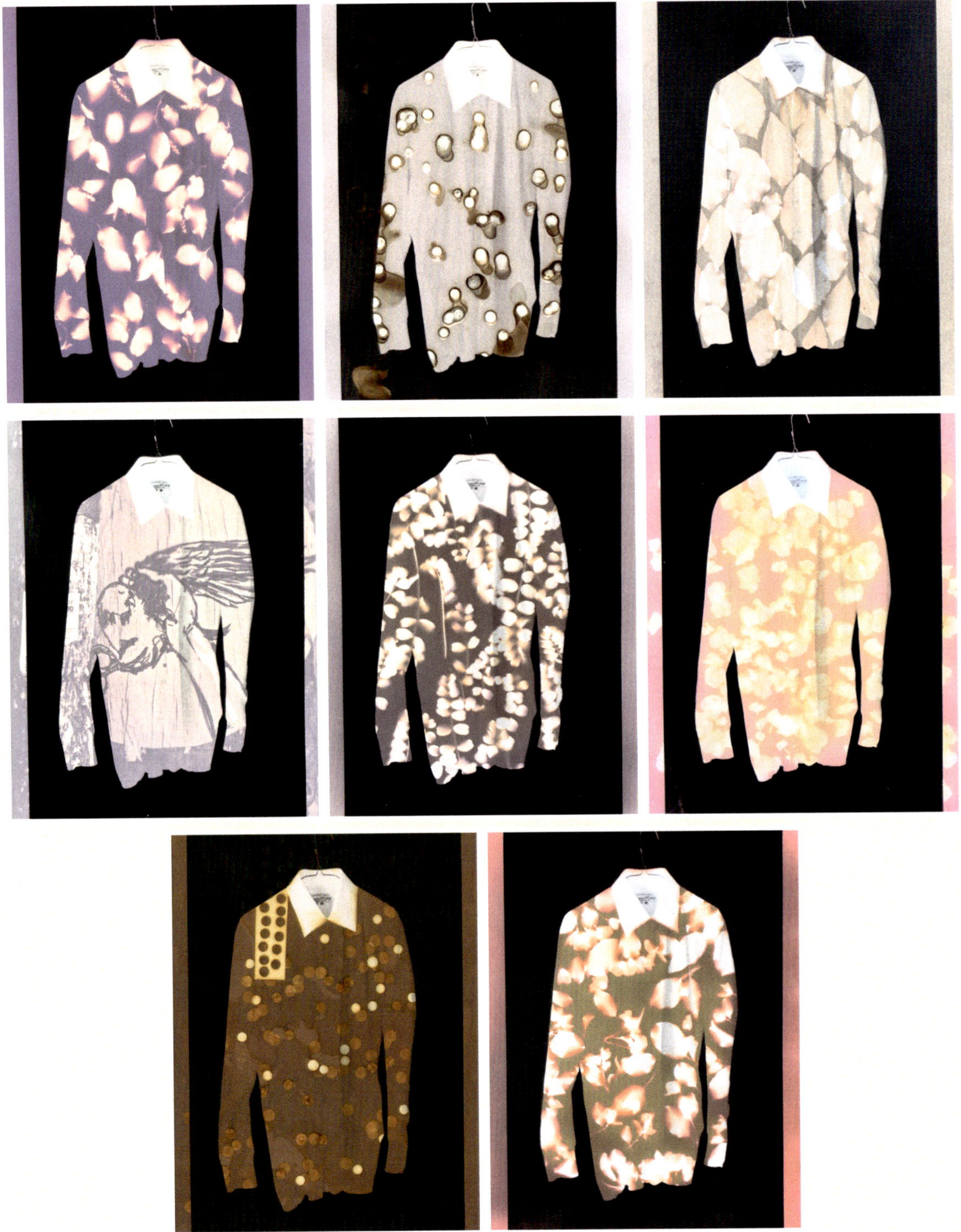

Figures 4.1-4.8. From top to bottom, left to right, *Sunday Shirt* on Fotokemika Emaks, *Friday Shirt* on Fotokemika Varycon, *Thursday Shirt* on vintage ILfobrom, *Tuesday Shirt* on Ilford Galerie, *Wednesday Shirt* on Fotokemika Varycon, *Another Sunday Shirt* on Forte Polywarmtone FB, *Monday Shirt* on Forte Polygrade FB, *Saturday Shirt* on Forte Polygrade, composites of a lumen print with a developed silver gelatin print © Tiina Kirik 2021. For directions see her work in the **Contemporary Experimental Artists** chapter.

Lumen Prints

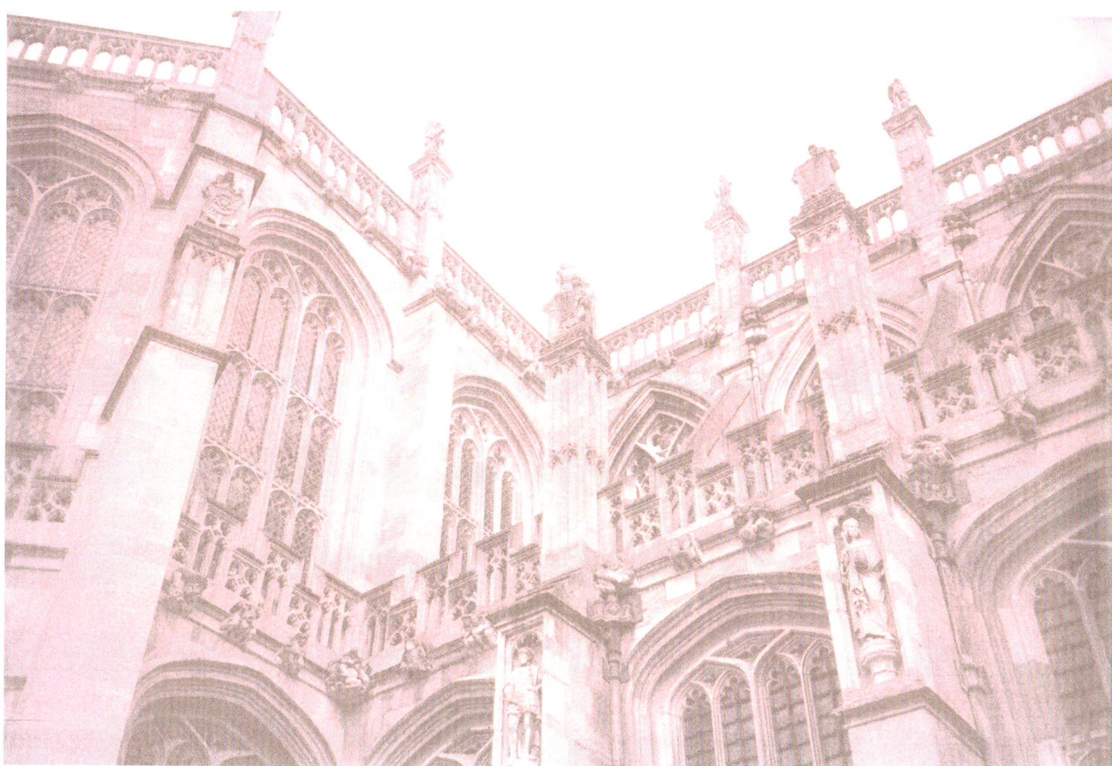

Figure 4.9. *St. George's Chapel*, lumen print on Ilford MGFB glossy paper, day long exposure under a QTR digital negative, 18.5″ x 13″ © Alyssa McKenna 2021. McKenna is a Colorado native completing her BA in Film and Photography at Montana State University. Her areas of photographic interest are alternative and experimental darkroom processes. To see more of her work follow her @alyssa_k.m and visit alyssamckenna.myportfolio.com

When silver gelatin paper is left out in light for long periods of time, it will turn various colors—yellow, pink, mauve, blue, purple, terracotta, peach, brown—a phenomenon most of us have witnessed over the years in darkroom trash cans. If the paper is fixed without developing first, the paper will stay colored. The master of this colored "printed out photogram"[1] who coined the term "lumen print" was Jerry Burchfield who made amazing photograms of Amazon flora under the hot South American sun. Jonathan Green states in the foreword to Burchfield's monograph, "...we have the accident, the gamble, the unexpected. This belief in the agency of chance and the uncontrollable visual discoveries of the photographic process derives both from the metaphorical photographers and from a third history that underwrites Burchfield's Amazon work: experimental work in alternative process and cameraless images."[2] Visual discovery is the primary reason to delve into this fascinating lumen print process. It is easy, and it is fun!

Lumen prints are technically so simple to do they don't require a chapter of explanation, though my research into the process may still be of benefit. Regular silver gelatin paper (or film) is exposed to sunlight for long periods of time, from twenty minutes to days depending on the weather, with various objects from translucent to opaque (or a negative) placed on top just as if one was doing a photogram (or a contact print) in the darkroom. When the paper color looks dark enough, the

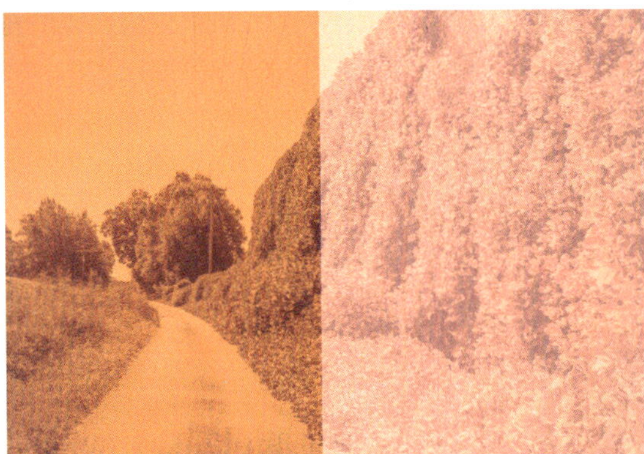

Figure 4.10. *Anderson Mill* © Christina Z. Anderson 2021, composite of two lumen prints on Ilford Warmtone. The left half was exposed all day under full sun, the right all day under cloudy bright conditions. The right side print is underexposed for my tastes, but for certain subjects a paler color works fine.

Figure 4.11. Four scans of the border of fixed Ilford Warmtone lumen prints. Each was exposed 8AM–5PM in conditions from cloudy to full sun. Note the color change from pink to terracotta to mauve to taupe gray, and also that at a certain point density reverses and solarizes on this paper with too much exposure. The pink border was from an underexposed print and the taupe gray from an overexposed print.

paper is fixed, washed, hypocleared, and archivally washed just like any silver gelatin print with one exception—the print never touches the developer.

Burchfield's exposures ranged from ½ hour to 5 hours[3] or longer, with one even as long as 94 days. When he felt the exposure was done, he put the print into a light tight box and fixed it when he returned to the United States. This illustrates that not only are lumen prints technically simple, they have amazing latitude in processing and handling. Even better, the lumen print process is perfectly suited for long-expired or fogged paper so not only is it easy and economical but also ecological.

Exposure time, intensity of light, humidity, moisture, chemistry and moisture from plants, choice of paper, age of paper, temperature, and added ingredients (lemon juice, baking soda, ascorbic acid, sodium carbonate, etc.) all affect the colors of the final print.

Err on the side of overexposure. Overexposure is rarely a problem with lumen prints. Underexposure is. All lumen prints experience major color shifts and lightening in fixer, and the most common problem is worrying that the exposure has gone on too long and then fixing too soon so that the image disappears to a pale yellow, gray, or brown. Think *hours* in full sun, depending on the opacity of the objects on top of the paper. Think *days* if it is cloudy.

Making a lumen print

1. Take a piece of silver gelatin paper out of its light tight black bag under safelight so the rest of the box of paper is not fogged. Once it is out of the packet it doesn't matter if that sheet is brought out into the light with no objects on it yet. Minimal light exposure will only produce the palest of colors when fixed. *Tip: save your light safe bags to transport silver gelatin paper to and from the darkroom; something as simple as a black garbage bag will also work.*
2. In pencil, label the back of the silver gelatin paper on one edge—paper name, RC or fiber, neutral or warmtone, paper surface, etc. *It is so important to do this!* You will find papers you love and papers that aren't so good, and five years from now you won't remember which ones worked well unless the paper has been labeled. Pencil is archival (don't use pen!).
3. Arrange the items of choice on top of the paper. It is especially good to have organics that are fresh and retain moisture because the moisture and chemistry affect color and design. Dip organics, if desired, in lemon juice, vinegar, diluted baking soda, etc. (see Phytograms, further for how certain substances react as "developers" to produce black on the lumen print). Moisture results in auras around objects.
4. If you want the objects to remain stationary put a piece of heavy plate glass on top. This might also be necessary if you have animals around and are using any sort of foodstuff. Be sure the plate glass is larger than the paper because the glass's edge will print an unpleasing line across the paper.

5. The longer the exposure outside, the more intense the color of the final print will be on most papers. Contrast is determined by how opaque the chosen objects are and exposure time. Winter exposures will take longer because the sun is weaker. Whereas in summer a full sun exposure from 10AM–4PM is plenty long, in winter this might translate to a couple days or more. The same for cloudy summer days; expect longer exposure times. Think in terms of UV light and sunburn; if you're not putting on sunscreen then the light output is low.

6. When the lumen print looks suitably exposed, take the paper out from under the glass and transport it back to the darkroom in a lightsafe bag.

7. In a separate tray of water wash off any substance on the paper to prevent contaminating the fixer if necessary. When the paper is rinsed well, transfer the lumen print to the fixer and fix just as if it were a normal print. You will notice an intense and immediate shift of colors in the fix. Don't panic. If the print has been exposed to enough light, the colors may shift from blues and purples to pinks, yellows and terracottas, for instance, but much of the density remains. The colors and density will shift again with drydown, darkening substantially—you can witness the drydown effect by sprinkling a dry lumen print with drops of water. There is an instant lightening of the colors underneath the water droplets, easily two stops of density. All of this is related to the Mie effect or light scattering (see the **Chromo** chapter for an explanation of the Mie effect).

It is said that using an alkaline versus an acid fix will minimize this drastic color shift and in my former books I have repeated this fallacy (never trust the literature without testing it for yourself!). Not only does an alkaline fix *not* minimize the drastic color shift, it actually often shifts a color duller and browner and a few papers lose their wonderful pinks. Any regular darkroom rapid (acid) fixer is just fine! *Tip: if desired, scan the unfixed lumen print just before fixing to preserve the unfixed colors for a digital print.*

8. Rinse, hypoclear, wash, and dry as per normal.

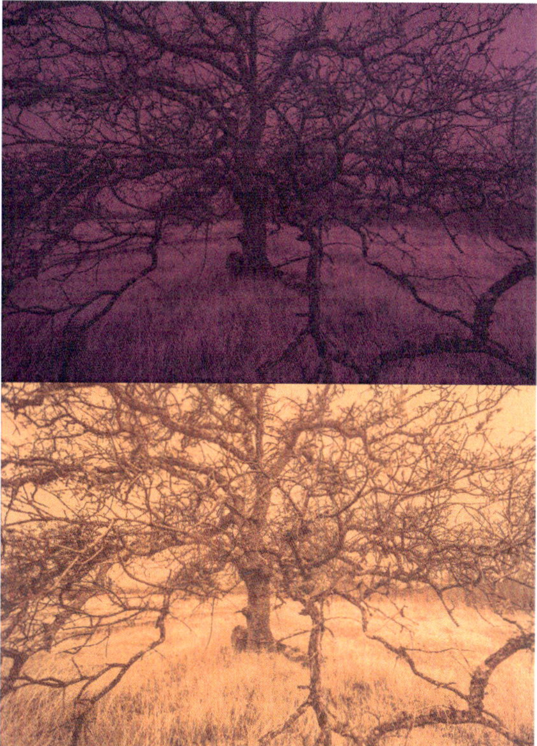

Figure 4.12. *Hooker Oak* © Christina Z. Anderson 2021. Note the color shift that occurs when fixing Ilford Warmtone.

Figure 4.13. A surprising difference between alkaline (left, pH 8) and acid fix (right, pH 6) on the same piece of paper, exposed at the same time. Acid fixing leans redder in color on certain papers. There is no reason to use anything but regular darkroom fix on lumen prints.

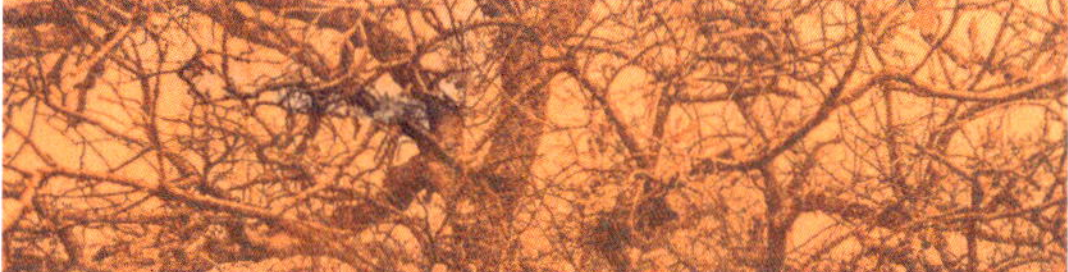

Figure 4.14. Note the black spot on the lumen print which sometimes happens during the water wash when an upside-down print rests touching the bottom of a tray. While washing agitate every once in a while and make sure the print is suspended in the water wash, not touching anything.

Figure 4.15. From left to right: untoned, gold toned, and selenium toned Ilford Warmtone.

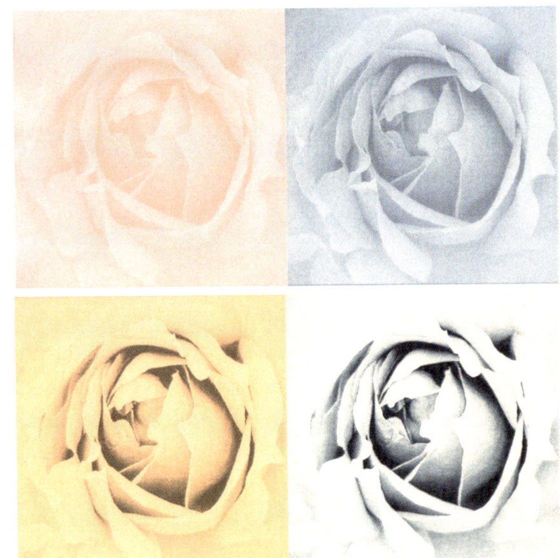

Figure 4.16. Top, Kentmere Bromide untoned and gold toned; bottom, Luminos Charcoal R untoned and gold toned. Gold toning adds density and is a way to turn a lumen print blue.

Toning

You can tone lumen prints just as any silver gelatin paper. See the **Toning** chapter for formulas. In my experience, I am not a fan of selenium toning of lumen prints because silver selenide is somewhat transparent and what it does to a lumen print is turn it a pale brown (Figure 4.15). I am also not a fan of sepia because it lightens the print considerably and does not produce a color better than the original lumen print itself. It is possible to gold-after-sepia for a peachy orange color, but again there is so much lightening of the print in the sepia step that it is probably only useful if the print is too dark to begin with, which is rare. If you are going to use selenium or sepia, use a weak dilution and very brief toning to avoid image fading as much as possible. Have a water tray ready to go so you can halt the toning action quickly.

Gold toning by itself works very well, though. Gold will tone from plum to gray-blue depending on the length of time in the toner (Figure 4.16).

Tips and ideas

- You can expose lumen prints under UVBL if outdoor exposure is not an option. Note that Leanne McPhee in Chapter 2 only exposes for ~10 minutes. When I have used UVBL, even 4 hours is not excessive, so I don't recommend UVBL because it's a waste of power when even cloudy exposure does a quicker (and free) job. However, in some climates UVBL may be your only choice. A benefit is not much heat is produced as is with a contact frame facing the hot summer sun.
- Warmtone papers result in warmer tones such as yellow, peach, brilliant pink and terracotta. Coldtone papers can be more neutral, pink to taupe brown, pink to deep lavender, or pale yellow to gray. Warmtone papers in general are more colorful.

Figure 4.17. These two fixed step wedge prints were both exposed on Ilford Warmtone under full sun (top) and UVBL (bottom) for four hours. The difference in color is attributable to more intense exposure (top) and less intense exposure (bottom). Ilford Warmtone goes from peaches and purples to terracottas with longer exposure.

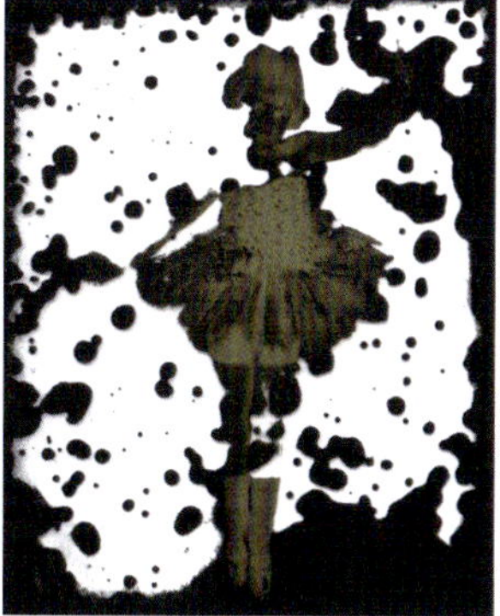

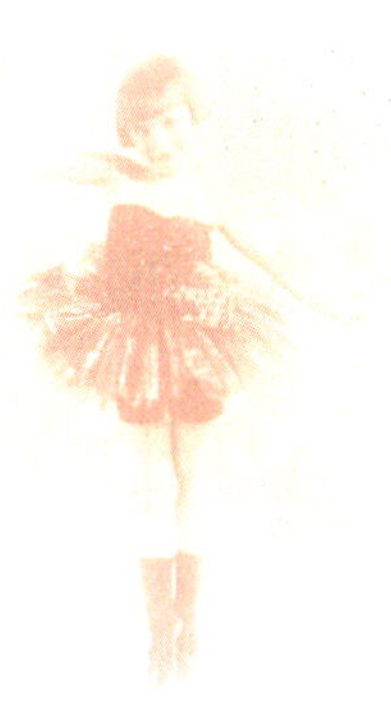

Figure 4.18. *Granny LaJean*, all day exposure of a digital negative on Ars Imago paper © Christina Z. Anderson 2021. When I pulled the negative off of the paper, half the ink stuck to the glossy paper surface. It did rub off in the water wash but the negative was ruined. In hot and humid conditions and with some smooth, glossy papers, use Dura-lar .003 mil polyester sheets between the digital negative and the paper.

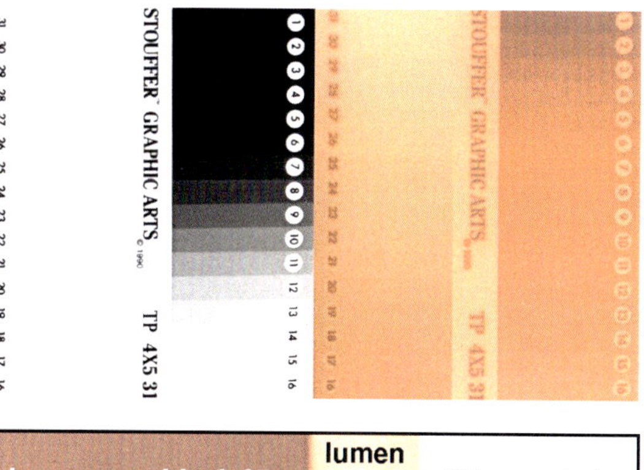

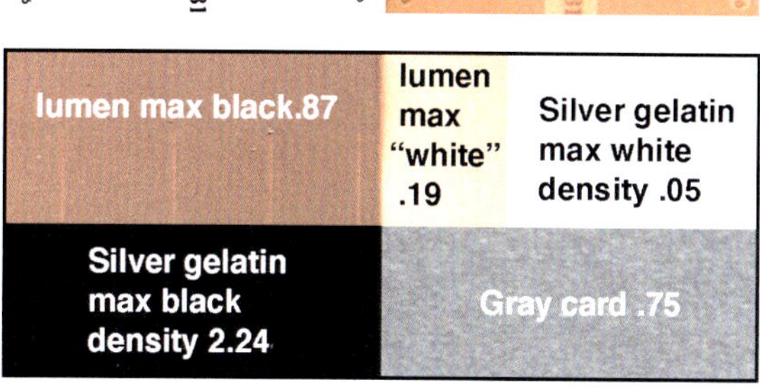

Figures 4.19–4.20. Top, a step wedge on Ilford warmtone paper developed out, side by side with the same paper as a lumen print. Bottom, comparison of a lumen print darkest dark and lightest light (max black and max white) on Bergger VCCM paper compared to a silver gelatin max black and paper white. The maximum density of the lumen print (.87 vs 2.24 on a densitometer) is much lighter than a developed silver gelatin print and the maximum white of a lumen print (.19 vs .05 on a densitometer) is darker than a fixed silver gelatin print. The perceived contrast of a lumen print and its intriguing color palette still works, but it will never have the density range of a traditional silver gelatin print.

Digital negatives and lumen printing

In the past I have attempted to print lumen prints with digital negatives and produced somewhat successful albeit low contrast results. The negative wasn't dense enough. It wasn't until I learned all things QTR which has the ability to control individual inks that only using the densest inks in a digital negative became possible. The negative substrate is not flooded with nonperforming inks when increasing negative density.

The lumen process benefits from a very dense but also contrasty negative. With enough of the exposure-blocking inks used, the necessary adjustment curve is almost straight line, enough so that you could probably get away without using a curve at all in the profile. See the **Digital Negatives** chapter for the lumen print QTR profile.

Keep in mind that the contrast of a lumen print will always be different than that of a normally developed out silver gelatin print. The deepest dark of a lumen print (maximum "black") will never be as dark as the black of a silver gelatin print (see Figures 4.19–4.20) because the print is not run through a developer. The darkest dark is equivalent to a deep gray. Highlights will never be as white as the white of a silver gelatin print either, but some form of pale color. Contrast is always perceived relative to its surroundings, though, and the digital negative works. An accurately prepared digital negative opens up new avenues of exploration for the lumen process, no longer centered upon photogram practice as has generally been the case.

Note that with some silver gelatin papers, like a glossy RC, the digital negative will stick to the paper with long, warm, sun exposures, especially in climates where humidity is higher. In that case use Dura-Lar thin, clear, polyester sheets in-between the negative and the paper to prevent this from happening. Dura-Lar or its equivalent is readily available from craft stores or Amazon.com. I have only had this problem on a few papers, and rarely on a fiber based paper. If it happens, the negative is ruined but the ink stuck to the silver gelatin paper is easily rubbed off in a water wash before the fix.

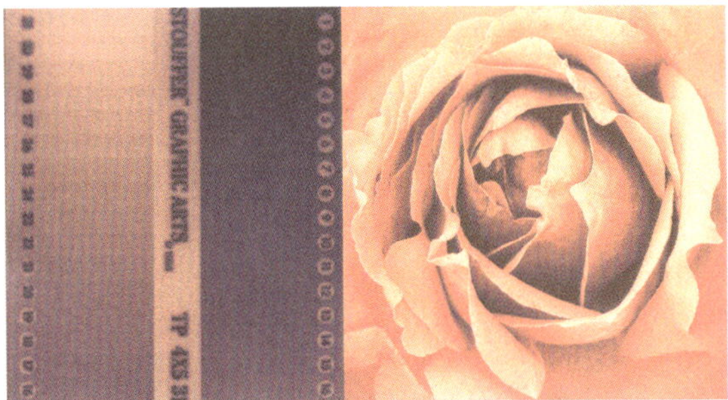

Figure 4.21. Fotokemika Emaks step wedge in comparison to a print on the same paper. Note how the dominant purple of the step wedge is only dominant in the shadows of the rose and the highlight peaches and yellows predominate.

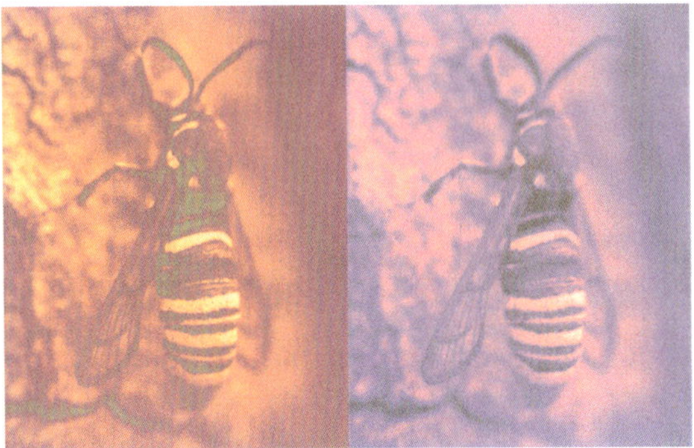

Figures 4.22–4.23. *Lunar Hornet Moth*, left, Ilford Galerie FB paper exposed over 2 cloudy days; right, Arista FB paper exposed to 10 hours of sun, 8″ x 10″ © Dani Hatfield 2021

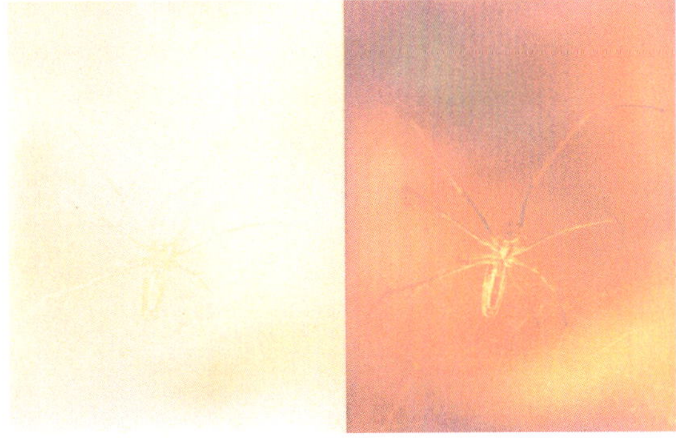

Figures 4.24–4.25. *Orb Weave Spider*, left, Kodak Polymax FD exposed to 10.5 hours of sun, right, Ilford Galerie exposed over 2 cloudy days, 8″ x 10″ © Dani Hatfield 2021

Lumen print step wedges

Following are a sampling from over 100 papers tested. Each was exposed outside for a day of sun March through September (10:00AM–4:00PM more or less) under a Stouffer 4″ × 5″ step wedge. Each step wedge print was then scanned before fixing (left) and after fixing (right) to illustrate the color shift that occurs with fixing. *I always fix my lumen prints.*

If the paper resulted in distinct steps from deepest darks to highest highlights without solarizing, it could handle lots of exposure. Some papers solarized at the dark end of the spectrum during that amount of time (Ilford Warmtone), which indicated less exposure could be used. Some papers produced bland, pale, mushy colors even with days of exposure so they did not make the favorites list, though results certainly may vary as nothing about lumen printing is cut in stone.

One discovery I made is that the resulting color of the step wedge may predict the general color "palette" of a lumen print on that paper, but when using digital negatives designed for lumen printing, much more of the highlight colors predominate than they do on the step wedge. This is because a digital negative is denser than the Stouffer film step wedge (a DR of 4.0 versus a Stouffer DR of 3.05 in photo geek speak) so the highlight part of the step wedge often predominates. Before judging a paper based on the step wedge alone, make an actual print. You can see this by comparing the following step wedge prints with the rose prints thereafter.

Favorite papers

- Adox Lupex
- Agfa BW 119 DW Glossy
- Agfa Luster RRS 119 3
- Agfa Record Rapid RRH 111 5 DW Glossy
- Agfa Record Rapid RRH 119 5 Lustre
- Arista Ultra VCFB Glossy
- Ars Imago
- Bergger Brom-240
- Bergger Fine Art Silver Supreme N

- Bergger VCCB and VCCM Warmtone
- Chicago Albumen Works New Centennial
- David Lewis Fine Art Bromoil
- Foma Retrobrom SP 151 and 152
- Fomabrom N111 Normal Glossy
- Fomatone MG Classic Warmtone 131
- Forte Polywarmtone FB Plus
- Fotokemika Emaks K888-3 DW Glossy G3
- Fotokemika Varycon
- Fotospeed Lith FB DW Semi-Matte
- Ilfobrom Galerie FB
- Ilford MG Art 300 FB Textured Matte
- Ilford MGFB Warmtone
- Ilford MGIV FB Glossy and Matte
- Ilford SP921P
- Kodak Elite Fine Art S3P/S4P
- Kodak Panalure II RC
- Luminos Classic Charcoal R FB
- Maco
- Oriental Seagull G2, G4 and G5 Bromide
- Oriental Seagull Portrait RP-R Warmtone
- Oriental Seagull VCFB II Warmtone
- Zone VI Brilliant VCII DW Glossy

Not so favorite papers

- Afga Brovira BN and BS 111-3
- Bergger Prestige VNB Neutral
- Ilford MG Cooltone FB
- Kenthene RC graded papers
- Kentmere VC Select
- Kodak Polymax RC papers
- Luminos Photo Linen
- Mitsubishi Gekko
- Oriental VC-RP II Glossy RC
- Tura VC-Plus RC
- Varydot RC

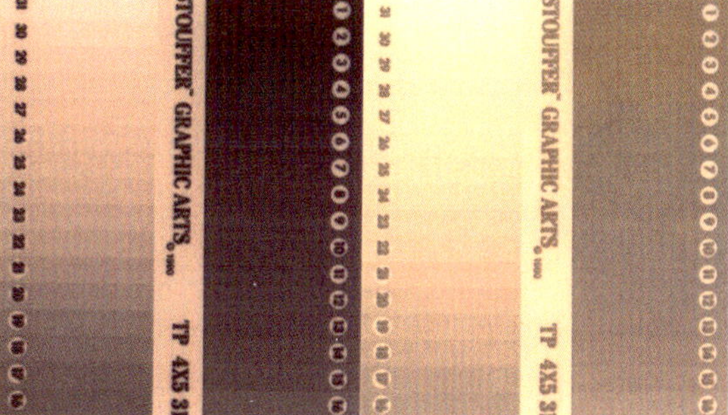

Adox Lupex. Distinct steps, caramel terracotta to yellow to pale cream, silver chloride paper.

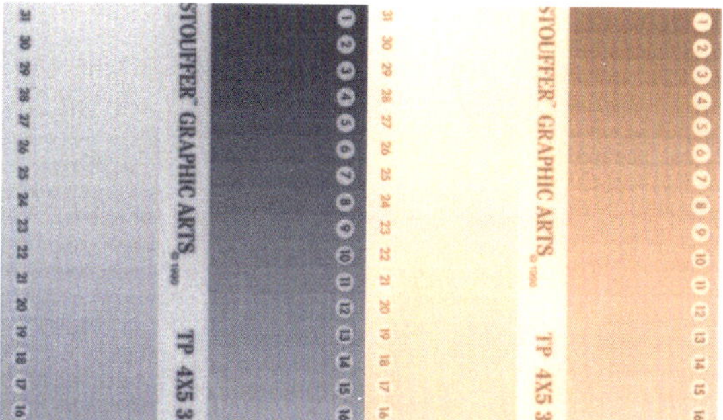

Agfa Brovira 119 DW Glossy. Unique woven texture, brick to cream, distinct steps, medium speed with excellent contrast.

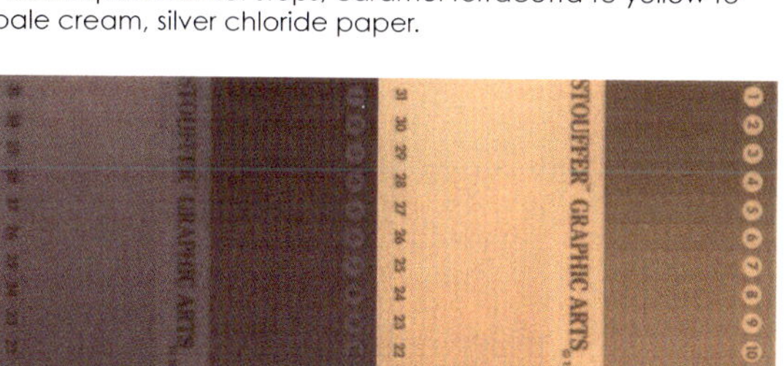

Agfa Luster RRS 119-3. Very warm brown to peach to yellow with various shades more yellow.

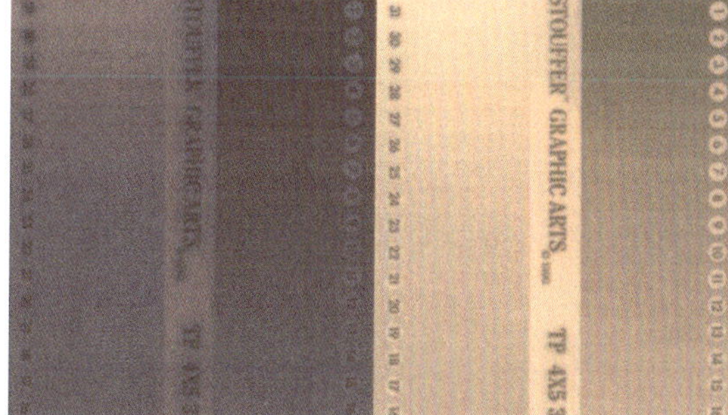

Agfa Record Rapid RRH 111-5 Glossy. Yellow to mauve to warm taupe, excellent contrast, didn't block up.

Figures 4.26–4.53. Here and on the next three pages are some excellent paper choices, scanned before and after fixing. "Don't fear the fix!" Tiina Kirik quips. Fixing makes a lumen print archival. You can scan an unfixed lumen and print it digitally, but I much prefer a "purist" approach which is to treat a lumen print as an archival silver gelatin print, which it is.

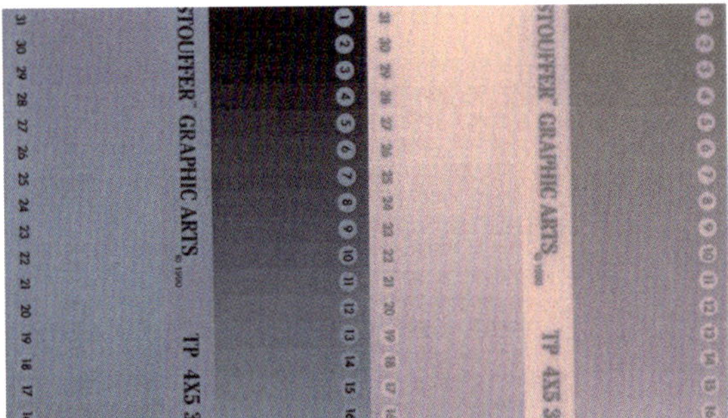

Arista Ultra FB Glossy. Cream to peach to pink to bright lavender to taupe. Fast, steps not so distinct.

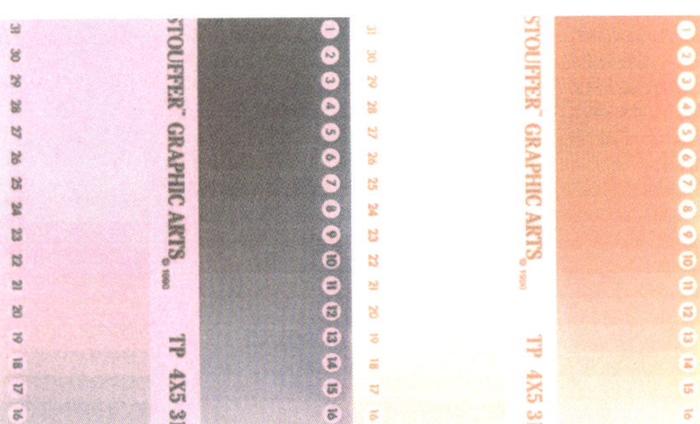

Ars Imago. Shimmery polyester base, hot pink is ortho coating, beautiful, distinct, bright peach steps, on slow side.

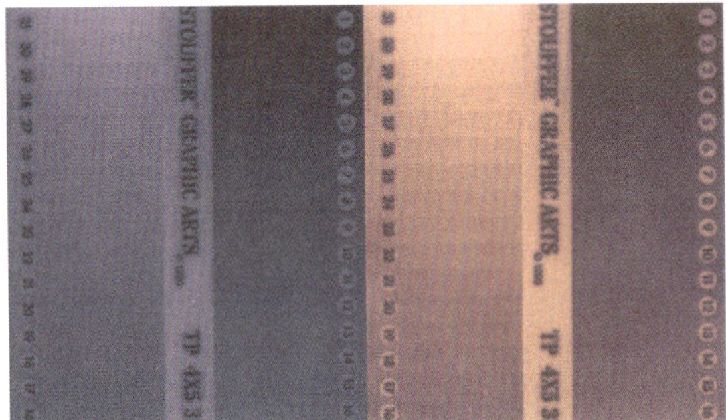

Bergger Brom-240. Lovely pinks and mauves, similar to David Lewis' Bromoil. Also Dmax is nicely dark.

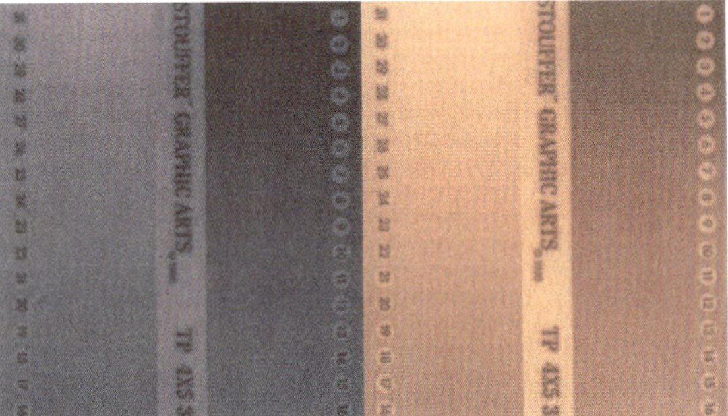

Bergger Fine Art Silver Supreme. Textured art paper surface similar to Ilford MG Art but colors more yellow to pale peach to deep roses and mauves to taupey brown.

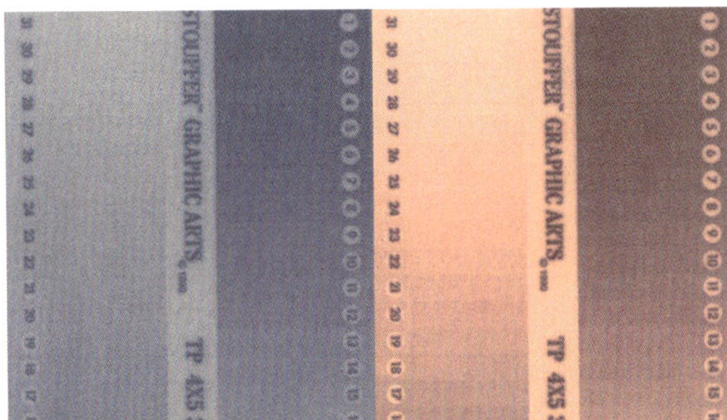

Bergger VCCM. Peach to rose to lavender taupe. Matte surface good for handcoloring. **Responds differently to acid and alkaline fixes; use acid fixes like Sprint**.

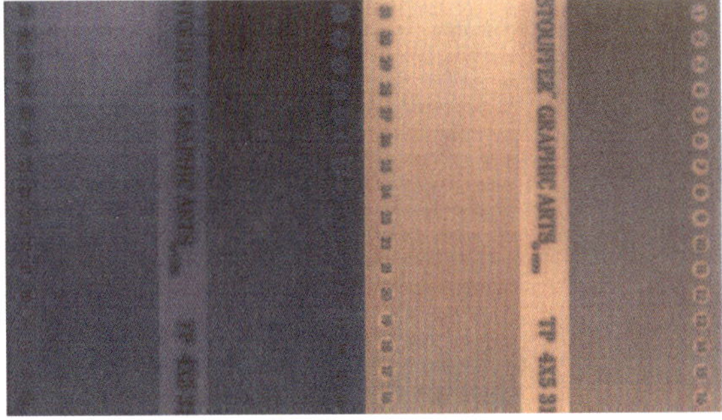

David Lewis Bromoil. Cantaloupe to orange to lavender gray, gets quite dark, fast, semi-matte surface, brilliant colors.

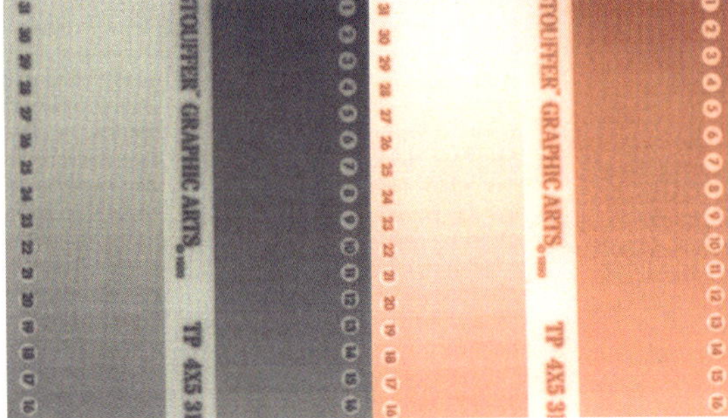

Foma Retrobrom SP151. Beautiful rosy peaches and creamy yellows. Favorite next to Forte.

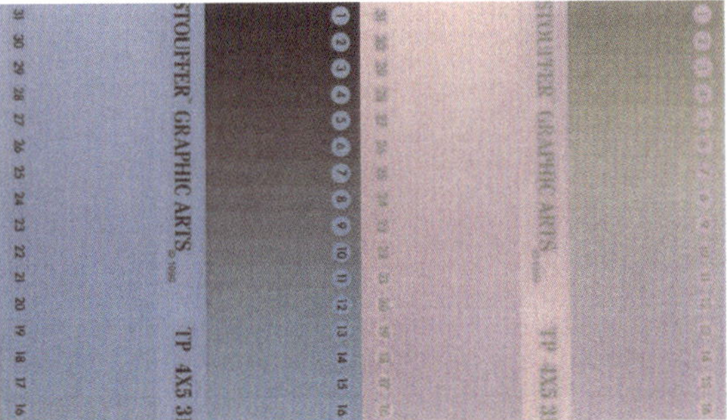

Fomabrom 111. Cantaloupe to pink to greenish taupe. Fast, silver chlorobromide.

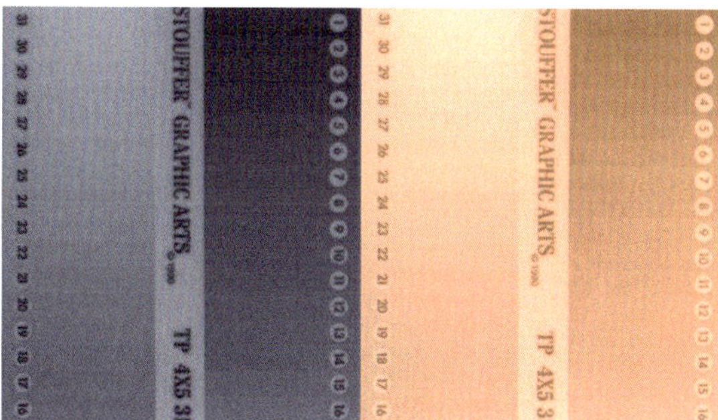

Foma Fomatone VC FB glossy. Way different than other two Foma papers. Evenly bright peach to terracotta.

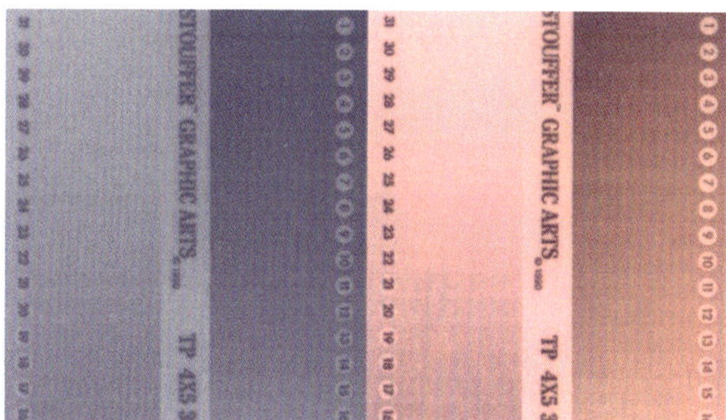

Forte Polywarmtone Elegance. Bright pinks or purples depending on fix; **use acid fix**. Watch uneven fixing/splotching.

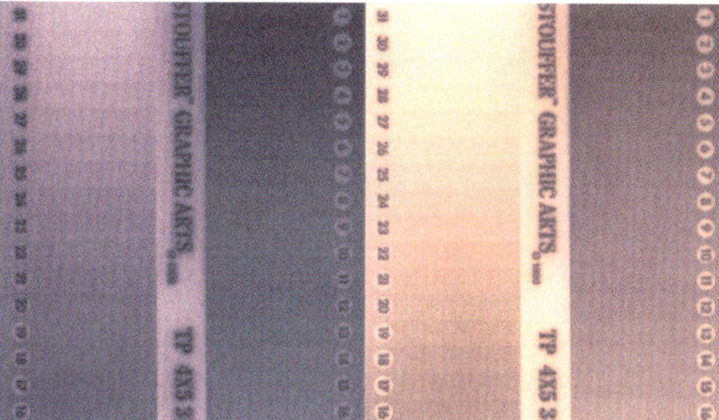

Fotokemika Emaks. Similar to Forte and Bergger, blue mauves to yellows, softer contrast and colors, **fix in acid fix**.

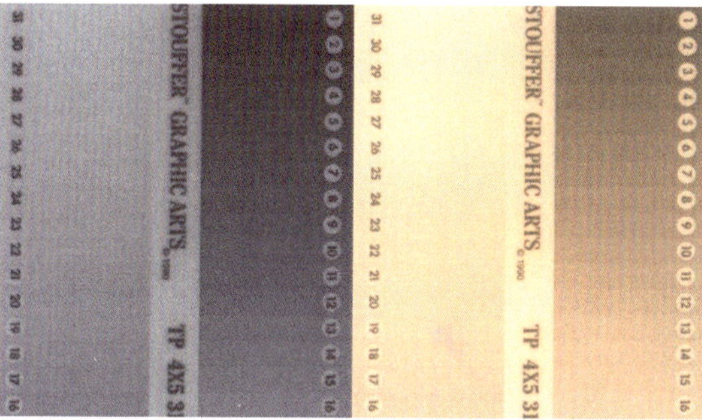

Fotospeed Lith FB DW Semi-matte. Caramel brown to peach to cream yellow, consistent color with no shifts. Slow.

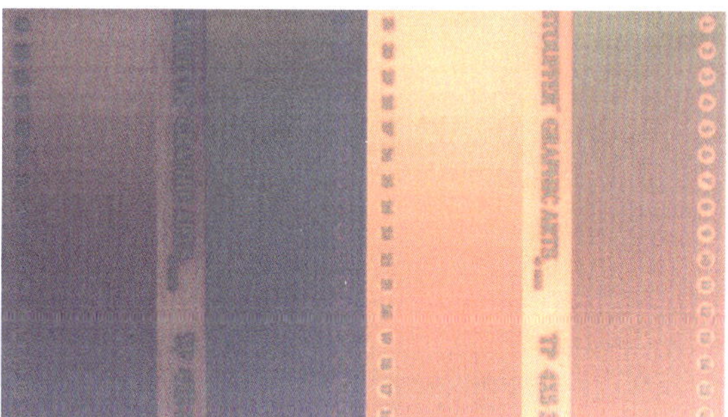

Ilfobrom Galerie G2 Glossy. Galerie is luscious, brilliant cantaloupes and mauves like MG Art.

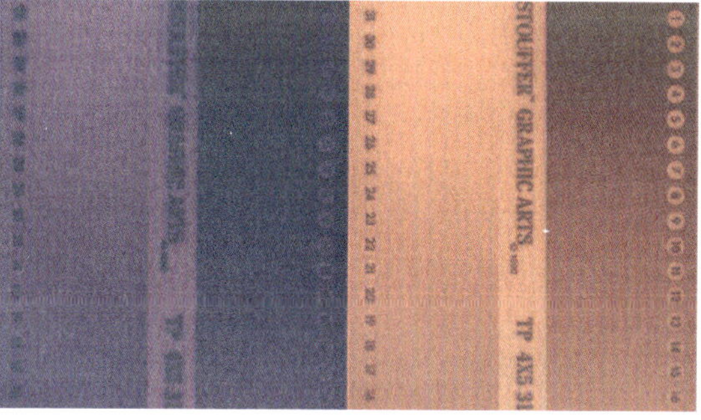

Ilford MG Art. Bright cantaloupe to ruby orange-pinks to deep rose. Excellent art texture. Solarizes with overexposure.

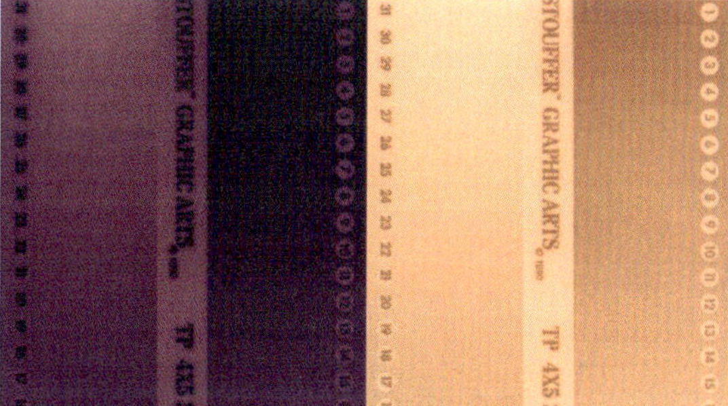

Ilford Warmtone Glossy. Brilliant yellows, oranges, deep terracotta. Saturated color. Fast to expose. Solarizes in darks.

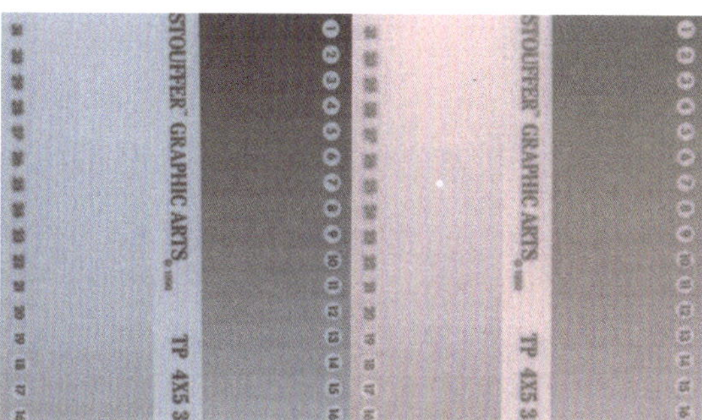

Ilford MGIV FB glossy. Matte and glossy similar pinks to purples to grays, also similar to Arista.

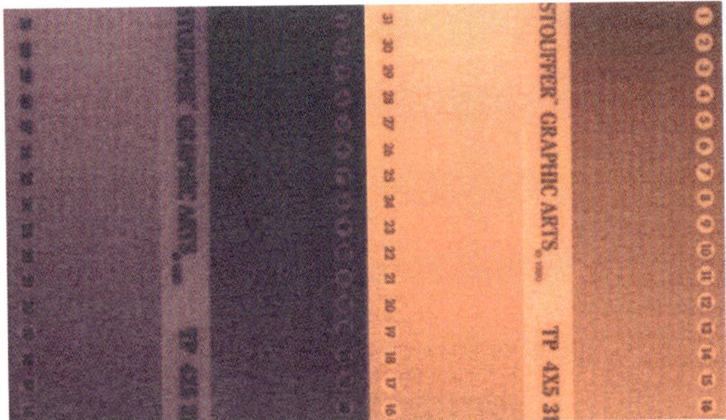

Ilford SP921P. I think this was a precursor to Ilford MG Art because it performs the same and has that beautiful texture.

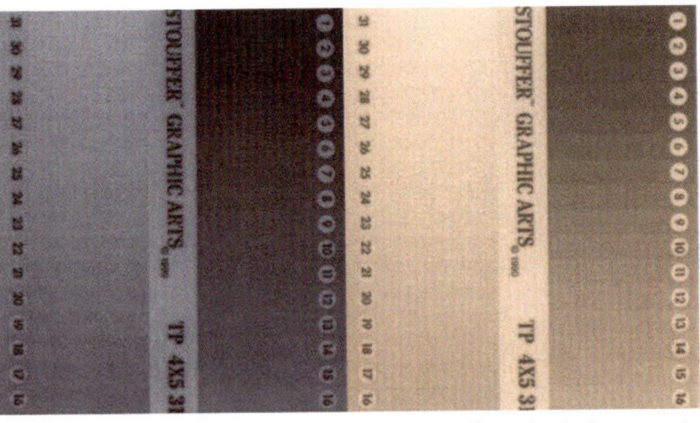

Kodak Elite S3. Beautiful browns, nicely delineated steps and retro color palette. Step wedge does not show the beauty of the paper. Thickest paper I've worked with, too.

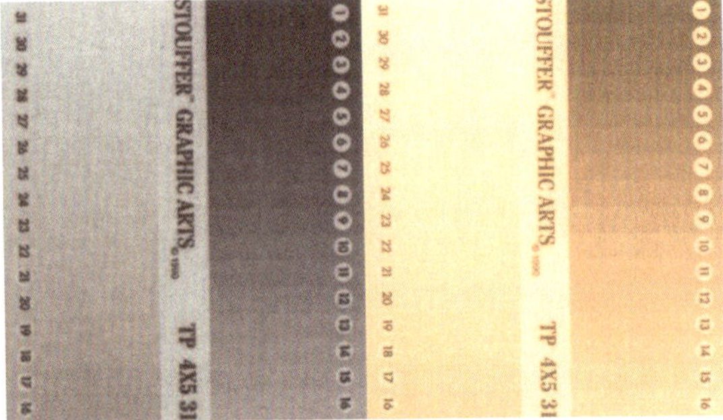

Luminos Charcoal R Warmtone. Textured art paper with more muted warm colors from pale yellow to brown. Slow.

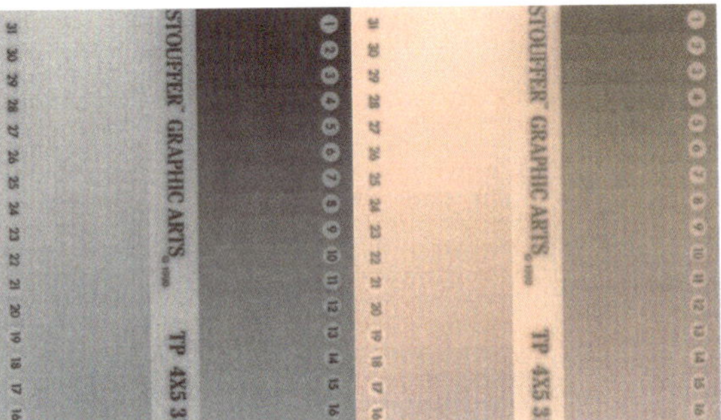

Maco. Greenish gray to lavender pink to peach pink, nice contrast and delineation of steps.

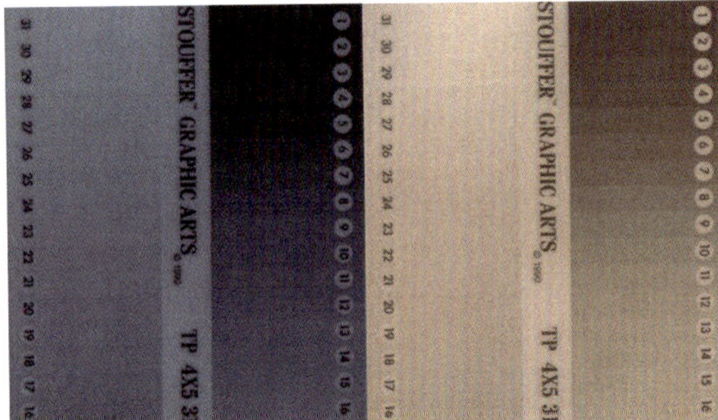

Oriental Seagull G5 Bromide. Beautiful creamed coffee colors and darks get dark.

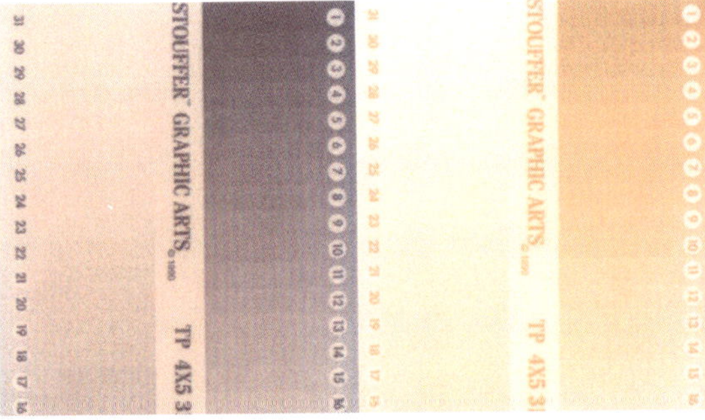

Oriental Seagull Portrait Warmtone Medium Contrast. Delicate, pale yellow peaches, good for certain subject matter.

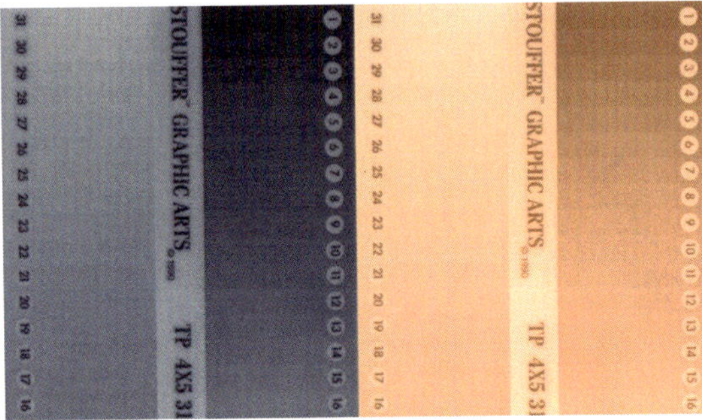

Oriental Seagull VC FB Warmtone. Nice even terracotta colors from peach to brown.

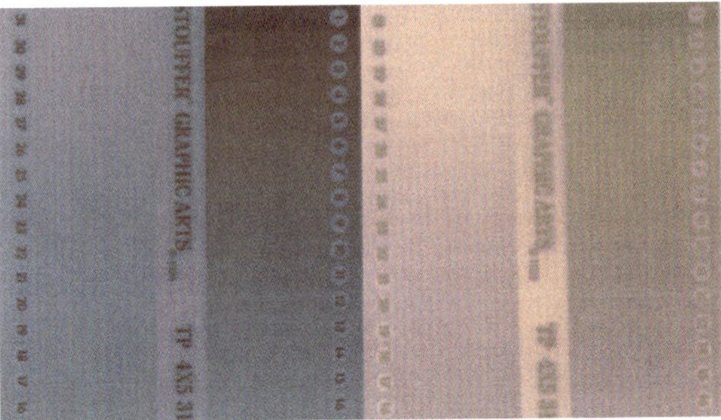

Zone VI Brilliant VCII DW Glossy. Muted lavenders and pinks; midtone lavenders flatten and almost reverse for an intriguing look.

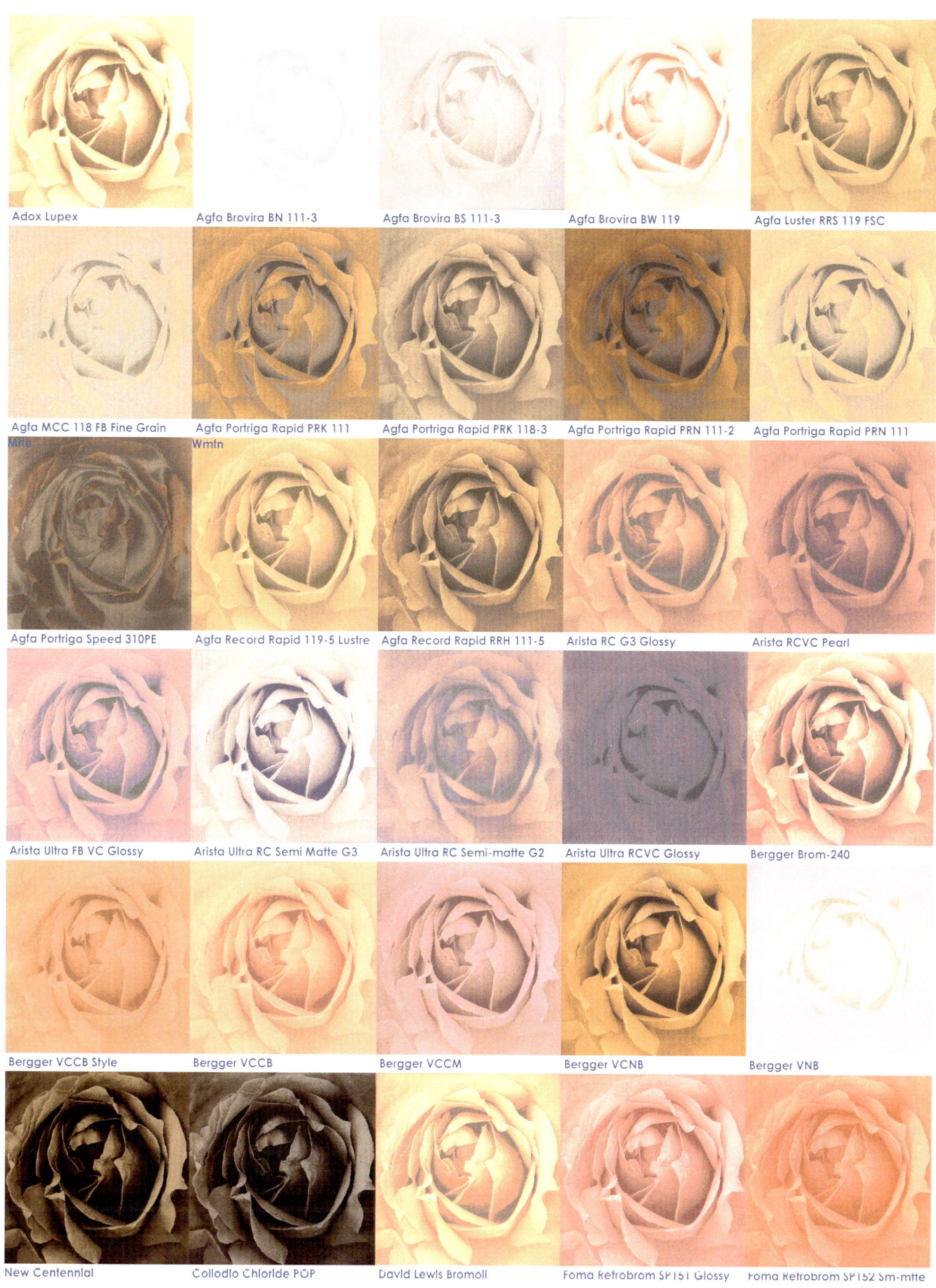
Adox Lupex
Agfa Brovira BN 111-3
Agfa Brovira BS 111-3
Agfa Brovira BW 119
Agfa Luster RRS 119 FSC
Agfa MCC 118 FB Fine Grain
Mtte
Agfa Portriga Rapid PRK 111
Wmtn
Agfa Portriga Rapid PRK 118-3
Agfa Portriga Rapid PRN 111-2
Agfa Portriga Rapid PRN 111
Agfa Portriga Speed 310PE
Agfa Record Rapid 119-5 Lustre
Agfa Record Rapid RRH 111-5
Arista RC G3 Glossy
Arista RCVC Pearl
Arista Ultra FB VC Glossy
Arista Ultra RC Semi Matte G3
Arista Ultra RC Semi-matte G2
Arista Ultra RCVC Glossy
Bergger Brom-240
Bergger VCCB Style
Bergger VCCB
Bergger VCCM
Bergger VCNB
Bergger VNB
New Centennial
Collodio Chloride POP
David Lewis Bromoil
Foma Retrobrom SP151 Glossy
Foma Retrobrom SP152 Sm-mtte

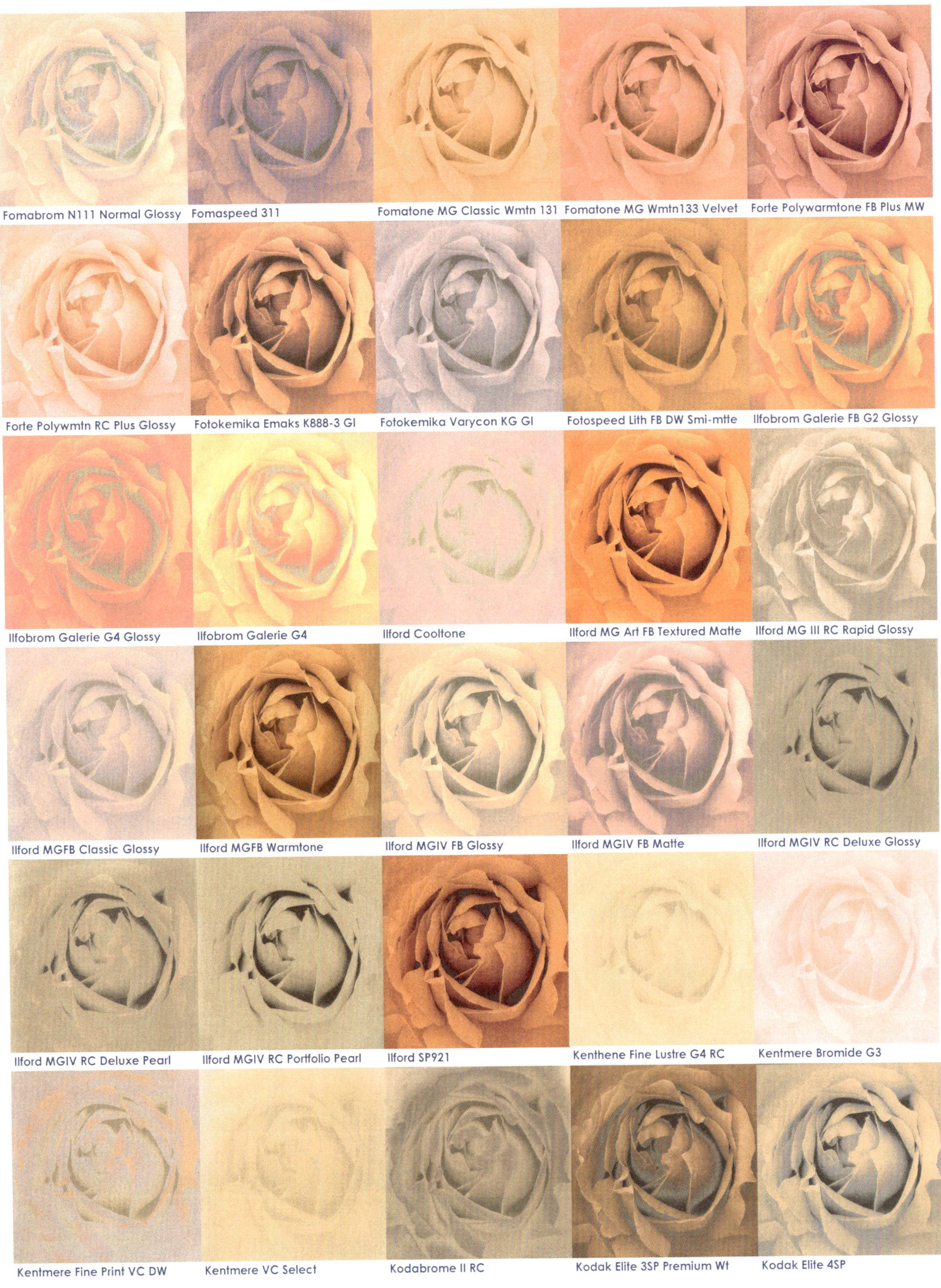
Fomabrom N111 Normal Glossy
Fomaspeed 311
Fomatone MG Classic Wmtn 131
Fomatone MG Wmtn133 Velvet
Forte Polywarmtone FB Plus MW
Forte Polywmtn RC Plus Glossy
Fotokemika Emaks K888-3 Gl
Fotokemika Varycon KG Gl
Fotospeed Lith FB DW Smi-mtte
Ilfobrom Galerie FB G2 Glossy
Ilfobrom Galerie G4 Glossy
Ilfobrom Galerie G4
Ilford Cooltone
Ilford MG Art FB Textured Matte
Ilford MG III RC Rapid Glossy
Ilford MGFB Classic Glossy
Ilford MGFB Warmtone
Ilford MGIV FB Glossy
Ilford MGIV FB Matte
Ilford MGIV RC Deluxe Glossy
Ilford MGIV RC Deluxe Pearl
Ilford MGIV RC Portfolio Pearl
Ilford SP921
Kenthene Fine Lustre G4 RC
Kentmere Bromide G3
Kentmere Fine Print VC DW
Kentmere VC Select
Kodabrome II RC
Kodak Elite 3SP Premium Wt
Kodak Elite 4SP

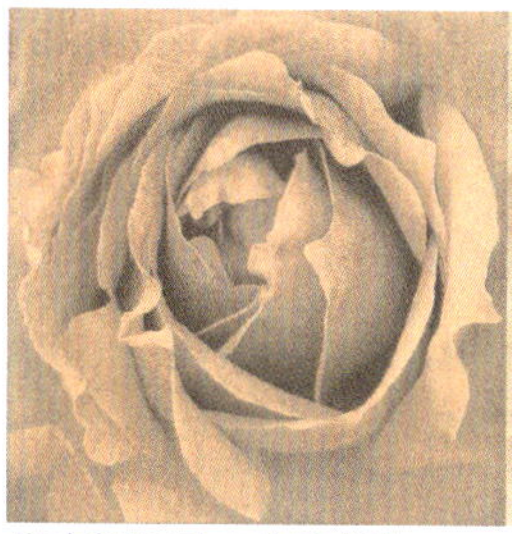

Kodak Panalure II RC F Glossy 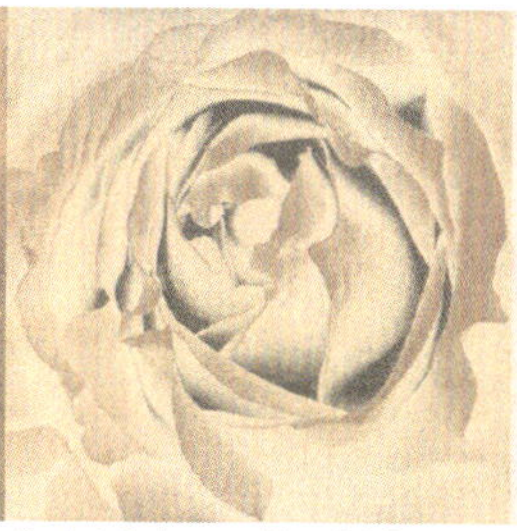 | Kodak Polymax Fine Art D 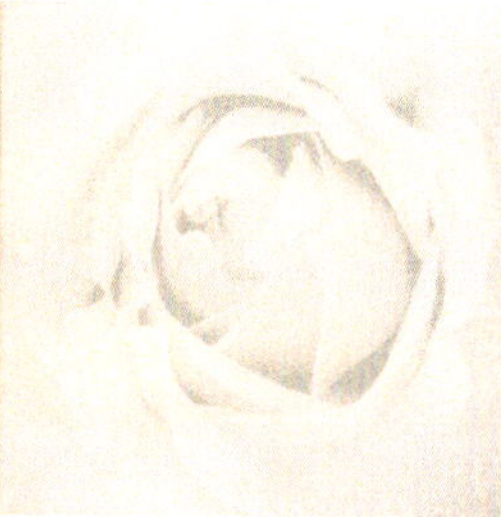 | Kodak Polymax 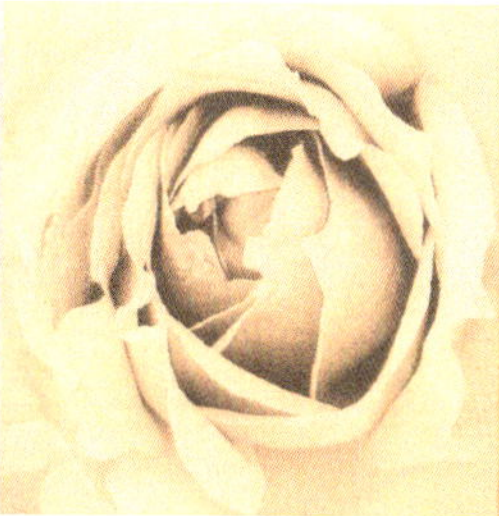 | Luminos Charcoal R Wmtn lt txtr 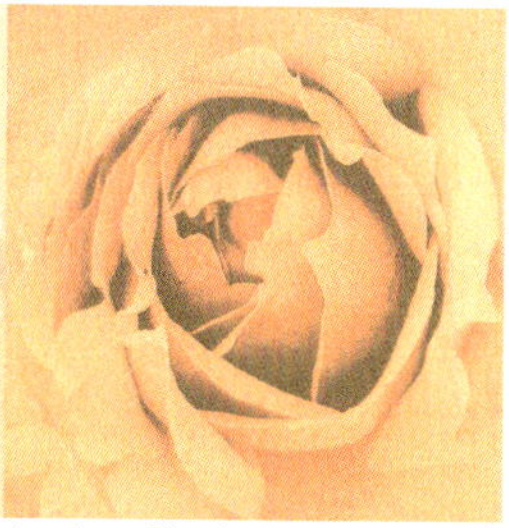 | Luminos Classic Charcoal R

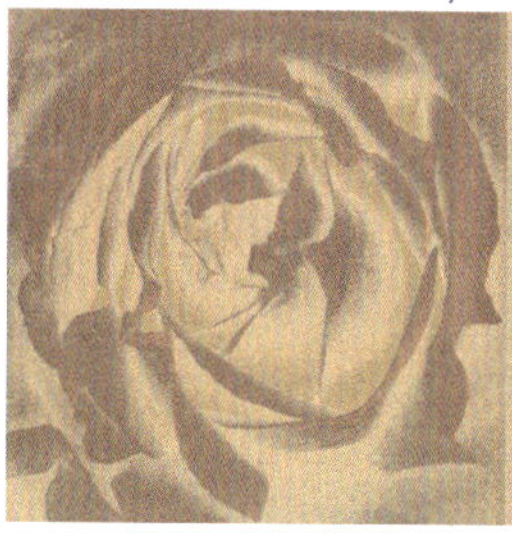

Luminos Flexicon VCRC SmMt 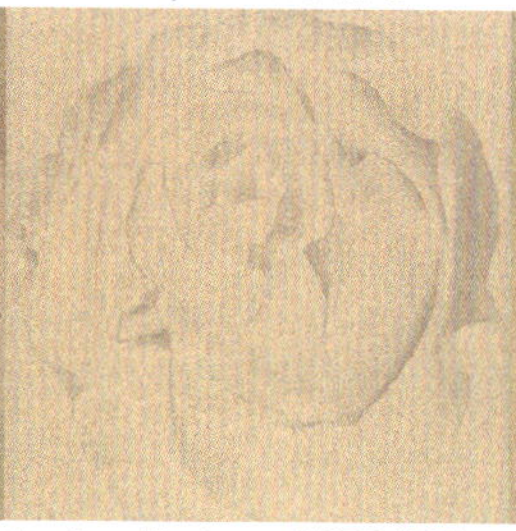 | Luminos Flexicoon VCRC VCF 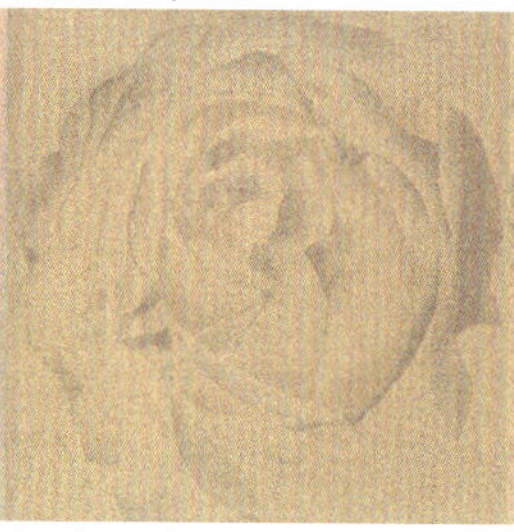 | Luminos RCR Rough G2 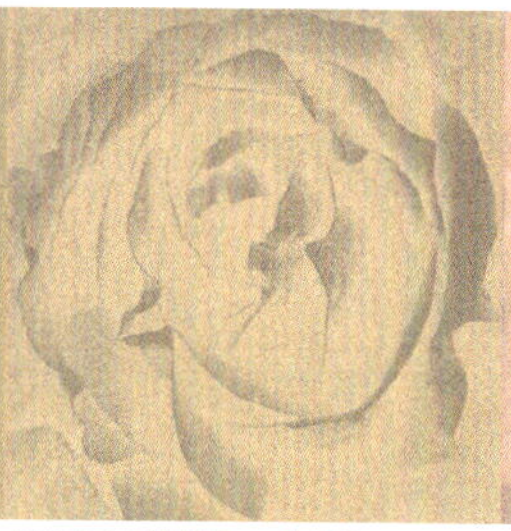 | Luminos RCR Rough G3 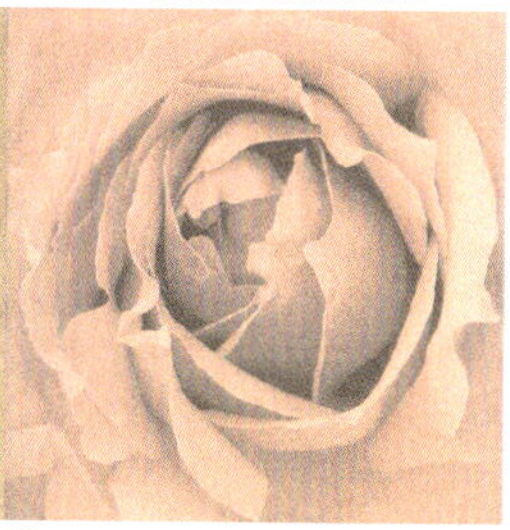 | Maco

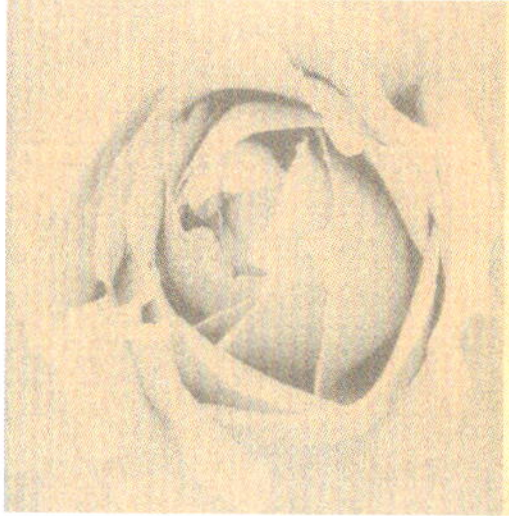

Mitsubishi Gekko Glossy RC 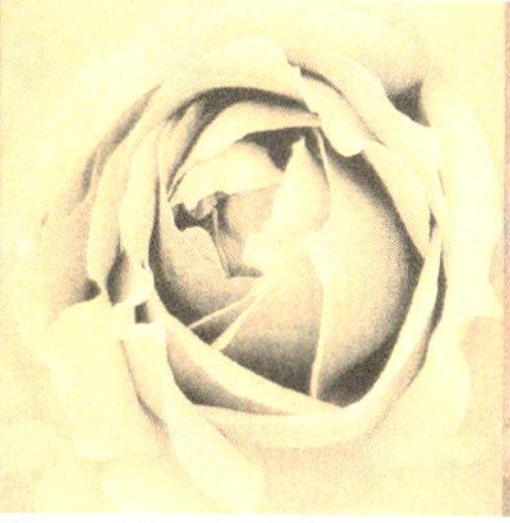 | Oriental Bromide G4 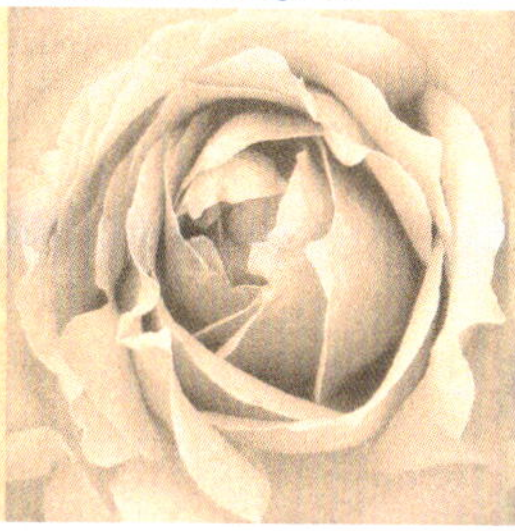 | Oriental Seagull Midgrd Wmtn 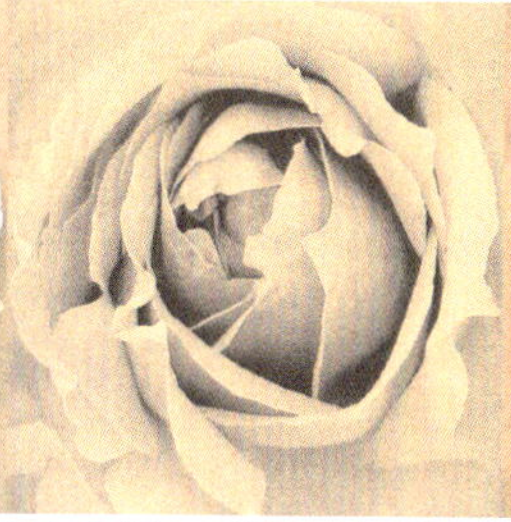 | Oriental Seagull Bromide G2 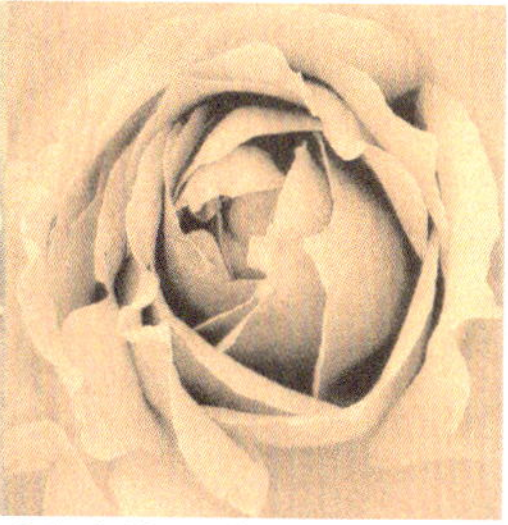 | Oriental Seagull Bromide G5

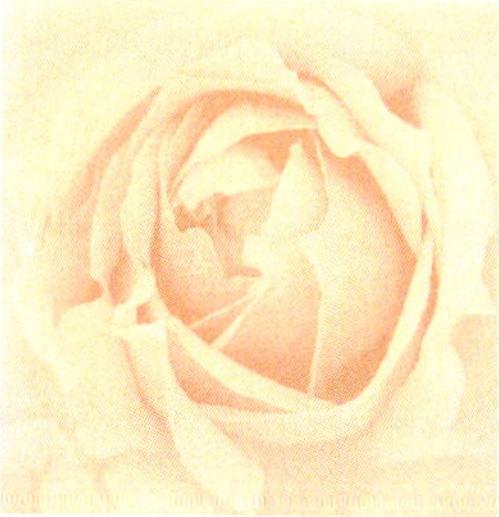

Oriental Seagull Prtrt Med Cont 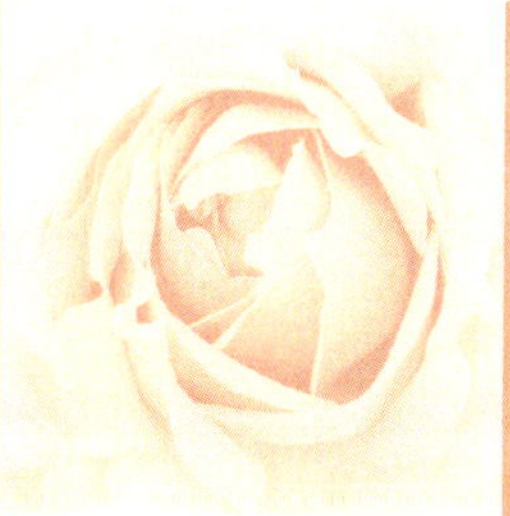 | Oriental Seagull Prtrt Soft Cont 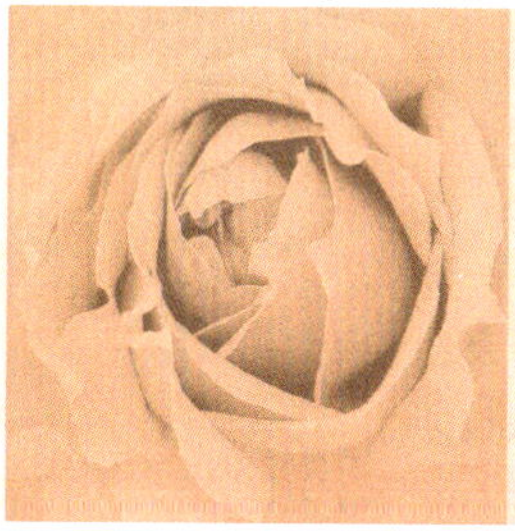 | Oriental Seagull VCFB II Wmtn 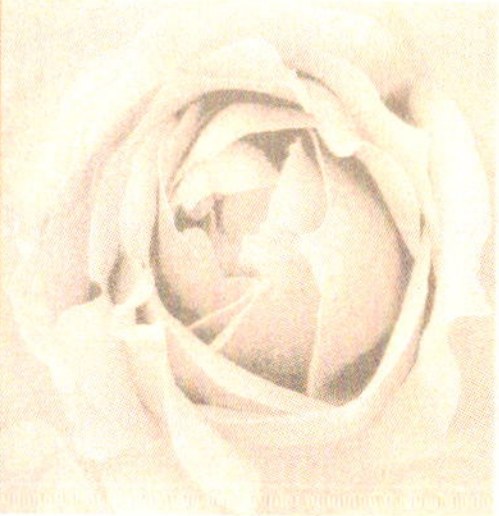 | Oriental VC Plus FB 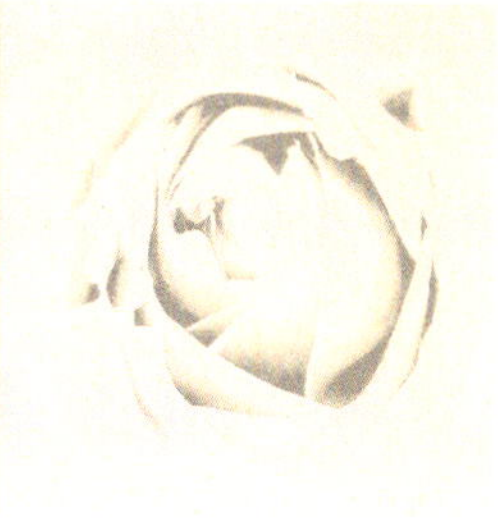 | Oriental VC-RP II Glossy RC

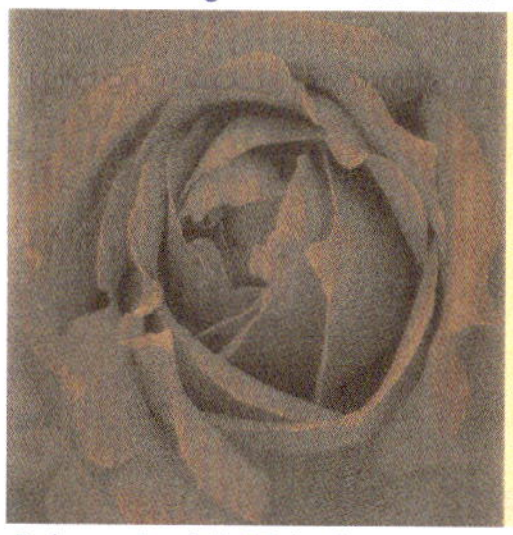

Polycontrast III RC Lustre 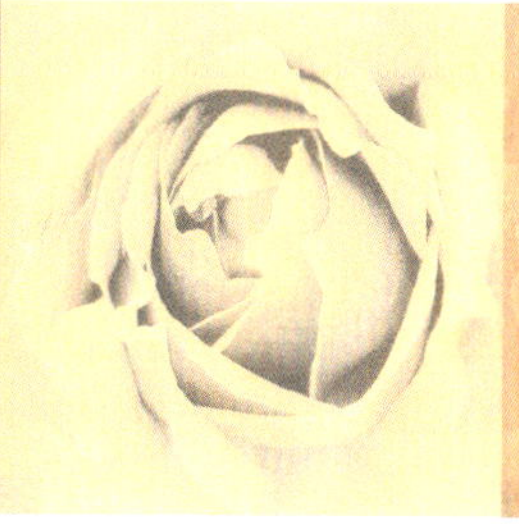 | Rapid PRK 111-3 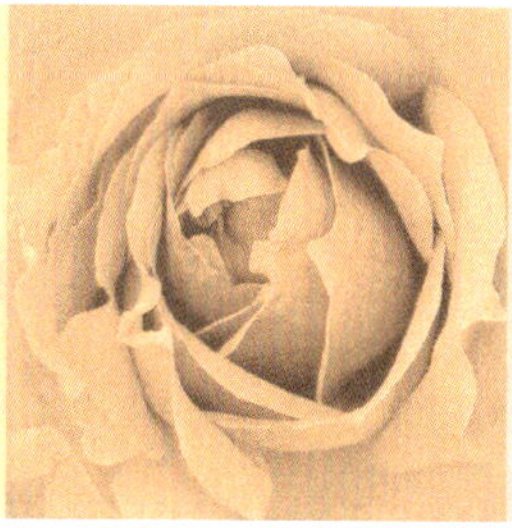 | Slavich Bromoportrait 80 FB G2 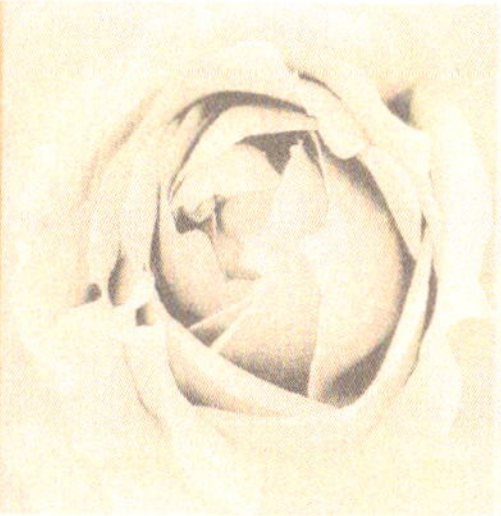 | Tura VC-Plus 12 PE RC Semimt 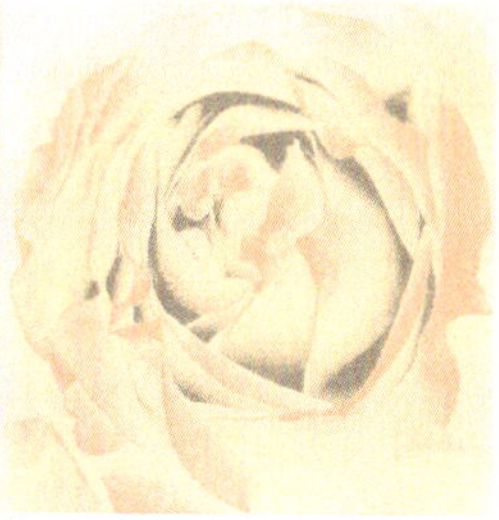 | Varydot

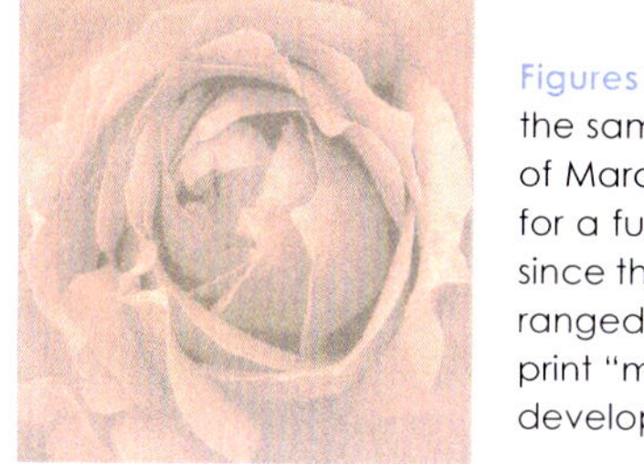

Zone VI Brilliant VCII DW Glossy

Figures 4.54–4.56. *Eighty-six Roses* © Christina Z. Anderson 2021. The preceding three pages are prints of the same QTR negative (profile in the **Digital Negatives** chapter) on 86 different papers over the months of March to September (three months on either side of the summer solstice). Each paper was exposed for a full day of sun (e.g. 10AM to 4PM) just like the step wedges. It's hard to compare apples to apples since the sun varies but the exposure times were roughly the same and the sun full sun to mostly sunny. UV ranged from 2–9. You can see from these prints that some papers print beautiful lumen prints while others print "mushy." Save the mushy ones for combination lumen/lith or chemigrams or other processes where developer will add dark tones.

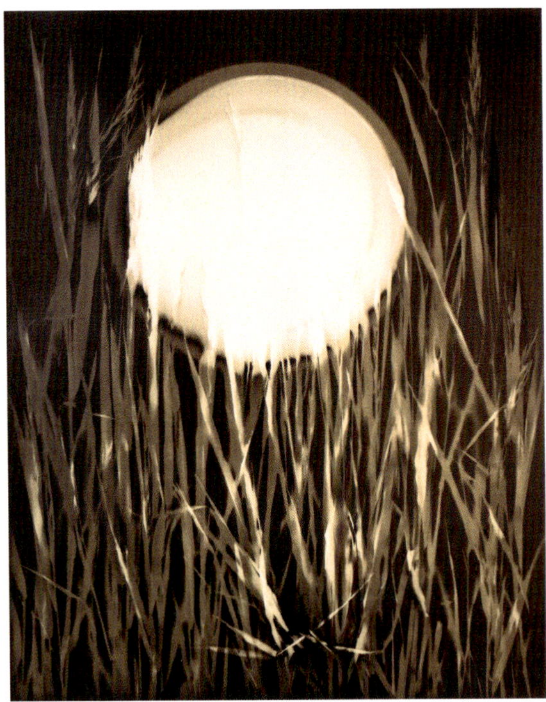

Figure 4.57. *Moonrise II*, lith lumen print © Tiina Kirik 2021

Using lith developer with lumen prints

As already said in this chapter, lumen prints are not developed in paper developer, only fixed, because if a print that has been exposing outside all day is put into paper developer you'll get a solid black print. There is an exception to this rule that first came to my attention from lumen expert Tiina Kirik (see the **Contemporary Experimental Artists** chapter) and the following are Kirik's words and directions:

"Lith developer is a special formula of print developer that is used in very dilute form for lith printing. Both lith printing and lumen printing are based on over-exposure. This dilute lith developer permits a print to be 'snatched' at the desired point of development. This can also be applied to lumen printing. The lith developer used at high dilution makes the process easier to manage and control. The lith lumen technique adds extra depth of color, a shift in color tone and a welcome touch of blacks to an otherwise colorful lumen print. Some solarization edge-effects may also occur. [Note: refer to the **Lith Printing** chapter for developers to purchase readymade and formulas to make your own lith developer if desired.]

1. Lith developer comes in two parts, Part A and Part B, combined just before use. The usual dilution is 15 ml Part A: 15 ml Part B: 970 ml water. At this dilution a lumen print will develop blacks in 1–2 minutes. Stronger dilutions tend to work too fast and uneven development may occur.
2. Have a pre-mixed stop bath of weak acid (e.g. 30 ml white vinegar in 1 liter water) handy to quickly arrest the action of the developer.
3. In dim room light, arrange materials on the silver gelatin paper. With lith development it is helpful to minimize light exposure of the paper outside of the time where image forming object(s) are in place.
4. Expose the lumen print as usual, and when exposure is done, bring the whole arrangement back into dim room light, or even darkroom safelight conditions before removing objects from the paper.
5. Rinse the paper to remove any plant juices or foreign materials from the surface of the paper if necessary (not necessary with digital negatives, of course).
6. Put your print into the dilute lith developer bath and keep the developer solution moving over the face of the paper for the whole development period. Watch carefully for the color shift and development of blacks.
7. When you see the print reach the level of black that you desire, snatch the print from the developer and put immediately into stop bath. At this point you can wash the print and take time to examine it briefly in very dim light. If the blacks are not sufficiently developed you can put it back into the developer. Note that if the developer becomes contaminated with acid from stop bath it will stop working, so rinse well before attempting any return the developer bath.
8. Fix, wash, hypoclear, wash, and dry as with any archival silver gelatin print."

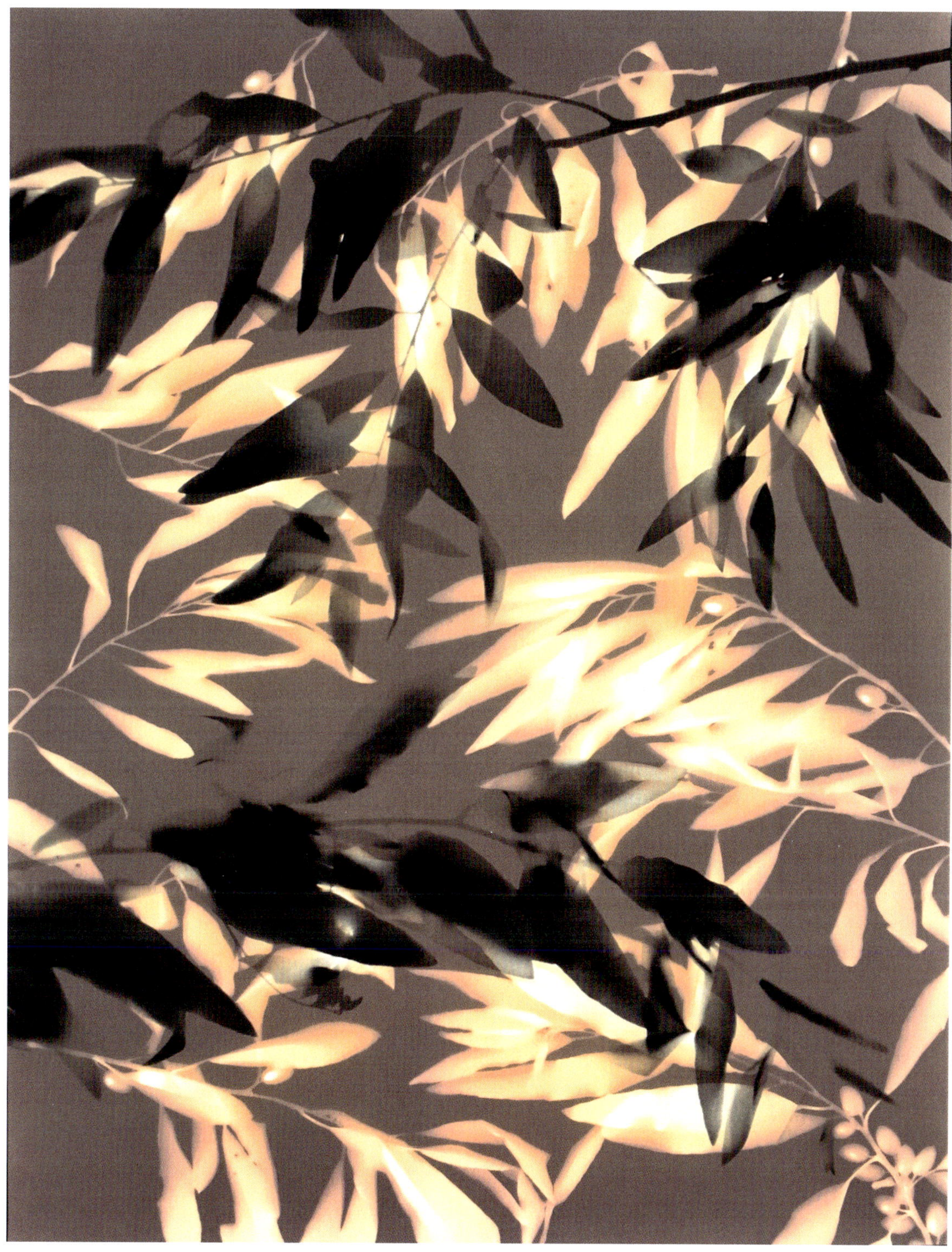

Figure 4.58. *Leaves and Shadows*, darkroom developed/lith lumen print, Ilford Warmtone © Tiina Kirik 2020

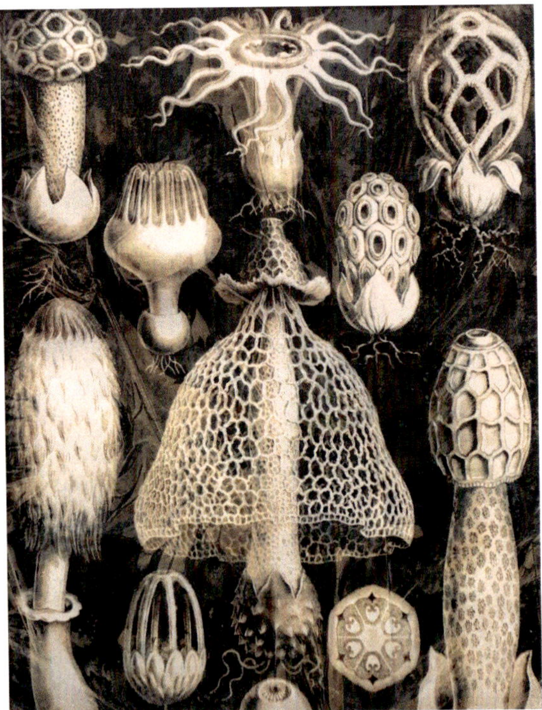

Figure 4.59. *Fungi, Ernst Haeckel* © Mary Thomas 2020, 8″ x 10″ Kentmere VC Select glossy paper, cyanotype solution sprayed on and exposed wet, sprayed with a diluted solution of baking soda, plastic wrap placed on top for texture under the negative, exposed in low spring sun for 45 minutes, rinsed in water, fixed in Ilford Rapid fixer for 30 seconds, soaked in a weak hydrogen peroxide bath for 30 seconds, then a final water rinse. Mary Thomas is a Welsh artist who began her alt photography journey after retiring from a teaching career in 2014. She started with cyanotype and then wet cyanotype. With her love of experimentation this ultimately led to the cyanolumen, a combination of silver gelatin paper, cyanotype solutions, and various household ingredients to create one of a kind works. Mary was drawn to the illustrations of Ernst Haeckel, a German biologist, as fitting for the cyanolumen process. Aside from sourcing Haeckel's illustrations she also uses her own digital imagery as well as organic material. Her work involves ongoing experimentation with adding kitchen cupboard ingredients such as turmeric, salt, baking soda and dilute vinegar, a sort of photographic alchemy that results in one of a kind works that cannot be replicated. For more of her work see @marytcyanolumen.

Cyanolumens

Cyanolumens are hybrid cyanotype-silver gelatin prints. Black and white (or color) paper is coated with cyanotype chemistry in the dimroom and then exposed like a lumen print outside for anywhere from 10 minutes to hours. The shorter the exposure, the more the cyanotype dominates the lumen, which stands to reason since the deeper colors of a lumen print require long exposures. The exposed paper is brought into the dimroom, washed, fixed, and washed again. The work you see here is from one consummate practitioner of the cyanolumen process, Mary Thomas (Wales). See the **Contemporary Experimental Artists** chapter for another artist, Annemarie Borg (London), working in this process, too.

1. If you have cyanotype on hand, mix Part A and Part B in equal amounts at time of use. If you have dry chemistry, merely mix in a tablespoon of ferric ammonium citrate and a teaspoon of potassium ferricyanide in 100 ml of water, enough for ten or more prints. *Tip: Generally cyanotype sensitizer is stored in separate A and B solutions, but mixing up a small amount such as this will most likely be used up before it goes bad. Plus this is experimental!*
2. Take a piece of gelatin silver paper out of the packet in the darkroom and coat or spray with the cyanotype solution and let dry. The solution can also be exposed wet if preferred, but if using a negative on top of a wet solution, protect it with a sheet of plastic wrap or Dura-lar in-between.
3. Bring the paper out into direct sunlight and expose for however long desired, a minimum of 10 minutes to hours. The brighter and hotter the sun, the shorter the exposure can be.
4. Bring the print into the dimroom and "develop" the cyanotype part of the equation by washing the print for a minute or two in a liter of water made slightly acidic with ¼ cup vinegar, stop bath, *or* ½ teaspoon citric acid.
5. Fix in an *acid* fixer (an alkaline fixer will bleach the cyanotype), wash, and dry as per a normal silver gelatin print, being careful of two things: do not over-fix—Mary fixes in Ilford Rapid Fixer for only 30 seconds—and do not overwash so the cyanotype disappears—5 to 10 minutes final wash is adequate, longer if desired if no fading of the print is observed.

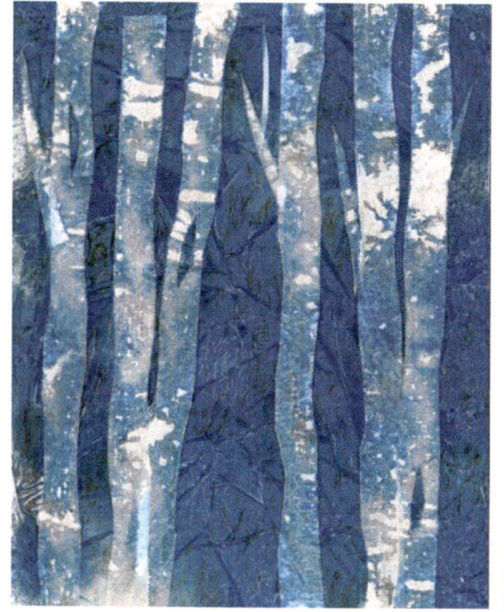
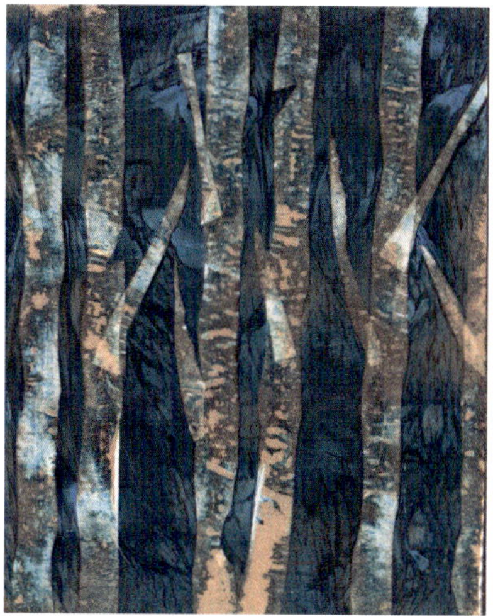
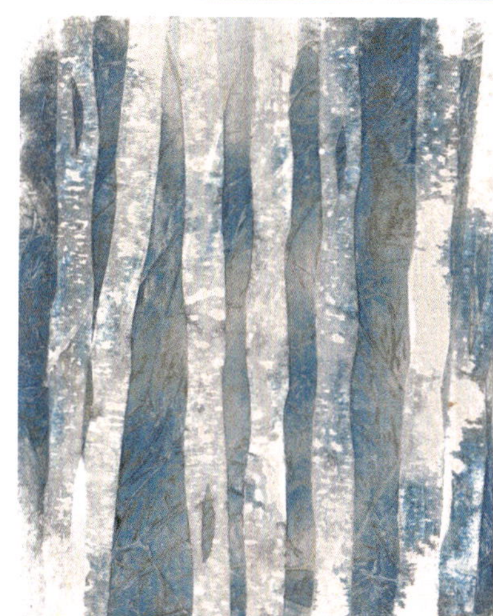
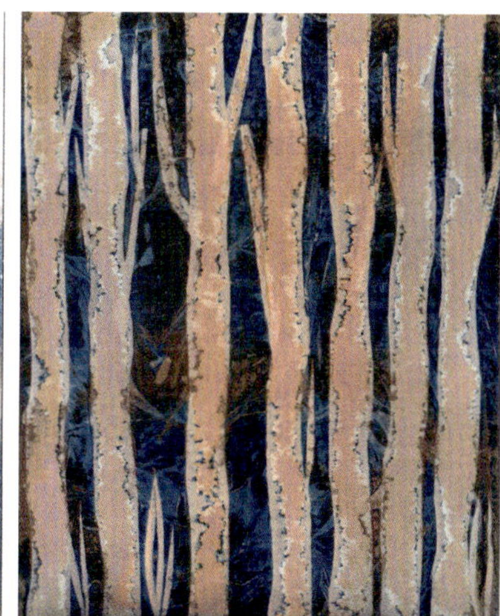
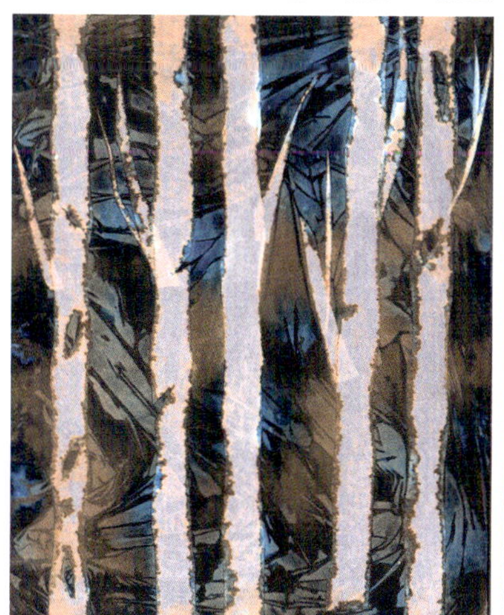
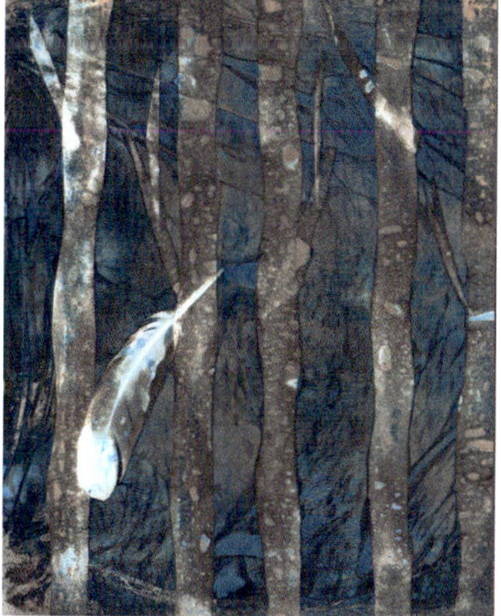

Figures 4.60–4.65. From left to right, top to bottom, wet process cyanolumens © Mary Thomas 2021. *Trees I*, 8″ x 10″, masking tape applied to Fujicolor Crystal Archive paper, sprayed with baking soda solution, then cyanotype solution, covered with plastic wrap, exposed to sun for 20 minutes, rinsed and fixed in Ilford fixer for 30 seconds, rinsed and dried. *Trees II*, 8″ x 10″, masking tape applied to Fotospeed RCVC glossy paper, sprayed with dilute vinegar, then cyanotype solution, covered with plastic wrap, exposed to sun for 20 minutes, rinsed and fixed in Ilford fixer for 30 seconds, rinsed and dried. *Trees III*, 8″ x 10″, masking tape applied to Ilford MGIV Deluxe glossy paper, sprayed with baking soda solution, then cyanotype solution, covered with plastic wrap, exposed to sun for 20 minutes, rinsed and fixed in Ilford fixer for 30 seconds, rinsed and dried. *Trees IV*, 8″ x 10″, masking tape applied to Ilford MG FB Warmtone glossy paper, sprayed with baking soda solution, then cyanotype solution, covered with plastic wrap, exposed to sun for 30 minutes, rinsed and fixed in Ilford fixer for 2 minutes, rinsed and dried. *Trees V*, 8″ x 10″, masking tape soaked in phytogram solution, applied to Kentmere Kenthene Stipple paper, cyanotype solution applied, covered with plastic wrap, exposed to sun for 30 minutes, rinsed and fixed in Ilford fixer for 2 minutes, rinsed and dried. *Trees VI*, 8″ x 10″, feather (Mary says the birds leave her gifts like this in her garden), masking tape applied to RCVC glossy paper, sprayed with dilute vinegar, cyanotype solution applied, covered with plastic wrap, exposed to sun for 20 minutes, rinsed and fixed in Ilford fixer for 30 seconds, rinsed and dried.

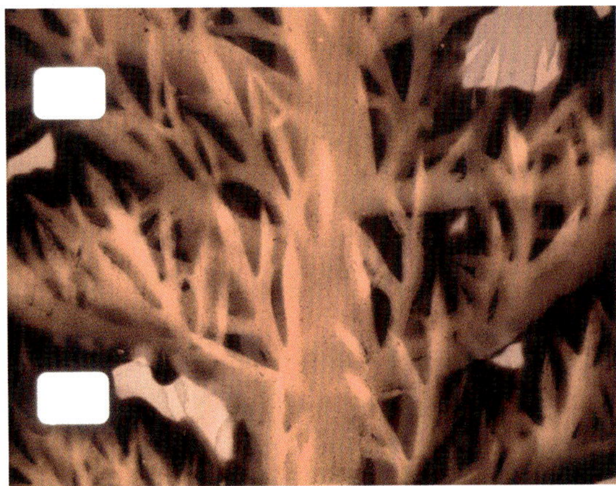

Figure 4.66. *Phytography*, phytogram made in direct sunlight, 34 x 25 cm © Karel Doing 2020

Phytograms

A phytogram[4] is a lumen print in which the organics put on the surface are presoaked in a mixture of washing soda and ascorbic acid (Vitamin C). The washing soda and ascorbic acid act as a mild paper developer to produce colors, dark areas, and sometimes silver. Everything otherwise proceeds as with normal lumen printing.

Around 2014 Karel Doing coined the term *phytogram* for this particular lumen print practice. He explains, "Industrial developers often contain the active ingredients metol and hydroquinone. These two chemicals are super-additive, they have a synergistic effect. Both can be classified as phenols, a group of chemicals containing one or two electron rich groups of atoms, which provide the necessary electron to initiate development. Coffee contains several phenols, making it suitable as a developer, especially in combination with Vitamin C, which provides the super-additivity similar to industrial products. This occurrence of phenols in coffee is the basis of caffenol developer. Many plants also contain some sort of phenol or polyphenol, especially in spring when the plant grows fast. By soaking the plant in the soda and Vitamin C solution, the phenol or polyphenol is released making the plant suitable as a developing agent. Still, this is a relatively weak developer, but by adding sunlight (or artificial light) the developing process is speeded up dramatically. The area where the plant makes contact with the photosensitive emulsion will darken and a careful application of a leaf or petal will result in a stain with a similar form. Sunlight that filters through the leaf or petal influences the process of staining, resulting in variations in tone revealing the internal structure of the plant in detail (thanks to Kevin Rice for getting this explanation straight). The results are dependent on the light conditions, temperature, and the prevalence of active chemistry in the plant species. In total darkness the process will be driven solely by the chemical reaction induced by the soaked plants. In bright sunlight the process will be driven by a combination of the chemical process and the effects of light (similar to a lumen print). In some exceptional cases the plants can produce subtle colour effects as well."[5] There is an excellent article available online in *Animation* (March 23, 2020).[6]

Plant soaking formula

2 tablespoons washing soda (sodium carbonate)
1 tablespoon Vitamin C powder
1000 ml water

1. Soak plants in the above solution for as long as desired; the longer, the softer the plant will become.
2. Drain the plants and place carefully on the film or paper and weigh down with plate glass if desired.
3. Exposure can be from several minutes to hours in full sunlight, just like with a lumen print but with the added element of chemistry. Peek underneath the edge of a plant and see if it is dark enough; that will be your exposure guide.
4. When exposure is complete, rinse off the paper or film, fix, wash, hypoclear, wash, and dry.

Note: plants add their chemical components to the end result but another avenue to explore is the use of non-plant or inorganic items soaked in the washing soda/ascorbic acid solution. *Tip: use a paintbrush or an Aquash pen filled with the solution for more markmaking possibilities.*

Endnotes

1. Burchfield, Jerry. *100 Lumen Prints of Amazonia Flora*. Santa Fe: Center for American Places, Inc., 2004, p. 118.
2. Ibid., p. xv.
3. Ibid., p. 120.
4. See phytogram.blog.
5. https://phytogram.blog/why-it-works/
6. https://journals.sagepub.com/doi/full/10.1177/1746847720909348full/10.1177/1746847720909348)

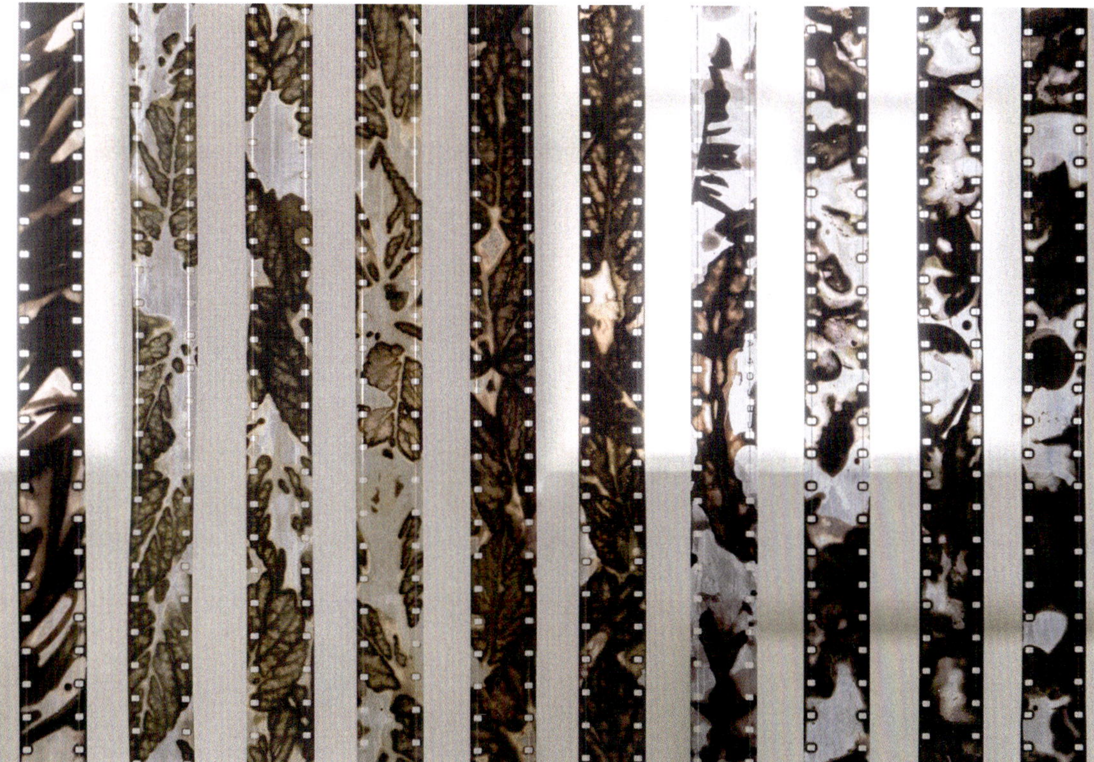

Figure 4.67. *Arachnophilia*, phytogram made in a dark garden shed, exposed over 24 hours, 200 x 250 cm © Karel Doing 2018.m"My practice is rooted in experimental photography and film. Photographic materials can be manipulated artistically in a number of ways during the developing process. A significant part of these alternative processes is based on a distortion or partial destruction of the image. This is especially true in experimental film. Many experimental filmmakers expose either their own camera footage or found-footage to aggressive chemicals such as bleach and acid. Other filmmakers bury, submerge or burn their footage or expose filmstrips for a prolonged time to the elements. My interest in this destructive approach was challenged during an artist residency that brought me to the tropical rainforest in South America. Inspired by the authentic ecological ways of making art that are practiced by the indigenous population I started looking deeper into my own understanding (and misunderstanding) of the relationship between nature and culture. Proceeding from this inquiry I asked myself if I could find a way to 'grow' an image instead of destroying it. I did set up a series of experiments with soil, salt, bacteria and fungi in my darkroom but only had limited success. Mostly, I was still destroying the photosensitive emulsion and although this yield-ed some interesting results, I was not anywhere near 'growing an image'. In parallel to my experiments, I was following online discussions about eco-processing and came across a recipe for mint based developer. Based on this idea, I hypothesized that it might be possible to use intact mint leaves as image makers by bringing the leaves directly in contact with film emulsion. After soaking a bunch of leaves in a Vitamin C and soda concoction I arranged the leaves across a filmstrip. To my delight the leaves imprinted themselves upon the film and after fixing the strip a string of leaf-like patterns was revealed. In the following years I have expanded upon this idea in multiple ways. Most importantly, I have taken my process out of the darkroom into the sunlight. By exposing my film and plant compositions to bright daylight the process is enhanced while colour effects emerge similar to those found in lumen prints. I have worked on silver gelatin paper, 16mm film and 35mm film while using a broad variety of different leaves, flowers and whole plants. Working with plants is inspiring, not in the least because of the sheer endless aesthetic qualities that plants offer but also because of the enormous variety of chemical components contained in plants. I have had many surprises and although I have gained much more control over this process, the outcome can still be quite unexpected. The benefit of this unpredictability is that the plants present themselves as true co-creators. It is not just me, the artist, who is at work creatively but my companions, the plants, contribute to the process in an inventive way as well."

Karel Doing is an independent filmmaker, photographer, writer and researcher currently based in Oxford, UK. In his practice he investigates the relationship between culture and nature by means of analog and organic process, experiment and co-creation. He studied Fine Arts in Arnhem, the Netherlands, graduating in 1990. In 2017, he received a PhD from the University of the Arts London. During his research he developed *phytography*, a technique that combines plants and photography. Doing's work has been shown worldwide. To see more of his work visit kareldoing.net.

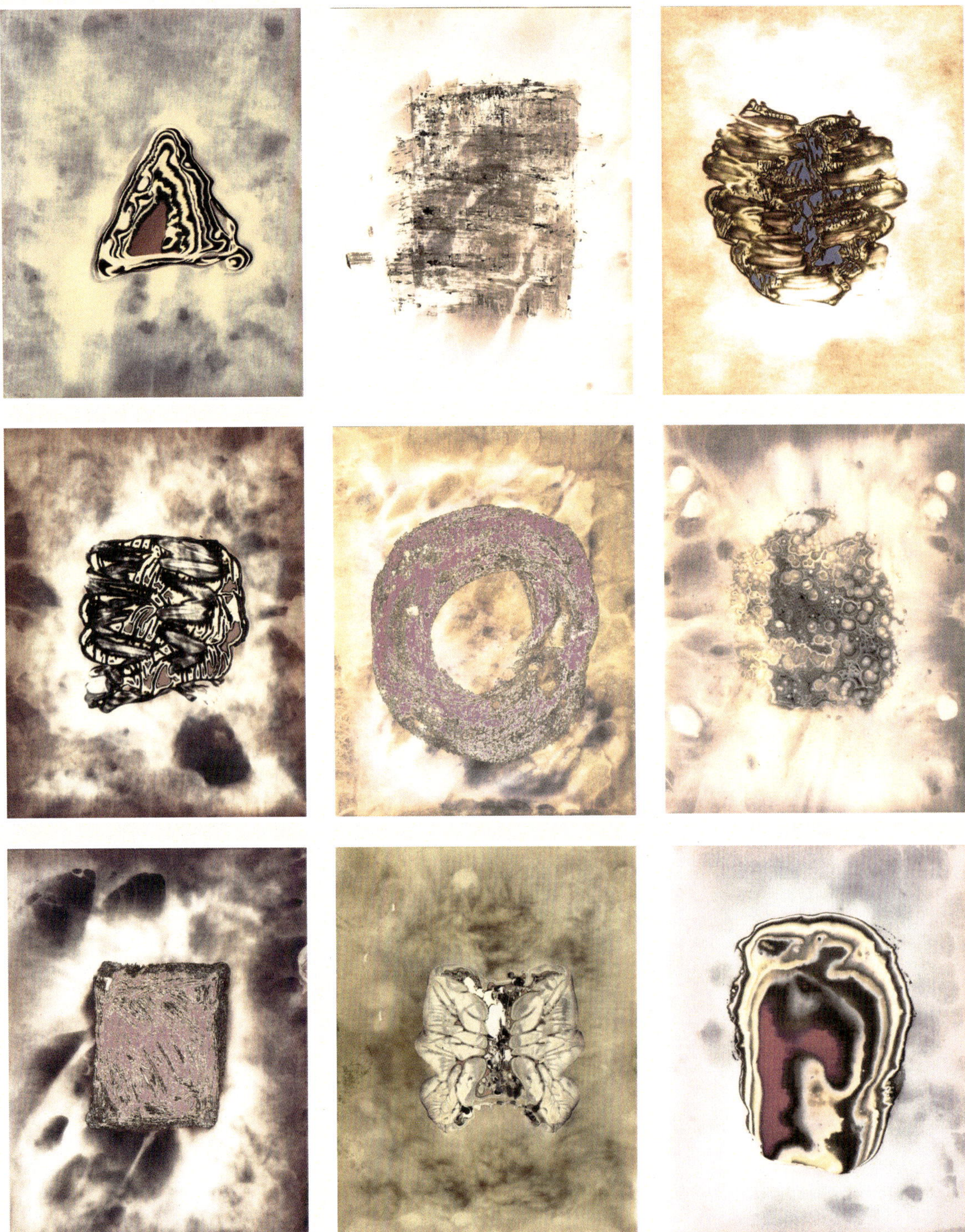

Figures 5.1–5.9. *Untitled*, soft resist chemigrams, 8″ x 10″ © Jesslyn Braught 2019. "From top to bottom, left to right, resists used were honey, bar soap, aloe gel, aloe gel again, butter, avocado oil + salt, chapstick, sunscreen, and agave syrup + salt. In full light, the substances were applied to gelatin silver paper and subsequently placed into a tray of fixer for about ten seconds, followed by a tray of developer for about ten seconds. This process of fixer/developer continued until the resist was gone. No final fix was applied; images were scanned 'as is'. " Jesslyn Marie is an adventure elopement photographer, specializing in back country weddings for the wildly in love. To see more of her work visit jesslynmarie.com.

Chapter 5

The Chemigram

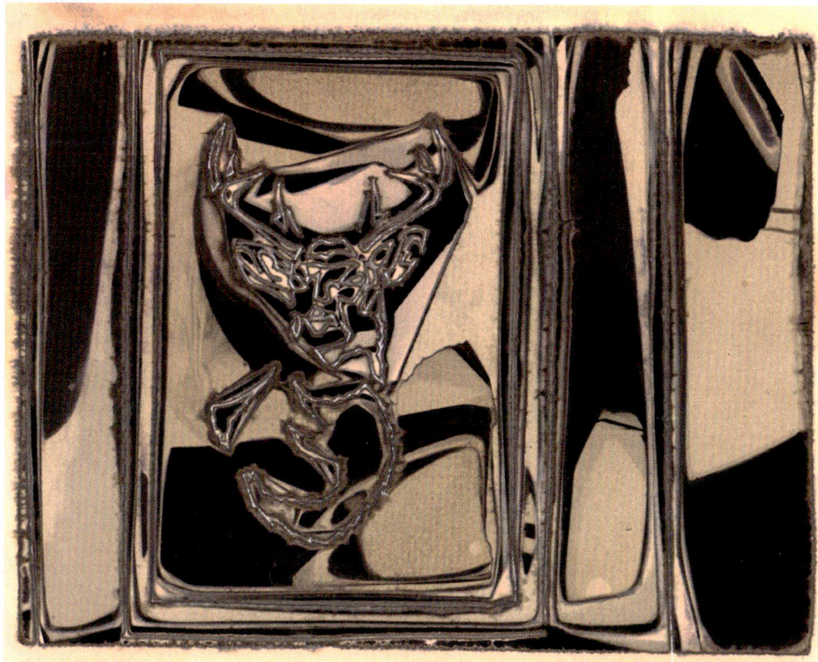

Figure 5.10. *Untitled*, hard resist chemigram using Golden MSA Varnish, 10″ x 8″© Kellie Swanson 2016. Kellie Swanson (b. 1994) is an alternative process photographer and artist based in Bozeman, Montana. She received a Bachelor of Arts in Film and Photography from Montana State University in 2018. After taking time off to travel and ski, she has refocused her work on handmade fine art printing and sustainable, one-of-a-kind, artistic fashion. In her KSX clothing line, Swanson explores the relationship between nature, photography, handmade prints, and self-expression. To see more of her work follow her @ksx-art and visit kellieswanson.com.

The chemigram is a unique process that uses **resists** on silver gelatin paper similar to the way wax is used as a resist in batik. The process was invented by Pierre Cordier on November 10, 1956. What Cordier discovered in 1956 was that a resist (in this case, nail polish) interferes with the chemical effects of developer and fixer on silver gelatin paper—for a time. Paper put into developer that has been exposed to normal room light for varying periods of time will turn black, except where a resist blocks the chemical reaction. The parts of the paper protected by the resist will continue to change color from extended exposure to room light. Likewise, paper put into fixer turns white, except where a resist blocks the chemical reaction. The parts of the paper protected by the resist continue to change color from the room light exposure, and suddenly there is the possibility of black, white, and colors in-between on normally monochrome paper.

With the back and forth from developer to fixer or fixer to developer, the resist begins to dissolve, so the next chemical bath either turns slowly exposing paper under the dissolving resist black (developer) or white (fixer) or some color in-between because of the now-lengthening room light exposure. With time this dissolution can be coaxed into creating beautiful, intricate, tree ring-like patterns.

Cordier calls the chemigram a "physico-chemical" process, because the physical nature of the resist—how it dissolves on the photo paper base when repeatedly immersed in developer and fixer—is made visible by the photographic chemistry.

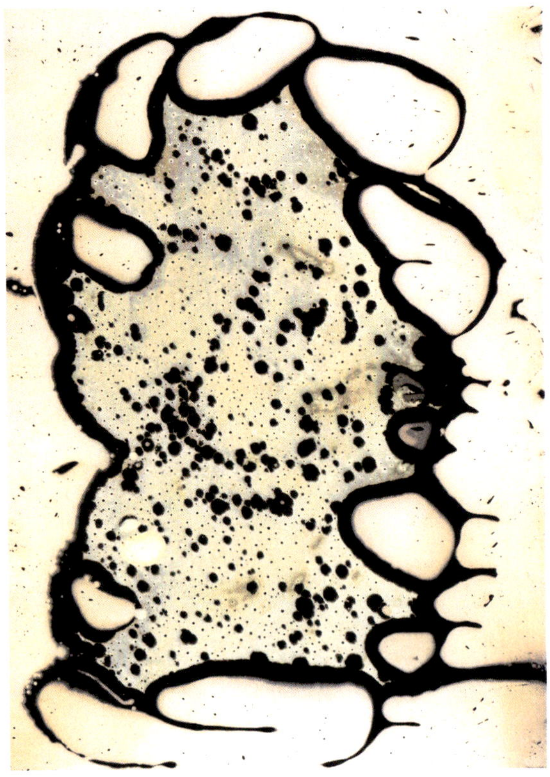

Figure 5.11. *Untitled*, chemigram on Ilford MGFB paper using olive oil as a resist © Danika Wolf 2021

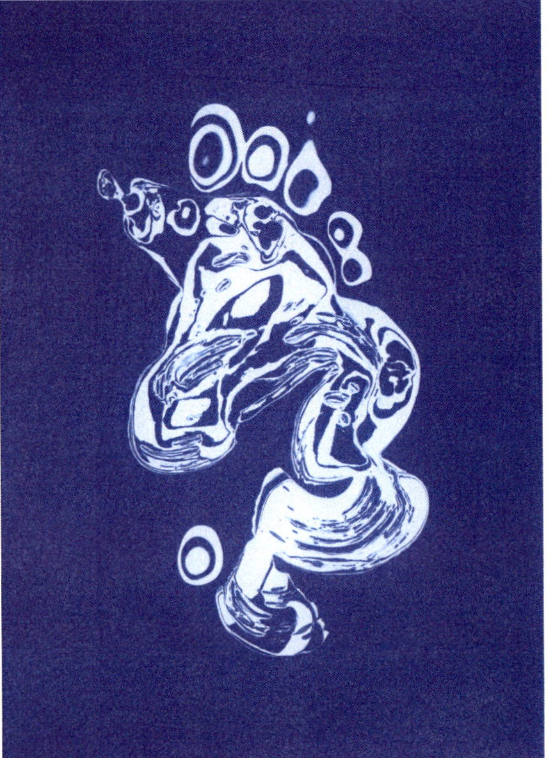

Figure 5.12. *Untitled*, from the *Micromanaging* series © Alyssa McKenna 2021. McKenna used soft resists on Ortho film and with the resulting chemigram negatives, printed them in cyanotype on watercolor paper.

Hard and soft resists

The first decision to make is what type of resist to use, because the resist directs the look of the chemigram. There are hard resists and soft resists, with the difference between the two more like a continuum than a clear separation. Think of a hard resist as something that takes time to slough off the paper and a soft resist as something that dissolves more readily in chemistry. It stands to reason, therefore, that a hard resist chemigram will take more time to complete, where a soft resist chemigram can be finished more quickly, sometimes in minutes.

Examples of hard resists

- Nail polish
- Cellulose varnish
- Acrylic varnish like Krylon (it crackles)
- Rust-Oleum
- Acrylic medium
- Lacquer or resin
- Golden MSA Varnish, spray or liquid (my favorite)
- Soluvar varnish diluted 1:1 with mineral spirits
- Epoxy enamel
- American Accents spray varnish (it crackles)

Examples of soft resists

- Wax
- Oil
- Honey
- Karo syrup
- Egg
- Water soluble glue
- Glycerin
- Spray oil like Pam
- Future or Pledge floor polish

You can mix in cornstarch or other thickening substances to change the way a soft resist works.

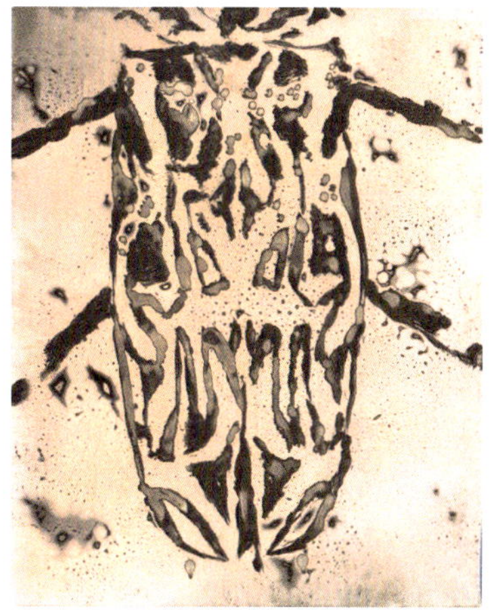
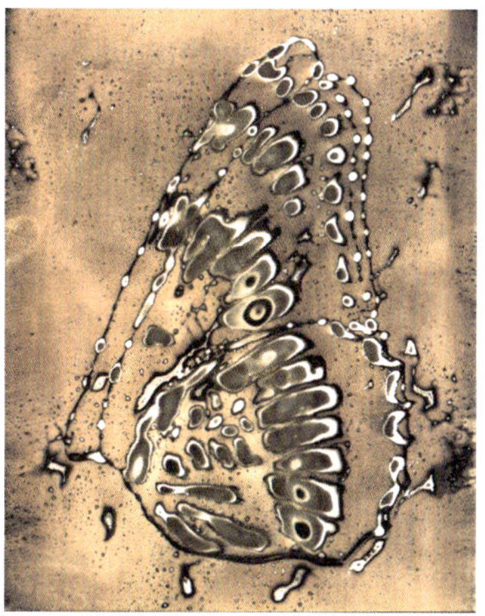
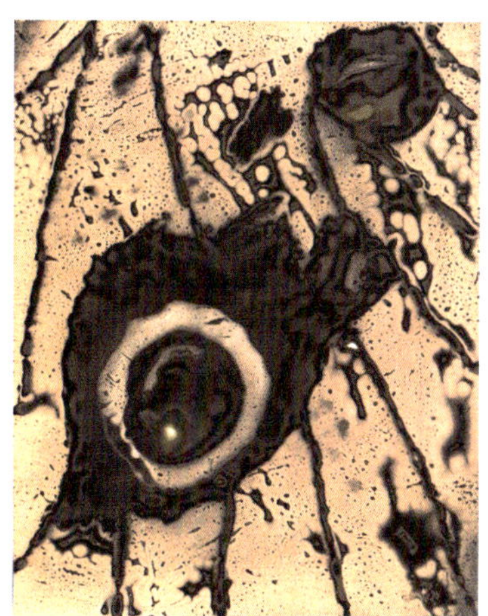

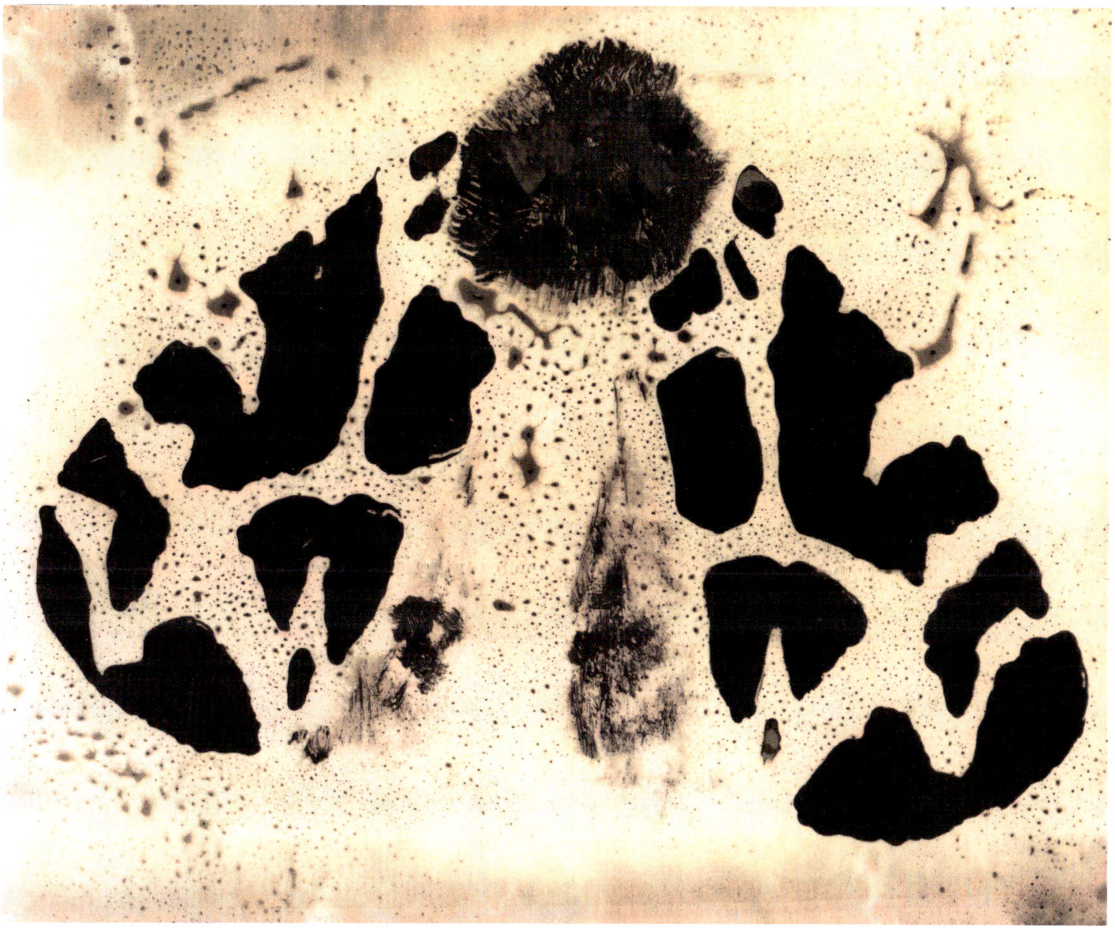

Figures 5.13-5.16. Top left, *Harlequin*; top center, *Limenitis*; top right, *Eye of Morpho*; bottom *Ornamental Tiger*, chemigrams on Kodak Polymax FD paper, 8˝ x 10˝ © Dani Hatfield 2021. "Down to the tiniest particles of matter, the universe is composed of patterns. In insects these patterns can be the functional series of ridges that allows a cricket to make its iconic song, or the beautiful alternating colors that allow a male beetle to attract a female. Using insects as the original patterns of my chemigrams, I use a variety of resists such as varnish, glue, honey, and oil to strip away the function of these patterns and show an abstraction of the insects themselves."

Other resists

- Felt tip pens
- Removable adhesive plastic
- Sticky labels
- Liquid mask or rubber cement
- Tapes, different kinds, which also can be used on the back of the paper to hold back chemical action through the paper base

Tools

There are numerous tools that will end up in your arsenal. An Xacto knife is necessary to incise lines into a hard resist. Tweezers are indispensable to carefully lift and peel off parts of a hard resist. One tool that is quite fun is a portable battery powered Dremel with a small round bit tip to draw curvy lines. A less expensive and smaller version of a Dremel is a battery operated micro metal engraving pen which costs under $20.

Examples of process choices

All choices affect the final look of the chemigram.

- Paper type and brand, warmtone or cooltone, bromide, chlorobromide, or bromochloride
- Paper age—outdated/fogged paper is excellent for chemigrams, even ones that don't perform well for lumen prints because developer and fixer are used to produce contrast and color
- Resist, from thick to thin, full strength to diluted, soft and syrupy to hard and water-resistant, etc.
- Additions to the resist—sugar, salt, for instance
- Resist applied in the darkroom or in room light
- Resist applied with a brush, spray, stencil, silk screen, roller
- Length of time the resist is allowed to dry before the developer and fixer baths
- Incising lines or drawing into the resist
- Fixer, diluted or full strength
- Developer, diluted or full strength
- Toners
- Strength of light, dimroom to outside sunlight
- Length of time under light
- Length of time in each bath (too much time in the fixer makes for weak blacks because the fixer comes through the back of the paper to partially fix all areas)
- Method of application of the baths, whether by tray, brush, spray, through a stencil, from a bottle, with a roller
- Which bath first, which bath second
- Sprinkles of dry chemicals from a salt shaker
- Nonfigurative versus photo-based or somewhere in-between—e.g. through a silk screen

Making a chemigram test strip

This low tech, easy test strip method is a perfect first foray into the chemigram process as well as a great way to learn how different resists react.

1. Take several different brands of BW photo paper out of their black plastic light-safe bags in the darkroom. With a pencil, label the back with each paper brand.
2. Place these sheets in a separate black plastic bag and label the bag something like "Chemigram Testing Paper." The rest of the test process can be carried out in room light.
3. Set up four trays: developer, water, fixer, and water, in that order. The developer could be normal strength to dilute. Likewise with the fixer, but for this first attempt, use both working strength.
4. Cut a simple shape out of a plain piece of typing paper. It can be a square, circle, snowflake, diamond, whatever comes to mind. This will be used as a low tech stencil.
5. Take one piece of paper from the Chemigram Testing Paper bag in full room light, tape it to a counter, and cover it with the typing paper cutout, taping that in place so both lie flat.
6. Take a resist of choice—start simple, e.g. butter, maple syrup, honey, Pam—and coat or brush inside the shape carefully and completely. Varnish works better thin. Syrup works fine thick. Cordier's "magic" varnish of choice is a metal polish because it will start lifting steadily off the paper base when submerged in a water bath.
7. Incise a few lines into the resist. When the resist goes back and forth in and out of the chemistry, the resist disintegrates faster around the line, the line becomes wider, more distressed, and chemistry will react with the successively exposed photo paper underneath that is no longer protected. The paper

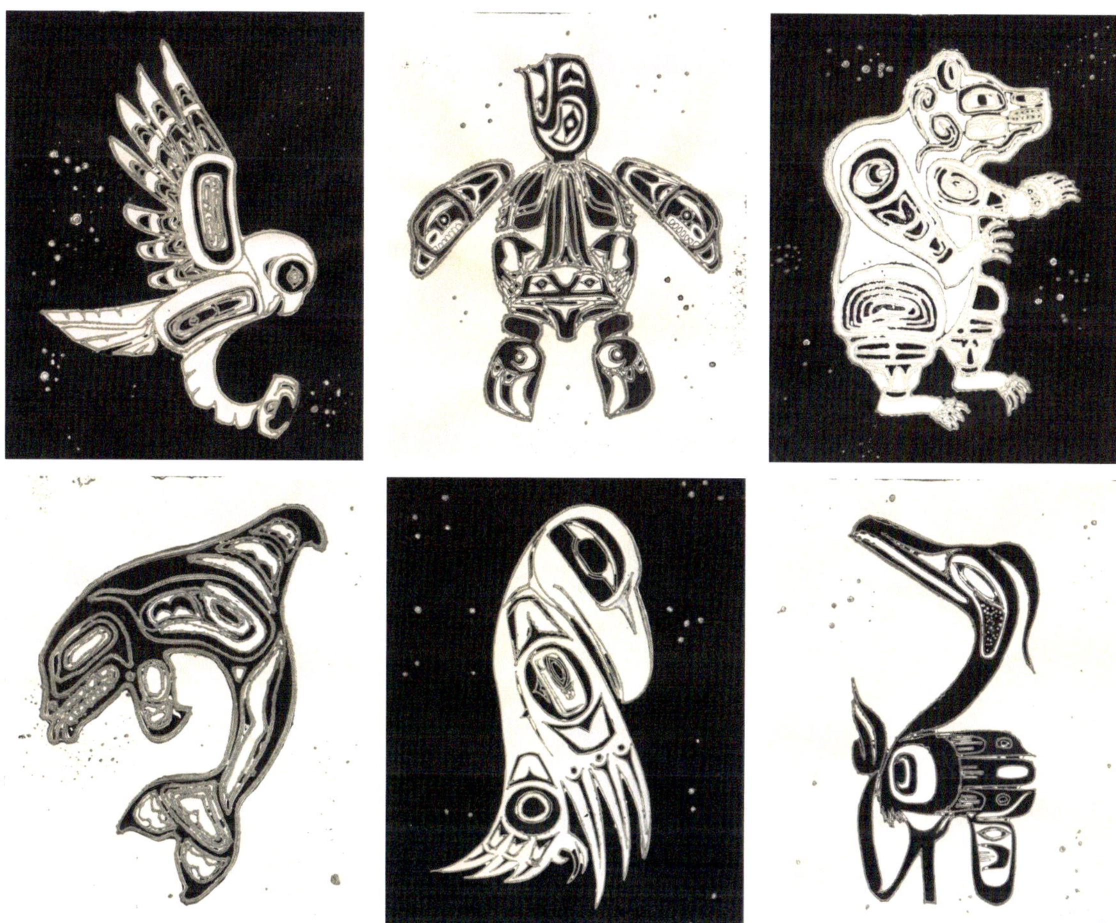

Figures 5.17–5.22. *Haida Chemigrams*, hard resist chemigrams created with Golden MSA varnish © Tara Medina Caplis 2019. "I've always been naturally drawn to creative and hands-on pursuits. I'm a kinesthetic and visual learner so naturally I chose a career in design and art. One of the most beautiful things about being an artist and designer is having the power to convey your thoughts and feelings in various media. What you create with your hands live on in the things you have made. Fall 2019 I was enrolled in an Introduction to Native American Studies course, where I drew much of my inspiration for this series—in particular, Northwestern Coast tribal art of the indigenous people of the Haida tribe. The creative embellishments, symmetry, and visual depictions of their culture in their art and work was beautifully captivating. I thought their designs would translate well in the chemigram process. I consulted with my Native American Studies professor, Dr. Walter Fleming, to be creatively conscious and sensitive while using Haida tribal designs. My intent was to celebrate their cultural symbols in a respectful way in my art." Tara Medina Caplis, landscape designer, graduated from Montana State University Spring 2021 with a B.S in Landscape Design and a Minor in Photography.

will develop a darker line and then a paler line every time the paper is put through the developer/fixer cycle.

8. With the trays all set up ready to go, slip the photo paper coated with the resist in either the developer to get a black background, or the fixer to get a white background. Meanwhile the paper will be turning color in room light—brown, yellow, mauve, blue, pink—that's OK. Don't touch the resist just yet.

9. Whenever the paper looks finished developing or fixing—a couple minutes for developer, brief seconds for fixer—move it to the water wash. Rinse well enough, still not touching the surface and marring the resist, and then put it in the opposite tray of fixer or developer, respectively. If the water wash is not used, there will be contamination between the developer and the fixer, which produces some nice colors and potentially silver through chemical fog, an option to consider.

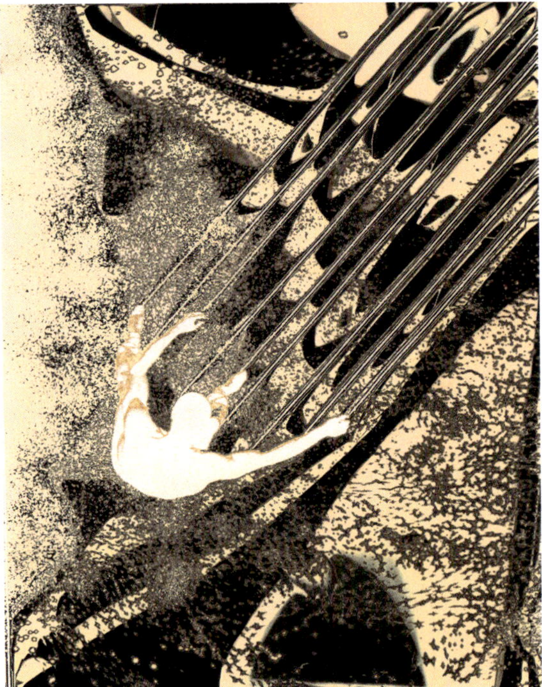

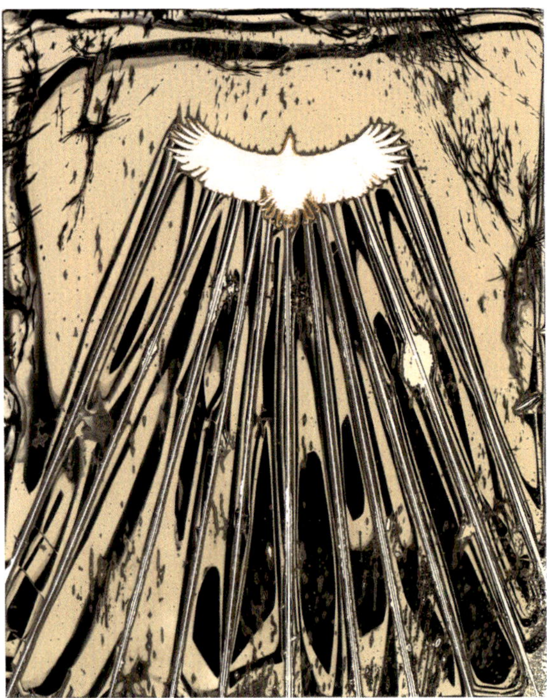

Figures 5.23–5.24. Left, *Untitled*, right, *Leviathan 17*, laser-etched chemigrams © Jace Becker 2015

10. The resist will start dissolving, some sooner than later. Butter doesn't dissolve too quickly. Honey does. Wherever the resist starts to dissolve, the underneath area will either turn lighter (fixer) or darker (developer), and with each back and forth, concentric areas of dark and light will begin to form like tree rings. Depending on the resist, the rings can have hard edges, mottled edges, or soft edges. Honey, for instance, produces soft and silky patterns.

11. The decisions are numerous. What the process teaches is patience, and going with the flow, both literally and figuratively. It is not necessarily quick.

12. The chemigram is done when all the resist has come off. At that point do a final fix, archival wash, and dry.

13. Do this same process with the remaining papers using different resists. Store these test strips in a notebook with copious notes on paper brand, resist used, time, order of chemistry.

The laser chemigram

Fall 2015 I taught the chemigram process to my Experimental Photography class at Montana State University, using both hard and soft resists. Tanner Houselog, a double-degree architect and photographer, familiar with laser printers, suggested a laser printer could be used to incise a hard resist. This type of laser printer is one using a computer aided design (CAD) program like Rhino and a laser beam to etch, score, or cut through materials, not what we typically think of as a laser printer. It can be adjusted to cut at different depths. Two students, Jen Marshall and Jace Becker, simultaneously produced promising results in November, showing that computer-aided design, the laser printer, and the hard-resist chemigram process could be happy bedfellows. The laser printer opens up all sorts of options from perfectly geometric drawings to the photographic (and conceptual discussions of hand *vs* machine!). It is yet one more way our digital world has added something of benefit to the analog/chemistry-based processes.

The laser printer has a characteristic look. The heat of the cutter can melt a varnish slightly and result in a minute furry or jaggy line quality to the line. A couple suggestions when using this printer is to use as high a resolution image as possible, and a vector-based image. Use simpler designs at first, too.

Tips and ideas

- Draw the design on top of a hard resist with a pen and then incise. Penmarks will disappear with the resist.
- Tape the design to a light table underneath the silver gelatin paper and trace it.
- Tone the chemigram with selenium 1+5 which will nicely boost contrast.
- Leaving the design face down or face up in the developer and fixer is a variable. Due to gravity of the resist falling down, the lines tend to be larger.
- The longer the print is left in either developer or fixer, the thicker the line of black or white respectively, but too long in the fixer can hamper the ability of the paper to turn dark in the developer as fixer will seep through the back of the paper to affect the front.
- Bleeding/marbling marks come from a quick dip in developer and then return to a dip in fix without rinsing between. It creates chemical flow patterns.
- Take parts of the chemigram and scan and put together digitally. Open the image in Photoshop, set the Photoshop noise filter to Dust and Scratches, Radius 2, Threshold 20, which cleans up most of the small stuff.
- See Douglas Collins, Bridget Conn, Eva Nikolova, and Nolan Preece in the **Contemporary Experimental Artists** chapter for detailed explanations of how they make their chemigrams.

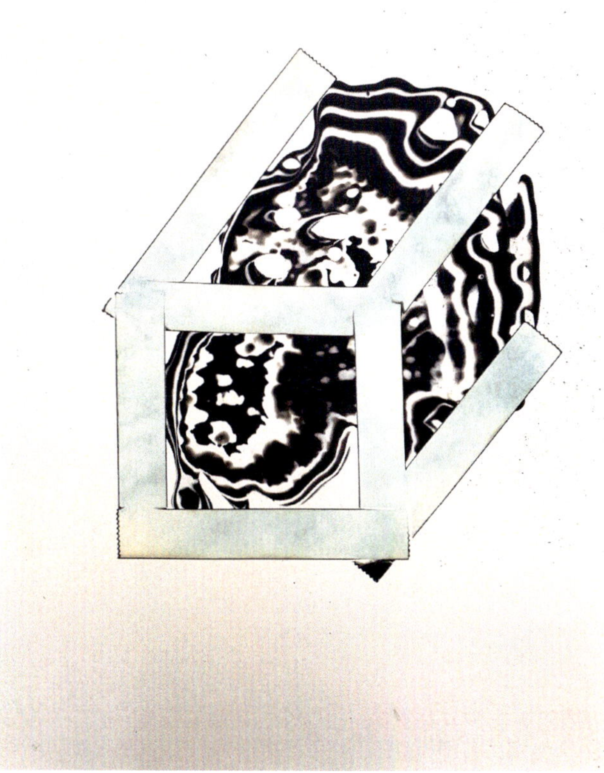

Figure 5.25. *Untitled*, © Sam Norsworthy 2021."To create this chemigram I used Ilford Warmtone paper, taped solid lines with Scotch tape, and then covered the inside shape with honey. I then submerged the paper in fixer until the background went off-white, followed by cool water and finally developer before washing the paper and repeating the process until the honey had been fully removed. Once the honey was fully removed I submerged the paper in hot water until I could remove the tape without damaging the print. I then used a fixer bath to complete the print. The green color is a mixture of water, fixer, and developer in my wash bath from transferring the paper back and forth." Sam Norsworthy has a background in graphic design and is currently pursuing a BA in Film and Photography at Montana State University. His photographic interests lie mainly in the landscape while also pursuing other avenues that will benefit his career in the visual field.

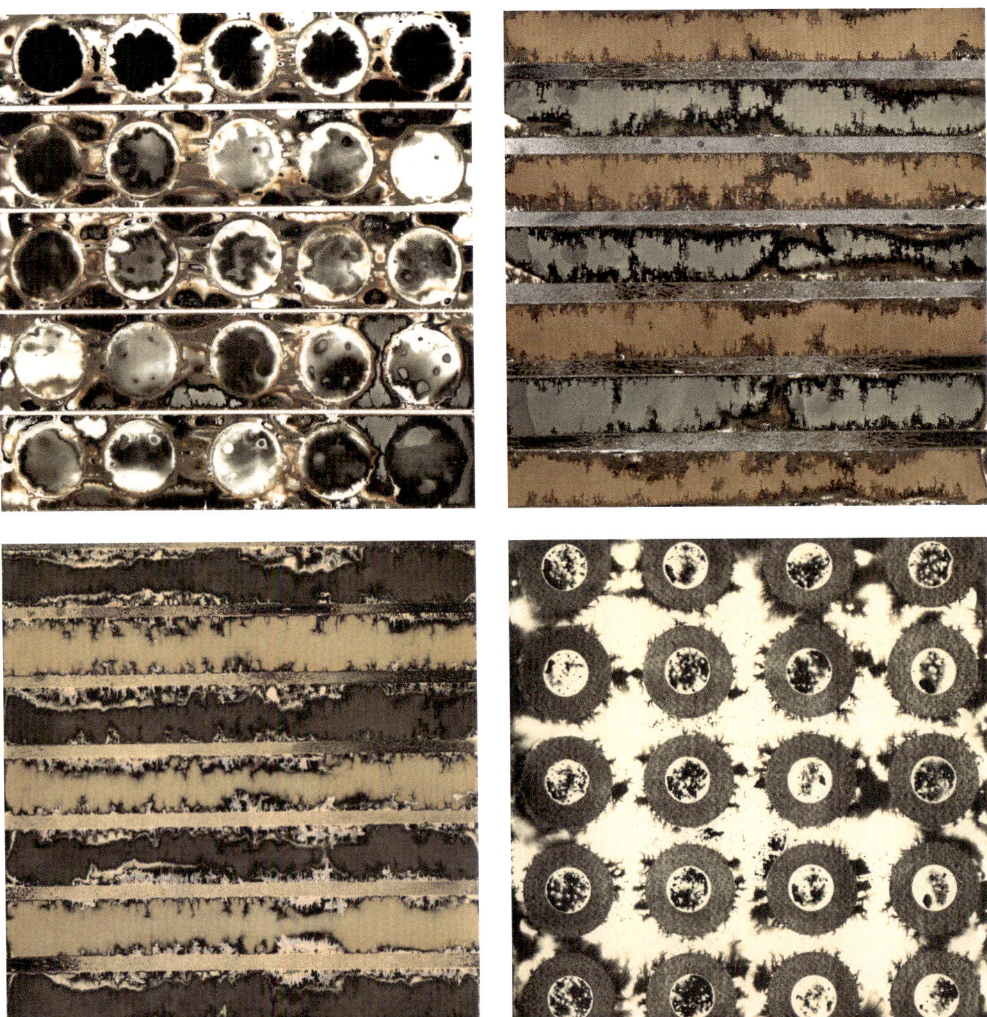

Figures 5.26–5.29. Clockwise, from top left, *Untitled*, 5″ x 5″ chemigram made on Ilford Direct Positive paper. The horizontal bands were formed by pieces of blue painter's tape and circular adhesive labels applied to the surface of the paper, then allowed to slowly lift off in successive immersions in developer, fixer and water © Richard Turnbull 2013. *Untitled*, 8″ x 8″ chemigram made on Ilford Direct Positive paper, horizontal bands formed by pieces of blue painter's tape and processed in the same manner as above © Richard Turnbull 2013. *Untitled*, 8″ x 8″ chemigram made on Luminos Classic Tapestry X paper. The circular motifs were formed by two sizes of adhesive paper labels applied to the surface of the paper, and processed in the same manner above © Richard Turnbull 2014. *Untitled*, 8″ x 8″ chemigram made on Adorama FB paper with standard Kodak black-and-white chemistry. The horizontal bands were formed by pieces of blue painter's tape applied to the surface of the paper, and processed in the same manner above © Richard Turnbull, 2013. "Although I did a lot of conventional black-and-white darkroom work in the 1990s, I eventually left the darkroom behind for the relative ease of digital photography. I began making chemigrams in 2010 as a way of investigating a hybrid form of photography and painting. I've worked on an ongoing series using readymade adhesives like tapes and labels to create grids and frames that bring a sense of order to the potential chaos of the only partially controllable chemigram process." Richard Turnbull is an art historian whose visual work includes chemigrams, artists' books, printmaking and assemblage. In his chemigrams he is drawn to grid systems that act as stabilizing frames for the unpredictable and unexpected results of the process. Turnbull uses the chemigram and other experimental photographic processes as a way of introducing the hand back into the photographic image. His visual work can be seen at furiousdaypress.com.

Figure 5.30. *Untitled*, soft resist chemigram using hydrocortisone cream and Ilford paper, washi tape, brushes, palette knife, tacks and rubber stamps © Claire M. Williams 2019.

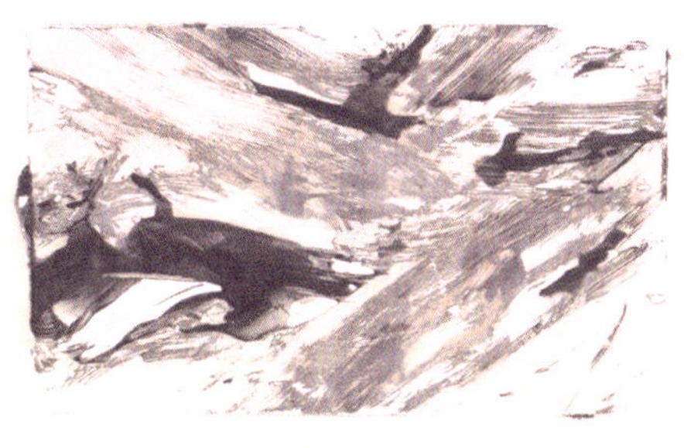

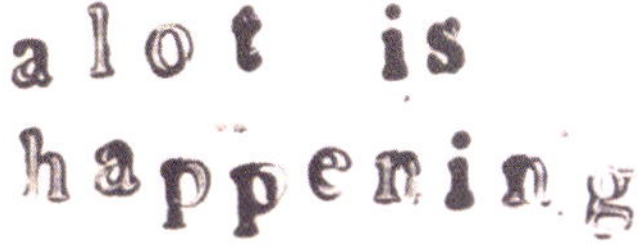

"Learning the chemigram process came at a pivotal time in my adolescent life. I was wrestling with the immeasurable loss of my sense of childlike security and overall general unbotheredness to the darker experiences of life. I was trying to catch a glimpse of what light and simplicity, even just being 'OK,' looked like in the midst of it all, and I'd like to think you can find the answers I got in these chemigrams. The chemigram process gave me a sense of control in the loss of control, if that makes sense. There are only certain outcomes willed by the chemicals to come out in chemigrams, no matter the effort, intent, or design, which paralleled with my world at the time. And in that willed, unruly chaos of an outcome, I found that simplicity could exist hand in hand with it—that light and dark are not mutually exclusive."

"For most of my chemigrams I used hydrocortisone cream as the resist and brushed it on with paint brushes and palette knives. I first used Washi tape to create a confined area for the hydrocortisone, and then rubber date and alphabet stamps that I also stamped in hydrocortisone cream. Before I placed the paper in the chemicals, I removed the Washi tape. The more abstract areas were created by selectively choosing certain areas to brush off (or keep on) the hydrocortisone cream in either the developer/fix."

Claire Williams grew up in Northern California, nestled between the coast and the mountains, and began making photographs at the age of eleven. High School brought her an education and love for the darkroom, where she decided to pursue a career in photography thanks to the encouragement and support of her parents and photography teacher, Mr. Frank Shields. Her heart for the outdoors took her to Montana for college, where she received a BA in Film & Photography and a BFA in Graphic Design from Montana State University. In her spare time, she enjoys taking slow walks, fly fishing, backpacking, and skiing. She currently resides in Bozeman, Montana with her husband, specializing in product photography and graphic design for small local businesses. To see more of Williams' work visit clairemwilliams.com.

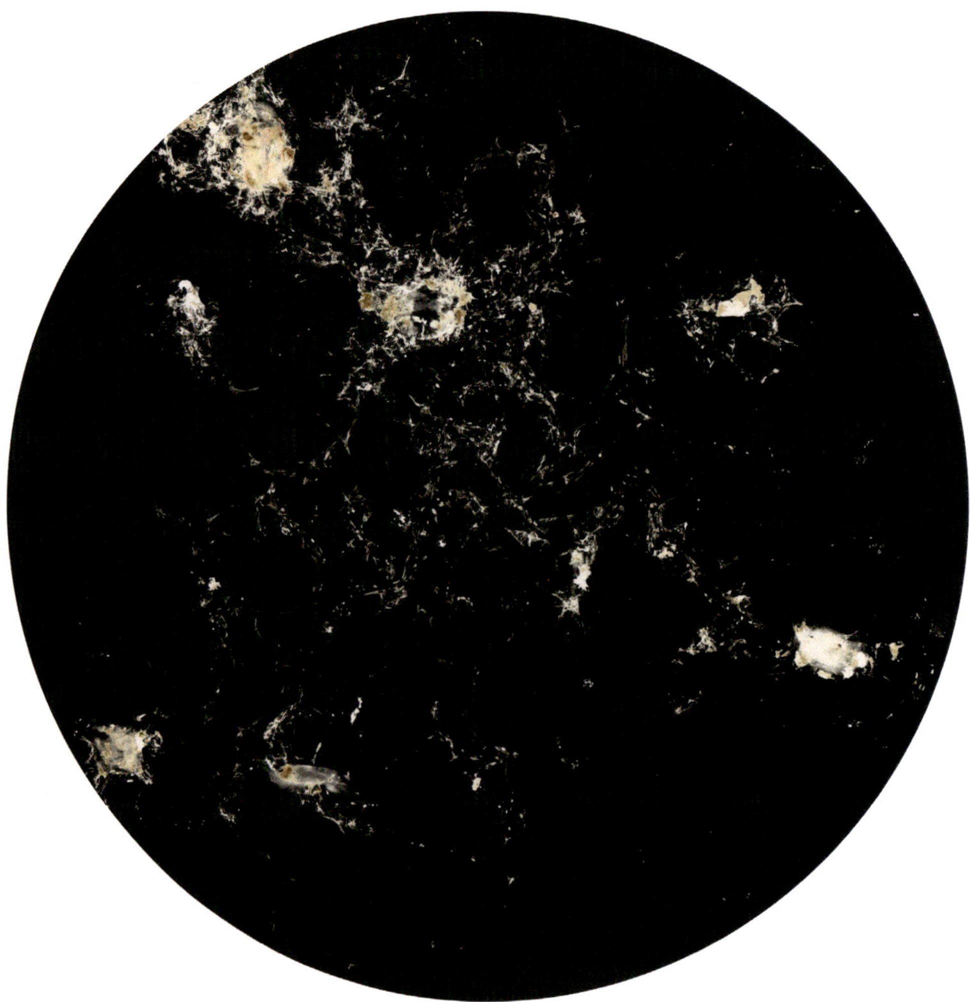

Figure P2.1. *Auric Object #5A*, silver gelatin photogram, 19.62″ diameter © DM Witman 2013. "From darkness, light and life emerge. Since the earliest of days, stars have acted as beacons home, simultaneously providing material for stories and fortunes. These celestial night images—my own nebulae and galaxies—aren't made from dark matter of the universe, but rather by the common slug. Delicate and persistent, the slug moves about from dusk until dawn on gelatin silver paper in my darkroom, making marks through their biology, creating something new. These images exist as microcosms of the cycles of life: feeding, defecation, sex, movement, life and death. I built a slug containment system in the darkroom using large trays. I collected slugs and placed silver gelatin paper in the trays emulsion side up. I allowed a faint light source to emit light. I placed the slugs on the paper, along with sponges for water (slugs need moisture to survive!). I had to make sure the slugs were contained and could not escape. I allowed the slugs to move about freely for several hours and then returned them to where I collected them. The paper was then processed normally and toned in selenium." DM Witman is a transdisciplinary artist working at the intersection of environmental disruption and the human relationship to place in the Age of the Anthropocene. Her creative practice is deeply rooted within the realm of the effects of humans on this world using photographic materials, video, and installation. To see more of her work visit www.dmwitman.com.

PART TWO

Camera Experimentation

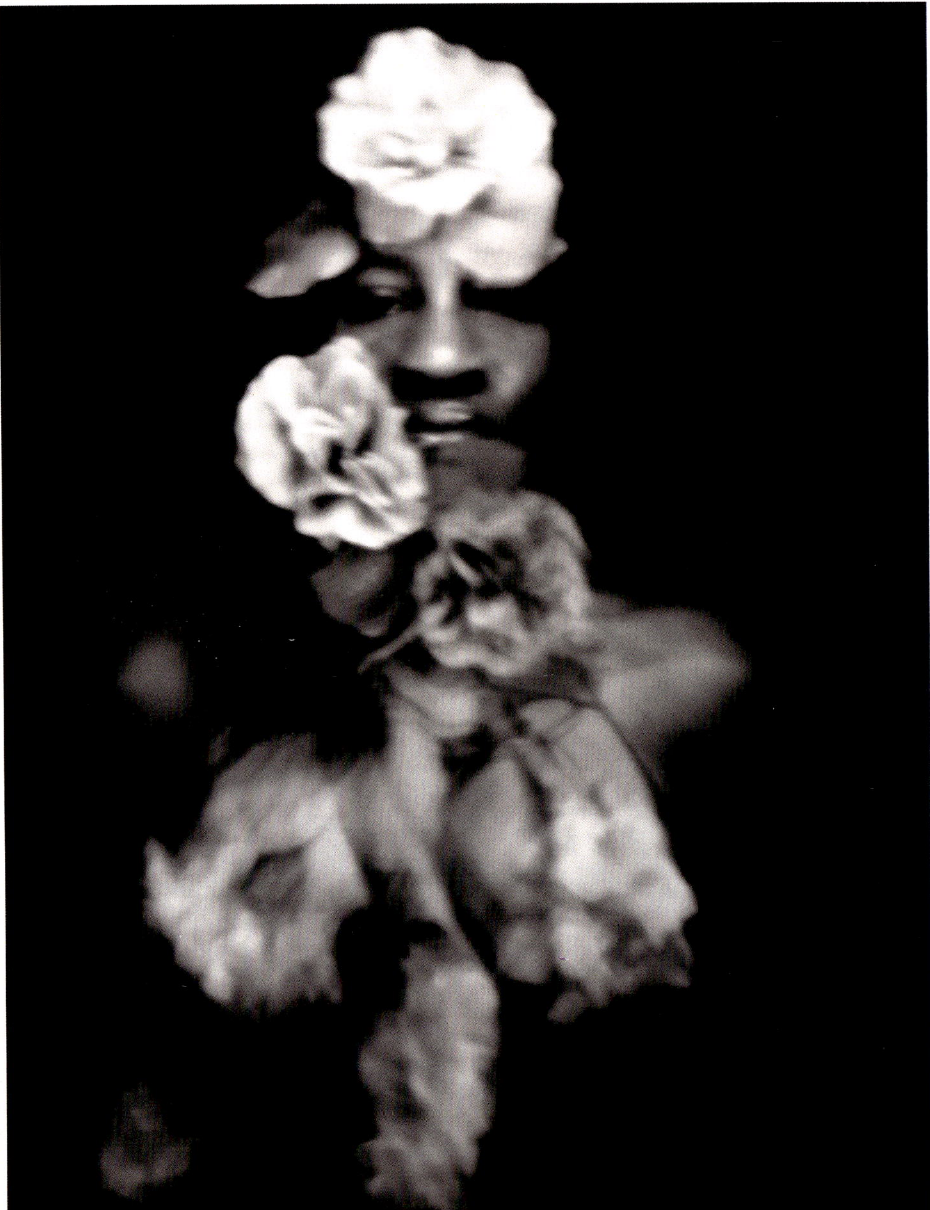

Figure 6.1. *Secret Garden*, 11″ x 14″ © Nicole Small One on One 2017. "An obsession with pinhole photography has opened the doors to limitless creativity and unique imagery. Most of the self-portraits were made using darkroom paper but also film. Each self-portrait was applied with a vision and title in mind. The idea of creating pinhole self-portraits began as an experiment. I began working with two 300 watt hot lights, which I had calculated as a total of 600 watts which I believed would be enough to work with. I was wrong. Exposure times varied between 8–13 minutes and the shorter times only happened when I had placed the lights just about two feet away, which included burning of the skin! I finally invested in continuous studio LED lighting which I now use for pinhole portraits of both myself and others." Nicole Small is an artist and photographer in Montreal, Canada specializing in fine art photography and self-portraiture. Exploration of the unusual and the non-mainstream are the generators behind her works of art through the use of historical photographic techniques alongside the dimensions of light and stillness in time. To see more of her work follow her on Instagram @nicolesmall_oneonone and nicolesmalljournalentries.wordpress.com; also YouTube: NicoleSmallOneonOne.

Pinhole and Zoneplate

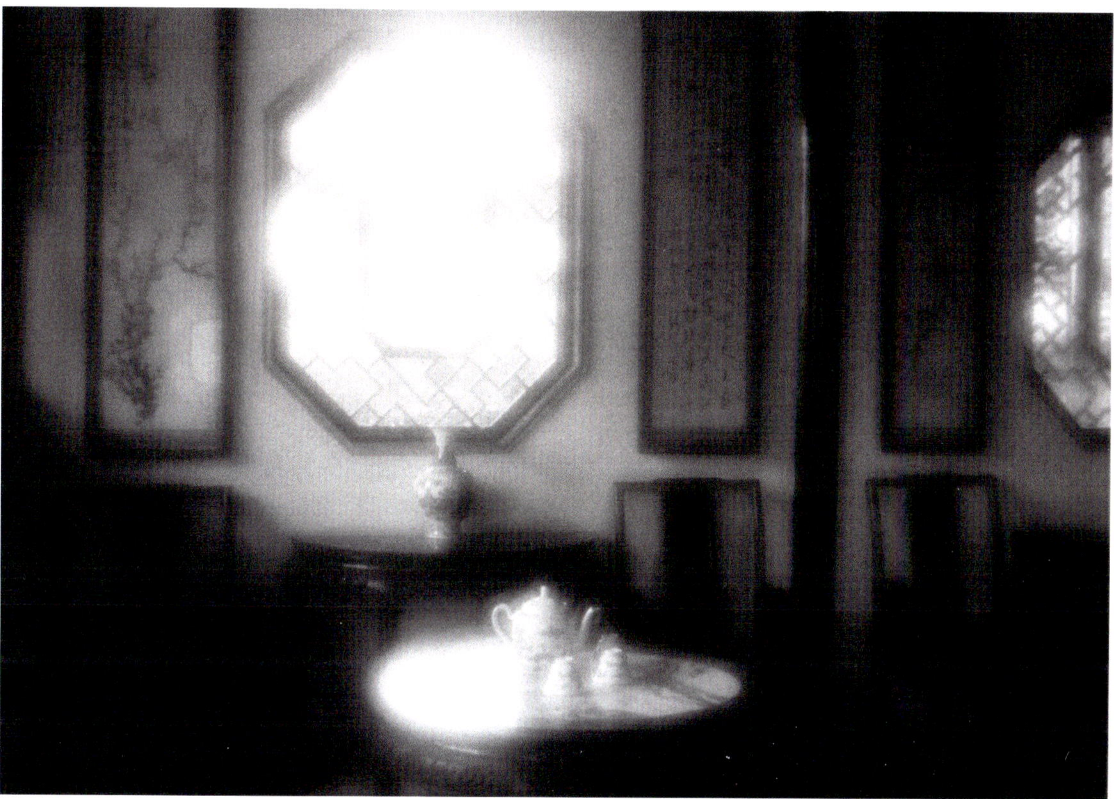

Figure 6.2. *Teapot*, digital zone plate, Kodak Azo paper printed with a QTR digital negative © Sam Wang 2021. Sam Wang retired in 2006 after teaching photography for 40 years at Clemson University, South Carolina. He has continued his photographic work in addition to locturing and publishing in tho US and China. His work is in the collections of numerous museums and art centers here and abroad. To see more of Wang's work visit www.samwang.us.

Pinhole cameras are the ultimate anti-technology. There's no lens to focus. There's no viewfinder to look through. A successful image becomes the result of the photographer allowing serendipity to happen, and not the sophistication of the equipment. It puts the play back into the process of picture making.

Instead of a lens, a pinhole camera has a minute hole for an aperture. This makes for longer exposures and softer images. There is no focusing since there is no lens, but no need to focus because a pinhole camera has almost infinite depth of field, or universal depth of field to use a more descriptive term. Something one inch away from the camera all the way to the farthest part of a landscape will all be equally sharp, or soft as the case may be.

The images remain rectilinear—there is no curvilinear distortion. Straight lines remain straight. This is most apparent at horizon lines.

Size, on the other hand, is very much distorted, and is something to capitalize upon. A little pebble close to the lens will appear like a boulder and a boulder in the distance will appear like a pebble.

The attributes of a pinhole camera, therefore, are a softer focus, universally "sharp," rectilinear, size distorted image.

Pinhole technicals

You could photograph with a pinhole and through trial and error figure out how to best make a picture. Or you could figure it out mathematically. There is this gamut of pinhole practice from flying by the seat of your pants to mathematical, and all ultimately result in good images. I will share the math in this chapter but don't let it prevent you from winging it if "being exact is not your thing." The four math-based calculations are:

- Calculating **optimal pinhole size**
- Calculating **f-stop**
- Calculating **exposure**
- Calculating **reciprocity failure**

Calculating optimal pinhole size

Depth of field is the area in a photograph where "circles of confusion" are perceived by your eye as being points and not blobs—where your eye registers focus. The pinhole needs to be big enough to allow the most light in so that exposures are as short as possible, but the pinhole needs to be small enough to keep circles of confusion small enough so that the eye perceives the image as being acceptably sharp.

There is a point where the pinhole image become too sharp and the resulting image looks like a normal image taken with an inferior lens. There is even a point where a too small pinhole is subject to light diffraction where the image becomes degraded, low contrast, and fuzzy. Somewhere in-between too soft and too sharp is the optimal pinhole size, and there is a formula for this, easy to calculate:

(The Square root of the Focal Length) × 0.007
= Optimal pinhole diameter (all in inches!)

The focal length is nothing more than taking a tape measure and measuring the distance between where the film (or paper) is from the back of the camera to the pinhole. If you make the optimal pinhole size for your camera and decide you want to have a softer focus image, you can easily use a larger pinhole diameter, up to double the size.

Finding the right needle

Once you've figured out the optimal pinhole size, you have to find a needle that will drill the hole for that diameter. Not all needle packages are labeled with needle size so it's guesswork. If you are lucky to find the needle size written on the package, like Clover brand, the diameter is in millimeters so convert it to inches by dividing the millimeters by 25.4. The smallest needle diameter in the Clover brand is the #10 quilting needle that has a diameter of .46 mm/.018″. This is optimal for a 6″ focal length camera (quilting needles are short and sturdy needles that don't bend much).

Needle size chart

Standard needle diameters/Optimal focal length:

Needle #6	.030	Around 16–18″
Needle #7	.027	Around 13–15″
Needle #8	.024	Around 10–12″
Needle #9	.021	Around 8″
Needle #10	.018	Around 6″
Needle #12	.014	Around 3½–4″
Needle #13	.012	Around 2¾″
Needle #15	.010	Around 1 ½–2″

If you are not the do-it-yourself kind of person, you can buy micro-drilled pinholes in all sorts of sizes! See **Pinhole Resources** at the end of this chapter.

Calculating the f-stop

Focal length divided by aperture = f-stop.

The focal length is a simple measurement from film plane to pinhole. The aperture is the diameter of the needle hole. As long as both are inches to inches or millimeters to millimeters, this formula is easy math division.

Calculating exposure

An easy way to do so is to use silver gelatin paper in the camera, make exposures, and develop the negatives as you would normally a silver gelatin paper, then assess. A more accurate method is to use a light meter, which even come on iPhones.

1. Set the light meter to F16.

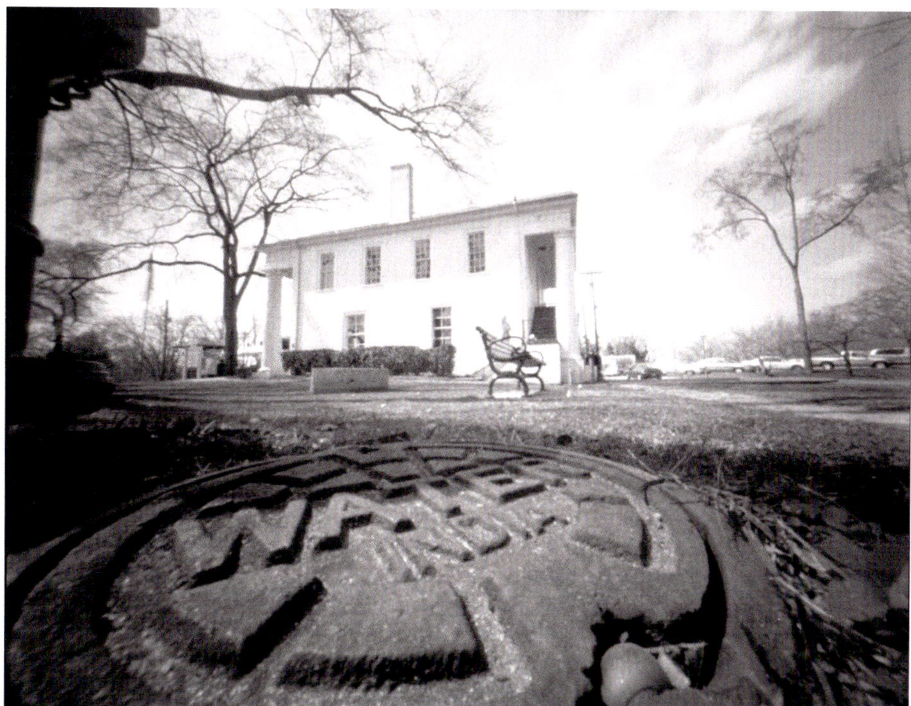

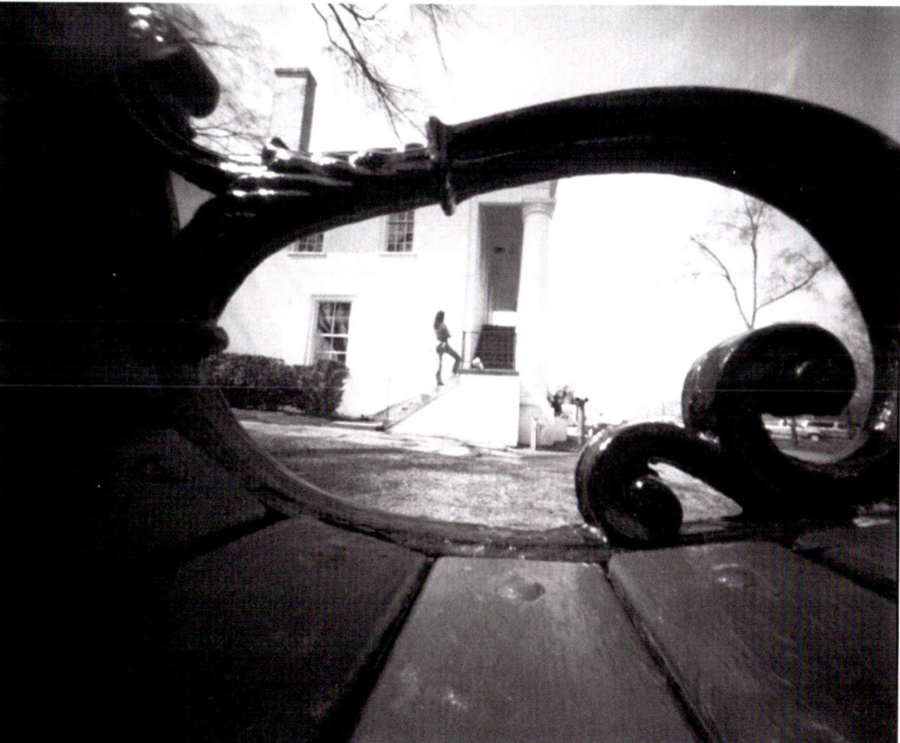

Figures 6.3–6.4. Top, *Farmers' Hall*, pinhole photograph from 4″ x 5″ sheet film exposed in a self-built extreme wide angle camera to take 4″ x 5″ film holders © Sam Wang 2006. Note the extreme depth of field where the camera is resting on the ground while exposing. Bottom, *The Wait*, pinhole photograph from 4″ x 5″ sheet film exposed in the same camera © Sam Wang 2006. The camera was resting on the park bench for this image.

2. Enter the film's ISO into the meter.
3. Take an incident meter reading with the meter facing the camera.
4. Figure out how many f-stops *smaller* from F16 the pinhole camera's aperture is. For instance, if a pinhole is F186, it would go like this: F22 to F32 to F45 to F64 to F90 to F128 to F180 or a little over 7 stops smaller than F16. Since each stop doubles the time of the stop below it, this would equate to 2 × 2 × 2 × 2 × 2 × 2 × 2 (*not* 2 × 7 = 14, but 2^7 or 128).
5. Multiply 128 × the shutter speed that the meter indicates. For instance, if the meter said F16 at 1⁄125th second, multiply 1⁄125th × 128 = 128⁄125 or about one second exposure.

In this example, 128 is the *exposure factor* relative to F16. Sometimes pre-made pinholes will come with an exposure factor, stated something like this: "Exposure time relative to F16," meaning the meter reading is always taken at F16. Some cameras will have an exposure time relative to F64, in which case the meter reading is taken at F64, etc.

Speaking of exposure factor

The charts at the end of this chapter are all based on the exposure factor formula. If one is Excel spreadsheet savvy, it is easy to build a spreadsheet to compute all exposures for all cameras with a simple entry of any f-stop number. The charts at the end of the chapter will handle most pinhole situations, but here's the math in case you want to know.

The charts are based on an exposure factor relative to F16, because most photographers understand the "Sunny 16" rule: on a sunny day, outside in full sun, a correct exposure will equal F16 at a shutter speed of 1/ISO. For example, using 3200 film, the exposure would be F16 at 1/3200. This is only a starting point for determining exposure factor, because of course all pinhole exposures are not taken outside on a sunny day. Following is the formula:

$$\frac{(\text{time @ F/16}) \times (\text{pinhole f-stop}^2)}{16^2}$$

To use the former example of F16 at 1/125 and an f-stop of F186, the formula would look like this:

$$\frac{(1/125) \times (186^2)}{16^2}$$

How would this math be done in a timely fashion in the field, though? It is way too complex. This is where the simple exposure factor comes into play.

There are two variables that *never* vary in the formula above. The *aperture* of the pinhole never varies (in this case, F186). The *aperture* to plug into the light meter never varies (in this case, F16), and thus the only variable is *time* which will always vary with changing light conditions.

Thus, the formula can be greatly simplified by separating it out to a simple number that is used to multiply the continually changing time variable, or as it is called, the "shutter speed" even though a pinhole technically doesn't have a shutter. That simple number is the *exposure factor*. When one's exposure factor is calculated one time for each camera, the only thing to do in the field is to take a meter reading at F16 with the correct film ISO and then multiply the meter-indicated shutter speed by the exposure factor. Here's how it works:

$$(\text{time @ F/16}) \times \quad \frac{\text{pinhole f-stop}^2}{16^2}$$

The right side of this equation = exposure factor, when using a relative aperture of F16. If using a relative aperture of F64, plug the number 64 in where 16 is currently.

Reciprocity correction for film

Using body caps on digital cameras is easy, because with one image capture you can quickly tell if you have exposed correctly. Digital cameras also do not experience the same reciprocity failure as do film cameras. Consult the film manufacturer for reciprocity data since films differ. Test a film before committing to an important project. Below are suggestions. When in doubt, err on the side of overexposure when using long exposure times.

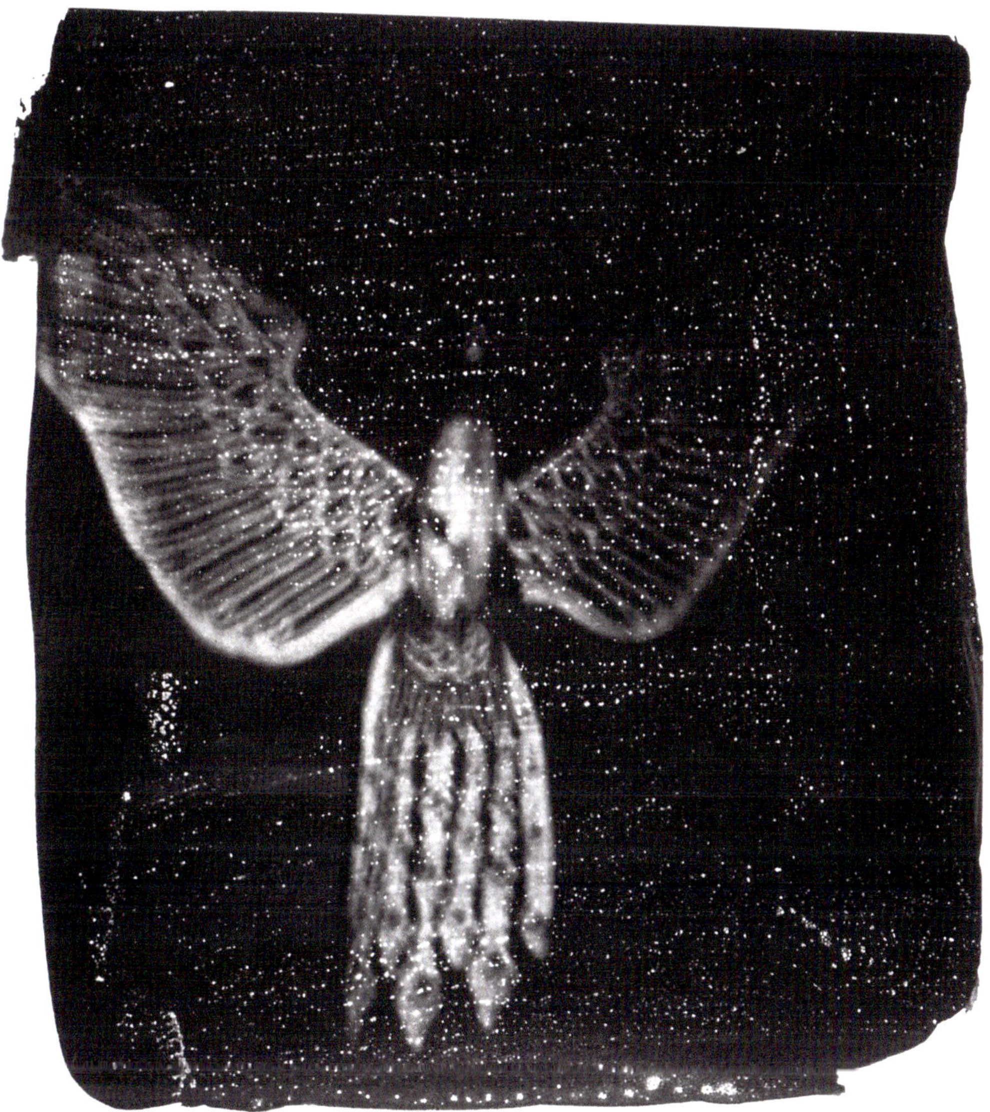

Figure 6.5. *Bird Kite*, pinhole image printed with hand coated Liquid Light emulsion on watercolor paper, 11″ x 11″ © Brenton Hamilton 2021. Brenton Hamilton's photography practice is centered upon traditional photographic materials. His work in silver processes and an array of 19th century methods—platinum, gum bichromate, paper calotype and cyanotype—have occupied him for over two decades. Hamilton is interested in experimenting with the materials of photography, unusual combinations of light sensitive materials and emulsions, and embellished printmaking. He exhibits regularly and internationally and has participated in over 100 exhibitions of his works. Recently a 25 year retrospective monograph, *Blue Idyll*, was published by Schilt publishing in Amsterdam. To see more of Hamilton's work follow him @BrentonHamilton and visit BrentonHamilton.com.

Exposure	Compensation
1–5 seconds	× 1¼
5–10 seconds	× 1½
10–15 seconds	× 2
15–20 seconds	× 3
20–40 seconds	× 4
40–60 seconds	× 5
1–2 minutes	× 6
2–4 minutes	× 8

Reciprocity correction for paper

1 minute	×	1.25
5 minutes	×	1.5
10 minutes	×	1.75
25 minutes	×	2
40 minutes	×	2.4
1 hour	×	2.75
2 hours	×	3
5 hours	×	4
10 hours	×	5
20 hours	×	6

Image diameter

The pinhole projects a circle of light 3½× the size of its focal length. Thus, a 6″ focal length produces an image circle of 21″. With light fall off around the edges—vignetting—this image area is not all exposed at the same strength of light. This is especially apparent when using enlarging paper in the pinhole camera. Since its speed is slow to begin with, there will be a good exposure in a small central area while the rest of the paper remains pure white. This works to one's benefit, though, when using these paper negatives in the enlarger; the small, exposed image area fits nicely in a 4″ × 5″ negative carrier.

Direct positive paper

Harman/Ilford now has a direct positive RC paper perfect for use in pinhole cameras or large format cameras or even Holga or "krappy" cameras because the image will not be a negative but a positive! It is a fixed grade, high contrast paper (3½–4 grade), fully compatible with conventional black and white paper processing chemistry. It is available in glossy and luster. Its speed is ISO 4–6. Paper is good for two years normal storage, much longer, of course, if stored in the freezer. Two caveats:

- The paper must be handled under red safelight.
- With direct positive paper, *less* exposure is needed to make the image darker, unlike conventional photo papers where more exposure is needed to darken the image.

Bright summer sun	1–2 minutes
Bright but not direct sunshine	2–3 minutes
Overcast (mixed sun/clouds)	4–5 minutes
Dull/cloudy	6–10 minutes
Interiors	1 hour

How to make a pinhole

Supplies

Small square piece of .003 or .002 brass shim stock or a piece out of an aluminum disposable pie pan or pop can
Pencil with an eraser tip, or a cork
Needle
400–600 grit sandpaper
Loupe

Any container capable of excluding light will work. There must be a way to get a piece of sensitized material into the container, and get it out after the exposure is made. Containers have ranged from small objects such as saltshakers, through very large items such as oil drums or luggage. Even trucks and rooms in buildings have been turned into cameras, as have red peppers, watermelons, and other unusual items.

Inside the camera, various materials such as black fabric, ultra flat black spray paint, or black tape should be used to eliminate internal reflections.

1. Insert the needle into the eraser-tip of the pencil, or into the cork. Be sure to get it straight so that when drilling the hole, the needle will be perpendicular to the metal.
2. Twirl this pencil/needle tool into the piece of metal to drill a straight hole. Have something underneath the metal piece to protect the table.
3. Keep twirling until the needle pierces through the metal. Pull the needle out, and on the opposite side there will be a little burr that will need to be sanded and flattened with the sandpaper. Do all this gently.

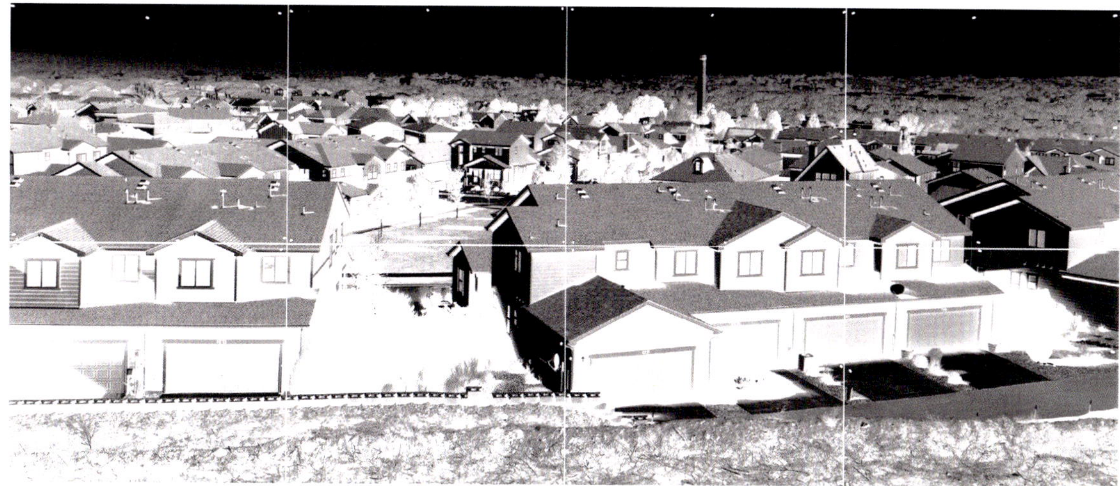

Figures 6.6–6.7. *Sprawl*, from the *Taking Time* series, silver gelatin print composite, 80″ x 32″ © Heather Oelklaus 2021. "The slow nature of pinhole photography alongside the desire to fit the world through a tiny hole are the inspirations for *Taking Time*, a series of ultra large paper negatives. Each piece in the series was photographed with my 1977 Chevy Box truck that has been transformed into a pinhole camera with an F1497 aperture. The truck is capable of photographing all the way up to 5′ x 10′ images. In this composite photograph the truck photographs the scene onto eight pieces of 16″ x 20″ Ilford Pearl RC Paper."

Heather Oelklaus lives in Colorado Springs where she explores unconventional photography. Photography as object and one of a kind photographic processes such as chemigram, lumen prints, pinhole, and cyanotype are her art making interest. Oelklaus explores themes of family, social roles, and abstract art. To see more of Oelklaus' work visit www.camerakarma.com.

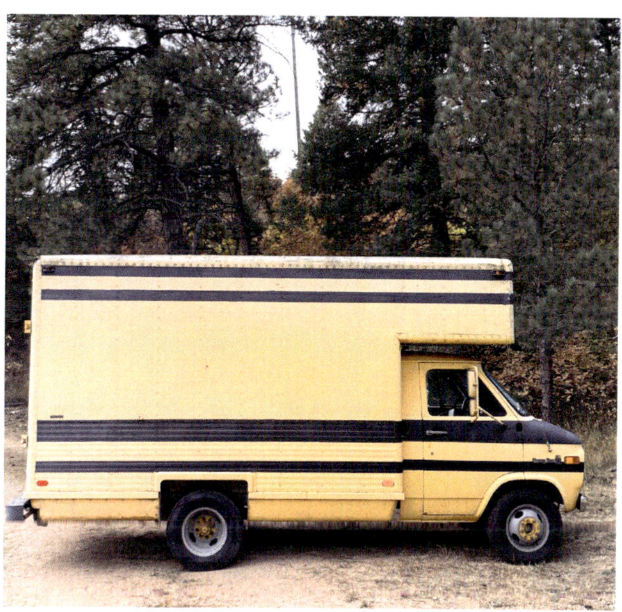

4. Drill the hole again with the needle, going in from the opposite side this time—the side that had the burr. Sand the opposite side when the needle has pierced through again. Keep twirling and drilling, and sanding the burrs off when the needle breaks through. Get out the loupe or magnifying glass and check to make sure the pinhole is nice and clean. The quality of the image will vary according to how the hole is made. Sometimes the ragged edges of the pinhole make for a unique image.

Oatmeal/ice cream pinhole camera

With an oatmeal box, all that is needed is black flat spray paint to cover the inside of the box, and black tape to cover any seams that might leak light. Spray the inside side of the pinhole plate flat black, being sure to cover the pinhole during the spraying process so as not to clog it with paint. When loading it with photo paper, tape the paper to the inside of the container so it does not wiggle. An ice cream container fits 8″ × 10″ nicely. RC paper can be used in the box. Matte paper is best for curved film

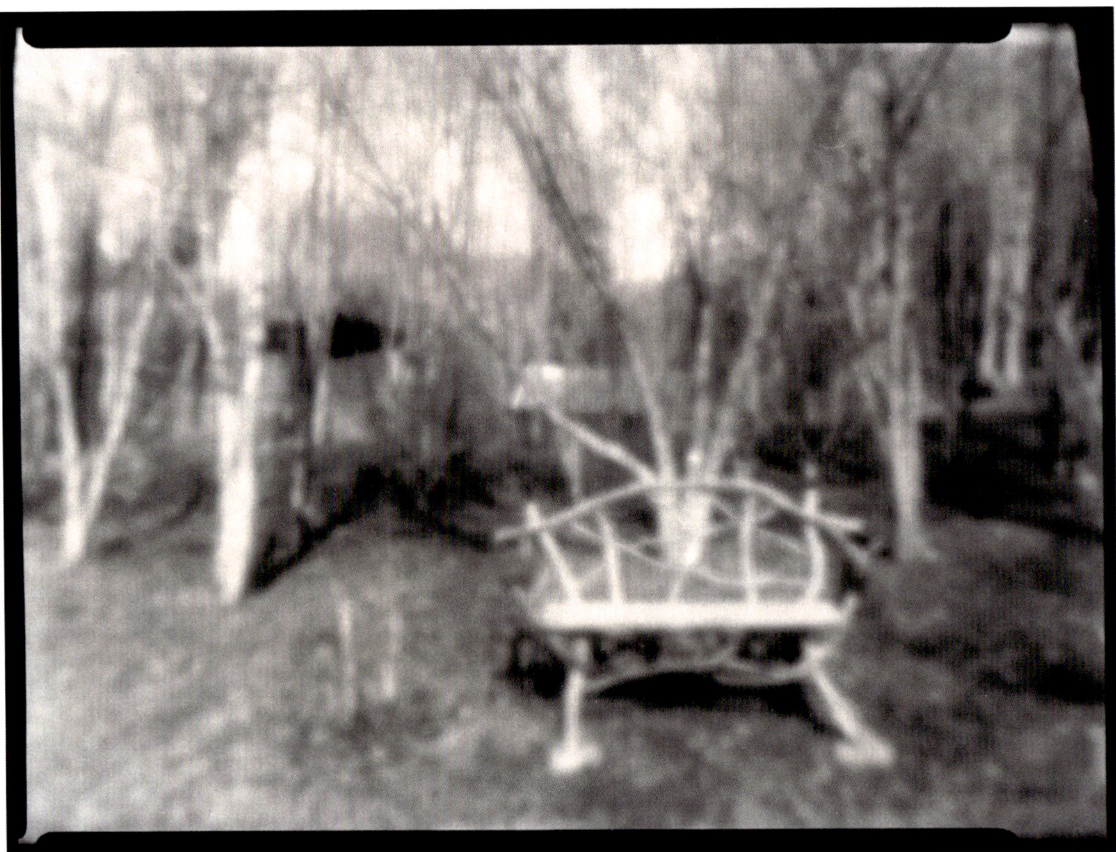

Figure 6.8. *Garden Bench by the Dogwoods*, silver gelatin print from a zone plate (~90 mm) in-camera film negative, Delta 100 5″ x 7″ film, Ilford MG Warmtone, toned with selenium and polytoner © J. P. Jackson 2021. "My picture making is a personal need that involves constant interactive perception of the world around me. It is like a 'call and response' that challenges me and sometimes brings me joy. I practice 'slow' photography because it suits my nature and the quality of analog photographic prints can be very beautiful." J. P. Jackson has been passionate about making pictures for over forty years. In the mid 1970s he had the good fortune to study photography with Jerry N. Uelsmann and Todd Walker at the University of Florida. In 2015, Jackson returned to darkroom work teaching himself cyanotype, platinum-palladium, gum dichromate, carbon printing and copperplate and photopolymer intaglio printing. Jackson works with analog film and prints by hand. To see more of his work, follow him on Instagram @jackson_john_p or visit ipernity.com/home/jpjackson.

planes because glossy will tend to show reflection marks. The paper is then processed normally and used as a paper negative. Photo paper is usually around ISO 1–12. Ilford paper is ISO 1–1.5, Arista ISO around 8.

Note that in a pinhole camera if the film plane is flat, there will be light fall-off or vignetting at the corners. The image may be overexposed at the center and underexposed at the corners. This vignetting, however, may be exploited consciously as an aesthetic effect. If light fall-off is not desired, the film plane can be curved so that the film at any point is roughly at the same distance from the pinhole.

Film canister pinhole camera

A quick pinhole camera could be an old film canister. Punch the plastic side with a paper punch hole and put the pinhole on top. Use a piece of electrical tape for the shutter, and cut little pieces of paper to fit inside. This will produce little paper negatives perfect for a 35 mm negative carrier. Paper texture will show in the enlarged image.

35mm pinhole body cap

A 35 mm camera body has a focal length of about 47 mm/1.85″. The needle size that would work best would be the #15, but can also be fudged a bit up to a #12. Buy a camera body cap to fit the camera. Drill a hole in the center. A Forstner bit works well for this because it has a pointed end to start the hole more quickly. Center the pinhole on this hole and tape in place. Easier yet, buy a readymade pinhole body cap from the resources listed in this chapter.

Zone plate

A zone plate pinhole is a piece of high contrast film with a miniscule bull's eye of concentric circles of dark and clear that is placed over a hole in a camera body cap or a lensboard. The zone plate bull's eye is the "pinhole" and exposes images that are soft focus, with a halo of light surrounding the edges of objects. It is a faster aperture than a regular pinhole of equivalent size (about 10×). However, the downside of a zone plate is the need to be more critical in matching the plate to a correct focal length, and considering the f-stop is around F64 to F128, a zone plate does not have infinite depth of field. Focus becomes more critical, especially in close-up work. Contrast in a zone plate image can be low but is easily corrected when using digital negatives. Zoneplate images have an intriguing mystical quality—quite addictive. Calculating exposure with a zone plate is the same as any pinhole camera. Zone plates can be found at PinholeResource.com. There is even a website to generate a zone plate: mrpinhole.com/zp.php.

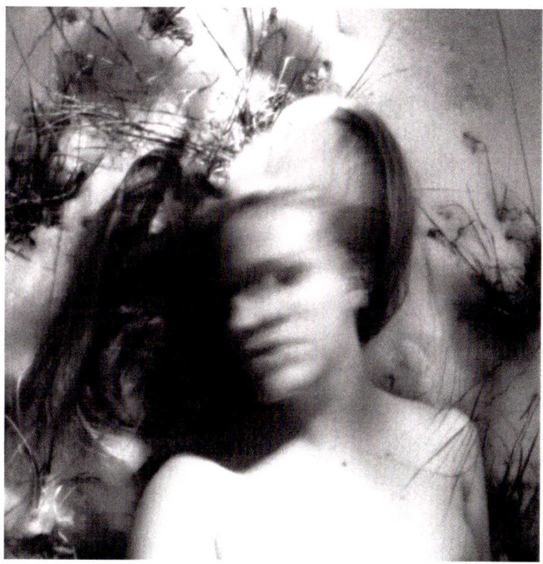

Figure 6.9. *Untitled Self Portrait*, silver gelatin print from a Holga pinhole negative, 10″ x 10″© Julia C. Martin 2019. To see more of Martin's work visit juliacmartin.com.

Tips and ideas

- Don't hand hold the camera.
- Do position the subject much closer to the camera than in "normal" photography, or the subject will be too small. Something can be positioned right next to the lens because there is no issue with depth of field.
- Do make sure the subject is in the picture for at least ½ the exposure time to get ghostlike images; if the subject is in motion, increase this time even more.

Pinhole resources

The Pinhole Resource: PinholeResource.com
Freestyle Photo: freestylephoto.biz
Wooden pinhole cameras: www.zeroimage.com
Pinhole math: pinhole.cz/en/pinholedesigner
Laser-drilled pinholes! daystarlaser.com.

Pinhole exposure tables

1. Xerox the following tables that match a camera's pinhole f-stop and tape them to the camera, so that when going out in the field the only thing necessary to bring is the camera and a light meter. If the chart f-stops do not match the pinhole camera exactly, use the closest f-stop that is a smaller aperture.
2. Set the light meter at F16 and the ISO of the meter to match the ISO of the film.
3. Set the shutter speed of the light meter to match the ISO of the film, 1/ISO. For instance—100 ISO film, set the shutter speed to 1/100 second. 400 ISO film set the shutter speed to 1/500 second. 800 speed film set the shutter speed to 1/800 second, and so on. The shutter speed should be as close a match as possible. If there is no 1/800, use the next shortest shutter speed (1/1000).
4. Take an incident light meter reading of the scene, pointing the meter toward the camera as is usual with an incident reading.
5. Record the f-stop the light meter says to use.
6. Find the vertical column on the chart for that indicated f-stop, and follow the column down to where the ISO of the film on the left hand side of the chart and that f-stop column intersect. That is your exposure time.
7. If the exposure time is 1 second or more, look at the Reciprocity Correction table on the left side of the chart and multiply the time accordingly. Some films such as Fuji film may not require any reciprocity correction up to as long as two minutes.

F64	Yellow highlighted numbers have been adjusted to minutes.								
Reciprocity Correction Suggestions	ISO	16	11	8	5.6	4	2.8	2	1.4
	3200	0.01	0.01	0.02	0.04	0.08	0.16	0.32	0.7
1 sec x 1 ¼	1600	0.01	0.02	0.04	0.08	0.16	0.33	0.6	1.3
5 sec x 1 ½	800	0.02	0.04	0.08	0.16	0.32	0.7	1.3	3
15 sec x 2	400	0.04	0.08	0.16	0.33	0.6	1.3	3	5
45 sec x 2 ½	320	0.05	0.11	0.20	0.41	0.8	2	3	7
2 min x 3	250	0.06	0.14	0.26	0.5	1.0	2	4	8
5 min x 4	200	0.08	0.17	0.32	0.7	1.3	3	5	10
10 min x 5	160	0.10	0.21	0.40	0.8	2	3	6	13
20 min x 6	125	0.13	0.27	0.5	1.0	2	4	8	17
40 min x 8	100	0.16	0.34	0.6	1.3	3	5	10	21
	80	0.20	0.42	0.8	2	3	7	13	26
	64	0.25	0.5	1.0	2	4	8	16	33
	50	0.32	0.7	1.3	3	5	10	20	42
	25	0.6	1.4	3	5	10	21	41	84
	12	1.3	3	5	11	21	44	85	3
	6	3	6	11	22	43	87	3	6
	3	5	11	21	44	85	3	6	12
	1.5	11	23	43	87	3	6	11	23
	1	16	34	64	2	4	9	17	35

F90	Yellow highlighted numbers have been adjusted to minutes.								
Reciprocity Correction Suggestions	ISO	16	11	8	5.6	4	2.8	2	1.4
	3200	0.01	0.02	0.04	0.08	0.16	0.32	0.6	1.3
1 sec x 1 ¼	1600	0.02	0.04	0.08	0.16	0.32	0.6	1.3	3
5 sec x 1 ½	800	0.04	0.08	0.16	0.32	0.6	1.3	3	5
15 sec x 2	400	0.08	0.17	0.32	0.6	1.3	3	5	10
45 sec x 2 ½	320	0.10	0.21	0.40	0.8	2	3	6	13
2 min x 3	250	0.13	0.27	0.5	1.0	2	4	8	17
5 min x 4	200	0.16	0.33	0.6	1.3	3	5	10	21
10 min x 5	160	0.20	0.42	0.8	2	3	6	13	26
20 min x 6	125	0.25	0.5	1.0	2	4	8	16	33
40 min x 8	100	0.32	0.7	1.3	3	5	10	20	41
	80	0.40	0.8	2	3	6	13	25	52
	64	0.49	1.0	2	4	8	16	32	65
	50	0.6	1.3	3	5	10	21	41	83
	25	1.3	3	5	10	20	41	81	3
	12	3	6	11	22	42	86	3	6
	6	5	11	21	43	84	3	6	11
	3	11	22	42	86	3	6	11	23
	1.5	21	45	84	3	6	11	23	46
	1	32	67	2	4	8	17	34	69

F128	Yellow highlighted numbers have been adjusted to minutes.								
Reciprocity Correction Suggestions	ISO	16	11	8	5.6	4	2.8	2	1.4
	3200	0.02	0.04	0.08	0.16	0.32	0.7	1.3	3
1 sec x 1 ¼	1600	0.04	0.08	0.16	0.33	0.6	1.3	3	5
5 sec x 1 ½	800	0.08	0.17	0.32	0.7	1.3	3	5	10
15 sec x 2	400	0.16	0.34	0.6	1.3	3	5	10	21
45 sec x 2 ½	320	0.20	0.42	0.8	2	3	7	13	26
2 min x 3	250	0.26	0.5	1.0	2	4	8	16	33
5 min x 4	200	0.32	0.7	1.3	3	5	10	20	42
10 min x 5	160	0.40	0.8	2	3	6	13	26	52
20 min x 6	125	0.5	1.1	2	4	8	17	33	67
40 min x 8	100	0.6	1.4	3	5	10	21	41	84
	80	0.8	2	3	7	13	26	51	2
	64	1.0	2	4	8	16	33	64	2
	50	1.3	3	5	10	20	42	82	3
	25	3	5	10	21	41	84	3	6
	12	5	11	21	44	85	3	6	12
	6	11	23	43	87	3	6	11	23
	3	21	45	85	3	6	12	23	46
	1.5	43	1.5	3	6	11	23	46	93
	1	64	2	4	9	17	35	68	139

F180	Yellow highlighted numbers have been adjusted to minutes.								
Reciprocity Correction Suggestions	ISO	16	11	8	5.6	4	2.8	2	1.4
	3200	0.04	0.08	0.16	0.32	0.6	1.3	3	5
1 sec x 1 ¼	1600	0.08	0.17	0.32	0.6	1.3	3	5	10
5 sec x 1 ½	800	0.16	0.33	0.6	1.3	3	5	10	21
15 sec x 2	400	0.32	0.7	1.3	3	5	10	20	41
45 sec x 2 ½	320	0.40	0.8	2	3	6	13	25	52
2 min x 3	250	0.5	1.1	2	4	8	17	32	66
5 min x 4	200	0.6	1.3	3	5	10	21	41	83
10 min x 5	160	0.8	2	3	6	13	26	51	2
20 min x 6	125	1.0	2	4	8	16	33	65	2
40 min x 8	100	1.3	3	5	10	20	41	81	3
	80	2	3	6	13	25	52	2	3
	64	2	4	8	16	32	65	2	4
	50	3	5	10	21	41	83	3	6
	25	5	11	20	41	81	3	5	11
	12	11	22	42	86	3	6	11	23
	6	21	45	84	3	6	11	23	46
	3	42	89	3	6	11	23	45	92
	1.5	84	3	6	11	23	46	90	184
	1	2	4	8	17	34	69	135	276

F256	Yellow highlighted numbers have been adjusted to minutes.								
Reciprocity Correction Suggestions	ISO	16	11	8	5.6	4	2.8	2	1.4
	3200	0.08	0.17	0.32	0.7	1.3	3	5	10
1 sec x 1 ¼	1600	0.16	0.34	0.6	1.3	3	5	10	21
5 sec x 1 ½	800	0.32	0.7	1.3	3	5	10	20	42
15 sec x 2	400	0.6	1.4	3	5	10	21	41	84
45 sec x 2 ½	320	0.8	2	3	7	13	26	51	2
2 min x 3	250	1.0	2	4	8	16	33	66	2
5 min x 4	200	1.3	3	5	10	20	42	82	3
10 min x 5	160	2	3	6	13	26	52	2	3
20 min x 6	125	2	4	8	17	33	67	2	4
40 min x 8	100	3	5	10	21	41	84	3	6
	80	3	7	13	26	51	2	3	7
	64	4	8	16	33	64	2	4	9
	50	5	11	20	42	82	3	5	11
	25	10	22	41	84	3	6	11	22
	12	21	45	85	3	6	12	23	46
	6	43	90	3	6	11	23	46	93
	3	85	3	6	12	23	46	91	186
	1.5	3	6	11	23	46	93	182	372
	1	4	9	17	35	68	139	273	557

F360	Yellow highlighted numbers have been adjusted to minutes.								
Reciprocity Correction Suggestions	ISO	16	11	8	5.6	4	2.8	2	1.4
	3200	0.16	0.33	0.6	1.3	3	5	10	21
1 sec x 1 ¼	1600	0.32	0.7	1.3	3	5	10	20	41
5 sec x 1 ½	800	0.6	1.3	3	5	10	21	41	83
15 sec x 2	400	1.3	3	5	10	20	41	81	3
45 sec x 2 ½	320	2	3	6	13	25	52	2	3
2 min x 3	250	2	4	8	17	32	66	2	4
5 min x 4	200	3	5	10	21	41	83	3	6
10 min x 5	160	3	7	13	26	51	2	3	7
20 min x 6	125	4	9	16	33	65	2	4	9
40 min x 8	100	5	11	20	41	81	3	5	11
	80	6	13	25	52	2	3	7	14
	64	8	17	32	65	2	4	8	17
	50	10	21	41	83	3	6	11	22
	25	20	43	81	3	5	11	22	44
	12	42	89	3	6	11	23	45	92
	6	84	3	6	11	23	46	90	184
	3	3	6	11	23	45	92	180	367
	1.5	6	12	23	46	90	184	360	735
	1	8	18	34	69	135	276	540	1102

F512	Yellow highlighted numbers have been adjusted to minutes.								
Reciprocity Correction Suggestions	ISO	16	11	8	5.6	4	2.8	2	1.4
	3200	0.32	0.7	1.3	3	5	10	20	42
1 sec x 1 ¼	1600	0.6	1.4	3	5	10	21	41	84
5 sec x 1 ½	800	1.3	3	5	10	20	42	82	3
15 sec x 2	400	3	5	10	21	41	84	3	6
45 sec x 2 ½	320	3	7	13	26	51	2	3	7
2 min x 3	250	4	9	16	33	66	2	4	9
5 min x 4	200	5	11	20	42	82	3	5	11
10 min x 5	160	6	14	26	52	2	3	7	14
20 min x 6	125	8	17	33	67	2	4	9	18
40 min x 8	100	10	22	41	84	3	6	11	22
	80	13	27	51	2	3	7	14	28
	64	16	34	64	2	4	9	17	35
	50	20	43	82	3	5	11	22	45
	25	41	87	3	6	11	22	44	89
	12	85	3	6	12	23	46	91	186
	6	3	6	11	23	46	93	182	372
	3	6	12	23	46	91	186	364	743
	1.5	11	24	46	93	182	372	728	1486
	1	17	36	68	139	273	557	1092	2229

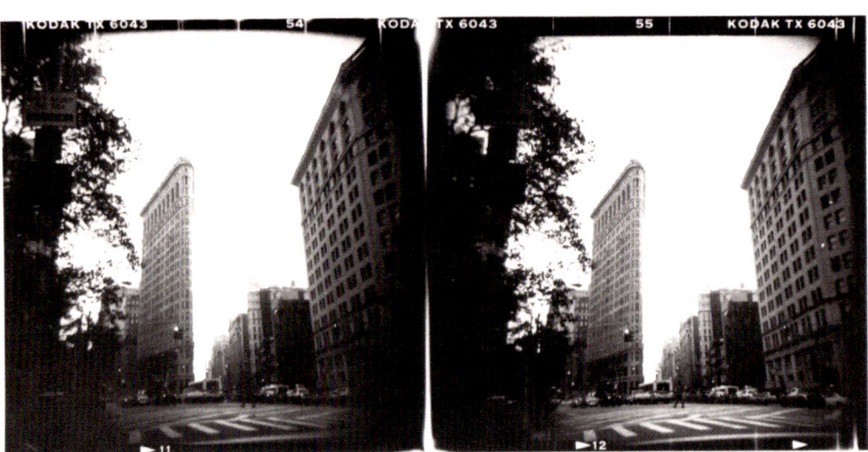

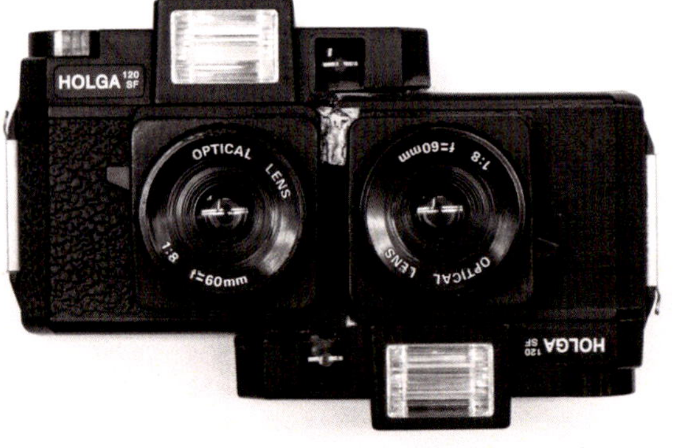

Figures 7.1–7.2. *Flatiron, New York*, silver gelatin stereo card, 7″ x 3.5″ © D. E. Todd 2022. "As a young artist I had the opportunity to go on a 'Grand Tour' following the tradition of European travel to study classical and Renaissance art. I've continued to explore historic formats central to the widespread popularization of travel photography ever since, including my homemade stereo-Holga and custom stereo cards. This homemade stereo camera was created by carefully measuring and sawing two Holga 120SF cameras with a hand-held jigsaw. The two pieces were first joined together with super-glue and duct tape before ritual upgrades led to epoxy and black gaffer tape in order to deter unyielding, yet affectionate, light leaks. The design allows a roll of 120 or 220 film to be loaded and advanced using the pre-existing spools and winding mechanisms. The lenses are spaced to the average distance between human eyes. The film is aligned to record a pair of corresponding left and right images side by side on the roll. The shutters are triggered independently, one with each hand, and one always upside-down. Each stereo card was printed in the darkroom using a custom negative carrier which allowed the corresponding left and right viewpoints to be enlarged and exposed simultaneously onto the photo paper." D. E. Todd is a photographic artist and educator known for his creative agility and hands-on approach to digital craft. His focus includes technical processes and photography's own pop-history. His works can be found in galleries, in print and online. To see more of Todd's work visit www.detodd.com.

The Holga

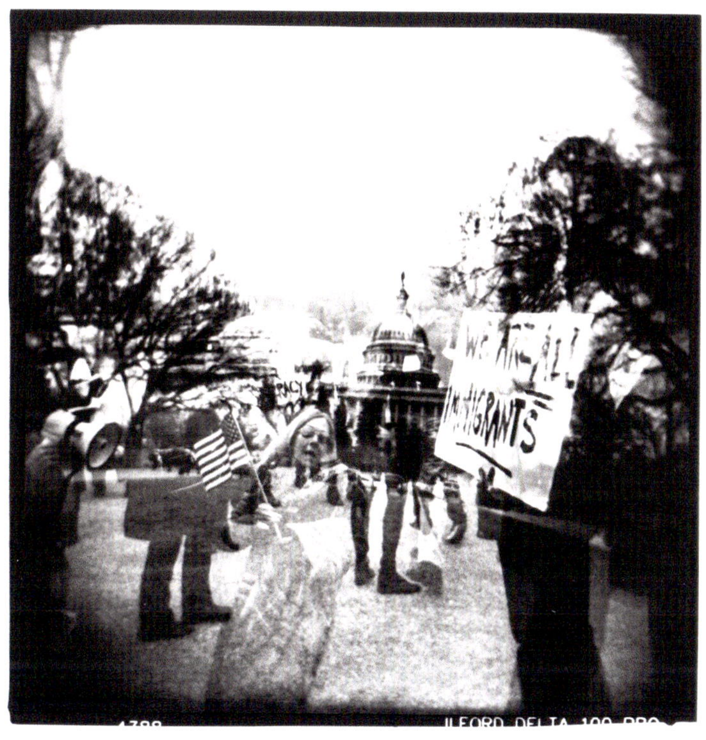

Figure 7.3. *We Are All Immigrants*, silver gelatin print from a Holga, 10″ x 10″ © Elizabeth Z. Pineda 2018. "*Caught between Two Worlds* is a work on immigration, identity, and belonging. The dual image offers a sense of past/present, old/new, cultural/political change, and traversing of borders. The photographs challenge truth, invert spaces, question logic, fuse landscape and people, asking one to carefully examine not just the images, but the issue itself. These prints are from in-camera, double-exposed images made with a Holga. The frames were sometimes held for days until the next image was found. Other times, the frames were captured instantly one after the other due to the nature of the event they were made in. The images are all split-filtered, printed on Oriental fiber base paper. Because the double-exposure tended to over-expose the negative, the light detail (including highlights) required extra exposure when printing, many times 100 % over base exposure. I carefully cut detailed boards stenciled with the image reflected with the enlarger to ensure that I did not lose important detail, or that I did not burn-in unwanted light, information onto the print." Originally from Mexico City, Elizabeth Z. Pineda is a photographer using traditional photographic processes. Her work resides at the intersection of time and memory. Branching off from her own story, she speaks visually of community and touches on barriers of language, culture, and society. Elizabeth is an MFA candidate in Photography at Arizona State University. To see more of her work visit phoenixtransect.org.

The Holga camera is a cheap (around $40 at the time of this writing) plastic-lens camera that has a certain charm and a cult following. The name originates from the Chinese word "ho gwong" meaning *very bright*. The Chinese started manufacturing this plastic camera in 1981 as a way for photographers to get into medium format photography cheaply. Then the type of photographs this cheap plastic camera produced—with light leaks, blur, vignetting and a vintage lo-fi look—became the rage. Today there are 120 mm Holgas, 35 mm Holgas, panoramic Holgas, pinhole Holgas, and if photographing with film doesn't interest you, buy a Holga lens to attach to a Nikon or Canon DSLR camera! The Holga proves that successful images do not depend on expensive camera equipment and lenses.

The Holga almost went out of production at one point, but Freestyle Photo resurrected it and is the primary supplier of Holgas in the US. Who would have thought the superiority of a camera lies in its inferiority as a picture making device.

The lens

The lens on the Holga 120 mm is a 60 mm lens—slightly wide angle for a medium format camera—and is equipped with a leaf shutter. The 35 mm has a 47 mm lens. Sometimes the shutter breaks; sometimes it doesn't work at exactly 1⁄100 second as it is supposed to, but this presents no problem if having fun with the camera is all that is expected.

The plastic lens is certainly not corrected for color or focus aberrations nor is it sharp. It gives low contrast and not much shadow detail. The edges of the image will tend to be a bit blurry, but this is all part of the Holga's charm.

Some Holga aficionados go a step further, thinking the lens is *too* sharp, and they modify the lens with sandpaper, Vaseline, nail polish, needle-scratching, or steel wool. Since the Holga is so cheap, buy several and modify each lens differently.

Focus

There are four focusing distances only, each indicated by a charming pictograph: a head and shoulders (3 feet), several people holding hands (6 feet), a group of people (18 feet), and a mountain (30 feet to infinity). Focus is somewhat inexact, and easy to forget, but many times the lack of focus adds to the charm of the Holga image.

Aperture

There are only two apertures, F8 and F11, and some say there is not much difference between the two. These are indicated by two more charming pictographs: clouds and sun, respectively. Quite low tech, but because there are only two aperture choices, exposure might be all over the board.

Shutter

There are also only two shutter speeds, a fixed one of 1⁄100 second and a Bulb (B) setting, which allows the photographer to keep the shutter open as long as the shutter button is depressed. The shutters aren't rocket science, and oftentimes who knows if the shutter is really 1⁄100 second or not! A test roll is always a good thing with every new Holga camera purchase. If using the B setting, a tripod and a cable release are recommended.

Film

The Holga 120 camera takes 120 mm film that will give either 16 6 × 4.5 cm negatives or 12 6 × 6 cm negatives by merely switching between two plastic insert masks that are included in the camera box (the Holga 35 mm does not have a mask). Each is labeled in a corner with a number 12 or 16. With either mask used, it is necessary to move the arrow on the back of the camera to point to either 12 or 16 correspondingly. Then it is a good idea to cover the red window with a flap of gaffer's tape because it isn't necessarily impervious to light. See further under **Taping your Holga**.

The plastic insert can also be completely removed, which is better for continuous multiple exposures while turning the film because the delineations between each exposure won't be so pronounced when the sharp edge of the insert asserts itself in the image. If the insert is removed, the film will not be quite so flat in camera and there may be more blur, but again, this is cultivated by many.

To prevent the film from jamming (this happens sometimes because the film take-up spool gets wound too loosely and then gets too big around so it jams), take a piece of cardboard from an end of a film box, fold it in half and jam it under the film spool on the left bottom side of the camera—jamming to prevent jamming.

400 ISO film is probably the best choice of film for a Holga. 100 ISO film is OK outside on a sunny day, but it is more common to underexpose with a Holga, and 400 ISO will help prevent that from happening.

Color film in a Holga is especially perfect because of color film's extreme latitude of exposure (one stop under and several stops over, essentially a 5-stop range of screwing up) and because color film gets less grainy with overexposure.

Another film that works well is Ilford XP2, a black and white film that is actually processed like color film in C-41 chemistry.

If it is overcast, use 800 ISO film. If indoors, 3200 ISO film is best.

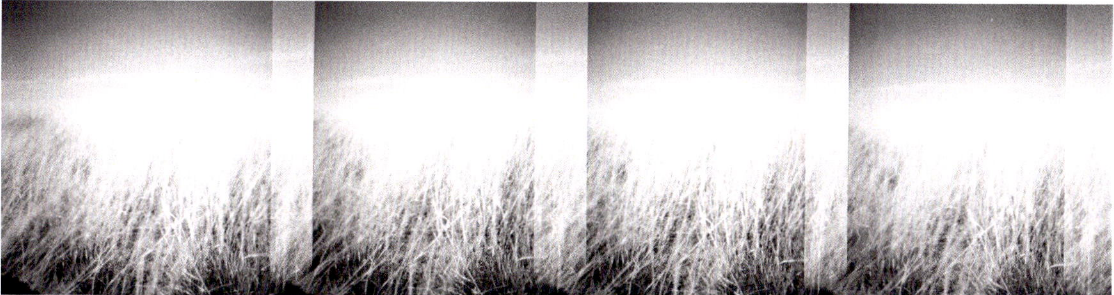

Figure 7.4. *Time Studies*, silver gelatin print from a Holga pinhole negative © Julia C. Martin 2020. Julia C. Martin is a photographic artist based in Phoenix, Arizona. Her work deals with themes of mortality, ephemerality, and time. In addition to photography, she also works in printmaking, papermaking, and book arts. To see more of Martin's work visit www.juliacmartin.com.

Flash

The Holga 120FN has a built in flash. Holgas that have built in flashes require 2 AA batteries. The Holga 120CFN has a color wheel filter in the flash. All other Holgas have a standard hot shoe mount which will accommodate most types of hot shoe flash units. After mounting the flash unit, flip the aperture knob to the "flash" setting. The aperture is now at F8.

The hot shoe also works with strobes. Use a hot shoe to PC adapter, or even an on-camera flash and photo slaves on strobes. However, with each shutter release, the Holga will trip the flash twice, once when pressing down and once when releasing. Therefore, with strobes keep holding down the shutter release so as not to damage the strobes by flashing them twice in a row so fast. Just make sure that the slaves are close enough to pick up the camera's flash.

Multiple exposure

Holgas are perfect for multiple exposures because it is a manual advance camera, meaning one can manually advance the roll film as little or as much as desired. One student calculated that about ¼ turn of the film advance knob equals ½″ of film, so if the knob is marked with quarter marks (use a permanent Sharpie) it becomes easier to judge what will overlap in the negative. As said before, multiple exposure does best when the insert is removed so the transitions between multiple exposures is softened. It is easy to forget to wind the film after a shot, too, but that can be when serendipity happens.

Loading a Holga 120 mm[1]

1. It is recommended to load and unload 120 mm film in subdued light to prevent any unwanted exposure.
2. Remove the clips from the sides of the camera to open the back.
3. Select the mask for either 16 images (6 × 4.5 cm) or 12 images (6 × 6 cm) and insert into the camera. Shooting without a mask yields 12 images and can lead to more intense vignetting.
4. If the Holga has a built in flash unit, install 2 AA batteries under the film mask on either side.
5. Slide the arrow on the back cover to point to the corresponding image count for the mask that was inserted.
6. Make sure there is a take up spool on the right side of the camera and break the seal on the new 120 roll of film and insert on the left side of the camera.
7. Place pressure on the bottom of the new roll of film and pull out the paper backing. Insert the tapered edge into the slot in the take up spool.
8. Turn the film advance knob a couple of turns keeping the film tight to prevent any slack.
9. Please note that it is important to keep 120 mm film tight to the spool. This protects the film from exposure since it is not in a canister. If you have an older Holga or the foam padding has fallen off, insert a piece of cardboard under the film spool to keep the film tight. Unlike 35 mm film, 120 mm film has no light-tight canister to protect from

exposure; the only guard against the sun is its thin paper backing. If your film is not rolled tightly, light can sneak in under the loose paper causing light leaks or even fogging.

10. Replace the camera back and make sure the clips are in place. Put a piece of gaffer's tape over the clips to prevent the back from slipping open. See further under **Taping your Holga**.

11. Turn the film advance knob until the number 1 appears in the counter window on the back of the camera. The Holga is ready to shoot.

Unloading the Holga 120 mm

1. After shooting the last frame, either 12 or 16 depending on the mask used, turn the film advance knob until the film and paper is completely rolled onto the take up reel.
2. Open the back of the Holga. The exposed film should now be in the right film chamber. An empty film spool will be in the left film chamber. Save the empty spool, as this is now the new take up reel for the next roll of film.
3. Extract the full take-up spool from the right side of the camera. Make sure that the film is wound tightly around the spool. Fold the tapered end under itself as directed on the paper backing and then seal the film with the provided adhesive tab.

Loading the Holga 35 mm

1. There are no masks included with 35 mm Holgas. To load the film, pull up on the film rewind knob. The back cover will pop open.
2. Insert a new roll of film in the film compartment on the left side of the camera.
3. Pull the film out of the camera until the tip of the film reaches the take up spool. Then insert the tip of the film into the slot on the take up spool.
4. Turn the film advance slightly so that the teeth catch the sprocket holes on the film.
5. Snap the cover back into place and turn the film advance knob to advance the film until it cannot turn any further and then press the shutter.
6. Repeat this until the number 1 appears in the frame counter window. The Holga is ready to shoot.

Unloading the Holga 35 mm

1. When the roll of film is finished, put the lens cap on the camera to avoid any double exposures.
2. Push down on the film rewind release button on the bottom of the camera.
3. Turn the film rewind knob clockwise. There will be some tension while turning the knob. Keep turning the knob until there is no tension, indicating the film is rewound back into the canister.
4. Pull up on the film rewind knob. The back cover will open and you can safely remove the film.

Taping your Holga

Many Holga owners look forward to the characteristic light leaks and anomalies of a Holga camera, but for those who are not a fan, taping up the Holga is the option. The best tape to use is black gaffer's tape or black photo tape which is readily available at most photo and studio lighting retailers and even hardware stores. Gaffer's tape does not leave a sticky residue like other tapes, and it is matte black. It is used in multiple ways with the Holga, not just to minimize light leaks. Follow these steps and all will be well.

1. Some run pieces of black tape along the seam where the back fits onto the body.
2. Since the metal strap holders also serve as the camera back holder, when the camera is set down on a table, the weight of the camera strap sometimes pushes the back holders down and the back falls off, exposing all the film. This is not a happy event. Cover the metal clips that secure the camera back and it will prevent the back from falling off the Holga.
3. If you have a standard Holga 120 mm and want to remove the mask inside the camera, there are two holes behind the mask and above the lens that can cause light leaks. A single piece of tape can cover them both. Perhaps for the first roll of film taken, don't tape anything and see how the light leaks perform.
4. The little red film counter window leaks light notoriously, especially with color film. A little black flap of gaffer's tape strategically placed there will solve this issue, and it can be flipped up quickly in lower light to see the frame number.

Long exposures

Long exposures are easily achieved when using the "Bulb" setting. Simply mount the camera on a tripod and set the exposure switch to the "B" position. Push down the shutter release button and keep it down as long as desired. Then, release the button to close the shutter to complete the picture taking cycle. When finished, remember to set the "B" exposure switch back to the "N" (Normal) setting or you may end up with blurry pictures, which may actually result in more serendipity.

Tips and ideas

- If all of a sudden your pictures are overexposed and you've had the Holga a long time, the shutter spring may have finally worn out.
- There are many Holga modifications that can be done, and websites devoted to modifications. There are also many Holga accessories for purchase; see FreestylePhoto.biz.
- The dark corners on a Holga image, vignetting, are one of Holga's many charms. If you prefer less dramatic vignetting try using the 6 × 4.5 cm mask.
- If pictures are blurry, make sure you don't have the shutter speed left on "B."
- Take an old UV, sky, or clear filter and coat it with Vaseline or clear nail polish to get a Holga-like effect with a normal camera lens. It is best to do so around the edges of the filter and leave it clear in the center.
- Shaking the camera while taking an image gives it an uncomfortable, eerie feel, especially with a scene that has strong darks in it.
- **Burning film:** with pliers on either end of a film strip, the strip can be held over a flame source such as a candle and pulled from each end with the pliers to stretch and warp the film. The strip should be kept far enough away from the heat source to prevent burning and bubbling of the plastic, unless this is what is desired. It is best to do this outside so as not to create plastic fumes. The final product may need to be printed in a glass negative carrier if the negatives are not flat.
- **Scratching film:** when scratching on the top/non-emulsion side of the negative, refraction will produce white lines on the print; when scratching on the bottom/emulsion side of the negative, the scratches will remove emulsion and produce black lines on the print. Using the smallest needle possible produces the most effective scratches. Even the tiniest scratch marks will become greatly magnified during enlargement, and thus fine lines, carefully executed, are best. Watch that the marks are not ragged, because the marks can appear contrived and elementary. A quilting "between" needle embedded in a pencil eraser is a good scratch tool. Some ideas to try: scratch words on top of the negative; write with a pencil on top of the negative, and the graphite density will print lighter; scratch an empty space in one negative and sandwich another negative with it when printing to print the second negative through the cleared area.
- **Distressing film:** step on it, grind it in the dirt, carry it around in a backpack unprotected, or take a piece of sandpaper to it.
- **Bleaching film:** Mix enough potassium ferricyanide in ¼ cup of water until it resembles the color of Mountain Dew. It doesn't have to be exact. With a small brush dipped in this bleach and a hose of running water at the ready, brush on the bleach in areas where image removal is desired. Watch carefully, being ready to spray water on drips at all times. Fix the negative, rinse, and dry.

What becomes apparent with the Holga is that the camera is no more than a light tight box, and hardly one at that. And the lens, even though plastic, still can lead to exotic images. Having such freedom and versatility with a camera and the advantage of medium format is a perfect combination for experimentation.

Endnotes

1.This information is from the Holga manual, a free download here: https://www.freestylephoto.biz/static/pdf/product_pdfs/holga/holga-manual.pdf

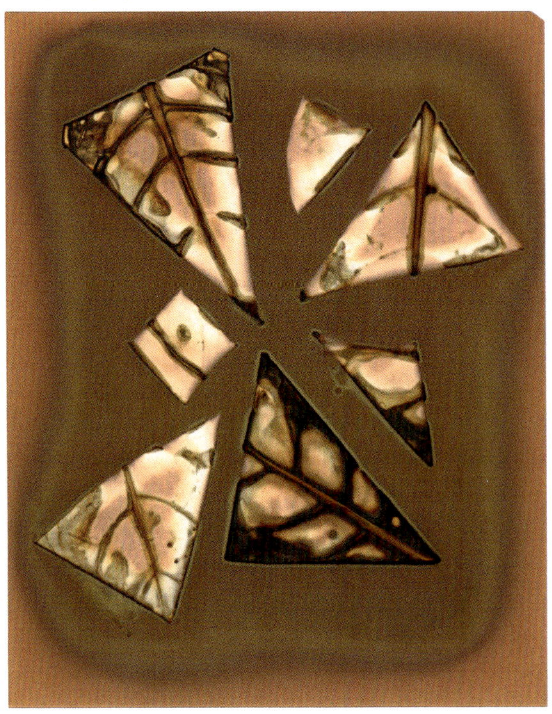

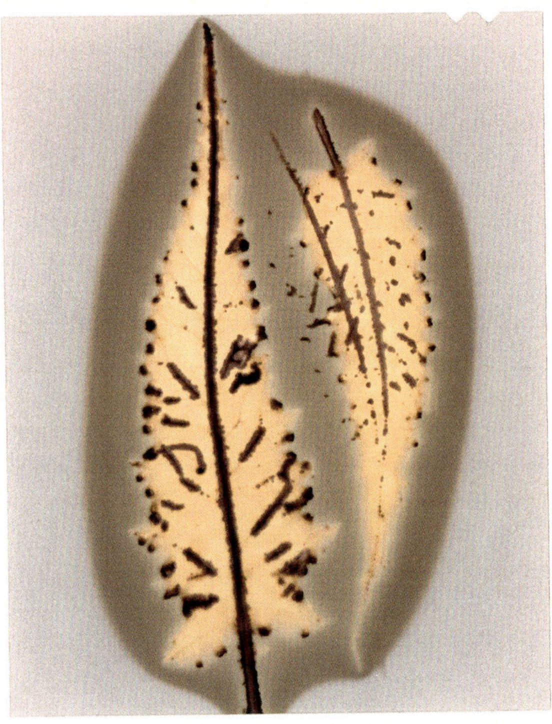

Figure P3.1-P3.2. Left, *Deconstructed* 3.9″ x 4.9″, gardenia leaves soaked in a developer made from ascorbic acid, sodium carbonate, and instant coffee, then placed on a sheet of Arista Ortho Litho film, exposed in the sun under glass, then fixed; right, *Canyon Ragweed*, leaves of Canyon Ragweed soaked in the developer above, placed onto a sheet of Adox black and white film, exposed in the sun under glass, fixed, both © Cyd Peroni 2020.

"My photographs explore the concept of *Mono No Aware*, a Japanese Shinto term, which contains the understanding that there is joy within the sad realization of the transience of life. I try to see moments and details in nature that are beautiful, but fleeting, and because of their impermanence hold a deeper significance."

Cyd Peroni is a fine art photographer working full time from her New River, Arizona studio where she experiments with alternative and digital photographic processes. Her work has been exhibited in solo and juried group exhibitions at Medium Festival of Photography, Light Art Space, Eye Lounge, A. Smith Gallery, FOUND:RE, Art Intersection, and Northlight Gallery. To see more of her work visit www.cydperoniphotography.com.

PART THREE

Printing Experimentation

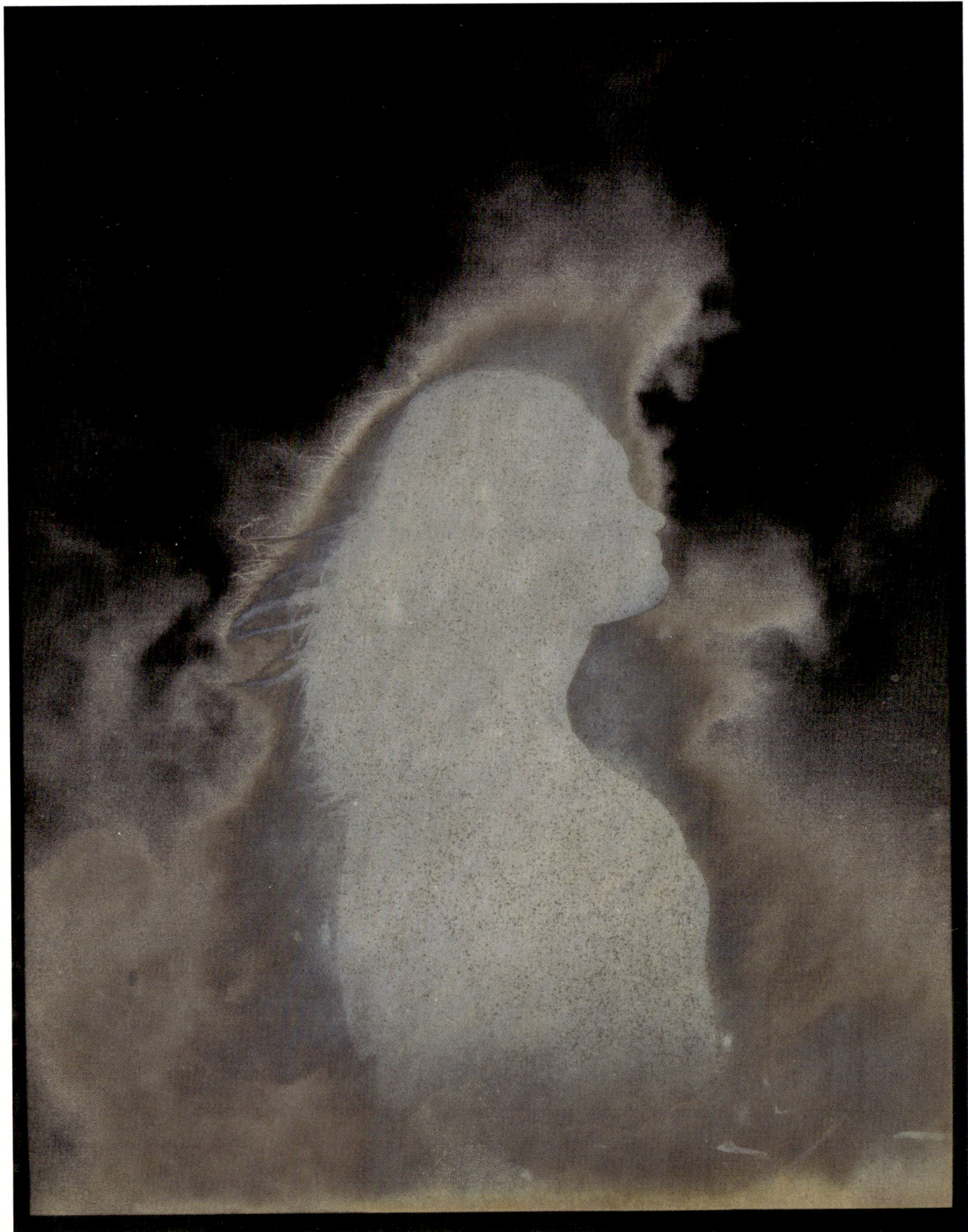

Figure 8.1. *Study in Silver*, chromo print, 8″ x 10″© Dani Hatfield 2021

Chapter 8

Chromo

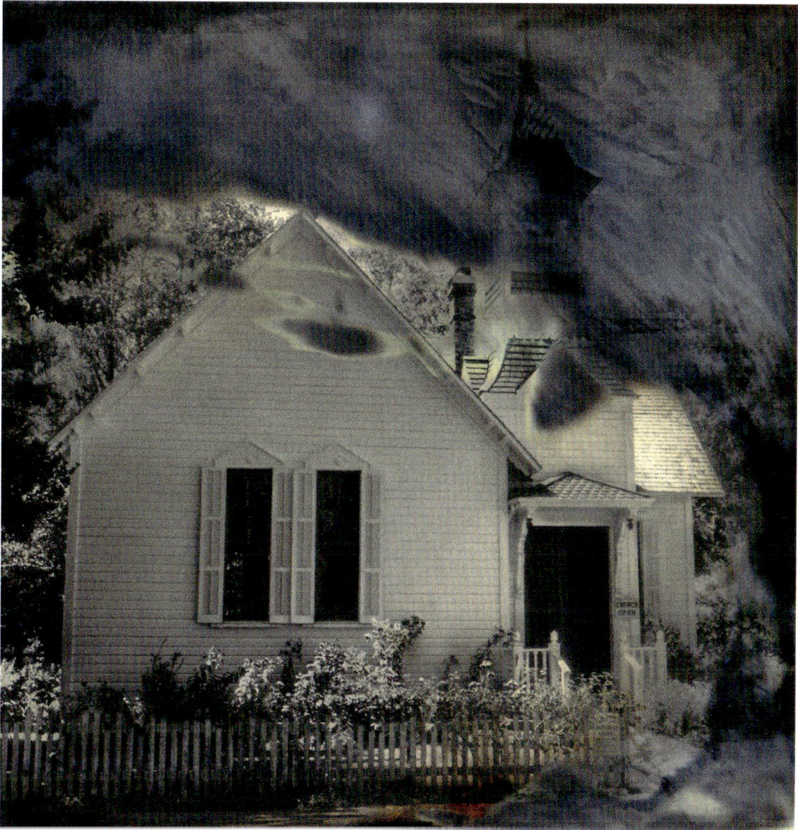

Figure 8.2. *Long Beach Church*, 10″ x 8″ chromo silver gelatin print © Brenden Scheller 2019. Brenden Scheller is inspired by the combination of abstract and landscape. He uses experimental processes to add a layer of atmosphere to his work. To see more of his work visit brendenscheller.com.

In the **Chemigram** chapter I describe a method of deriving black, white, and colors on silver gelatin paper while using **resists**. One offshoot of the chemigram process is "chromoskedasic sabattier" or "chromo" as it has come to be known. The chromo process is often figurative: a negative is exposed to silver gelatin paper in the normal way, but then special chemistry—Chromo Activator and Chromo Stabilizer—is used to create colors and plated silver on the paper. Light is not necessary to create the colors and generally resists are not part of the process.

In my former *Experimental Photography Workbook* I titled this particular chapter Photo+Chemigram but the chapter title created confusion in readers. Freestyle had come out with their Arista *Chromo* Activator and *Chromo* Stabilizer in March of 2009 so by 2012 when the book was published most everyone was referring to the process as chromoskedasic sabattier or "chromo" for short.

The process has been called by other names, too—chemogram, painting with light, duotone solarization, silver mirror printing, chromoskedasic duotone pseudosolarization. I have seen a photographer or two, unaware of the history of the process, think they were the inventors of this unique method of silver gelatin printing, and unfortunately sometimes this lack of giving credit where credit is due was intentional. Imagine my dismay, after helping one well-known photographer with his chemigram prints, to read in his gallery catalog description that he invented the process himself.

When the Arista Chromo Activator and Stabilizer chemistry are used along with normal darkroom chemistry, *chemical fog*, as opposed to light fog, can be induced on photographic paper. The chemical fog produces colorful monochromes and one extra benefit if done in a particular way—plated out metallic silver. The chemical fog can be induced with or without any light exposure to the paper. This can be easily demonstrated in the darkroom by putting an unexposed piece of black and white paper into the chromo tray; the paper will plate out with metallic silver in a minute or two.

The use of Activator and Stabilizer chemistry, (Kodak S2 and S30 at that time) was the result of Dominic Man-Kit Lam's experimentation. Lam was a professor of Ophthalmology and Director for Biotechnology at the Texas Medical Centre in Houston (not a photographer). He was developing silver gelatin pictures of eye images. One of the images had brown stains. Lam was curious about the stain and decided to play with it. He worked out a method of creating these colorful monochromes without giving it a name.

In 1989 Dr. Bryant Rossiter, who worked for Kodak, saw Lam's prints and suggested that the colors were the result of the "Mie" effect which is light *scattering* as opposed to light *reflecting*. Mie scattering is named after Gustav Mie who first described it in 1908. Lam's prints were scanned under an electron microscope at Kodak, and the Mie effect was found to be the cause. Rossiter is the one who told Lam he should name the process "chromoskedasic," Greek for "color by light scattering." Man-Kit Lam called it "chromoskedasic painting," not solarization or sabattier.

To explain the Mie effect, a black and white print is normally monochromatic because the silver particles that remain in the print after fixing absorb all color and reflect black. In the colorful monochrome processes the silver particles are carefully managed with different chemicals, with or without exposure to light, to become different sizes. These different sized silver particles scatter light in different ways to produce the different colors. Smaller particles will look yellow; larger particles will look red. The process becomes even more fascinating when bright, shiny metallic silver plates out on the surface of the print where the whites once were—like a "poor man's daguerreotype."

Lam and Rossiter published a two-part article in *Scientific American* shortly thereafter which inspired a number of practitioners, two of whom were Alan Bean and William Jolly.[1]

Bean read Lam's article on a plane, got home and tried the process right away. He brought his prints to Houston's Photofest, where he met a woman from *View Camera* who then asked him to write an article on the process.[2]

At about the same time, on the opposite side of the country, a chemistry professor at the University of California, Berkeley, William Jolly, began researching the process. Jolly had seen the 1991 *Scientific American* article by Man-Kit Lam and Rossiter and surmised that the chemistry, specifically thiocyanate, promoted developmental fog which was responsible for the colors and silver, because thiocyanates are in the Stabilizer.[3] Jolly published his results in *Darkroom & Creative Camera Techniques* (Nov/Dec 1992). Jolly also published an article in July/August 1993 and September/October 1993, and then his article on "Silver-Mirror Printing" in January/February 1999 (under the magazine's new name *PHOTO Techniques*).[4]

Jolly concluded one of his articles with this statement: "I have not worked out all the details of this method, but I feel that it is such an exciting process that I should not delay in letting the readers know about it, even in its present imperfect state."[5] It was Jolly's and Bean's articles that inspired me to teach this process beginning in 2001 at Montana State University.

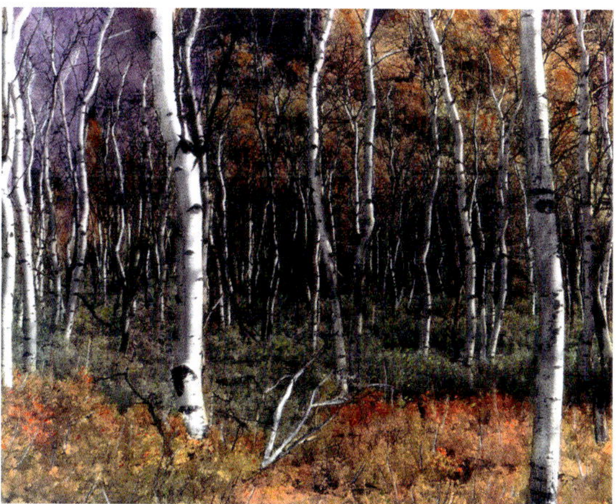

Figures 8.3–8.4. *After Wolf Kahn*, left, hand colored silver gelatin print, 14˝ x 11˝; right, *Aspens*, chromo silver gelatin print from the same negative, 10˝ x 8˝ © Christina Z. Anderson 2005 and 2010 respectively.

Discoveries

Silvering out was elusive for me. Jolly's explanation for silver plating was: "The fogging developer contains thiocyanate, which dissolves the silver halide by complexation. The complexed silver ion then undergoes so-called 'physical development' on the emulsion base, much as silver is plated out on a glass surface in the traditional chemical method of making silver mirrors. The rate of silver deposition is enhanced by making the second developer highly alkaline with potassium hydroxide."[6] Knowing the "why" was helpful; a darkroom mistake led to the "how."

To make a long story short, in the spring of 2009 I discovered two ways to make the silver plating predictable. One is the use of EcoPro developer instead of Dektol. EcoPro is an ascorbate developer with no hydroquinone. I have no idea if the absence of hydroquinone is the ticket, or the sodium isoascorbic in EcoPro, but it works. Two is the use of warm to hot water in the solution. My chemist friend Alberto Novo from Italy led to the latter discovery when he told me warm solutions were used to plate mirrors with silver. With these two factors, in twelve years I have yet to have the process fail me.

Following is my fail-safe process I have taught for over a decade. It is a perfect method for your first foray into chromo. If further experimentation is desired, see the **Appendix**. In the Appendix are Bean's and Jolly's processes, the latter's extensively described, as well as other practitioners' methods.

Materials needed

All items are available from Freestyle Photo; Arista is Freestyle's signature brand name. If you can't locate the chemistry and you are handy with mixing chemistry in the darkroom, I've included the MSDS ingredients in this chapter.

Arista.edu Ultra or Ilford Multigrade Warmtone glossy paper, only
Arista Premium B&W Chromo Activator
Arista Premium B&W Chromo Stabilizer
LegacyPro EcoPro B&W Paper Developer
Normal darkroom chemistry

Image type

Colors only appear where there is white (undeveloped silver halide) in the print. The image must have large areas of white or not much color will occur. This is easy with digital negatives—fill in areas you want to silver out with white even if they don't occur in the original image—or print any image with a high contrast filter so that highlights in the image "blow out."

The chromo tray method

You will be taking an exposed, freshly developed but not yet fixed silver gelatin print and putting it in a combination of "Activator" and "Stabilizer," in the darkroom only, or in the darkroom and out under room light. The Activator is a dilute potassium hydroxide; the Stabilizer is an acetate buffered thiocyanate.

Tray 1

Note this is an easy to remember formula: 4 parts warm water + 2 parts Activator + 1 part Stabilizer + 1 part EcoPro or 4/2/1/1.

500 ml warm water (86–105°F/30–40°C)
250 ml Arista Premium B&W Chromo Activator
125 ml Arista Premium B&W Chromo Stabilizer
125 ml EcoPro developer stock solution

In a liter container, add 500 ml warm water.

1. Add 250 ml Activator.
2. Add 125 ml Stabilizer.
3. Add 125 ml EcoPro stock solution (undiluted).
4. Cap and lightly shake. The solution will smell strongly of ammonia.
5. At time of use, pour this in a tray large enough to allow a print to be picked up by the edges with tongs. Better yet, use nitrile-gloved hands to move the print from tray to tray. An 11″ × 14″ flat-bottomed tray is best for 8″ × 10″ prints. If doing prints larger than this, use a 16″ × 20″ tray and two liters of mix.

Tray 2 (if desired)

900 ml warm water
100 ml Arista Activator

1. Add 100 ml Activator to 900 ml water in a tray, or enough to be able to submerge the print under a thin layer of solution.

Tray procedure

1. Expose the paper to a negative and develop the print in any paper developer until darks are suitably dark and there is detail in the midtones to lower highlights—perhaps a minute.
2. Drain, rinse in water, and slip face up into Tray 1. Agitate for the first 30 seconds or so and then watch for silver to plate out over the whole surface. This will take up to several minutes. In the darkroom it will appear as a creeping, massive gray fog. Look at the print obliquely in the tray to see if it fluoresces silver. It works best when the solution is warm (80–105°F).
3. Remove it and place it face up in Tray 2. If the print looks perfect after Tray 1 there is no need for the Tray 2 bath (I actually never use Tray 2).
4. Bring Tray 2 with the print submerged in the solution out into room light for however long desired. Color shift will occur—pinks, mauves, peaches, and even blues. This part of the process moves somewhat slowly. Plan time to nurse the print along while watching.
5. When done, stop, fix, wash, and hypoclear the print as usual. Never touch the surface of the print until dry or it will mar permanently! This means either separate trays to wash each print or an archival washer with individual print slots, and no squeegeeing.
6. Dry face up. Once the print is dry, if it tarnishes it can be delicately polished with a soft cloth.

The chromo brush method

10 ml Arista Stabilizer in 90 ml water (10% solution; can use 10–20%)
20 ml Arista Activator in 80 ml water (20% solution; can use 10–20%)
15 ml EcoPro Developer in 85 ml water (15% solution)
Assortment of brushes, small to large; fat calligraphy brushes work well
Three separate plastic cups

EcoPro is very concentrated. Working strength is mixed using 1 + 9 parts water. Dektol is less concentrated. Working strength Dektol is mixed using 1 + 2 parts water. Both can be used in the brush method, but more Dektol stock than EcoPro stock may be required, e.g. 50 ml Dektol and 50 ml water.

Brush procedure

1. Expose and develop a print for about a minute, or until all highlight detail is present.
2. Drain developer off, rinse with water, and bring out into room light in a flat bottom tray.

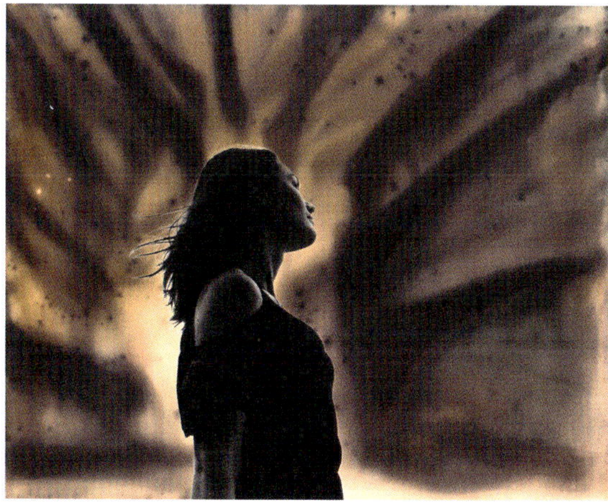

Figure 8.5. *Autumn Sun*, 10″ x 8″ chromo silver gelatin print © Dani Hatfield 2021. This image is made from the same negative as in Figure 8.1, but whereas Figure 8.1 is a tray method chromo print this is a brush method chromo print.

3. Immediately paint a thin layer of 10% Stabilizer over the entire print and watch the darkening print color turn to pale yellow.
4. After a bit, paint on 20% Activator in places where a dark brown shift is desired. It will shift slowly. The amount of each solution used will determine that—for instance, more Activator and less Stabilizer on the print, quicker change. If it moves too quickly, paint on more Stabilizer.
5. Paint on some EcoPro 15% solution. Usually silvering out occurs at this point where the three chemicals are layered on the print.
6. The rest of the process is a repetition of these three steps, with these three solutions. Move slowly and pay attention to brush strokes to insure they are contributing to the image, and be careful because they will be very dominant. Note: if the Activator gets dark and grungy, don't dump it, just replenish it with fresh Activator and keep on brushing. There's good stuff in there. Silver deposits will happen gloriously with the brush method if the Activator gets grungy brown. The Stabilizer, for the most part, will stay clear.
7. When the print is done, rinse, stop, fix, hypo-clear, wash, and dry as with any black and white print, being careful with the tender surface. Do not squeegee or touch the surface of the print until it is dry.

Tips and ideas

- Stick with Ilford Warmtone glossy or Arista Ultra—they are perfect for the process. After getting a handle on the process, try out other papers.
- Temperature is important; if the process is not going well, increase the Tray 1 temperature by either pouring back the mix in a jug and putting the jug in hot water, or putting the tray in hot water, or using hot water to mix it in the first place.
- Stabilizer leans toward yellow.
- Activator leans toward orange.
- Developer leans toward red-brown.
- Stabilizer does just that—slows down things.
- Activator does just that—speeds up things.
- The spectrum from yellow to red is produced fairly easily with these chemicals. The spectrum from green to blue, a bit more difficult to induce, is usually accompanied by silver.
- Most often, Stabilizer to Activator is in a 1:2 proportion.
- The more concentrated the solutions, the deeper the colors.
- The less concentrated the solutions, the paler the color.
- Color obtained is related to pH to some extent. High pH leans toward the red end of the spectrum and low pH leans toward the blue end of the spectrum.
- Activator increases the pH, hence redder colors.
- To increase pH use add 10–50 ml Activator to the tray or even some sodium carbonate powder.
- To decrease pH add 3–10 ml 28% acetic acid stop bath to a tray.
- If color forms too slowly, raise the pH (more Activator).
- If color forms too quickly, reduce the pH (more Stabilizer).
- There is a drastic color shift when the print is fixed as well as when the print is dried, just like with lumen prints. Drydown is easily a stop denser. It is easy to see the effect: just wet half the finished print again and see the difference between the wet half and the dry half in both color and density.

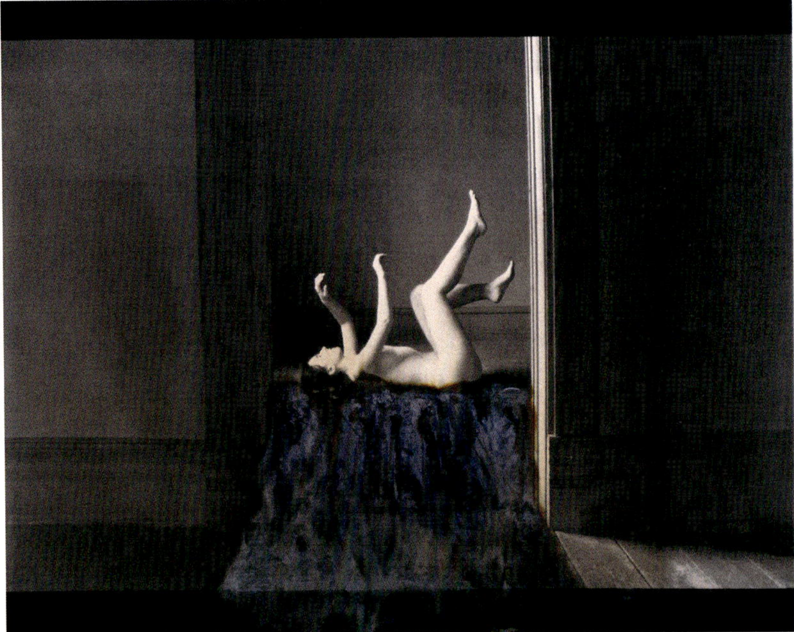

Figure 8.6. *Pedestal*, silver gelatin chromo © Jessica Hays 2019. "These images explore trauma in relationships, loss, and the experience of overcoming and regaining power afterwards." Jessica L. Hays is a conceptual photographer, alternative process printmaker, and curator from Bozeman, Montana. Her work focuses on human relationships, issues of mental health, trauma, personal memory, and places of healing. Born and raised in Montana, Hays has bachelor's degrees in Photography and Liberal Studies from Montana State University, and is an MFA candidate at Columbia College. To see more of Hays' work visit jessicahaysart.com.

- Make sure the Tray 1 Chromo remains fresh or a layer of amorphous, black, sludge silver will precipitate on the surface of the print. This can be wiped off *gently* with dampened cotton balls and alleviated somewhat by chromoing the print face down; or, use smaller amounts of chemistry in the tray one-shot, dumping after use.
- Try selective development of a print, using a brush to paint on developer on only parts of the image. This will give more white area for the colors to appear. To do this, expose the print to a negative as per normal, and then place the print on a level piece of glass. Wet a brush with paper developer and brush it on in the image area. When the image starts appearing, brush more developer on where it is needed until the image is fully there. At this point rinse and either place the paper in Tray 1 or brush with Stabilizer and then bring it out into room light to use the chromo brush technique.
- The wide, white border areas between the darks and the chromo colors are sort of pseudo-Mackie lines and you can make them more dramatic by painting on the chemistry and then hanging the print vertically. You will see streaks of color descending from these wide white areas, another visual element to cultivate.
- Mix a solution of 50 ml each of working strength paper developer, full strength Activator, and full strength Stabilizer, and pour it directly on a print or brush on a print. It will plate out dark blueish silver.
- Buy several Aquash fillable pens and fill them with the chemistry so you can draw with it.
- Polish the surface of a chromo with a soft cloth to clean and shine.
- If an oily fingerprint gets on the silver, the print will require a brief rinse in rubbing alcohol to try and get rid of it, or live with it as the artist's touch.

Chemistry of the solutions

EcoPro (pH 10.35)

Weight %	Chemical Name
10–25	**potassium carbonate**
7–10	**sodium sulfite**
5–10	**sodium isoascorbic**
1–5	**triethanolamine**

Arista Activator (pH 14)

Weight %	Chemical Name
5–10	**potassium hydroxide**
5–10	**sodium sulfite**

Arista Stabilizer (pH 4.85)

Weight %	Chemical Name

15–20	**ammonium thiocyanate**
5–10	**sodium metabisulfite**
1–5	**acetic acid**

Kodak Dektol, for comparison (pH 10.2-10.4)

Weight%	Chemical Name
50–55	**sodium carbonate, mono**
30–35	**sodium sulfite**
5–10	**hydroquinone**
1–5	**bis (4-hydroxy-N-methylanilinium) sulfate**
1–5	**Polyphosphoric acids, sodium salts**
1–5	**potassium bromide**

Freestyle can't ship Chromo Activator and Stabilizer to Europe, but try making your own solution of Activator (75 g potassium hydroxide, 75 g sodium sulfite, water to 1000 ml) and Stabilizer (175 g ammonium thiocyanate, 75 g sodium metabisulfite, 25 ml glacial acetic acid, water to 1000 ml).

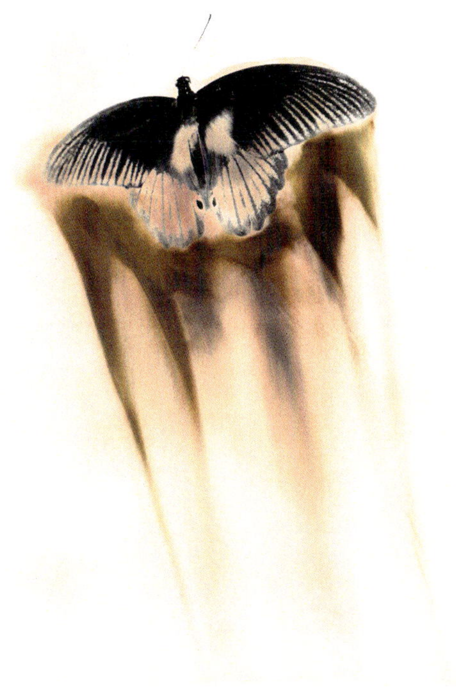

Figure 8.7. *Metaphor*, brush chromo © Christina Z. Anderson 2009

Chromo sources

See the **Appendix** for more chromo formulas.

"Brushes with Light; Photographs by Denny Moers" and "Brushes with Light, Explained" in *Camera Arts*, November/December 1981.

Lam, Dominic Man-Kit and Bryant W. Rossiter. "Chromoskedasic Painting" in *Scientific American*, November 1991, pp. 80–85, 136–137. Also here: http://www.dominiclam.net/LAM_science/Chromoskedasic1991.pdf

Bean, Alan W. "The Black and White Corner. Chromoskedasic Painting" in *View Camera*, September/October 1992, pp. 40–43.

Jolly, William L. "Chromoskedasic Duotone Pseudosolarization Using Development Fogging" in *Darkroom & Creative Camera Techniques*, November/December 1992, pp. 30–31.

Jolly, William L. "Dramatic Duotone Solarization" in *Darkroom & Creative Camera Techniques*, July/August 1993, pp. 19–21. This article is a sabattier technique; see the **Sabattier** chapter.

Jolly, William L. "Chromoskedasic Pseudosolarization Update, Popular Technique Improved" in *Darkroom & Creative Camera Techniques*, September/October 1993, pp. 28–31.

Jolly, William L. *Solarization Demystified, Black and White Chemistry of William L. Jolly* (Chapter 6), 1997. https://www.wljollysolarizationchemistry-photography.org/book-solarization-demystified

Jolly, William L. "Silver Mirror Printing and Other Unusual Black-and-White Print Development Processes" in *Photo Techniques*, January/February 1999, pp. 32–36.

Jolly, William L. "Silver Mirror Printing Update" in *Photo Techniques*, July/August 1999, p. 11. https://www.wljollysolarizationchemistryphotography.org/

Endnotes

1. Lam, Dominic Man-Kit, and Bryant W. Rossiter. "Chromoskedasic Painting," and "Painting in Color without Pigments," *Scientific American*, November 1991, pp. 80–85, 136–137.
2. Bean, Alan W. "The Black and White Corner. Chromoskedasic Painting" in *View Camera*, September/October 1992, pp. 40–43.
3. Jolly, William L. "Chromoskedasic Duotone Pseudosolarization Using Development Fogging" in *Darkroom & Creative Camera Techniques*, November/December 1992, pp. 30–31.
4. Jolly, William L. "Chromoskedasic Pseudosolarization Update; Popular Technique Improved," pp. 28–31, September/October 1993; "Silver Mirror Printing and other Unusual Black and White Print Development Processes," pp. 32–36, January/February 1999; "Silver Mirror Printing Update," p. 11, July/August 1999, all in *Photo Techniques*.
5. Jolly, William L. "Chromoskedasic Duotone Pseudosolarization Using Development Fogging," pp. 30–31.
6. Jolly, William L. "Silver Mirror Printing and Other Unusual Black-and-White Print Development Processes," p. 35.

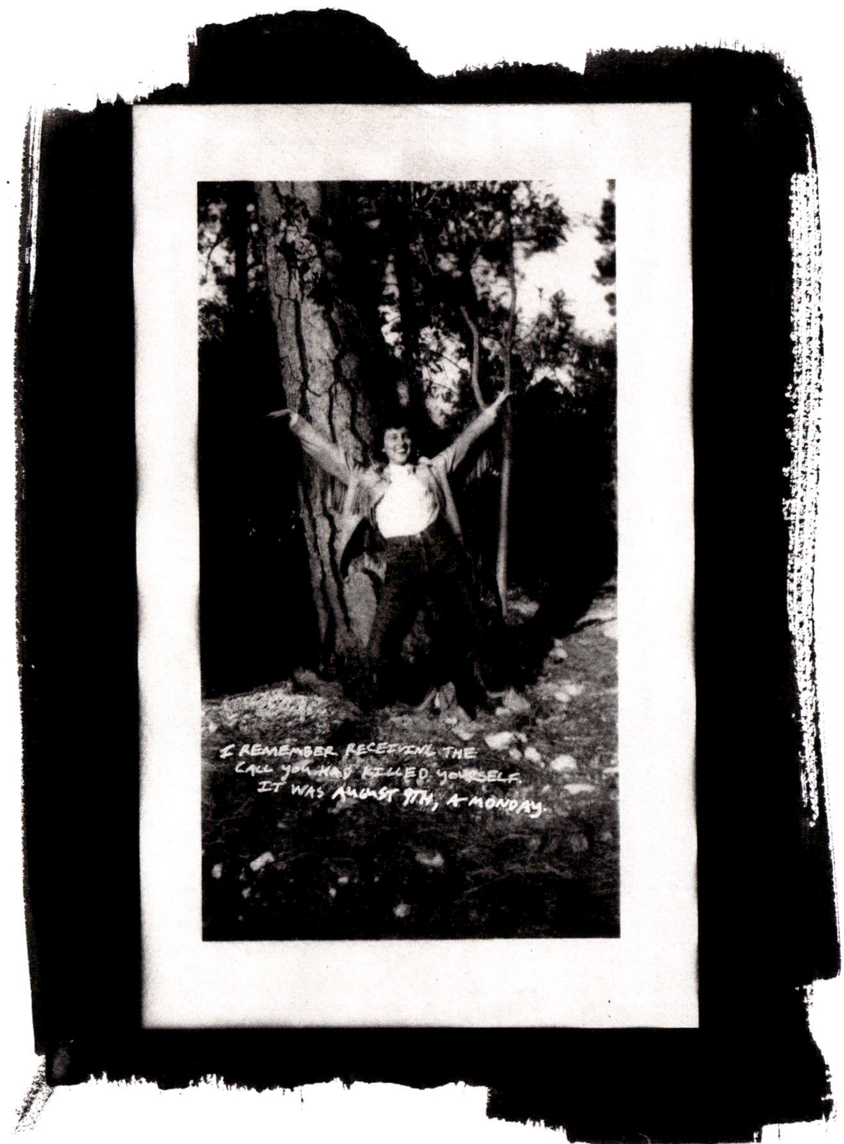

Figure 9.1. *Elenor 01*, from the *Elenor* series, liquid emulsion print © Zachary Begler 2021. "My grandmother, Elenor, was a private woman who only talked about herself in great detail towards the end of her life. Over the summer I told myself I was going to visit her at Christmas and give her art I made during the semester to liven up her home décor. On August 9th, she killed herself. Elenor is a series of eight images, a repurposing of past photographs translated into a story of who my grandmother was and whom I believed her to be: a friend, a mother, lively. Who she was and who I want her to be are two separate entities that hold similar weight. This work explores how she and my idea of her collide. All images originate from Elenor's collection of photographs spanning from her early 20s in the 1950s to the last image I captured of both Elenor and her husband Terrence in 2018. The images were printed in liquid emulsion on Fabriano Artistico watercolor paper. Transcribed upon the images is a letter I wrote to her in the months surrounding her passing. The letter creates a story when all eight images are lined up correctly." Zachary Begler (b. 1995 Helena, Montana) moved to Bozeman, Montana in 2014 to pursue a BA in Film and Photography at Montana State University. Midway, Begler took a break, bought a van, and traveled the West Coast to photograph homelessness and gangs, mostly in the Los Angeles area. Begler takes pride in getting to know his subjects prior to taking their images. Two exhibits of this series *A Lens to the Streets* resulted at the Holter Museum of Art, Helena, Montana, and at the University of Montana Western, Dillon, Montana. Begler returned to MSU and completed his degree in May 2022.

Chapter 9

Liquid Emulsion and Modern Tintype

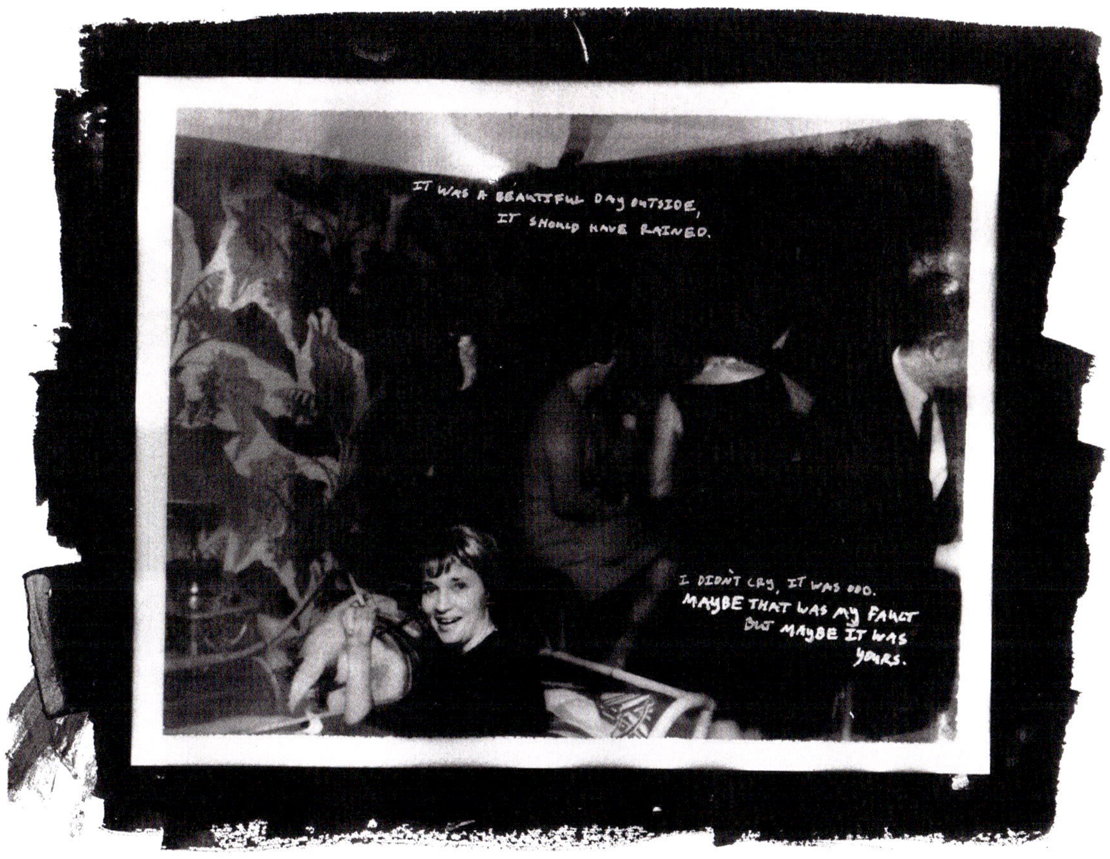

Figure 9.2. *Elenor 02*, from the *Elenor* series, liquid emulsion print with text © Zachary Begler 2021

Liquid emulsion is a liquid form of the same light sensitive emulsion that is on silver gelatin paper. It can be used on all sorts of surfaces to make them photo-sensitive. As a first foray into liquid emulsion, watercolor paper is easiest. Then explore other surfaces once you are familiar with its use.

There are contrast graded liquid emulsions that do not need filters nor respond to filters as they print at a fixed contrast, usually like a grade 3 paper. There are variable contrast liquid emulsions that respond to filters and print at different contrasts from low to high. Choose variable contrast so you have choices.

There are speed differences between liquid emulsions. Some expose slower and some faster. Liquid Light is slower than the rest, but it does not require red safelight while the others do. If your darkroom is not equipped with a red safelight, use Liquid Light. Otherwise purchase other brands and use red safelight so fogging does not occur.

The brands of liquid emulsion available at the time of this writing are Rollei Black Magic Variable Contrast or High Contrast, Rockland Liquid Light, and Fomaspeed. Rollei High Contrast, Fomaspeed, and Liquid Light all are similar to a grade 3 paper. I prefer Rollei Black Magic because it is fast and variable contrast.

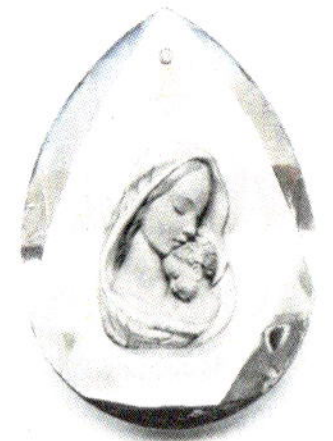
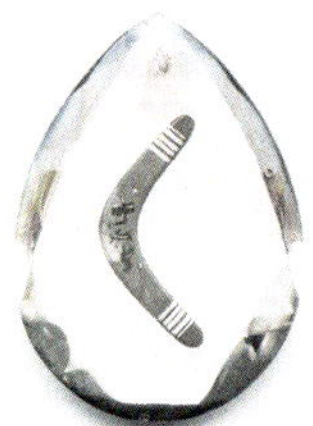
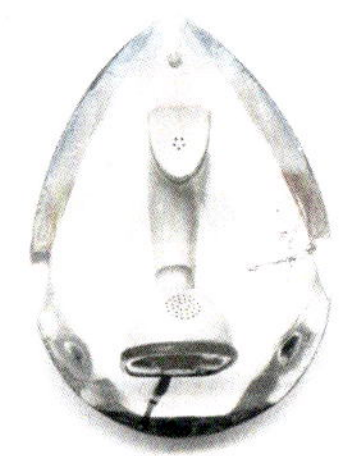
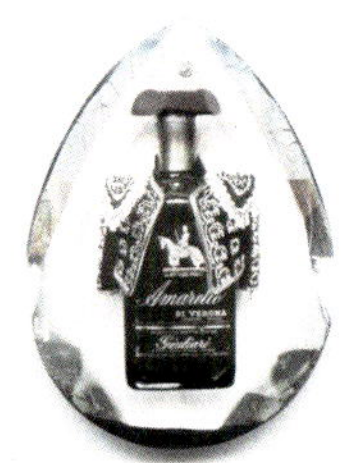
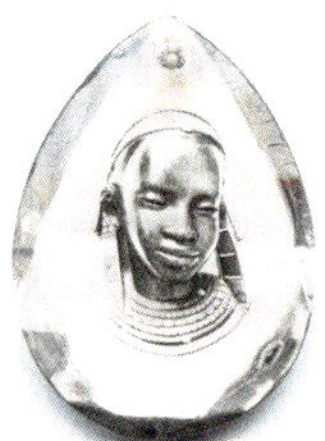

Figures 9.3–9.7. *Grandmother's House*, crystal drops from a chandelier coated with liquid emulsion, 6.5 x 5.1 cm © Laura Corrado, 2015. "The pictures are part of a project aimed at creating a portrait of my grandmother's house, made through still life photos of the most significant objects I could find in it. Each picture is darkroom printed on a crystal drop taken from her livingroom's chandelier." Laura Corrado was born in Naples, Italy. After graduating from the Academy of Fine Arts in Rome, she pursued her masters in professional photography. To see more of her work visit www.lauracorrado.it.

Emulsion hardener

There is no need for a hardener when using liquid emulsion on paper. However, on other surfaces this may be necessary. Rollei and Fomaspeed both make a hardener available for purchase. The Rollei brand is called RBM5 and is a glutaraldehyde hardener, so take care in its use as with any aldehyde.

Surface preparation

If the support is paper or cloth, there is no surface preparation needed. Other surfaces need preparation.

Semi-matte or matte (not glossy) non-yellowing *oil based* polyurethane varnish is a good choice for metal . If an opaque coat is desired, oil-based gesso, primer or paint works. *Do not use acrylic*—the liquid emulsion will not adhere well. Note that some metals react with the photosensitive emulsion and fog it; aluminum presents no problems. Copper does.

Plastic should be varnished, as should wood. A cheap foam disposable brush for painting on the varnish works great because it is disposable and saves a brush cleanup step.

All these surfaces need to be well cleaned before use. Soap is not a good cleaner—it leaves a residue. Instead, use something like Arm and Hammer Washing Soda and clean and scrub well until water sheets off the surface instead of beading up, which is an indication there may still be a film of oil, grease, or something else on the surface.

Gelatin-alum subbing solution for glass

A gelatin subbing solution for use on glass or tile is as follows.

2 packets of Knox gelatin (4 teaspoons)
475 ml of water
2 g (½ teaspoon) chrome alum crystals
25 ml warm water

1. Clean the glass in hot water containing sodium carbonate or Arm and Hammer Washing Soda, then scrub with a cloth. Rinse well. See how the water flows off the surface. It should form a barely visible film, and not make droplets or bead up. If necessary, continue scrubbing until the surface is clean.
2. Sprinkle the gelatin on 475 ml of cold water. Let it stand for 15 minutes until dissolved.
3. Heat gently on the stove until melted, about 140°F.
4. Meanwhile, add the chrome alum (hardener) to 25 ml warm water and let it dissolve.
5. Add this solution to the hot gelatin.
6. Pour this solution, still warm, over the clean glass surface, drain thoroughly and allow it to dry at least 4 hours or overnight.

Coating

Coated paper lasts, just like photo paper, so coat a batch of sheets at once and then store.

1. In the darkroom (do *not* open up the bottle of liquid emulsion in room light) put the unopened bottle of emulsion in a container of warm water

at a temperature of 100–120°F until it liquefies. Higher temperatures may fog the solution. It will take about 45 minutes to liquefy a whole bottle, but if just a little is needed, better to transfer a smaller amount of liquid emulsion to another light safe container and heat that up, always under red safelight. A smaller amount will probably be heated and ready to go within 15 minutes.

2. Pour out the necessary amount of emulsion first into a small graduate so the bottle of emulsion can be recapped and returned to the hot water bath. Replenish the graduate with the warmed bottle solution when needs be, but never return poured out solution to the bottle because it may fog the entire contents.

3. Coat the paper/support under red safelight, being sure not to touch metal to the solution at any time, which may fog the solution. Fogging is the most frequent problem with liquid emulsion. A soft-haired stitched-ferrule hake brush works well for liquid emulsion.

4. Don't be shy with the brushing. Brush in one direction, then the other. Push down on the brush to make sure the emulsion sinks well into the surface irregularities, even on hot pressed paper. Pop any bubbles that may appear. Glance at the paper in the light, looking for any stray brush hairs that may be stuck to the emulsion.

5. When done coating the paper, let it dry completely in the dark making sure there is no stray light leaking into the darkroom. *Tip: use a hair dryer on cool to speed it along.* When completely dry, mark the uncoated side with an X, and put in a photo-safe black bag. Before doing this, to be sure the paper is dry, run fingers along the edges because that is where a thicker layer of emulsion may bead up and not be quite dry.

6. Agitate the brush in fixer for 5 minutes and then wash for 10 minutes. If emulsion is left on the brush it can fog the next batch. Black streaks and specks in the print can be caused by a previously used and unclean brush.

Exposure

Reserve one piece of coated paper for test strips. It is also possible to use regular black and white paper, make a comparison between liquid emulsion and that paper, and then use it instead of the liquid emulsion to test. Black Magic is close to the same speed as Ilford MGIV. Liquid Light is up to two stops slower (4× the time).

Processing

1. Develop the exposed print for 2–3 minutes.
2. Use an acid stop bath or a water stop bath. There is disagreement over whether to use an acid stop bath; some say it causes the emulsion to bubble and lift. I recommend a stop bath because if the print has any developer remaining in it—which happens without a thorough rinse in between developer and fixer—the print will smell like fish and turn brown. The thicker the paper, the longer the stop bath and the more rinsing at every single step.
3. Fix for twice as long as you normally do with regular enlarging paper. It takes a long time for watercolor paper to fix. It is best to lengthen times for all steps of liquid emulsion except the developer.
4. Hypoclear and wash for 40–80 minutes if hypo cleared, 60–120 minutes if not.

Tips and ideas

- Don't shake the bottle because bubbles will develop that will mar the image. To get rid of bubbles, blow on them gently, or poke them with a brush. Or cut emulsion 50% with distilled water and coat twice.
- Do not freeze the emulsion; keep it cool or refrigerate it. As it ages, the emulsion produces rich blacks, but too old an emulsion will fog or turn black. Use it up within 6 months of opening.
- A bottle of liquid emulsion can be reheated several times, but after that it may fog.
- If you have them lying around from your analog film days, a plastic film canister holds 1 ounce (30 ml) of solution and will coat up to 6 8″ × 10″s which is about what can be cut out of a 22″ × 30″ sheet of watercolor paper.

- When coating glass, keep it warm on top of a heating pad, or blow on it with a hot hair dryer, so that the emulsion does not instantly harden when it is poured on the glass surface. Some thin the emulsion with water and do two coats instead of one on glass.
- Make sure a print is completely dry before flattening it in a dry mount press. Any moisture left in a print will cause it to stick to the press and rip.
- If the substrate is delicate, buy fiberglass screening from the hardware store and make a cradle for the print with which to transfer the print from solution to solution when developing.
- Add mica, metallic or colored pigments to the emulsion before coating. Some pigments will change color in the fix, though—red is one that is worthless. Pigment may affect the exposure time of the emulsion.
- Make a poor person's orotone by backing a liquid emulsion print on glass or plastic with gold acrylic pigment.
- Try Yupo, a plastic frosted translucent paper. Use hardener in the emulsion, though.
- Use Thai Mulberry paper—spray the back of the paper twice with Krylon Crystal Clear Matte Acrylic to prevent bleed through before coating.

Modern tintype using liquid emulsion

Tintype is traditionally a wet plate collodion process on a blackened metal plate exposed in camera. The black background camera *negative* that results appears *positive* because it is against black. There are many still practicing the collodion version of tintype. In this chapter the process is done with liquid emulsion under an enlarger. A positive, not a negative, is required for exposure—simple with digital negatives—and the paper developer has additives to make it a fogging developer. The fogging developer turns the layer of liquid emulsion lighter so that it shows up on the black surface.

Supplies

Rockland Colloid tintype kit
(www.rockaloid.com, www.freestylephoto.biz)
or
Trophy plate aluminum #108 buffed bright or #308 opaque, .025″ or .020″ thickness
(www.maintrophysupply.com)
or
Metal sprayed with flat black spray paint
Tintype developer
Liquid emulsion
Darkroom chemistry (fix, hypoclear, etc.)
Oil based glossy polyurethane varnish

Tintype developer I

1 liter packet of Dektol
300 g sodium sulfate
125 g ammonium thiocyanate
25 g sodium carbonate
Rollei Black Magic hardener, if desired

1. Heat 3 liters of water to 110°F.
2. Add packet of Dektol and stir until completely dissolved.
3. Add sodium sulfate and stir until completely dissolved. Cool.
4. When room temperature, add ammonium thiocyanate and sodium carbonate.
5. Pour into a gallon container and add enough water to make 1 gallon.
6. Allow to ripen for a few hours before first use. Working strength developer will last several weeks.
7. Add two capfuls of the Black Magic hardener to each 1000 ml developer at time of use to harden emulsion if desired.

Tintype developer II

To one liter of *working* strength Dektol add 75 g (about ¼ cup) sodium sulfate and 40 g (about 3 tablespoons) ammonium thiocyanate. Stir thoroughly until dissolved.

Quickie tintype developer

3 parts Dektol
1 part exhausted rapid fix
At time of use add fixer to working strength Dektol.

Rockland tintype developer

1. Heat 3 liters of water to 110°F.
2. Add the packet of Dektol (Part 1) and stir until completely dissolved.
3. Add the Part 2 powder and stir until completely dissolved. Cool.
4. When room temperature, add the Part 3 liquid. Pour into a gallon container and add enough water to make 1 gallon. This will last several weeks.
5. Add two capfuls of the Black Magic hardener to each 1000 ml developer at time of use if a hardener is necessary.

Tintype directions

1. Remove the plastic sheet of protective material from the trophy aluminum plate.
2. Buff with 600-grit sandpaper or fine steel wool if desired.
3. Clean the plate with sodium carbonate, Arm and Hammer Washing Soda, or Windex until water sheets off instead of beads off. Dry well.
4. Spray or brush with glossy or semi-gloss polyurethane *oil-based* varnish and let dry 6 hours or longer to enhance adhesion.
5. Heat the liquid emulsion until liquefied a crock pot is perfect for this to keep it warm at a low temperature of around 110–120°F. Never shake the bottle as this will create bubbles in the coating. Pouring smaller amounts in light-safe containers is a good idea to avoid reheating and overheating, both of which may contribute to fogging of the emulsion.
6. Put the dry and cleaned plate on top of a small tray (smaller than the plate) filled with hot water which will keep the plate warm. Have this in another tray so the excess emulsion can drip into the outside tray.
7. When the emulsion is liquid, pour a generous amount on the plate. With gloved fingers or a brush, spread the emulsion evenly, letting excess pour back off a plate corner into the container. All of this is done under red safelight only! It may help to dilute the emulsion up to 10% with water so it spreads better, or brush on two coats, drying in between. A hair dryer is useful for warming the plate before coating, too.
8. Dry the plate flat *overnight* in the dark—the longer the better. The emulsion adheres better if the plate is not exposed right away. It also adheres better if a hardening fix is used.
9. Expose the tintype to the positive. All exposure times should be worked out beforehand as discussed in the **Digital Negatives** chapter. One plate reserved for a Stouffer step wedge is useful, and you can even clean off the liquid emulsion with hot to boiling water and reuse that plate.
10. Develop in the tintype developer for 2 minutes. Always have the plate face up. Never touch the surface because it is very fragile.
11. Wash for 30 seconds in water.
12. Fix for 3 minutes in a hardening rapid fix.
13. Wash, hypoclear, and wash again.
14. Dry vertically.
15. Once dry, spray with a coat of Krylon Crystal Clear polyurethane varnish, or use the traditional varnish recipe below.

Lavender varnish recipe

200 ml Everclear or methylated alcohol
30 g gum sandarac
20 ml oil of lavender

1. Dissolve the gum sandarac in the alcohol.
2. Filter debris out.
3. Add the oil of lavender.
4. Store in a glass bottle.
5. Heat before use and pour on.

Troubleshooting modern tintype

- If the tintype is too light, it is overexposed.
- If the tintype is too dark, it is underexposed.
- If the tintype is blueish, it was coated too thinly.
- If the tintype has bubbles, either the emulsion was shaken or the brushing was too vigorous.

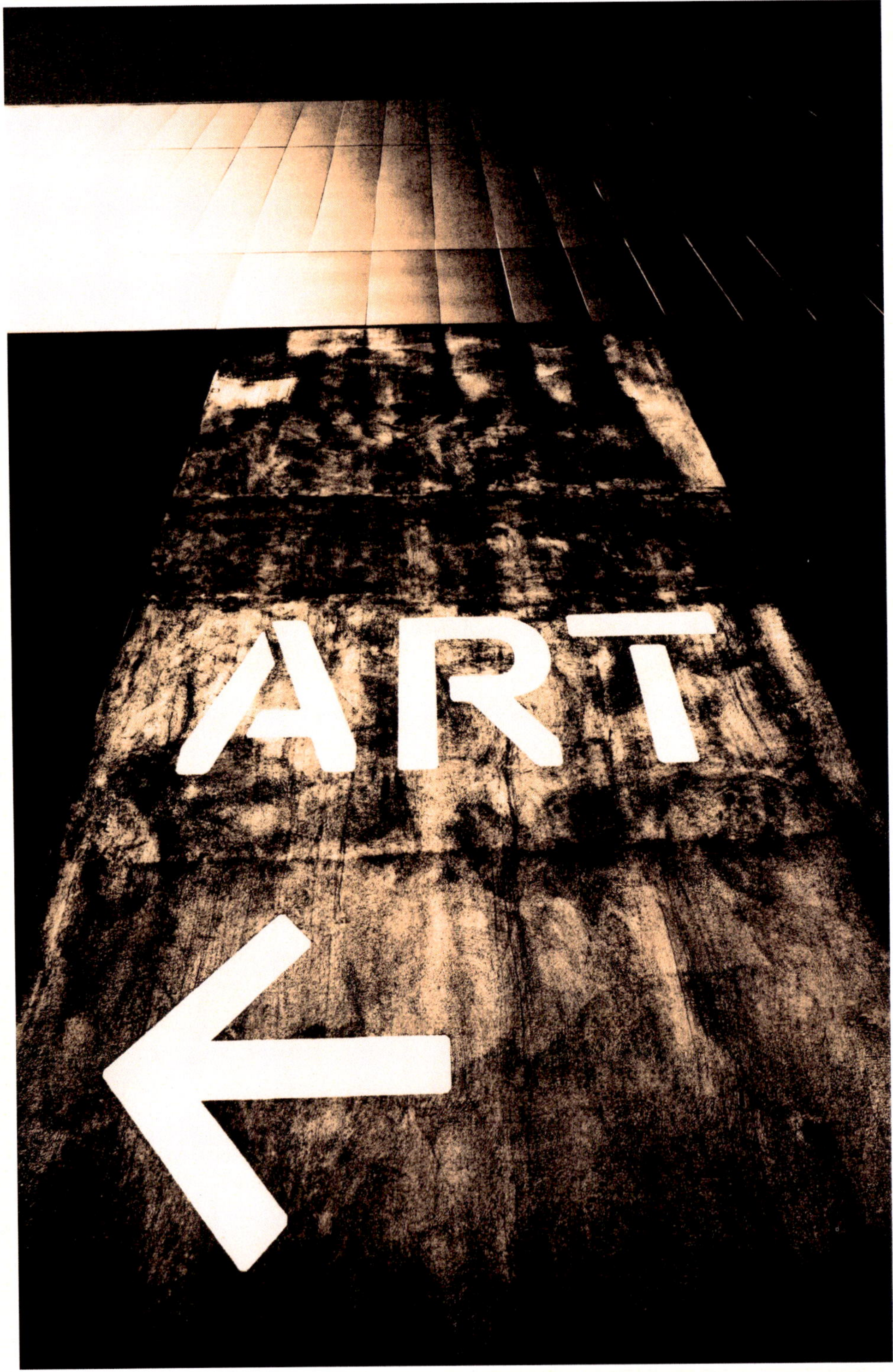

Figure 10.1. *Tacoma Art Museum Parking Lot*, lith print on Fomatone MG (current), Arista Liquid lith developer 150 ml Part A + 150 ml Part B + 3 liters water, print #8 through the developer © Douglas Ethridge 2021

Lith Printing

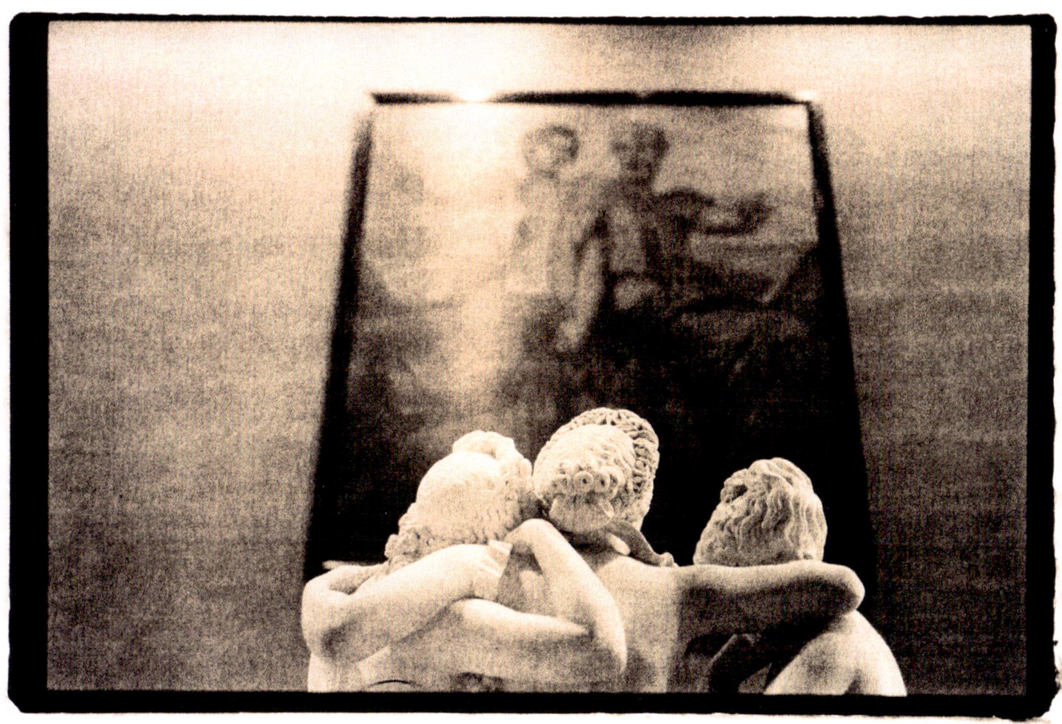

Figure 10.2. *Best Friends, Louvre,* lith print on Forte Polygrade V using Fotospeed LD20 lith developer, 50 ml Part A + 50 ml Part B + 2 liters of water, first print through the developer © Douglas Ethridge 2021

Lith printing is a unique method of printing silver gelatin paper wherein the paper is overexposed 2–3 stops and then developed in a highly diluted lith developer for a long period of time. Images result in gritty, grainy blacks with creamy highlights that are uniquely colored from pale yellow and pink to deep caramel and terracotta. With the right image and patience for a slower development process, lith printing is flexible, infinitely variable, and also quite fun. Note that with the length of time it takes to expose and develop lith prints, red safelight is best to prevent fogging. [I thank Douglas Ethridge for editing and adding his well-seasoned experience to this chapter.]

Papers for lith printing

The hardest thing about lith printing today is that there are few suitable papers for lith. The most reliable papers on the market are currently Fomatone MG Classic 131, 132, 133 and Foma Retrobrom 151 VC. All other contemporary papers are generally limited to use for Second Pass lith.

Lith developers

Arista Premium Liquid A and B Lith Developer

This developer comes in quart bottles and is very economical. Mix at a 1:24 dilution. A tray of two liters of this will lith about 8 prints before snowballs appear, in which case mix up a fresh batch.

Arista Powder A&B Litho Developer

This developer works well and is a different formula than the liquid.

Moersch Easy Lith

Though it is pricier than Arista Lith, this can be purchased in smaller quantities from 100 ml bottles to 500 ml bottles. It is mixed up 1:15–1:30.

Moersch SE5 Master Lith Kit

This is a four solution mix with two extra additives to the normal Part A and Part B. If lith printing becomes your process of choice, this is a next step.

Each developer will provide a different looking result with any given paper, and some paper/developer combinations are more prone to artifacts such as pepper fog. Consequently experimenting with different developers is always good. Two reliable combinations are Fomatone MG with EasyLith and Fomatone MG with Arista Liquid.

One important aspect of lith development is that the developer is chemically changing with each print that is run through. As each printing session proceeds, there will be a gradual but noticeable increase in contrast and this can be offset to some degree by slightly increasing exposure times (5–10%) from one print to the next. There will also be an increase in "grit" or "texture," and often in color. The trend of these chemical changes is relatively consistent from session to session. This means that, for example, if you like a print that was made in the middle of a session, the best chance of making a print with a similar look in a later session is to make it again in the middle of the session, not at the beginning nor at the end.

Lith Developer ID 13

Some refer to this as Ansco 70.

Solution A

750 ml water at 125°F
25 g hydroquinone
25 g potassium metabisulfite
25 g potassium bromide
Water to make 1000 ml

Solution B

750 ml cold water
50 g potassium hydroxide (care!)
Water to make 1000 ml

1. Mix chemicals for Solution A in the order given and store in a separate container from Solution B.
2. Mix Solution B carefully! Potassium hydroxide produces heat when it goes into solution—hence the cold water and slow mixing or it can explode in one's face. Potassium hydroxide is the same as Red Devil Lye from the grocery store, a very caustic chemical!
3. At time of use add 1A+1B+4 or more parts water. Development times will be 2½–5 minutes or longer.

Lith Developer ID 85

ID 13 is a good developer, but ID 85 is even better. Where ID 13 might not produce a good lith print until several have gone through and seasoned the developer, ID 85 has, in my experience, lithed the first print through. The downside to ID 85 is the use of formaldehyde which is a bit sickly sweet smelling and a known carcinogen (even though it is in all kinds of products). Therefore, proceed with caution in the mixing of this chemistry, as is true of any of the formulas in the book.

Solution A

500 ml water at 125°F
36.5 g sodium sulfite
9.4 g boric acid crystals
28 g hydroquinone
2 g potassium bromide
Water to make 1000 ml

Solution B

500 ml water @ 90°F
11 g sodium bisulfite
1 g sodium sulfite
37.5 g paraformaldehyde
Water to make 1000 ml

1. Mix chemicals for Solution A in the order given and store in a separate container from Solution B.
2. Mix chemicals for Solution B in the order given and store in a separate container from Solution A. At time of use mix 4A+1B+10 parts water.

How lith works

Lith works on the basis of **infectious development**: the darker a tone becomes the faster it develops, and the faster it develops the darker it becomes, and so on. It may take as long as 25 minutes to get to this point, during which time it is necessary to watch development closely, because once infectious development takes hold, things can move quickly and the image can easily become much darker than you may like. Snatch the print when you like it and place immediately into the stop bath with no drain time.

The dilution of the developer allows a larger window of opportunity for this snatch time. The more dilute the developer, the more lith-y the print, i.e. the greater difference between the shadows and highlights.

It is best to use a large volume of developer to get the biggest window of opportunity. A gallon of developer in a 16″ × 20″ tray for 8″ × 10″ work is ideal. Keep on hand fresh developer to prime the developer if snowballs appear.

Since the developer is continually aging, lith results are not exactly repeatable. This is another benefit to using larger amounts of developer in the tray—more consistent results.

Rule 1: exposure governs the highlights while development governs the shadows. If darks block up before highlights appear, increase exposure 50–100%. If darks don't show by the time highlights are dark enough, decrease exposure. Not all papers react this way, but many do.

Highlights determine exposure. If they are too dark, less exposure is required. If they are too light, more exposure is required. This seems to follow normal black and white paper.

The development length of time relates only to the shadows, not the highlights, in the following way: if the shadows of the print are blocking up before the highlight detail comes in, more exposure and less development is needed, perhaps a 50% or 100% increase. If development time is too short to allow a good snatch point between the darkening of the darkest areas and the midtones, less exposure and more development time is needed.

Rule 2: contrast, color, and shadows are controlled by development time and exposure: the longer the development time, the higher the contrast. If you need higher contrast: cut exposure, develop longer. If you need lower contrast: increase exposure, develop shorter. If you are using a variable contrast paper, applying filters at the far end of the scale such as Grade 0 and Grade 4 will also make a noticeable difference.

This stands to reason—somewhat. If it takes a longer time to develop a print it seems logical that the highlights would be taking their time printing in. Actually, it follows expansion and contraction principles of film exposure and development to a T: to increase contrast, decrease exposure and increase development. To decrease contrast, increase exposure and decrease development. Less exposure gives higher contrast, more exposure gives lower contrast.

The lith process

1. Mix the lith developer 1A + 1B + 4–30 parts water and pour it into the tray. Dilution of developer is dependent on the rules above, the paper, and the lith developer brand.
2. Calculate your standard printing time for the paper at hand in regular developer and add 2–3 stops. For instance, if the correct printing time is 10 seconds, adding two stops is 10×2×2=40 seconds, 10×2×2×2=80 seconds.
3. Develop the exposed paper in the lith developer anywhere from 5–30 minutes, with a suggested time to shoot for being about 10 minutes or so. This depends on exposure and how much the developer is diluted.
4. Watch the print closely the entire time, and agitate well. A handy tool is a mini mag light equipped with a night vision red filter. Unfortunately the color of the highlights are not very visible in the darkroom so the only thing to be watching for is the development of the shadows. Watch that there is no safelight close to the developing tray so fogging does not occur.
5. As soon as the shadow areas go black as you would like them, pull the print and immediately slide the sheet into the stop bath to stop the development. Earlier snatches produce softer images, later snatches produce bolder images. Remember—more development, more contrast, because the development is making the darks go darker faster

TROUBLESHOOTING

INCREASE CONTRAST
- Decrease exposure and increase development

DECREASE CONTRAST
- Increase exposure and decrease development

TOO CONTRASTY
- Underexposed

HIGHLIGHTS BLOWN OUT
- Underexposed

TOO FLAT
- Overexposed
- Safelight fogging
- Exhausted developer

BLACKS NOT RICH ENOUGH
- Exhausted developer
- Wrong exposure
- Snatched too soon

BLACKS BLOCKED UP
- Underexposed
- Overdeveloped
- Snatched too late

UNEXCITING LITH EFFECT
- Unsuitable paper
- Developer too fresh or too strong
- Exhausted developer

than making the highlights go darker.

6. Fix the print as usual. When a lith print hits the fix it immediately appears to lighten drastically because colors change. Most of the time these colors are not visible in the darkroom, and the true color of a lith print doesn't really appear until the print is completely dry.

7. Wash, hypoclear, wash again, and dry as per normal archival procedures.

Second Pass lith

Since the majority of modern papers do not work for the traditional method of lith printing, Second Pass lith makes it possible to explore this printing method with many readily available papers. See Tim Rudman in the **Contemporary Experimental Artists** chapter for examples of this process.

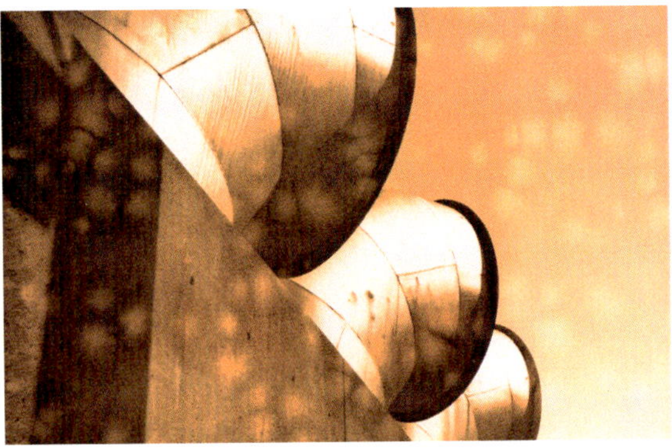

Figure 10.3. Note the "snowballs" due to exhausted developer, lith print on Arista ultra, Arista liquid lith developer © Douglas Ethridge 2022

Take a previously exposed print and bleach it completely in the Standard Bleach, further. Rinse well and redevelop in a lith developer, just as if doing a lith print from scratch. This is a great way to use old prints that were not well printed as long as they are not too light. If development is carried too far, the print reverts to a normal silver gelatin print, but if this happens, the print can be lithed again. When the print is to one's liking, rinse, fix, wash, and dry. The process works better on some papers than on others. Ilford MGIV does a nice pink/purple split.

Standard bleach formula

100 g (5 tablespoons) potassium bromide
100 g (6.5 tablespoons) potassium ferricyanide
Water to 1000 ml

This makes a liter of stock solution. At time of use, dilute 1 part stock with 9 parts water (1+9). Chemistry doesn't have to be exact, which is why the tablespoon measures are used here.

1. Place the print in a tray of working strength bleach and watch the print while it bleaches.
2. Rinse and redevelop the print in dilute lith developer.
3. Wash as normal for an archival print.

Bleach-back lith

A gritty, lith look alike can be achieved by overexposing a print a couple stops, developing it normally, and then bleaching it back to normal density. The print will have slight brown tones. Fix, wash, and dry.

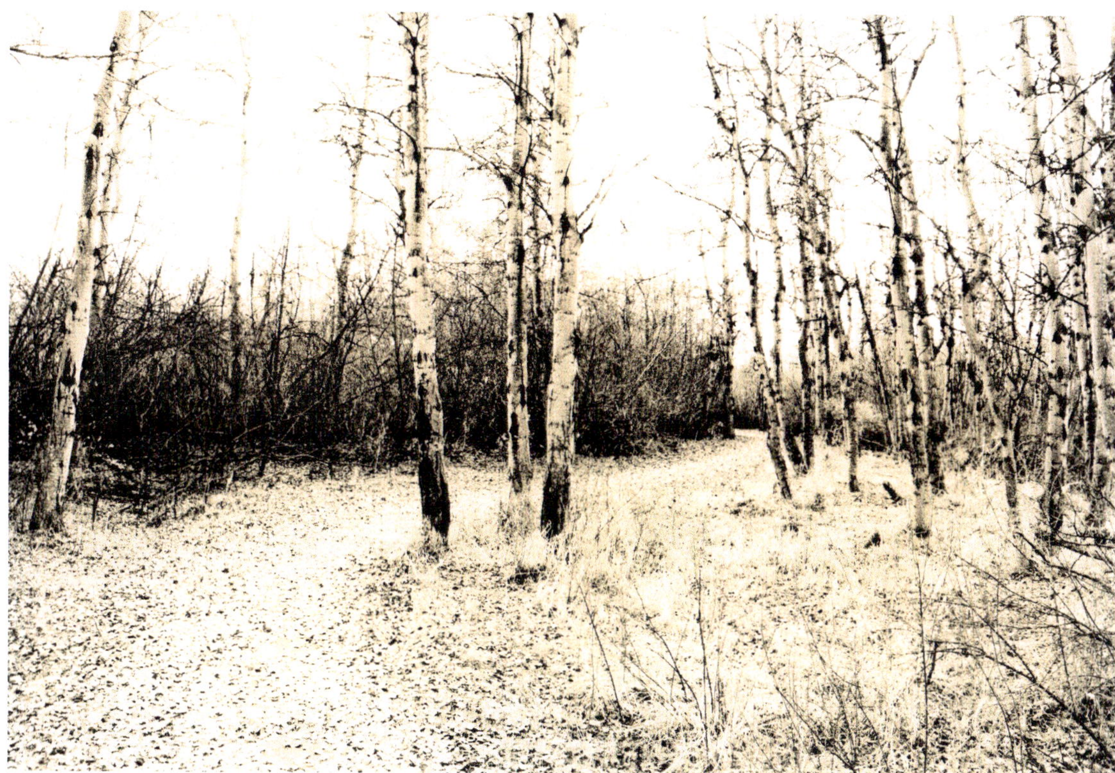

Figure 10.4. *Lost in the Trees*, lith print on Fomatone MG 131 Classic in Arista Lith 1A+1B+18 water © Emma Culwell 2021

Troubleshooting

- There are several common developer artifacts caused by exhausted developer. The appearance of any of these is a sign to either mix fresh developer or add extra developer concentrate. These artifacts include pepper fog, tiny perfectly round pinpoints of black, snowflakes, which are fairly good sized spots of white, and snowballs, which are white billowy masses. If you see any of these artifacts near the beginning of a session, it's a good sign that the paper you are using would be a better match for a different developer.
- Many workers find that the onset of developer artifacts such as snowballs as well as the gradual lengthening of development times can be alleviated by using a replenishment approach. Mix up the developer normally, and then reserve ¼–⅓ of the mixed developer in a beaker. After each print, add 80–100 ml of the reserved developer to the tray.
- If edges of a print are darker than the center, agitate the tray less vigorously, use a tray one size larger so that there is less edge turbulence, and make sure the edges of the print are always submerged, because the exposure of corners and edges of the paper to air may enhance the activity of the lith developer in those areas by increasing the rate of hydroquinone oxidation.
- Fomatone MG starts with warm brown print results which then move toward bright orange or as Doug Ethridge says, "nuclear holocaust territory." This is probably a result of the fact that a used developer gives more color than fresh so if it is not to your liking use fresh developer.
- Toning with selenium or gold is excellent; gold will go from red to blue. Selenium toner tones shadows first, then highlights; gold tones highlights first, then shadows. Some interesting split tones can happen.
- Two exposed prints can be placed back to back in the lith developer and continually flipped to do two prints at once.
- Try higher temperatures of developer, up to 100°F to shorten the development time.

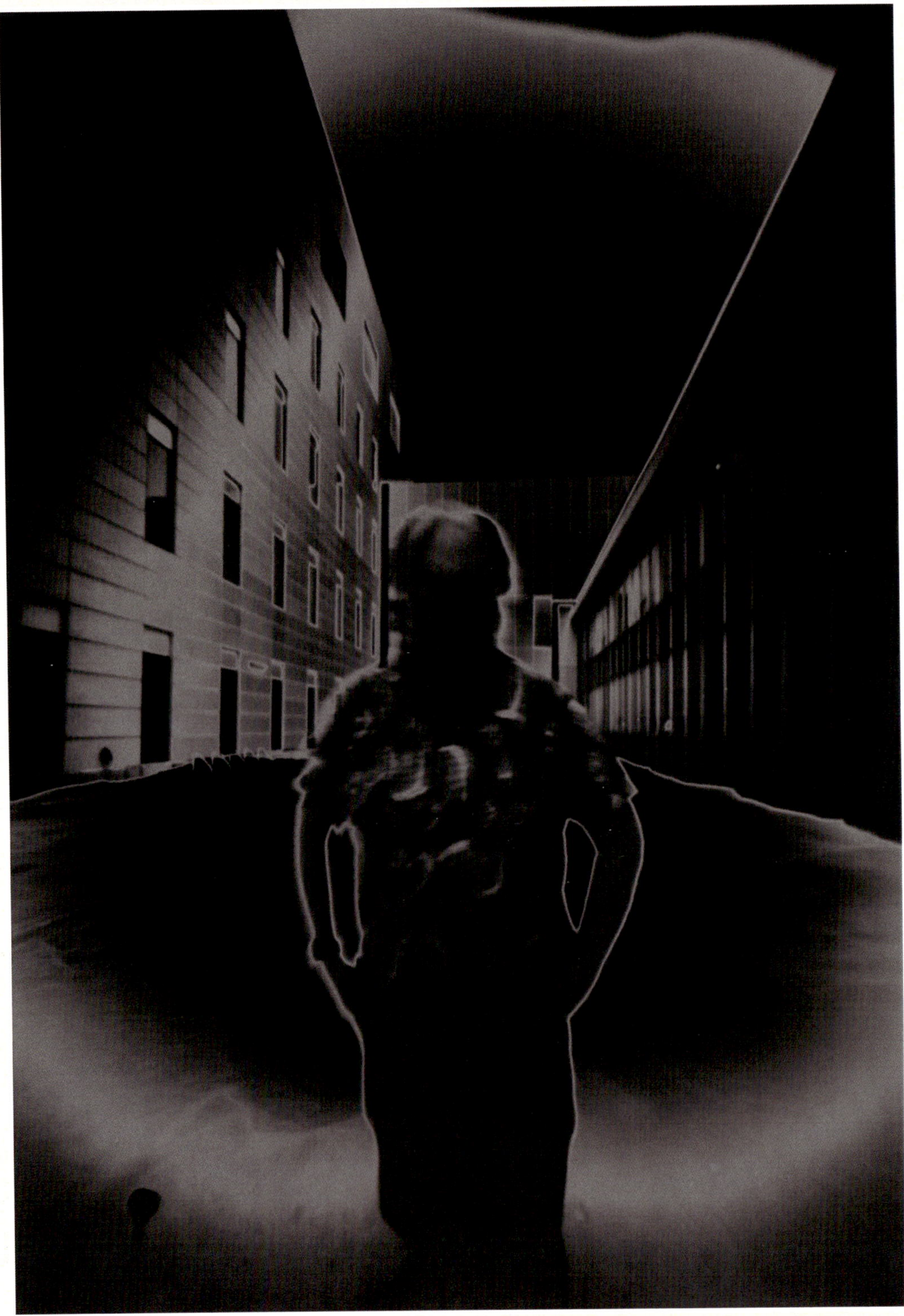

Figure 11.1. *Making the Most of a Pandemic and a Snowstorm*, sabattier pinhole image, 4″ x 6″ sabattier print © J. Jason Lazarus 2021

Sabattier

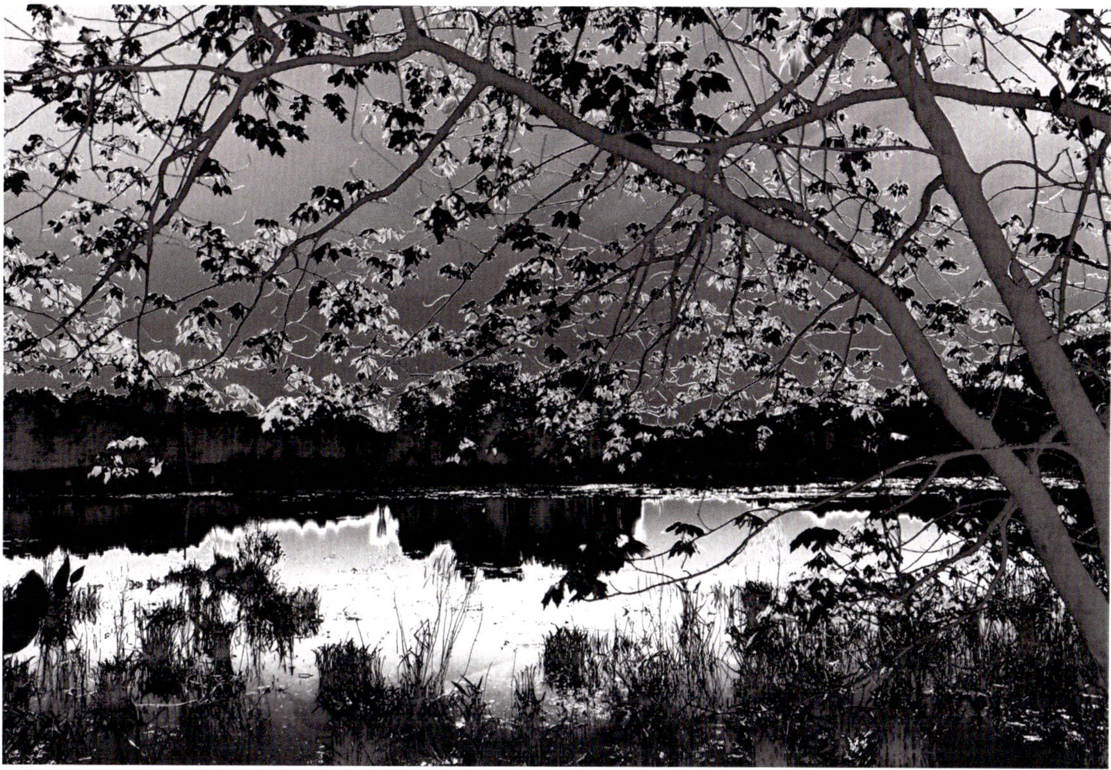

Figure 11.2. *Untitled*, silver gelatin sabattier, 10″ x 6.5″ © Mark L. Eshbaugh 2020. "This print is exposed normally in the enlarger with a high contrast filter and processed in Sprint chemistry. During the developer stage the print is pulled from the chemistry at about 30–45 seconds and placed in a dry flat bottomed tray. I then expose the print using a second enlarger with the aperture stopped down to its limit and re-expose the print with the timer set to 2 or 3 seconds. The print is then replaced in the developer for about a minute (I pull the print based on visual inspection rather than time). On rare occasions, I pull and expose the print an additional time, but that either works well or results in too dark of an image. The remaining processing is done as per normal." Mark L. Eshbaugh is an artist, author, and musician. His work has been exhibited in museums and galleries worldwide. Mark teaches photography and digital art at several colleges. He has written about photographic subjects, and contributed to several textbooks about art. He lives in Massachusetts with his wife and son. To see more of his work visit www.markeshbaugh.com.

In 1862, Armand Sabattier discovered something from a mistake. He had accidentally exposed his wet collodion plate to light while developing it, and noticed the partial reversal of tone that occurred. The rest is history. Or so Armand Sabattier says. First of all, his name is actually spelled with one "t," not two. That was history's mistake. Second, his first name was not Armand—history got that wrong, too. Third, he was not the discoverer of the process. According to William Jolly, the originator of the process was William Jackson of Lancaster, England, who reported on the process in a letter to the editor of the *Journal of the Photographic Society of London*, in 1857. And finally, sabattier has forever incorrectly been referred to as "solarization" throughout the photographic community even to this day. Solarization is when film is subject to gross overexposure and density reverses to clear. If the sun is in an image, for instance, it will result in a clear spot on the negative which will print black in the final print. In this chapter "Sabatier" will be spelled incorrectly as "sabattier" because the horse has left that barn decades ago, but never referred to incorrectly as "solarization."

About sabattier

A print is exposed to light somewhere during the development process, before fixing. This brief re-exposure of light will have a greater effect on the highlights in a print than the shadows which have mostly developed out. Density will increase rapidly in the highlights to a full black, the midtones will partially reverse to a lighter tone, and the dark areas of the print will remain somewhat the same. Lending to the graphic effect of the image is a phenomenon called "Mackie lines"—white lines that rim objects in the print. These Mackie lines occur where light and dark areas meet at the areas of higher contrast.

Paper and developer to use

Use **glossy fiber base paper**. In practice, matte papers and warmtone papers do not work as well.

The old method of sabattier employed exhausted developer nicknamed "old brown." It was thought that old brown was necessary for the process, but Jolly discovered that sabattier works best in the absence of hydroquinone, which is depleted in old brown. A fresh, hydroquinone-free developer therefore works beautifully.[1]

Clarence Rainwater's R77

60 g (8 teaspoons) sodium sulfite
13 g (4 teaspoons) catechol
48 g (8 teaspoons) sodium carbonate monohydrate
2 g (1 teaspoon) phenidone
7 g (1 teaspoon) potassium bromide
Water to make 4000 ml

Mix the chemicals in the order given into warm water, stirring well after each until dissolved. Use full strength.

Sabattier the quick way

Rule of thumb: the longer the initial exposure of the print, the more positive the final print. The shorter the initial exposure, the more negative.

1. Expose the paper under the enlarger with a high contrast filter, and give it about ¼ to ½ stop less exposure than it requires.
2. Place the paper in the developer for ⅓–⅔ the normal development time—around 50 seconds, for instance. Make sure the midtones have come up.
3. Flash the paper while in the developing tray with a 25 watt bulb several feet above the tray for about ⅒ second. A shorter, brighter flash increases contrast, a longer, dimmer flash reduces contrast. It is easiest to have this light attached to a timer to measure time accurately. ⅒ second is a starting point, but by no means the best time for every print. It is also possible to flash more than once. Be sure there is no other paper out in the open that may be fogged by this exposure.
4. Leave the print to develop until the full development time is complete. Then process it in stop, fix, etc., as per normal.

Duotone sabattier

Duotone sabattier has cold shadows and warm midtones and highlights. The print is flashed in a second tray of developer that has potassium bromide added to it. Potassium bromide warms up the tones of the print but it also slows development.

1. Prepare a tray of Dektol or Rainwater.
2. Prepare a second developer tray of Dektol or Rainwater, with 10–50 g potassium bromide added per liter of developer. The more bromide, the yellower and lighter the brown. The less bromide, the redder and darker the brown. 2 tablespoons of potassium bromide per liter of developer works well.
3. Install a light source over the second tray. A 100-watt light bulb about 2–4 feet above the tray works well.
4. Expose the print under the enlarger and develop it in the first tray of regular developer for 50 seconds.

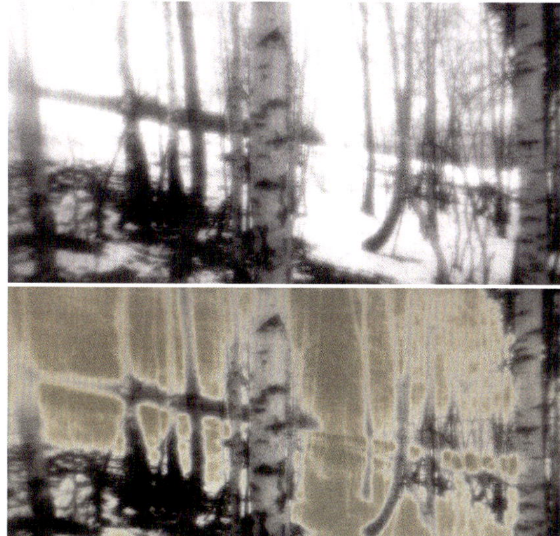

Figures 11.3–11.4. Top, *Birches*, silver gelatin print from a zoneplate camera, 18 x 24 cm © Danilo Pedruzzi 2018. Bottom, *Birches*, silver gelatin sabattier print from a zoneplate camera, 18 x 24 cm © Danilo Pedruzzi 2018. Danilo Pedruzzi (b.1956 Bonate Sotto, Italy) opened his photographic studio in 1991. Over the years he has experimented with many alternative processes as well as pinhole photography. Pedruzzi is a member of Rodolfo Namias Group, Italy, since 2008. His works have been published and are held in museums and private collections. To see more of his work visit danilopedruzzi.blogspot.com.

5. Remove the print from the first tray of developer and place in the bromide-enhanced developer tray; agitate 15–20 seconds and then let it set in the center of the tray. While submerged in the bromide-enhanced developer, flash the tray for 5 seconds. The lower the bromide in the second developer, the shorter the flash. The higher the bromide, the longer the flash.
6. Leave the print in the tray until development is complete and the brown tones look good, and stop, fix, hypoclear, wash, and dry.
7. The print can be toned with Kodak Rapid Selenium toner, diluted 1:7 for 5–10 minutes to develop the color more fully, if desired.[2]

Thiosulfate sabattier

1. Expose and develop a print for 40–50 seconds, drain it for 10 seconds, and then transfer it to a tray containing 200 parts water, 90 parts Dektol stock, and 35 parts 10% solution of sodium thiosulfate.
2. Develop for 2½ minutes while agitating, and then expose the print to a 40 or 60-watt light bulb 3 or 4 feet over the developer tray for 3–6 seconds. Agitate for another minute, and process as usual in stop bath and fixer. Essentially this fogs the paper with the addition of sodium thiosulfate.[3]

Tips and ideas

- Print contrasty: #3½–#5 filter
- Print bolder subject matter.
- Keep extensive notes; no two prints will be exactly alike, but good notes will aid in an attempt to replicate an effect.
- If the print is overexposed in the enlarger, the image will not reverse much but will have the Mackie lines and tonal gradation in the highlights. If the print is flashed later on in the first development time, this will hold true, too.
- The longer the developing time before re-exposure to light, the stronger the Mackie lines, but the greatest sabattier occurs earlier in development. The shorter the initial exposure, the less pronounced the Mackie lines, the less detail in the blackened highlights, and the print will be less contrasty. If a normally exposed print is flashed too early in the first development, this will hold true, too. Let the image completely appear in the first development time before flashing.

Endnotes

1. Walker, Sandy, and Clarence Rainwater. *Solarization*. Garden City New York: Amphoto, 1974.
2. Jolly, William. "Dramatic Duotone Solarization" in *Darkroom and Creative Camera Techniques*, July/August 1993, pp. 19–21.
3. Jolly, William L. "Silver Mirror Printing and Other Unusual Black-and-White Print Development Processes" in *Photo Techniques*, January/February 1999, pp. 32–36.

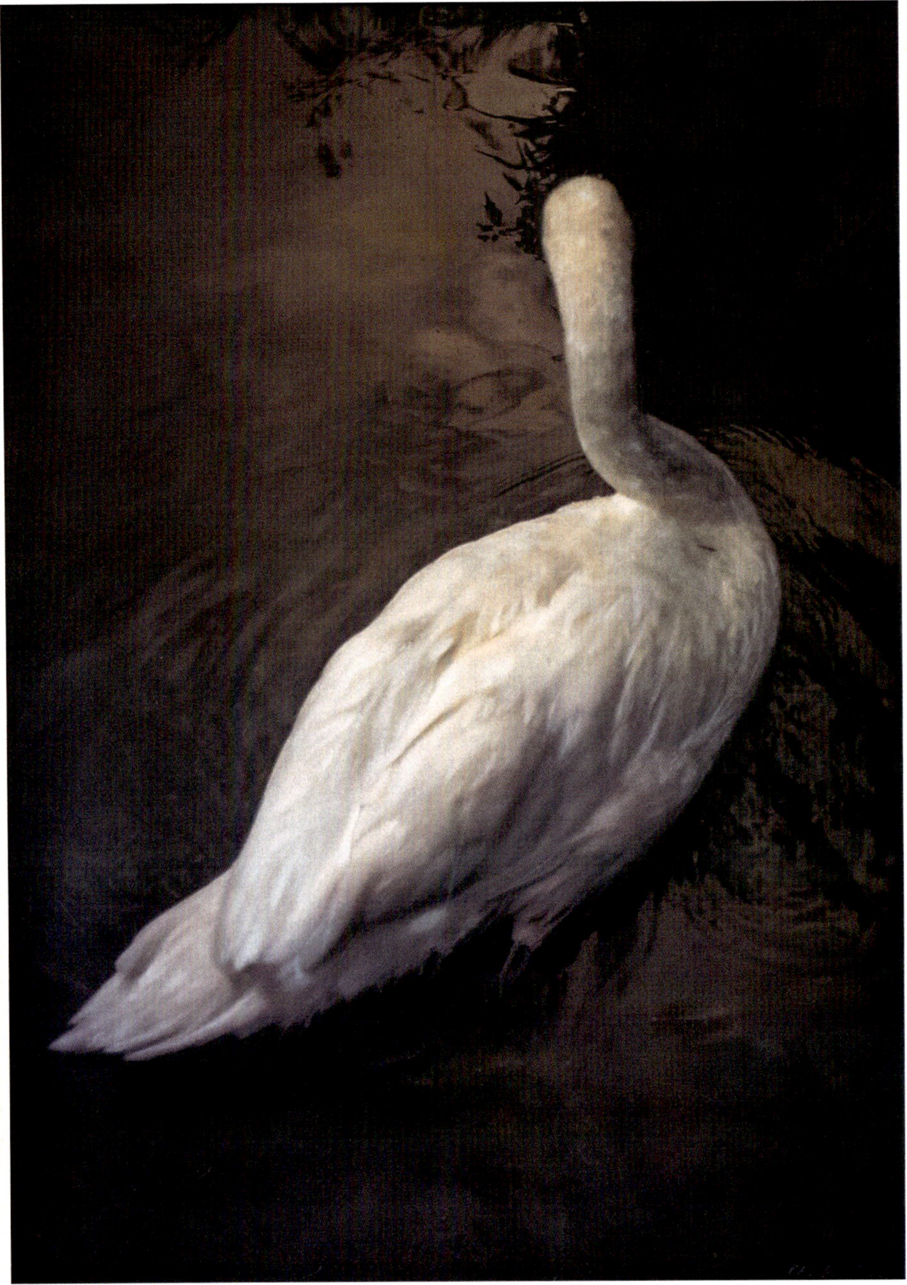

Figure P4.1. *Swan*, from the series *Ghosts of Love*, silver gelatin print handcolored with pastel and pencil, 24″ x 32″ © Kate Breakey 2018. Kate Breakey is internationally known for her large-scale, richly hand-colored photographs. Since 1980 her work has appeared in more than 120 one-person exhibitions and in over 60 group exhibitions. A native of South Australia, Breakey moved to Austin, Texas in 1988. She completed a Master of Fine Art degree at the University of Texas in 1991 where she also taught photography in the Department of Art and Art History until 1997. Her collections include the Houston Museum of Fine Arts, the Center for Creative Photography, Tucson, The Australian National Gallery, The Wittliff collections, and the San Diego Museum of Photographic Arts, as well as various private collections. She has resided in Tucson, Arizona for 22 years. She regularly teaches workshops nationally and internationally. To see more of her work visit www.katebreakey.com.

PART FOUR

Finished Print Experimentation

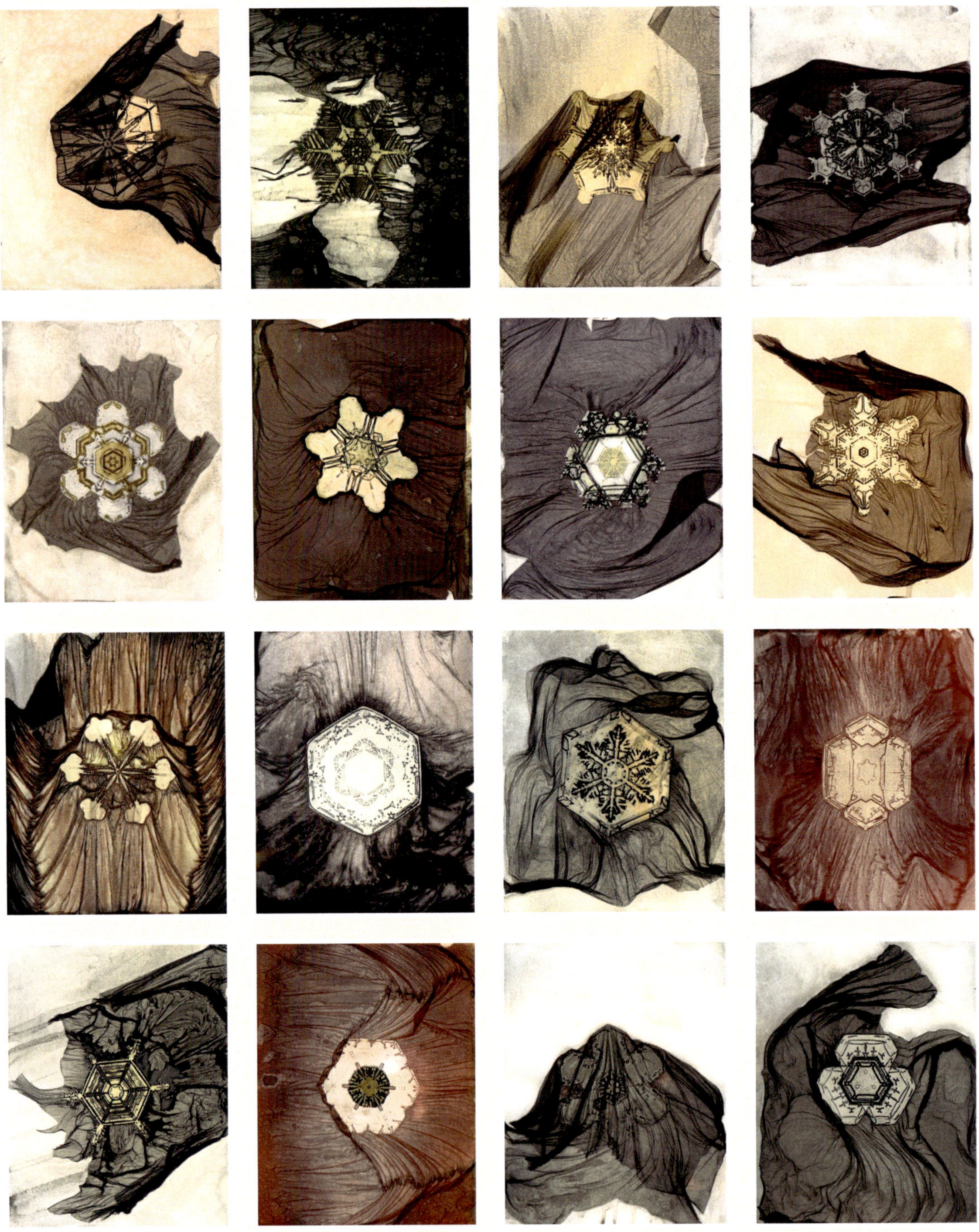

Figures 12.1–12.16. *Bentley Snowflakes*, 8˝ x 10˝ silver gelatin mordançage prints © Christina Z. Anderson 2010. Over a century ago a nineteen-year-old Vermont farm boy named Wilson Alwyn Bentley began a 46-year love affair with the typology of snow crystals. Summer 2010 the Jericho Historical Society granted me permission to use Bentley's archives. Bentley's snowflakes with their black backgrounds were perfect for mordançage. The backgrounds would veil and dissolve in the caustic bath—a fitting visual metaphor for the floating and ephemeral nature of a snowflake. Because each mordançage print is completely unique, how equally fitting to the uniqueness of snowflakes. I created contact negatives from 52 of the 5000+ snow crystal images, which I then printed onto silver gelatin paper. Bentley's snow crystals are beautiful in their pristine, white, perfect surfaces. The beauty of my work lies in their darkened imperfections.

Mordançage

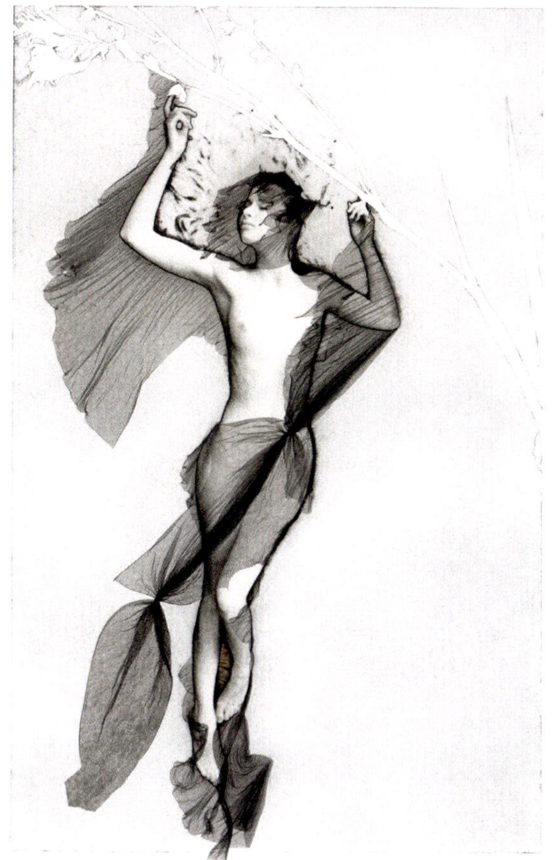

Figure 12.17. *Changer la Femme Version I*, mordançage on 11″ x 14″ silver gelatin paper © Elizabeth Opalenik 2016. For more of Opalenik's work, see the **Contemporary Experimental Artists** chapter.

The bleach-etch process, now generally called *mordançage*, dates from the late 1800s. It has had various other names, too: etch-bleach, gelatin relief, and reverse relief. The process was originally used on film, not paper (see the **Appendix** for further formulas). It was a way of reversing a film negative to a positive, and often that film positive was colored with dyes. Liesegang was the discoverer in 1897 (see **Bibliography**). Then Andresen improved upon Liesegang's formula in 1898 by substituting hydrogen peroxide for the ammonium persulfate in the original formula. Hydrogen peroxide is still what is used today.[1]

I saw my first mordançage print in 1999 at Savannah College of Art and Design. My guess is the student who created the print learned from Craig Stevens, who knew the master of mordançage, Jean Pierre Sudre. Stevens met Sudre in 1981 and was introduced to the process along with other photographers, one being Elizabeth Opalenik. Sudre started using the process on prints instead of film. His protégé Elizabeth Opalenik carried his process further when she chose to retain the delicate gelatin veils on the surface of her prints, the first to do so. Since meeting Sudre and being introduced to this process, it has been Opalenik's signature life work. Because of Sudre, Opalenik, and Stevens, bleach-etch/now mordançage was turned into an art form and is much more widely practiced today. Sudre died in 1997, but his memory, process, and prints live on.

When I saw those prints at SCAD I began my mordançage treasure hunt, wanting to teach the process to my Experimental Photography class. My research was made easier by generous people such as Jon Bailey, Judy Seigel, Nate Apkon, and others on the alternative process list-serv who directed me to patents and articles as well as shared their own mordançage notes.

Jean-Pierre Sudre is the one who originated the term *mordançage*. This term confused my initial research, because the French word translates to "mordanting" as in making a print (or fabric, etc.) accept dye. Denis Brihat said the process should really have been called *grignotage* because the bleach-etch solution "nibbles" away at the print instead of mordants it. However, that horse has long left the barn and mordançage it is.

Mordançage is probably the most difficult process to use effectively. It is visually dominant. The process can command more presence than the image. The image should be well chosen for the process and the two integrated into one whole. Couple this visual dominance with a certain amount of lack of control (sometimes serendipity) while doing the process, and it becomes even trickier. Nevertheless, with forethought, practice, and patience, it is unrivaled.

In the mordançage process an acidified copper bleaching solution is used to simultaneously bleach and dissolve away parts of a silver gelatin print, leaving behind a relief-maplike texture. The dissolving occurs proportionately to the darks—the darker the area, the more dissolution. With a little rubbing, the solubilized metallic silver gelatin layer lifts off of the print and leaves behind whites in reverse relief where the darks once were. Then with redevelopment, toning, or dyeing, the image reappears.

The chemical reaction that is taking place is that the gelatin in contact with metallic silver is chemically "etched," or dissolved away, by the hydrogen peroxide. "Hydrogen peroxide gives up its oxygen when reacting with the silver, and this nascent

Caution! Caution! Caution! Caution! Caution!

This caution applies to film as well as paper, and to copper sulfate as well as copper chloride: this process requires excellent ventilation, and must be done outside. Do NOT breathe in the fumes. Use this process at one's own risk and mix chemistry *exactly as described and in the order described*. If hydrogen peroxide is poured on copper chloride powder, toxic chlorine gas will result, which is why copper chloride is first added to water. The solution is caustic and will eat through a stainless steel sink so store in plastic bottles and nowhere near metal. Always protect eyes from splashing. Wear old clothes or an apron, because the solution will discolor and ruin fabric. Wearing gloves is an absolute must. Latex gloves are permeable to chemicals, so nitrile gloves are the best choice. Remember: AAATW—always add acid to water, never water to acid! Consult the MSDS documentation before using any chemical. It is the reader's responsibility to find the necessary information about a chemical before using it. It is the reader's responsibility to take any appropriate measures of caution in respect to the health and safety of themselves and anyone around. Chemicals no matter how innocuous should always be treated as if dangerous. Avoid contact with skin, eyes, mouth, and other body parts. Do not ingest any chemical. Glacial acetic acid is 99% pure acid and should not come in contact with skin. It is corrosive. It is also irritating to the mucous membranes, eyes, and respiratory system so do not splash it or breathe it in. Copper chloride is a strong oxidizer and corrosive. Avoid light, air, and moisture. If you are unable to follow any part of this caution, do not do this process.

oxygen attacks the colloid."[2] Copper chloride is in the formula to bleach and to increase hydrogen peroxide's oxidizing potency. The more oxidizing power the solution has, the faster and greater amount of dissolution happens. Increasing either hydrogen peroxide or copper chloride will speed things up, but too much is overkill and will dissolve most of the print.

There are choices at every stage of the process. One of the first choices is whether to rub the surface of the print after the bleach-etch bath wholly, partially, or not at all. If the print is rubbed wholly, any black areas that have dissolved will be removed. Upon redevelopment, those areas remain white and the print looks more negative than positive. If the print is rubbed partially, the image will be some measure of positive and negative. If the print is not rubbed at all, and you are careful to leave the gelatin veils intact, the veils will create a beautiful flow to the image and the image looks more positive. These veils, tenuously attached to the points of contrast between highlights and shadows, upon drying will re-adhere to the print surface and stay put. Most often, the highlights and midtones remain unaffected by the chemistry.

The process can be used on any silver gelatin print (untoned), whether years old, freshly processed, or even right after developing and before fixing.

The best images for this process are ones with a good measure of deepest black, such as black backgrounds or intricately detailed patterns like black lace or wrought ironwork. It is easy to add black to an image digitally, even if there is none, so today is the best of both worlds, analog and digital, for the mordançage process.

Mordançage is not a process for beginners but for those who have good knowledge and employment of safety measures. For one, the solution is caustic, pH below 3. Two, the process requires excellent ventilation. I only do it outside, in my garage because of its potential causticity to the lungs and I would never recommend it be practiced in an enclosed, poorly ventilated darkroom. Wearing eye, clothing, hand, and skin protection goes without saying. Most importantly, mix the chemistry **exactly and only as described** by adding each chemical to water, one by one, stirring thoroughly before adding the next, and **AAATW—always add acid to water**. I can't *imagine* why anyone would do this, but **if you were to pour hydrogen peroxide on dry copper chloride powder you would release toxic chlorine gas that would kill you**. That hopefully puts the fear of God in you and in this process. This is why I always mix the formula in front of my students while they watch or else they are not allowed to participate in the class. I also have all sign a release waiver if they want to do the process. One can't be too cautious.

Coote formula[3]

Solution A

750 ml water
10–30 g copper chloride (1–2 tablespoons)
80–110 ml glacial acetic acid (can also substitute 10–20 g citric acid; can also substitute 300 ml 28% stop bath in place of 220 ml of the water; make sure the stop bath is not colored)
Water to make 1000 ml

Always protect eyes from splashing and always wear gloves. Latex gloves are permeable to chemicals; nitrile gloves are your best choice. Remember: AAATW—always add acid to water, never water to acid!

1. Add copper chloride slowly to the water and stir.
2. Add acetic acid slowly to this mixture and stir.
3. Add water to make 1 liter.
4. Store this solution, correctly labeled POISON, in a plastic liter container—never metal. This solution is usable indefinitely.

Solution B

10–20 volume hydrogen peroxide

Peroxide is mixed in equal proportion to Solution A at time of use. Regular strength drug store peroxide will work fine. It is about a 3%/10 volume solution. If the process is slow to bleach-etch, keep on hand a 20v (6%) hydrogen peroxide from a beauty supply store (buy the clear kind, not the creamy) and prime the working tray solution with a glug. I used to also buy 40v (12%) but I never use it now; 20v is even a bit much.

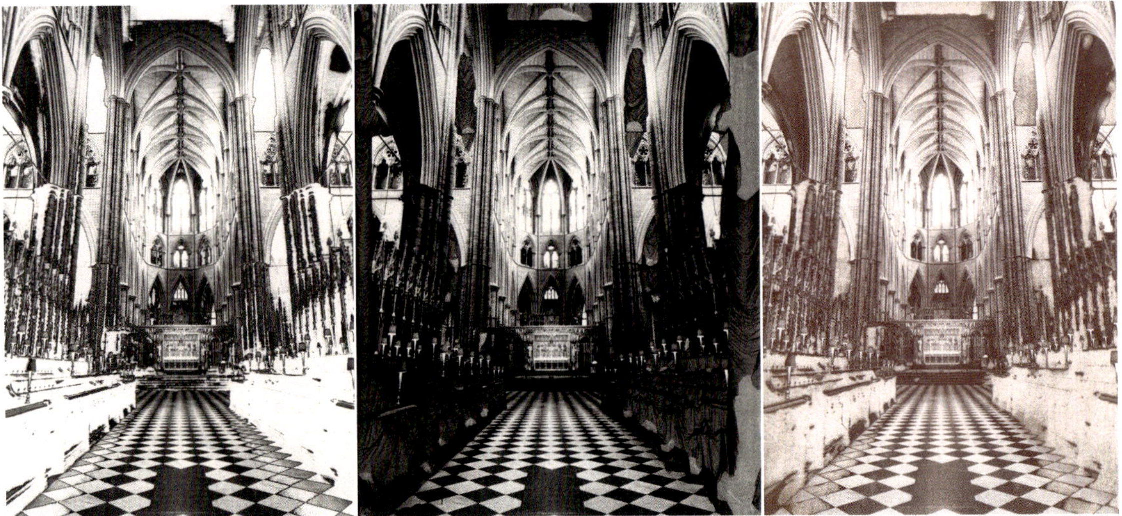

Figures 12.18–12.20. *Westminster Abbey*, from left to right, rubbed mordançage, mordançage with veils, and mordançage with sun exposure "redevelopment," 8″ x 10″ silver gelatin prints © Alyssa McKenna 2021

There is no need to use a stronger hydrogen peroxide. Some formulas call for 135v hydrogen peroxide. I used to be able to buy it at the beauty supply store, but it is hazardous, explosive, the container will bulge at the bottom as it expands, and you just generally don't want it around. When 135v hydrogen peroxide is used in a formula it is always used in small amounts in the water, and it is just as easy to use more hydrogen peroxide of a lesser strength.

Papers to use

All brands of papers work. However, the easiest paper to etch is Ilford MGIV glossy because it dissolves rapidly.

RC paper has some advantages in this process, despite its inherently unpleasing plastic quality. It rinses quickly between steps, and remains more impervious to the chemicals, so it doesn't have the yellowing problem that fiber paper sometimes does. However, veils slip off easily and are hard to control. It is easy to rub too much emulsion off with too vigorous rubbing, so be careful.

Mordançage process

Wear gloves at all times! Do the process outside! Have I said this already? Do I seem like a broken record?

1. Mix Solutions A and B together in equal parts to produce the amount of working solution needed. 500 ml in a flat bottom tray works well. Once A is mixed with B, this working mixture will last a number of days, though it is best to mix right before use. If it weakens, add more or stronger hydrogen peroxide; also, add more glacial acetic acid if the pH has gone above 3.0. A box of pH strips are invaluable. I have stored old solution and reactivated it with hydrogen peroxide and it works fine. Precious chemistry is not wasted. Remember to store this working strength solution in its own labeled *plastic* jug, not metal.
2. Set up trays, from left to right in this order: mordançage solution, plain (warm) water, working strength or weak developer, plain water, toner(s) if desired and a final tray of plain water for rinsing. Have sheets of Plexiglas on hand to transport delicate prints from one tray to the next if desired.
3. Bleach a wet or dry print in the mordançage solution for twice as long as it takes to fully bleach. This can take from 1–15 minutes, depending on the print, paper, strength of hydrogen peroxide and

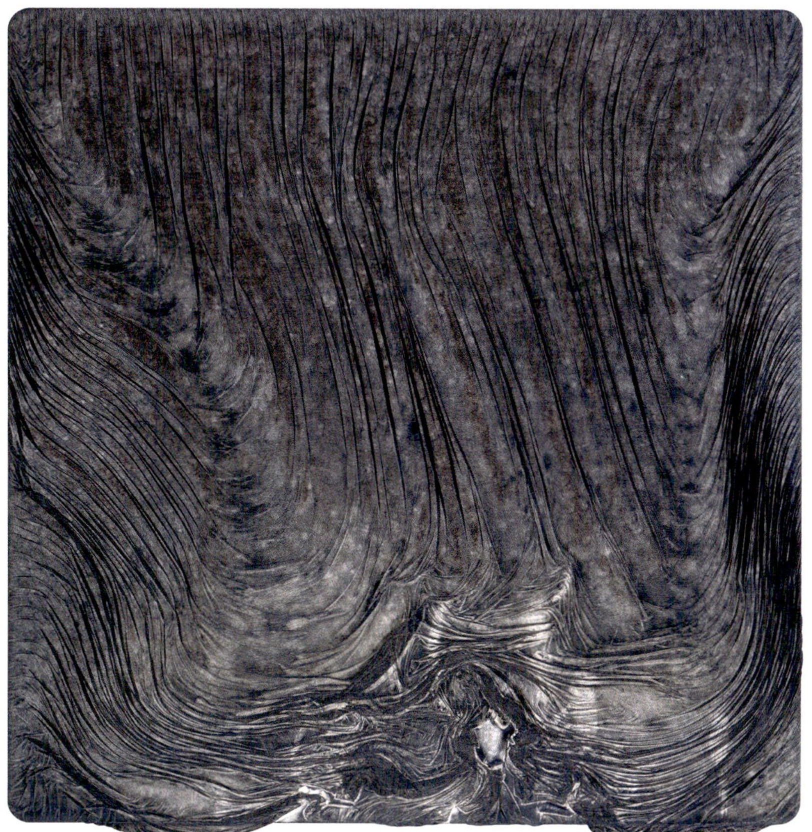

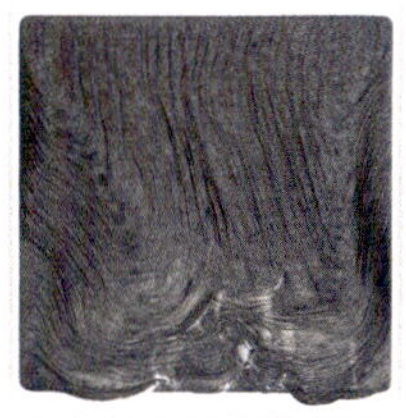

Figures 12.21–12.22. *Mordançage Gelatin Silver 7*, © Brittany Nelson 2021. Left, original. Top, installation. For more of Nelson's work, see the **Contemporary Experimental Artists** chapter.

amount of copper chloride. The more hydrogen peroxide, the greater dissolution. The more copper chloride, the faster the bleaching. Papers used to take this long but lately Ilford MGIV takes a minute or so to complete the bleach etch.

4. Nudge a dark area of the print to see if it is lifting off and bubbly. If the darks dissolve too much, use the weaker strength hydrogen peroxide. If the print bleaches too fast before it etches, decrease the amount of copper chloride.[4]

5. Take the print carefully out of the bleach-etch tray and place it in the next tray of water to rinse off as much chemistry as possible before it goes into the developer. The water in this tray can be hot (Coote recommends 120°F[5]). The hot water cleans the print of chemistry more effectively, and it speeds up the bleach-etch immediately. It also allows one to do mordançage in the garage during winter. If the bleach-etch solution gets too cold it slows down or stops working. With hot water, voilà.

6. Rinse well in this tray, especially with fiber paper. Be cautious with the veils that float around. Never touch the surface of the print with tongs. If the veils are too delicate, it may be that rinsing well is not possible, should you desire to leave veils attached. Should you desire to remove veils, it is at this point you rub off the disintegrating emulsion carefully with cotton balls. Do this under water, with the print on a piece of Plexiglas if the trays are not flat-bottomed.

7. Redevelop the print in any of the following:
   - Paper developer, either working strength or diluted up to 1:5
   - Part B of a sepia or thiourea toner
   - Film developer such as Pyro or D76

   or

   Expose the print to direct and strong sunlight for as much time as it takes for an image to appear fully. This will give warm tones such as pinks, magentas, and red-browns.

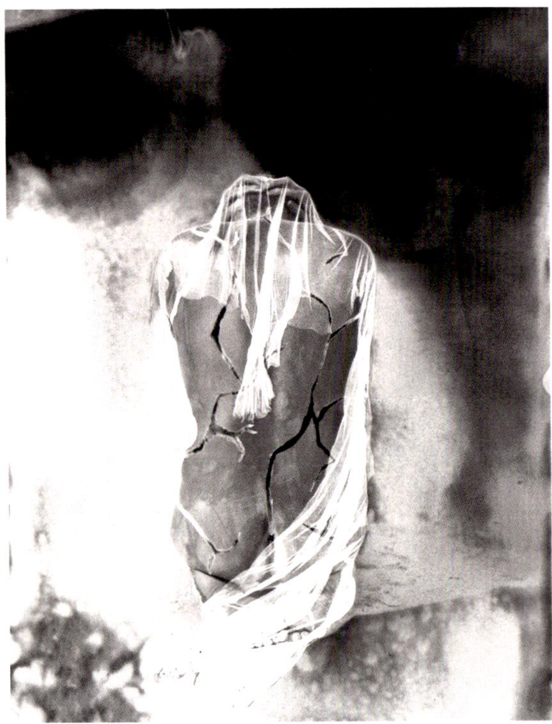

Figure 12.23. *Liminal III*, silver gelatin print from a mordançaged film negative © Jace Becker 2016

8. Remove, rinse carefully and fully, and inspect. If the print needs more dissolving, repeat the bleach-etch bath and redevelopment again. Sometimes the gelatin may not budge until it hits the developer for the first—or second—time. It is rare with this formula to have to re-bleach and redevelop, especially with Ilford MGIV paper, unless the print has been previously toned or if the bleach-etch bath is too cold.
9. Wash. If there are veils attached, the print will be difficult to wash well. It is best to use a separate tray for a finished print to sit and carefully soak in plain water; change the water a number of times over the course of an hour.

You can use the following bath for one minute, followed by a short rinse, if desired, to return the print's acidity to normal.

Baker's Neutralizing Bath[6]

1 part sodium bicarbonate (baking soda)
16 parts water

10. Dry. Don't use a normal drying cabinet because the print will contaminate the screens.
11. Once dry, drymount-press between two dedicated pieces of mat board so as not to contaminate the dry mount press. A great aid is a couple Teflon sheets placed on top and underneath the print in the dry mount press; the softened gelatin will not stick on the press or the mat board.
12. Scan the print at high resolution on a flatbed scanner to preserve a digital copy of it (if it is too big to scan, take a photograph of it). It is improbable you will achieve the same mordançage twice and this way you can make multiple copies if desired.
13. Take the print outside and spray it with one or two coats of Krylon Crystal Clear Non-Yellowing Acrylic Varnish. The varnish does two things for the print: It evens out the non-glossy and glossy parts of the image to one glossy whole, and it protects the image from the environment by reducing the amount of air that can get to the print. I have heard of prints losing their beautiful ruddy tones over time. That has not happened to me and I surmise the Krylon prevents that from happening.

Mordançage negatives

Even though mordançage's original purpose was for use on the negative, I have found it difficult to use the Coote formula on negatives. The negative dissolves and sloughs off from its plastic base in seconds. Speck's formula, which uses the milder copper sulfate in place of copper chloride, works great. Copper sulfate is cheap and available at a garden store. The process proceeds the same as with prints, above, but the negative has to be watched cautiously.

Speck formula I[7]

I've written the formula easier than the original. All cautions in this chapter must be followed.

750 ml water
33 g copper sulfate
10 g potassium bromide
4 ml glacial acetic acid (or 13 ml 28% stop bath)
Water to make 1 liter

1. Add copper sulfate to 750 ml water.
2. Add potassium bromide to the water.
3. Add acetic acid to the water.

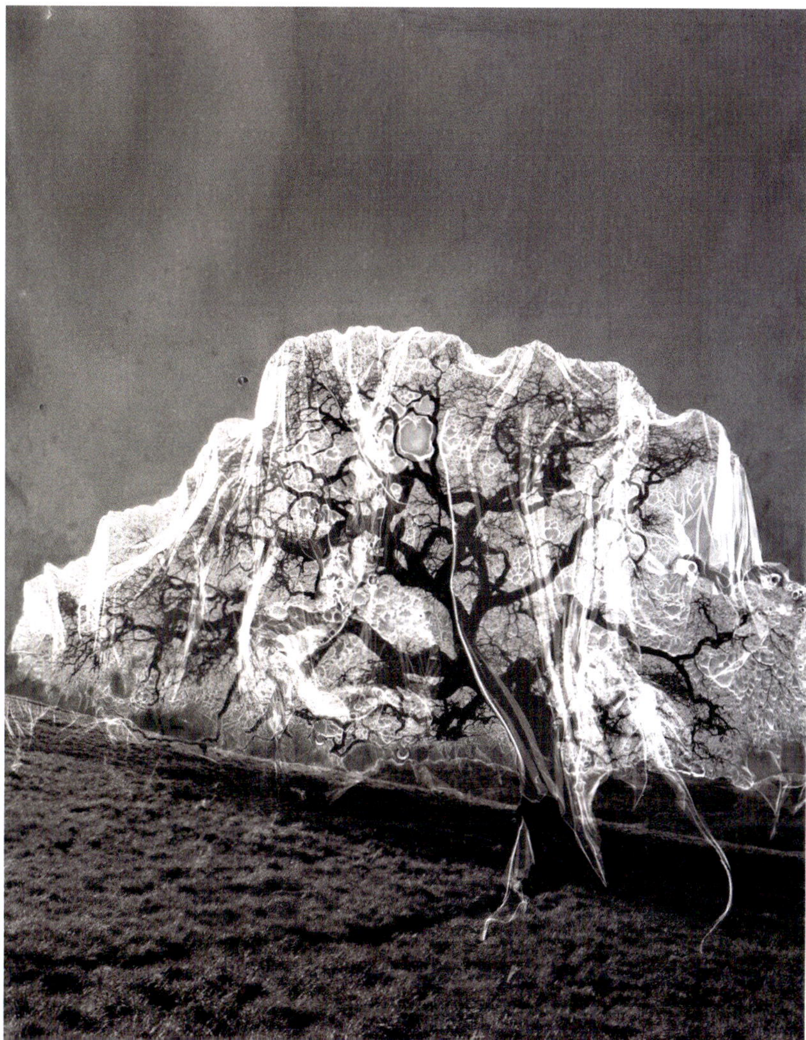

Figure 12.24. *Trees III*, silver gelatin print from a mordançaged film negative © Jace Becker 2013. Jace Christian Becker, 38, of Pittsburgh Pennsylvania died peacefully on November 4, 2021. Jace was talented, funny, smart and creative. He received his BA in Photography from Montana State University and an MFA from Arizona State University. Jace was honored with many accolades and awards for his creative work. His thought process in his approach to everything in life, whether artistic accomplishments or scaling a difficult mountain, always took a different route. His way of visualization led him to scale El Capitan and mountains all over the world as well as develop new and creative artistic concepts. He wanted to explore the route never taken. Tales of Jace's exploits will live long after him. He laughed loud, never slept, and conquered heights. His approach to his art and his life can be summed up in his favorite quote.... "Be excellent to one another!" Climb High, Jace!

4. Add water to make 1000 ml.
5. At time of use mix equal parts of this formula with hydrogen peroxide strength of choice. First try drug store strength and if necessary use 20v.
6. Immerse the negative in the solution. Softening of the emulsion takes place in approximately 1½ minutes at room temperature.
7. Wash the negative for a minute in 110°F water to wash off the softened gelatin, if desired, or leave it veiled.
8. Redevelop in toner, developer, or dye. Complete rubbing will make the negative positive.

Troubleshooting—the paper is stained

Fiber paper can stain yellow to brown in the highlights and borders of the print, which is beautiful, in my opinion, but if this look is not desired, try the following steps.

- Rinse the mordançage solution off very well before redevelopment to prevent chemical stain resulting from contamination between copper bleach and developer.
- Reduce the copper chloride in the solution. The lowest I've seen is 5 g copper chloride per liter.
- Use the lesser strength hydrogen peroxide—10v or 20v. The higher the volume of peroxide, the

more it softens the gelatin and helps it to accept developer in places you may not want it to go.

- Mordançage under dim light.
- If the print has been rinsed really well, so that there is no chemistry left in the paper and the print has returned to a less acid/more neutral state, you can fix the print. Some of the literature doesn't say to fix after the mordançage process, some do. I no longer fix because when the print goes into the fix it releases a sulfurous smell that is not good and even possibly toxic. When I heard that, coupled with the contradicting advice in the literature, I decided to no longer use fix. Do not use fixer if you are doing the process indoors.

Troubleshooting—mordançage not working

If the mordançage is not dissolving as it should, there are a number of causes to address:

- Give the print more time in the mordançage solution.
- Make sure the mordançage solution is room temperature. When the bleach-etch gets cold, the hydrogen peroxide slows down doing its "thing."
- Use hotter water after the mordançage bath, up to 120ºF.
- Use a stronger volume of hydrogen peroxide. Instead of drug store 3% use 20v from a beauty supply store.
- The hydrogen peroxide may have exhausted so add a glug of a stronger volume of hydrogen peroxide to the mordançage bath. I keep a gallon of 20v on hand. A shot of that stuff will revive the soup. The stronger the hydrogen peroxide, the greater the softening of the gelatin (the greater the risk of stain on fiber paper, though).
- The acidity of the mordançage solution needs to be between 2.6 and 3.0,[8] so measure the solution with a pH strip and add more glacial acetic acid if necessary (or citric acid also).
- Paper used to be so stubborn I had to heat the print in a dry mount press before using it in the process, a practice recommended in one patent (heating the film to 180ºf made the gelatin more malleable).
- Be sure your print has not been previously toned as the chemistry doesn't work as well or at all with previously toned prints.

Tips and ideas

- Spray paint a clear gloss stencil design on top of the print before the process. The spray paint will protect areas from disintegration.
- Make a print and develop it, but do not fix. Rinse briefly, and put it in the bleach-etch bath. Remove from the bleach-etch bath, rinse in water, and turn on the room light. Either rub the emulsion off at this point and then put the print back in the developer with the room light still on, and redevelop. Or, redevelop, and then rub off the emulsion. This produces a completely black and white negative image of the original.
- After mordançaging a print, instead of redeveloping, put it out in direct sun like a lumen print to turn colors. You can also use a small brush with developer and develop only parts of the image.

Endnotes

1. Wall, E. J. *Practical Colour Photography*, 2nd edition. Boston: American Photographic Publishing Co., 1928, p. 90–94.
2. Ibid.
3. Coote, Jack H. *Ilford Monochrome Darkroom Practice: A Manual of Black and White Processing and Printing*, 3rd ed. Oxford: Focal Press, 1996, pp. 299–304.
4. Marriage, A. "Notes on Etch Bleach Baths" in *British Journal of Photography*, April 21, 1944, p. 142.
5. Coote, p. 302.
6. Baker, E. N. "Photoink Printing", Patent #2,058,396, March 13 1933.
7. Speck, Robert. "Photographic Relief Image," Patent #2,494,068 Jan 10, 1950, called by Robert Speck, assignor to Eastman Kodak Co, Rochester, NY.
8. Ibid.

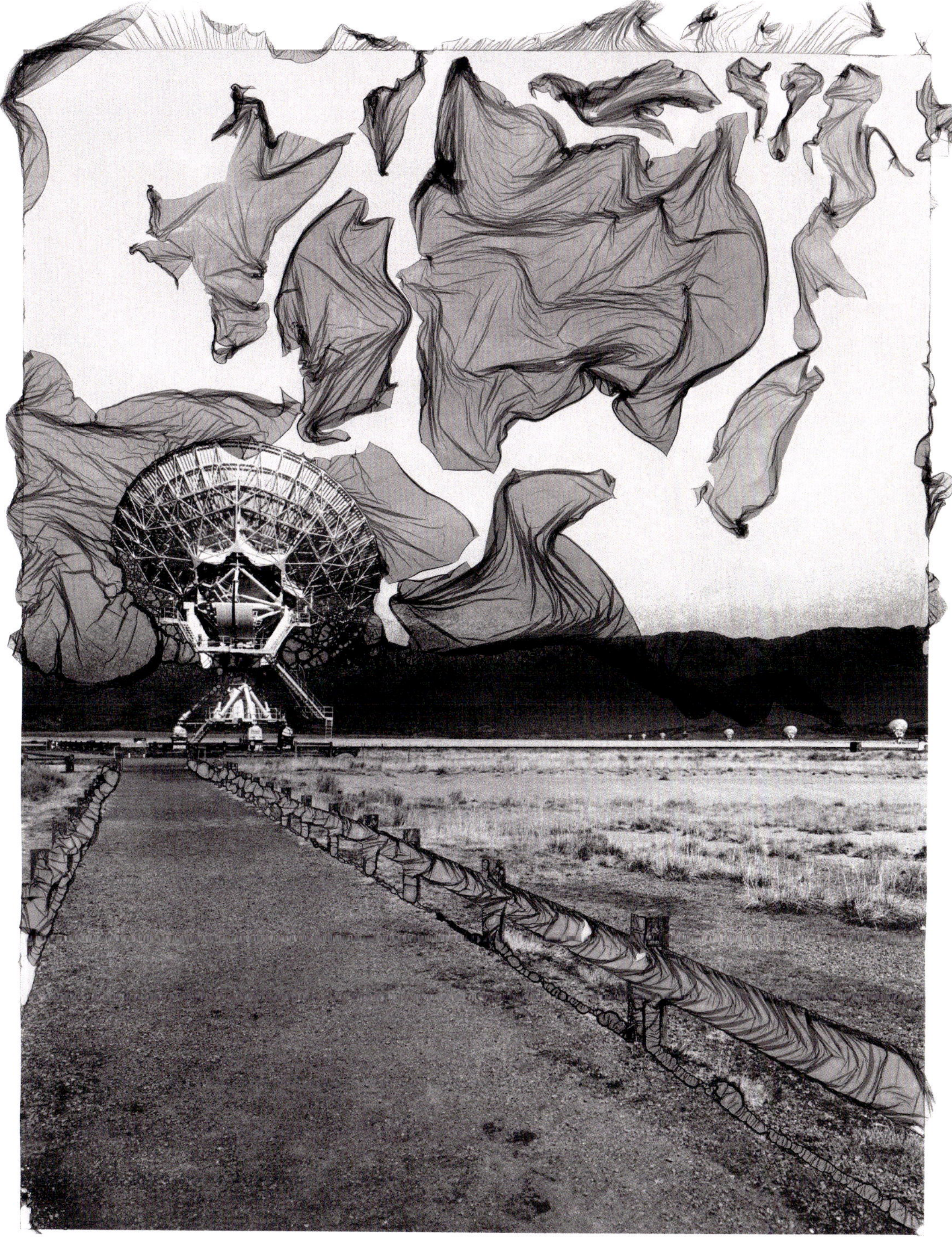

Figure 12.25. *Very Large Array, Soccoro, New Mexico*, mordançage print, 11″ x 14″© J. Jason Lazarus 2020, J. Jason Lazarus is an Alaska-based photographer and educator who creates narrative-driven photographic work utilizing a wide range of alternative and historical photographic processes. Lazarus has served as a photographic educator at the University of Alaska Fairbanks since 2005, teaching and developing a wide range of courses in digital, alternative, and traditional darkroom photography. His alternative process work ranges from abstract chemigram prints that discuss the complex historical legacy left behind by World War II to darkroom-printed mordançage images that show a fragile Western American landscape decaying under the pressures of resource development, economic failures and climate change. To see more of his work visit obscura-works.com.

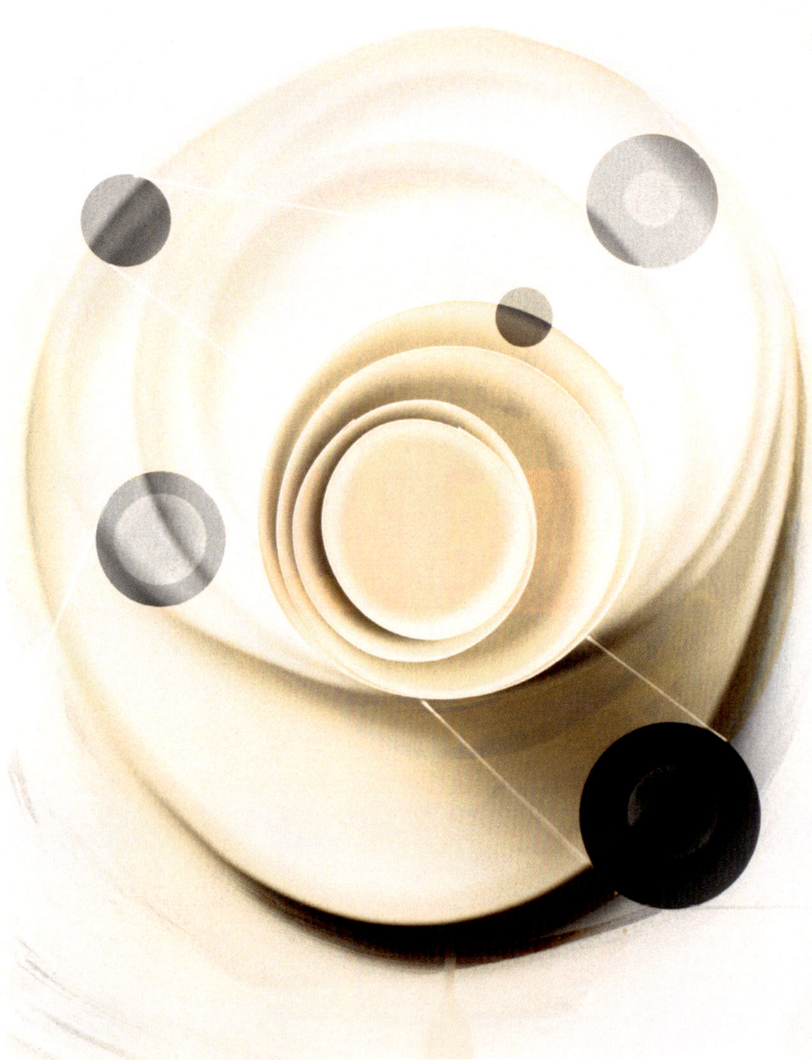

Figure 13.1. *3A.2015*, from the *Fabrication of Space* series, 19″ x 23″ © Andrew Sovjani 2015. "The *Fabrication of Space* series is an investigation into our perception of space and light within the unified surface of the two-dimensional silver gelatin print through a combination of photographic imagery and post-exposure photochemical mark making. I create and photograph arrangements of white paper using a view camera and monochromatic film. The corresponding straight silver gelatin print then becomes the launching point for spatial play, illusion, and interpretation by employing unique toning methods and hand drawn chemical line work in an iterative bleach/redevelop process that embraces chance and premeditation simultaneously. I have chosen to retain the purity and integrity of the print surface, constraining the mark making to those that only alter the silver particles within the surface of the print. By maintaining the unified surface, I am placing the photographic imagery on the same plane as the post-exposure alterations. This self-imposed limitation encourages the development of new ways and tools to work the print, blurring the lines between photography and printmaking. Each final print is a unique record of this printing performance.

"All work in this series uses the following process: Either one or two B&W negatives, sometimes sandwiched together, are exposed onto silver gelatin paper. An additional exposure is often given through masks to create dark shapes. The print then goes through multiple selective iterations of bleach/thiourea tone/fix/redevelopment using calligraphy pens, paper shape cutouts, brushes and rags. The final print is often selectively gold toned." Andrew Sovjani (b.1967) is a visual artist recognized for blurring the boundaries between photography, printmaking and painting. Raised in a family of working studio artists, Sovjani has drawn from his life experiences in the scientific world and living in Asia to create transcendent bodies of work that are often quite peaceful. His award-winning photographs have been shown in exhibitions throughout the United States, Europe and Japan and are held in public and private collections. He has won awards of distinction at top fine arts festivals in the nation and has been a finalist for multiple Critical Mass book awards. To see more of his work visit andrewsovjani.com.

Bleaching and Bleachout

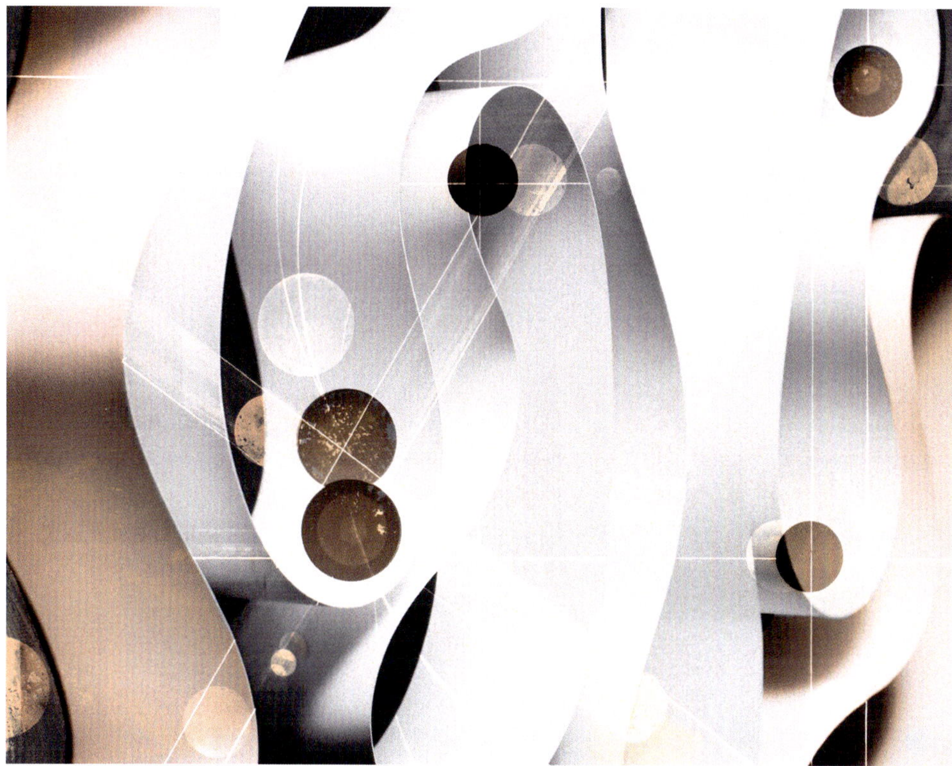

Figure 13.2. *4A.2015*, from the *Fabrication of Space* series, 19″x23″ © Andrew Sovjani 2015

Photographic bleach is a most useful tool in the darkroom. For one, it can be used to correct a too dark print. Two, it can be used to lighten selective areas of a print for emphasis. Three, it can be used in more creative ways, in a unique line-drawing process called "bleachout." The bleach formula is so easy to mix, doesn't have to be exact, and lasts forever, so mix up a liter and keep it on your shelf at all times.

Standard bleach formula

100 g (5 tablespoons) potassium bromide
100 g (6.5 tablespoons) potassium ferricyanide
Water to make 1000 ml

1. Add the potassium bromide to 750 ml water and stir until dissolved.
2. Add the potassium ferricyanide to the water and stir until dissolved.
3. Add more water to make 1000 ml total.

This is a *stock* solution. At time of use take 1 part bleach and mix with 9 parts water to make a *working* strength. 1 liter of stock will make 10 liters of working strength bleach.

Bleach as a corrective or selective tool

Bleach can be used as a corrective tool or in more creative ways. For instance, it can be used selectively on parts of a print you want to stand out.

1. Have a hose of water directed right below where the bleaching is to be done.
2. Load a calligraphy brush with the working strength bleach solution and with the print

supported on a piece of Plexiglas at an angle, paint the bleach on the area with the brush in one hand and the running water from the hose directed exactly below the brushed area to catch any unwanted drips and prevent streaks below the area.
3. Bleach for a bit, not until completion, and then fix the print. Assess the bleached area—if it is still too dark, a good thing, go back to the Plexiglas and do the process again.
4. Bleach and fix the print bit by bit, slowly lightening the area in baby steps.
5. Stop bleaching *just* before it looks perfect because the final fix will lighten the bleaching a bit more, and if it looks perfect before bleaching it will be too light when fixed.

If at any time the print has been over-bleached, return it to a paper developer *before fixing* and the bleached-but-not-yet-fixed silver will redevelop. Once it is fixed, this is no longer possible because the rehalogenated silver has been removed.

Farmer's Reducer bleach formula

Farmer's Reducer is a mixture of bleach and fix in one solution. The good news is that fixing of the print goes along with bleaching of the print so at the end the print just needs to be hypocleared, washed, and dried. The bad news is there is no ability to turn back and redevelop a print when you have accidentally gone too far with bleaching like there is in a two-step bleach/fix process. Farmer's Reducer uses two separate solutions mixed at time of use and discarded after the session.

Part A 20% Thiosulfate

100 g sodium thiosulfate
500 ml water

Add the sodium thiosulfate to the water and stir until dissolved. Store this in its own separate bottle.

Part B 10% Potassium Ferricyanide

50 g potassium ferricyanide
500 ml water

Add the sodium thiosulfate to the water and stir until dissolved. Store this in its own separate bottle.

1. At time of use mix equal parts of A and B and use immediately. It only keeps working for a short time.
2. A weaker solution of this is mixing 100 ml of Solution A with an equal volume of water and then add 5 ml of solution B.

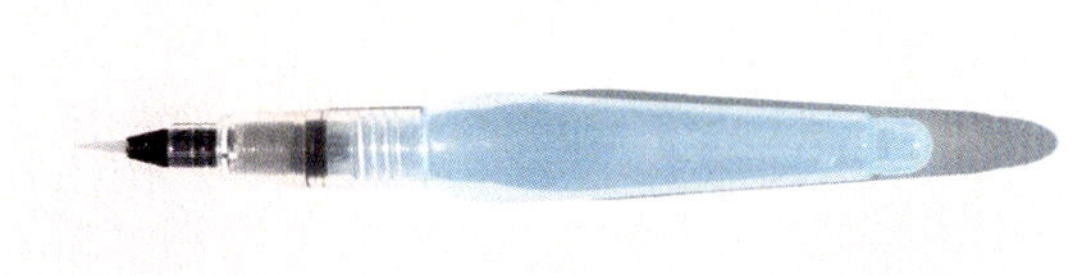

Figure 13.3. Pentel Aquash pen. The blue plastic barrel can be filled with the bleach solution. Just squeeze the flexible plastic to feed the solution to the nylon fiber tip. The pen comes with a variety of tip sizes.

Bleachout

This technique is merely drawing on a print with permanent ink of some sort and bleaching away the photographic image in part or in whole. The final image is part drawing and part photograph or all drawing and no photograph.

1. Expose, develop, dry, and flatten a print in a dry mount press if it is fiber. The surface should be very flat for drawing.
2. Use a Sharpie ultra permanent pen (the kind that is permanent on glass or plastic), an India ink pen, or a permanent ink tech pen for the drawing. Test the different pens to make sure the bleach does not remove them, as it does some permanent inks. While the print is going through wet processing, the marks should not be touched. *Tip: the subject matter of the print can be followed accurately with the drawing, or other subject matter that is not in the image can be added.*
3. When the drawing is finished and the ink is thoroughly dry, bleach the print by either brushing working strength bleach on with a soft brush and a gentle touch or submerge the whole print in a tray of working strength bleach.
4. When enough bleaching has occurred, rinse the print in water, fix, hypoclear, wash, and dry.
5. Touch up any lines that may have weakened in the wet stages with more permanent pen.

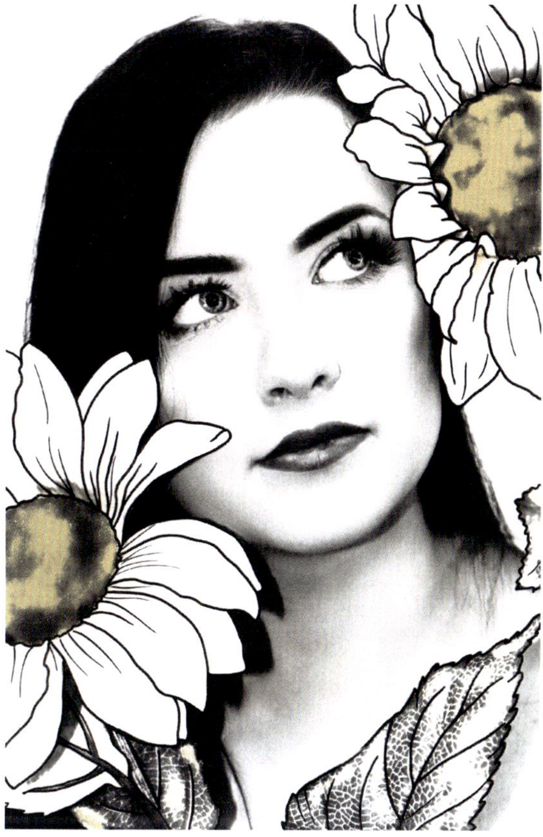

Figure 13.4. *Sunflower*, bleachout © Maddison Fritzler 2019

Tips and ideas

- If the print is too dark overall, it can be bleached lighter in stages as follows: first soak the print in water for 10 minutes. Then transfer it to the bleach tray for 5–10 seconds with continuous agitation. Check to see if it has lightened enough by pulling it out and rinsing it off with a hose. If not, give it 10 more seconds. Keep doing this back and forth until the print looks almost light enough and rinse well. Fix (it will lighten up somewhat in the fix), wash, hypoclear, and wash again for 30 minutes.
- If there are black spots in a print, they can be bleached out with a tiny brush dipped in the bleach formula. Once the black spots are removed, the print must be fixed again because the silver that has been bleached becomes re-sensitized to light. Or use the Aquash pen pictured above which can be conveniently filled with bleach.
- Overexpose a print, develop, stop, fix, and wash as usual. Then bleach it to the desired lightness and fix, wash, hypoclear, and wash again. This produces tones from blacks to browns in the print, and works well with grainy images.
- Overexpose a print and bleach out only what you want to highlight.
- After bleaching, rinse the print well until all the yellow stain of the bleach has disappeared. Put the print flat on a piece of glass or Plexiglas, pat gently with a paper towel to remove as much moisture as possible, and with a paintbrush filled with either Part B of a sepia toner, or just regular paper developer, selectively brush parts of the image so that those parts reappear. The sepia toned parts will come back in shades of brown; the paper developer parts will come back in shades of black. This is easiest carried out in room light. When done, fix, etc., as usual.
- Use pencil/graphite and draw on the print before bleaching; the drawing acts as a resist.
- Stencil bleach on a print. Either buy or make a stencil out of plastic or removable sheets of frisket film which has low tack adhesive on one side. Alternately, use rubber cement on one side of the plastic to make it adhere to the print if you don't have frisket film. Then, with a *full* strength bleach take a minimally soaked brush or sponge and pounce the bleach onto the print through the stencil. Be careful that it does not get underneath the plastic or the pattern will be sloppy. When done, immerse the whole print in fixer, stencil and all. Rinse, remove the stencil, and finish processing.
- A print can be scratched wet or dry, but a wet print is easier. Soak the print in water for 5–10 minutes and then squeegee. Take a sharp instrument such as a needle, an Xacto blade, scalpel, etc. Scratch the print surface to distress the print. Watch that scratches aren't ragged and ugly, but fine and appropriate. Color can be rubbed into the scratches for emphasis once the print is dry.
- With an Xacto knife, cut and peel away parts of a print from the paper base below. RC paper is best for this technique. See Leah Schretenthaler in **Contemporary Experimental Artists** for another take on this, using a laser etching printer.

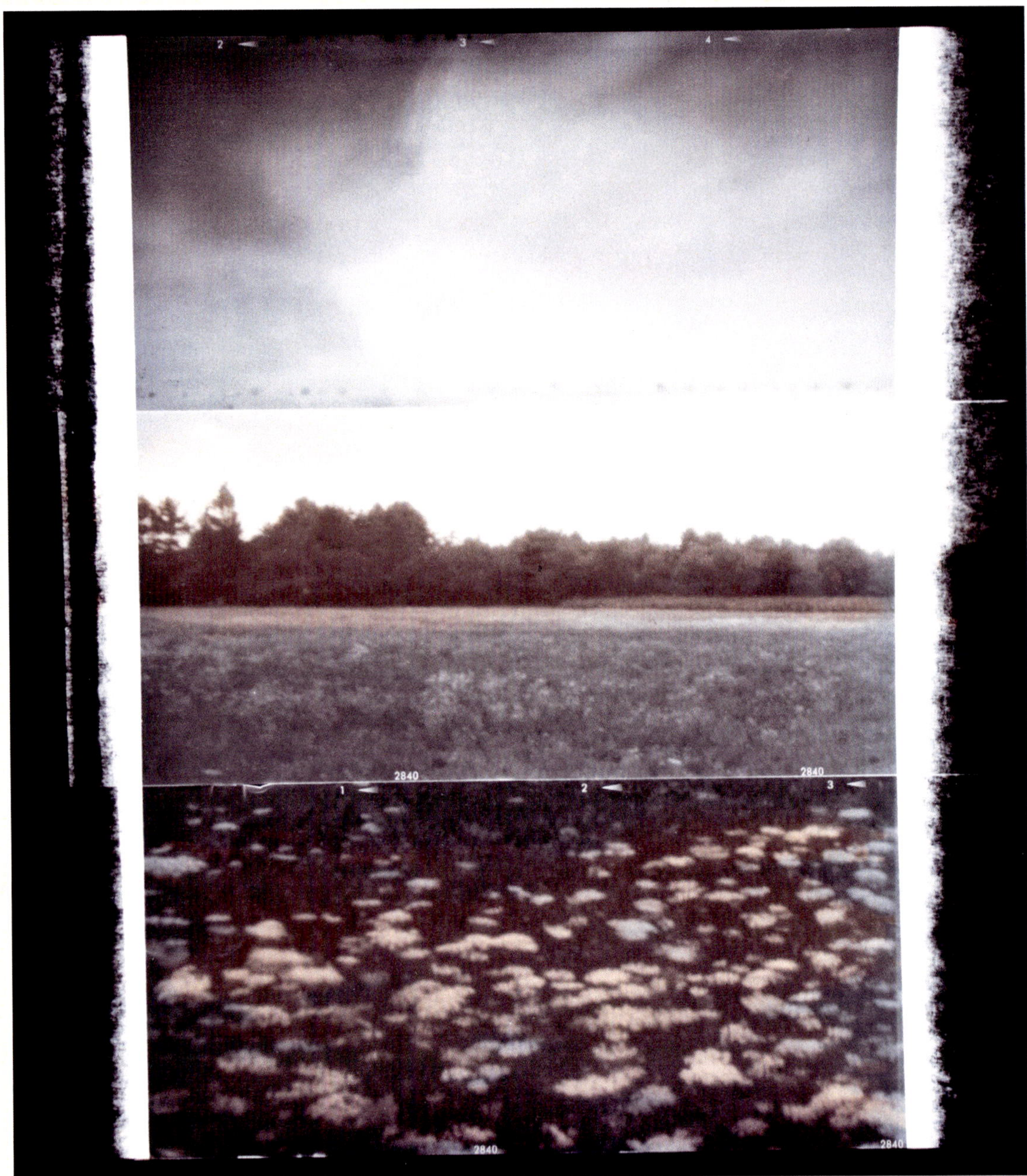

Figure 14.1. *Untitled #255* from the *Day's End* series. 16″ x 20″ © Mark L. Eshbaugh 1999. "The fractured imagery reminds of the limitations of the medium and the limitations of our own memories. We cannot capture a complete moment of time with a photograph, just as we can never remember a complete moment of time accurately. As time moves on memories are either romanticized or denigrated. This series of work is shot with a pinhole aperture. The multiple rolls of 120 mm film were shot simultaneously in the camera I designed and built specifically to be able to load multiple rolls of film at once. This image is printed on Ilford Warmtone fiber-based paper and then split-toned with selenium 1+10. Using a hake brush soaked in distilled water it was then selectively toned with Copper toner (Pt. A: copper sulfate 7 g, potassium citrate 28 g, water to 1 liter and Pt. B: potassium ferricyanide 6 g, potassium citrate 28 g, water to 1 liter). I wring the brush out, dip it into the copper toner and paint it over the areas I want to change color. It takes several applications alternated with gently running water from a hose to feather the color into the image naturally."

Toning

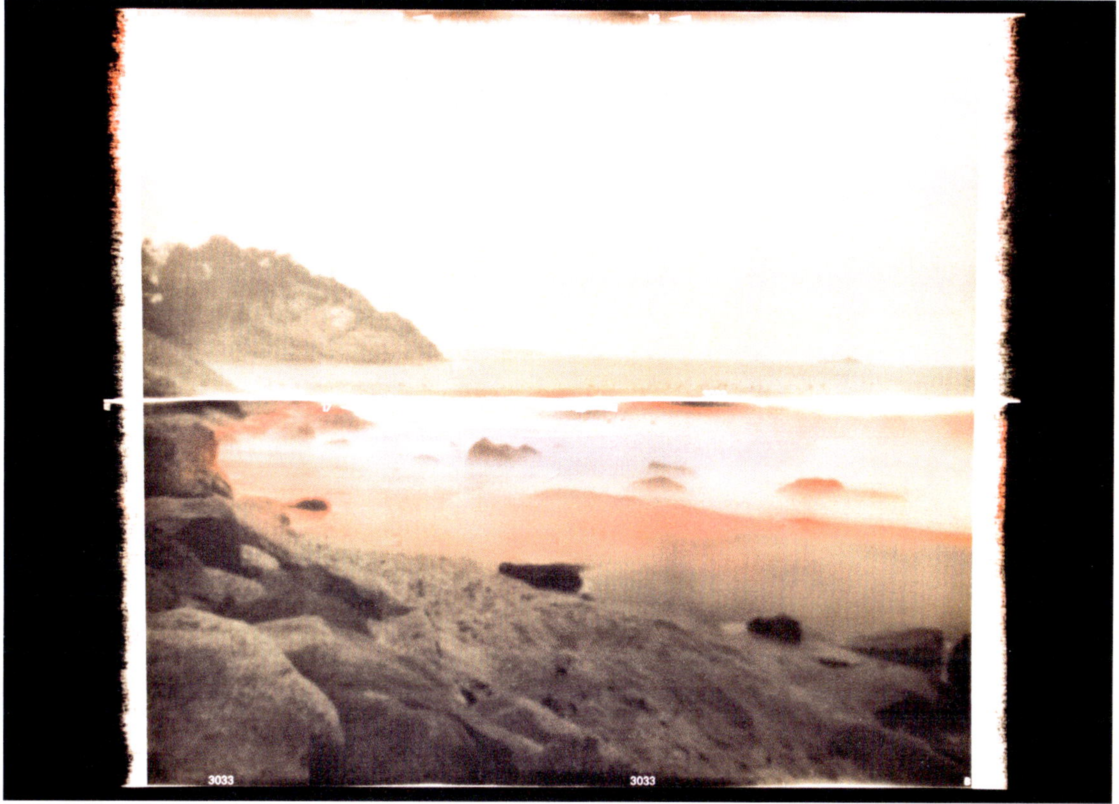

Figure 14.2. *Untitled #281* from the *Day's End* series, 14″ x 10″ © Mark L. Eshbaugh 2001. "This image, like the one left, is shot with a pinhole camera loaded with multiple rolls of 120 mm film. The image is printed on Agfa Classic fiber-based paper, split-toned with selenium 1+10. The image was then partially bleached, and then toned back with the thiourea 3 g and sodium hydroxide 6 g to 1 liter of water. The print was then washed for 30–45 minutes and dried. To get the red tones the print was then soaked in a saline bath (1 tablespoon salt to 1 liter water) and then put into GAF 231 gold toner. The center area that shifts back to a slate gray was created by using a medicine dropper to put a 1% gold chloride solution directly on the print surface. This step is done carefully with gently running water from a hose at the ready. If the gold solution is left on the print too long it will cause permanent stains."

Toning a silver gelatin print has traditionally be used for two primary reasons: to make the print more archival and/or to alter the print color. Silver gelatin prints react to sulfur in the atmosphere and deteriorate over a period of time. Toning with selenium, sepia, thiourea, or gold changes the chemical makeup of the silver to a more stable form which resists deterioration. As far as color goes, warmtone (chlorobromide) papers show the toner color more than coldtone (bromide) papers. Ilford MGIV in selenium, for instance, shows little color change. Ilford warmtone in thiourea toner shows noticeable color change. However subtle the color change is, though, the toner has still done its work of making the paper more archival.

One bath *vs* two bath toners

Selenium, gold, copper, and blue toning are all one bath toners. Sepia and thiourea are two bath toners, with the first bath being some sort of bleach and the second a redeveloper. We will cover both kinds of toners in this chapter.

Print preparation for all toning

- Prints first need to be archivally processed in all chemicals with great care toward cleanliness.
- Prints can either be toned right away, after the final hypoclear and wash, or toned years later.
- If a fiber print is dry, soak it in water for a good 10 minutes to get it thoroughly and evenly wet; RC paper only needs a several-minute soak.
- It is best practice to have a good border around the image area because tong marks or gloved fingers can leave evidence. Otherwise, hold the print with gloved hands only by its edges when transferring it from tray to tray.
- For some toning processes, it is best to print a bit **darker** before toning: thiourea, sepia, copper can lighten a print ⅓–½ stop.
- For some toning processes, it is best to print a bit **lighter** for toning about ⅓ stop: selenium and iron blue for example.

Selenium toning

Warning: Wear gloves! Toners, like selenium, can be toxic and should not come in contact with skin. Also, unexposed enlarging paper should always be kept in its black plastic bag when sepia/sulfide toning because sulfide fumes fog unexposed paper.

Selenium is easy. It comes in liquid form, and the only requirement is to dilute it. Selenium toners on the market are made by Berg, Ilford, Moersch, and Kodak (Rapid Selenium Toner or KRST). Selenium can be used full strength for maximum effect but most photographers dilute it from 1+5 to 1+9 (1 part toner + 9 parts water). For archivalness, a 1+9 or stronger concentration should be used for a minimum of three minutes at room temperature.

Prints can be selenium toned in room light because no silver in the process is resensitized/rehalogenated.

Selenium toner can be reused numerous times. Dilute the toner to the desired strength, pour it into the tray, and immerse the print in the toner for 3–8 minutes or much longer if desired. Keep another copy of the same print next to the tray to see the change occur because it can be subtle on some papers. When done toning, return the diluted toner to a plastic storage bottle and label it with the dilution.

Selenium-toned prints should be washed, **hypocleared**, and washed again because the toner contains fixer (ammonium thiosulfate, sodium sulfite along with sodium selenite) which has to be removed.

Split toning with selenium

Selenium begins toning the shadows first and then the highlights. At a certain point, the highlights are still cool gray when the shadows begin to shift to the characteristic warm red-brown of the toner. At this very point the print can be snatched from the toner and immediately immersed in a tray of water to preserve this cool/warm split. Split toning gives the prints a subtle 3D effect that is hard to describe. Unfortunately, the papers that split tone well are dwindling, but you can always try for the effect anyway, with warmtone papers being your best bet. I have heard Ilford MG Art 300 works well. If you want to achieve this effect watch the print continuously as it tones for that snatch point.

Bleaching after selenium

Bleach doesn't have as much effect on silver selenide as it does on silver halide, and thus a bleached selenium toned print reveals the reddish tones of the selenium that are usually masked by the larger, dark, incompletely toned bromide molecules. It is ruddy and quite beautiful. Note: you cannot bleach before selenium toner because the fixer in the toner will fix away the image permanently.

Standard bleach formula

100 g (5 tablespoons) potassium bromide
100 g (6.5 tablespoons) potassium ferricyanide
Water to 1000 ml

This Standard Bleach is something that should be on hand in the darkroom always because it is so useful for many different processes. It doesn't go bad. This makes a liter of **stock** solution. At time of use, dilute 1 part stock with 9 parts water (1+9). Chemistry doesn't have to be exact, which is why the tablespoon measures are used here.

1. *Fully* tone a print for 15 minutes in a **strong** 1+5 selenium dilution. The print should show toning throughout the shadows and the highlights. Rinse well.
2. Place the toned print in a tray of working strength bleach and watch the print while it bleaches.
3. It is helpful to remove the print from the bleach and rinse from time to time to check the progress. If too much detail has been removed from the highlights for some reason, it is always possible to return the print to paper developer to redevelop the print back to normal. It is also possible to redevelop the print to normal in sepia or thiourea toner.
4. The print can be bleached again, redeveloped again, rebleached again, and so on and so forth until it looks right.
5. Fix the print if the print has not been redeveloped to completion in either sepia, thiourea, or paper developer, because there may be remaining rehalogenated silver in the print that will be light sensitive.
6. Wash, hypoclear, and wash again as normal for an archival print. Hypoclear is always necessary after selenium toning to rid the print of the fixer chemistry in the toner itself.

- If selenium toning results in stains, this can be because a) there is remaining acid in the print from fixing, b) the print was not fixed well, or c) the print was fixed in exhausted fixer. Make sure to process prints archivally, and to do a 2-minute hypoclear before toning.
- If there is a milky residue on a finished print, soak the print in a normal stop bath and swab gently with cotton balls to remove the residue.

Gold toning

As can be imagined, gold is expensive. One gram of gold chloride is $49 at the time of this writing. However, it is used in a 1% solution in such small amounts that one gram goes far. It is so easy to mix your own gold toner that there is no reason to buy it, especially since commercial gold toner is pricey. The stock 1% gold chloride solution below is kept on hand separately and then mixed with other chemistry at time of use.

1% gold chloride solution

This is the basis for all gold toning formulas.

1 g gold chloride
100 ml distilled water
150 ml plastic or glass container

1. Pour 100 ml of distilled water into the container.
2. The gold chloride comes in a small glass vial. Remove the cap carefully, empty the gold chloride into the container of water, and *dump both the vial and the cap into the water also*. This way any little speck of gold chloride stuck to the cap or vial will go into the solution. The vial and cap can stay there forever, clinking around, or be removed later, if desired.

Gold sodium bicarbonate toner[1]

Mix only the amount you need because it doesn't keep.

5 g (1 teaspoon) sodium bicarbonate
7 ml 1% gold chloride solution
500 ml distilled water

1. Just before a printing session, add the sodium bicarbonate to the water and stir.
2. Add the 1% gold chloride solution to the water and stir.
3. Test the acidity of the solution with a litmus strip. It should be slightly alkaline, about an 8 pH. If it is alkaline enough the toner will be clear in color. Immerse the print in the toner and agitate it until it reaches the desired tone, 3–15 minutes.
4. Wash and dry as usual.

Gold thiocyanate toner[2]

This two-solution gold thiocyanate formula produces beautiful orange-reds when used to tone a previously toned sepia/thiourea print. It uses a 0.2% gold chloride solution (one fifth the strength of the 1% described earlier) but more of it, in equal proportions with a 2% ammonium thiocyanate solution. Solutions, stored separately, last indefinitely.

Solution A

1 g gold chloride
500 ml distilled water

1. Mix the gold into the water as instructed previously. This is a more dilute formula than a 1% gold so if you have 100 ml of 1% gold chloride solution on hand dilute it with 400 ml water (or 10 ml diluted with 40 ml water, etc.).

Solution B

10 g ammonium thiocyanate
500 ml water

2. Mix the ammonium thiocyanate into the water and stir until dissolved.
3. At time of use mix equal parts of A and B and brush on a print or submerge the print in a tray.
4. Wash, hypoclear, wash, and dry as usual.

Gold thiourea toner

12 ml gold chloride (1% solution)
12 ml thiourea (1% solution)
12 ml tartaric acid (10% solution)
5 g sodium chloride
Distilled water to make 500 ml

1. Make the 1% gold chloride solution by adding 1 g of gold chloride to 100 ml distilled water.
2. Make the 1% thiourea solution by adding 1 g of thiourea to 100 ml distilled water.
3. Make the 10% tartaric acid solution by adding 10 g of tartaric acid to 100 ml distilled water.
4. At time of use, add 12 ml of the thiourea solution to 12 ml of the gold chloride solution and stir until the precipitate that forms is dissolved.
5. Add the 12 ml tartaric acid solution to 150 ml of the distilled water.
6. Add the gold/thiourea solution to the tartaric acid/water solution and mix thoroughly.
7. Add the 5 g sodium chloride and water to make a final 500 ml.
8. Solution is ready for use immediately, but also keeps well.
9. Immerse the print in the toner and agitate it until it reaches the desired tone, 3–15 minutes.
10. Wash, fix, wash, hypoclear, wash, and dry as usual.

Blue toning

Blue toning comes in a number of brands by Foma, Berg, or Photographer's Formulary. It is good in combination with sepia. The toner is mixed in a one-liter solution. A print is submerged in the toner until the desired depth of blue is achieved. The print can be toned again if it is not blue enough, and even washed longer if it is too blue, so it is a loose and forgiving toner. Three caveats:

- Agitate carefully and don't touch the surface while toning because it mars
- Wash carefully until the yellow is gone but don't overwash or all of the blue will wash out
- Although entrancing, blue toning is not archival.

Blue toner is mixed at time of use and discarded after a toning session; I do store old solution and continue to use it for experimental purposes.

Iron blue toner

An easy to mix one-bath iron blue toner.[3]

8 g ferric ammonium citrate
8 g potassium ferricyanide
75 ml glacial acetic acid (or 265 ml 28% acetic acid like a Kodak stop bath)
1000 ml distilled water

1. Add the ferric ammonium citrate to the water and stir until dissolved.
2. Add the potassium ferricyanide to the water and stir until dissolved.
3. Add the acetic acid and stir until mixed.
4. Pour into a tray.
5. Soak finished prints to be toned in water until saturated.
6. Place the prints one at a time in the toner.
7. Tone until the print looks good, 3–15 minutes. Agitate continuously and don't touch the surface while toning because it mars. Watch carefully because if left too long in the toner, uneven stains can result, also if too many prints are run through the solution.

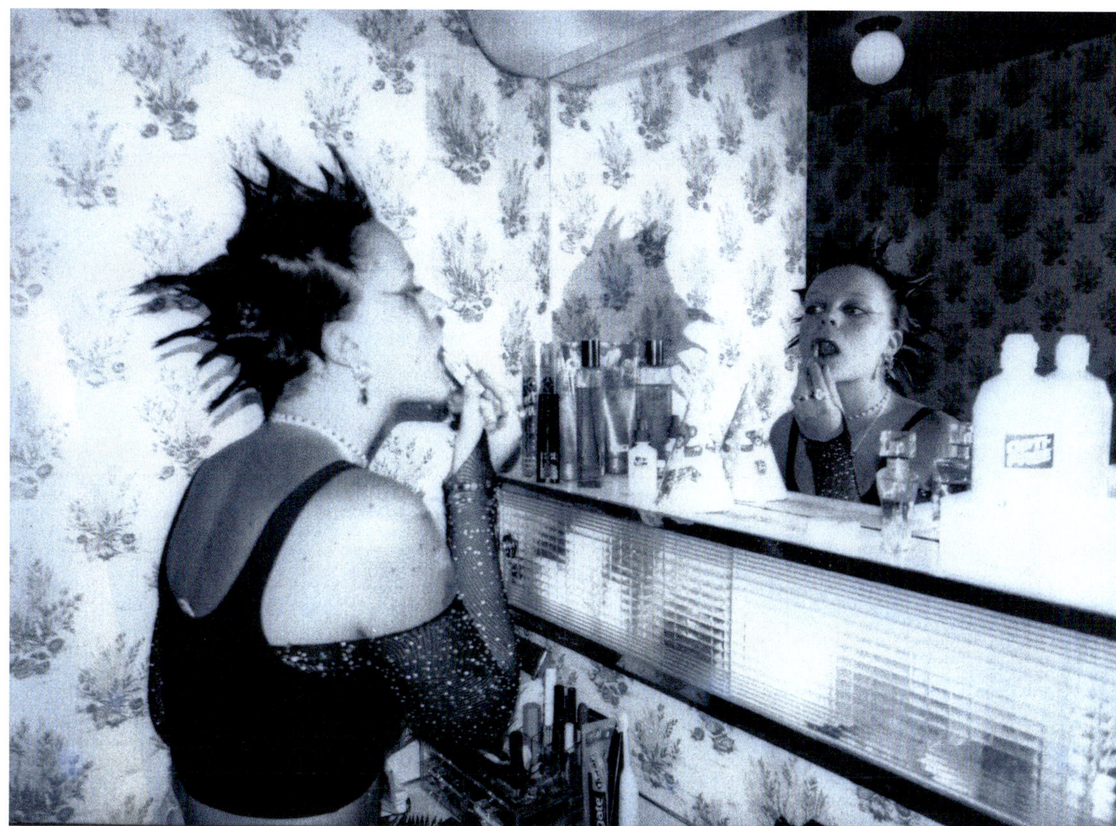

Figure 14.3. *Punk Rock Blues*, blue-toned silver gelatin print from a QTR digital negative, 10″ x 8″ © Danika Wolf 2021. Danika Wolf is pursuing her BA in Film and Photography and BFA in Graphic Design at Montana State University, with an expected graduation of 2023. Her photographic style runs the gamut from analog to digital practices.

8. Transfer the print to a tray of water and rinse until the yellow in the highlights clears, but watch that you do not overwash or the blue can wash out.
9. Hang the print to dry.

Copper toning

Copper is a one bath toner just like blue toner and behaves in much the same way. The longer the print is left in, the more toning occurs, to the point that the shadows of the print become velvety and plated-out. Copper results in colors from slightly pink to deep red-orange.

Two brands of copper toner are Formulary and Berg. Copper toner is mixed according to package directions and stored in two parts, A and B. The parts are mixed into one solution in equal portions at time of use. Once mixed, the solution is used immediately and is discarded after the toning session, though for more experimental toning methods I have stored it for later use.

1. Soak finished prints to be toned in water until saturated.
2. Pour equal parts A and B into a tray and mix.
3. Place the prints one at a time in the tray of toner.
4. Tone until the print looks good, 3–15 minutes. Agitate continuously and don't touch the surface while toning because it mars. Watch carefully because if left too long in the toner, uneven stains can result, as they do when too many prints are run through the solution.
5. Transfer the print to a tray of water and rinse for 15 minutes and hang the print to dry.

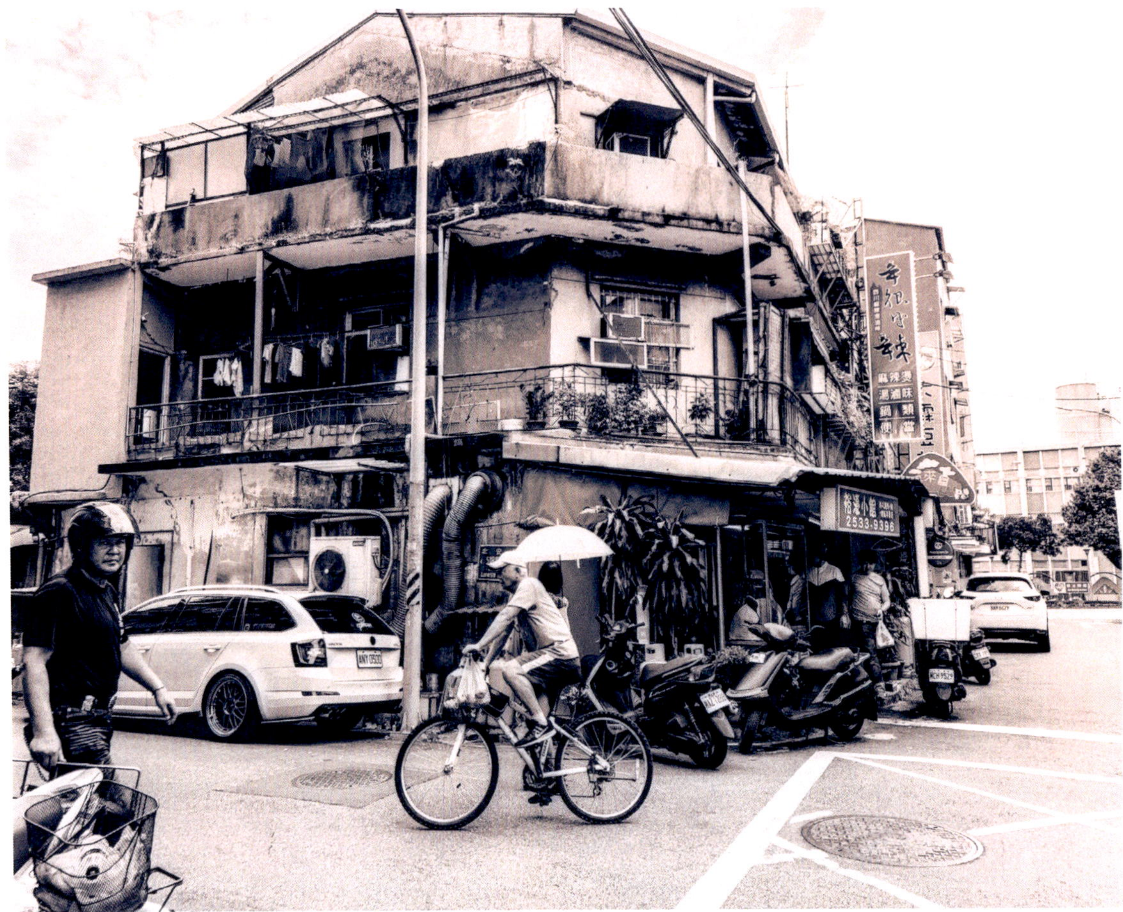

Figure 14.4. *Taiwan Abode*, silver gelatin print toned with copper and blue toners, 8″ x 10″ © Brenden Scheller 2019

Ferguson's copper toner

This toner gives colors from pale brown to deep red-orange.[4] Toning is done after fixing or to a previously dry and completed print. Sodium citrate can be substituted, too.

Part A
6 g copper sulfate
24 g potassium citrate
Water to 1000 ml

1. Add the copper sulfate to the water and stir until dissolved.
2. Add the potassium citrate to the water and stir until dissolved.
3. Store in a liter container, marked Part A. The container does not need to be light tight.

Part B
5 g potassium ferricyanide
24 g potassium citrate
Water to 1000 ml

4. Add the potassium ferricyanide to the water and stir until dissolved.
5. Add the potassium citrate to the water and stir until dissolved.
6. Store in a liter container, marked Part B. The container does not need to be light tight.
7. At time of use mix equal parts of Part A and Part B and pour into a tray. Once Part A and Part B are mixed together, the combined solution does not keep past one toning session.
8. Immerse the print in water until evenly soaked.
9. Drain the print and immerse in the copper toner.

10. Tone until the color desired is reached, which can be anywhere from a few minutes to really long (30–90 minutes). Some fun stuff can occur with long toning if you desire, such as plating out of copper on the print. However, watch carefully and don't leave the print unattended or staining can occur.
11. After toning, rinse the print for 15 minutes in running water and dry.

Tea toning

Toning with tea is not a *proportional* toner. It's more of a *staining* toner, not a true toner, giving an evocative, antique look to a print. Different teas give different colors. Darjeeling tea is yellow orange, Ceylon orange red, Assam dark red, Kenya bright red, and green tea pink.

1. Immerse a print in water at least 10 minutes to thoroughly and evenly wet it. This ensures the print tones evenly.
2. Boil 750 ml water and pour over one tea bag. Steep the tea bag for a few minutes, add some cool water up to a liter, and the toner is ready. This toner should be used "one shot" and discarded after a print is toned. Otherwise staining or uneven toning of the next print can occur. One tea bag per print is not too great an expense.
3. Immerse the print in the tea solution all in one fell swoop so it tones evenly. Agitate continuously.
4. Watch the print as it tones. Take it out of the toner when it looks half there and put in a tray of water. Tea toning darkens considerably upon drying. Toning may take seconds to minutes, perhaps even up to one half hour. The longer the toning the greater the effect.
5. Once the print is fully toned, remove it and rinse well and dry.

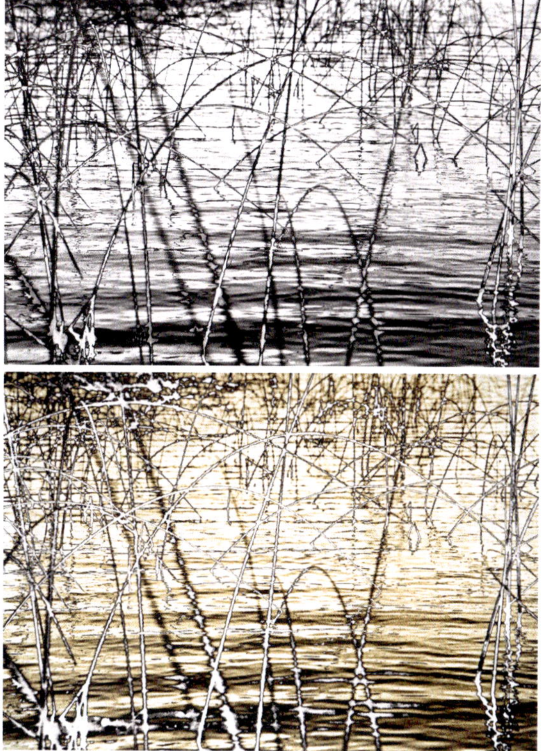

Figures 14.5–14.6. *Mollie Lake Reeds I* and *II*; top, untoned silver gelatin mordançage, bottom thiourea-toned silver gelatin mordançage, 13˝ x 9˝ © Christina Z. Anderson 2005

Walnut or other nut toning

Walnut husks can be purchased where basket making supplies are sold, because they are often used to dye baskets.

1. Put a scoop of walnut husks in water to cover and boil for a while until the water turns dark brown. Remove from heat and let the liquid cool.
2. Drain the liquid from the husks into a container (husks can be frozen and reused).
3. Presoak the print in water for 10 minutes so it is fully and evenly wet.
4. Place the print rapidly in the walnut husk solution.
5. Just as with tea toning, agitate vigorously and continuously and remove the print before it looks sufficiently dark because it will darken when it dries down.

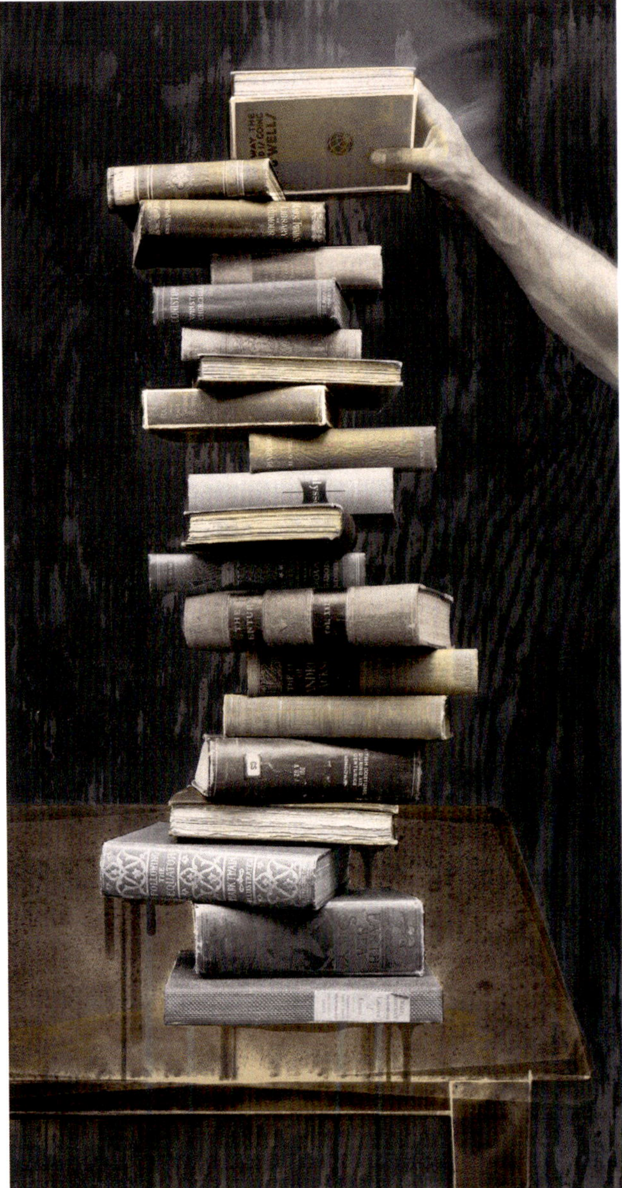

Figure 14.7. *Just One More On Top*, from the *Off the Shelf* series, 15″ x 23″ © Andrew Sovjani 2016. "For me, physical books are the poster-child for things that are on the verge of disappearing as we adopt more technological devices. The side effect is that we are losing many multisensory experiences. An old book has many visual qualities as well as a certain heft, a memory inducing smell, a texture in the paper acknowledged by our fingers while turning each page, etc. This series pays respect to the book experience. Large format black and white negatives are exposed onto silver gelatin paper. The print then goes through multiple selective iterations of bleach/thiourea tone/fix/redevelopment using calligraphy pens, paper shape cutouts, brushes and rags."

Sepia toning

Sepia is the one toner most people know about, with one drawback: a rotten egg odor from the sodium sulfide (think sulfur). It can also fog unexposed paper. There is a non-smelly brown toner made from thiourea that is much more pleasant to work with (shared further on) and is the one I use.

Bleaching can be done fully, until there is only a faintly visible yellowish image left. The more the bleaching, the warmer the sepia tones will be in the final print. The less the bleaching, the blacker-brown the print will be. A slight bleach that lightens just the highlights of the prints without affecting the blacks will give a subtle, lovely split tone effect.

Sepia is a "tone to completion" toner, meaning the toner will tone until it is done toning all silver that has been resensitized by the bleach bath, and at that point the print will go no darker even if the print is left in the toning bath for hours. No worries about toning time, therefore, as long as it is enough.

Part A Standard Bleach

100 g (5 tablespoons) potassium bromide
100 g (6.5 tablespoons) potassium ferricyanide
Water to 1000 ml

At time of use, dilute 1 part stock strength solution with 9 parts water (1+9).

Part B Toner

50 g sodium sulfide
Water to make 1000 ml

1. Bleach the print for 2–5 minutes, until only a faint image remains. It is not possible to over bleach. Ilford papers take long to bleach.
2. Rinse the bleached print in a tray of water until the yellow stain is gone—about 2–10 minutes.
3. Place the print in the toning solution, and tone until completion or when noticeable image change stops, usually 1–2 minutes.
4. Wash for 30 minutes and dry. There is no need to hypoclear after sepia toning because no fixer is used.

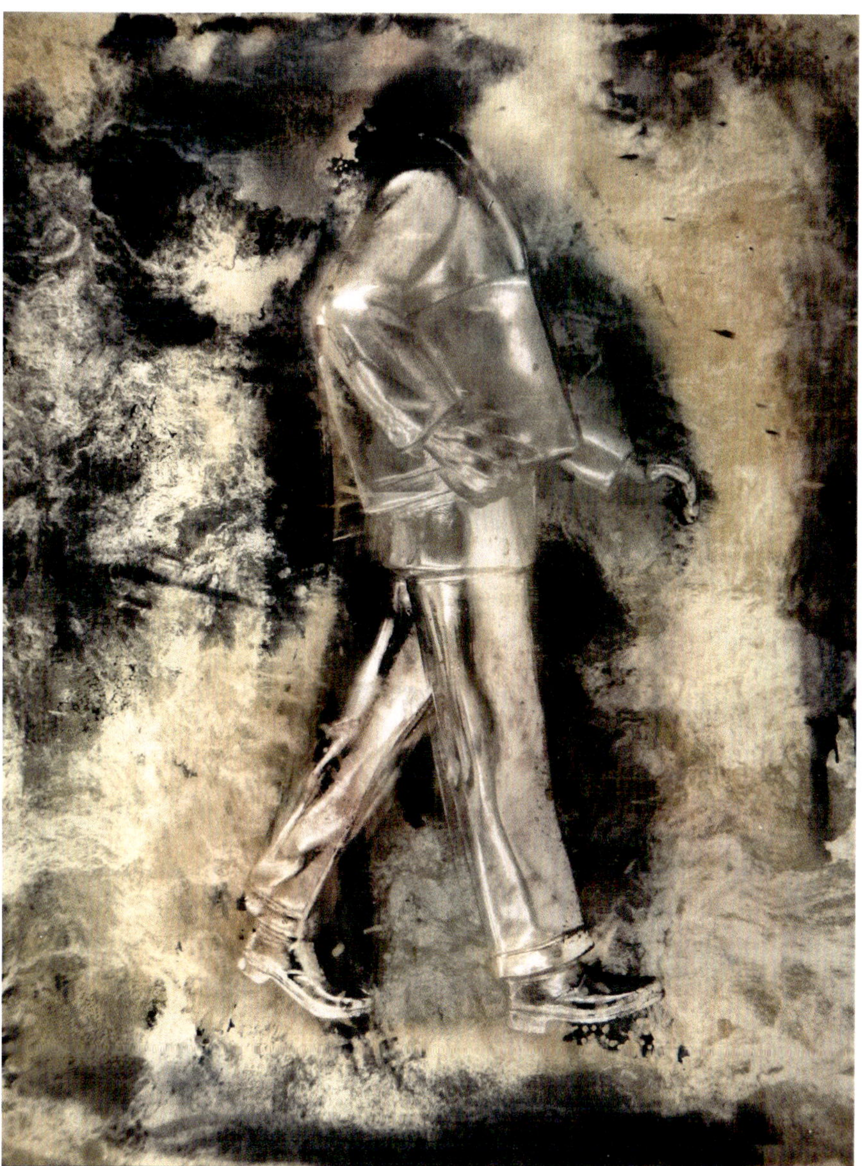

Figure 14.8. *Trophy Man*, toned gelatin silver print on Ilford paper from a 4″ x 5″ negative, 16″ x 20″ © Melanie Walker 1995. "This image is part of a group of images made using artifacts that I have collected and photographed over the years. Arrangements of old objects on textured backgrounds serve as metaphors for human emotions and psychological states. Inspired by "object reading," the supposed ability to discover facts about an event or person by touching inanimate objects associated with them, the objects photographed are intended to transcend their material nature and evoke the mysterious presence of the past. After printing this particular image, I experimented with Berg copper and blue toners along with potassium ferricyanide bleach. I went through a number of bleaching and toning steps, finally settling on an image that was mostly bleached out and not fixed."

Melanie Walker has been a practicing artist for over 50 years. Her expertise is in the area of alternative photographic processes, digital and mixed media as well as large scale immersive photographic installations and public art. In her photographic practice she has been driven by contemporary sensibilities as applied to historical photographic processes and hand-made prints along with new ways of presentation. Her work is a collision between installation, photography, sculpture, textiles, puppets and sometimes sound. Her practice is haptic and multi-sensory, being born visually impaired. In recent installations she works with images on sheer fabric to emulate the double vision she experiences with her visual challenges. She lives between sight and blindness hoping to serve as a bridge to empathy and compassion. To see more of her work visit melaniewalkerartist.com.

Thiourea toning

Thiourea toner is a brown toner just like sepia, but without the rotten egg odor. It uses the same bleach step as other two-part indirect toners, but Part B of thiourea toning has two solutions that can be mixed in varying proportions to enable colors from yellow-brown to red-brown. It requires three separate liter containers, one for the stock bleach, and one each for Solutions B1 and B2, but all solutions last indefinitely until mixed together.

Part A Standard Bleach

100 g (5 tablespoons) potassium bromide
100 g (6.5 tablespoons) potassium ferricyanide
Water to 1000 ml

1. Add potassium bromide to 500 ml water and stir.
2. Add potassium ferricyanide to the above solution and stir.
3. Add water to make 1000 ml.
4. At time of use, dilute 1 part stock strength solution with 9 parts water (1+9).

Part B1 Thiourea Solution

100 g thiourea
Water to 1000 ml

1. Have 750 ml water in a graduate, and slowly add the thiourea. Stir carefully with a plastic rod, and then add the remaining water to bring the amount up to 1000 ml. Store in its own plastic liter container.

Part B2 Sodium Hydroxide Solution

100 g sodium hydroxide
Water to 1000 ml

Caution with mixing this chemical: always add acid to water (AAATW)! Have water cold because sodium hydroxide gives off heat (exothermic) and the cold water suddenly gets warm. Also, sodium hydroxide spatters and burns if it touches the skin. I learned that the hard way!

1. Slowly add the hydroxide to 750 ml water in a graduate, protecting eyes, body and clothing. Stir carefully with a plastic rod, and then add the remaining water to bring the amount up to 1000 ml. Store in its own plastic liter container.
2. At time of use, mix a combined 120 ml of Parts B1 and B2 per every 1000 ml water. The more B1, the yellower the brown; the more B2, the redder the brown.
3. Bleach the print in the standard bleach bath, diluted 1+9.
4. Rinse the print in water until all yellow of the bleach is gone (about 2–10 minutes).
5. Tone in the Part B1/B2 thiourea/sodium hydroxide/water bath until no more change occurs (1–3 minutes).
6. When toning is complete, wash fiber prints for 30 minutes, RC for 4. There is no need to hypoclear after thiourea toning.

Clay Harmon's one-shot thiourea toners

Steps proceed as above under thiourea toning.

Formula I (medium brown tone): for the bleach, mix 7.5 g potassium ferricyanide and 7.5 g potassium bromide in 1000 ml water. For the toner, mix 3 g thiourea and 100 g sodium carbonate in 1000 ml water.

Formula II (cooler purple-brown): for the bleach, mix 20 g potassium ferricyanide and 10 g potassium bromide in 1000 ml water. For the toner, mix 3 g thiourea and 9 g sodium hydroxide in 1000 ml water.

Selective toning

Selective toning is simply toning only parts of an photograph. Tools to have on hand to make the process go smoothly are a hose with a continuous water supply and a piece of Plexiglas or glass propped up at a 45° angle to support the print. Also, triangular cosmetic wedges, Q-tips, cotton balls, brushes, and masking solution can be used.

Bleach is applied to the print in certain areas. The hose is kept running just underneath the area to be bleached at all times to catch any drips that run outside the bleaching area. If drips occur, redevelop the print in paper developer and start the bleaching process again. Once the area is sufficiently bleached, sepia or thiourea toner is used. It will tone the bleached area only. You can mask the untoned area surrounding the bleached area with masking fluid prior to bleaching, and then when the print is finished the masking fluid can be rubbed off, but masking fluid will leave a sharp edge. Nowadays you can buy masking pens like Masquepen or bottles of masking fluid with non-clogging tips.

Multiple toning

Experimentation begins with multiple toning. Here are some possible combinations of toners:

- Sepia/thiourea then selenium
- Sepia/thiourea then blue
- Sepia/thiourea then gold (oranges)
- Sepia then gold then blue
- Selenium (strong) then bleach then sepia
- Selenium then blue
- Selenium then gold
- Copper then blue
- Blue then copper
- Bleach then paper developer then sepia

Favorites are a combination of warm and cool tones of thiourea and blue. It is best to warm tone first and blue tone next.

The one caveat: after a bleach bath a print can not be directly toned in selenium. Selenium toner contains fixer and will fix the print to a nice blank.

Mortensen's metalchrome

William Mortensen named this toning process "metalchrome" because of gold chloride—the metal part—and watercolors—the chrome part. However fancy the name may be, it is really only selective toning with gold chloride over a previously sepia/thiourea-toned print. The gold toner changes the warm browns of the sepia toner to a pale peach to deep orange tone. Watercolors (optional) can be used to tone down the intense peach tone if necessary. The peach tone is perfect for flesh or Southwestern landscapes where red clay abounds.

Part A:

1 g gold chloride
250 ml distilled water

Gold chloride solution keeps indefinitely. Take the little glass vial with the gold chloride powder, uncap it, and put the entire vial in the bottle of distilled water to make sure to get every grain of gold powder out of that vial and into solution. Leave the glass vial in the bottle permanently. This is just a more dilute form of gold chloride than the 1% recommended in this chapter, so you could merely add 15 ml water to 10 ml 1%.

Part B:

20 g sodium thiosulfate
11 g thiourea
250 ml distilled water

Add the thiosulfate to the 250 ml water. Add the thiourea and mix completely and store.

1. At time of use: mix equal parts of A and B together in very small amounts. A little goes a long way.
2. Use a warmtone paper such as Ilford warmtone, and semi-matte or matte if the print will subsequently be hand colored.
3. Tone the print first in a two step process sepia or thiourea toner as instructed in this chapter. Wash well, and squeegee excess water off the surface. Lay flat on a piece of glass.
4. Mix a small amount of equal parts of Part A and Part B together, starting with perhaps 10 ml of each. With a small watercolor or calligraphy brush, apply to the area to be toned. Keep reapplying, having on hand a water source to pour on top of the print to stop the process when it looks complete. If the toner seeps outside the lines of the area being selectively toned, immediately douse the area with water to stop the toning. The process moves slowly enough that there should be time to think and adjust.
5. When finished gold-toning, rinse, hypoclear, wash for 30 minutes, and dry.
6. The print can be hand colored with a neutralizing color to tone down any areas that may have become too orange. Only a very thin wash is necessary, if at all. The intensity of the peach tone is proportional to the depth of the tone in the print, and highlights are rarely too peachy.

Endnotes

1. Harrison, W. Jerome. "The Toning of Photographs, Considered Chemically, Historically, and Generally" in *The Photographic Times and American Photographer*, Vol. XXI. New York: The Photographic Times Publishing Association, 1891, "Alkaline Toning Baths," Ch. VII, pp. 243–244.
2. Rostagni, Jean-Christian. "French Photographer Denis Brihat: Spiritual Heir to Edward Weston" in *Photo Techniques*, January/February, 2003, pp. 27–29.
3. Anchell, Steve. *The Darkroom Cookbook*, 3rd ed. Burlington, Massachusetts: Focal Press, 2008; 4th ed. New York: Routledge, 2016, p. 303.
4. Jones, Bernard E., ed. *Cassell's Cyclopaedia of Photography*. New York: Funk & Wagnalls Company, 1912, pp. 414–415.

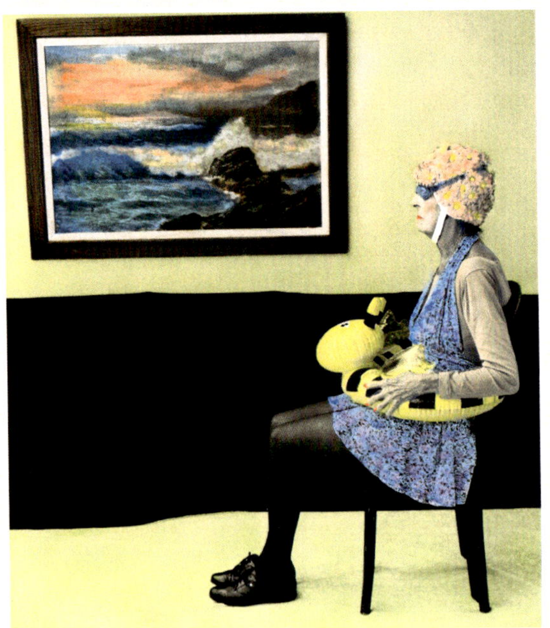

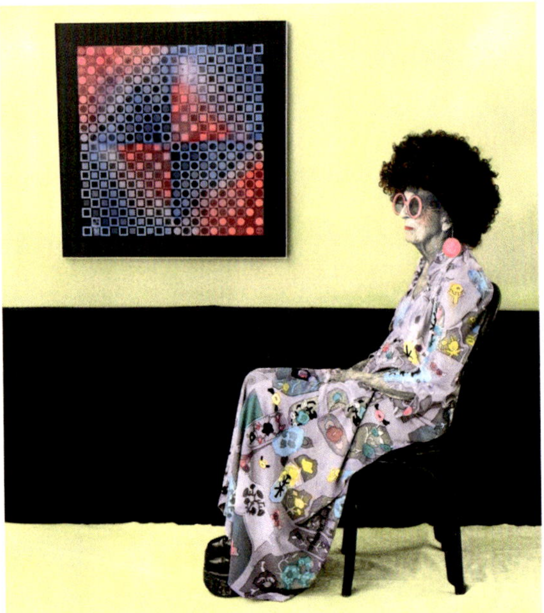

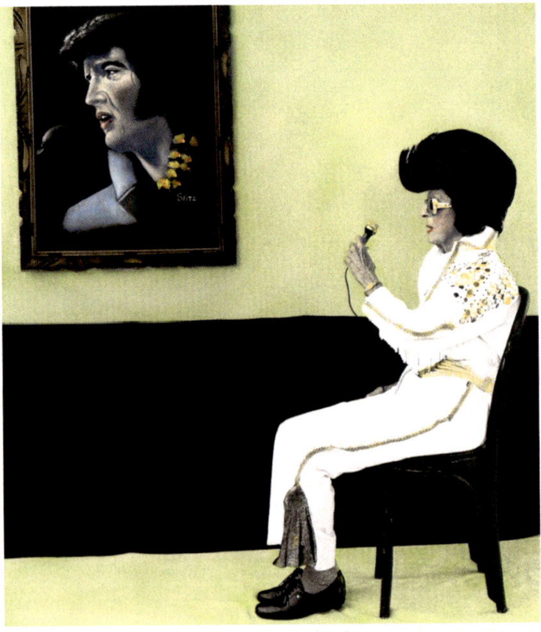

Figures 15.1–15.3. Clockwise from top left, *Arrangement #3*, *Arrangement #12*, *Arrangement #14*, handcolored silver gelatin prints © Aline Smithson 2005. "With my *Arrangement in Green and Black* series, I am using hand painting in a more contemporary way, not the typical landscapes and children in bonnet images that were popular in the 1980s. I have been greatly influenced by the Japanese concept of celebrating a singular object. I tend to isolate subject matter and look for complexity in simple images, providing an opportunity for telling a story in which all is not what it appears to be. The poignancy of childhood, aging, relationships, family, and moments of introspection or contemplation continue to draw my interest. I want to create pictures that evoke a universal memory. The most joyful part of the journey is making the work—having time to play and experiment. It's important to make messes and revel in the creative process." Aline Smithson is a visual artist, educator, and editor based in Los Angeles, California. She is best known for her conceptual portraiture and a practice that uses humor and pathos to explore the performative potential of photography. She has exhibited widely including over forty solo shows at a variety of international institutions. Smithson's work has been featured in publications including *The New York Times*, *The New Yorker*, and *PDN*. She is the Founder and Editor-in-Chief of *Lenscratch*, a daily journal on photography. The Magenta Foundation published her monograph, *Self & Others: Portrait as Autobiography*. The Smithsonian Air and Space Museum commissioned her to create a series of portraits for the upcoming *Faces of Our Planet* exhibition. In 2018 and 2019, Smithson's work was exhibited in the National Portrait Gallery in London as part of the Taylor Wessing Prize. Kris Graves Projects commissioned her to create a book on Los Angeles, *LOST II: Los Angeles* and Peanut Press will be releasing her monograph, *Fugue State*, in Fall 2021. To see more of her work visit **www.alinesmithson.com**.

Applied Color and Abrasion Tone

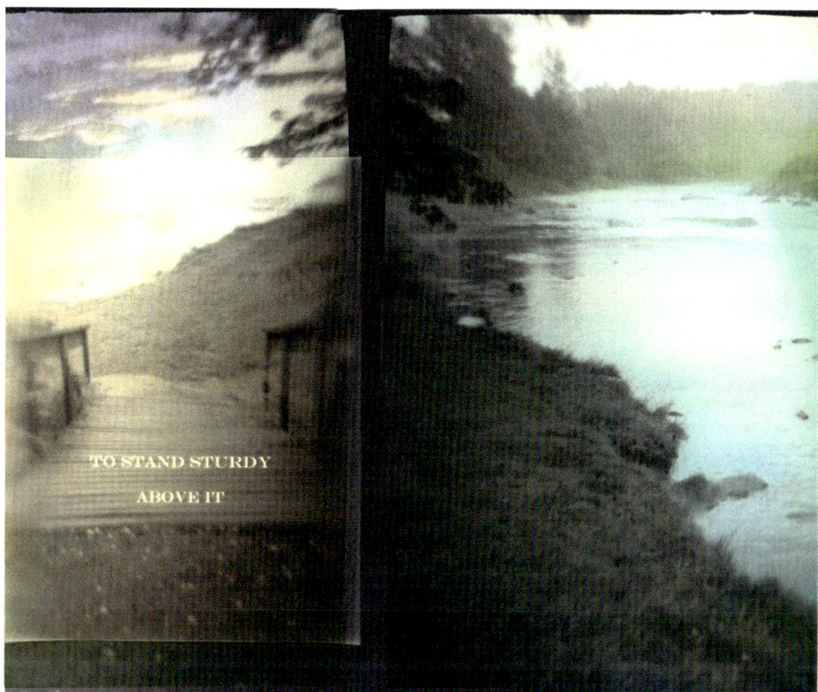

Figure 15.4. *To Stand Sturdy,* from the *Shadows and Stains* series, handcolored silver gelatin print © Aline Smithson 2008. "In the *Shadow and Stains* series,work created with a toy camera where I can extend the frame, I break all the rules of the darkroom—cutting negatives, overlapping images, adding text. I create the collages in the dark and have a typed phrase ready to place as the top layer to my efforts. Later I instinctively add washes of color with oil paint. This is the opportunity for play and for failure in the darkroom. Losing precision in the darkroom was liberating and took away the onerous task of creating perfection. Not knowing the outcome was much more exciting."

The hand colored black and white photograph possesses a unique aesthetic. In the very beginnings of photography when color film and paper did not exist, there was a strong tradition of hand colored black and white prints, because that was the only way to achieve realistic color with a photograph. With the advent of color film and paper, the need for hand coloring dwindled to the purview of fine art photographers who appreciated the muted, retro look. Some handcolorists follow the photograph carefully and subtly. Some color only parts of the image—selective coloring. Some use color sumptuously with a velvety application. Some obliterate much of the photographic information with very painterly markmaking. With no longer the need to merely represent reality as in the 1800s, hand coloring is wide open for experimentation.

There are few brands of photo oils on the market now. The original (my favorite) is made by Marshall and is available from dickblick.com and other places. There are several sets at different price points. The larger kit is the one to buy if committing to the process long term. The oils last forever.

Freestyle sells their brand of photo oils called Arista Photo Oils (freestylephoto.biz). The oils are made by Gamblin and come in little jars instead of tubes as do the Marshall oils.

It is possible to use regular oil paints for hand coloring, the ones that are high quality and highly pigmented, but the amount of color needed is so minimal—the size of a pea—that having a whole set of little tubes of Marshall's paint is very economical, with far more color choices than if one had to buy normal sized tubes of oil paint.

The cleaning solution with the Arista kit is mineral spirits and not the Marlene solution that comes with the Marshall's kit. Marlene is trichloroethylene, a chemical that dries instantly with no residue. It is apparently used in the dry cleaning industry. It is a miracle cleaner with hand coloring because it removes pigment instantly and leaves

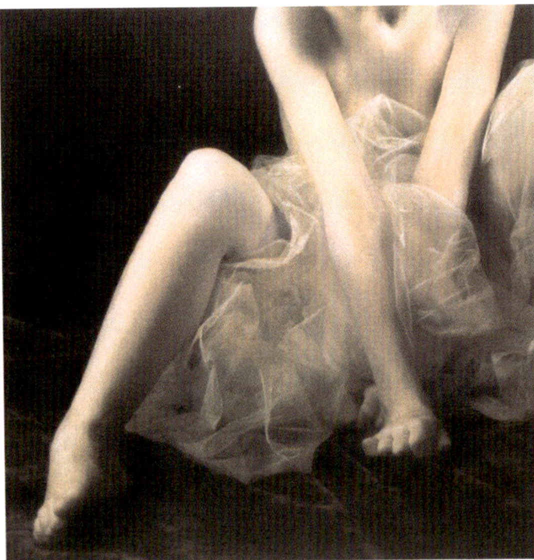

Figure 15.5. *Dancer I*, handcolored silver gelatin print, 16″ x 16″ © Brigitte Carnochan 2003

no oily residue behind to muck up the rest of the pigment on the photograph. Unfortunately, trichloroethylene is banned in many states for its toxicity. In future times it may be that the only available cleaners are mineral spirits or naphtha. If hand coloring becomes a process of choice it would be wise to stock up on Marshall's Marlene. Or, make friends with a dry cleaner and see if it is possible to get some from them. Otherwise naphtha or mineral spirits will have to do.

Starting with photo oils and then a matte or semi-matte paper will make the hand coloring process easy. Glossy photo paper has such a slick surface that the paint does not grab enough. Whether the paper is RC or fiber doesn't matter as much as whether the surface is matte or glossy.

Some print a bit lighter (⅓ stop) and lower contrast, because if the image is too dark or contrasty, the oils can appear muddy. Some don't do this. In either case, the print should have good detail in both highlights and shadows.

Second, if possible, toning the print warm with a mild sepia toner or even split-toning the print so just the highlights are brown but the shadows stay black makes the final print look better. Oils on top of warmer tones look better than oils on top of cooler tones.

Once the print is completed, it is easiest to drymount it onto an archival mat board so it will stay flat for the handcoloring process or, at least, tape it to a support that can be rotated.

Supplies

100% cotton balls (real cotton is a must)
Q-tips
Toothpicks
Marlene, naphtha, Arista cleaner, or mineral spirits
Extender (if desired)
Krylon Crystal Clear glossy acrylic spray
Wax paper
Frisket removable film
Antistatic cloth or disposable antistatic sheets such as Pledge Grab-its
White vinyl eraser to clean up small areas

The P.M. Solution, Duolac Varnish, and drier that come in the kit are not particularly necessary. The drier, mixed 1:2 with the oils, dries the paint in less than 24 hours. The P.M. Solution is used by hand colorists who color with pencils. They coat the entire print with a layer of P.M. Solution, wipe it almost dry, and then let it absorb and evaporate for a bit. It prepares the print to receive the pencil or paint in a less grabby fashion. After applying the pencil, the marks are rubbed with cotton to blend. Alternatively, the pencils can be dipped in the P.M. Solution while coloring the print.

P.M. solution can be used to clean the entire print if the coloring process is not working well and one needs to start over, but mineral spirits will do that as well. Otherwise, Marlene is used to clean up small parts of a print while in process of hand coloring or at the end of the process to clean up minute highlights or areas where the color looks messy. Marlene leaves a perfectly clean, dry surface. P.M. leaves an edge halo as the oil/turpentine mixture creeps into other colors and dissolves them.

Extender is used to extend pigment to a weaker color. It makes the paint greasier, and pigment can be made weaker by merely rubbing it off with cotton balls. I personally never use it.

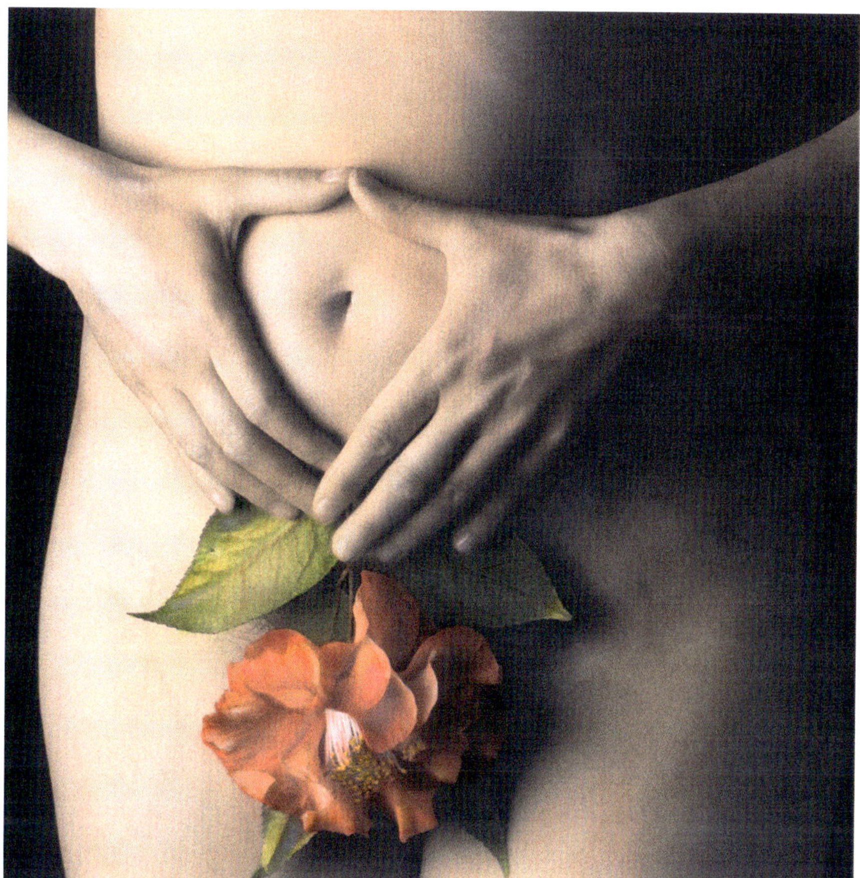

Figure 15.6. *Nude with Camelia*, handcolored silver gelatin print, 16″ x 16″ © Brigitte Carnochan 1997. More of Carnochan's work and process is in the **Contemporary Experimental Artists** chapter.

Steps

Plan on hand coloring the print from start to finish in one sitting. If this is not possible, put the partially hand colored print in a sealed plastic bag to keep it from drying out. The sooner the print is finished the better, because trying to color over partially dry paint creates unevenness. If it dries partially before completion, better to let it dry completely (3 days to a week) before working on it again.

1. Prepare the print. Mount a fiber base print onto archival mat board so it will remain flat. RC paper usually remains flat so this dry mounting is optional for RC.

2. Protect the print. Cover the white borders with cut strips of Frisket film to preserve the whites and save on cleanup time. Don't use tape—it'll rip parts of the print off upon removal unless it is a low-tack variety such as Kleenedge brand tape. Frisket Film is low tack and removes nicely. It is worth its weight in gold, and Frisket strips can be reused after the excess paint dries on them.

3. Prepare a makeshift paint palette. Tape a double thickness of wax paper onto the table to use as a disposable palette. Make this about 4″× 6″ at least, large enough to mix colors on. Freezer paper works well for this, too.

4. Prepare the paints. Squeeze out colors onto the palette—for larger areas use the size of a pea, for smaller areas such as lips use just a smudge from the top of the tube. It is easy to replenish the palette with more paint, but once the colors are squeezed out, they will dry overnight and be unusable. It is possible to cover the pigments with another piece of wax paper to keep them moist longer, but if a skin forms on top of the pigments, it can leave bits of crud in a handcolored layer.

5. Mix the colors either on the wax palette or on the print itself by dabbing the different colors where they will belong and then mixing them with the cotton. Flesh tones should probably be mixed on the palette first, and then bits of yellow, blue, and

red can be added on the print to warm up or cool down highlights and shadows. With skies, walls, or other larger areas just layer the colors on the print directly and then rub gently together.

6. Start the color application. When applying colors to the print, remember to over-color at first and then rub down to the desired strength. If the initial color application is too dark, it can always be rubbed down with cotton to a lighter shade.

7. The hand coloring mantra: Go from larger to smaller, top to bottom (if possible), messy to clean. Translated, this means to color the skies and background larger areas first, without worrying about overlapping color into smaller areas. Since the next application of color will displace and, in essence, clean the messed up color from that area (within reason) do not worry about edges much in the beginning. When the background larger areas are complete, work on the next smaller areas and on down, until the last elements that are hand colored are such things as gold rings, lips, eyes, fingernails, etc.

8. Painting is begun with larger tools and finished with smaller tools: cotton balls at the beginning, then Q-tips, and then finally small details are colored with toothpicks wrapped in teeny bits of cotton. To make the latter, wet the end of the toothpick, pick up a smidgen of cotton, and wrap it around the moistened toothpick by spinning the toothpick.

9. Color with variety. The secret to hand coloring is twofold: don't use large areas of unmodulated, straight color but mix, mix, mix with a pinch of this and a pinch of that. (The second secret is perfect cleanup, discussed below.) Avoid using solid color which can be boring, too "raw," or amateurish unless carefully done. Thus, a sky might contain several blues along with a bit of yellow or sepia if warm is desired, or Payne's gray, neutral tint or purple if cooler tones are desired.

10. The same goes for water. Water has ultramarine blue and purple and viridian and chromium oxide green and cadmium yellow and red and Payne's gray—all kinds of colors. Flesh is never just straight flesh tone, but flesh mixed with white or yellow, or red to warm it in touchable areas, or a tad of blue or brown for the shadows.

11. Whenever shading an object, use its complement in the shadows—a blue box, for instance, could be shaded with orange mixed in with the blue. In fact, using a complement of a color will tone down a too bright or too raw color and make it appear more natural (yellow/purple, blue/orange, red/green). This all follows color theory. Hand coloring a photograph is the same as painting a canvas.

12. Some suggestions for color combinations are as follows:

- Blonde hair: raw sienna, white, and Verona brown; or try khaki. Blonde hair is actually ash toned and thus leans toward green.
- Brown hair: Verona and sepia for the highlights.
- Black hair: neutral tint.
- Red hair: Verona brown and burnt sienna.
- Gray hair: sepia and white.
- Skin: there are several different flesh paints. One leans more towards red, one more towards yellow. They range from light to dark, but straight flesh tone is an unpleasing Band-Aid tan, and must be highlighted with other colors as said above. Example: basic flesh and white for midtones, straight flesh for the shadows (or use Verona brown), and add raw sienna for the highlights.
- Darker skin: Verona brown and red.
- Darkest skin: Verona brown and flesh.
- Eyes: use a toothpick and make sure not to cover up the catchlight; wipe it clean with Marlene or dot it with titanium white at the 11:00 or 1:00 position. A tad of cheek color in the corner of the eye white will warm up the eyes. Use neutral tint on the pupil, never black. Or use a touch of a black pencil for the pupil.
- Lips: for men's lips use Flesh 3, for women's lips, Lipstick Red in the Marshall's kit.
- Grass: oxide green or tree green mixed with browns, blues or reds for shadows and yellows for highlights.
- Skies: mix extender in with the blue oil if needing to dilute the color. Keep the horizon sky area less blue and grade to more blue toward the top of the print. Rub color over the complete sky, even over tree branches; afterwards, just color branches right over the blue, and even use colored pencils to do tiny detailed branches and

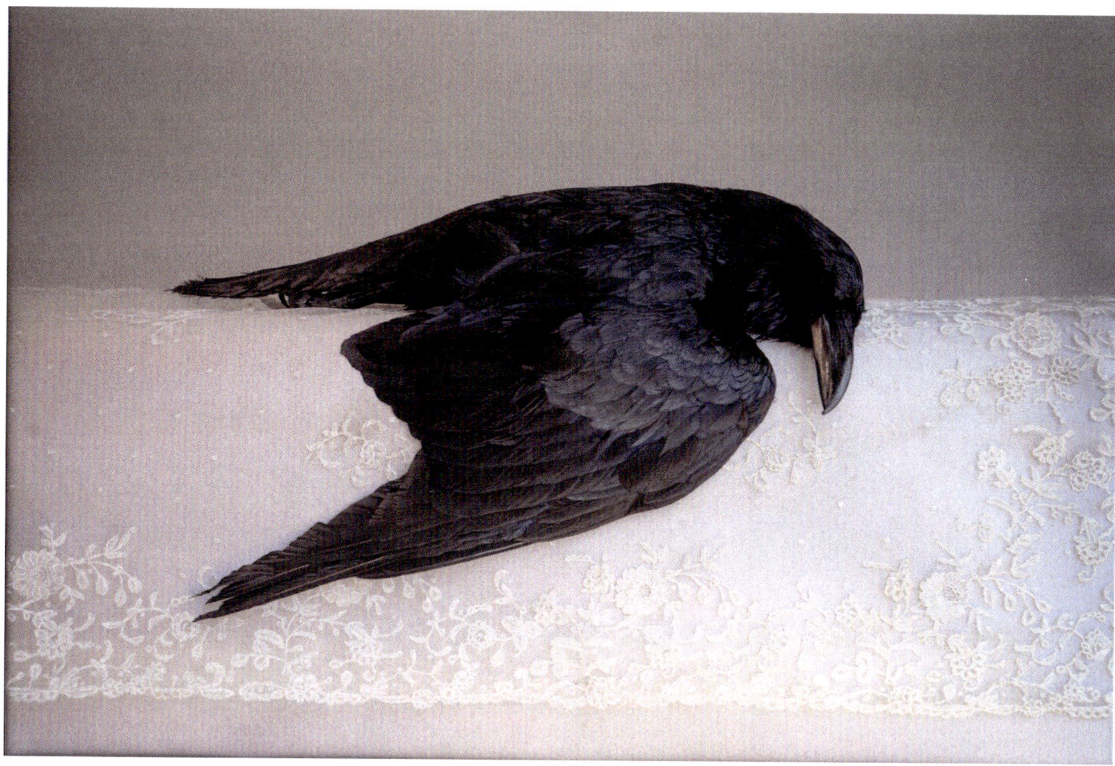

Figure 15.7. *Common Raven on Lace*, digital archival inkjet print hand-colored with pencil and pastel, 36″ x 24″ © Kate Breakey 2022. "Several studies have found that bird populations are rapidly declining. In North America alone we have lost 1/3 of all birds in 50 years—3 billion of them. The primary cause is habitat loss, but window collisions, vehicles, power lines, communication towers, domestic cats, pesticides, and extreme weather events due to climate change are all responsible. As pollinators and insectivores, birds are utterly essential to a functioning ecosystem. Their disappearance is an indicator, a clear and sobering signal, that what we have done spells immeasurable trouble for the health of our planet, and therefore our own wellbeing. Can we imagine a world without birds? Quite apart from everything else, without them, our souls would surely die."

leaves. Remember, as things recede they get bluer due to atmospheric perspective; thus, distant mountains are bluish and closer mountains will appear greener and warmer.

13. When the coloring is complete, the final and most important step is cleanup. How good a hand colorist is can be told by the attention they pay to cleanup. Any mistakes become even more noticeable if published in books.

14. Investigate the print with a loupe, scrutinizing it closely for any bit of color that is out of place. Take a toothpick with cotton, dip in cleaning solution, and clean the stray color up. Rub the area lightly with a dry cotton-covered toothpick to clean off the cleaner (oily residue from mineral spirits, or the little dot of color left by the Marlene). Clean up eye whites, teeth, any highlights such as catch lights in the eyes and specular highlights on jewelry or lights. Blue and red are hard to remove so these two colors should be carefully applied.

15. Dry prints at an angle leaned against a wall face side down so that dust will not collect on the surface and dry into the paint. Another idea is to dry the print inside a dust free plastic bag with a cardboard bridge to keep the bag from touching the surface. Or dry inside a box.

16. When completely dry, wipe off the print with the antistatic cloth and spray with a coating of Krylon Crystal Clear glossy acrylic spray. This will even out the glossy and non-glossy areas of the print and deepen and enrich the colors. It is amazing how nicely the spray makes the finished print look. It glows!

Tips and ideas

- Don't color the whole print, but color selectively to establish a focal point.
- Use titanium white to put highlights in the print, create delicate almost invisible patterns, or to recede areas of unimportance to make the focal point pop out more—a kind of false atmospheric haze.
- Experiment with colors not natural to the image—green skies and pink trees.
- Hand color liquid emulsion on water color paper. Watercolors are perfect for this.
- Color with pastel, charcoal, pencil, gouache.
- Create stencil patterns with a fabric pattern as the basis. With a piece of mylar or other form of plastic sheeting, and an electric pen from a craft store, the fabric pattern can be traced onto the mylar and burned out. Place the fabric underneath a sheet of glass, the plastic sheet on top of the glass, and trace the design with the heat pen tool.
- Coat the paper with a thinned solution of shellac and methylated spirits of alcohol. Shellac is an actual natural substance created out of ground up beetles that has an odd smell and looks like a transparent cockroach color. Thinned with methylated spirits, it is a unique antique yellow color, and accepts waxy colored pencil and oils quite well.

The bottom line is, hand coloring is no longer some prissy old fashioned portrait technique, but a contemporary method of fine art making. It can be subtle or strong, kitschy or elegant. Most important, it is just plain fun!

Abrasion tone

William Mortensen was an avid print manipulator from the first half of the 20th century. Today he might be termed a post-visualizer. Mortensen did kitschy work at a time when Ansel Adams and straight photography reigned. In fact, Adams was highly critical of Mortensen.

The abrasion tone process was Mortensen's creation. His version of abrasion tone consisted of laborious print abrading with pumice and a razor blade and then toning the print by rubbing such colorants as pencils, chalk, and pastel into the scratches. He also scratched off entire parts of the photograph. I will share a much simpler method that doesn't require abrading; think of it as merely hand coloring a print with pastels. I will outline his complex process for posterity.

Abrasion tone (without abrasion)

- Ivory black and burnt sienna pastels, ground to a powder in a blender or coffee grinder. Use high pigmented pastels or conté chalks. Mix in a 2:1 proportion of ivory black to burnt sienna.
- Graphite pencils or graphic powder, if desired
- Erasers such as kneaded gum and pencil
- Cotton balls and Q-tips
- Gelatin silver, matte-surface print
- Krylon Crystal Clear matte/gloss acrylic spray

Merely use the colorants such as powdered pigment, pencils, etc., and erasers to add tone to the print, *without* scratching. Graphite give a beautiful silvery shimmer to the print surface. Then fix with the Krylon spray to seal the pastels/handiwork.

Mortensen's abrasion tone

- Ivory black and burnt sienna pastels, ground to a powder in a blender or coffee grinder. Use high pigmented pastels or conté chalks. Mix in a 2:1 proportion of ivory black to burnt sienna.
- Erasers such as kneaded gum and pencil
- Carton of powdered pumice
- Cotton balls and Q-tips
- Architect's drafting brush
- Print spotting solution and spotting brush
- Carbon drawing pencil, BB (carbon black, not shiny gray graphite)
- Xacto knife and blades of the sharpest, pointy kind, or a traditional razor blade
- Silver gelatin, matte surface print
- Krylon Crystal Clear matte/gloss acrylic spray

1. Dip a cotton ball in the powdered chalk/pigment, shake off, and rub over the entire print so that the print is completely covered with a spare layer of the pigment but not noticeably darker.
2. Take another cotton ball and wipe the surface evenly so that there is no loose powder showing.

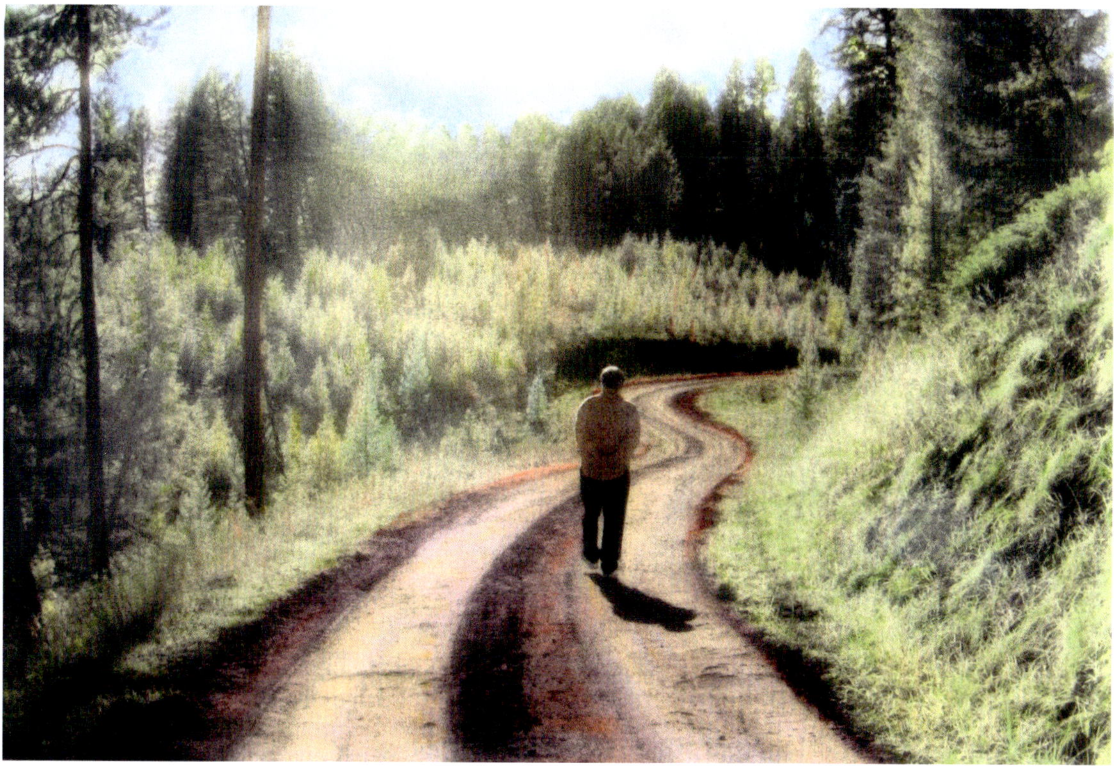

Figure 15.8. *Contemplate*, infrared, hand-colored silver gelatin print, 13.25″ x 10.25″ © Christina Z. Anderson 2007

With the kneaded eraser, remove the pigment from the light areas of the print. Don't worry about unevenness at this stage.

3. Sprinkle a small amount of pumice over these lightened areas, and with another cotton ball, blend in the unevenness with the pumiced cotton ball until the edges between light and dark are blended.

4. If there is pigment in the previously lightened areas, clean up again with the kneaded eraser in the very lightest parts of the lightened areas, in essence creating a greater tonal range.

5. Add specular highlights with the pencil eraser.

6. Sweep off remaining pumice and pigment with the drafting brush.

7. Take the carbon pencil and add touches of dark in larger areas and the deeper midtones. This step can be used for enhancement of darker areas or correction of unwanted light tones or details. Do not use the pencil as a line drawing tool but a tone adding tool.

8. Blend the carbon pencil with a cotton ball and pumice. Brush off.

9. With the Xacto knife, using a gentle, ⅛″ long stroke, scrape away bits of the emulsion to remove or lighten or even take parts of the image away. Do not dig into the paper, but gently scrape, with the blade held at a 90° angle to the print, and scrape away from one's body in tiny strokes, with the blade continually moving back and forth so that it does not scrape in one place for so long that the print gets gouged. Blow off any resulting crumbs.

10. Spot any corrections with photo spotting solution and a brush.

11. Spray with Krylon Crystal Clear matte or gloss acrylic varnish to protect the print and mark making.

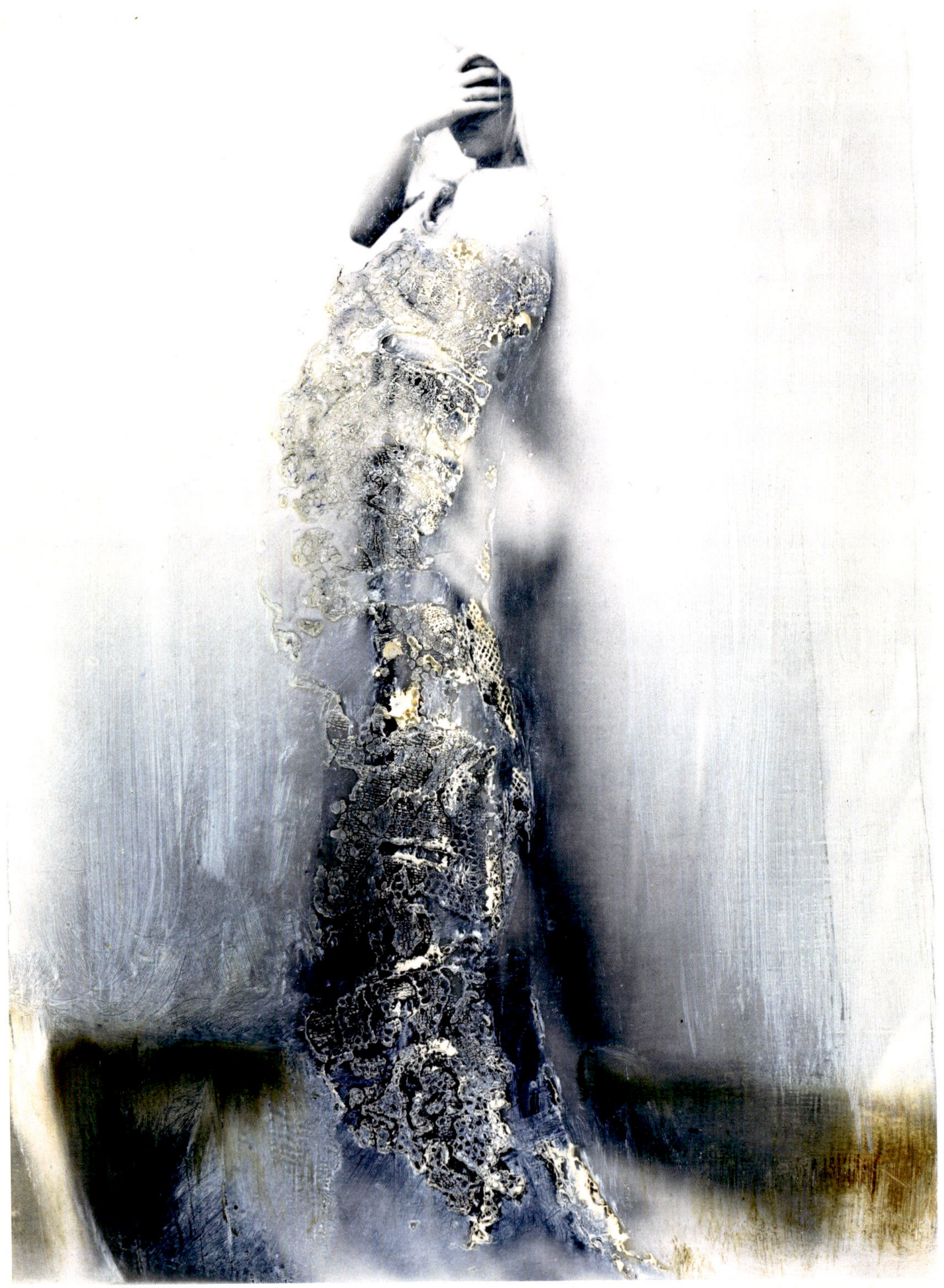

Figure 16.1. *Lace Robe*, 7″ x 9″ silver gelatin print with encaustic © Leah Macdonald 2018. More of Macdonald's work and process are in the **Contemporary Experimental Artists** chapter.

Chapter 16

Encaustic, Collage, Photomontage

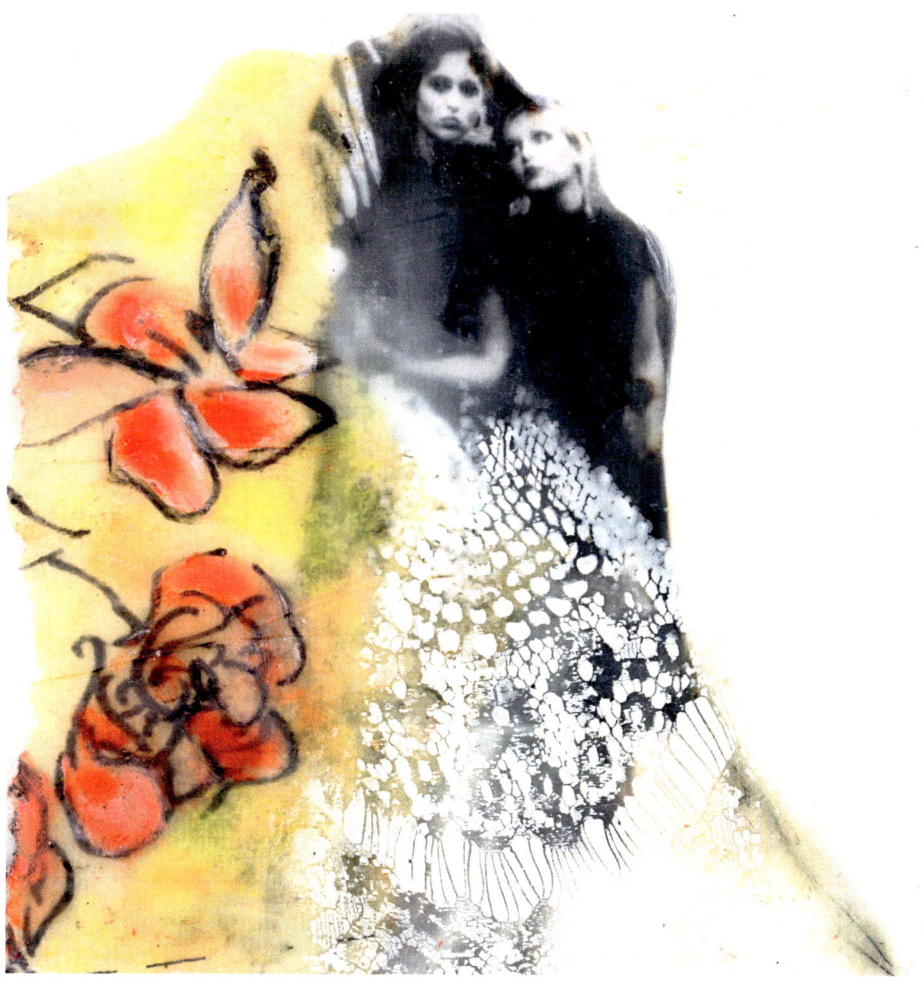

Figure 16.2. *Flower Girls*, 7.7″ x 7.8″ silver gelatin print with encaustic © Leah Macdonald 2021

Encaustic is a method of painting with wax that is extremely archival. Different colors of encaustic paint are derived by mixing powdered pigment into wax. Encaustic supplies are available for purchase or can be made with a few supplies. This chapter will touch on the creative use of encaustic specifically in relation to photographic images (e.g. encaustic was first and foremost a painting technique). Even something as quick and easy as saturating a photograph in beeswax acquires a beautiful translucence and antique feel.

Supplies

- Unrefined beeswax: this comes in blocks that are yellowish in color, available at most hardware stores. Unrefined beeswax still has pollen and propolis in it, which gives it its characteristic yellowish color. Refined white beeswax, sold in pastille form, has the pollen removed.
- Encaustic medium: encaustic medium is a mixture of beeswax and dammar resin. You can make your own, or buy it readymade from the sources included in this chapter.

- Heat gun: the heat gun bonds, fuses, heats, and reheats layers of wax which are added one after the other. If a heat source is not used to fuse each layer together, the encaustic will not work. With the heat gun, wax can also be reheated and moved around at any time after application. Heat guns now come with digital temperature readouts, and multiple temperature settings from low to high, also attachments to direct the heat flow as well as variable fan speeds. A heat gun, an essential tool for encaustic, represents some investment.
- Frying pan or griddle: this is used to heat up wax paint and keep it warm.
- Muffin tin: this is a handy tool to place on top of the heat source, in which different colors of pigment can be stored and heated all at once.
- Brushes: natural bristle brushes are the ticket; synthetic bristles cannot be used; they melt. A good brush would be a Japanese hake brush.
- Palette knives
- Paper or other support: many encaustic artists use cradled wood panels as their support. Photographs can be affixed to these supports with PVA archival glue or acrylic gel medium, and dried overnight. A photograph can also be the support because paper absorbs wax. Whatever the case, the final encaustic has to stay rigid because flexing will crack the wax.
- Other: if really pursuing encaustic, there are lots of tools specifically designed for hot painting such as brass bristle brushes and hot wax pens. These are beyond the scope of this book, but an excellent description of these tools is in Rankin's book cited under **Sources** in this chapter.

Low tech encaustic

- Soak smaller photographs in wax heated up in a frypan until the paper is impregnated with wax through and through. Remove and let the wax harden. The print will look more translucent and antique, especially if natural beeswax is used. This simple encaustic works well with water color paper. Try soaking liquid emulsion on water color paper in wax.

Medium tech encaustic

- Dip the whole print in wax first to get it impregnated with wax through and through, and then heat, drip, palette knife, or brush more wax on top. Each additional layer of wax will have to be fused to the layers below with a heat gun.
- Buy powdered pigments and add them to the wax. A little goes a long way. Don't add too much because it'll become too opaque.
- Use metallic powdered pigment for shimmer.
- "Glazing" is done by mixing very minimal amounts of pigment into a layer of wax for mere hints of color.
- You can mix oil paint with wax, but this will take longer to dry, depending on how much oil pigment is added.

The encaustic process

Most of the information in this chapter comes from the wonderful website rfpaints.com.

1. Purchase encaustic paints and mediums readymade from the sources in this chapter, a wood panel, and PVA glue. If you want to make your own medium, have 2 parts Dammar resin + 9 parts beeswax ready to go.
2. Glue the photograph to the wood support with PVA and let it dry overnight.
3. To make your own beeswax/resin, heat the beeswax only in a pan until melted at about 160°F. Then add the Dammar resin and bring the mixture to 180°F, stirring well. Cool.
4. Melt either the purchased or homemade dammar/wax medium and apply a first layer with a brush, palette knife, or by pouring or dripping. Let cool.
5. Heat and fuse the layer with the heat gun.
6. Apply the next layer of medium, then heat and fuse it to the layer below, and so on and so forth with each layer. The thicker the layers of wax, and the cooler the wax applied, the more important it is to properly fuse each layer to the one below. Otherwise they will separate down the road. It is best to do thinner and more frequent layering.
7. When the encaustic is finished and completely cool, it is done and requires no further work other than a mild buffing. Do this with a soft cotton cloth.

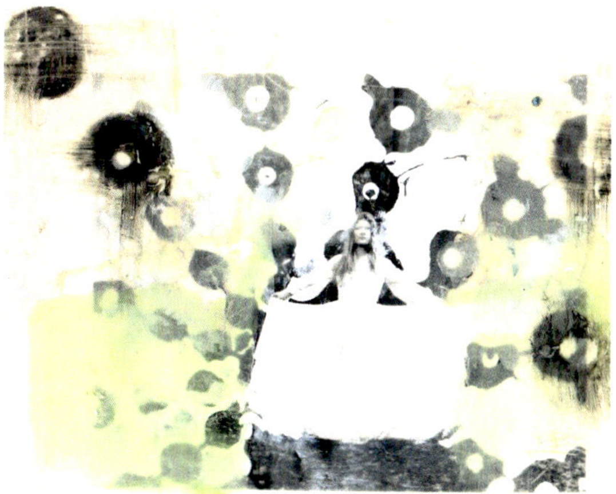

Figure 16.3. *Circles*, 6.8″ x 5.3″ silver gelatin print with encaustic © Leah Macdonald 2021

8. Cleanup: most tools can be heated and the wax wiped off. Mineral spirits can be used for cleanup as well. It is best, though, to dedicate a set of tools to encaustic, eliminate the use of mineral spirits, and keep them cleaned with just heat and paper towels.

9. For several months after the last melting of the paint, the wax/resin will go through a curing process in which the surface continues to harden. During this time moisture or other impurities that have gotten into the paint while hot may work their way to the surface and cause a slight haze. Buffing will restore the high polish.

10. Encaustic does not need to be varnished or protected by glass. A temperature of 40–110°F (4–44°C) is fine. Do not put an encaustic in sunlight or a hot car in the summer or it will melt. On very hot days in a house the paint can soften somewhat, but no real damage will occur. If any dulling occurs, the surface can be buffed when the encaustic is cooler.

11. In very cold temperatures wax will shrink slightly. If layers have not been fused well they will separate or crack. If any parts break off, add more wax and fuse again. In fact, you can return to the encaustic years later and do additional work if desired, or even heat and scrape off any previous work and start anew.

The ivorytype

The ivorytype is a handcolored photograph that is affixed to a piece of glass with warm wax. The glass is first cleaned and then warmed, then covered with a layer of melted white beeswax or the Dammar/beeswax encaustic medium. While the wax is hot and evenly layered on top of the glass, the print is carefully lowered and embedded into the heated wax, from middle of the print to the edges. A flat-edged ruler or similar tool is used to press and smooth down the print to the glass plate. Hopefully there will be no air bubbles trapped in the sandwich or it'll have to be reheated and sandwiched once again. When the ivorytype is dry it is backed with something white to make it brighter and framed.

Tips and ideas

- Encaustic medium contains 8–15% Dammar resin and produces a harder layer and more shine.
- Dammar *resin* is not the same as Dammar *varnish*, which is the resin mixed with turpentine.
- The addition of Dammar resin to encaustic paint raises its melting point, allows the wax to cure and harden over time, adds gloss, and prevents bloom which is a whitish haze caused by hydrocarbons in beeswax. Encaustic paint made from beeswax without resin can develop this bloom, or clouding, which can only be removed by reheating the wax, so this is why it is best to use resin in the mix or buy an encaustic medium that includes the resin already.
- Because wax is an adhesive, encaustic can be impregnated with papers, foils, strings, fabric, or found objects of almost any material. Objects can be placed in layers on top of each other, or they can be separated by layers of wax to give the effect of floating.
- Fabric can be saturated with wax and integrated with the photograph.
- The preservative quality of wax allows the use of organic materials, protected from deterioration when imbedded in the wax away from oxygen. Newspapers will not yellow, for instance.
- The melting point of beeswax is about 145°F.

- The melting temperature of R&F encaustic paint is approximately 162°F (72°C). The working temperature does not need to be much higher.
- If too high a temperature is used, the wax and pigments will be adversely affected and fumes can result. Keep the palette temperature around 200°F (93°C). The paint should be well melted and fluid. If it does get too hot (about 275°F/ 148°C), the beeswax will start smoking. Too high a sustained temperature can decompose the wax and some pigments, making them toxic.

Sources

For encaustic paints check out:
Rfpaints.com; DickBlick.com; Fineartstore.com; EvansEncaustics.com; Encausticsupplies.com. Two recommended books are *The Art of Encaustic Painting* by Joanne Mattera and *Encaustic Art: The Complete Guide to Creating Fine Art with Wax* by Lissa Rankin.

Collage and photomontage

Collage and photomontage are methods of image making that have been around for over one hundred years. Even though the terms are often used interchangeably, there are differences. Historically, collage differs from photomontage in that glue is used (the name *collage* comes from the French *coller* or "to glue"), it doesn't have to be photographic, and its construction is not necessarily hidden. Photomontage is photographic, doesn't have to be glued, and its construction is often hidden.

In practice collage is like a treasure hunt, finding beauty in cultural fragments. An indispensable modern convenience is acrylic medium which doubles as a glue and a protective coating. With that, a few magazines, and a piece of watercolor paper for support, collage is a fun and inexpensive way to make art.

Possible supports

- Untempered hardboard like Masonite
- Cardboard
- Bristol board
- 300 lb watercolor paper and watercolor board
- Poster board
- Mat board
- Archival foam core
- Stretched canvas and canvas board
- Photographs

Possible materials

- Fabric
- Purchased papers: bond, charcoal, color-coated (Color-Aid), printmaking, rice, metallic leaf, foil
- Found papers: from delicate toilet paper to roofing paper; consider all the junk mail and magazines
- Prepared papers: painted, silk-screened, drawn
- Color or black and white photocopies
- Photographs
- Rubbings
- Typefaces: from magazines, books, newspapers, Xerox, posters, bulletins, stamps, labels, calendars, flyers, ticket stubs, candy wrappers, can labels
- Organic material: sand, leaves, flower petals, twigs

Adhesives

- White glues (PVAs) like Wilhold, Elmers, Sobo, wheat paste, wallpaper paste, Yes™ glue
- Acrylic gloss medium (used as an adhesive and as the first protective coating of the support)
- Acrylic matte medium (used as an adhesive and to make the final collage non-glare)

Tools

- Brushes, small and large
- Scissors
- Xacto knife
- Plastic container for water
- Towel
- Freezer paper is handy
- Old wooden spoon to rub pieces in place
- Tapes, brayers, sponges, scrapers, and sandpapers

Five steps to collage

1. Coat the support on both sides with undiluted **gloss** medium (or gloss gel thinned 50/50 with water). Let dry.
2. Coat the support again with matte medium and let dry.
3. Arrange collage pieces and adhere them with matte medium. Wipe off excess medium. Let dry.
4. Seal the completed collage with a coat of gloss or matte medium or gel. Dry thoroughly. Put weights on top to flatten.
5. Before storing, dust the finished collage with cornstarch.

Photomontage

Photomontage, layering photographic imagery, preceded collage. Almost as soon as photography was discovered, images were layered in camera or in the darkroom. Layering has continued in full force into the 21st century with the advent of Photoshop. It is so easy to combine images in Photoshop that doing it the "old" way in camera or in the darkroom is unnecessary. However, combining bits of images by hand still has merit.

1. Cover the work area with protective paper such as freezer paper or newsprint.
2. Choose a support for the background such as watercolor paper or a photograph as a base.
3. Cut out the elements that will be added to the background, making sure to do smooth, continuous cuts with the scissors. Use an Xacto blade in smaller areas. Cut at a canted angle, slanted in toward the back of the piece, so the paper base of the photograph will not show white around the object. If dry mount tissue and a dry mount press are to be used, the elements must be affixed to the dry mount tissue before cutting.
4. Color the cut edges to match the piece or the background it will be placed on. If the background is white, don't color.
5. Apply adhesive to the pieces. If spraying little pieces, pin them down before spraying so they don't blow around.
6. Working from top to bottom, affix the pieces to the support. If using dry mount tissue, use the tack iron to tack them to the background and then dry mount the whole image when all pieces are attached correctly.

Tips and ideas

- Wax paper or the waxy side of freezer paper provides a perfect place to coat pieces with matte medium and dry.
- Encase pieces of collage in matte medium: coat one side on top of freezer paper, let dry, peel off of the freezer paper and coat the other side. Dust pieces lightly with cornstarch when dry for storage to prevent sticking together.
- Use stick pins to keep pieces in place.
- Sort and store different colors in Ziploc baggies; sort according to color, subject matter, or texture.
- 2 L-shaped pieces of mat board work great to frame the image while working out compositions.
- Heavier materials may require a mixture of acrylic modeling paste/gel medium mixed half and half.
- Yes™ glue will not wrinkle magazines or photos.
- Use matte medium for a final coat on the collage to cut down on glare.
- When done with the collage, lightly dampen the back of the support with a sponge and water, weight it overnight with books, and flatten.
- Rinse brushes continually before any acrylic hardens in the bristles.
- Coat the neck of acrylic medium jars with a bit of Vaseline to keep them from sticking.
- Text often dominates the image and structures its meaning—text trumps image in other words. Its use in collage can provide humor and irony. Add text with pencils, markers, colored pencils, inks, crayons, paints, pastels directly onto the print.
- Add magazine words pasted on with acrylic medium.
- Use words printed out on transparency and sandwiched with the image while exposing.
- Use words written on the negative directly, or scratched into the negative, or added in Photoshop to a digital negative.
- Text can be suspended above the paper while enlarging to make it less distinct.
- Try exposing a print through a personal letter.
- You can also write words on the object being photographed.

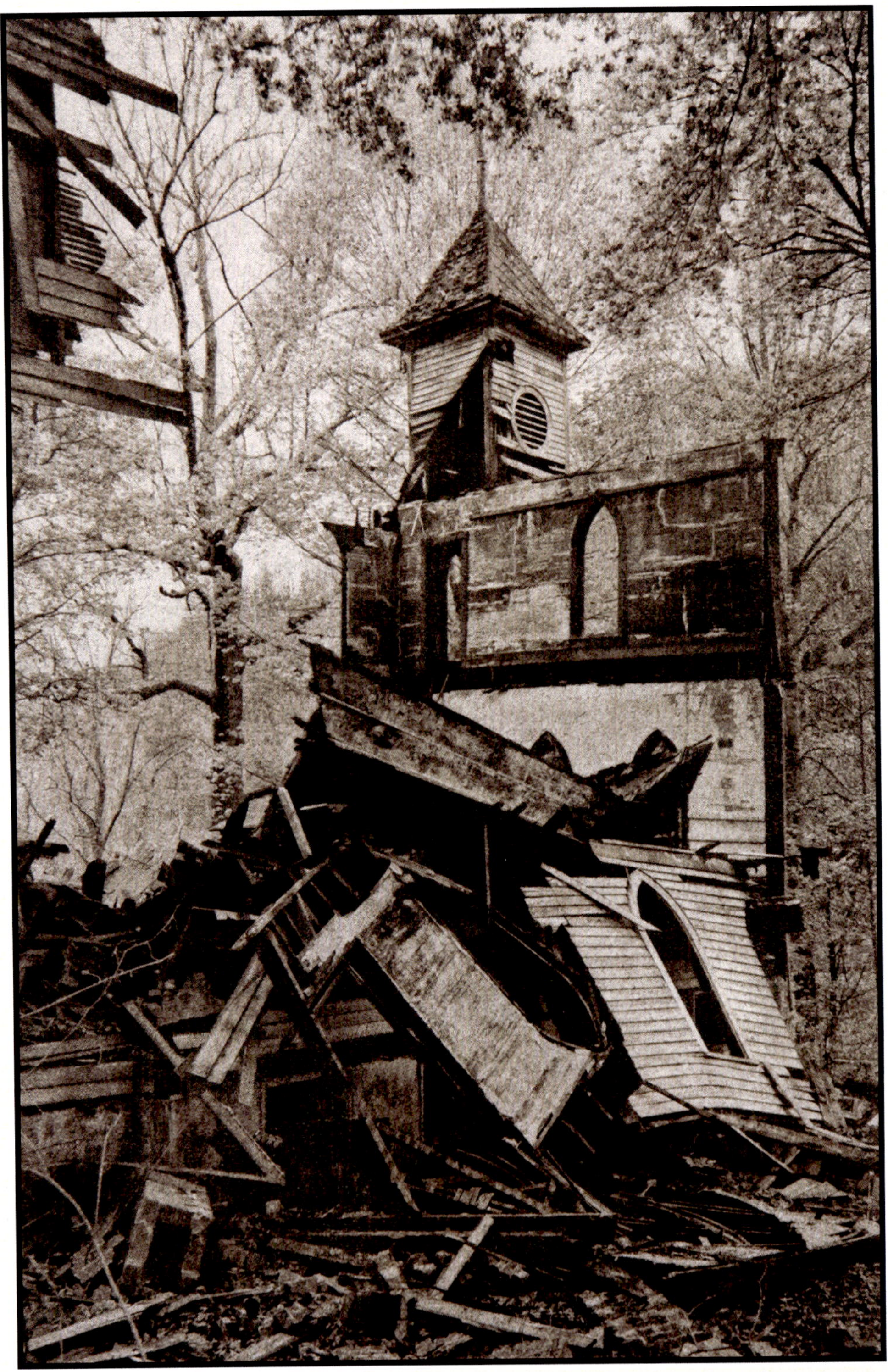

Figure 17.1. *St. John's Baptist Church, Stotesbury, West Virginia*, bromoil print, 8″ x 12″ © David W. Lewis 2010

Bromoil

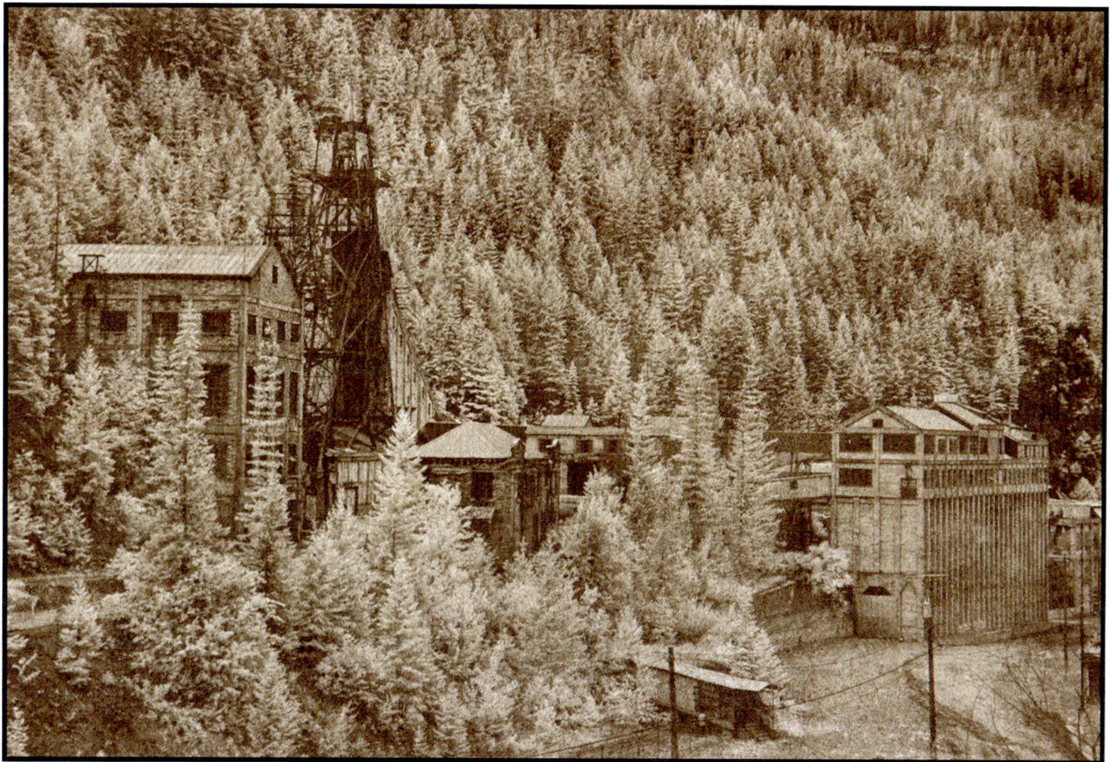

Figure 17.2. *Star Mine, Burke, Idaho*, bromoil print, 12″ x 8″ © David W. Lewis 2018. David Lewis is a master of oil, bromoil and transfer. For much of his 50+ year career his work has centered upon de-industrialization throughout North America. Lewis documented the loss of rural farming communities such as Keppel Township from the 1970s to 1980s, many long abandoned industrial sites, permanent closures of North American forestry and mining industries (coal, gold and silver mines), and current resource companies. This five-decade long journey has resulted in the preserving of an important part of culture and reflects on the humility of our society. Lewis manufactures materials required for the bromoil process including bromoil non-supercoated paper, brushes, and pigment inks. To see more of his work or purchase products, visit www.bromoil.com.

In the bromoil process a silver gelatin print is bleached away and replaced with oil-based ink. During the bleaching, the gelatin surrounding the silver grains is tanned and hardened by the chemistry, specifically potassium dichromate. It is tanned proportionately to the amount of silver present. The shadow areas of the print containing more silver are the most tanned and hardened and the highlights containing less silver are the least tanned and hardened. When it comes time to make the bromoil, the silver gelatin print is soaked first in a tray of water. The softer highlights absorb more water and swell more than the harder shadows. This results in a differential rejection of oil-based inks. The more water accepted into the print, the more an oil based ink is rejected. The less water accepted into the print, the more the ink is accepted. It stands to reason, then, that the shadows will be ink accepting, the highlights ink rejecting, and a proportionately tonal print will result.

There are two tools used to ink up the print: brush or brayer, or a combination of the two. The brush method is the traditional method that produces a softer, sometimes grainier and certainly more painterly image. The brayer produces a more photographic image with less texture, so much so that it can be hard to tell if the print is a silver gelatin print or a bromoil. The brush method takes more time and less ink. The brayer takes less time and more ink—too much if one is not careful and the print will take months to dry. Either method becomes personal preference.

With bromoil there is an infinite range of results possible. An image can be coarse or fine grained; detailed or painterly; monochrome or colorful; low contrast or high contrast; subject matter minimally altered or drastically altered; and so on and so forth. That is the fascination of bromoil—the print is not locked into one look.

Even though bromoil seems a bit daunting at first, it has many benefits, such as this one: it is possible to print and bleach a large number of prints in a darkroom session and then save them for inking up later, even years later. Some bromoilists, in fact, do all the darkroom work in a day or two and spend the rest of the year inking!

There are three good books on bromoil: *The Art of Bromoil and Transfer* by David Lewis; *Bromoil 101* by Gene Laughter for a loose method; and *Bromoil: A Foundation Course* by Derek Watkins which has good instructional images. This short chapter on bromoil is an introduction to the process. These books are important to have if wanting to progress to the next level of expertise.

An easy way to get into bromoil is to buy a bromoil bleaching kit from Bostick and Sullivan (www.bostick-sullivan.com). It is very easy to mix the three solutions and they keep indefinitely.

Two caveats: one, the process is a bit messy with its use of lithographic ink. Simple Green™ is a perfect nontoxic cleaner for brushes and the work area. Two, the process takes time to perfect. It may take a couple hours to make one print and a lifetime to be an expert. Start small— a 4″× 5″ or 5″×7″ print on 8″×10″ paper at first—for less frustration.

Paper choices

Silver gelatin papers today are surface-hardened so they don't scratch. Fixer often has hardener added to prevent print surfaces from damage during the wet processing. Both of these add up to a paper that is difficult to ink up. It is best to use non-hardened papers and non-hardening fix where possible. A bromoil paper is available from David Lewis (bromoil.com). It is not terribly expensive—at the time of this writing, around $1.25 an 8″ × 10″. Lewis' paper is about 1 stop slower than Ilford MGIV, and a fixed grade 2; keep in mind that graded papers don't respond to filters like variable contrast papers. You can also use Ilford MGIV or Ilford Warmtone matte or semi-matte.

Other supplies

- Lithography ink such as Graphic Chemicals Senefelder's Crayon Black litho ink #1803 (stiffer) or Graphic Chemicals #1796 Lithographic Black (softer)
- Palette knife
- 6″ cheap glazed ceramic tiles, 2 or more
- Brayer, 2″ hard rubber and 4″ hard rubber
- Brushes: men's old-fashioned shaving brush cut flat and on an angle like a stag foot, David Lewis' bromoil brushes available at bromoil.com or other brushes like stencil brushes, pastry brushes
- Soft, white, 4″ foam brayer with rounded edges
- Cosmetic foam wedges or 1″ flat nylon brush
- Chamois cloth (synthetic from auto supply store)
- Naphtha, lighter fluid, mineral spirits or Simple Green to clean the brush and tiles
- Bromoil bleaching kit from Bostick and Sullivan or 100 g copper sulfate, 100 g potassium bromide, and 10 g potassium dichromate
- Large piece of glass to support the print
- Distilled water
- Blotting paper
- Paper towels

Bromoil bleach formula

Mix and store these three solutions separately:
100 g copper sulfate (5 tablespoons) added to a total volume of 1000 ml distilled water
100 g potassium bromide (4½ tablespoons) added to a total volume of 1000 ml distilled water
10 g potassium dichromate (1½ teaspoons) added to a total volum of 1000 ml distilled water
At time of use mix:

- 70 ml of the copper sulfate solution
- 70 ml of the potassium bromide solution
- 30 ml of the potassium dichromate solution
- 830 ml distilled water.

One liter will bleach/tan ten 8″ × 10″s.

Making the print for bromoil

When printing for bromoil, be sure to leave at least a 1″ border around the image for ease of picking up the wet print during the inking process.

The first tricky part is to find the correct exposure for the print that gives full detail in the highlights and full detail in the shadows when light is transmitted through the print, say, on a light box. When the print is viewed by normal light, it will look dark, dull, and unacceptable. If highlights don't have detail they will swell too much with water and not accept pigment. If shadows don't have detail they will accept too much pigment and block up.

The increase in exposure needed to make a print this way is image and paper dependent but easily done with digital negatives. Just think, dark and dull and full detail everywhere. Flat. A starting point may be ½ stop more exposure (divide your standard exposure time by .7) and one contrast grade softer filter. (a 0 or 1 filter). You can use a normal digital negative and make these two adjustments with variable contrast paper.

1. Overexpose the print the decided amount of time and one contrast grade softer so that there is complete detail in the highlights and shadows even if the print looks dull.
2. Develop for the full three minutes with constant agitation, stop bath for 30 seconds, and fix in a non-hardening fixer. If the print is fixed in a hardened fixer, it has a harder surface so it will ink up too easily. However, it will still work.
3. Wash, hypoclear, wash again, and dry thoroughly as with any normal print.
4. Heat the print when it is completely dry in a dry mount press at 250°F for 2–3 minutes. This is termed *super-drying* and is said to soften the gelatin and to make inking easier. If you don't have a dry mount press, skip this step.

A bit quicker bromoil

It is possible to make the print, above, and bleach it in the bromoil bleach bath after the stop bath (without rinsing) and before fixing. In other words, expose and develop the print, then stop bath for 10 seconds and place the print directly into the bromoil bleach bath. Bleach for 10 minutes, rinse for 5, and then fix, wash, and hypoclear as per normal. This is the "short form" of bromoil and saves time. The enlarging and bleaching steps all occur together in the darkroom and then the matrix is complete. Some, even, take the wet print from the darkroom and begin the inking process immediately!

Bleaching the print

Insure temperatures of the baths do not exceed 70°F. If the initial water soak is too warm, the print will absorb too much water and the surface will reject ink. Unfortunately it will always return to this "blow out" stage when resoaked.

1. Soak the print in water for 5 minutes.
2. Mix a liter of the bleach (use distilled water; one liter of bleach will do a dozen 5″ × 7″ prints) and bleach the print for 8–20 minutes, but normally 8–10 minutes. It is fine to bleach two at once back to back with continuous agitation as long as the prints are always submerged under the bleach solution. If the print is not bleaching completely, it has been printed too dark, so expose less next time.
3. Wash the print for 5 minutes, fix for 5 minutes, wash again for 5 minutes, hypoclear for 5 minutes, run the print through a final 10-minute wash, and dry (generally just like the normal print cycle).
4. Super-dry the print once more in the dry-mount press at 250°F for 2–3 minutes to make inking easier.

Inking the print with the brush

The bleached print is now referred to as the "bromoil matrix."

1. Soak the matrix for 10 minutes in 68°–70°F water. Some papers require a longer soak, some a shorter soak. This will be found by trial and error. If a paper is soaked too much for that particular paper, the highlights will swell too much and not accept as much ink as they need to. If the paper is not soaked enough, the highlights will accept too much ink and be dull. Some papers will show a gelatin relief on the surface where the highlights swell greater than the shadows with the intake of water. Highlights will also feel more slippery and shadows more "grabby."
2. While the paper is soaking take a pea size of the ink and work it with the palette knife onto one of the tiles to soften it up a bit. Ink should remain surprisingly stiff, barely workable with a palette knife. After working the ink, use the knife to spread a thin 3″ square of ink on the tile.
3. Use the 2″ brayer and brayer a layer of the ink onto another tile. This is the paint that will be used to ink the brush or the 4″ foam brayer. The only part of the brush that is inked is the toe; the heel of the brush is never used in the inking process, and the brush is inked by lightly stippling it on the brayered ink square.
4. Remove the print to blotter paper and let it set to dry for 90 seconds, during which time use the wet chamois to gently pat away moisture. When ready to ink there should be no visible wet spots. It is easy to spot these when the print is viewed at an oblique angle. If any wet spots are visible on either the front or back, blot again with the chamois.
5. Put the print on the glass, and do what is called a "walkabout": brush ink on with a press-drag downward motion from top to bottom of the print and then from side to side. Re-ink the brush and do this again and again until the whole surface is covered with a very thin layer of ink. Turn the print 90° and do this again, and again and again until the print has been inked four times and looks like a gray square. Return to the water for a 2-minute soak.
6. Remove the print from the water, blot the back of the print with the damp, wrung-out chamois, place it on blotting paper and gently blot the face of the inked print free from all water and visible wet spots.
7. Take the non-ink-charged brush and hop the surface of the print to move the ink around a bit. The ink will be picked up from the highlights and repositioned into the shadows.
8. At this point, charge the brush with ink again, stipple the print with ink, charge and stipple/pounce until the print is completely inked, and return to the water for another 2-minute soak.
9. The inking and wetting process is carried out as many times as is needed to fully ink the print. In low humidity there will be more need to return to the water. In high humidity, the opposite will be true. Time from start to finish can be as quick as 7 minutes to as long as hours for a large print. The walkabout that is first done is done only once; the hopping and stippling is done together and in that order every time the print is removed from the water, dried and inked up again. Hopping should only take about 45 seconds. Stippling will take longer.
10. The very last step is to take a cosmetic wedge or a small, flat ½″ or 1″ nylon bristle brush and gently, under water, remove all pigment from the white borders of the print. Then hang the print to dry. The print will dry in several hours but the ink will still be wet perhaps for several weeks, so allow the bromoil time to dry before dry mount pressing and matting. With the brayer process or when using more ink on the print than necessary, the print can take months to dry. I found this out the hard way with my first ever brayered prints.
11. Clean all tools and tiles with cleaner of choice.

Inking the print with the brayer

1. Ink the 4″ foam brayer lightly, and ink the print in one direction with the brayer, rotate the print, inking again, and rotate twice more so the print has been fully inked in all four directions. If the print dries out, resoak it and blot it as above.

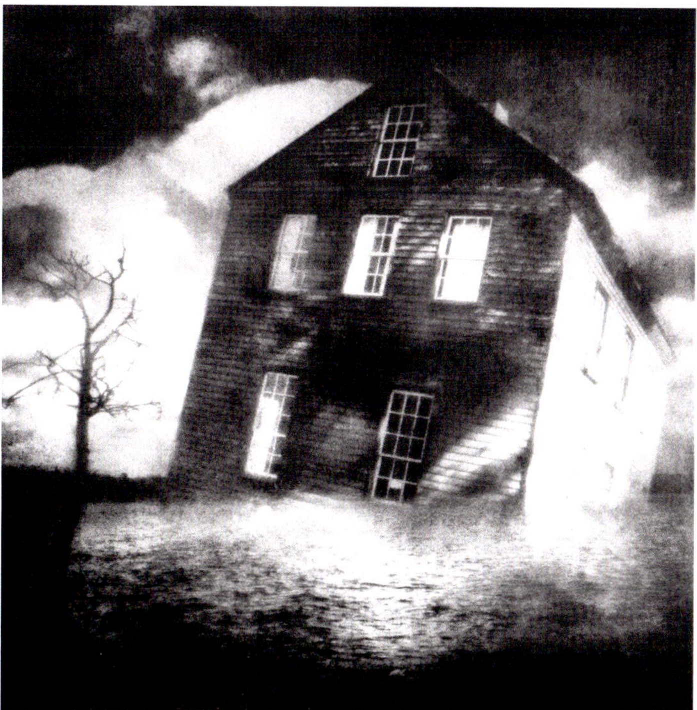

Figure 17.3. *Ocean of Baseness*, from the *Hereafter* series, bromoil print, 10″ x 10″ © Rebecca Sexton Larson 2014

2. Clean off the brayer on a bare tile, and brayer with a non-charged brayer to remove excess ink from the print. Then ink again with a charged brayer.
3. With a brayer that is not loaded with ink, pigment is removed when brayering and contrast is increased. With a brayer that is inked, pigment is placed and contrast is decreased.
4. If brayer marks develop they can be brushed/pounced/hopped out with a brush.
5. Repeat this process of brayering, soaking, and blotting, until the print looks complete.
6. Clean up the edges of the print carefully with a damp cosmetic wedge or a flat 1″ synthetic nylon brush.
7. Clean all tools and tiles with cleaner of choice.
8. Let the print dry in a dust-free environment for several days to several weeks for a correctly inked bromoil print. If too much ink has been deposited, it will take far longer than this.

Oleobrome

The oleobrome process is a variation of bromoil, invented by F. J. Shepherd and F.F. Renwick. A soft rubber roller and a hard gelatin coated photographic paper is used. The bleached and dried print is inked up while it is *dry*, with a roller, leaving an overall grey ink deposit on the paper. Then it is put in a water bath tray with a flat bottom (or a piece of glass on the bottom of the tray) and a soft foam roller is used to gently "develop" the print under water by rolling it back and forth on the surface of the submerged print. The ink will adhere in the swelled, shadow areas of the print better than the unswelled highlight areas as per above. If it is not dark enough, ink again out of the water and redo the rolling process in the water until enough density is built up. The print can also be initially inked up and left to dry a couple days and then soaked and rollered.

Bromotype

Instead of bleaching and fixing to make the bromoil matrix, the print is bleached and then returned to the developer to develop to completion. The print is then fixed, washed, hypocleared, washed, and dried as per normal, and then soaked and inked as if it were a normal bromoil matrix, except this time the image is completely visible. The added ink reinforces the image, but can also be used to introduce a completely different color to the image.[1]

Troubleshooting bromoil

- If the print is not looking good, resoak, clean off all ink under water, and start over.
- If there is no deposit of pigment during the first stage of the walk about, the ink is too hard, so soften it with a slight drop of linseed oil.
- If the print is accepting ink too readily, the ink

may be too soft so stiffen it with some magnesium carbonate powder or powdered pigment such as a warm brown to warm up the black.
- White spots all over the print surface are from water that rises to the surface of the print during the pouncing or hopping of the brush and/or a brush that has gotten wet. Return the print to the water tray and give it a good soak and try again, after having towel-dried the brush or switched to a dry one.
- A blotchy bromoil print is caused by too much ink or too much pressure.
- If the water dripping from a print streaks it, the water temperature is too high or the ink too soft.

Tips and ideas

- Williams Sonoma sells a round pastry brush that with a little trimming to get it flat-bottomed, works great.
- Home Depot sells a Ralph Lauren fitch brush in the faux finish section which is great for hopping, according to bromoil expert Jill Skupin Burkholder.
- Dick Blick sells Escoda natural bristle brushes that are also cheap (dickblick.com).
- The traditional bromoil brush is one that is cut like an angled hoof. The full bottom of the brush bristles is never used for inking, just the toe.
- To trim a brush, soak the brush in a solution of bone glue in warm water several times to build up a coating. Let dry until hard. Trim the brush shape with something like a mini circular saw on a Dremel tool. Once the brush is shaped to one's liking, it can be soaked in warm water to dissolve the bone glue and return the brush to softness. This is an old Dutch technique.
- Simple Green diluted with water is a great brush cleaner; use and no need to rinse.
- Ink and hop with the toe of the brush and do not pound away on the matrix; re-soak frequently as the matrix dries out quickly unless there is very high humidity.
- Use continuous agitation in all baths.
- When bleaching a set of prints, put the first print in the bleach face down, the second face up, and so on until 8 are in the bleach bath at once. Then interleave continually.
- The soaking temperature and time of immersion in the water bath varies, depending on the degree of hardness of your water, but a temperature of 68°F for 10 minutes is an excellent starting point.
- If the print does not look like what is envisioned, don't toss it. Keep working with it and it may become something completely unique.
- If there is no non-hardening fix available, buy some sodium thiosulfate crystals and mix up a 10% solution for fix. 2 liters of this divided into 2 trays will fix ten 8″ × 10″ prints.
- Brighten up a print with a damp cotton ball under water as a final step before drying.
- Believe it or not, a dried bromoil print can be inked again. Re-soak the print and ink as per normal. If one wants to vignette the print, for instance, it is easy to pounce ink around the edges.
- Prints can be spotted with the same ink color, thinned with a touch of naphtha, mineral spirits, or lighter fluid. Moisten the brush with the naphtha and then dab it in the ink and then the ink to the print.
- Prints can be retouched to remove ink with a hard pencil eraser or the tapered rubber end of a clay shaper tool (tip from Derek Watkins).
- Gene Laughter was known to use steel wool judiciously to remove pigment and add texture!
- Bromoils can be hand colored, once dry, with oils, pastels, or other coloring agents.
- Lewis has a great technique for printing a clean-edged border when making a print from a digital negative: he selects the image, then chooses Edit/Stroke/10/Inside/Opacity 100% and foreground color set to black. It creates a nice clean very minute border of black around the image which will accept ink readily and contrast with the borders of the bromoil print that remain white.

Endnotes

1. Watkins, Derek. *Bromoil: A Foundation Course*. Lewes, East Sussex: Photographers' Institute, 2006, p. 153.

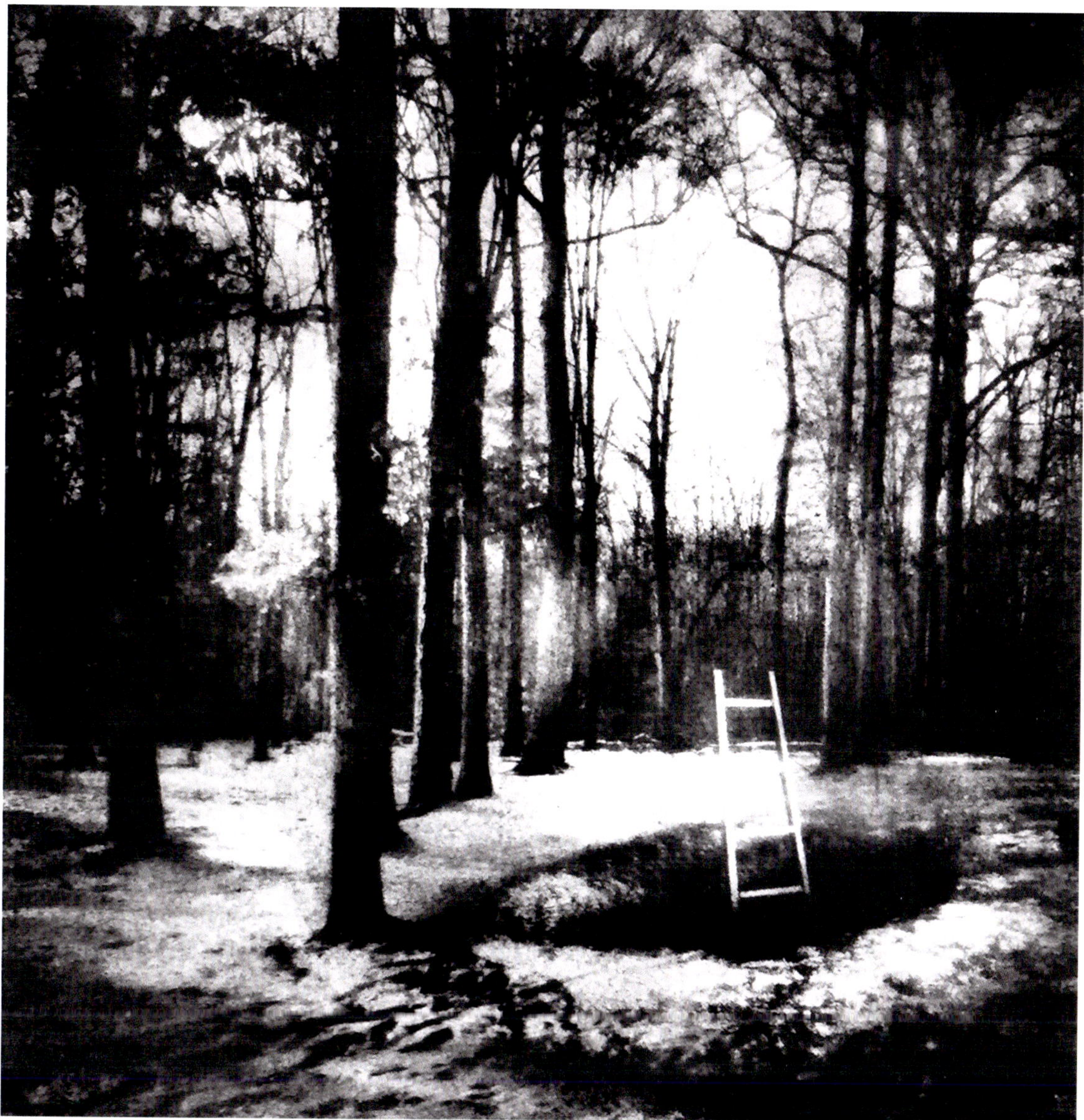

Figure 17.4. *Curiouser and Curiouser*, from the *Hereafter* series, bromoil print, 10″ x 10″ © Rebecca Sexton Larson 2014. "*Hereafter* echoes the contemplation of the impermanence of life. Frequently dark and isolated, the photographs draw the viewer into reinvented landscapes reflective of an implied narrative. The objective is not to directly document physical surroundings but to imagine environments we have yet to understand or see. The deep contrasting tones of the works illicit a darkly romantic and somber mood mirroring the passage of time, environmental space, and mortality." Rebecca Sexton Larson is a Tampa based studio artist working with photographic processes. Sexton Larson has been awarded three Florida Individual Artist Fellowships (1998, 2002, and 2008). In 2006, she received an Artist Enhancement Grant from the State of Florida and, in 2005, was commissioned by the City of Tampa as its Photographer Laureate. As Photo Laureate, she documented from her perspective the visual poetry of Tampa using a pinhole camera combined with one-of-a-kind hand-painted black and white photographs. Sexton Larson's photographs are in numerous significant collections throughout the country, including Polaroid; Progressive Corporate Art; Graham Nash (Crosby, Stills, Nash & Young); Museum of Fine Arts (St. Petersburg); the Tampa Museum of Art (Tampa); and Historical Museum (Santa Fe). To see more of her work visit sextonlarson.com.

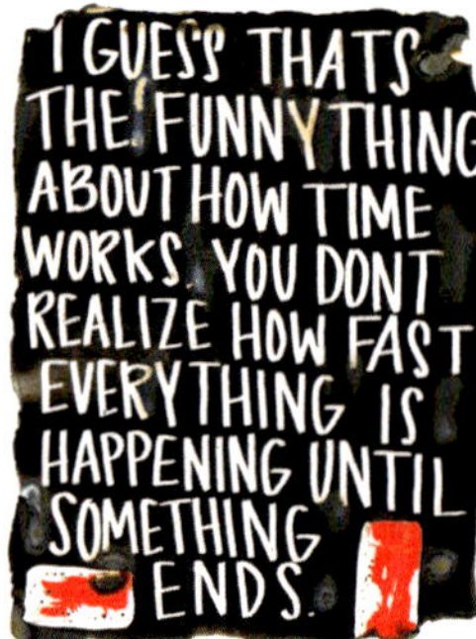

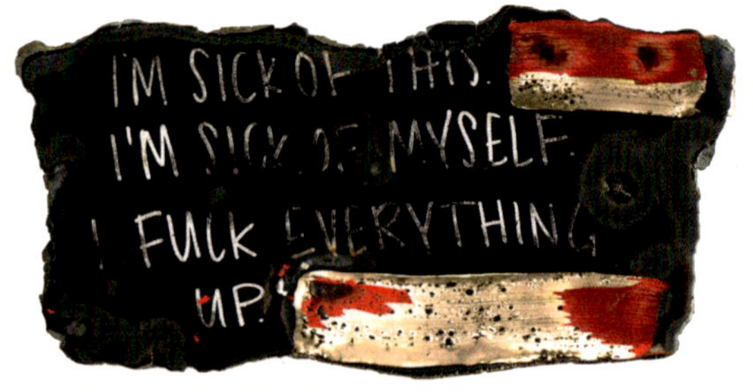

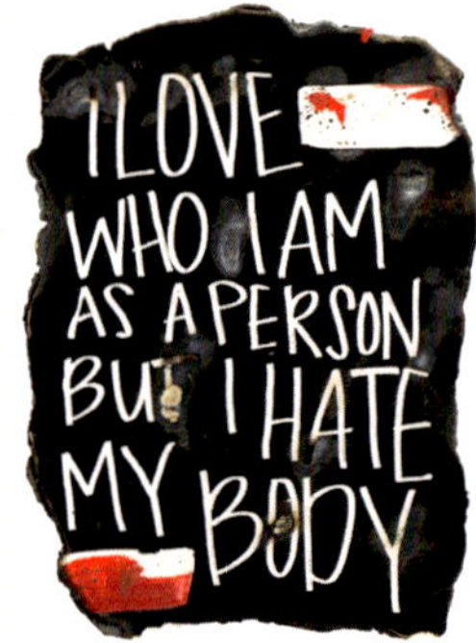

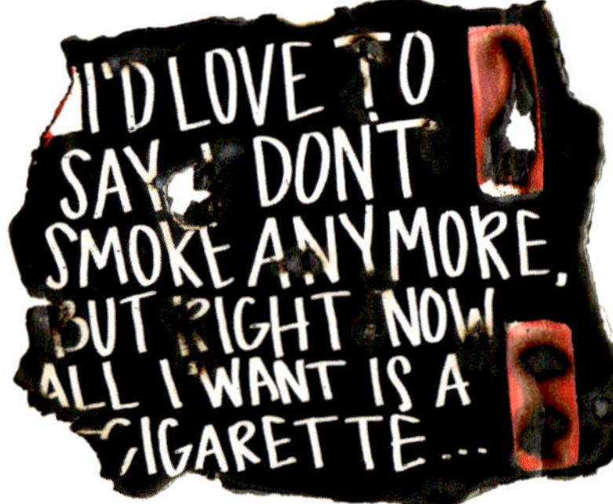

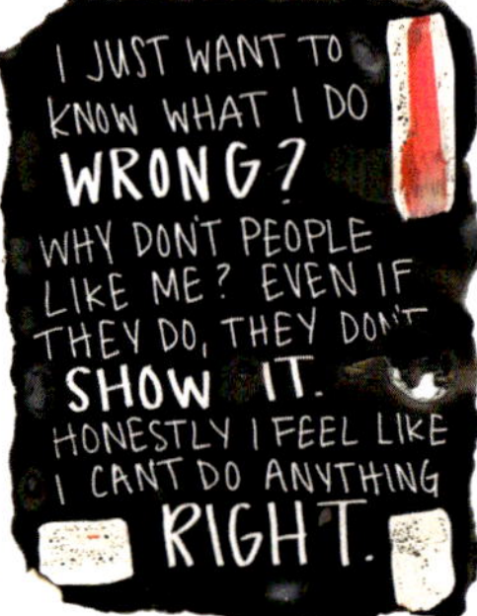

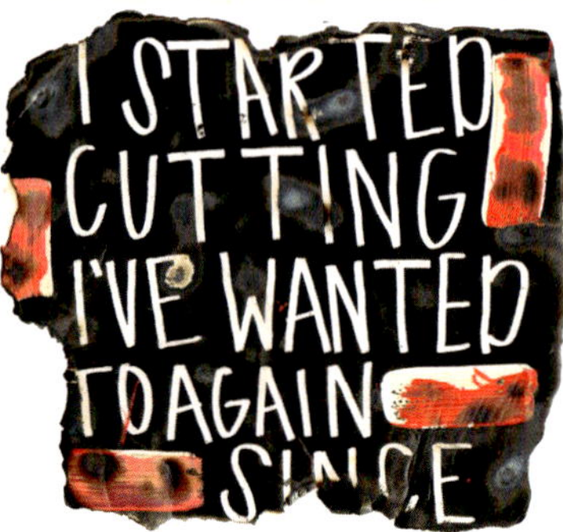

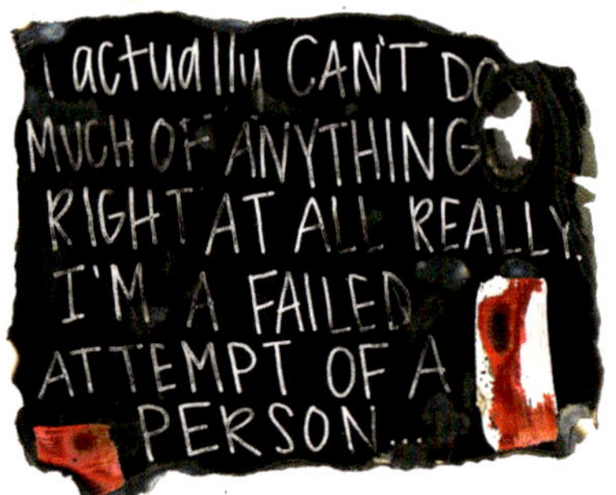

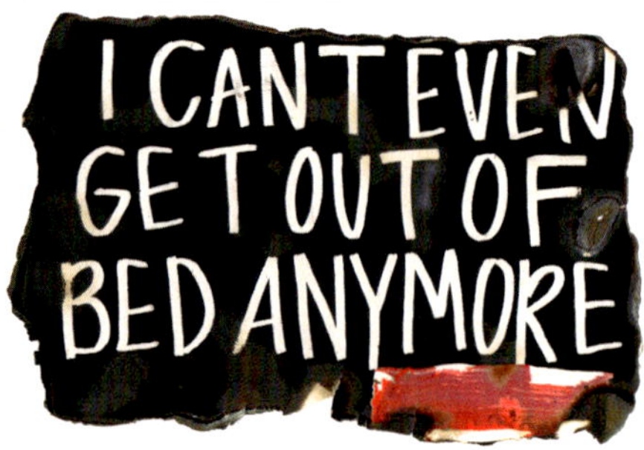

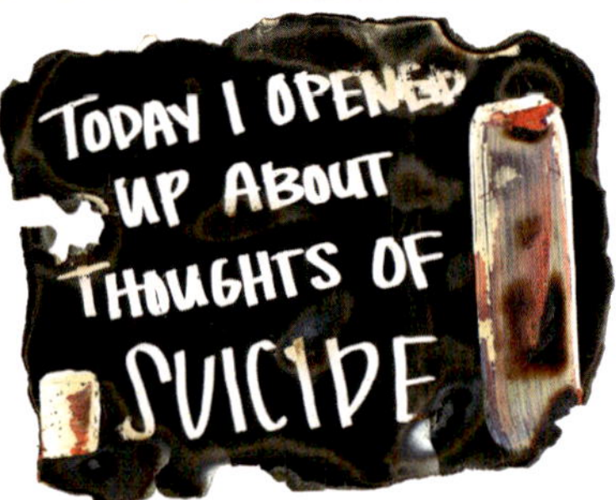

Figures P5.1–P5.10. *Burnt Out*, hand colored chemigrams © Maisy Hoffman 2021. "The concept of a photograph has always seemed very straightforward, but when introduced to chemigrams my idea of what is a photograph changed. A photograph can be anything that captures a specific moment in time, and these specific moments in time were initially captured in my high school journal. With red paint as a hard resist, and lighting the edges of the photograph on fire with a torch, I was able to use the chemigram process as part of my therapeutic journey." Maisy Hoffman is an alumna of the School of Film and Photography at Montana State University. Hoffman uses personal experience in her work to talk about complex and sensitive topics dealing with the realistic portrayal of life and emotions.

PART FIVE

Contemporary Experimental Artists

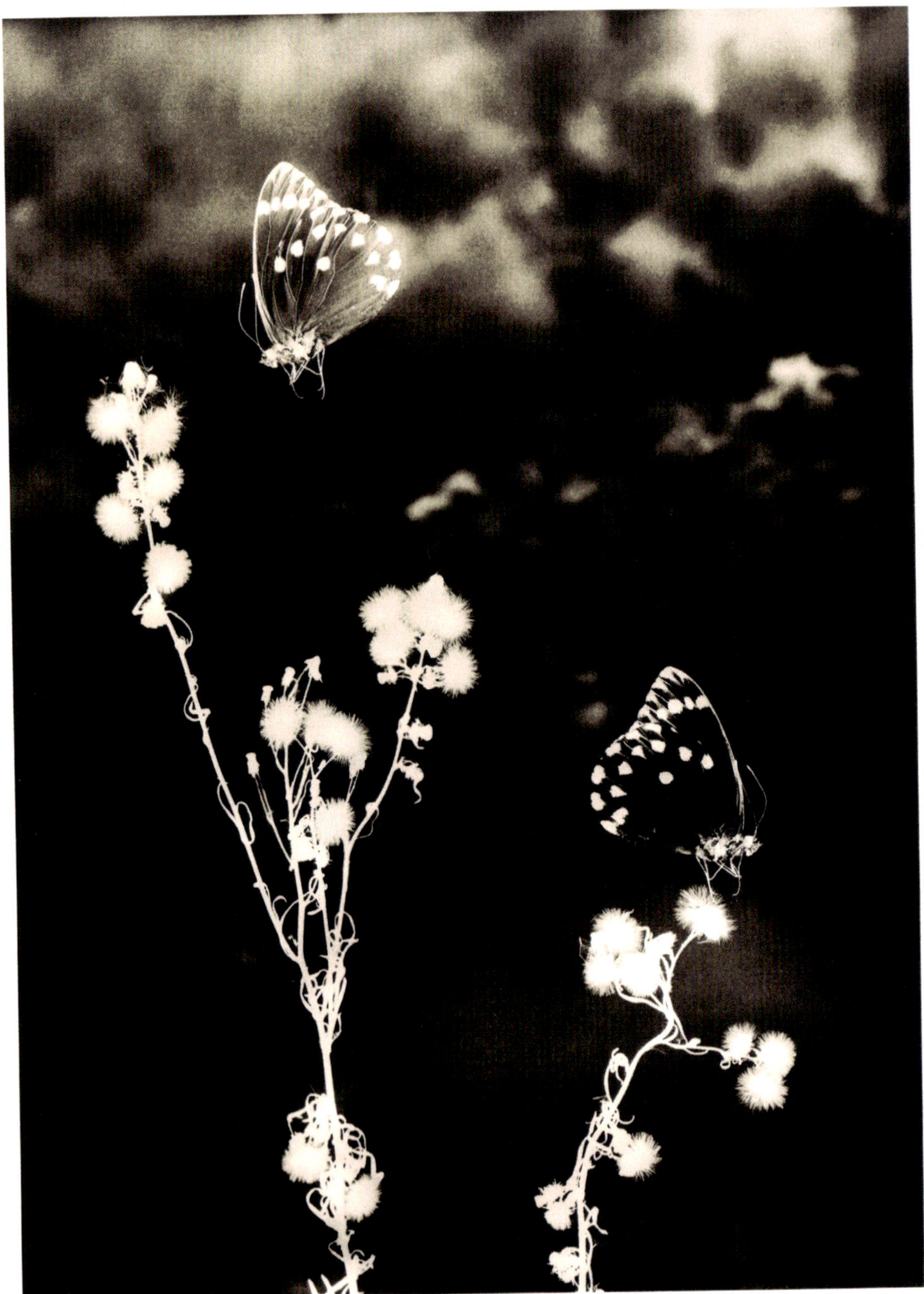

Figure 18.1. #6, lith print, 12″ x 16″ © C. Reid/Bianco Negro. Chris Reid came to Australia from Belfast, Northern Ireland in 1994. His darkroom experience began in the Netherlands in 1989 and he has been in the dark ever since. Reid has been running Blanco Negro since January 2000 and recently relocated to an off grid darkoom in the Lower Hunter Valley four years ago. His main occupation has been specializing in all aspects of silver gelatin fine art exhibition printing. From lith printing to the liquid emulsion process his skills also emcompass toning techniques as well as teaching these processes. Blanco Negro works for most of Australia insitutions as well as many fine art photographers, both local and international. His Devere digital enlarger also allows the printing from digital files onto traditional silver gelatin papers. Reid continues to expand his knowledge in historical photographic processes and by taking on commissions that challenge his skill sets.

Chapter 18

Contemporary Experimental Artists

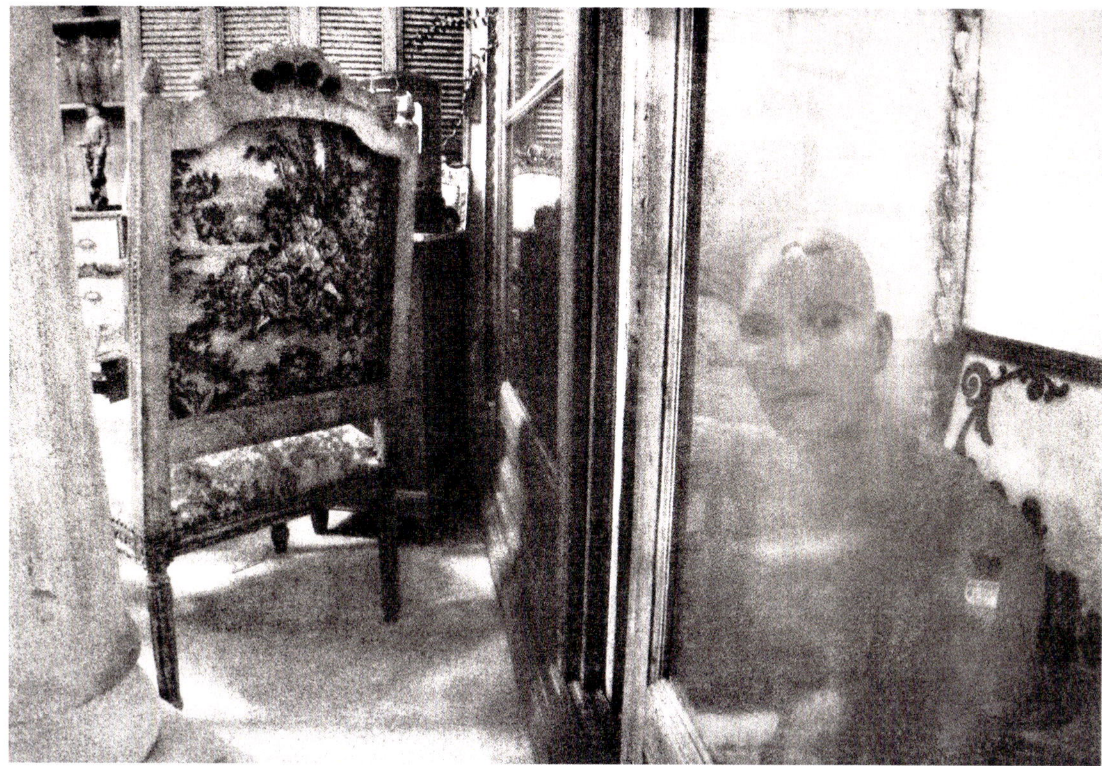

Figure 18.2. *Man in Glass*, from the *Circus of Memories* series, bromoil print, 9″ X 6″ © Jill Skupin Burkholder 2004. Jill Skupin Burkholder is a photographer/artist whose work includes handcrafted techniques such as bromoil and encaustic. She began working with photography in 1985 and studied both traditional and digital photography, experimenting with various alternative photography techniques. Recent work includes the series, *Hidden Worlds*, ethereal photographs of animals taken using a motion-activated trail camera. She teaches workshops across the country and in her home in the Catskill Mountains of New York. Her prints are included in private and public collections. To see more of her work visit www.JillSkupin.com.

Each artist who appears in this chapter was sent a questionnaire asking about the hows and whys of their process of choice. When editing their questionnaire I intervened minimally in their words to preserve their characteristic voice and syntax. Artists are presented here democratically, in alphabetical order, in 2-, 4-, or 6-page spreads, length dependent on how much they wrote and how many images they submitted.

I resisted the temptation to highlight all the tips and ideas in these pages; suffice it to say there are many!

I thank these artists for taking time out of their lives to share their passion, as I know it is yet one more commitment in their already busy lives, and with no remuneration besides the pleasure of seeing their creative talents come to fruition in print. There were many more artists that I would have liked include in this book, but the page count was limited and the subject matter in the how-to portion of the book is very broad.

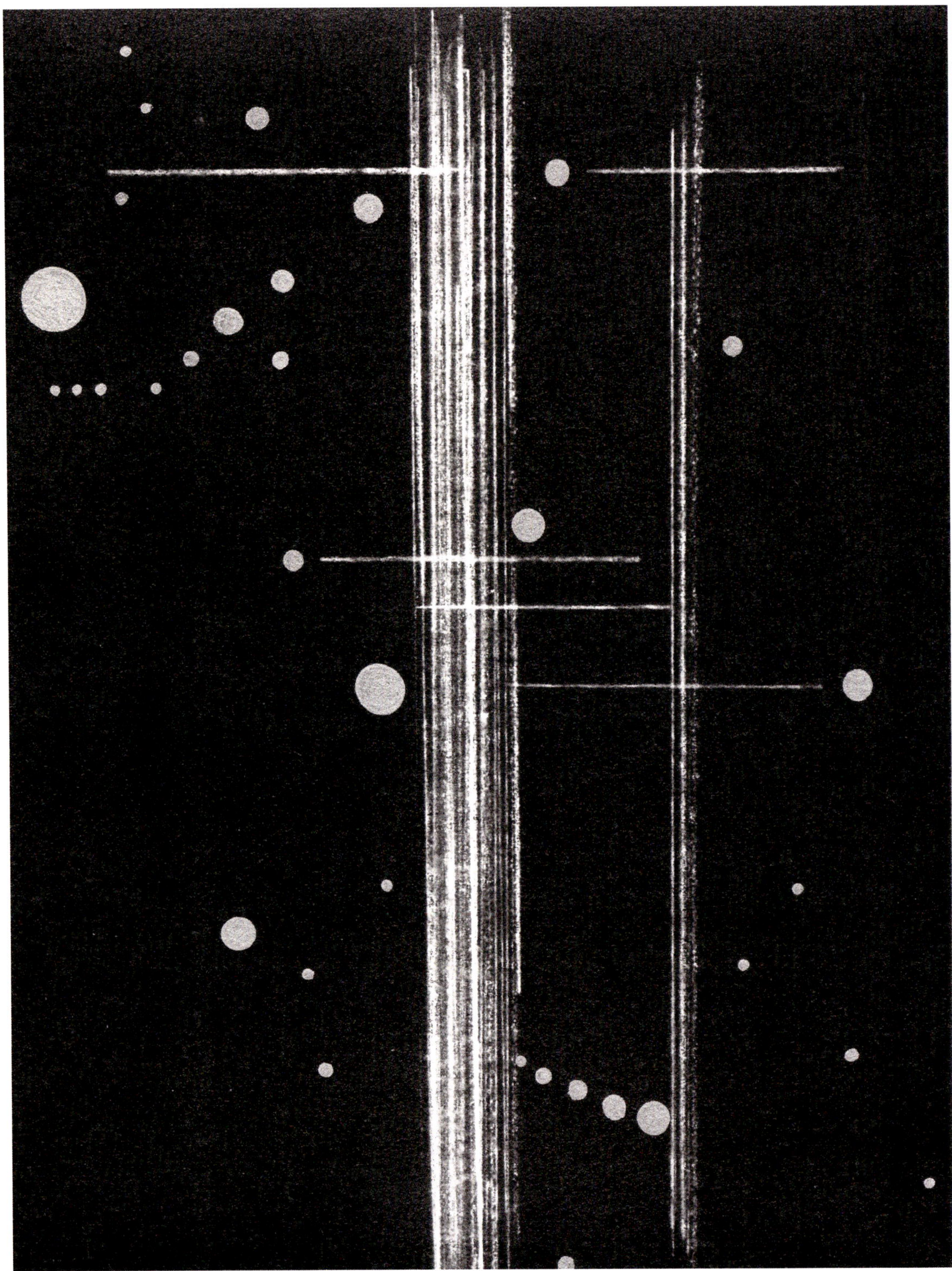

Figure 18.3. *Geometry 136*, unique oxidized gelatin silver cliché-verre print with ink, 8″ x 10″© Patricia A. Bender 2018

Patricia A. Bender

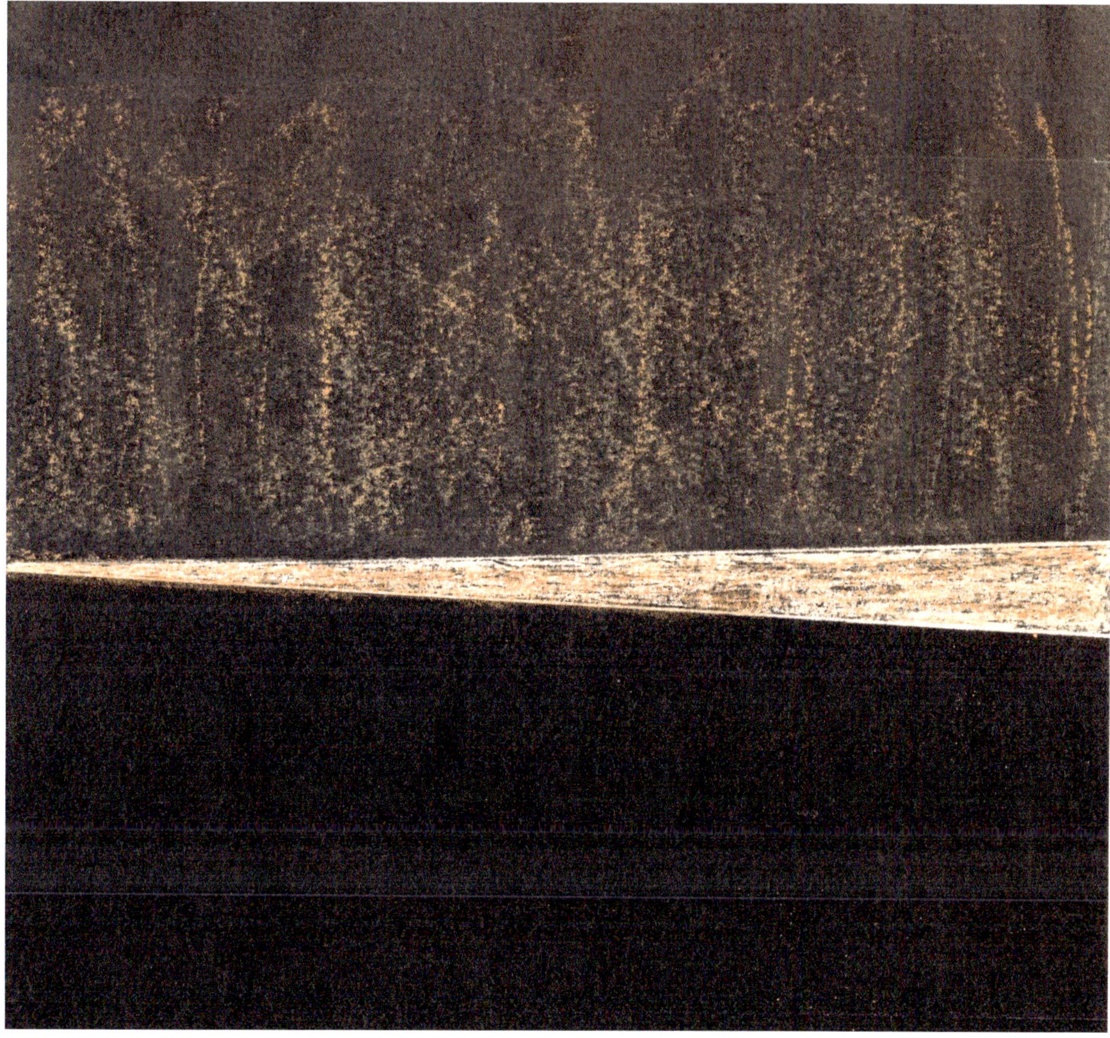

Figure 18.4. *Geometry 218*, unique oxidized gelatin silver photogram with colored pencil and pastel, 9″ x 8″© Patricia A. Bender 2018

Creative process

I am strictly an analog photographer, both film and paper. For the past several years I have been experimenting extensively with new ways to work with silver gelatin paper. It began when I decided to use silver gelatin paper as my negative in an 8″ × 10″ view camera in order to teach myself how to use the camera without going bankrupt buying 8″ × 10″ film. I discovered that I loved the look of paper negatives and the way that the texture of the paper can become an interesting and beautiful part of the image. I then began to experiment with

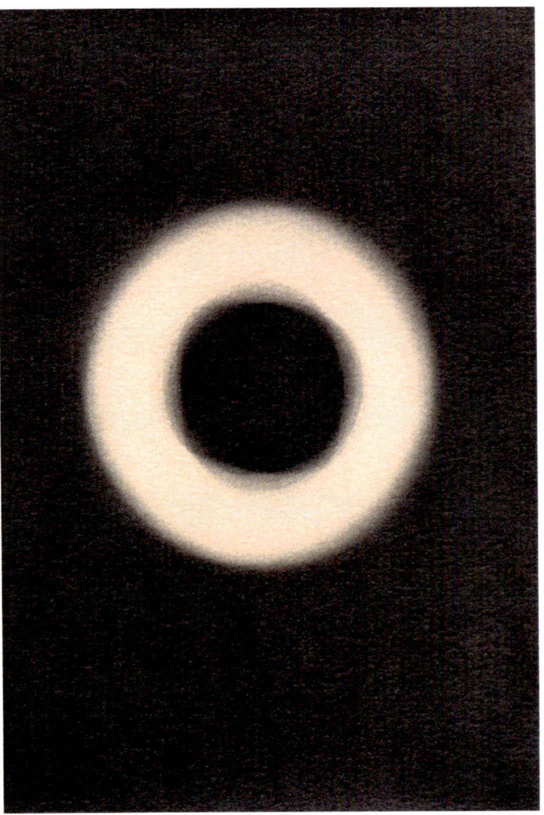

Figure 18.5. *Enso*, unique oxidized gelatin silver photogram created by spinning glass, 4″ x 6″© Patricia A. Bender 2017

using papers of all types, shapes and sizes to create photograms. I have stacked, folded, torn, rolled and mangled papers, burned papers, and then placed them on top of the gelatin silver paper for exposure, sometimes with glass on top, sometimes not. I have also experimented with moving the papers during exposure to see what kind of layering and depth this movement can create.

My experiments with photograms next led me to try drawing on paper and then using that drawing as a negative in the darkroom. Again, I use many different types of papers and drawing media to create the drawings for my negatives. Each paper and each tool for drawing—pencil, pen, charcoal, etc.—has its own unique look. While I initially thought of these images as photograms too, I later learned they are more accurately considered to be cliché verre prints.

Lately, I have begun to experiment with sewing, painting, folding and drawing on the gelatin silver print itself. As you can tell, each experiment has opened the door to a new one. Who knows where this will lead next.

In all these experiments and iterations, I generally oxidize my final print, as I like the look of age this lends to the image. To oxidize a print, you expose your image and place it in the developer as normal. Once it has developed, you take the print out into the light. This exposure to light, either natural or artificial, will gradually change the highlights from white to a peachy orange to brown and finally to a deep purple. The blacks will continue to darken a bit as well. You then return to the darkroom and stop and fix the print as normal. The fix will lighten the overall effect of the oxidization.

Oxidization is a process you have to play with over time in order to learn how to achieve the effect you are looking for, as the gelatin silver paper you use, the strength and type of light you expose the print to, and the length of time you leave your print in the light will determine the final results.

My go-to papers are Ilford Warmtone semimatte and Ilford Art 300, both multigrade fiber papers. I particularly love the tones and texture of the Art 300 paper. When I first began darkroom photography nearly twenty years ago, there was a plethora of interesting papers to choose from. With the advent of digital, those papers rapidly disappeared from the market. As a result, I collect, horde and use sparingly any and all old photo papers I can get my hands on. Because I only create unique work, I am happy to use expired papers just to discover what might happen. If the paper doesn't work because it is too old or because it has been previously exposed to light, so be it.

I primarily use Ilford and LPD paper developers, though I'm happy to experiment with other developers that may come my way. I also experiment with various dilutions, and with reusing spent developer that I juice up with new. I like to experiment with staining my prints with natural liquids like coffee, fruit juices, tea or wine. One day I'll give Kool-Aid a try.

Photograms: I want to see what everything looks like as a photogram, so I collect objects, papers, plants, you name it, bring them back to my darkroom, place them on top of gelatin silver paper in various arrangements, expose them to light and see what emerges in the developer bath. I have a kind of mad scientist approach to photograms, constantly trying new things and experimenting to see what will happen. I float things in water under the enlarger. I spin objects during exposure. I get the gelatin silver paper wet before placing objects on it and exposing it to light. Anything goes in my darkroom because you never know where it will lead you.

Cliché verre: I make a drawing using any combination of paper and drawing media to serve as my negative in the darkroom. The drawing is placed on top of the gelatin silver paper and exposed to light to produce a contact print of the drawing. It is then processed as you would any black and white print. I sometimes use different filters and diffusion screens while exposing the print to achieve certain effects, and I have experimented with layering drawings to create "double exposures." I also combine the cliché verre paper negative with photogram objects to create a hybrid image of both. Again, I am willing to try just about anything to see what will happen.

Creative practice

I think one of the most important discoveries I have made while creating this work is to give myself permission to go wild in the darkroom. Nothing is off limits or too crazy to try. When you first learn the photographic process you are overwhelmed by the rules. Develop your film this amount of time. Invert the development tank so often. Make sure the water temperature is exactly so many degrees. Develop your print for this many seconds. These are things you must learn and master. But once you have done so, it is important not to let these rules hold you back from trying new things. Maybe that expired paper developer you were going to throw away has some oomph left in it, and will result in something strange and interesting if you just give it a try. Perhaps that old, moldy gelatin silver paper you stumbled upon at a flea market will produce an interesting image (it can!). What will happen if you place crumpled wax paper on top of gelatin silver paper during exposure? I have found that the mad scientist approach works well for me, always leading me down new and interesting paths of discovery and creativity.

I have found that many of the "problems" I've encountered are not really problems, they are actually road maps to a new discovery. For example, when I first began creating cliché verre prints I discovered that using a graphite pencil to draw negatives resulted in rather blurry, diffuse lines when the drawings were contact printed onto gelatin silver paper. I was not happy with this look, so I began to go over the graphite lines in my drawings with ink pens. This resulted in photographic prints with crisp lines that had a kind of halo effect around them. I loved this look.

Through an ongoing process of experimentation, I have learned how to combine many types of drawing media with different papers to achieve the look I want in my final cliché verre print. If you embrace your "mistakes" and try to work with them rather than against them, it frequently leads you in unanticipated directions with interesting and exciting results. The trick is not to get discouraged.

When I first began to experiment with drawing on my gelatin silver prints I quickly learned that the plastic like coating on the print causes many inks to smear and some graphite not to adhere. To overcome this problem, I experimented with sanding areas of the print before drawing on it. I also tried embossing and debossing the print and then drawing on the raised or lowered lines. I experimented with many pencils, pens, inks and paints and discovered some actually worked. I love this process of experimentation and discovery. It's one of the things that keeps me coming back for more, day in and day out.

Curiosity, a willingness to embrace chance and serendipity, and an openness to experimentation are the critical elements in my creative practice because they allow me to lose myself in my work and be surprised by what I create.

I am a strong proponent of mastering your craft. Once you have done so, the real fun begins. You can test the limits of what you've learned, break all the rules you've been taught and set out on your own unique path of artistic expression. Along the way, drink up all the art you can see, read, hear and experience. Some of it will leave you cold, but much of it will inspire you to think in new ways and try new things.

I keep a journal/sketchbook with me at all times for recording ideas, quotes, sketches, the names of artists that inspire me, the titles of books I want to read, and, in this day and age, links to the Instagram pages of artists, galleries and museums. A journal allows me to create something new every day, because I believe a daily practice, no matter how small or inconsequential an entry may be, is critical to artistic growth.

Artist statement

From the first day I began to make photographs seriously, I was drawn to creating abstract images. Using black and white film, I initially photographed in the manner of Aaron Siskind and Harry Callahan, seeking the abstract in reality: weather-worn rocks, torn bits of paper stapled to telephone poles, bare twigs breaching deep snow.

In the past several years I became restless; no longer content hunting abstracts in the real world, I wanted to create them myself. Drawing and cliché verre prints, where my drawings serve as the negative in the darkroom, seemed the perfect fit for this pursuit. I could experiment with lines on paper and light in the darkroom to construct my own abstractions. To paraphrase the artist Dorothea Rockburne, I wanted to create images that were of themselves and not about something else.

The mysterious ability of abstraction to move the human heart and mind has always fascinated me. When I photograph a beautiful tree I understand why people respond. It's a beautiful tree. When I create an image of a simple circle bisected by a line I have no understanding why it moves me or others, but it can. I love the cryptic nature of the conversation between abstract art and emotion.

In the work presented here, I explore geometric abstraction. The process is completely intuitive. I add and subtract objects, shapes and layers until somehow it feels complete. A simple circle can spawn endless images. Seems I'll be at this for some time to come.

Biography

Patricia A. Bender is a photo-based visual artist living and working in New Jersey and Michigan. She began studying photography in the early 2000s, and was hooked from the moment she shot and developed her first image. She works exclusively in the darkroom with black and white media, and personally creates each image from the moment it is conceived through the finished gelatin silver print. She has recently added drawing to her artistic practice, and often uses her drawings as paper negatives in the darkroom to create unique cliché verre prints. Bender has exhibited in solo and group exhibitions throughout the United States and internationally. She is an artist on the curated White Columns artist registry, and is the recipient of numerous awards for her work, including being named to the 2018 Critical Mass Top 50 and as a 2020 Critical Mass Finalist. Bender's work has been published in *Harper's Magazine*, *The Hand Magazine*, *Lenscratch*, *The O/D Review* and *Analog Forever Magazine*, among others, and is held in the permanent collection of the Philadelphia Museum of Art and Michigan State University, as well as many other public, corporate, and private collections. To see her work, visit www.patriciaAbender.com.

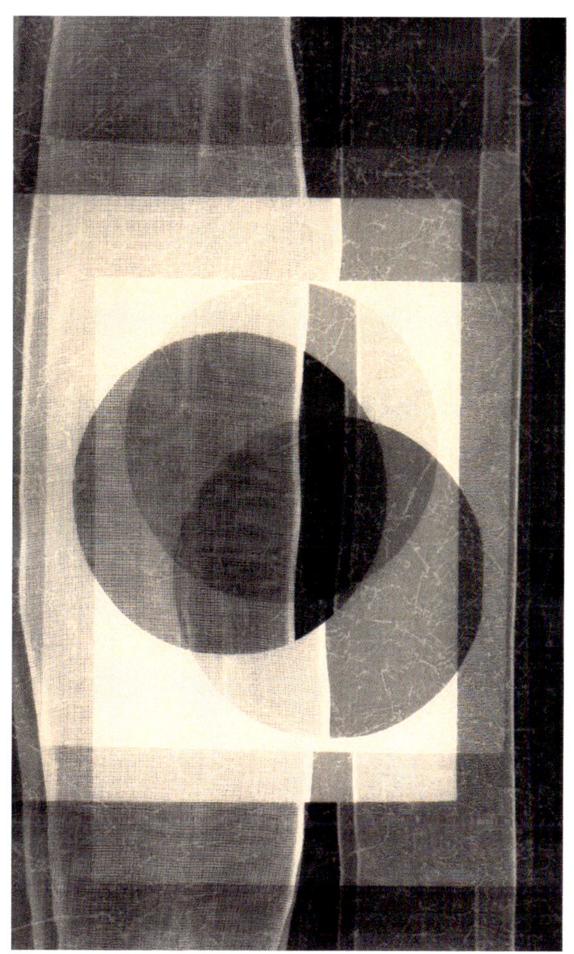

Figure 18.6. *Untitled 131*, unique oxidized gelatin silver photogram created with paper and ribbon, 4″ x 6″© Patricia A. Bender 2017

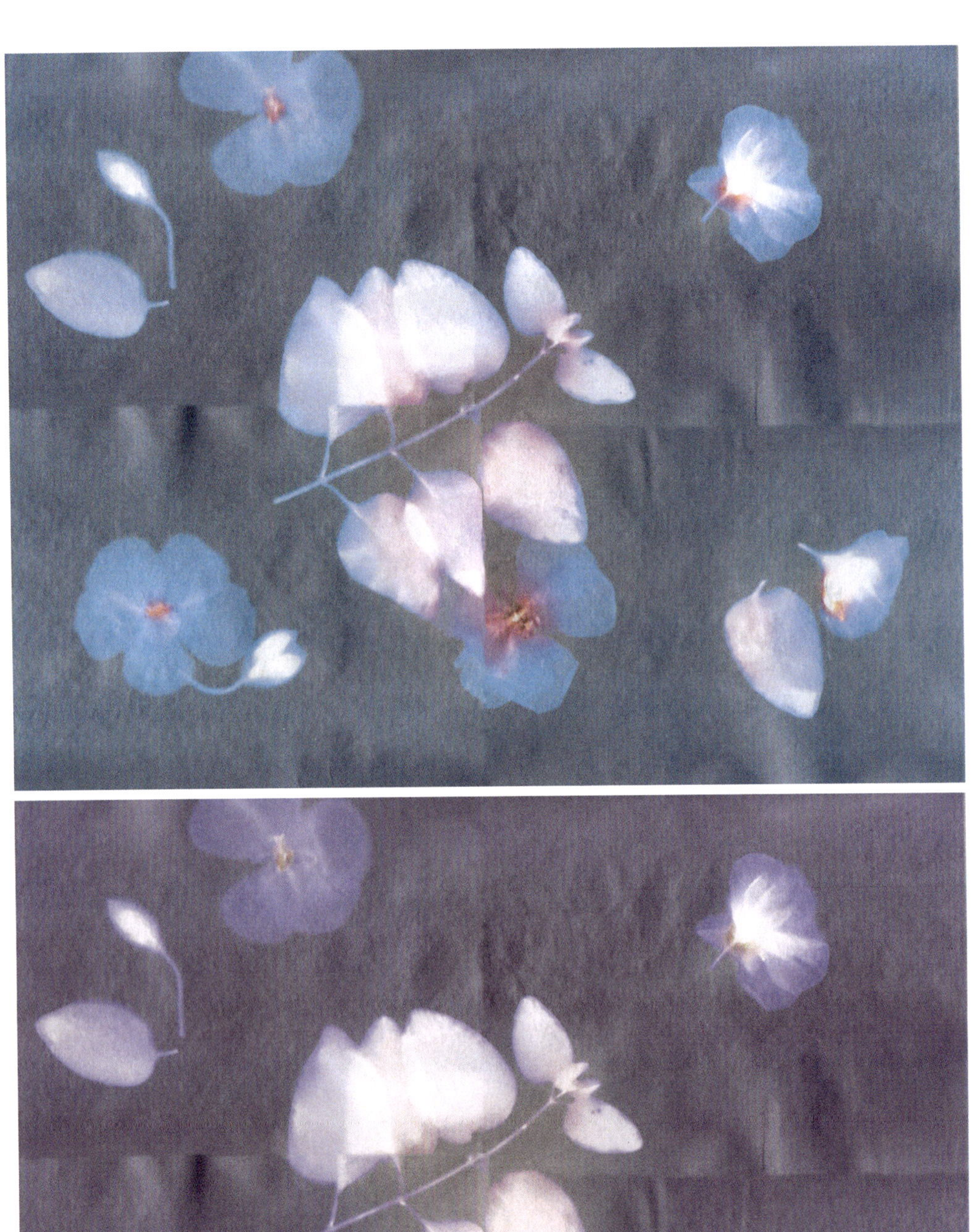

Figures 18.7–18.8. *Japonica Collage I* and *Japonica Collage II*, lumen on film washi, 10″ x 8″ © Annemarie Borg 2021

Annemarie Borg

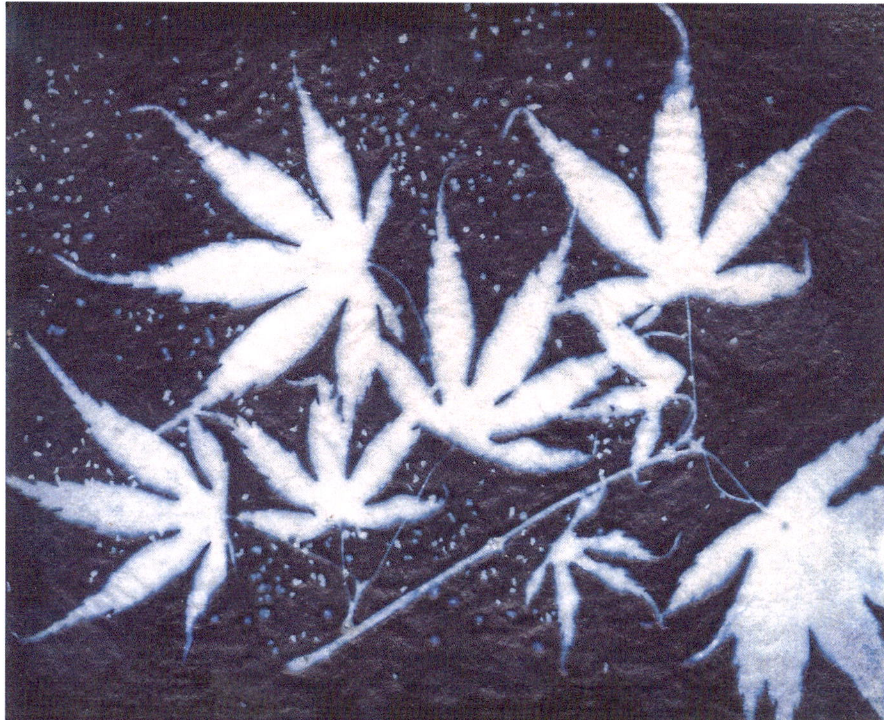

Figure 18.9. *Blues in the Night*, cyanolumen on film washi, 5″ x 4″ © Annemarie Borg 2021

Creative practice

I am French Swedish based in the United Kingdom. I studied business law and maritime law in Paris, opera and psychology in London. I am a composer, performance coach, visual artist and ocean preservation speaker, as well as a Fellow of the RSA. What has this to do with photography and alternative processes? Nothing and everything. I am essentially an observer and a maker. Our natural world is the main focus in all I do. These last fifteen years I have been trying to express my concerns about how important it is to show the beauty and generosity of nature. I have, for a long time, realised that there is a feeling of information fatigue concerning how damaging our behaviour is to our environment. I made the decision to focus more on the beauty of all we could lose instead of harassing people with depressing facts. My approach is more about what to do than about guilt and reproach, without denying facts. I present talks and workshops on ocean preservation illustrated by my live music and visual art or films. This has brought me to many places and conferences around the US and Europe.

On one of these trips, this time to Fairbanks, Alaska, my encounter with alternative processes happened. At the University of Alaska, Fairbanks, I was introduced to Professor J. Jason Lazarus by Dennis Moser, also a professor there. This encounter started my journey into cyanotype and lumen processes. They allowed me to realise that I could actually print with a modicum of space and materials and have a physical representation of what I was seeing and imagining. I had a natural feel for this new adventure in visual arts.

I stayed with cyanotypes for a few months and then discovered lumen printing. Another door opened. Different papers, different approaches, different exposure times were producing such

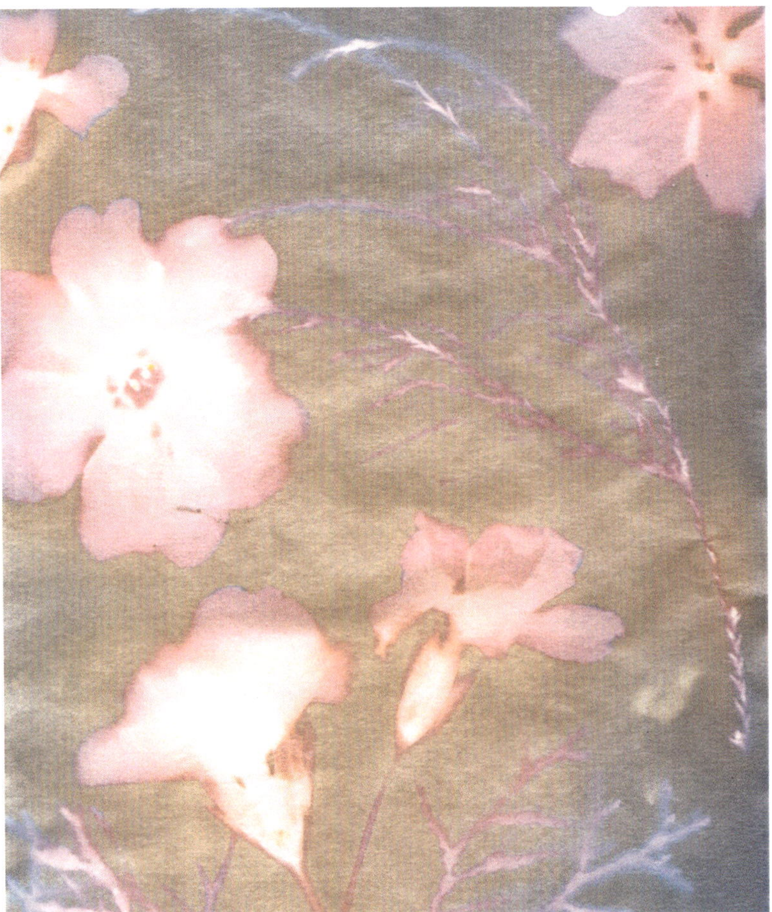

Figure 18.10. *Try a Little Tenderness*, lumen on film washi, 4″ x 5″ © Annemarie Borg 2021

print would take it. This idea of colour led me to wonder about a cyanotype-lumen combination, sometimes printing from wet and with organic materials, or dry with digital negatives. Then I wanted to see what would happen if I combined a digital negative and organic material on the same black and white paper coated with cyanotype solution, leaving it wet and applying a piece of cling film under glass to create various shapes and lines, or bubble paper which left some unusual markings, or letting the solution dry off before creating a print. So many options were fascinating and the results very varied and exciting, especially when I found a source of vintage black and white photographic papers online.

What I enjoy in this combination is its spontaneous style. I have found it very stimulating because of how

different results—how exciting! In Bellingham, Washington, we frequented a particular photographic shop where I was offered a box full of expired black and white photographic papers—different provenances, different sizes, different ages. This started me on a deeper quest into what was possible with the lumen process.

On my return to London I set up my small photographic studio, taking over a spare bathroom in my apartment. I stayed with the cyanotype and lumen processes separately until early 2016 when it occurred to me that I was missing colour. I had started painting discreetly in a rather Japanese style over my lumen prints, adding some other colours or sponging some intaglio ink when the surface of the

you use your imagination and intuition to experiment. It has something fairly unpredictable and that is part of the adventure, at least for me. Can I exactly reproduce them? Not really, though there are constant parameters to respect to get a certain result (paper, how to coat, let dry, or not, how to expose, elements to add, exposure time, etc.). But no cyanolumen for me will be exactly the same. Each has its own uniqueness.

Late 2016 I began investigating another type of "paper," film washi produced in France by Lomig Perrotin. I have always loved washi in general, its thinness and fragility, the different and unusual textures. My curiosity was rewarded by some lovely results, colours coming alive before fixing and after.

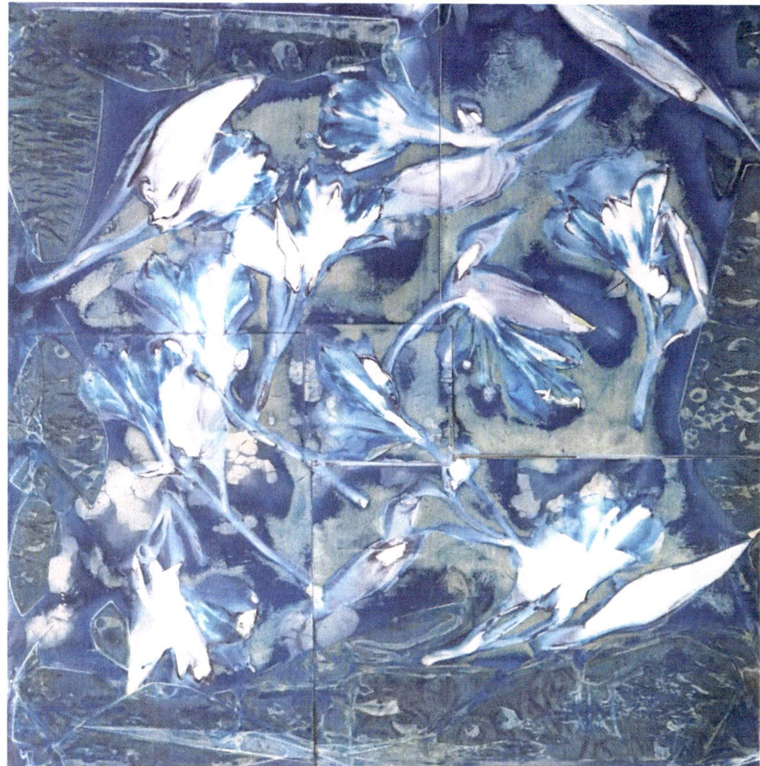

Figure 18.11. *Summer Extravaganza*, cyanolumen composite of four tiled sheets of Ilford MGIV RC Glossy Deluxe intertwined with a small square in the center, coated and exposed, 12″ x 12″ © Annemarie Borg 2021

I had to investigate how cyanolumen would take to film washi as well—tricky because of the nature of the paper, tricky to coat and to handle without tearing the print, but very rewarding.

I have since added one or two elements to the cyanolumen process. I call it *au doigté* because it involves the idea of finger manipulation. With the addition of finely distributed *encre de chine* in droplets and a layer of cling film, I create shapes by moving the ink in the fold of the film. It is a very intuitive and spontaneous way of almost finger painting your vision onto the cyanotype coated photo paper. I compare this to improvisation in jazz, and yet it follows certain rules. It is a process which would be good in art classes, especially for young children, to learn how to use their imagination freely. Like music, it enhances the ability to concentrate and enjoy learning and creating. After all, learning should be fun and exciting.

Biography

Annemarie Borg is a Fellow of the Royal Society of Arts. She is a professional musician, classically trained singer, and ambient music composer with five album releases. For Borg, visual art is a natural extension of her passion for music and the environment. Her work encompasses theatrical and street photography, landscapes, wildlife, and black and white macro photography in a series entitled *The Intimate Language of Flowers*. Borg approaches her visual work and professional commitments with a deep passion for Nature. Through trial and error she finds her way through these processes, from cyanotype to lumen, and her personal combination of cyanolumen. Her experimentation with cyanotype continues, now introducing ink as well as different substrates, which she terms *au doigté*. Borg believes creativity and imagination are tools for change, and that to be static is not an option. To see more of her work visit https://www.antara-project.com/annemarie-borg/.

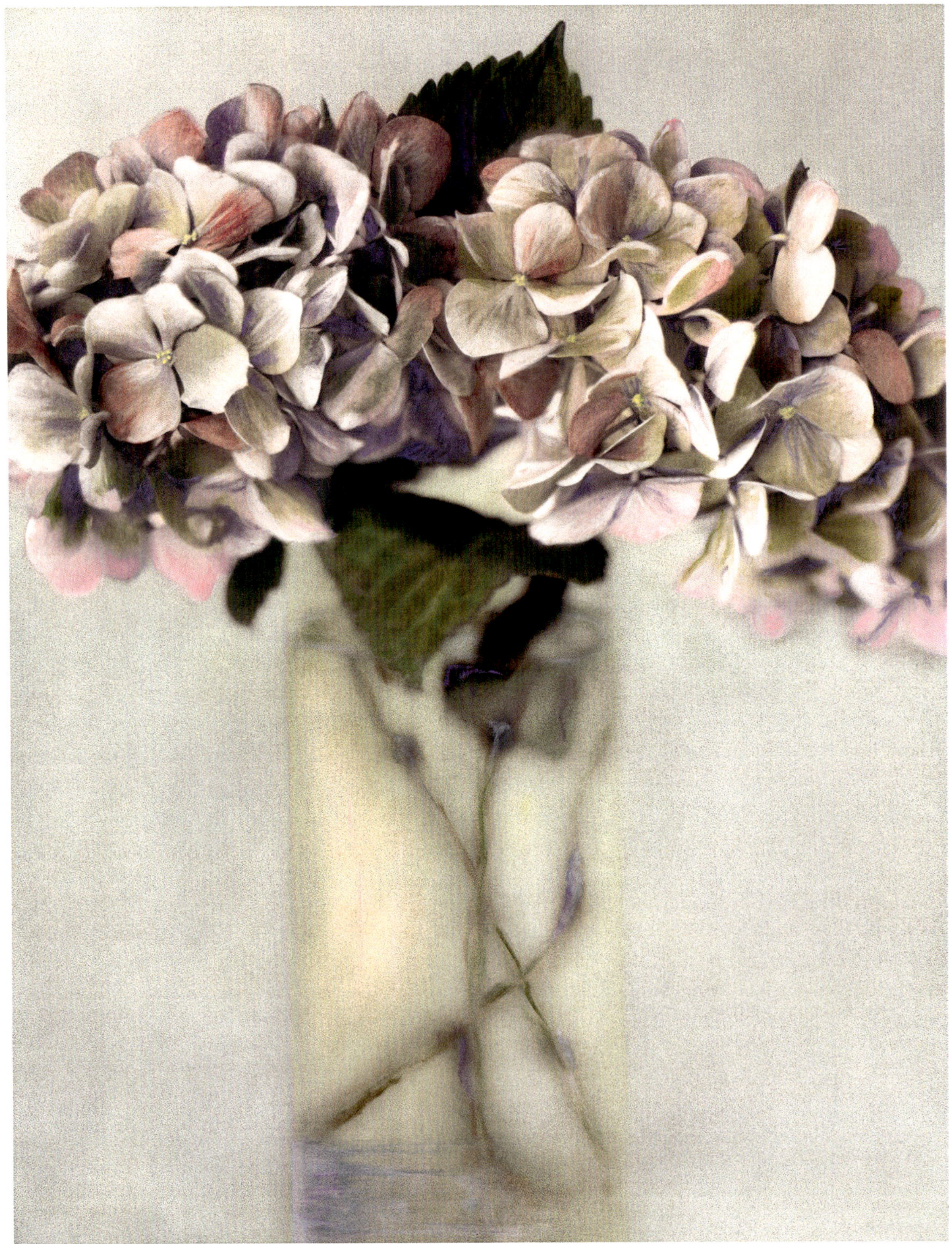

Figure 18.12. *Hydrangea*, hand colored silver gelatin, 16″ x 18″ © Brigitte Carnochan 1999

Brigitte Carnochan

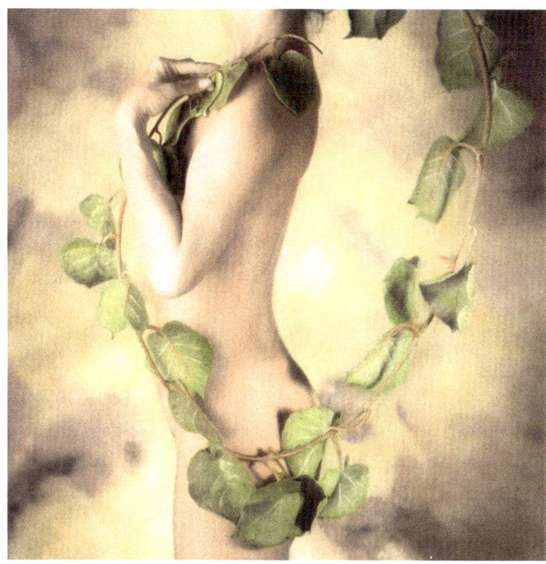

Figure 18.13. *Dryad*, hand colored silver gelatin, 16″ x 16″ © Brigitte Carnochan 2001

Creative process

When I make silver prints for painting, I print them as I would ordinarily—not lighter and not sepia-toned. I mount the flattened print with paper corners to mat board so I can turn it on an angled drawing table when I'm painting. I mask the image with quick release tape because I like the look it gives edges—paint gets pushed under the edges, builds up irregularly in the different colors used in the image, and makes for an interesting "frame." The most important aspect is the choice of color palette. After I've settled on a color scheme (which I almost always alter or refine) I squeeze paints onto a palette of waxed paper in a plastic container with a tight-fitting lid (found in art supply stores). This allows paint to be stored in the freezer between painting sessions, where it stays wet and reusable.

I began using Marshall's photo oils but discovered that many kinds of oil paints are effective. When I begin applying paint, I almost always begin with the background and work to the foreground. I find that my backgrounds (even if they're black) play an important role. Not only color but variations in tone give life to an image. Fortunately, the photo itself gives you most of the clues you need to adjust. Knowing the relationships between dark and light colors—dark colors recede and light colors come forward—or between cool and warm colors can be learned by trial and error, by taking a painting class, by visiting galleries and museums, by learning color theory.

These painted images start out as silver gelatin prints on Agfa 118 paper. Deciding when and how to paint an image is intuitive for me–some images lend themselves to the transformations of oil paint and others don't. Using cotton swabs of varying sizes, I apply paint and remove bits of it with an art eraser to create highlights and other effects. There's a magic for me in applying the paints—moving them around on the image, layering them, deepening the shadows and opening the highlights.

Biography

Brigitte Carnochan (b. 1941) came to the United States in 1947, where she fell in love with ballet and the idea of being a dancer. Instead, she became a high school and later university teacher and administrator with a love of gardens and gardening. When her interest in photography, dating from the childhood gift of a brownie Hawkeye, culminated in a decision to make photography her career, flowers and dancers' bodies became her natural subjects. Carnochan's photographs are represented nationally and collected globally by museums and corporate and private collectors. She has had solo exhibitions in Latvia, Italy, Chile, and Hong Kong as well as in New York, Albuquerque, Houston, Boston, Palo Alto, Los Angeles, Santa Fe, Ketchum, Woodstock, Albuquerque, Carmel and San Francisco. There are five published monographs of her work, *Bella Figura* (2006), *Shining Path* (2006), *Floating World* (2012), *Imagining Then* (2012), and *Brigitte Carnochan* (2014). Carnochan taught workshops and classes at University of California Santa Cruz and Stanford University. To see more of her work visit www.brigittecarnochan.com.

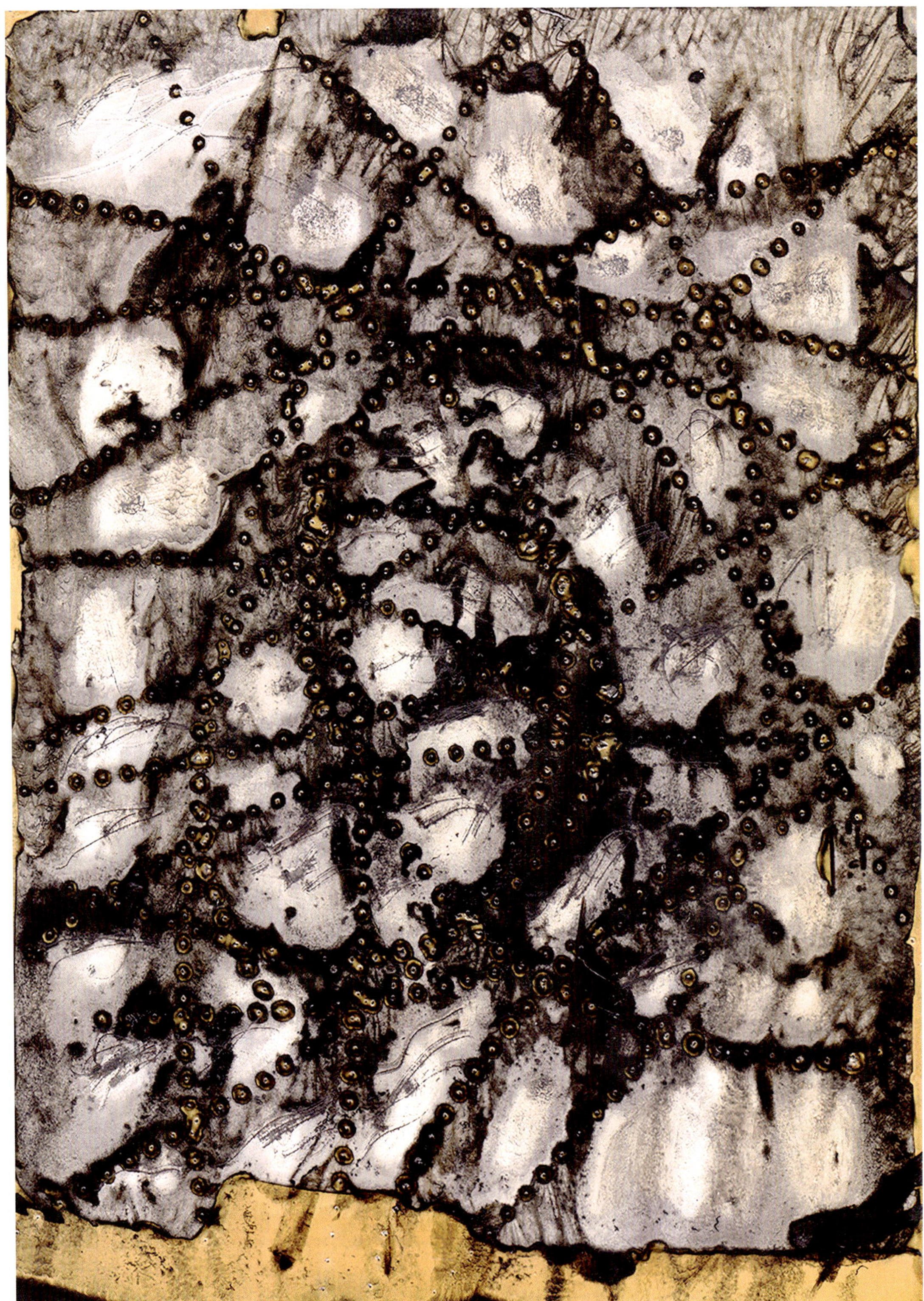

Figure 18.14. *Nazaré # 8* © Douglas Collins 2019

Douglas Collins

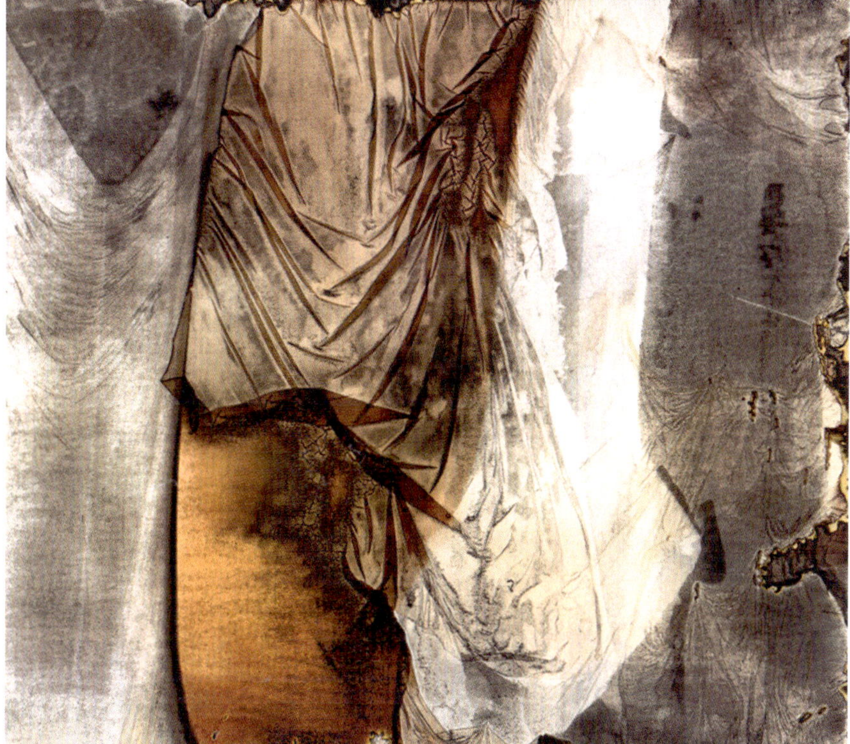

Figure 18.15. *70914* © Douglas Collins 2014

Creative practice

I came to cameraless photography from a background in etching. The style I was most attracted to was to use as subject matter the physical line or mass itself, rather than images pulled from daily life in the external world. When a studio colleague of mine suggested I might want to try doing something in an abandoned darkroom on our premises, just for the fun of it, I was intrigued. It brought back long days developing film and making photographic prints as a young man in a makeshift closet darkroom in Brooklyn, and I relished the thought of possibly reliving those experiences.

The darkroom had an enlarger, trays, tongs, running water, a timer, a safelight, and even photo paper, rather outdated, a curse which later would turn out to be a blessing. But without a camera, I seemed to lack a way to deliver an image to the paper. It soon dawned on me that I could draw with markers on acetate, set these drawings under the enlarger over a sheet of photo paper and expose it. That worked like a charm. I found these were called clichés verre and had a rich history dating to the Barbizon school of French painting in the 19th century. I discovered, to my astonishment, an artistic legacy of photograms and luminograms and other inventions that went back to the Bauhaus in 1920s Berlin and even earlier, all using basically light and shadows to create images. I studied these techniques and soon incorporated them into my work. I was off and running into the world of cameraless.

One day a student—I was teaching these methods then—came to me and asked if we could bring color into the mix, a reasonable request. I began experimenting with gum bichromate. Wonderful

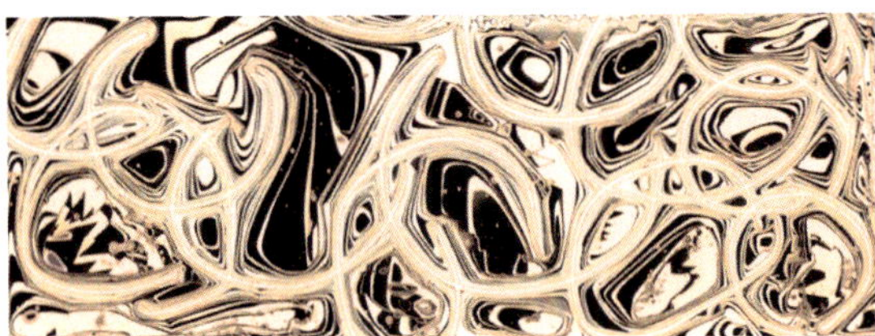

Figure 18.16. *Pierresque # 3* © Douglas Collins 2011

and moody though it was, it was too literal for my tastes, and too difficult as well. Looking further, I stumbled on what a Belgian photographer named Pierre Cordier had dubbed *chemigrams*. The images I was presented with oozed with mauves, oranges, reds, blues, ochres. This was it. The chemistry in the development of exposed paper was being somehow subverted and sent on other errands to produce these colors. I resolved to find out how, and how I could exploit it. I pored over textbooks of photographic chemistry and patents as well as early descriptions by Cordier himself. I ran experiments for a full year trying to reverse engineer what was going on in chemigrams, until at last I felt I could comfortably reproduce the steps and make a chemigram. Here's what I found.

- First, you should consider the darkroom as just a place where an infinite number of possibilities can and will occur, not just those handed down by photographic convention. For instance, chemigrams can be created in broad daylight; there's no need for a darkroom except as a room to store chemicals and paper in.
- Second, the shop-worn sequence of developer to stop bath to fixer to wash should be tossed out.
- Third, you will treat parts of your paper differently from other parts through the use of resists, or masks, such as varnishes, tapes, lacquers or pastes—anything that sticks for a while and then wears away, cracks, melts, peels or dissolves.

Creative process

I first select a photo paper, most often, in my case, Foma fiber grade, though Ilford RC (resin coated) or Arista RC are equally valid choices; Foma over the years has given me the most interesting results. Each paper has its own character and demands. There is no wrong paper.

I lay the paper on a work table, exposing it to light. Depending on the paper, it will begin to color slightly—rose, lavender, beige, or then it may not—but it will not turn completely dark until immersed in developer, which I will prevent until a moment I select, by applying a resist to all or part of the paper. The use of resists in this connection is a key technique in chemigrams of the type exemplified by Pierre Cordier's work, and represents a significant advance because resists give you a way to create figures and shapes, since we are going to carve into the resist.

Although I've experimented with an endless variety of resists, my workhorse is Golden MSA (mineral spirits acrylic) varnish. Apply it in a well-ventilated area; it has a strong smell. Application can be done with brush or sponge brush and you should let it dry for at least an hour, depending on how thick a coat of varnish you put down. You can use it right from the can, or you can thin it up to 50% with mineral spirits or paint thinner from the hardware store. Avoid 'odorless' mineral spirits, a product which has the xylene stripped out and will not perform well in chemigrams.

Once the resist is coated and has dried thoroughly, you're ready to begin. Fill a darkroom tray with developer and another with fixer, and finally a third with running water. A tray for stop bath is not required, though some chemigramists do use it. I never do. The reason will become clear in a moment.

In passing let's mention the most important tools you will need to create your chemigram. There are just two: a fine-blade utility or craft knife such as X-acto or Olfa (my favorite) and a pair of tweezers. With the knife, draw freely on the coated areas of the paper. Make lines, circles, squares, whatever, but do not penetrate through the paper, only through the resist, so that a slender line of underlying emulsion is exposed. We are now at a decisive moment: do you want the line you've just carved to be black, or white? If you want it black, plunge the paper into developer. Leave it there for 20, 30 seconds, or maybe one minute, maybe two. You will notice the line has become black, because developer has begun reducing the silver halide of the emulsion to pure silver. The areas around the

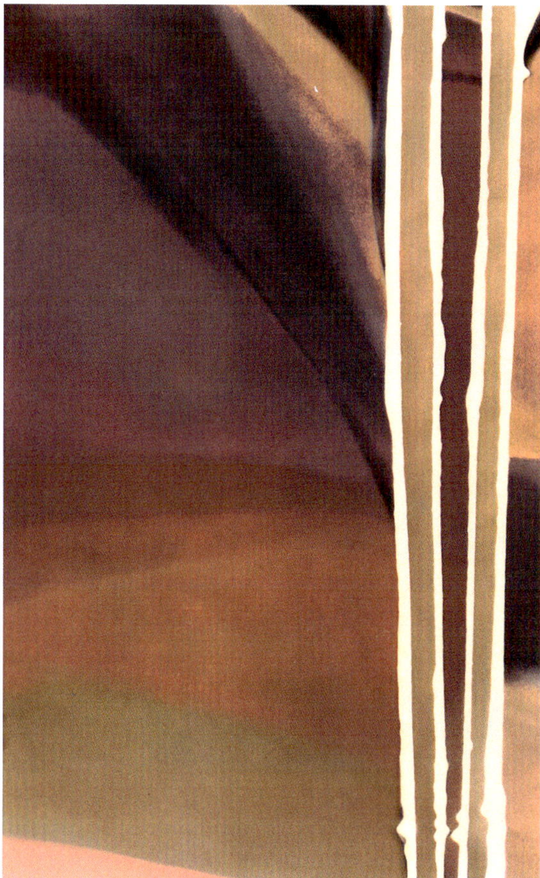

Figure 18.17. *60811-1* © Douglas Collins 2011

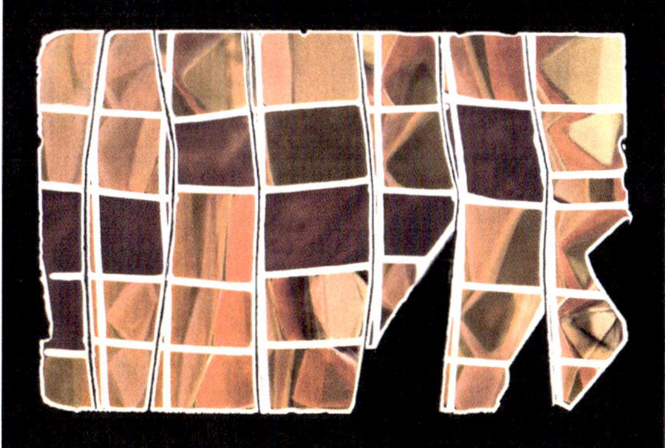

Figure 18.18. *71611-4* © Douglas Collins 2011

line are unaffected since they are still protected by the resist. Now pull it out, shake it off, dip it in fresh water briefly and immerse it in fixer. The action of fixer is to block developer action, so it makes things white. If you leave the paper in fixer for a minute or two, your black line will soon be accompanied by a pair of thin white lines, one on each side of the black one. What becomes white is irrevocable: it will stay white no matter how much longer you put the paper back into developer. But that's exactly what we will do next; we reverse the process, shaking off the paper that was recently in fixer, and go in the opposite direction by placing it once again in the developer bath. After another minute or two you begin to see two more black lines emerging alongside the white ones, which themselves still enclose the original black one. What's happening is crucial to this sort of chemigram: the developer, eroding the edge of your original incision, is creeping beneath the resist a short distance to plant its blackness there. Earlier, in fixer, the same process had occurred, only with fixer.

Continue going back and forth, swapping trays of chemistry, briefly rinsing off on each trip so as not to overly contaminate the trays. In time, say 20–30 minutes, you get a whole pattern of black and white stripes, in principle not unlike what's happening in *Pierresque #3*.

Meanwhile other things are going on that need our attention. We notice that constant soaking of the paper in liquids is beginning to weaken the resist's grip generally, not just along the incision but in broader areas of coating. How to handle this? We must make choices. We can let it happen by itself in random fashion—this has its own charm—or we can encourage the spontaneous shedding of resist by tugging at it further with our tweezers, pulling it off entirely and thereby coloring it with whatever tray we're in, developer or fixer. Or we can pull it partially, then rinse and dip it back in the other tray, giving it the opposing color. You can see a bit of this in my pictures *60811-1* or *71611-4*. Of course by now the trays are growing rather contaminated with the chemistry of each other, so that the coloring will not be pure black or white but decidedly mixed, and this is where it gets interesting—you start to see appear red, orange, yellow, blue and shades of other colors, some exotic with no name at all. How this happens concerns interactions between the degrading silver salts and partial products of developer and fixer. This is one of the great fascinations with chemigrams. At this

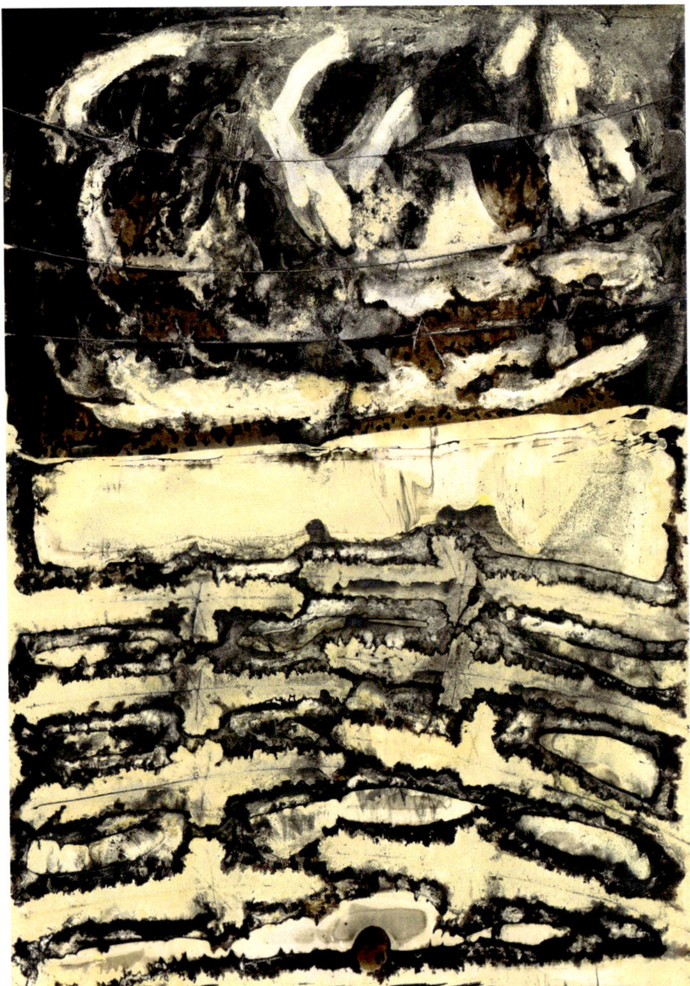

Figure 18.19. *Nazaré # 7* © Douglas Collins 2018

point the chemigramist may want to refresh her chemistry. Go ahead, throw the old stuff out and pour in new. Events in the trays will gain definition and, because so much chemistry has already soaked into the paper, you will not lose the ability to generate those wonderful colors.

By now you probably understand that making a chemigram is a time-limited activity, controlled by the erosion or removal of the resist. As you reach the end, this activity, once fairly passive, now becomes hectic, as you grab this or that piece of resist with tweezers before it's too late and it sloughs off by itself in a way you didn't intend. In any case once all the resist is off, your work is done. Put it in the soak tray to rid the paper of any chemicals lurking there, up to an hour for fiber-base paper and much less for RC. Hang to dry.

If you want to go further, there are things you can do: toning for example, although it's true that some toners don't work well with chemigram colors. I've used selenium and gold toning to good effect in my work. Another thing you can do is make your chemigram the basis for further creation in another modality, and here you can let your imagination be the guide. In recent years I always begin with a chemigram strategy but pass quickly into a modified bleach-etch mode, also called mordançage, leaving the appearance of a pure chemigram behind. My pictures *Nazaré #7* and *Nazaré #8* are examples of this. On the other hand, chemigrams can and are being done without using any resists whatsoever, profiting solely from the mixing of developer and fixer. My earliest attempts were of this kind, image *12110* remaining a favorite still.

Biography

Douglas Collins' photographic work is based on the cameraless modes of mordançage and the chemigram. He has taught chemigrams at the International Center of Photography in New York for 10 years. His work has appeared in several books and he has exhibited in Europe, North America and Asia. He created and directed the influential blog Nonfigurativephoto (nonfigurativephoto.blogspot.com). To see more of his work visit douglascollinspictures.com.

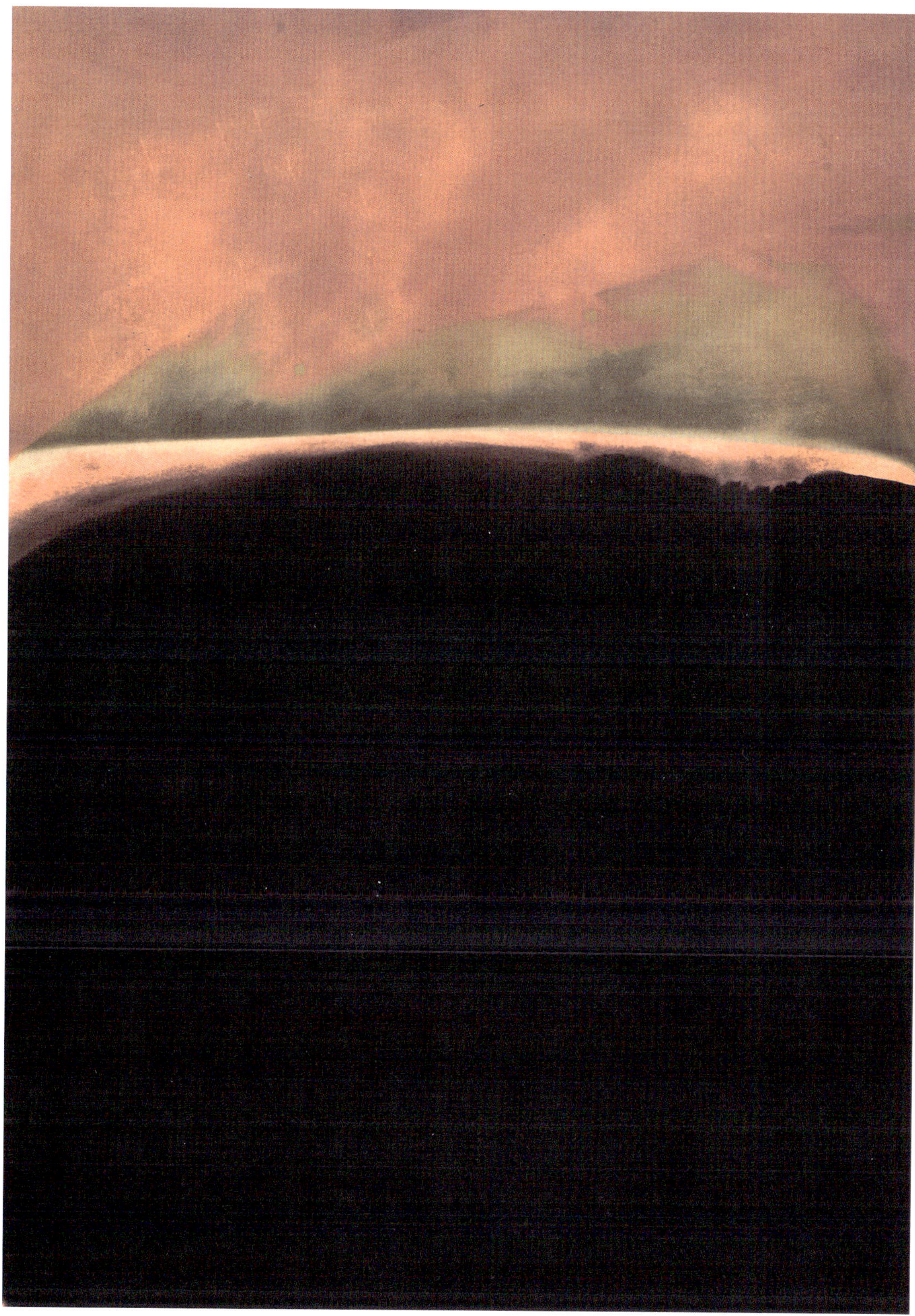

Figure 18.20. *12110* © Douglas Collins 2010

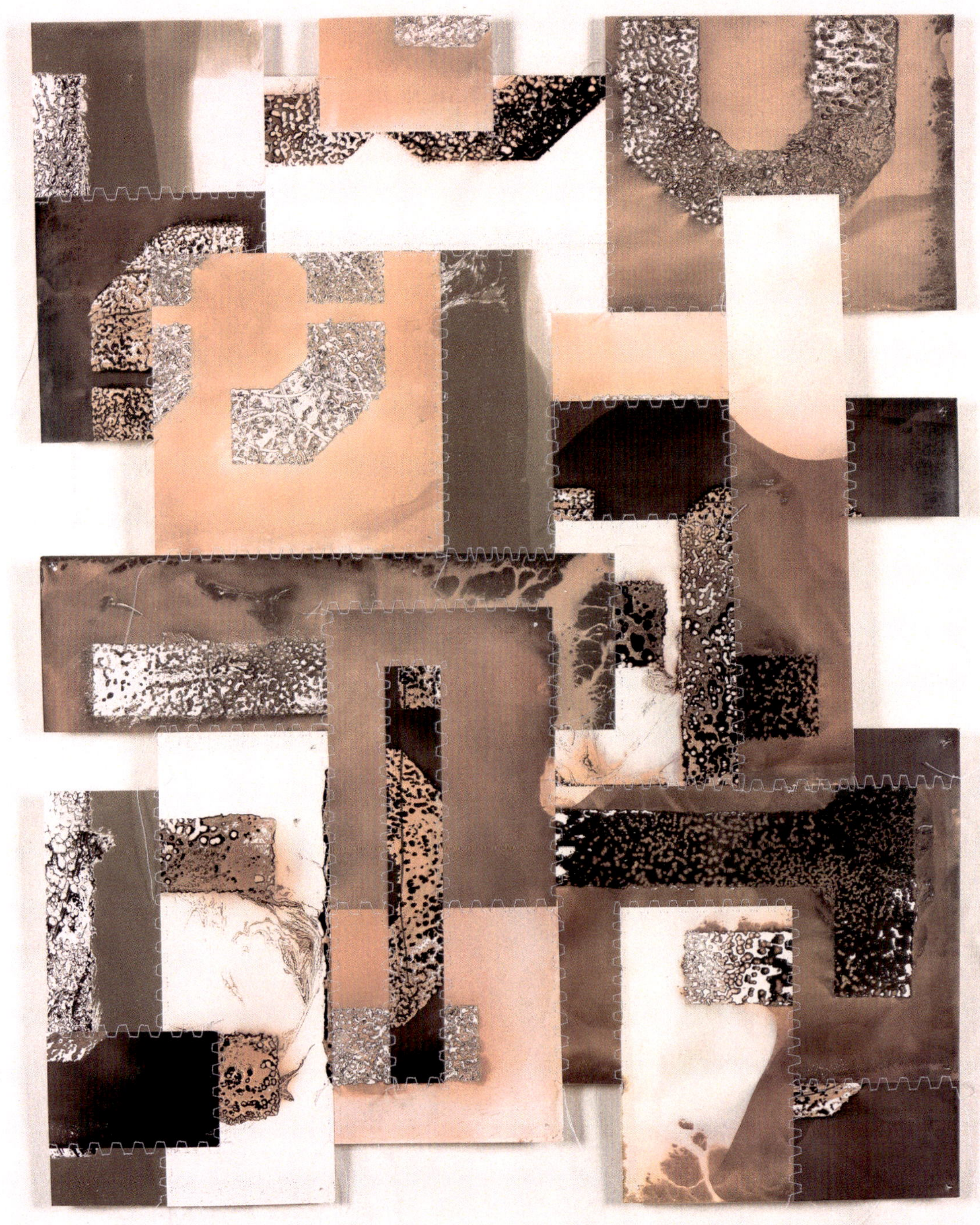

Figure 18.21. *Mantra #7 (Persist)*, silver gelatin chemigrams, thread, 16″ x 20″ © Bridget Conn 2020

Bridget Conn

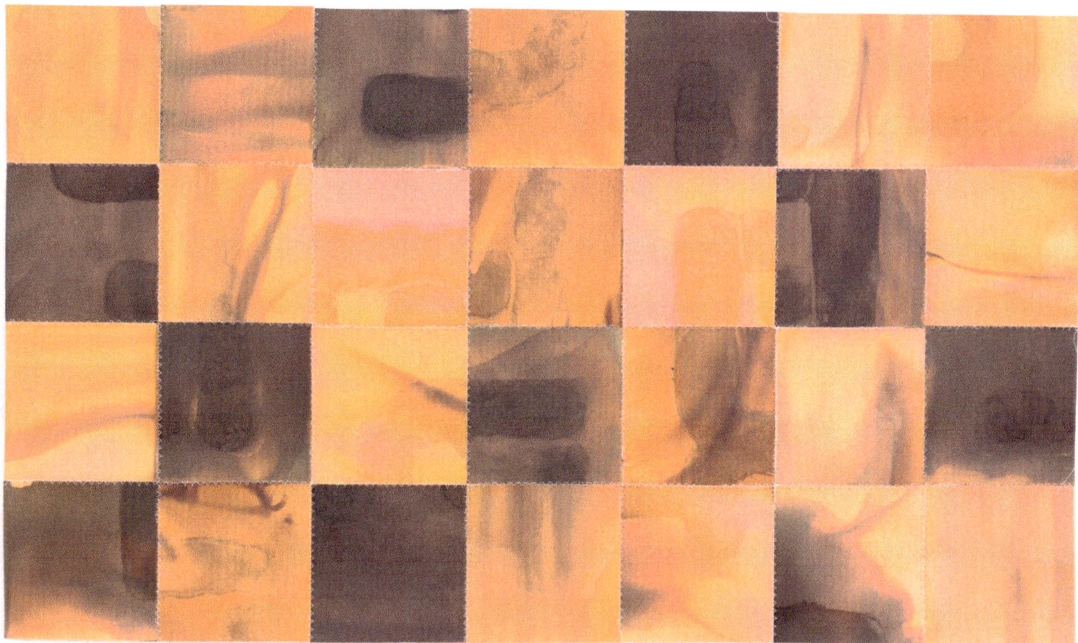

Figure 18.22. *Box Breathe (13 Moons)*, detail #10, silver gelatin chemigrams, thread, 28″ x 16″ © Bridget Conn 2020–2021

Creative process

I use whatever papers are available. Ilford Multigrade RC Pearl gives predictable results and a wide range of possible hues so it's been a standard go-to. My process is as follows:

1. Set up four trays from left to right: developer (half strength), water, fixer (full strength), water. I cycle between these and a fifth tray of a water holding bath.
2. Apply the resist in any number of ways, drawing with a stick of butter, spraying through stencils with cooking spray, breathing onto the paper, passing butter through a silkscreen, etc.
3. Decide what the predominant color or value will be for the background, which dictates whether to go through the fixer or developer first. It's usually the fixer first as that opens up the most possibilities.
4. I cycle through the four trays from left to right until no more resist remains. Depending on the stubbornness of the resist, this could be one pass, or it could take 20+ hours over three days of printing, cycling through the trays repeatedly.
5. Once all the resist is gone, the print sits in the holding bath until I am ready for a final running water wash. If resists are oily/sticky, I will do a direct wash with a sponge and dish soap, and then an additional "clean fix" tray to make sure the chemigram is fixed and stable. I then wash the prints for at least 10 minutes.
6. Once the prints are dry, that might serve as the end point, or I may cut them up and spend several hours rearranging them as I consider various possible compositions. Some sculptural wall pieces are already sketched ahead of time and are placed into a pre-determined form. From there I construct the final object by sewing the prints with my sewing machine.

Figure 18.23. *Modes of Breathing, Spring 2020*, chemigrams created with breath, thread, 20″ x 24″ © Bridget Conn 2020

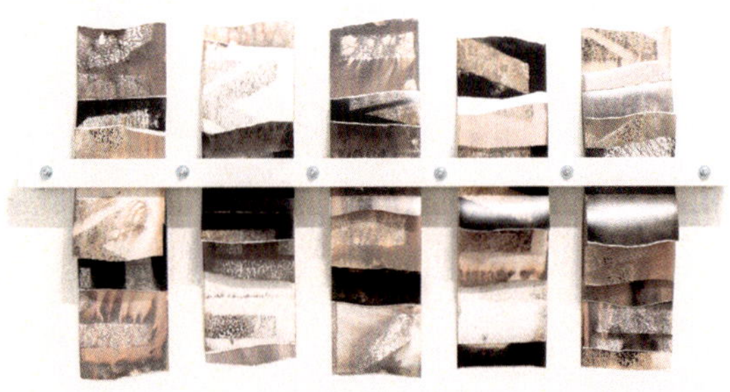

Figure 18.24. *Mantra #3*, chemigrams, wood, metal, 39″x 20″ x 3″ © Bridget Conn 2019

Some of the more basic problems arise from temperature—if a resist is receding too quickly or not quickly enough to provide a certain type of look, I either have to put my trays of chemistry within hot water baths, or concede to the elements that it may be too hot to work with a certain resist at that time of year (the only downside of having an outdoor "darkroom" workspace!). More of my problems arise from my sewing machine.

Creative practice

I identified as a writer before I did as an artist. Words were never a problem for me, until the last few years, where phenomena such as "information exhaustion" and "doomscrolling" seemed to take their toll and silence me. I found myself unable to verbalize the onslaught of personal and political events. I began to distill my reactions into a singular word. I use stencils to create a resist onto silver gelatin photo paper, and process the prints to create chemigrams. I then cut these prints, rearrange them to disrupt the letterforms, and either sew them into singular physical pieces, or construct them into sculptural works. The abstraction of the stenciled letters mirrors my inability to find words that fully represent my emotions by rendering the language indecipherable.

I began by making chemigrams as a way to record spontaneous, gestural marks. This evolved into cutting up chemigrams and mounting them into collages on wood panels, as I began to explore the paper as a material on par with the wood. I introduced thread via sewing machine and began to make standalone chemigram collages, some presented floating in frames, some nailed directly to the wall and pulled out along the nails to emphasize their 3D properties. My most recent works use the paper more fully as a 3D sculptural material, sewing it and sculpting it so that it comes more directly off the wall and onto the floor. My newest upcoming series is using silkscreen to create photo-based chemigrams.

In some cases, the resists are used conceptually, such as moisture from my own breath or from hand-sanitizer, and I have to accept what that gives me visually, and adapt the final chemigram construction to make it visually compelling.

Chemigrams became a natural progression for me to explore photographic paper as a physical medium unto itself, more than simply the substrate on which an image taken from the outside world rests. The silver gelatin paper is freed to accomplish its essential property—record the presence of light.

My formal concerns with this work have evolved into using wood and thread to equate the photographic paper with a sculptural material. I look to

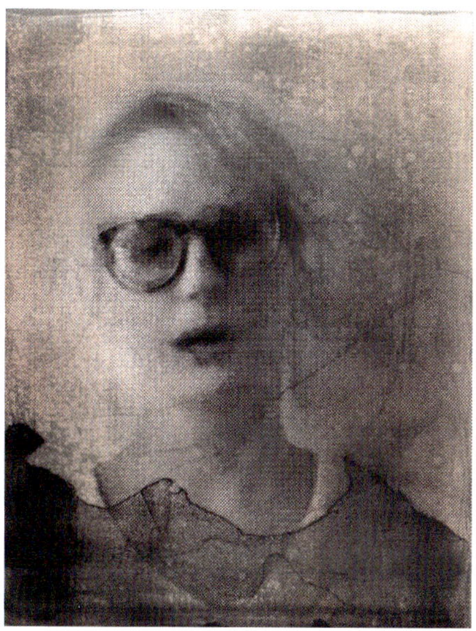

Figures 18.25–18.26. Left, *Deep Breath (Nadine #1)*; right, *Deep Breath (Teake #1)*, 11″ x 14″ silver gelatin photographic chemigrams created with silkscreened peanut butter © Bridget Conn 2021

parallels between sewing and analog photography, in that both sewing machines and silver gelatin prints were once considered more automated technologies, but nowadays are viewed as involved in the creation of "hand-made" objects. By stitching the paper with thread, I am claiming it as an object and not solely an image. By returning to camera-based imagery through the use of silkscreen, I am coming full circle in my photographic path, but still clinging to a unique print, and rejecting photography's reproductive nature as we have come to know it.

In a world where all the correct answers exist in my pocket, it has become rare and beautiful to temporarily exist in a space of unknowing, of wonder—to take pause and explore a medium in which I do not have full control. There is no nostalgia in my use of the darkroom; it's simply the venue in which I currently choose to do my exploring, as the sculptor, painter, and printmaker all do in their respective environments. None of them are expected to give up their tools and surrender to Photoshop. For much of my life, I made art by calculation, with plan, heavy with objects to photograph that reside in my studio and psyche for months, or years. While the comparative instant gratification of chemigrams is seductive, what calls to me even more is the mystery of this process. I find myself performing a delicate dance between the known and unknown—seeking control over composition, yet enjoying the discovery of what color or value will emerge from the photographic paper and when (and why). The resulting sense of discovery and awe is one of the strengths of analog photography over the precision of its digital counterpart.

Biography

Bridget Conn received her BFA in Studio Art from Tulane University (2000) and MFA from the University of Georgia (2003), focusing in photography, mixed media and installation. Conn lived in Asheville, North Carolina for seven years, where she founded The Asheville Darkroom in 2012, as well as worked as an arts writer, designer, and independent artist. Her work has been shown in over 150 national and international exhibitions as well as featured in publications such as *Lenscratch*, *Light Leaked*, *Analog Forever*, *Focal Plane Journal*, and *The Hand*. She is an Assistant Professor of Art at Georgia Southern University in Savannah, Georgia, where she teaches numerous forms of photography. Her work explores the potential of photography as a chemical and physical medium through the process of chemigrams. To see more of her work, visit www.bridgetconnartstudio.net.

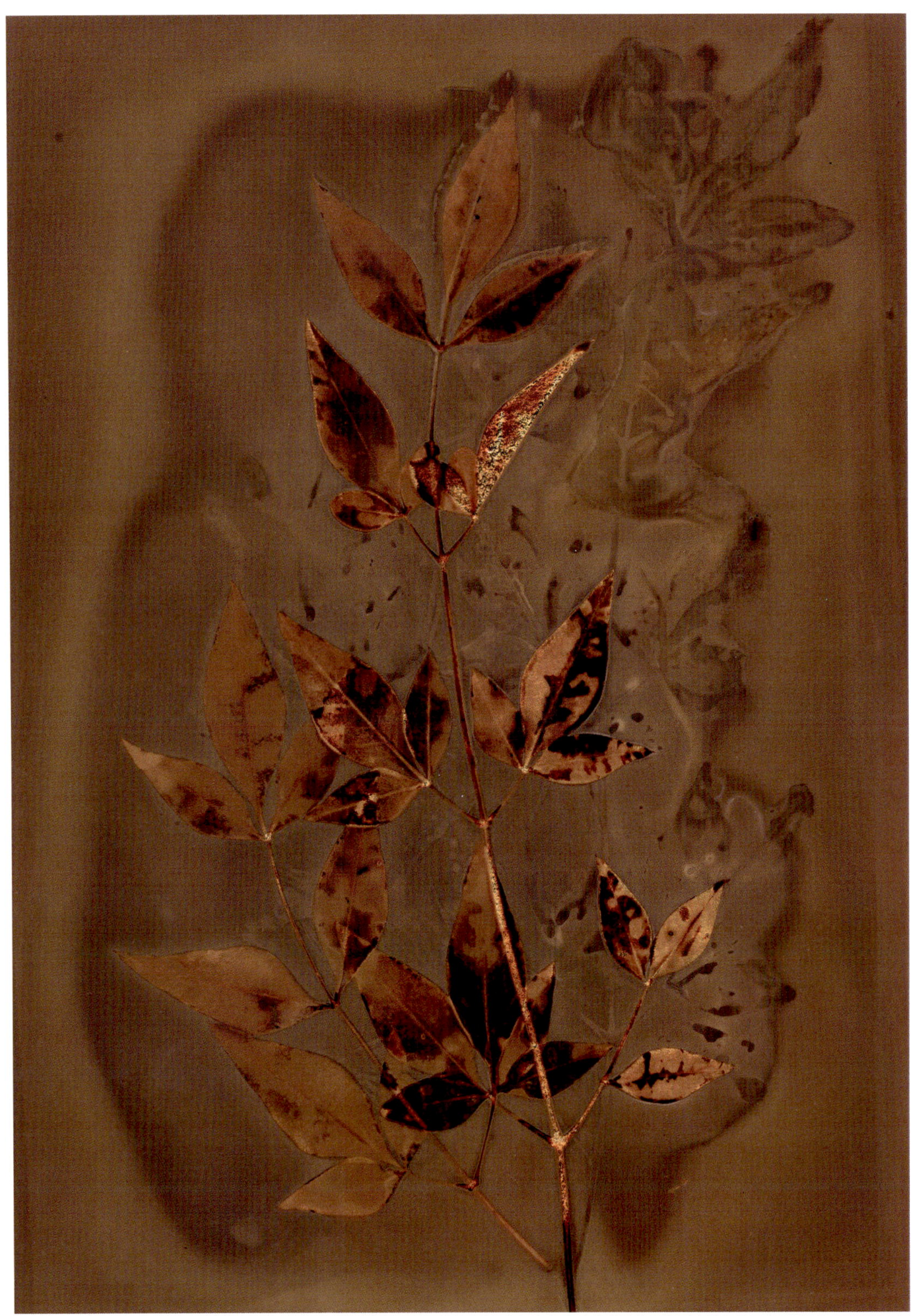

Figure 18.27. *Phytogram 13*, from the *Botanicals* series, phytogram on Arista ortho lith film backed with gold leaf, 5″ x 7″ © Karen Hymer 2021

Karen Hymer

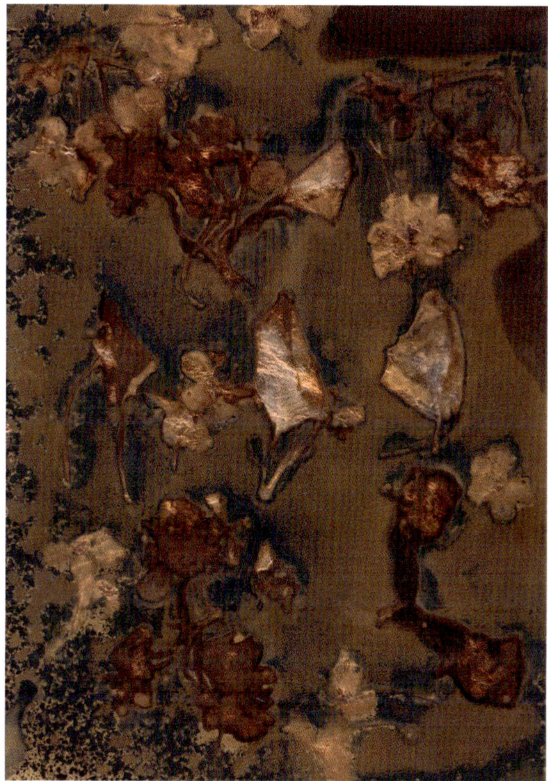

Figure 18.28. *Phytogram 7*, from the *Botanicals* series, phytogram with cyanotype on Arista ortho lith film backed with copper leaf, 5˝ x 7˝ © Karen Hymer 2021

Creative process

My recent explorations involve using ortho and other outdated black and white sheet film to make *phytograms*, cameraless images using organic matter. After processing I apply metal leaf to the back of the film. The process is as follows:

1. Select the botanical matter to be used.
2. Mix the developer: dissolve 2 tablespoons washing soda (sodium carbonate) and 1 tablespoon ascorbic acid (vitamin C) in 1 liter of warm water. Pour the developer into a tray.
3. Mix fixer: Dissolve 2 tablespoons sodium thiosulfate crystals in 1 liter of water. Pour fixer into a second tray.
4. Lay botanical matter in the developer tray and soak for 15 minutes or longer. Alternatively, you can put developer in a spray bottle (fine mist is best, like one used by hairstylists) and spray the plant matter.
5. In complete darkness open the film box (if using Ortho film it can be handled under a red safe-light) and remove the sheet of film to be used. Close the remaining film in the box securing it in the light-tight box. The film to be used can then be handled in a dim room.
6. Remove the plant matter from the developer and blot plants to remove excess developer. Lay plants on the emulsion side of the film and place glass on top to secure in place.
7. Expose to UV light; in spring in southern New Mexico, midday, exposures are around 20 minutes.
8. After exposing, remove the film from under the glass and place in the fixer tray, agitating gently. Film should clear in about 15 minutes.
9. Wash the film for 20 minutes and hang to dry.
10. Once dry, if desired, the film can be backed with gold or other leaf. I spray the back of the film with Odif Metal Leaf Adhesive and then apply gold and other leaf (copper, white gold, silver) to the film. I then spray the leaf with Krylon UV-resistant clear acrylic gloss, to protect it.

Tips

- Cyanotype can be combined with this process. I have sprayed cyanotype chemistry on the plant matter and/or applied it to the film with a brush before exposure. It is hard to control and the cyanotype chemistry does not want to stick to the smooth film, but the results can be interesting. Small amounts of cyanotype can produce a nice cool contrast to the warm tones of the film. Applying too much cyanotype chemistry can make a real mess! I found using a fine mist spray produced the most interesting results. Be sure you protect your work space or you will have cyanotype chemistry everywhere
- Each film type produces different colors and

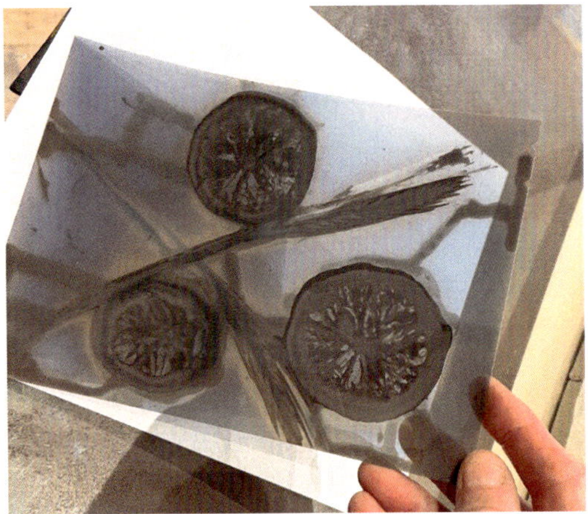

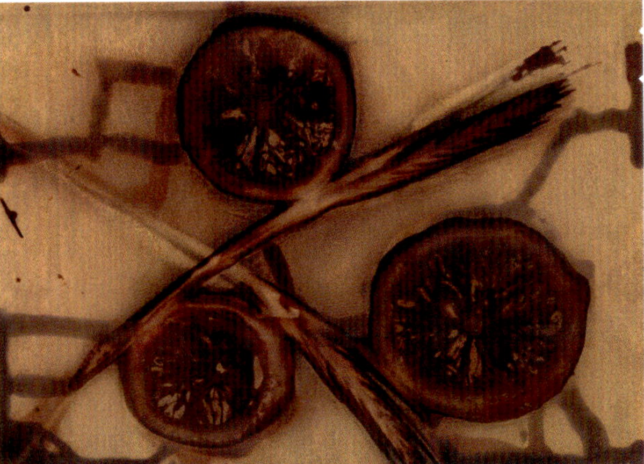

Figures 18.29–18.30. Left, *Phytogram 25*, from the *Botanicals* series, phytogram on outdated Kodak Tri-X pan film (1986), 5″ x 7″; right, *Phytogram 25* backed with gold leaf © Karen Hymer 2021

levels of translucency. When soaked in the soda/vitamin C developer the plant matter releases phenols that interact with the film. This affects the colors produced. Each plant reacts differently and the amount of developer used determines areas of the film that will turn dark. The applied leaf is visible through the clearest parts of the film, shifting the color and adding a richness to the image.

- Determining exposure can be difficult since there are many variables. At first, I was over exposing so the film was too dense and no areas were translucent or even semi-clear.
- Too much developer will produce large areas of darkness, which was not my desired result. Blotting the plants more or only spraying lightly worked better.
- Gold leafing is expensive but produces beautiful results. If you want to gold leaf the film then you need clear areas for the leaf to show through.

Creative practice

Although trained as a photographer and educator, my approach to image making explores the blending of photosensitive materials, digital media, and printmaking. I work with various photographic processes including photopolymer gravure, cyanotype, lumens, phytograms, palladium over pigment, gum dichromate, and photo-encaustics. The handmade print is important to me.

Artist statement

The *Botanical* series reflects my interest in the flora of places I live. While exploring my environment, I observe, photograph, and collect specimens. In some cases the final work includes camera images while others are made with direct contact with the plant matter. Playing with light sensitive processes, working with a variety of papers and fabrics, hand applying emulsions, and using the sun for exposures lends itself to unpredictable results. Letting go of control and observing the alchemy before me offers a welcomed relief from modern life. My intention is not to replicate nature but rather to create unique, beautiful impressions.

Biography

Karen Hymer's work is photo-based and often involves the blending of multiple processes. She is fascinated with how the passage of time affects the human body and other natural elements in the world. Her work has been exhibited widely and is featured in numerous publications. She relocated to Silver City, New Mexico in the summer of 2018 to open and operate Light Art Space. The space features galleries, a sculpture garden/event space, wet darkrooms, a printmaking studio and teaching space. Workshops are offered in alternative photographic processes and other media. To see more of her work, visit karenhymer.com and lightartspace.com.

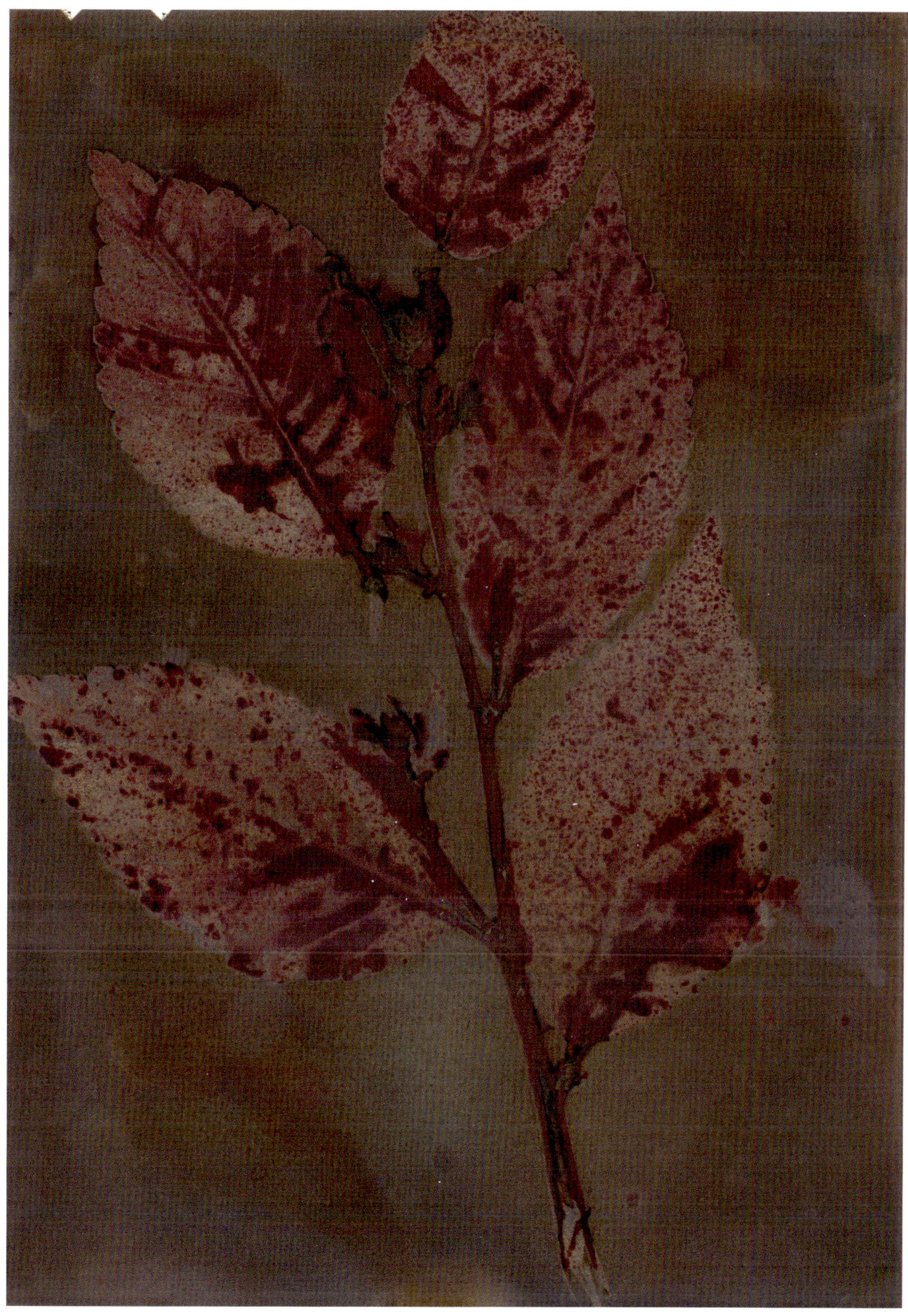

Figure 18.31. Phytogram 26, from the *Botanicals* series, phytogram on outdated Kodak Tri-X pan (1986) backed with gold leaf, 5″ x 7″ © Karen Hymer 2021

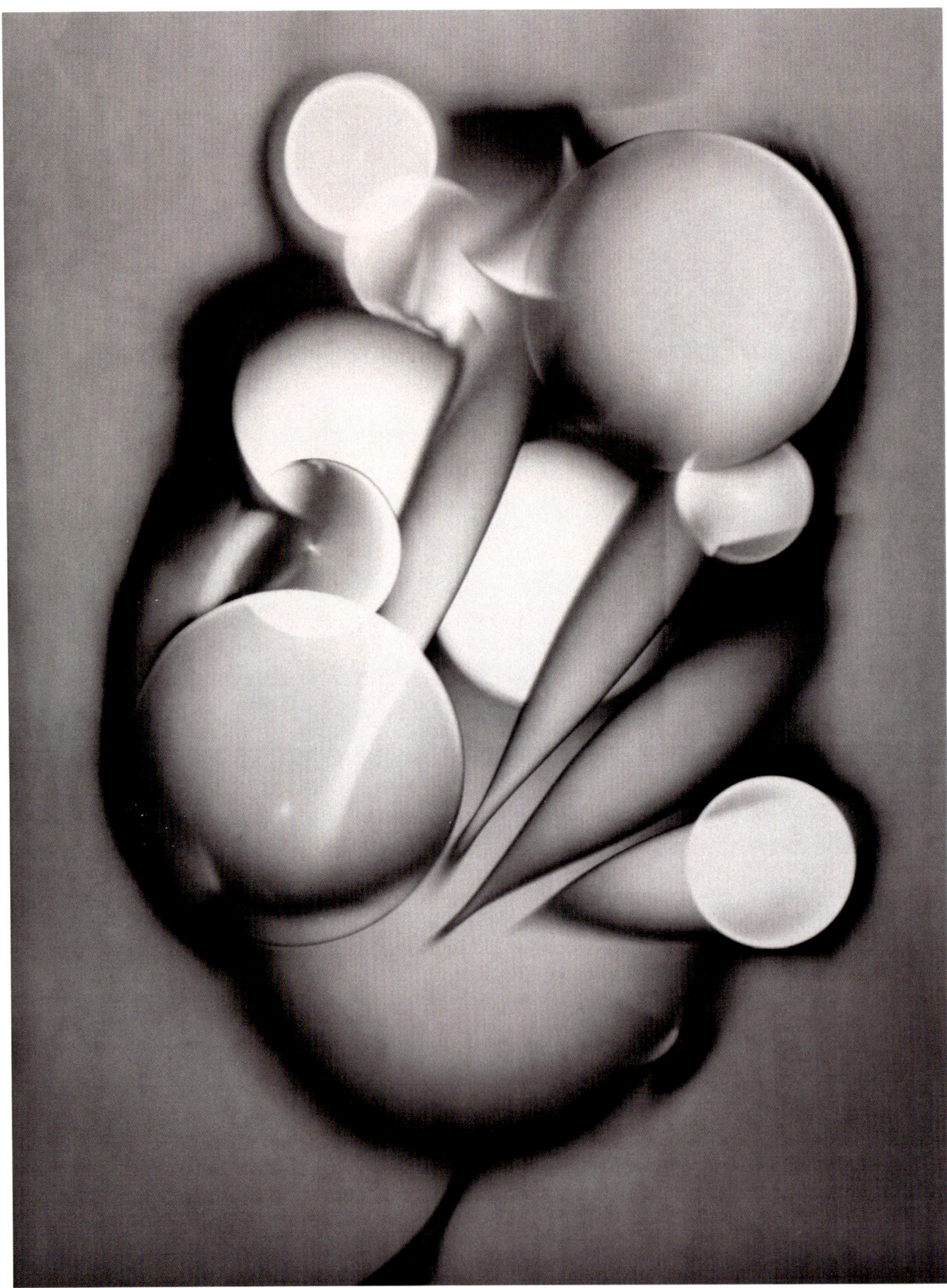

Figure 18.32. *Luminogram #540*, unique luminogram on silver gelatin paper, 12″ x 16″ © Mike Jackson 2016

Mike Jackson

Creative process

I try to approach the use of silver gelatin paper in the same way that a sculptor would approach rock or clay. I want to transform the paper rather than to add marks to it. That way of thinking really helps when it comes to making the work. It is a starting point that pushes me into the right direction. I see the paper as a medium that is transformed the same way as solid materials are. Rather than the medium being added to a canvas like paint or pencil, silver gelatin paper *is* the medium and it physically changes at a chemical level the same way that a solid material is sculpted. Instead of a chisel, light is used to magically transform the paper. I think in terms of carving and shaping and transforming, and eventually the work begins to look the way that I think.

I use standard Ilford fibre silver gelatin paper and standard developer, stop and fixer. The way that I apply marks to the paper has changed over the years. I constantly take what I know and try to move into what I don't know so the process used last year will not be the same this year. I also try to mix up processes. I have a saying that goes, "Purity of process is the death of progress" meaning that if you can do something to a piece of work that will make it better, then it is always best to do it rather than worry that it does not fit into the ordinary. I would do anything to a piece of work if it helped it move along. If I didn't I would be restricting myself.

I have made many discoveries since working with cameraless photography—how the paper reacts to different situations, how I react to different situations, how the chemicals need to be treated with respect and how all needs to be in sync to get a good result.

Before I worked with cameraless techniques I spent eight years solely photographing a beach in Wales—Poppit Sands. That long period of constant attention to a single place has been the basis of everything that I do.

It took me over a year of experimentation with the luminogram process before I managed to get repeatable results. The more problems I had the more unique solutions I had to figure out. The more unique my solutions, the more unique the results. There were no courses online! I believe strongly that ideas and processes should be fine tuned and figured out on one's own. That is the best way to get a unique voice.

I work full time, five days a week in my darkroom at home. I have a shed in the garden that gives me the space and time to think, make decisions and then dive in. My creativity solely comes from that learning during my eight years in Wales on Poppit Sands. Even though my work now is so very different from my work then, the fundamental way of thinking is the same. I still follow the same voices in my head that I did then. I call them my 'little doors of happiness" that open up when I am onto something good.

Biography

Mike Jackson was trained as a painter at West Dean College in England. He has since explored avant-garde darkroom ideas creating a unique cameraless process using controlled light with silver gelatin paper. Jackson's past twenty years of work are founded in part upon the desire to record experiences of everyday events by mirroring them with marks made on silver gelatin paper using controlled light. His work is an "objective response to a subjective response"—the initial response is subjective and captured objectively onto paper. Jackson exhibits internationally, with works held in permanent collections at The National Gallery of Art in Washington and the University of Minnesota. To see more of his work visit www.mgjackson.co.uk.

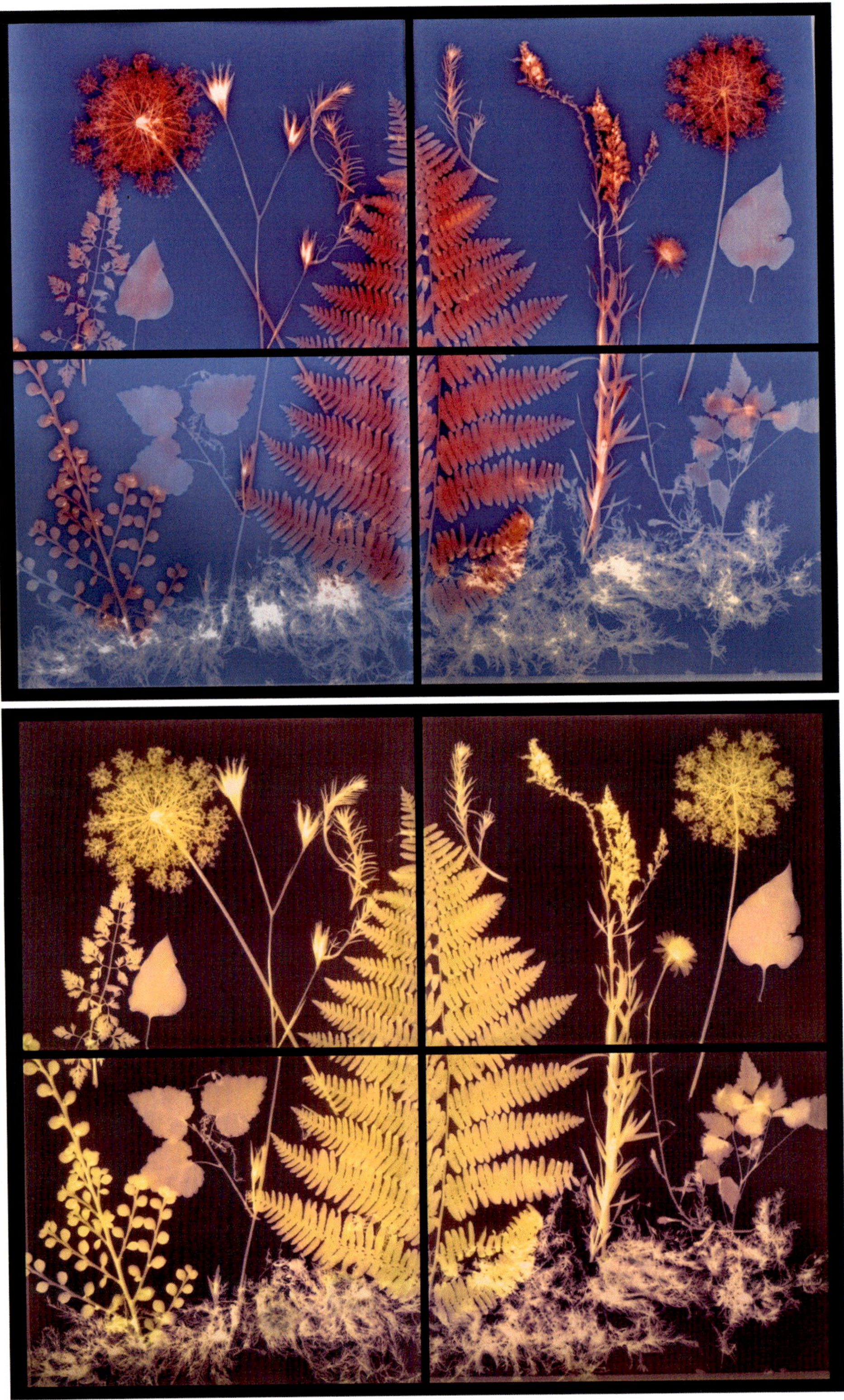

Figures 18.33–18.34. *Willow Lumen: Four Corners 01*, 20˝ x 16˝, lumen print exposed in sunlight for 1–4 hours using four 8˝ x 10˝sheets of Forte silver gelatin paper, scanned before and after fixing © Geir & Kate Jordahl True North Editions 2020

Kate Jordahl

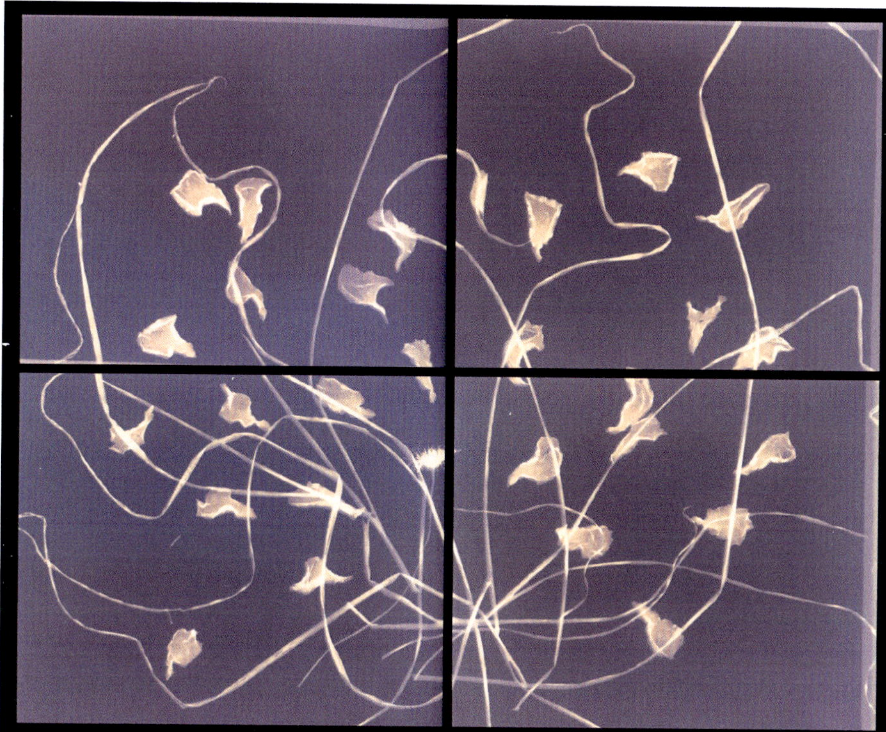

Figure 18.35. *Willow Lumen: Dried Rose Petals*, 20″ x 16″, lumen print exposed in sunlight for 1–4 hours using four 8″ x 10″sheets of Forte silver gelatin paper, prints scanned before and after fixing © Geir & Kate Jordahl, True North Editions 2020

Creative process

I use silver gelatin as a palette for my artwork, with both digital negative and plant materials. I find lumens a unique and magical re-imagination of the potentials of silver gelatin paper.

I print digital negatives using QTR on an Epson P800. I let the negative cure/dry overnight and then expose for 6–8 hours to full sun. I scan both the unfixed and fixed (Kodak Rapid Fix) versions. Depending on my next project (book, collage, framed piece) I might use the scan or the original silver lumen print as the final artwork. I like the opportunity to rethink the interpretation that working with a blending of digital and physical paper gives me. Serendipity is added to the mix of my creative process.

With organic lumens, the interaction of the plants with the photo paper—both the unexpectedness of the outcome and the range of colors sparks me to explore more. Some plants are too thick, so I have a range of contact printing frames for this. Some older contact frames that are too loose for negatives, are great for bulky plants.

Creative practice

I am very interested in the grid as a form and the continuation of the frame and the line from block to block. My grid lumens call up for me both windows onto the world and a need for the viewer to complete the line from frame to frame. The increase of the unexpected as I work on these grids is what interests me. I lay out my found plants and then decide to use a grid of paper or a single piece. I respond and then scan and then fix and then scan, once again giving me a mix of interpretations.

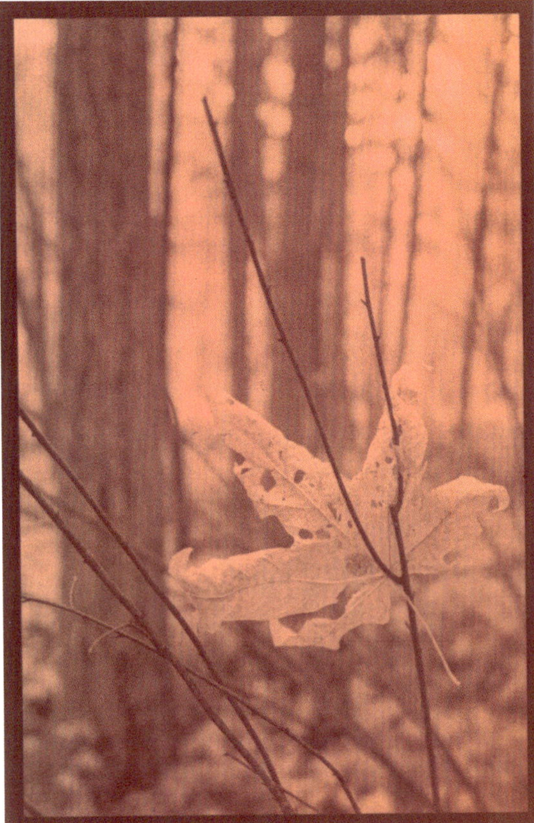

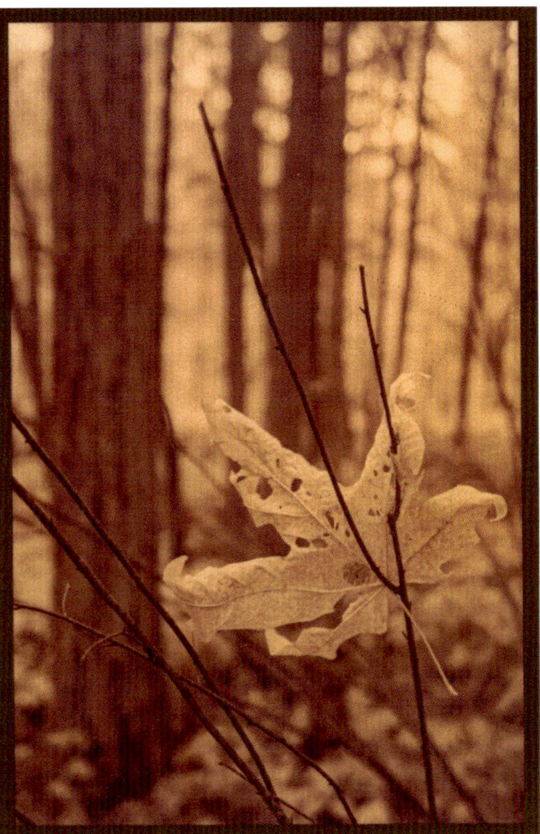

Figures 18.36–18.37. *Leaf, Hundred Acre Wood, Bellingham*, 4.25″ x 6.5″, printed with a QTR digital negative on Pictorico Ultra Premium OHP using an Epson P800, exposed six hours on Bergger (left) and Forte (right), fixed in Kodak Fixer. © Kate Jordahl, True North Editions 2021

I find it important to being open to both the control and the role of chance in my work. I love working digitally, but I also need the physical world. Working with paper and process is satisfying and increases my creativity.

Artist statement

I am dedicated to excellence in craft and vision and the melding of the traditions of art and photography with the new technologies. I believe art heals and leads our way to understanding. In the making of books, collages, and singular images, I strive to create a pause and an opportunity for reflection. Threading my way between the technical and the philosophical, I make quiet work that beckons viewers to contemplate.

Biography

Kate Jordahl is an educator, photographer, editor and curator. She is a Professor of Fine Arts and Communication/Photo at Foothill College, California, and co-owner of True North Editions. Her photographs are in numerous collections including the Bibliothéque Nationale de France, Paris, Santa Barbara Museum of Art, University of Texas at Dallas, San José Museum of Art, and the Yosemite Museum. To see more of her work, visit http://www.jordahlphoto.com and http://www.truenortheditions.com.

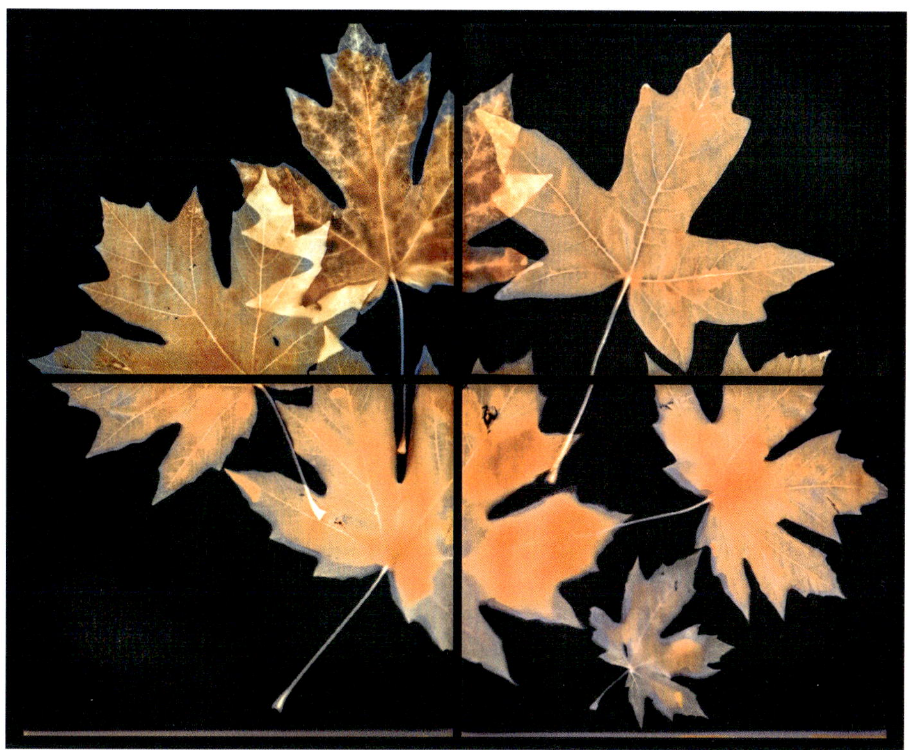

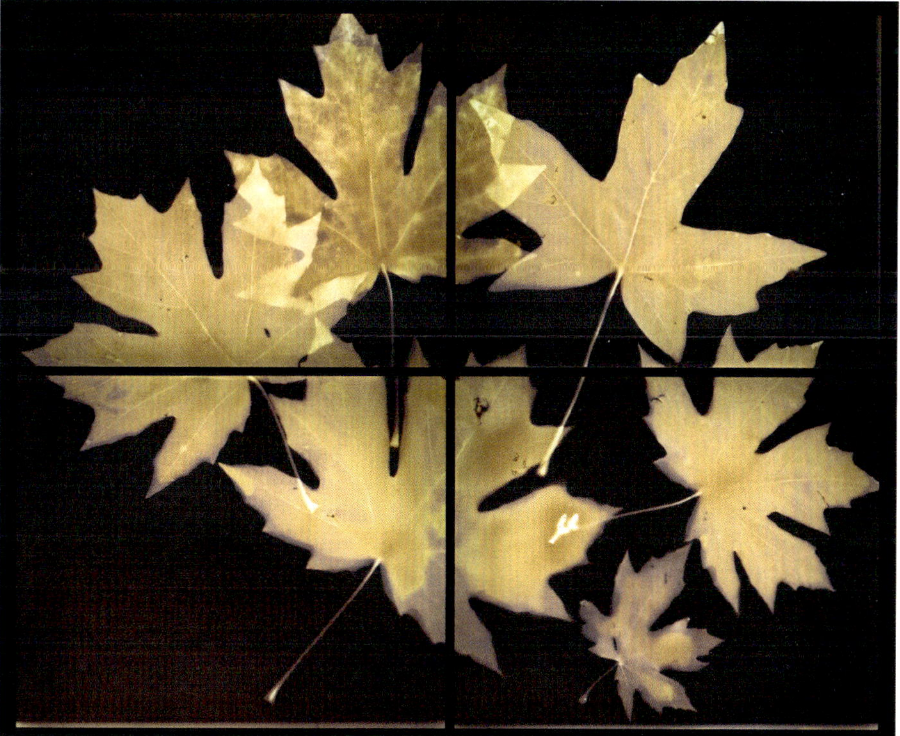

Figures 18.38–18.39. *Bellingham Lumen: Maple 01 and 02*, 20″ x 16″, lumen printed in sunlight for 1–4 hours using four 8″ x 10″ sheets of Forte silver gelatin paper, scanned before and after fixing © Geir & Kate Jordahl, True North Editions 2021

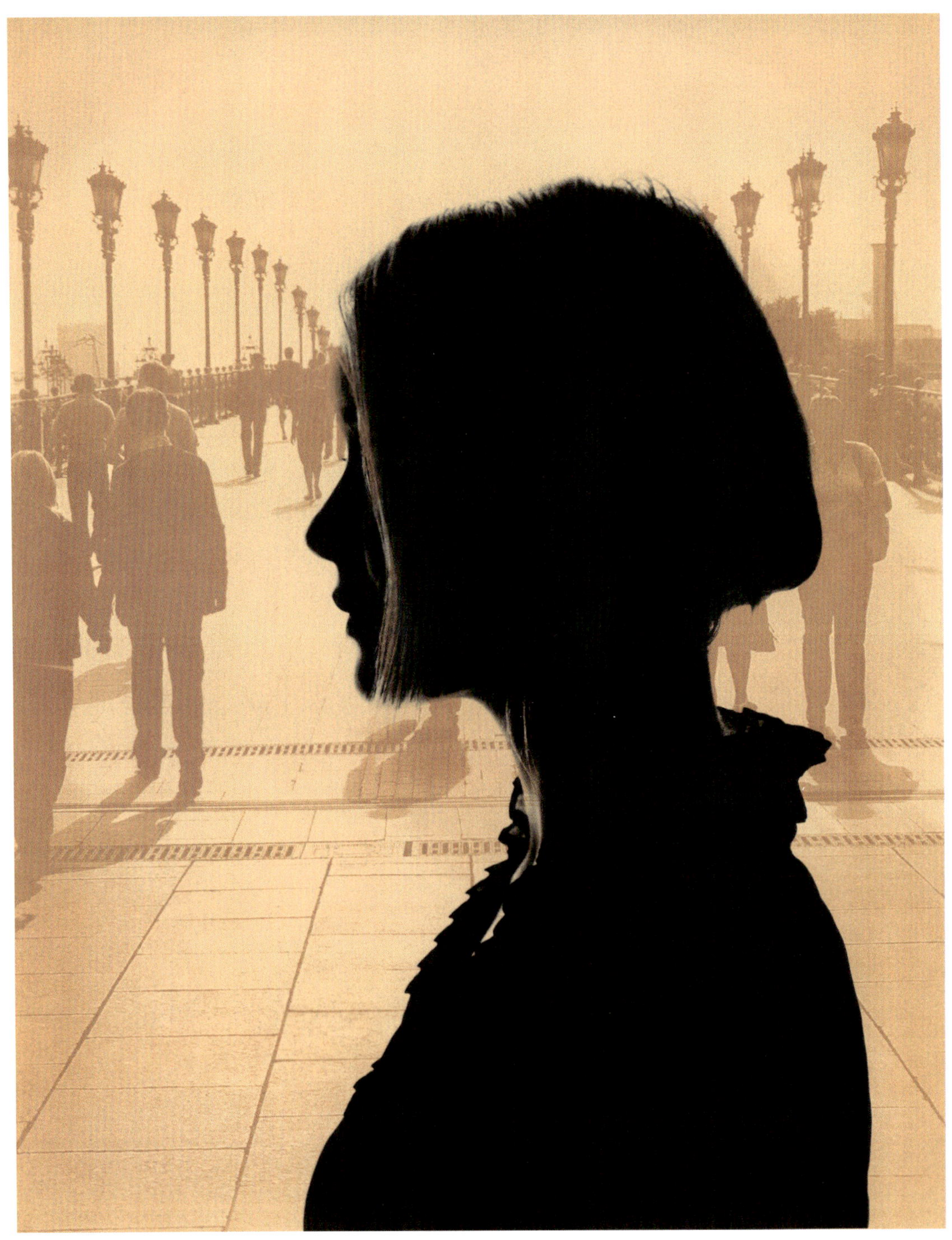

Figure 18.40. *Sarah in the City*, developed silver gelatin print composited with lumen printing, Forte Coldtone RC, 8″ x 10″ © Tiina Kirik 2020

Tiina Kirik

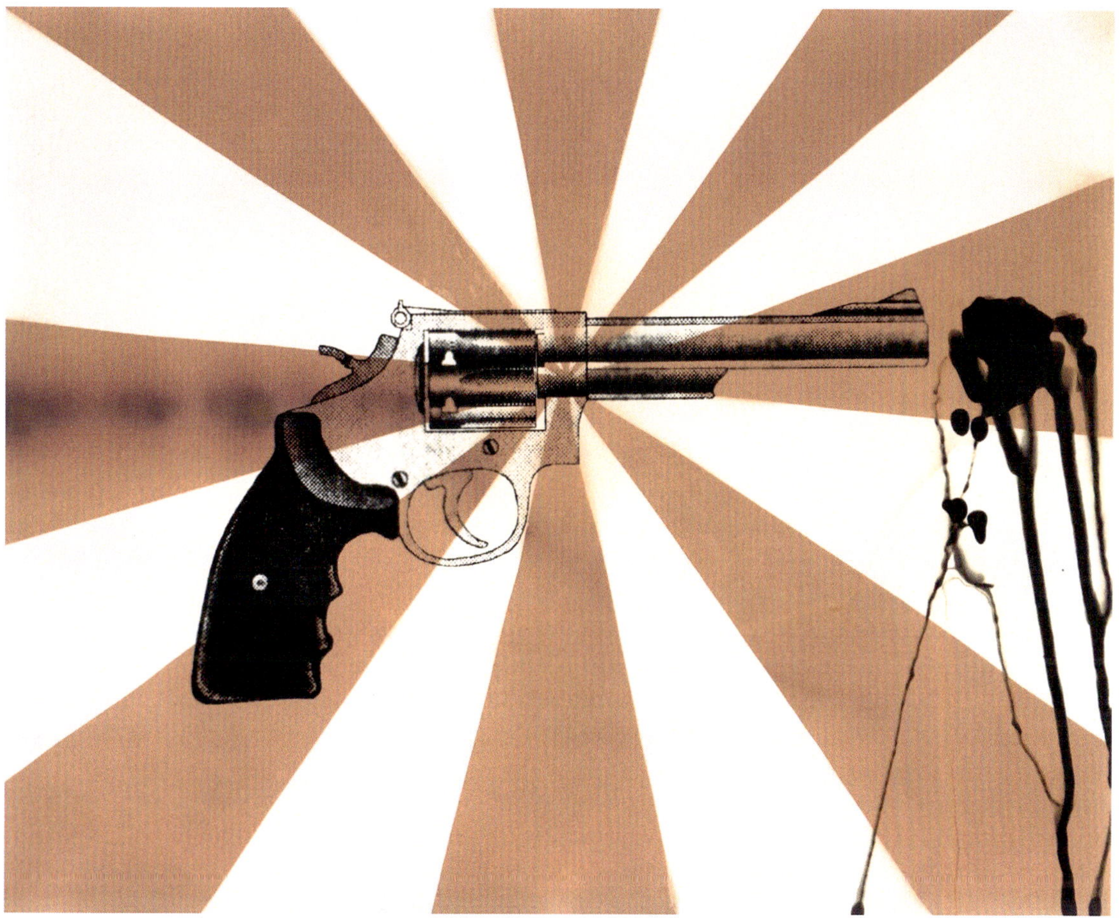

Figure 18.41. *Shoot*, developed silver gelatin print composited with lumen printing, Forte Polygrade FB, 14″ x 11″ © Tiina Kirik 2021

Creative process

There are many ways one can combine a black and white print with the colours obtained by the lumen process. Perhaps the easiest is by making a normal black and white darkroom print, but process it only to the stop bath stage. Then make your lumen exposure before fixing the final print. The composite images shown here were made using this method.

1. Expose the paper under normal darkroom conditions. You may do this with a film negative, a paper negative, or make a direct photogram image. Try whatever strikes your imagination.
2. Develop the print, and stop development as usual in a mildly acidic stop bath. Keep the print moving during the entire stop bath stage, for 10–15 seconds.
3. Wash the print very well to remove any traces of developer. This will require 2–5 minutes wash of resin-coated papers, or 10–20 minutes wash for fibre-based papers. You may let your print dry in dim tungsten light, protected from any ultraviolet light. These unfixed prints may be stored, away from light for periods up to several months, before making the lumen part of the exposure.

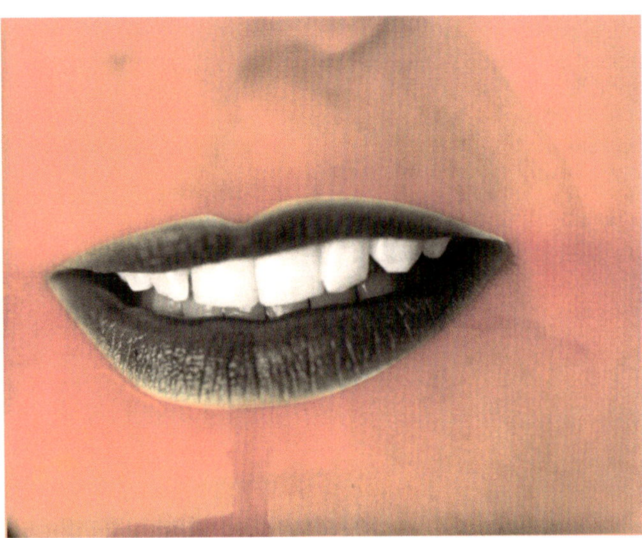

Figure 18.42. *Grin*, developed silver gelatin print composited with lumen printing, Forte Polywarmtone FB, 14˝ x 11˝ © Tiina Kirik 2020

4. Any parts of the print that you wish to keep monochrome, should be carefully masked by light-opaque material before any exposure to UV light or sunlight. Arrange materials over the paper and make your lumen exposure. A sheet of glass, or use of a contact printing frame keeps objects in close contact with the paper for a sharper image.
5. Fix and wash the print as normal. All lumen prints are more stable once fixed and carefully washed. "Don't fear the fix."

Tips: The lumen part of your composite image may be made using plant materials, digital negatives, paper, or other objects. You might like to do some chemigram work on the image, before fixing it, such as selectively "painting" it with photographic developer. You can also choose to bleach out your black and white print, before doing a lumen exposure (see the **Bleaching and Bleachout** chapter for the bleach formula). When a lumen exposure is made after bleaching an unfixed black and white print, the image made in the darkroom makes a ghostly reappearance behind the lumen image and this can be quite intriguing.

The colours obtained through the lumen process are largely related to the emulsion type of the paper used. If you are not happy with the colours you obtain, first check that you are using a suitable light source and giving adequate exposure time. Fixing your print will inevitably change the colours, but they should be no less brilliant than those of an unfixed print once washed and dried. Warm tone papers tend to be more colourful than neutral tone papers, and some resin-coated papers give better colour than fibre papers. Vintage papers, long past their expiration date, often give the most beautiful colours with the lumen process but they are prone to age-related fogging. To make a good darkroom print with these papers requires more advanced chemistry. Use of antifog agents such as benzotriazole, a high-contrast developer and an over-expose and snatch technique are helpful. Photographic paper emulsions are constantly changing. Even papers of the same name can show completely different results with lumen, even though the papers may be identical when processed as a normal black and white darkroom print.

Lumen printing is an exciting and colourful photogram technique, that does not require access to a photographic darkroom. It is expanded in potential and scope when combined with other silver gelatin based processes such as darkroom black and white practice!

Biography

Tiina Kirik is an artist and educator who works primarily with traditional silver-based photographic printing techniques. Although largely self-taught in both darkroom and alternative processes, the mentorship of many colleagues has been instrumental in honing her unique vision. Kirik has been teaching darkroom skills through workshops at the School of Photographic Arts in Ottawa Ontario. She is completing an artist-in-residence and filling the role of darkroom technician at the Ottawa School of Art. As part of her residency, she has written instructional books about lith printing (*Lith: The Secrets of Lith Printing in the Darkroom*), and lumen printing (*Lumen: Exploring Beyond the Boundaries of Lumen Process*) available through Blurb.com. Kirik is working on her third book about photogram techniques to be released in 2022. To see more of her work visit byetiinakirik.wordpress.com.

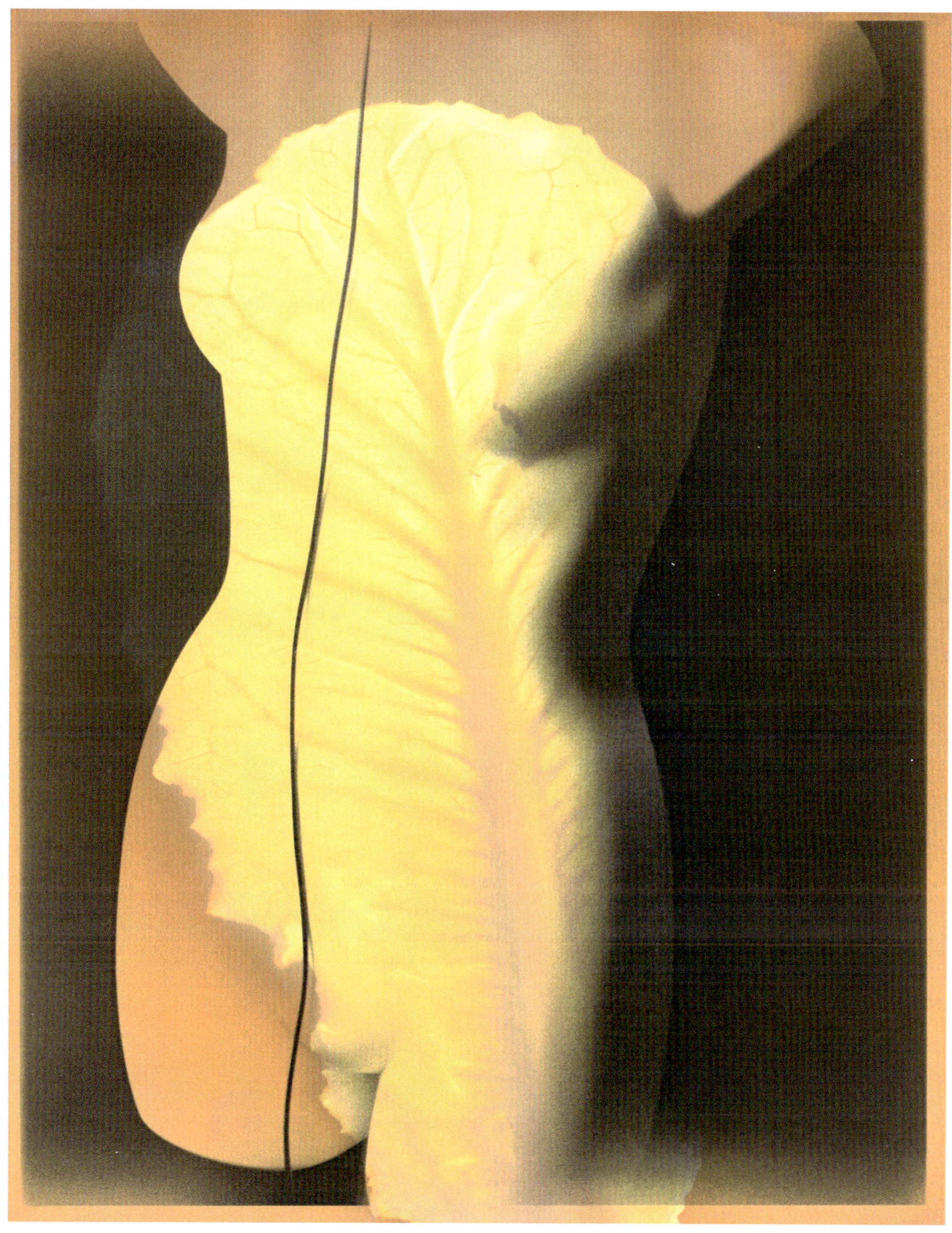

Figure 18.43. *Mannequin*, developed silver gelatin print composited with lumen printing, Ilford Warmtone RC, 8″ x 10″
© Tiina Kirik 2020

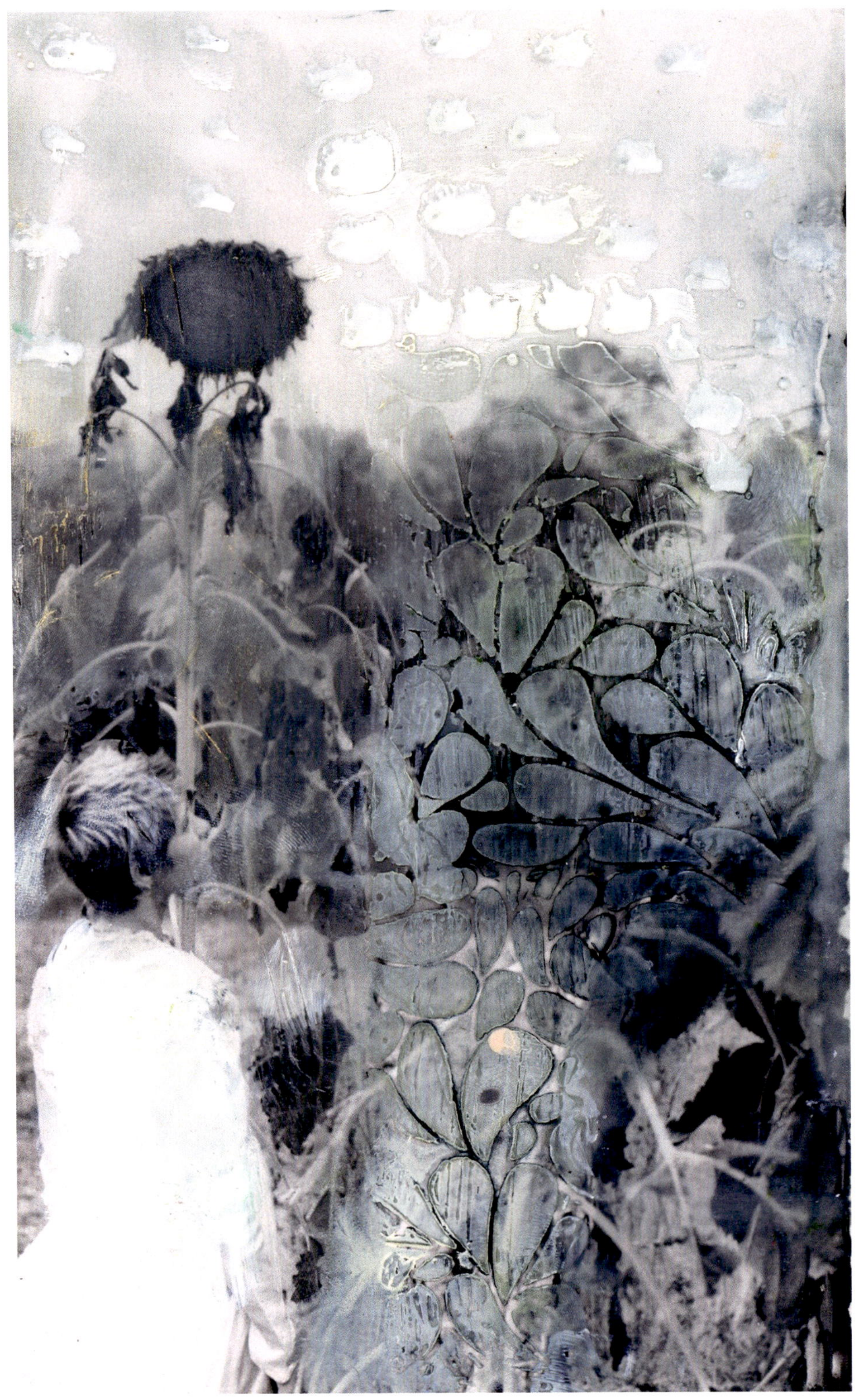

Figure 18.44. *Kali*, 5″ x 8″ silver gelatin print with encaustic © Leah Macdonald 2018

Leah Macdonald

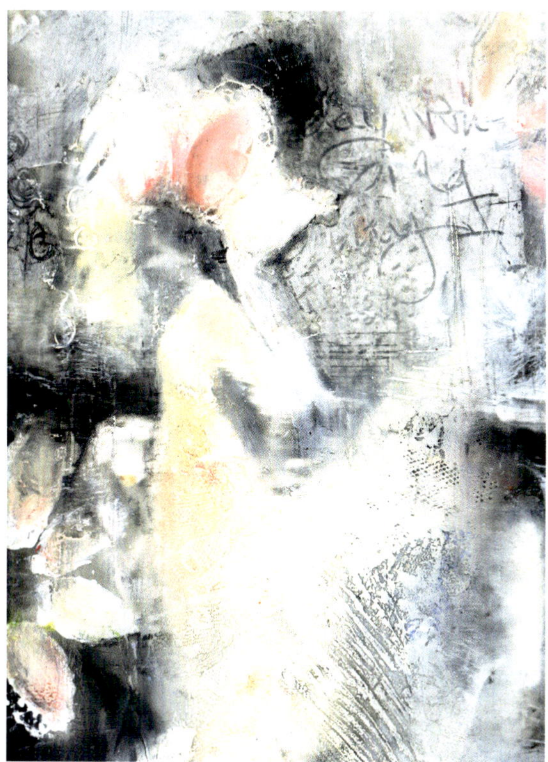

Figure 18.45. *Run Girl*, 7.5″ x 10″ silver gelatin print with encaustic © Leah Macdonald 2019

Creative process

I photograph with medium and large format cameras. I use mostly Ilford matte paper. I melt wax medium on the griddle and brush it onto the photograph. I use a variety of texture making techniques including adding lace, stencils and string. I add colored encaustic wax or pigment paint sticks to enhance the colors. For me, encaustic was the answer to my desire to have texture and a surface layer to the photographs. The wax has a matte surface but can be buffed to be more shiny. It can also be colored and show off the dimension by adding paint into the 3D spaces. Sometimes I use too much wax and the wax then becomes opaque instead of translucent. Learning about translucency and how to use the wax to look integrated with the imagery and not just put on was challenging. I think the layers of medium have to speak to each other and work together. The process is a layering technique so I learned to add and subtract medium to make the work balanced.

Creative practice

I was an MFA student at the California College of Art. I worked with Larry Sultan, Todd Hido, Linda Conner, Ken Miller, and Charles Gatewood. Many of my peers were interested in story telling and narrative with their photographs. I was, too, but also I was interested in texture, painting and poetry. I went out on a limb to try to develop my own language and style with my work. It started in college and continued to graduate school when I was working with the paper in ways that other people were not. I used sandpaper and pens and developers and toners to disrupt the normal process of my printing and to try to make unusual colors and tones and surfaces appear on my prints. I actually discovered beeswax by accident. Looking around the art store, I had been collaging a lot and I was using Cutrite kitchen wax paper as a layer over my black and white images. I really liked the way it looked, so I bought the beeswax and I have been using it ever since. That was 1995. I think it was 2005 that I was curated into a National Encaustic Conference and I had to ask the curator what was encaustic! I had been using it for a long time before I realized the importance of encaustic and the history of the medium.

Biography

Leah Macdonald's work centers on the feminine narrative in the natural landscape, an outcome of her experience living a life closely connected to nature and emotions. Macdonald's work has been exhibited at galleries in Philadelphia where she currently resides. She is represented by Cerulean Arts and teaches workshops nationally and internationally. To see more of her work visit www.Leah-Macdonald.com.

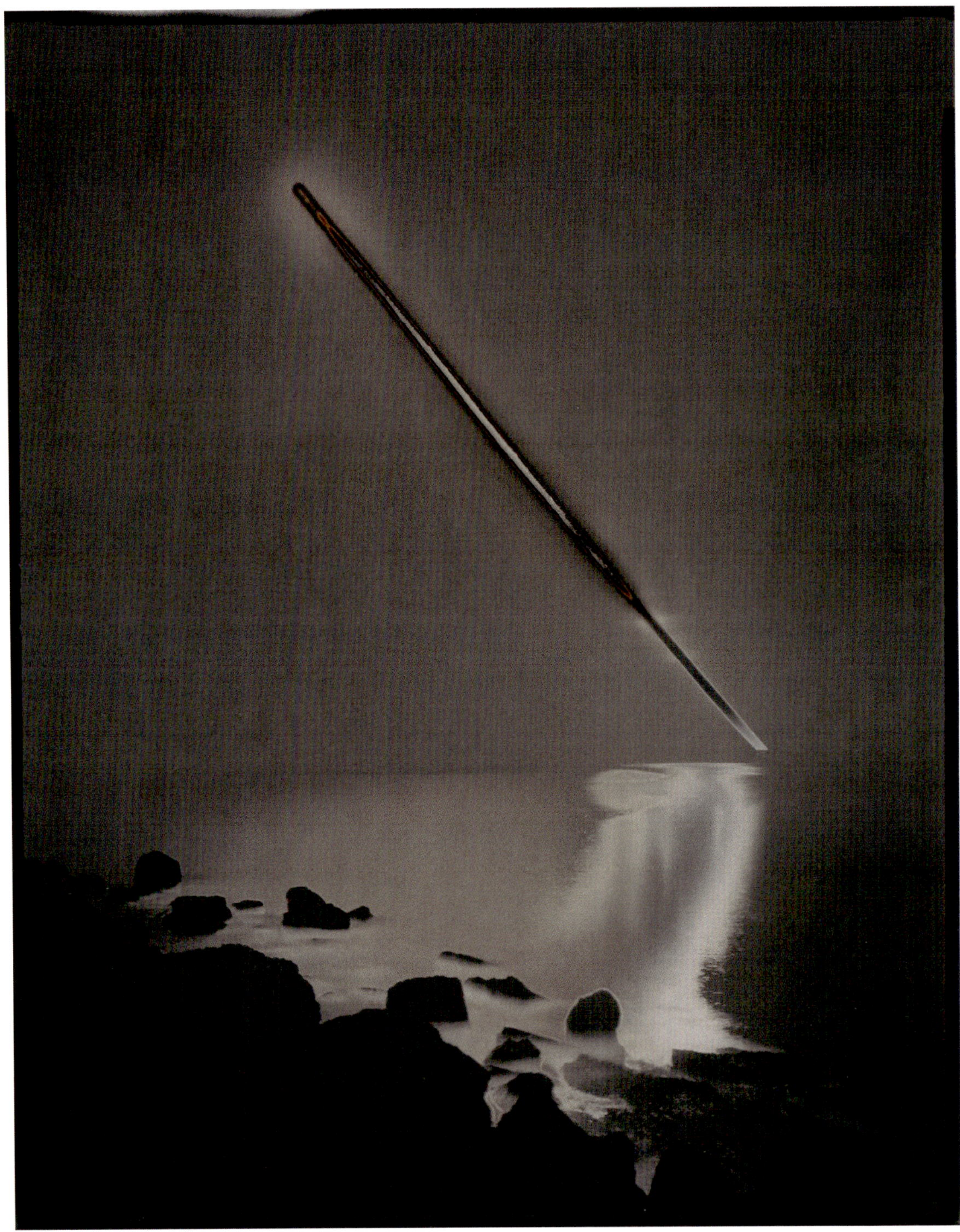

Figure 18.46. *Sunburned GSP#676, San Francisco Bay*, 8″ x 10″ unique silver gelatin paper negative

Chris McCaw

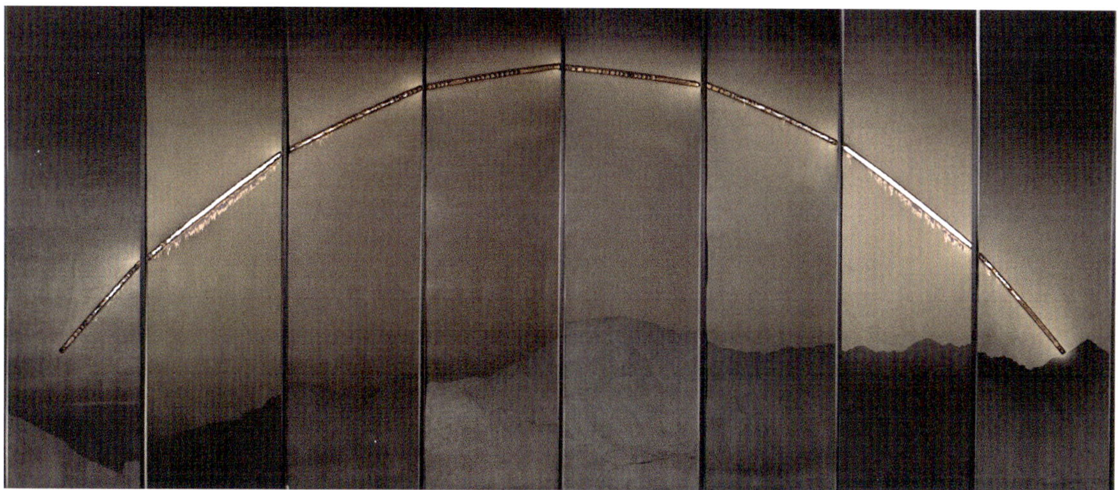

Figure 18.47. *Sunburned GSP#900, Mojave Full Day*, eight 12″ x 41″ unique silver gelatin paper negatives
© Chris McCaw 2016

Creative process

I use a variety of silver gelatin papers from the 1960s to the 1990s in place of film, exposing the paper directly in large format cameras. I have tested decades of these papers, learning about all the beautiful surfaces no longer manufactured and the various weights of paper, more than just double and single weight. With the paper inside my large format camera, I photograph the sun's apparent path in the sky (we are the ones moving) using the lens of the camera much like how you use a magnifying glass to start a fire. The aperture is wide open, with fast optics, which ignites the paper inside the camera. The paper, due to the extreme overexposure, exhibits true solarization where image tonality reverses from negative to a unique positive image.

As my subject is the sun, I am at its mercy. I have to follow it literally to the ends of the earth, from the equator to well within the Arctic Circle. Certain works are only able to be made during certain seasons. All-day pieces not in the Arctic Circle need to be made in winter, a time of year it can be tricky to find clear skies. I am getting a better sense of how seasons vary through the year and how they vary with location on the planet.

Biography

Chris McCaw has been getting his hands wet in the darkroom from the time he was thirteen. Since then his personal and photographic life are one and the same. From that early age, McCaw has been continually producing photographic work while remaining excited about the medium. Through the mid- to late1980s McCaw was involved in skateboarding/zine/punk scenes with a fisheye lens and Tri-X. After high school he fell in love with the simplicity of large format cameras. In 1992 McCaw got his first 4″ × 5″. In 1993 he discovered platinum/palladium and went on to build even larger cameras. After working the boundaries of analogue photographic mediums with his *Sunburn* project, McCaw continues to rethink the traditional use of photographic materials, now working with instant pack films. Still building his own cameras, he is currently manipulating the mechanics of how cameras record time. His work is held in over twenty-five public collections both nationally and internationally. To see more of his work visit www.chrismccaw.com.

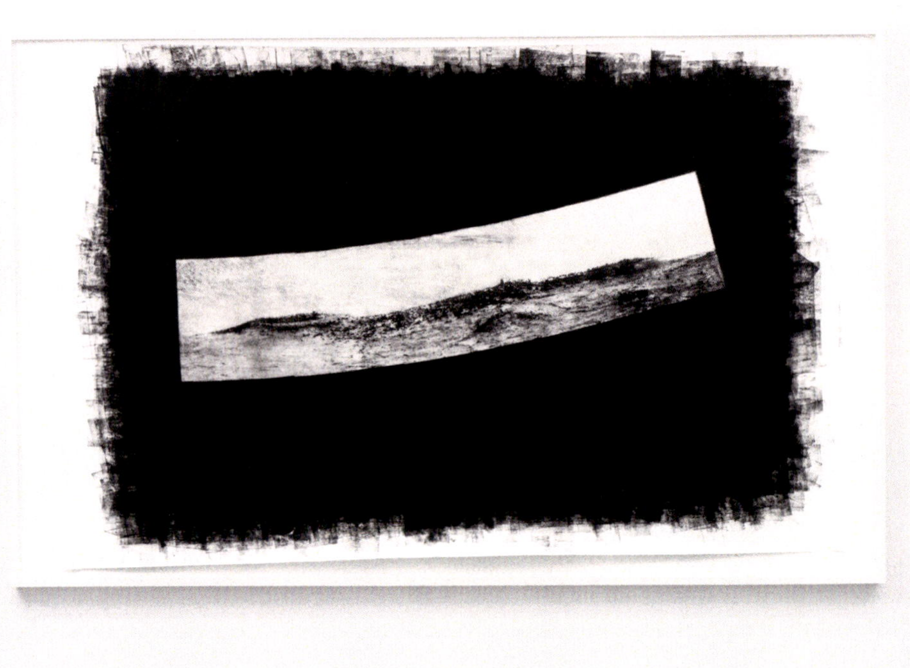

Figure 18.48. *Wharton Ridge*, bromoil print, 69″ x 42″ © Brittany Nelson 2019

Brittany Nelson

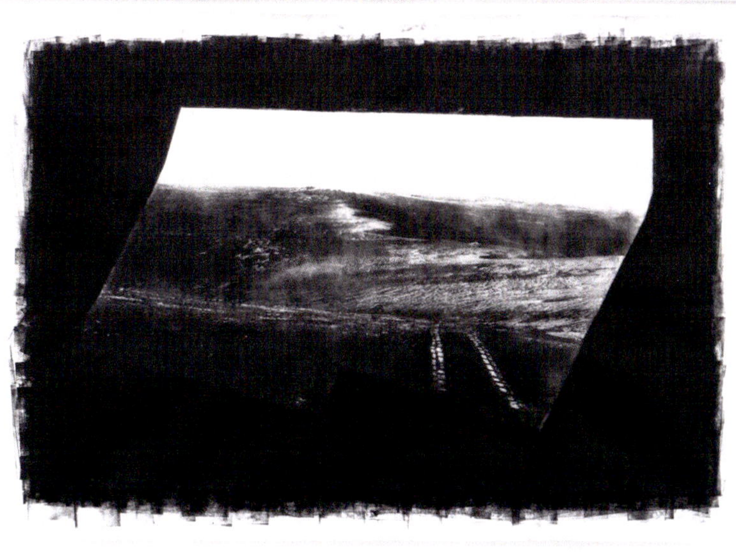

Figure 18.49. *Tracks I*, bromoil print, 67″ x 42″ © Brittany Nelson 2019

Creative process

I use Ilford MGIV matte paper in a 42″ roll. My bromoil solutions are copper sulfate (10%), potassium bromide (10%), potassium dichromate (1%); also I use Kodak Dektol, Ilford Rapid Fix, and Heico Perma Wash.

The images from the Mars Opportunity rover are downloaded from the NASA website archive, desaturated (from enhanced or false color images) then printed digitally on Moab Entrada bright paper, copy-slide photographed to 35mm film, and then exposed to gelatin silver paper.

After the prints are exposed, developed, fixed and archival washed, they are left to dry, usually in the sun, to make sure no moisture is remaining. Back in the darkroom the prints are then dried thoroughly again with a hair dryer before bleaching.

I will bleach 2–3 prints maximum (the print sizes are around 42″ × 75″) in a large bleach bath at one time, and then the bleach must be disposed of and remixed due to exhaustion. The prints are then washed, fixed again, and then archivally washed and dried in the sun a second time.

To prepare the matrices for inking, I use a hair dryer on the prints again before resoaking thoroughly in water and then hanging on a drying line to let most of the water run off. I will then use shop towels to dry off the excess moisture front and back. Then the print goes on a large table where I further towel dry the surface until no beads of moisture remain.

I will then roll a medium-light coating of ink on a brayer. I prefer spreading the ink on a sheet of glass for this step to get an even distribution. I use

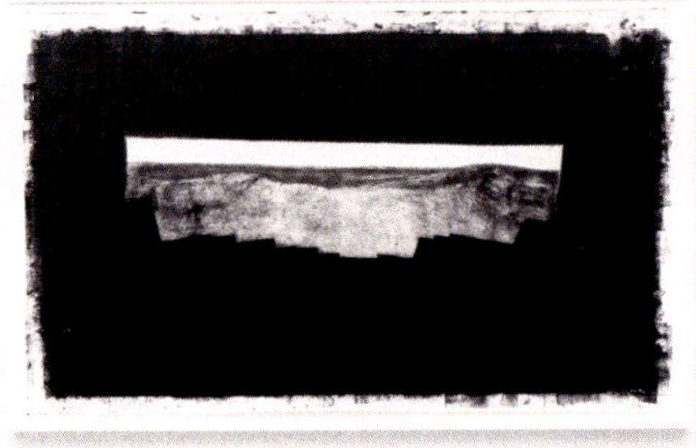

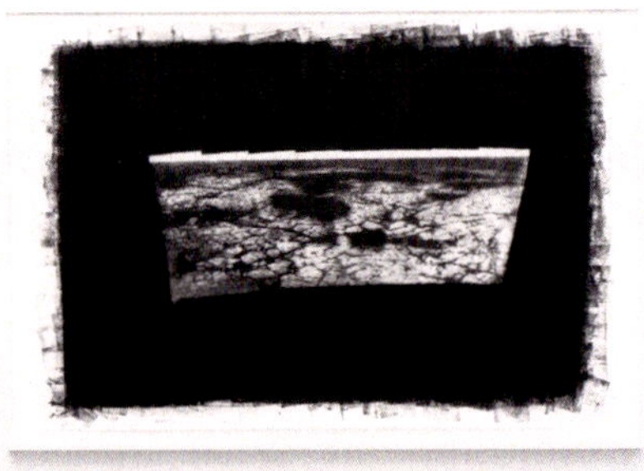

Figures 18.50–18.51. Left, *Endeavor Crater*; right, *Olympia*, bromoil prints, 70″ x 42″ and 67″ x 42″ respectively

the brayer to apply ink over the entire surface of the image. Then I will use large brushes for bromoil to excavate the details of the images out of the ink. While it is recommended to do a "hopping" motion, I do more of a stab. I will switch between applying ink over the entire image with brayers, and then doing detail work with the brushes until I start to reach the desired density in the shadow areas. After several hours of this, I will then hang the print up on the wall using magnets, and do all of the finishing and detail work this way. I use wet shop towels, cotton swabs, and cotton pads to re-wet areas where the highlights are, and a variety of brushes to work out the shadows and midtones. I will do a single print start to finish in one day, usually taking around 8–11 hours.

When working on a bromoil print this large, and because of the nature of the process, it became very important to constantly take a step back while working on it. It became an exhausting dance to work on rendering small details within the print and then walking across the room to look at it from a distance. To avoid disaster, I would never absorb myself in up-close work for more than a few minutes before moving backward to observe it in its entirety, more or less a physical manifestation of how one should edit in Photoshop, constantly zooming out and zooming back in.

It is recommended that you "super dry" bromoil prints between steps, making sure that all of the moisture is completely evaporated from the paper. For drying giant bromoil prints between developing, bleaching, and inking, I unrolled the prints in the back of my Jeep on top of screens pulled from a darkroom drying rack, and parked the car in the sun with the windows up. This heated the prints very quickly and efficiently, which helped combat any issues with very humid weather in Richmond, Virginia where they were made.

In order to develop, fix and bleach prints this large, I had trays manufactured specifically for this project in a variety of sizes, the largest of which are 75″ × 51″. The trays are made from aluminum to minimize the weight and I had them powder coated with a chemical resistant finish. They also contain a simple drain valve that screws into the side of the trays.

Artist statement

The bromoil works depict the desolate landscapes taken from the Mars rover Opportunity, who roamed the planet alone for 14 years, her twin rover dying seven years previously. Only intended to live 90 sols (about 90 Earth days), Opportunity outlived her lifespan many times over, and was in unscheduled missions for almost the entirety of her 14 years, traveling the farthest of any off-planet vehicle. Only referred to with she/her pronouns by NASA, the lonely robot became heavily personified by the public. The combination of conducting hard science experiments, traveling far distances never to find a mate, and taking contemplative photographs looking back at her own tracks, portrays Opportunity as a classic lesbian trope. Using the

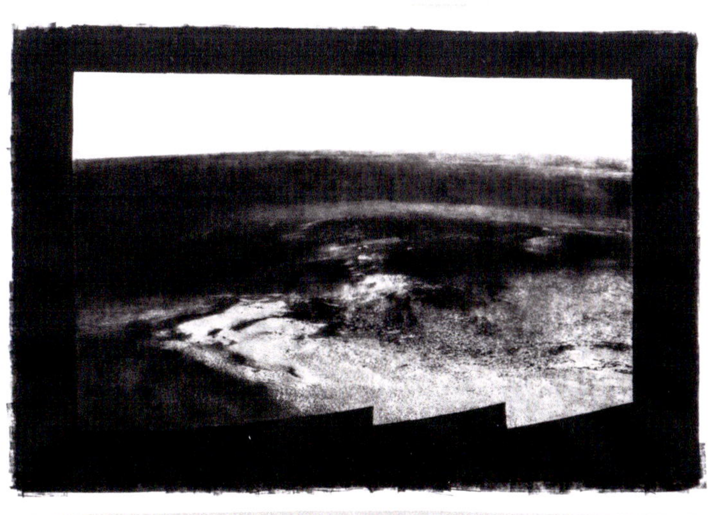

Figure 18.52 *Greeley Haven*, bromoil print, 67″ x 42″ © Brittany Nelson 2019

vastness of the NASA archives, I appropriate imagery from Opportunity's cameras and then translate them into bromoil, a heavily romantic Pictorial era process that replaces the silver in a photographic print with hand layered lithographic ink, an attempt to touch the landscape of a faraway world. I made all these works in 2019 for two exhibitions, *10,000 Light Years From Home*, at Patron Gallery in Chicago, and *Kosmologiska Pilar* (Cosmological Arrrows) at Bonniers Konsthall in Stockholm, Sweden.

Biography

Brittany Nelson (b. 1984, Great Falls, Montana) works with 19th century photographic chemistry techniques to address themes of queer and feminist science fiction. She is the recipient of a Creative Capital Foundation Grant in Visual Arts and a Theo Westenberger Foundation Grant for advancing women in the arts. Her work has been exhibited at Die Ecke (Santiago, Chile), Sonnenstube (Lugano, Switzerland), Bonniers Konsthall (Stockholm, Sweden), The Museum of Contemporary Art Detroit (Detroit, Michigan), The Brooklyn Academy of Music (New York, New York), The International Print Center (New York, New York), among many others. Her monograph *Out Of The Everywhere* was released in 2019 by Mousse Publishing (Milan, Italy), and her sculptural book *Monuments to the Conquerors of Space* was released in 2017 and published by Small Editions (New York, New York). Nelson is currently an Artist in Residence with SETI (Search for Extraterrestrial Intelligence) and was a 2017 artist in residence at the Headlands Center for the Arts (San Francisco, California). Her work has been featured in publications such as *Art in America*, *Frieze*, and *The New Yorker*. Nelson is currently based in Richmond, Virginia and Trondheim, Norway. To see more of Nelson's work visit www.brittanynelson.com.

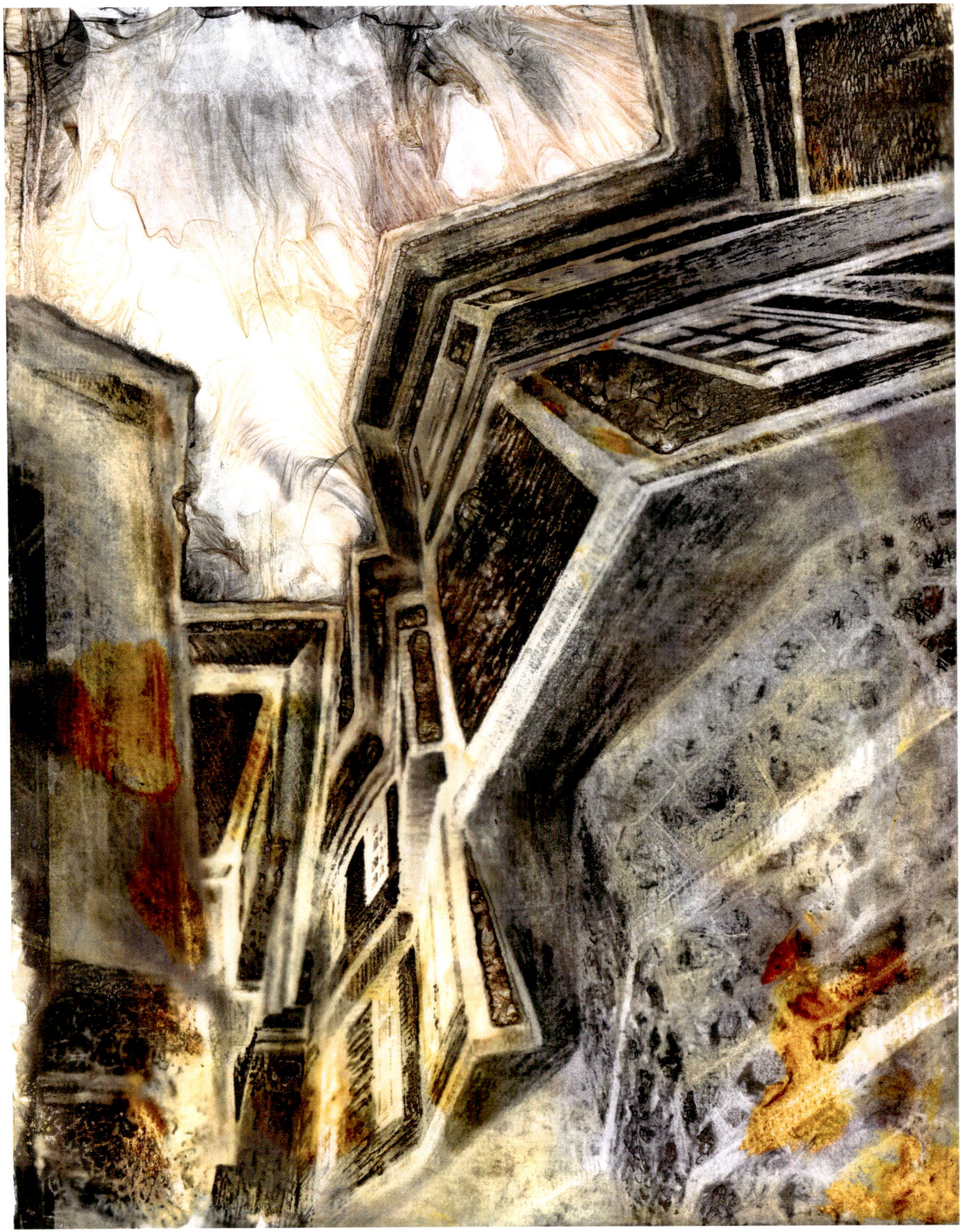

Figure 18.53. *Projections I*, 8″ x 10″ printed as a 24″ x 30″ pigment print © Eva Nikolova 2019. All of Nikolova's works in this section are cameraless prints inspired by Balkan vernacular architecture. They began as drawings which were contact printed onto silver gelatin paper. The resulting clichés verre were bleached in a mordançage solution and selectively redeveloped with a brush.

Eva Nikolova

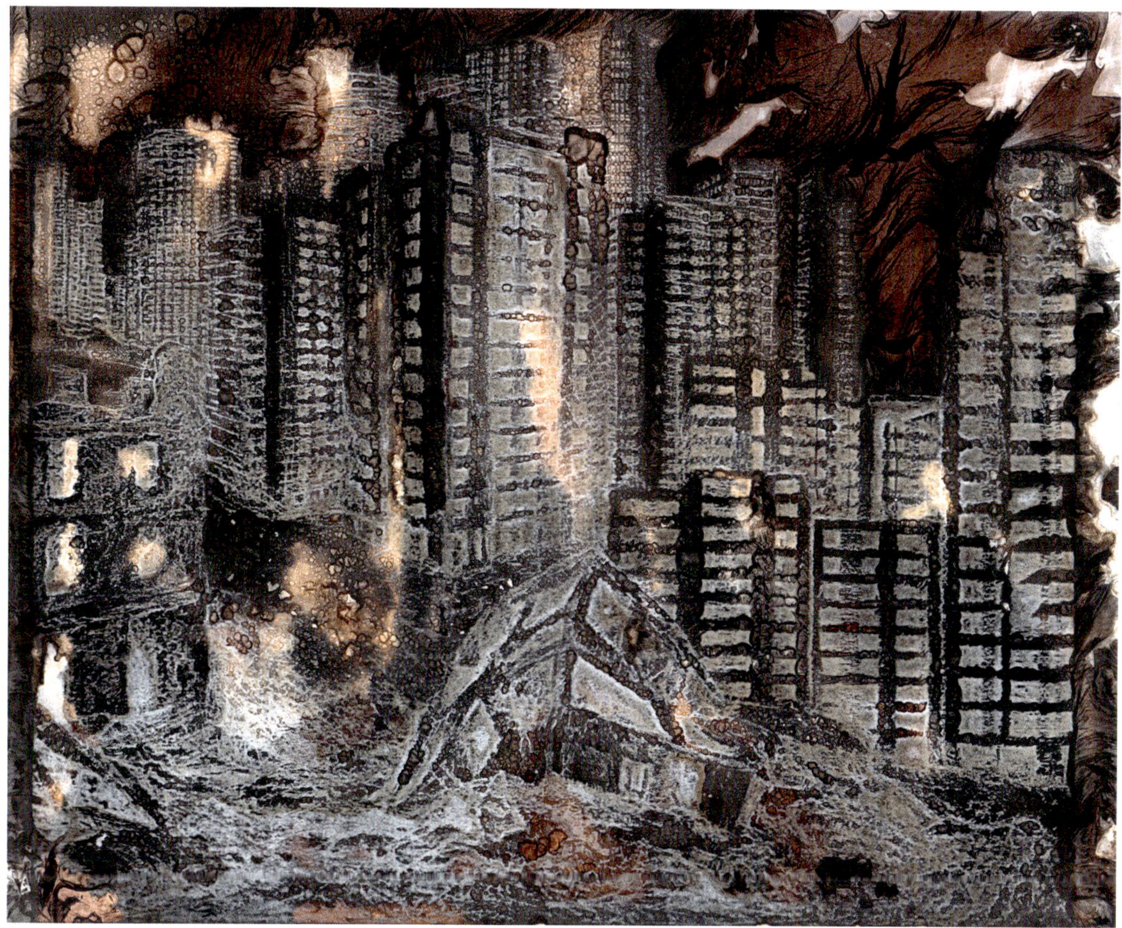

Figure 18.54. *21 Fragments of Yesterday and Tomorrow XVI*, 10″ x 8″ printed as a 18″ x 15″ pigment print © Eva Nikolova 2016

Creative practice

The relationship between geography and memory has been the central preoccupation in my work ever since moving to the US from my native Bulgaria in 1992. When past and present are geographically discontinuous, as they are for the immigrant, remembrance is forever bound up with place, with what must be the meaning of home. And so it is that in my cameraless photography, drawing, printmaking, and animation, I am drawn to images of land and dwellings, and to narratives of displacement, loss, longing and remembrance.

In *21 Fragments of Yesterday and Tomorrow*, I set out to create a suite of works as a meditation on the radical metamorphosis of the place I grew up in, then left, then revisited after a decade's absence. What I found was the landscape of my youth being transformed into a sort of building site without prior history, where development and obliteration were effectively indistinguishable. And yet it became apparent to me that even when all traces of a past are erased, landscape is haunted by memory no less than memory by landscape.

To arrest this erasure, I might have reached for my camera, that device seen as the conserver of memory. But for me—this will seem paradoxical to some—nothing can erase the experience of the past quite like a photograph, which replaces what it purports to preserve. To create photographs that would not rob me of the subjectivity of lived experience, I would have to go back to the dawn of the medium before the tyrannical ubiquity of the camera, when it was still an outgrowth of a free experimentalism with materials, of unfettered curiosity, and of a fascination with the making of marks on paper.

I began the works in *21 Fragments* with drawings from memory, which then went through various transformations spanning media and technologies both historic and contemporary. As a printmaker by training and mindset, who processes experience through drawing and who has dedicated the last decade to cameraless photography, I turned to the cliché verre, an obscure cameraless technique in which a hand-designed matrix (as in printmaking) is traced by means of light onto light-sensitive paper (as in photography).

Cliché verre has remained a practice on the fringes of both photography and printmaking and as a graphic medium has been seldom used since the mid-19th century. My own discovery of it came about in 2011 at Manhattan Graphics Center in New York City thanks to Douglas Collins, who also introduced me to chemigrams which comprise the bulk of my work in alternative photography. Collins later also showed me bleach-etch *aka* mordançage—that mysterious process which I use in conjunction with cliché verre in this series and the series *Projections* from 2019.

While the original cliché verre matrix was a glass plate onto which a drawing was made with an etching needle through a smoked etching ground or printmaking ink that had been dusted white, contemporary approaches use a wide range of drawing substances and tools. To make the matrix, I drew on 8″ × 10″ paper with graphite, charcoal, black and white ink, white chalk and oil pastel. Because I mixed a variety of materials, whose visible tones do not coincide with their opacity—which is what matters when making a negative to print from —I photocopied the drawing onto thin printer paper often re-working this copy by scratching through the toner with a blade for textural effects. This then was contact-printed under the enlarger onto Ilford Multigrade RC Glossy paper developed with standard darkroom chemistry to yield cliché verre prints, that would constitute a sizeable edition, were the process to end here. But rather than the end point, each cliché verre was merely the stage for a series of further interventions, scanned and output in its final state as a 15″ × 18″ archival pigment print.

In a precarious process, where creation takes place on the edge of ruination, the clichés verre were bleach-etched in a solution of copper chloride, hydrogen peroxide and citric acid until the image disappeared and the emulsion began to lift off. The fragile emulsion was in places rubbed away, and in others painstakingly rearranged with a needle, while the prints were selectively redeveloped with a brush and Dektol in various dilutions. In this process owing more to painting and alchemy than to photography, chosen parts of the vanished picture were resurrected, imparting color to the black and white prints solely through chemical interactions. Some of the colors were further intensified by drying the prints in direct sunlight. The silver gelatin emulsion, equally a site of creation and dissolution, became the embodiment of the themes of the work—the nature of transformation and the interchangeability of construction and destruction within the unstable and fragmentary edifice of memory itself.

Artist statement

Imbued with the singularity of the process that gave rise to them, the prints in *21 Fragments of Yesterday and Tomorrow* endeavor to reclaim a stereotypical Balkan landscape. Alternately understood as site of genocidal brutality, exotic getaway, or iconic object of nationalistic pride, the depicted locale instead became the locus of a deeply personal connection to a place and its past. While they may signify the

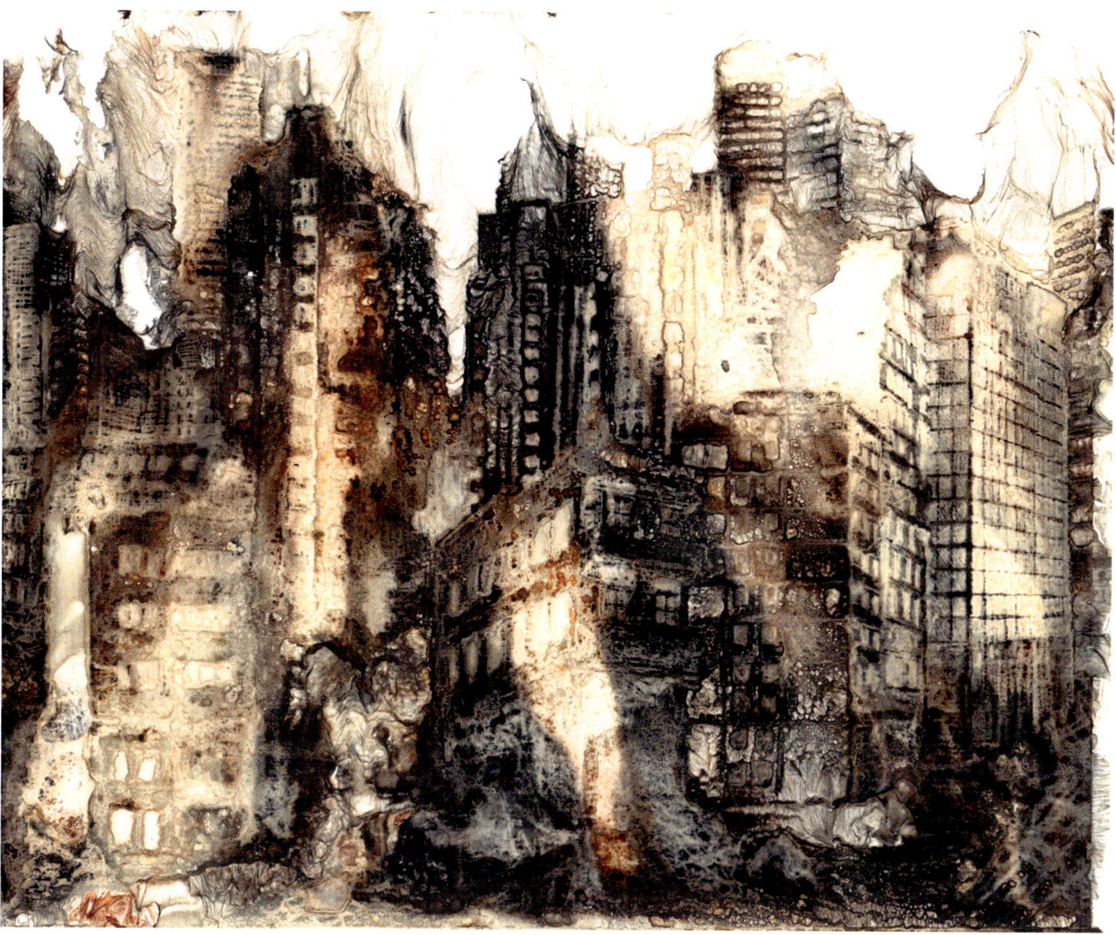

Figure 18.55. *21 Fragments of Yesterday and Tomorrow VI*, 10″ x 8″ printed as a 18″ x 15″ pigment print © Eva Nikolova 2015

region's history of war and its current predicament of speculative development, the works transcend the specificity of the context from which they arise. Ruins evoke not only their own site, but resonate with other images of decay and catastrophe, functioning as a trope of global trauma fraught with the ever-increasing wreckage of modernity.

Biography

Eva Nikolova is a Bulgarian-born, New York City-based artist who works in alternative photography, drawing, painting, and printmaking exploring themes of memory and identity in relation to place. Since 2012 she has been creating hand-drawn, cameraless silver gelatin photographs that blur the lines between drawing and photography. Experimenting with a wide array of substances, chemicals, and vintage gelatin silver papers, her prints contemplate transformation and destruction through the prism of architecture and landscape. Nikolova is the recipient of over thirty scholarships, fellowships, grants and awards, and has participated in fully funded residencies at Virginia Center for the Creative Arts, Millay Colony, Brush Creek Foundation for the Arts, Vermont Studio Center and Kimmel Harding Nelson Center for the Arts. Her work has been exhibited nationally as well as in Germany, England, Canada, Scotland, and India. Nikolova holds a BFA in Painting/Printmaking from Southern Illinois University and an MFA in Printmaking from Indiana University, Bloomington. To see her work visit: www.evanikolova.com.

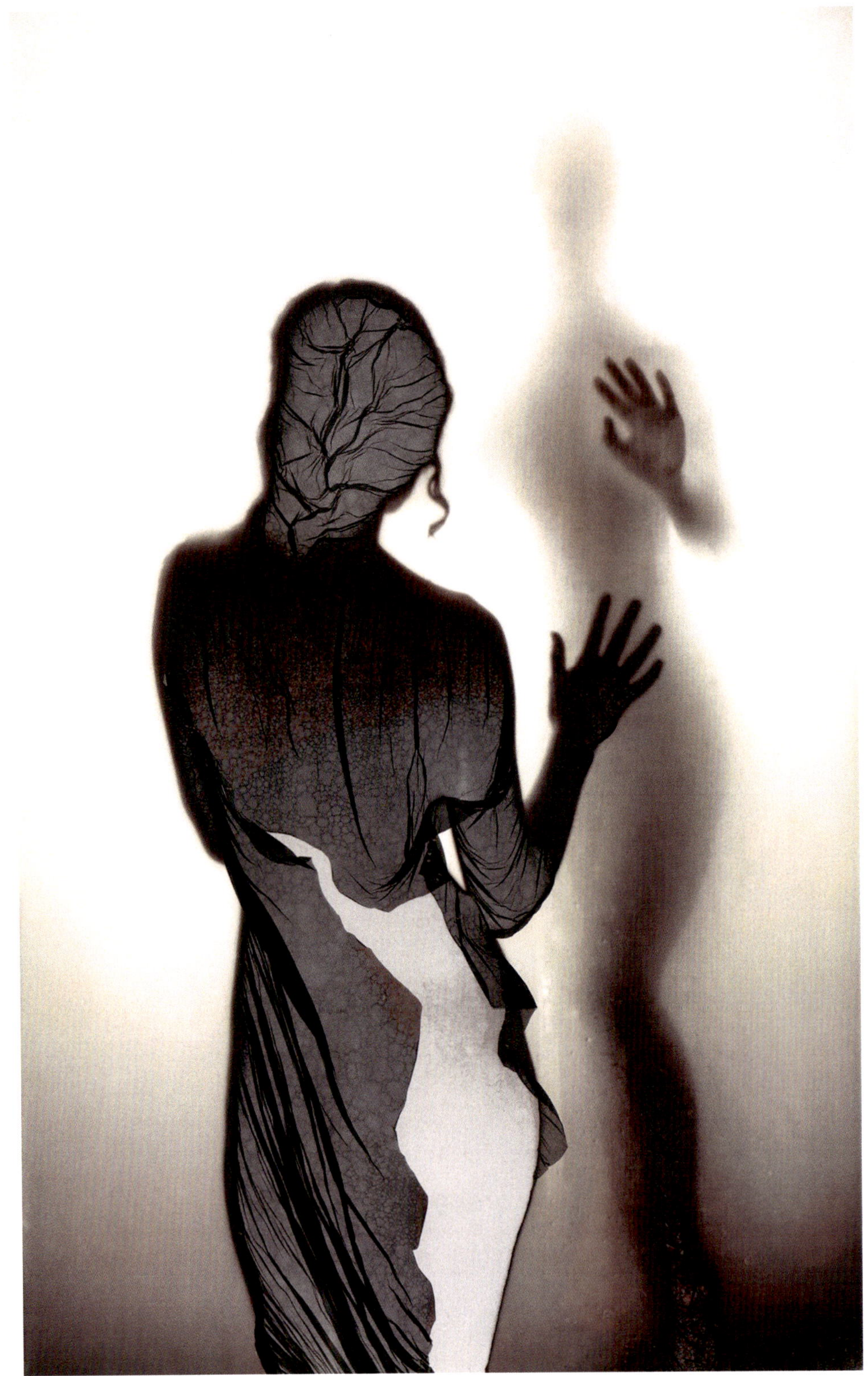

Figure 18.56. *Finding Self*, mordançage on 11″ x 14″ silver gelatin paper © Elizabeth Opalenik 2010

Elizabeth Opalenik

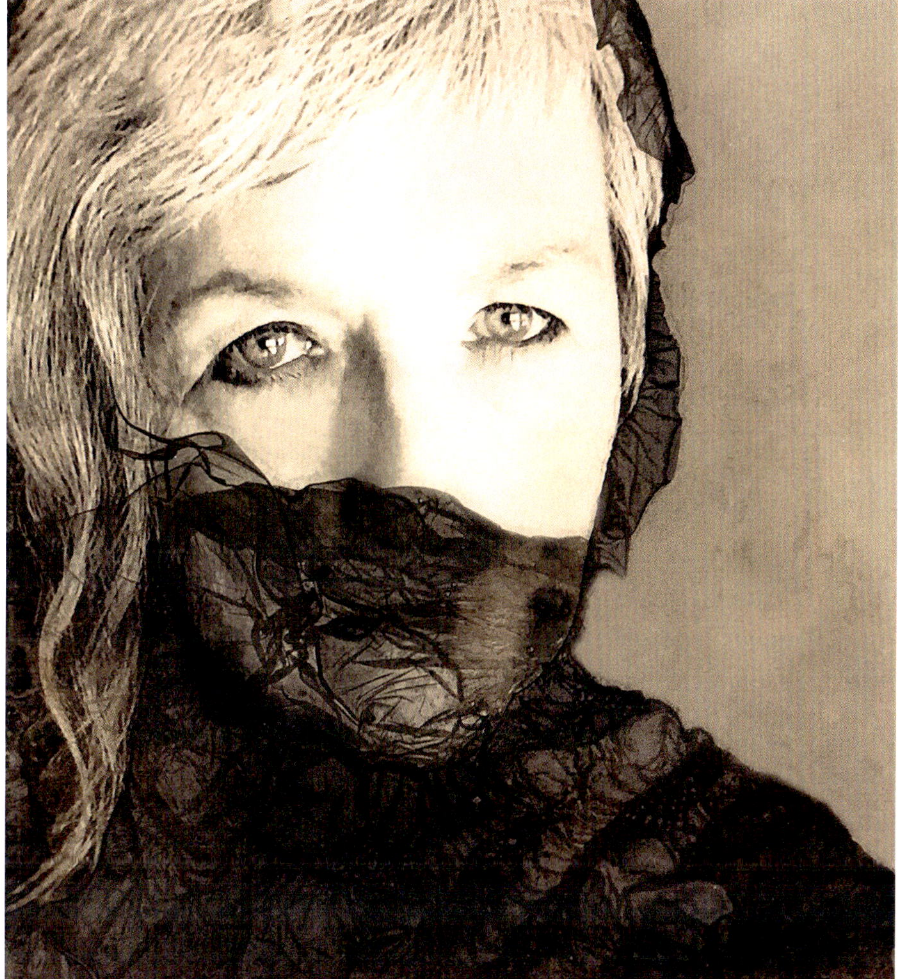

Figure 18.57. *Masked Mordançeuse, Pandemic Self Portrait,* mordançage on 11″ x 14″ silver gelatin paper © Elizabeth Opalenik 2021

Creative practice

In 1983 I met the French artist Jean-Pierre Sudre and was introduced to his practice in mordançage. I knew instantly that I had come home photographically and sought to further understand his process through annual visits to his studio to view his work. In a 1991 workshop with him in his Provence studio I learned the basics. My advice is to learn from a master and then make it your own. By print # 5 in that workshop I began saving the veils of emulsion on the road to my style in the process, which also incorporated the figure.

Creative process

My preferred darkroom process involving silver gelatin is the mordançage technique and experimenting with all its possibilities. From the beginning, the lifted veils of silver emulsion in the shadow areas of the photographic paper were a fascinating element. Normally, they would cling to the highlights and be washed or rubbed away. I had not previously seen mordançage images in the style of saving those veils, and exploring how to manipulate the floating emulsion to cloak the figure in veils as delicate as silvery spider webs became my

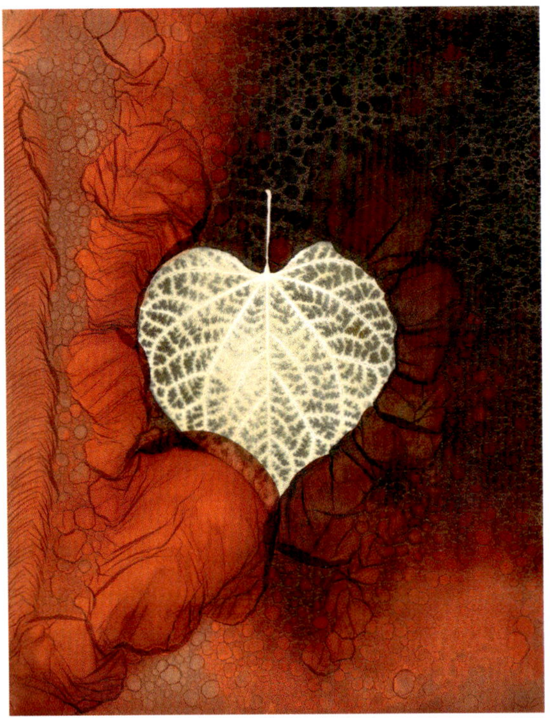

Figure 18.58. *Centered in the Universe*, mordançage on 11″ x 14″ silver gelatin paper © Elizabeth Opalenik 2008

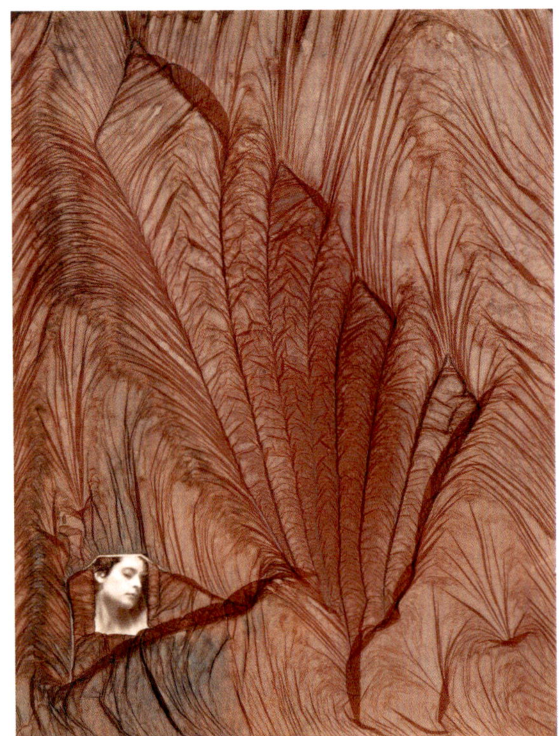

Figure 18.59. *Flight of Dreams*, mordançage on 11″ x 14″ silver gelatin paper © Elizabeth Opalenik 1994

mission and my contribution to the process. The process of controlling the veils by gently rocking the mordançaged image in a tray of water, using an eyedropper or my breath, is akin to a meditative practice for me.

I have a freezer full of saved older papers and use them when possible for their high silver content, like Agfa warmtone and Ilford. Papers on the market today—Ilford, Bergger, Foma, Arista and Adox—also work well. Each offers a different look to mordançage, some better for the veiling of the silver emulsion that I favor and some for the tonal variety. Different images "ask" for different treatments and combinations.

My normal developer for mordançage is Dektol, always available, but for redeveloping in the process, just about everything is tried, often mixing my own developers from powder. Even film developers work for redeveloping, and with the right combination of paper, redeveloper, or toner, I have achieved some of my best image colors. The most beautiful image for me has been *Centered in the Universe, 2008*, and took a few weeks to 'develop' to that red color. One of the redevelopers was very old D-76. The image was kept in the darkroom space, under safelight or lights off, to oxidize. I believe all these factors contributed to the final color, but there is no way to test for that.

In mordançage the key to success is experimentation and patience. Each piece is unique. Without preserving the veils, you could perhaps derive similar results.

I start with a basic formula of distilled water, copper chloride, 30–35% hydrogen peroxide and glacial acetic acid. I have found, while teaching at various locations, that regular tap water can cause problems because of varied ground water chemicals, so best to eliminate that possibility by mixing the formula with distilled water. Each paper can require an adjustment to the amounts in the formula and age of the hydrogen peroxide. One only knows

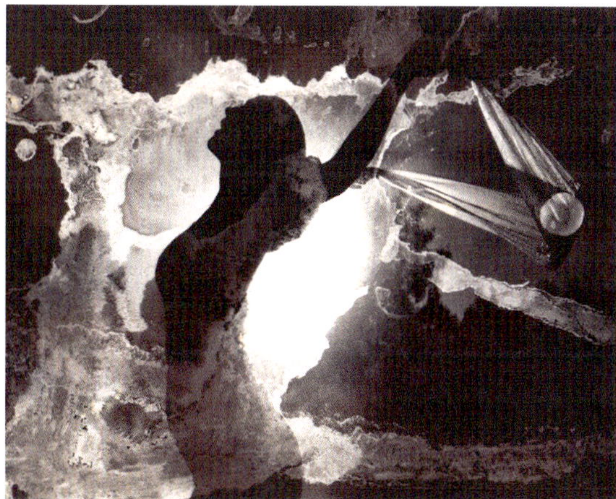

Figure 18.60. *Catching the Crystal Moon*, mordançage on 11″ x 14″ silver gelatin paper © Elizabeth Opalenik 2012

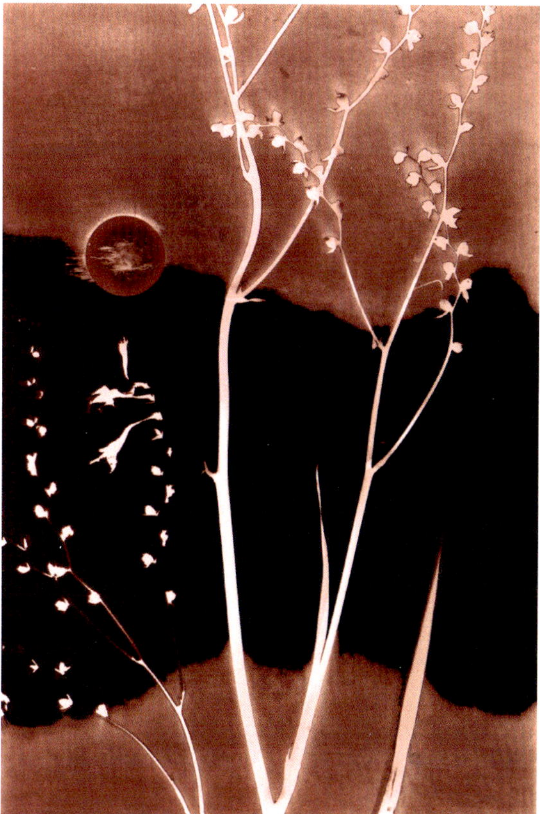

Figure 18.61. *December Moon*, mordançage on 11″ x 14″ silver gelatin paper © Elizabeth Opalenik 2009

that through testing. Doing test bands each time is one of the most important parts of the process and is the one, sadly, most people will try to skip. It is where you will learn the most about how the process will work. From test bands one gathers information on controlling how quickly the emulsion will lift and at what stage or contrast that will happen. Then use the test bands for redeveloping in various ways to see coloration variants.

If just beginning in the process, photograms are a good place to start. To eliminate variables, I have used a heart shaped leaf for most of my thirty years working in mordançage each time I want to test something new.

Until recently I used only film negatives. Today, digital negatives offer a lot more possibilities to adjusting contrast and any other issues before you begin. This allows more control though I have always liked the surprises I got from a film negative and accepting all I could not control. That challenged me to think outside the box. I create with just veils of emulsion (see *Flight of Dreams*) and also use crystallizations on glass as my negative, much in the style of Jean-Pierre Sudre, my mentor. To those I might add collage of the figure or some other element (see *Catching the Crystal Moon*). Photograms and scratching into the softened emulsion offer possibilities where a cat's eye marble on the shelf can become a moon on the paper (see *December Moon*). Imagination is a wonderful resource and also helps save some of those test prints after you have dedicated a few hours of going through all the wash cycles in the process (see *Tulip #1*, following page, a photogram of a tulip in vase where a ghost vase is created by leaving the silver haze in place of the over exposed test print where the glass vase disappeared in the wash cycle).When using a digital negative, leave the step tablet on the bottom of the paper, at least for the first image, so that you can gather information about the emulsion lifting in various zones. It is also important to leave a white border around the image so that the veils, which stretch, have a surface to dry back onto. If you have no edge, it is harder to hold the print and the stretched veils will rip as they wrap around the paper, causing problems

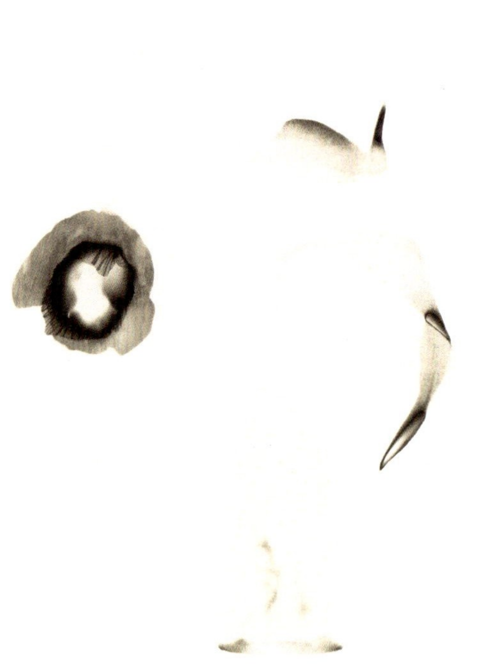

Figure 18.62. *Tulip No. 1, Westport, Connecticut,* mordançage on 11˝ x 14˝ silver gelatin paper © Elizabeth Opalenik 1992

when trying to remove the paper from the tray. To avoid this problem, I often work on Plexiglas, which makes lifting the image out of the water easier, especially if I am saving the veils.

Just because you can save veils, doesn't mean you always should. Like any process, each step along the way should complement the final image.

Controlling the process takes observation and ingenuity. I often work in just water to help finesse the silver emulsion—hot for lifting, cold for slowing down the process. I will employ a hypodermic needle to release water under the veil to avoid tearing while rocking the tray during a wash cycle. Because washing 15–20 minutes between each step is key to creating an image as archival as possible, this is all very important to me. If you are not saving the veils, but removing them with jets of water or a ball of cotton, then the washing process becomes much easier. The hypodermic needle can also be used to remove veils or bits of silver emulsion on the wet image.

Some images with veils can take all day to make. I may dry between steps and then continue to wash. I have learned the hard way that it is easier to stay with each image until the end; it will result in a higher success rate especially if you keep good notes. It is a dance and why Sudre called me a "mordançeuse." Always remember, what takes time to create, time respects.

Biography

Elizabeth Opalenik has a forty year career teaching or making images on six continents seeking the beauty and grace that exists within all things. Her "what if" approach, whether digital or darkroom, has her using photography as the visual voice for stories left behind. Opalenik prefers working in mordançage with her signature veils of floating emulsion or other handmade processes such as carbon, platinum/palladium or hand painting. Her work is collected and exhibited internationally. Following a life long dream, she published her first monograph, *Poetic Grace: Elizabeth Opalenik Photographs 1979–2007*. In 2021 she conjured into existence *Workshop Stories: Changed Through Photography*, with stories and images from over 100 of today's iconic photographers. To see more of her work visit elizabethopalenik.com.

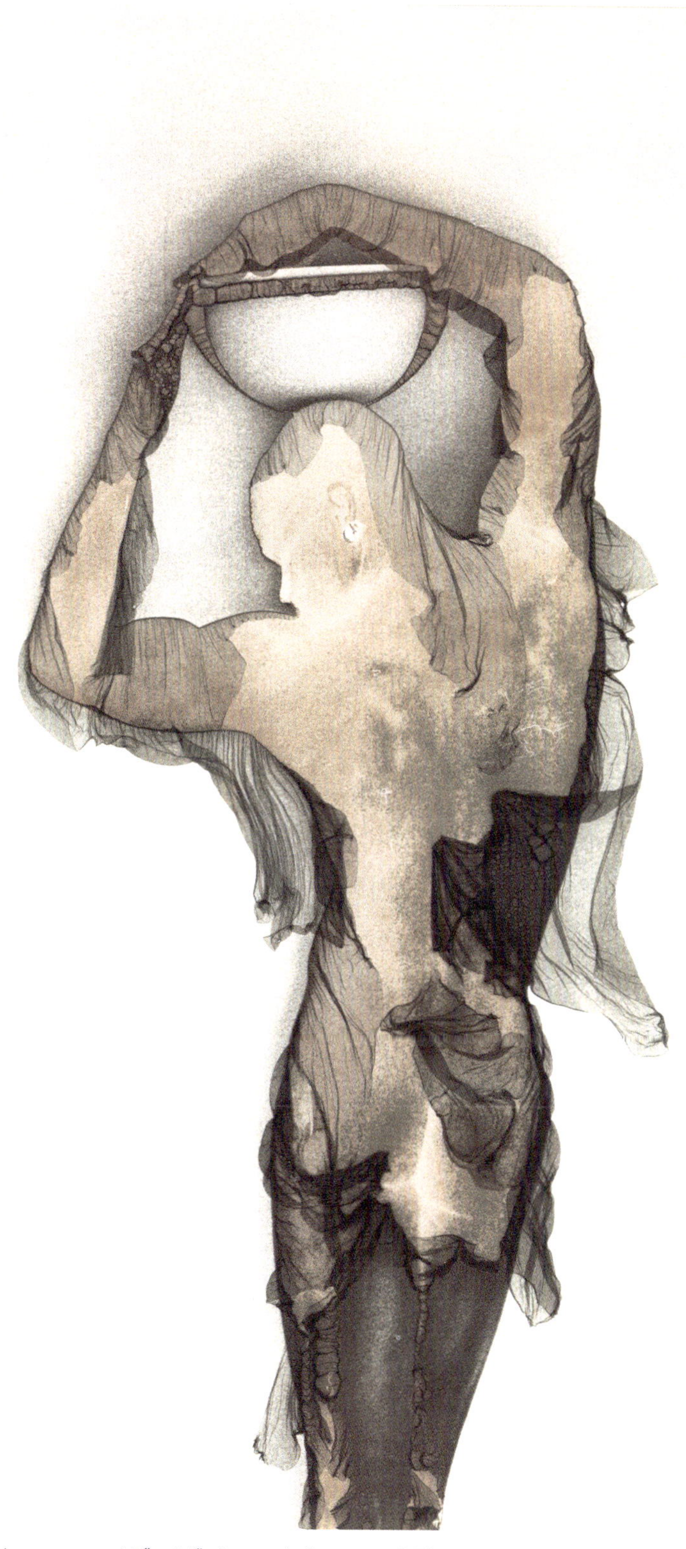

Figure 18.63. *Revelations*, mordançage on 11″ x 14″ silver gelatin paper © Elizabeth Opalenik 1996

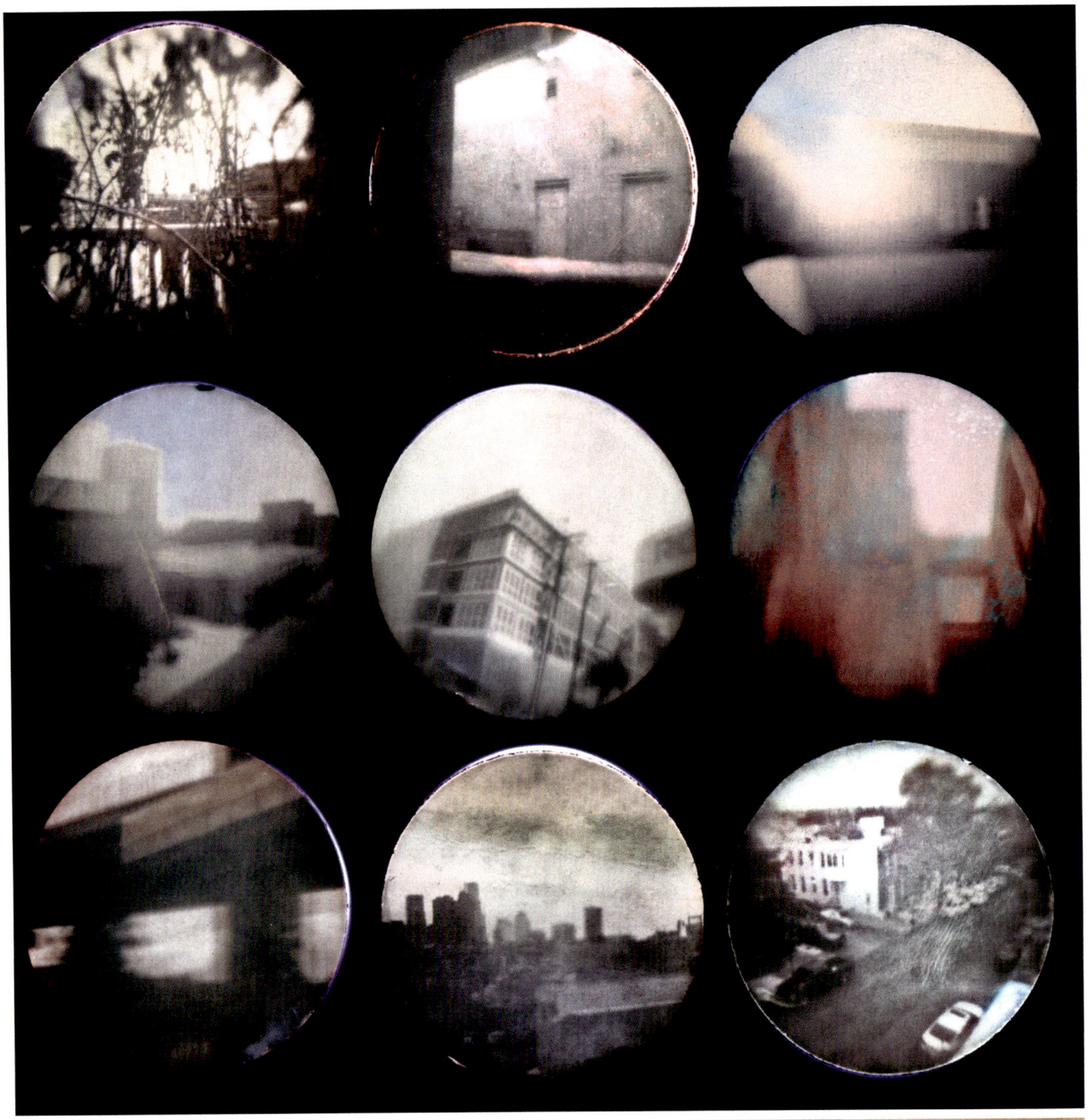

Figures 18.64–18.65. *Time Capsules*, 24″ x 24″archival pigment print from lumen box camera images © Chris Peregoy 2021. To the right is a lumen box camera that Peregoy constructed from a 35 mm film canister on which he puts a lens. The top to the film canister is filled with a tiny circular cut piece of silver gelatin paper. Exposures are from ten minutes to eight hours. Then Peregoy scans the individual images to print larger archival pigment prints.

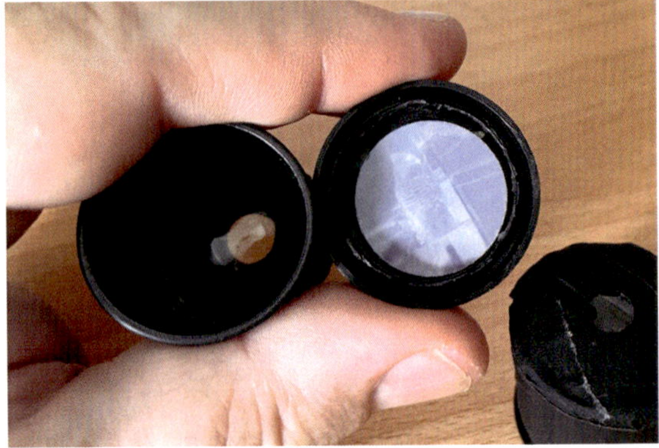

Chris Peregoy

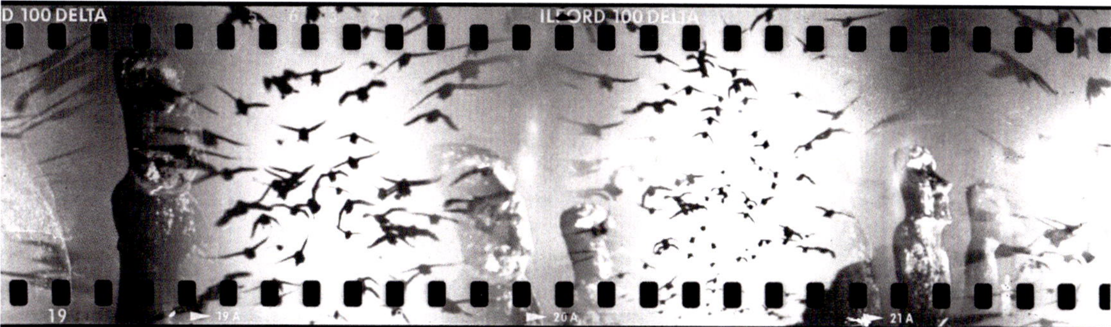

Figure 18.66. *Eastern Gaze*, 20″ x 6″, archival pigment print from blending pinhole camera © Chris Peregoy 2004

Creative process

I heard about Lumen Box images on a podcast where black and white photo paper is exposed in a camera between 10 minutes to over an hour. My first Lumen Box was a size 14 shoebox with diopter lenses which are usually used to change a normal lens so that it can focus closer. By themselves, they will focus light like any other lens. A +1 focuses light at 1 meter, a +2 at half a meter. Each diopter power is divided into one meter to give its focal length. For my shoebox I used a +1 and a +2 to make a 333 mm lens (about 13 inches).

My current project with this process uses 35 mm film canisters with either a 25 mm or a 45 mm focal length lens. I cut one-inch circles out of black and white paper and stick them in the lids. These lumen camera exposures are between 10 minutes and 8 hours depending on the light. I consider these time capsules since I'm capturing time while working or doing other activities.

I have a lot of Kodak Polycontrast RC paper that I'm using for the lumen cameras. For darkroom printing I prefer Forte Elegance and Kodak Azo or homemade potassium chloride contact printing paper. I also make my own silver gelatin glass plate in 2.5″ × 3.5″ and 5″ × 7″ for lens and pinhole images. I process glass plates and x-ray film and my homemade silver gelatin paper in Kodak HC110 and print using Sprint chemicals.

My negatives are scanned and used to make QTR negatives for alternative printing processes and for black and white darkroom printing. I find that computer imaging software can help control my exposures and compensate for my contrast, retouching and defects in my process. QTR negatives allow me to not have to make camera film originals that are only suited for one process.

The camera I used for my 9 pinhole image was constructed from a 4″ × 5″ film box that I taped onto a Graphmatic 6 sheet film holder. A pinhole will spread light to a 3½″ circle for every inch of pinhole to film distance. I used a 10 sheet 4″ × 5″ box which gives about 2½″ image circles for each pinhole. Instead of arranging the pinholes in a grid I flipped coins into the box and marked where they landed. After nine flips I thought I had enough. Each was exposed after moving the camera. I use tape as the shutter.

In Eric Renner's *Exploring Pinhole Photography* he wrote about David Lebe's convex curved cameras that blended frames together. I had been intrigued with multiple framed blends for a long time so this idea really appealed to me. In my camera my film passes over a piece of plastic pipe to make a curved film plane. This was attached to an old folder camera in which I had cut the film guides away so that the film could wrap around the pipe. The outer box was from a bulk Kodalith film

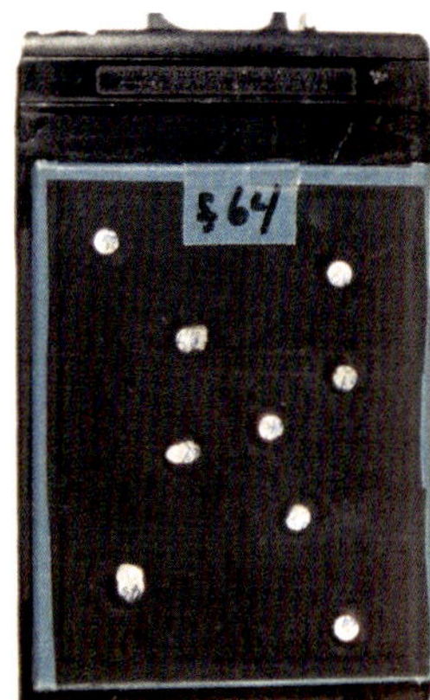

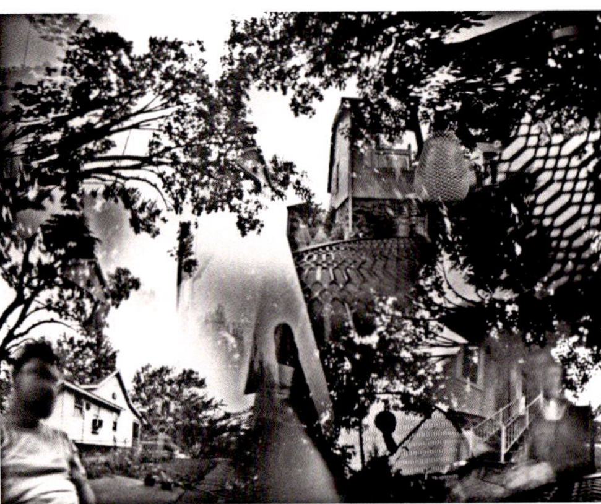

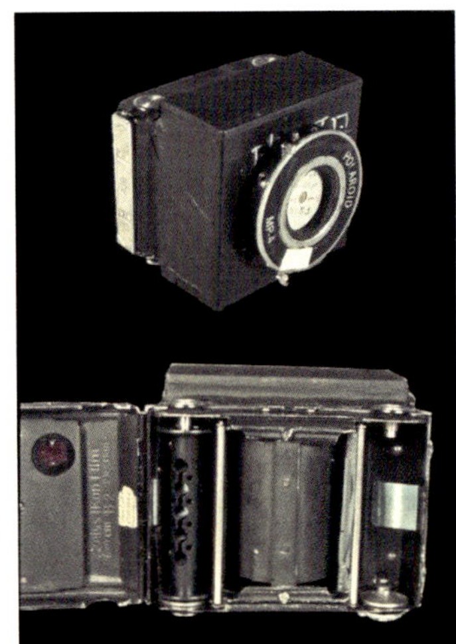

Figures 18.67–18.69. Left, nine pinhole camera, 7″x 5″ x 2″, made from a film box, film holder, tape, and aluminum pie tin. Middle, *Dinner with Mia*, 8″x 10″, silver gelatin print from the nine pinhole camera © Chris Peregoy 1998. Right, blending pinhole camera, 4″ x 5″ x 3″, made from a folding 120 camera, PVC pipe, bulk film box, Polaroid MP4 shutter, and brass shim stock © Chris Peregoy 1999. See images on next page.

container. I figured out how many revolutions I needed for the amount of overlap I wanted. I later used this concept to make a 3-pinhole camera in a cookie tin. I marketed these cameras as Pinhole Blenders.

Creative practice

Camera making is a process of discovery that brings me back to the early history of photography. I enjoy reading about historic technology. Pinhole was a good starting place that led me to making my own lenses, making wet and dry plates and repairing and using plate cameras from 2.5″ × 3.5″ up to 11″ × 14″. I like to tinker and to work with primitive cameras but I also see the value of my imaging software, scanner and inkjet printer. All of these have opened up new ways to work. One of the discoveries I stumbled upon while working with collodion dry plate (a wet plate that's been preserved in tannic acid) is that if you scan them in color, the pyro stain from the developer inverts into some amazing colors. When this process was used in the early 1860s there was no way to see this effect. I still print these in black and white but I love the colors of the scans and use them as inkjet prints as well.

One of my favorite things to do is to walk the aisles of any hardware store to discover new objects for cameras. It could be a neat container for a pinhole or a plumbing part that could become a helical for a focusing lens. I once turned a 3-foot section of sewer pipe into a blending camera that could expose a whole roll of 35 mm film at once. Even a coconut can be a camera with a hole added to it.

Biography

Chris Peregoy has been working in and exhibiting photographically derived work for the past forty years. Originally trained in traditional photographic practices, his current work crosses the boundaries between digital, traditional and primitive photography and marries digital image making with historic photographic processes. Many of his images deal with forgotten or imagined memories. His work has been shown in North and South America, throughout Europe, and in Japan. Peregoy's work with pinhole photography led him to form his own company, the Pinhole Blender Company, which sells his uniquely designed cameras throughout the world. To see more of his work, visit chrisperegoy.com and @pinholeblender.

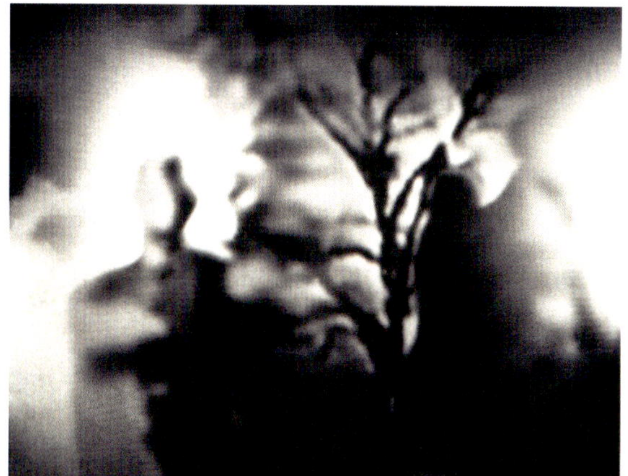
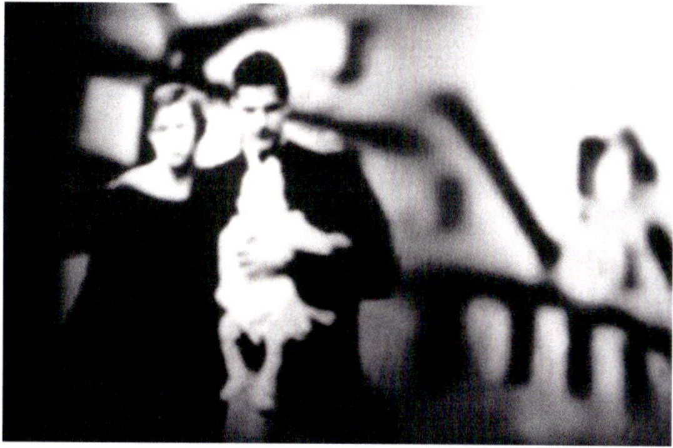
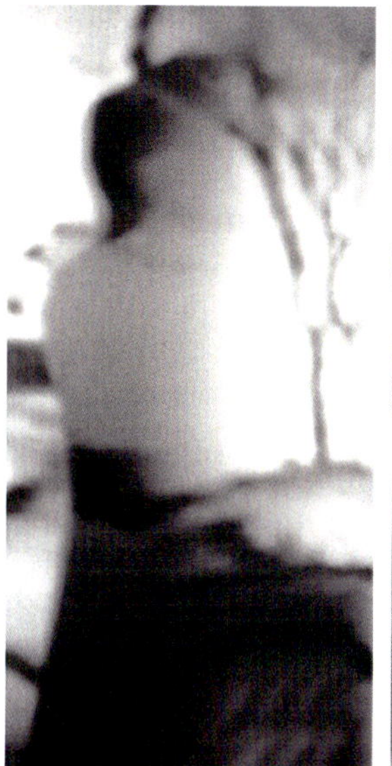
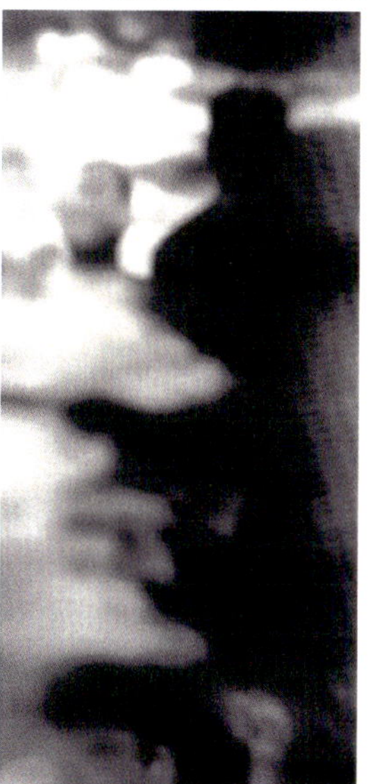
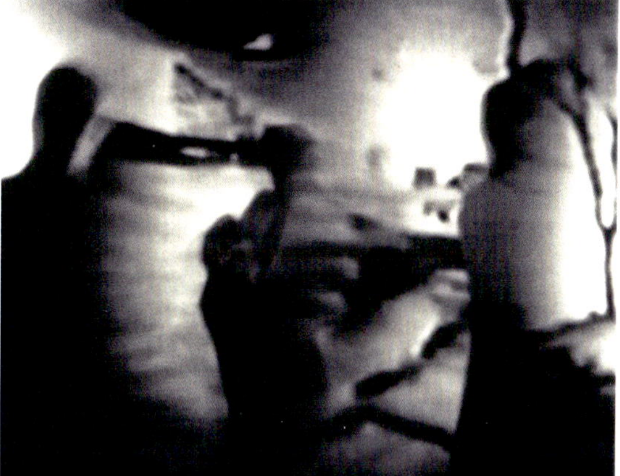
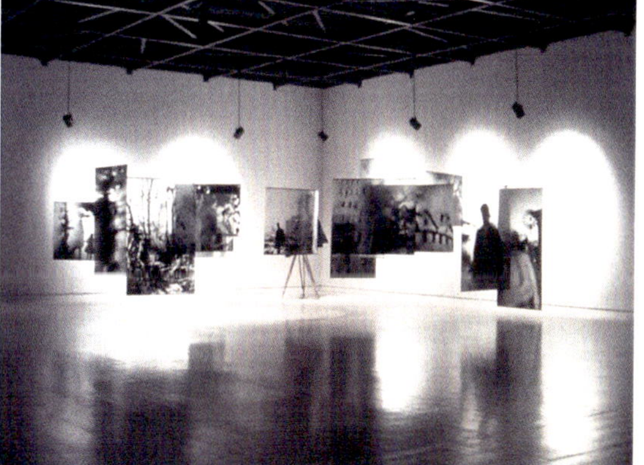
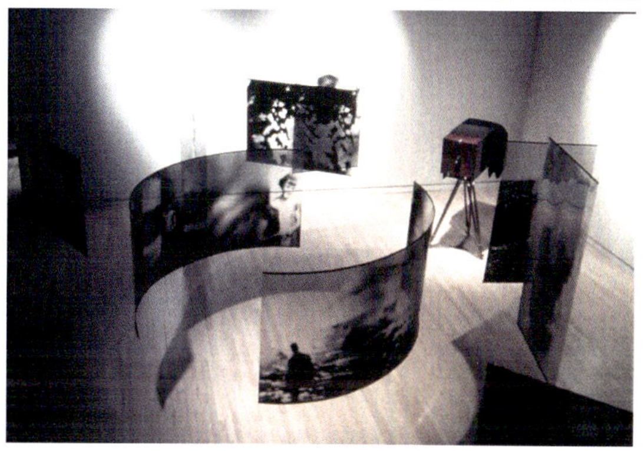

Figures 18.70–18.76. From the *Blurred Boundaries* series, all images in-camera collage using a blending pinhole camera, printed onto mural size lith film, processed for continuous tone, images hung in an installation © Chris Peregoy 1999. "In *Blurred Boundaries* I (re)construct personal memory to establish a sense of 'home,' grounding and identity, woven together from both visual and oral family histories. In the countless times that I have perused the family album, from childhood through adulthood, a host of stories have been told surrounding this picture or that. I work to rearrange these anecdotes in a way that creates a reasonable sense of family background, and through that, a clearer self-identity. The installation consists of 15 black and white transparencies and a looping video projected onto the ground glass viewing screen of a camera. The images were reconstructed from a found family album by layering family members from the depression over video footage and rephotographing them with pinhole cameras. The resulting images were printed on lith film that ranged in size from 36″ × 48″ to 36″ × 96″. The video was composites of the pinhole images with images from the album and prose written about forgotten and imagined memory."

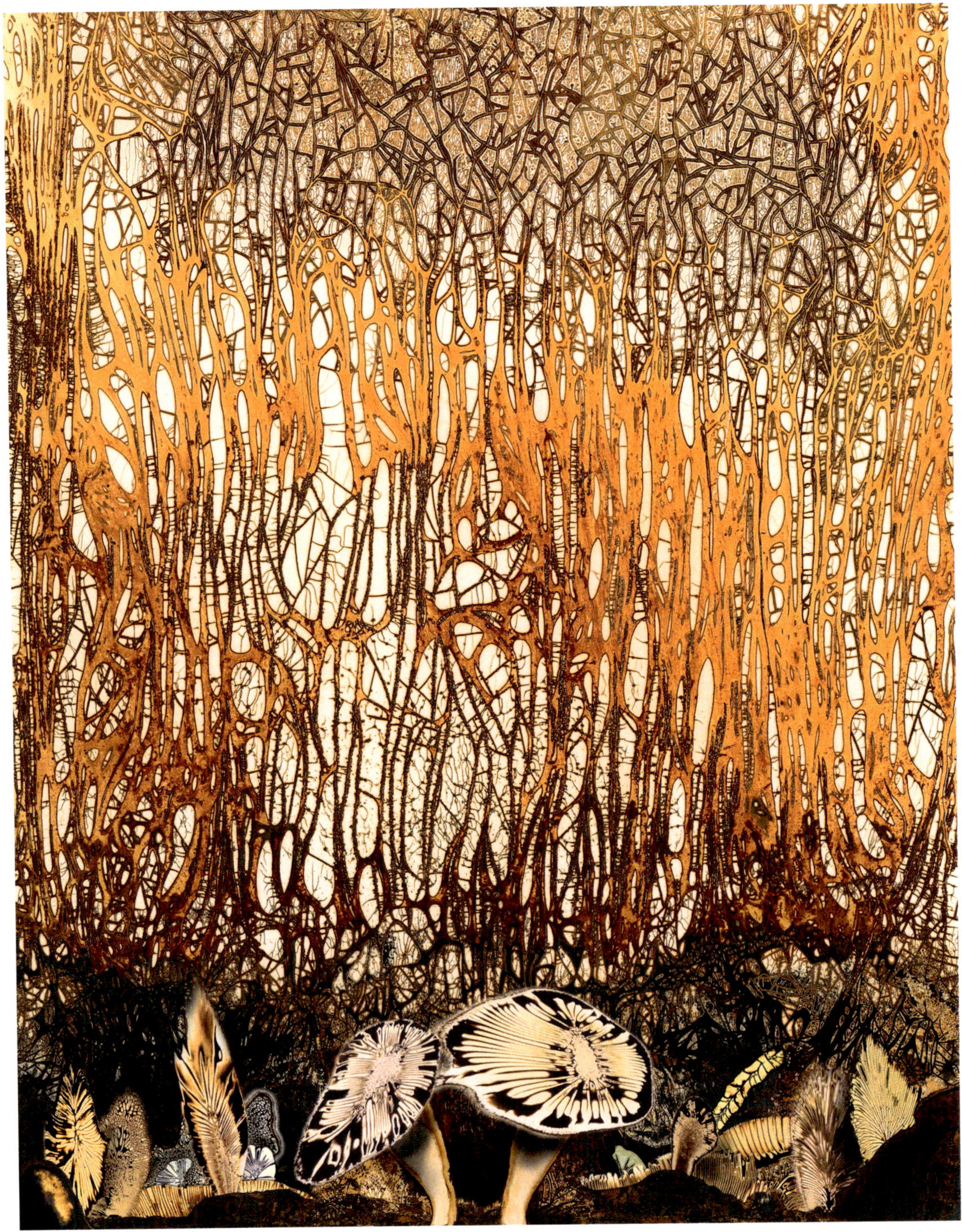

Figure 18.77. *Bramble*, 16″ x 20″ © Nolan Preece 2017

Nolan Preece

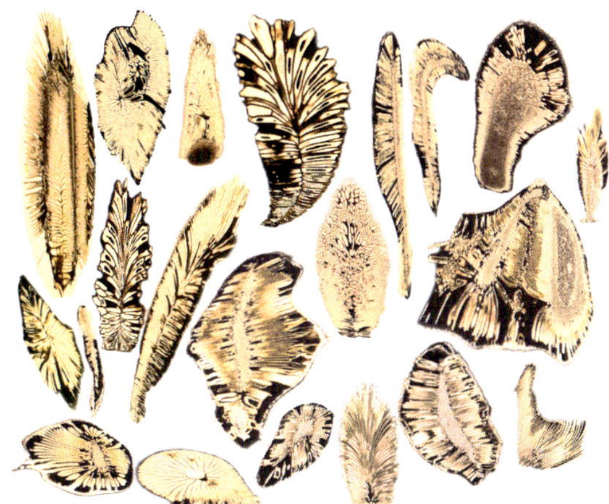

Figure 18.78. *Flora*, 20″ x 16″ © Nolan Preece 2019

Creative process

I am both a photographer, having spent many hours in a darkroom throughout my life, and a chemigramist, having also spent many hours since 1981 making chemigrams in full light. A chemigram is an equal mix of photography, printmaking and painting. Photographic materials, such as silver based papers or films, provide the substrate and photographic chemistry produces the image. Printmaking plays a role through the use of resists, substances that hold back the photographic chemical action to create the image and textural effects, much like a hard or soft ground. Examples are paint, varnish, wax and my own preference, acrylic floor finish. Painting performs the task of adding color to the image through the use of selective chemical coloration, much the same as toning. Coloration and other painting effects can also be achieved digitally by using Photoshop.

I have become a photographic paper hoarder of sorts. I have zeroed in on the Kodak developer formula D72 that I mix myself. For my fixer, I always mix Kodak fixer formula F24, a nonhardening fixer. Both formulas hold up well under the cycling back and forth needed to make a chemigram.

When I start to make a chemigram, I think in advance about the effect I want to create. The paper and surface of the paper are so important to the result. I try to previsualize how I will apply the resist. For a landscape, I may use a puddle pusher or PVC pipe and a syringe. I blue tape the paper all the way around about 1/8″ into the paper. My resists consist of a range of floor finishes: Mop and Glow One Step; Quick Shine Multi surface Floor Finish; First Street Super-Crylic Floor Finish; Bona Stone Tile & Laminate Floor Polish; Pledge Floor Care Finish, a great one but no longer available. If I want the resist to crack and peel, I check the room temperature and if it is below 65°F and 30% RH, I can use all these resists. Above 65°F, Quick Shine and perhaps Bona will work to about 75°F.

I load the syringe and apply a generous bead as I push the puddle pusher across the paper. With the end of the puddle pusher part way down the paper I can form mountain ranges with a lake and a few clouds if there is some resist left on the puddle pusher.

When the floor finish is dry in about an hour, I start to think about processing it in the developer and fixer solutions. Temperature is not so important—not too hot and not too cold. There needs to be a tub of water (1–2 gallons) between the two solutions to rinse the print between cycles. If white is critical to the image, as in sky, I start with the fixer. If black is the desired starting point, the developer will be first.

It is intuitive as to how long to leave the print in each solution. Fixer takes less time to remove the silver halides, but developer is an alkaline solution that starts to break down the acrylic after a couple of cycles. Each resist is different. I plan on an average of 10–30 minutes total time for the print, i.e. 3 minutes in the fixer; then 1 minute in the developer, then extend the times for each until the acrylic starts to flake off and the image is

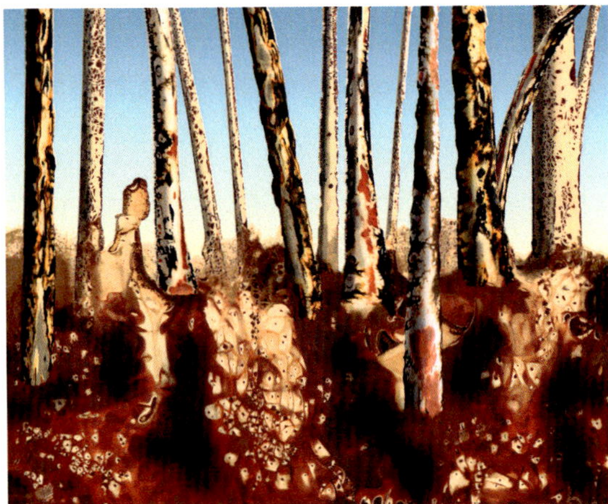

Figure 18.79. *Rimfire*, 20″ x 16″ © Nolan Preece 2020

resolved to satisfaction. First Street can take quite a bit longer; it is very tenacious, but I like it for certain subjects. Hot water or a diluted ammonia solution will remove the remainder of the acrylic. I then process the print as normal.

The issue of the acrylic resist cracking and peeling while drying and leaving beautiful patterns is still a mystery to me. I think humidity and possibly temperature are the reason. I will never forget the first time the resist cracked and peeled. It happened in September, 2014 on a Kodak Medalist J 1953 paper and with a Pledge resist. After that experience I set out to unlock the secret and I have partially succeeded at my lab in Reno.

Mop & Glow threw me a curve. After some pooling with a test, I discovered I could make clay dams out of modeling clay mixed with a bit of motor oil and attach a coil circle to the paper. I then poured just enough of Mop & Glow inside to cover the bottom. In a few days it dried to a beautiful floral pattern. I then removed the clay dam and processed it as described above.

I tried letting the resist dry in the refrigerator and a whole new world opened up. However, drying in the freezer didn't work.

It is no secret that I use Photoshop with my chemigrams. I feel that this creative digital tool has expanded the range of the chemigram tremendously. There is nothing that says you can't make several different chemigrams and combine them, or change the perspective, or add color, or remove, replace, and rebuild a chemigram.

Recently, I've explored making trees, bushes, rocks, and logs. It requires a brush and a natural sponge to create trees and bushes. Logs can be made using tape. Rocks can be fashioned using a cork or a brush. All are made using acrylic floor finish.

Creative practice

My mother had an artistic side and she taught me to paint and draw when I was a child. My father was an amateur photographer who taught me how to use a camera and how to compound my own photographic solutions. So it was easy for me to take up printmaking from my mentor, Moishe Smith, in grad school. These influences have come together to shape my current work.

I've been an industrial photographer, a press photographer, a photographer of scientific methodology and a fine art photographer with large format cameras. When I wasn't working at one of these, my interests fell to alternative photo processes. The chemigram offers lots of territory to play in and I've taken advantage of this. I have been playing with chemically formed imagery on silver-based photographic materials since about 1981. At first I used different toner solutions as painting media to enhance or to simply try and come up with some sort of visual vocabulary, with or without a printed image from a negative. This procedure hasn't changed much from when I first started. Since 2010, I've also been using acrylics as a resist to hold back the chemistry, much the same way Pierre Cordier, father of the chemigram, uses paint, varnish and wax as resists.

Out of necessity, I began teaching Photoshop in my photography classes in 2003. After teaching this platform for about 10 years, I automatically shifted to scanning in my small chemigram matrices so that I could enlarge and retouch them digitally. I usually try to keep the original coloration of the chemigram, but to intensify it a bit. The scanner has become the photographic enlarger.

My work has been tied to environmental issues for almost 40 years now. I have tried many approaches to illustrate the need to change the way we view the planet. The chemigram provides a unique visual vehicle to carry that message. My

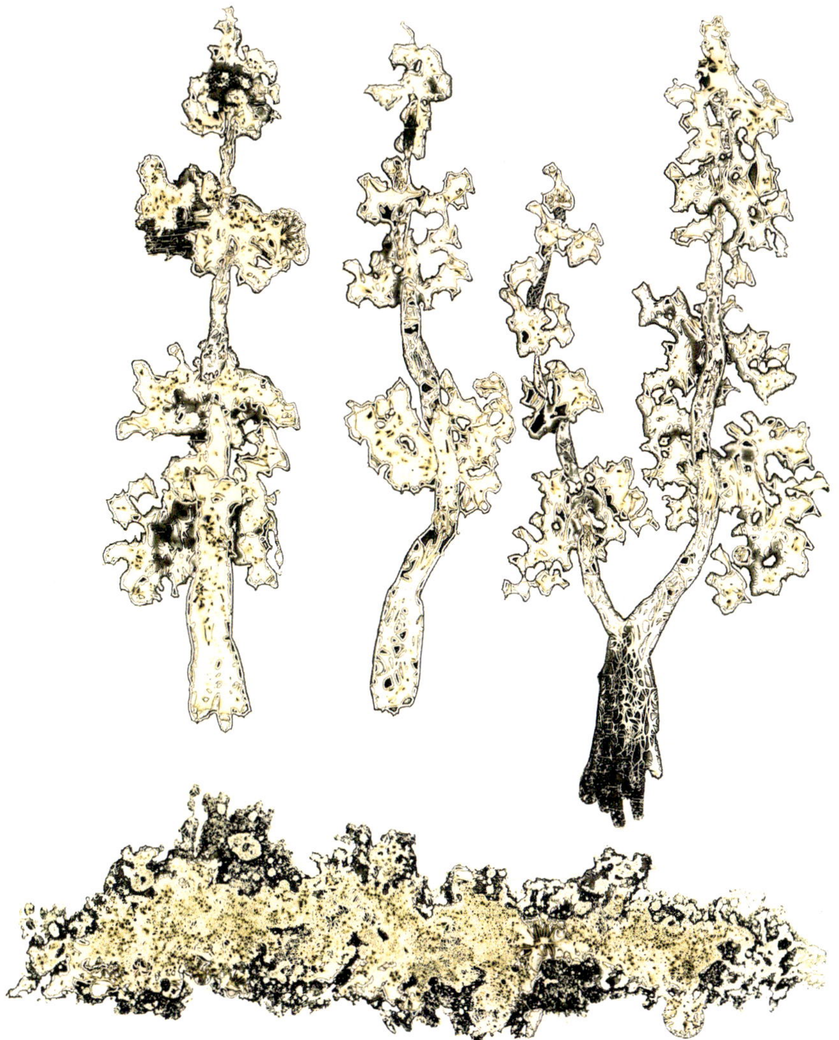

Figure 18.80. *Trees and Bushes*, 8″ x 10″ © Nolan Preece 2021

first attempts at Enviro Chemi Art were quite literal. However, as my work has progressed and evolved, I've come to realize that a more nuanced approach may be more effective. These chemigram landscapes have a post-apocalyptic feel to them with their color and texture.

Biography

Nolan Preece received his MFA in photography and printmaking from Utah State University in 1980. Working in a range of media including photography and intaglio printmaking over the past forty years, Preece employs both traditional and experimental techniques with an intuitive balance between process and concept. Preece's work has appeared in more than 100 juried, invitational, and solo exhibitions throughout the country and he is in thirty-seven permanent collections including those of the Utah Museum of Fine Art; Western Illinois University; The Nevada Museum of Art; The Snell and Wilmer Collection, Phoenix, Arizona; and the Southeast Museum of Photography, Daytona Beach, Florida. Preece has had solo chemigram exhibitions at numerous museums across the U.S. He is represented by Stremmel Gallery in Reno, Nevada and by the Walter Wickiser Gallery, New York City. Preece is an emeritus photography professor and gallery director at Truckee Meadows Community College in Reno, Nevada. To see more of his work visit nolanpreece.com.

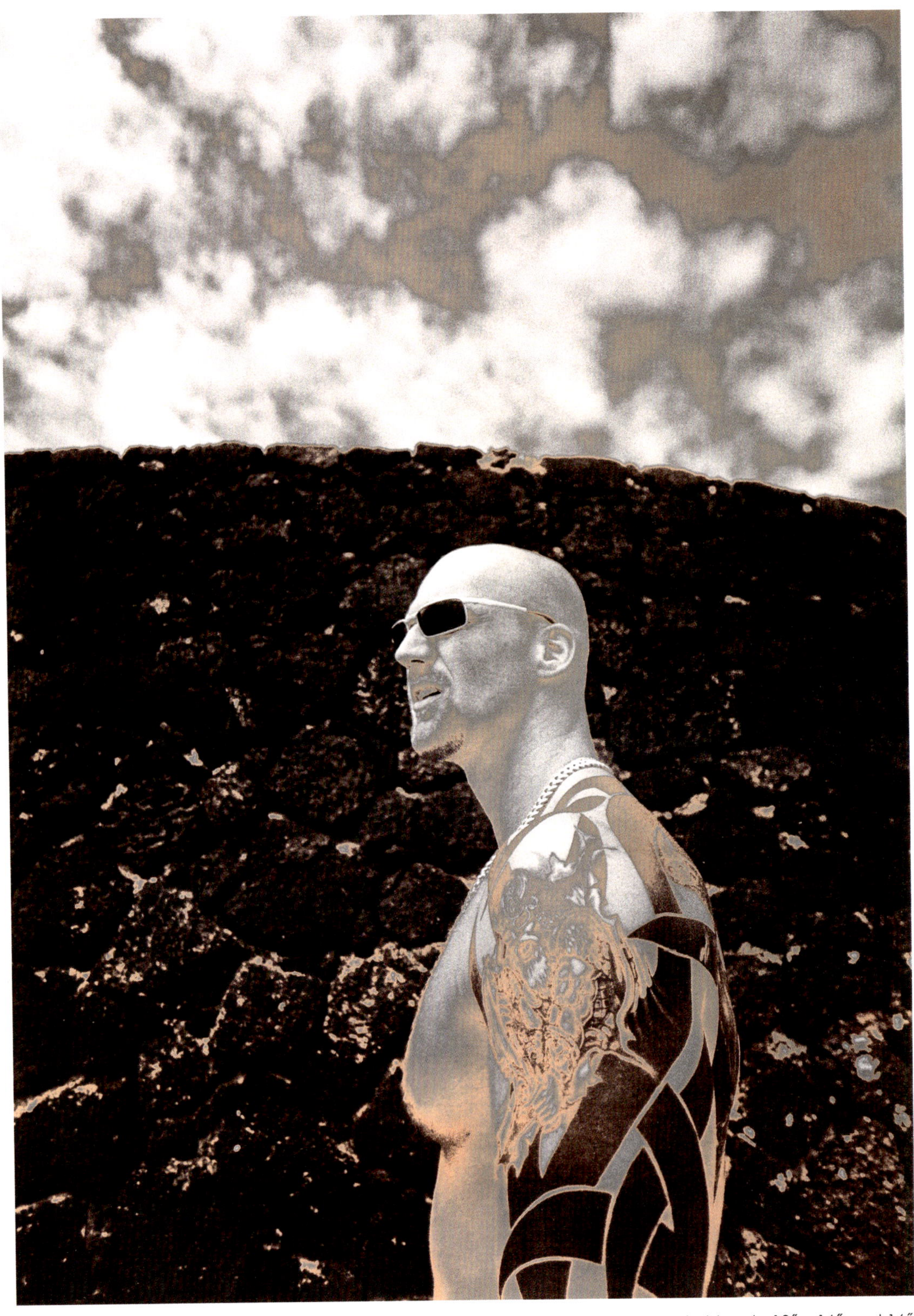

Figure 18.81. *Man of Steel*, Second Pass lith on Foma Fomatone using copper sulphate bleach, 12″ x 16″ and 16″ x 20″ © Tim Rudman 2021

Tim Rudman

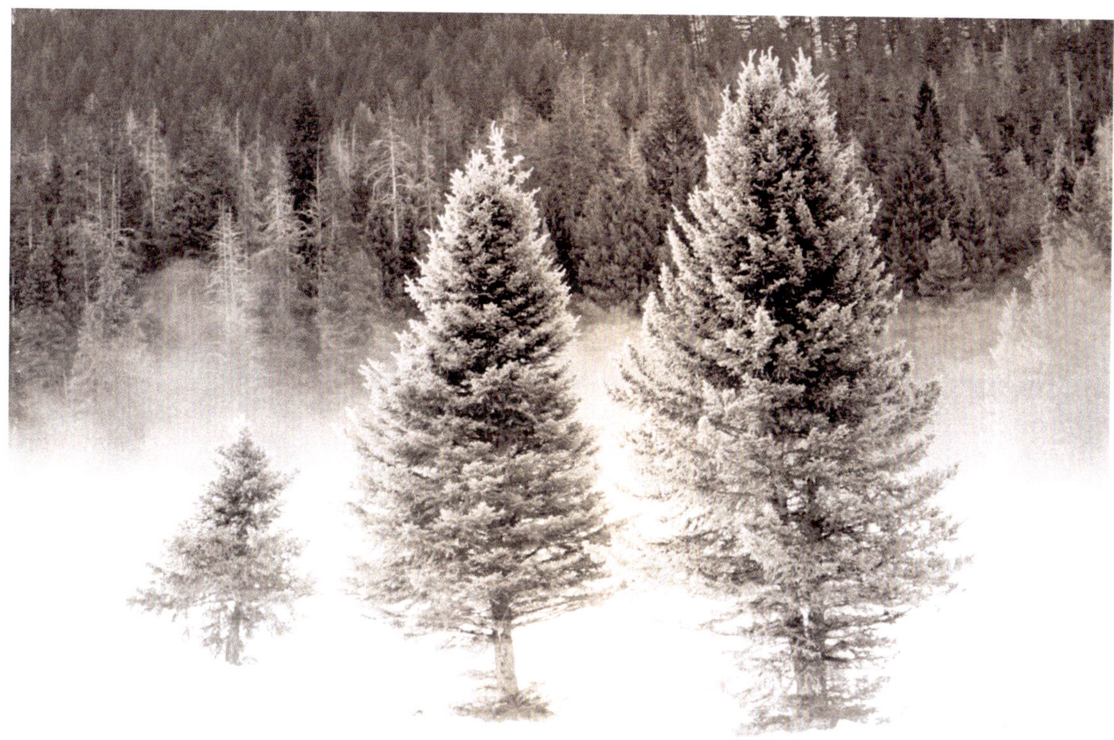

Figure 18.82. *Family of Trees, Yellowstone*, Second pass lith on Ilford Multigrade Warmtone using ferricyanide bleach and LD20 lith developer, 16″ x 20″ and 16″ x 12″ © Tim Rudman 2021

Creative process

I work with conventional black and white silver gelatin papers and negatives and use specialized lith developers, reducers (bleaches) and/or chemical toners to alter tonal relationships and introduce false colour.

Lith developers were originally designed for the graphic arts industry of the pre-digital era to produce extreme two or three tone high contrast results with film. They achieve this through a unique process of *infectious development* by which light tones and dark tones develop at different rates. Lith printing on paper exploits infectious development by heavily overexposing the paper, usually by two or three stops, and then snatching the print part way through development as light and dark tones diverge with different grain size properties.

I use Moersch Lith developer and old stocks of Kodalith and Fotospeed's LD20, which keep surprisingly well with the separate A and B solutions. I generally use Fotospeed's ST20 ferricyanide-halide redevelopment bleach and occasionally homemade copper sulphate/halide bleach. See further on for the formula.

The choice of paper is a major factor as every paper has its own individual emulsion characteristics. In addition to currently manufactured papers, I have a substantial stock of old discontinued lith-capable papers in cold storage, notably the old 1980–1990 era Oriental Seagull variants, Kodalith, Agfa's Record Rapid etc., Forte Polywarmtone and Bromofort, Sterling Lith paper, Fotospeed Lith paper, Kodak Transtar TP5, Kentmere's Kentona, Art Classic, Tapestry and other favourite papers

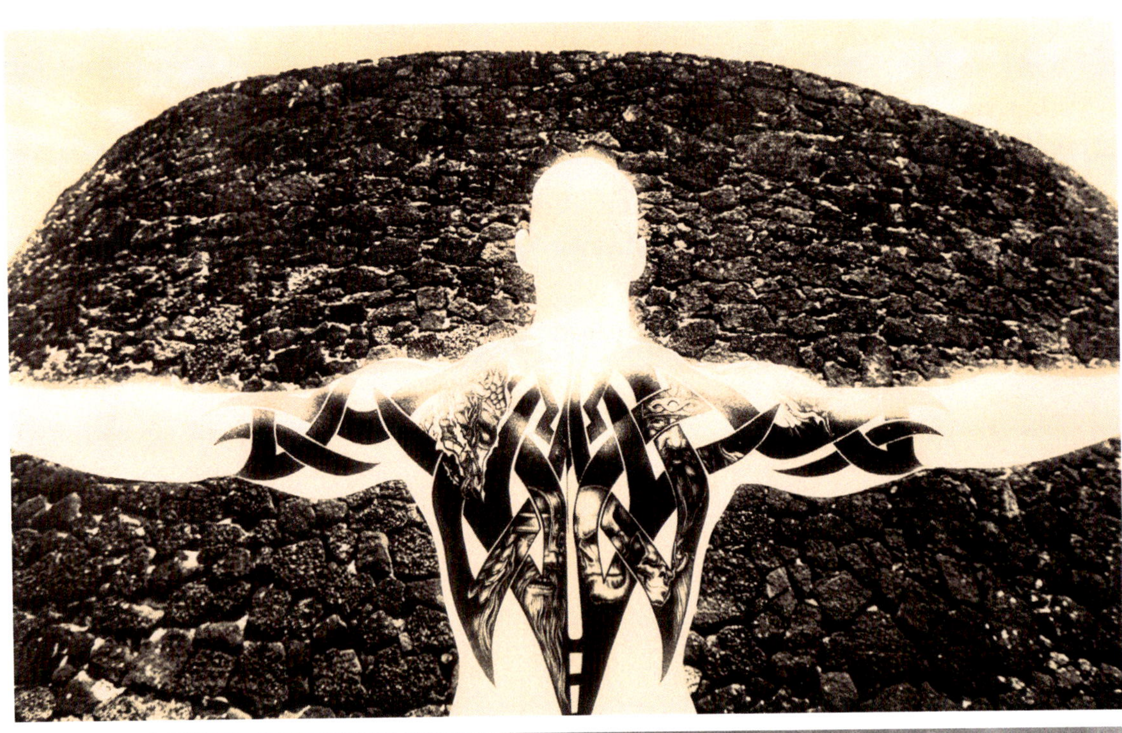

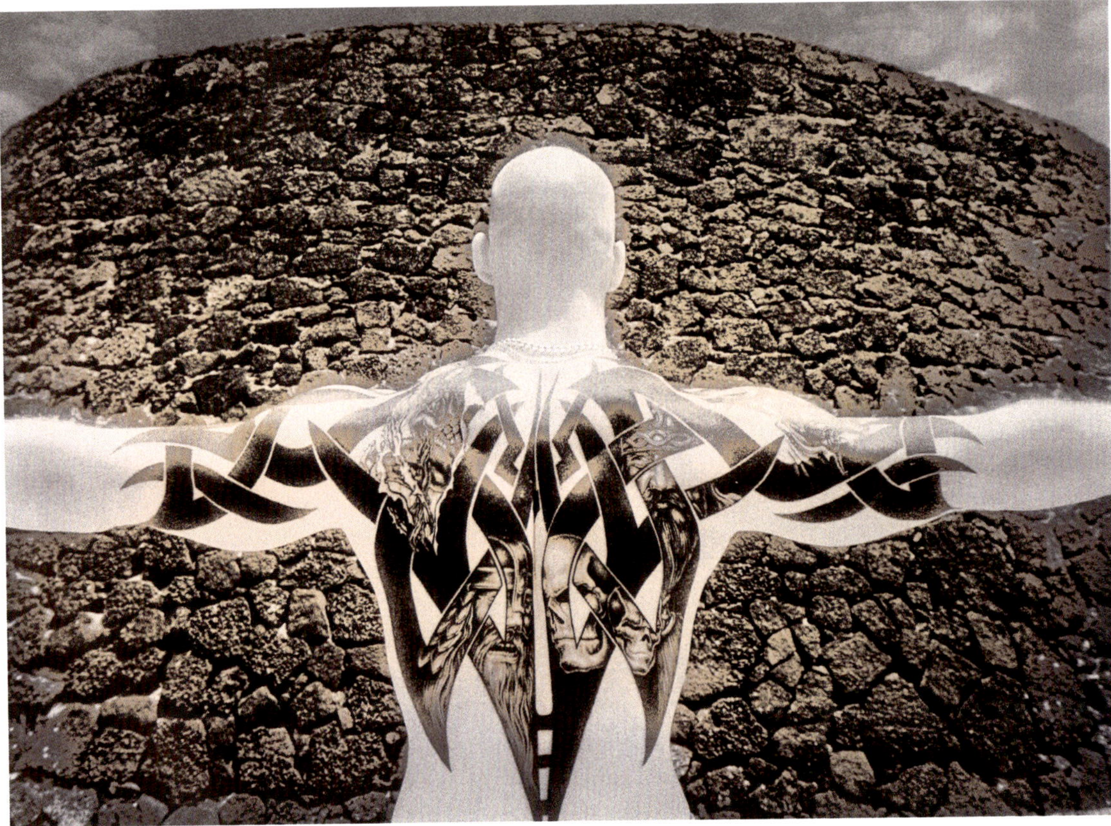

Figures 18.83–18.84. Top, *Man of Steel 2*, bleach-back using ferricyanide bleach on Foma Fomatone, 20″ x 16″; bottom, *Man of Steel 2*, 2nd pass lith on Foma Fomatone paper using copper sulphate bleach, 20″ x 16″ both © Tim Rudman 2021

of yesteryear. Many of these contained the now banned element cadmium and were/still are spectacular in lith developer.

Sadly, only a few currently made papers show convincing true infectious development in lith developer, notably Foma's Fomatone emulsion papers and Slavich's Unibrom (recently unavailable at the time of writing). Some others will yield lith-like colours in lith developer, but lack the same distinctive juxtaposition of fine grain/large grain properties and the control that infectious development permits.

However, the use of a re-halogenating bleach effectively recreates a new paper emulsion with different properties in lith developers—enter *Second Pass lith*. Any paper is worth experimenting with and many current papers work well.

Second Pass lith and Bleach-back

I coined the term *Second Pass lith* in the 1990s in order to distinguish this process from other bleach/redevelopment procedures and the term has since become part of the established lith printing lexicon. *Second Pass lith* refers to a development/bleach/redevelopment sequence in which the first developer can be any developer, but the second developer is a lith developer. It also has the advantage that the lith development stage can be done in normal room light, which makes the snatch point easier to judge. Second Pass lith printing allows the lith process to be applied to a much wider selection of current silver gelatin papers and can produce a greater permutation of possible outcomes.

Bleach-back uses various bleaches after conventional processing to *simulate* a lith look but without the use of a lith developer. For Bleach-back I use a dilute ferricyanide plus hypo bleach after conventional processing, or a strong iodine bleach after selenium toning to completion. No redevelopment is involved. In either case another final fixing bath is required.

For Second Pass lith the first step is to make a conventional black and white silver gelatin test print using any paper and developer combination. The print should then be overexposed, commonly ¼–½ stop, depending on how early it will need to be snatched from the second (lith) developer in order to achieve the desired result. It is helpful to make two or three variously overexposed prints to allow for experimentation. As with normal lith printing, the print is never developed to completion in the second (lith) developer but is snatched as it progresses through development. It will therefore always be lighter than it was after the first development and like a lith print will need some degree of overexposure to compensate. This affects density and colour depth.

These untoned prints should be fixed and well washed in the conventional manner because any residual fixer left in the paper will react irreversibly with the bleach in the next step and result in loss of tone and density.

The next steps of bleach and redevelopment can be undertaken in room light or subdued daylight straight away, or at any later date, in which case the dry print must be thoroughly re-soaked before proceeding. The print is bleached—either fully or partially—washed and redeveloped in dilute lith developer and snatched when a desired result is reached; otherwise it will redevelop fully, usually back to black and white. In order to arrest development quickly, the print must be moved swiftly to the stop bath without draining off. Washing and fixing is as usual.

Every stage of the Second Pass lith process can be varied to affect the outcome to one degree or another and then (with practice) can be reproduced with reasonably predictable results. Note that the initial choice of black and white developer for developing the original print can have a considerable impact on the end result.

The simplest type of bleach to use for Second Pass lith is a ferricyanide/halide formula (see the **Bleaching and Bleachout** or **Toning** chapters). Several variations exist and each can give a slightly different result with lith redevelopment. They are all based on potassium ferricyanide plus a halide (bromide, chloride, iodide) or a mixture of halides, which together with the silver in the print will effectively reconstruct the new paper emulsion. Fotospeed's ST20 is a good example. It works very well and is available separately without the toner.

Another interesting bleach is this copper based formula:

Copper sulphate/halide bleach
50 g cupric sulphate
6.5 ml sulphuric acid 96% (or 13 ml 48%)
50 g sodium chloride (pure)
Water to 1000 ml

1. Caution! Always add acid to water—never the other way round. Add the cupric sulphate to 750 ml water and stir until dissolved.
2. Add the sulfuric acid and stir.
3. Add the sodium chloride and stir.
4. Add water to 1000 ml.

For full bleaching I use the solution full strength. For better control with part bleaching I dilute the concentrate 1+5 or 1+10 with water. The action of this bleach is quite unlike the action of ferricyanide bleaches. Initially nothing much seems to be happening, then suddenly changes appear in the midtone band, with colours shifting and maybe some solarisation and colour/tone reversal, so snatch point is really important here too. This bleach can also be used for bleach-back without redevelopment.

The choice for a lith developer is now quite limited but will affect outcomes. Moersch lith developer (with optional additives) is widely available. Ultrafine and Arista lith are available in the US. See **Lith Printing** for other formulas.

Snatch point(s): the snatch point with lith developer (and with copper bleach) is that critical moment of intervention to interrupt and stop the very rapidly accelerating progress. This involves an element of anxiety! Would the image be even better if left longer? Or would it be spoiled? Initially, the only way to know is to press on and see the full cycle. Hence it is a good idea to start with two or three identical prints and note the sweet spots and times with the first print. The snatch point is one of the most significant steps for personal expression, affecting as it does contrast, grain size, visual texture, colours and density.

It often comes as a shock and a disappointment that when the Second Pass lith print enters the final fix much of the colour fades, but it changes again on drydown and even these more gentle colours can be very attractive. Increasing the initial exposure may help this, especially with earlier snatch points.

Creative practice

Like many old school photographers and printers in the 1960s, I began my journey using black and white film and coldtone bromide paper. As I was studying medicine, my photography was entirely self-taught with little or no guidance and I soon developed a methodology of playful experimentation to see "what happens if." This inevitably led to the kissing of a lot of fairy tale frogs and the discovery of just an occasionally exciting princess. The first of these was the introduction of highlight colour change by using a bleach reducer as a bath rather than applied locally as liquid sunshine. *Bleach-back*, as it was often known, seemed to transport the image almost into the realms of fantasy and imagination.

The survival of black and white photography in this digital era, where the default is colour, is more than historical accident. It is still cherished as an art form because it abstracts the image one step from reality, focusing the viewer on the relationship between tone, texture, form and light alone. However, as for many years it was the main form of image reproduction, people became inured to it, almost as reality. The introduction of false colour removes the image unambiguously from reality, freeing the viewer as well as the printer to form their own interpretations. The expressive use of false colour informs much of my work. It provides a link between me and the viewer, but also allows the viewer permission to explore their own reactions to the work more freely.

Whilst serendipity plays an important part in this journey, so for me does reproducibility and I find I can only do this by keeping records rather than relying on memory. Play-discover-record-repeat has become my mantra.

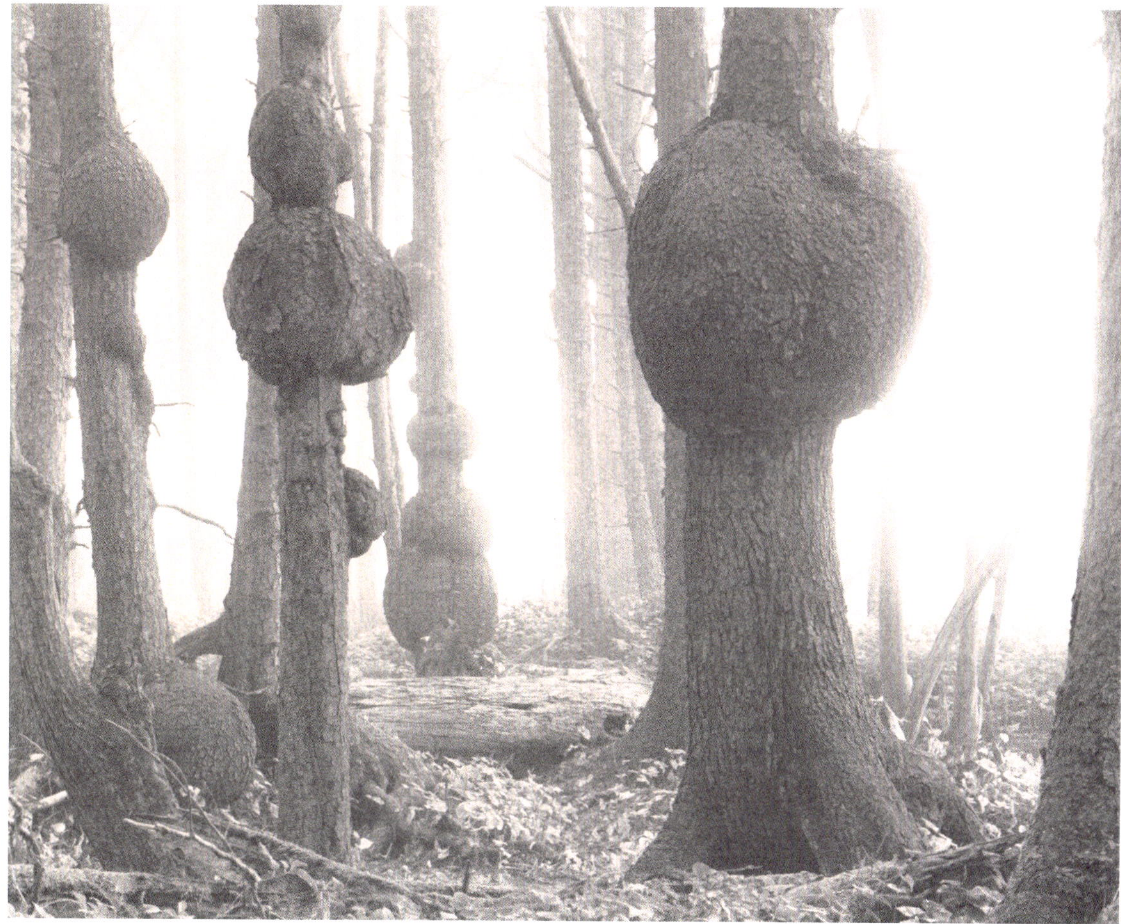

Figure 18.85. *Burls,* 2nd pass lith on Kentmere Document Art using ferricyanide bleach and Moersch lith developer, 16″ x 12″ © Tim Rudman 2021

Biography

Tim Rudman has an international reputation as a photographer, printer and expert on darkroom techniques. His four acclaimed books on printing, toning and lith printing are widely regarded as essential reading in their fields. His later book and exhibition *Iceland, An Uneasy Calm* was released in September 2015. Rudman has conducted darkroom workshops in the UK, Ireland, Spain, Canada, America and Australia. He is widely published and exhibited, and his prints are held in public and private collections around the world, including the permanent collection in London's V&A Museum. To see more of his work visit www.timrudman.com and www.iceland-anuneasycalm.com

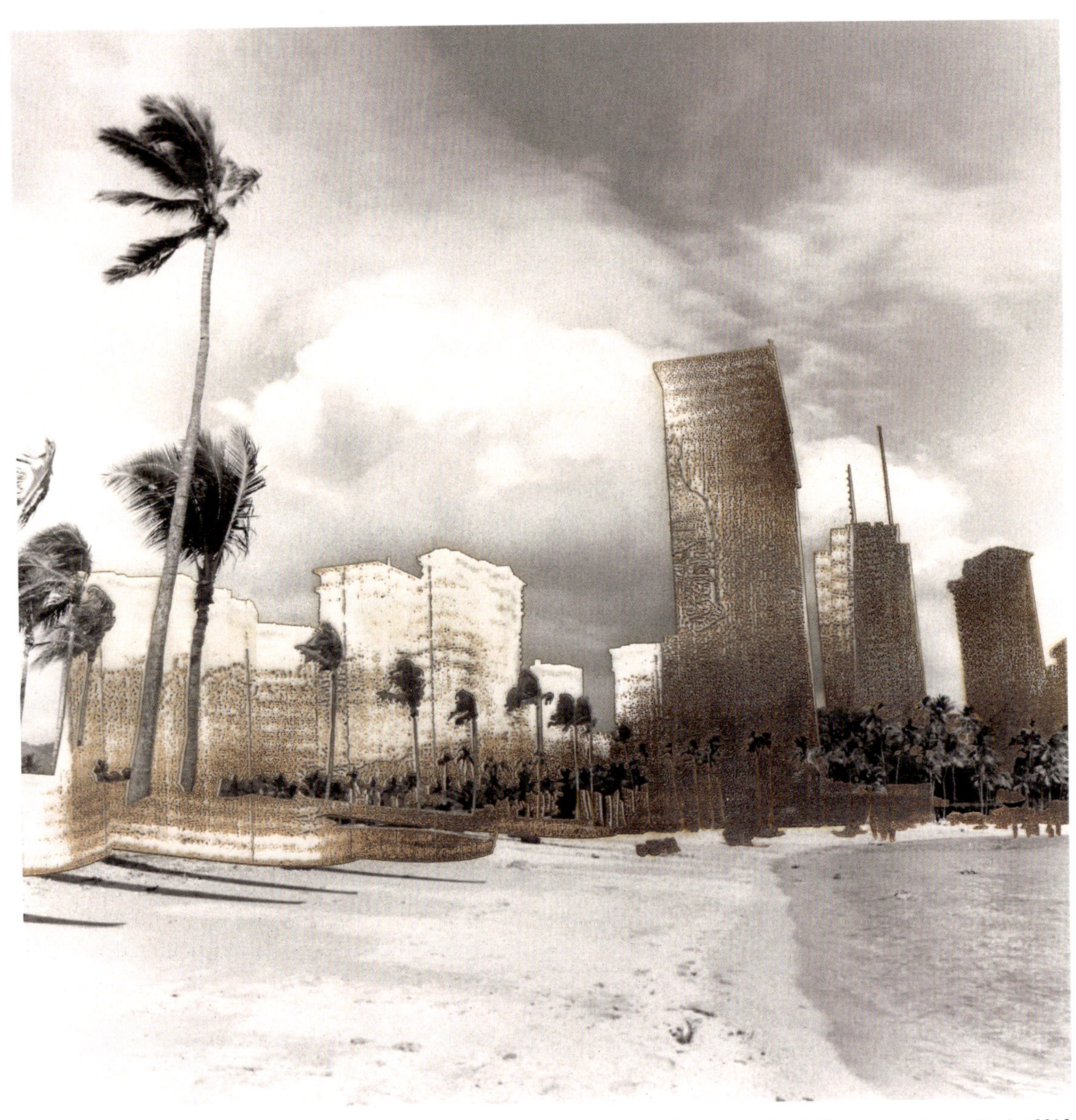

Figure 18.86. *Waikiki*, from the *Invasive Species* series, laser-etched silver gelatin print, 9.5″ x 9.5″ © Leah Schretenthaler 2019

Leah Schretenthaler

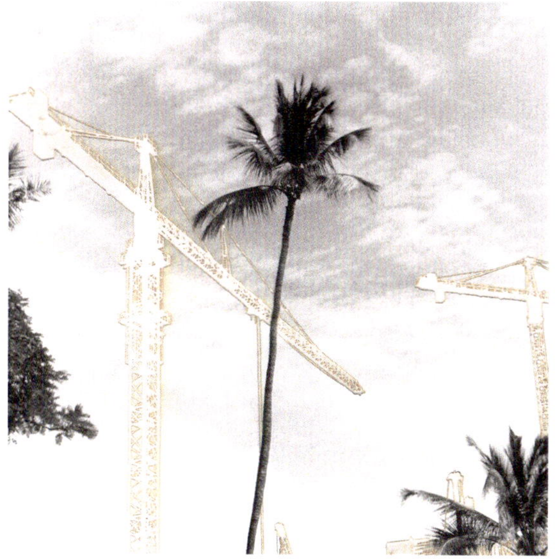
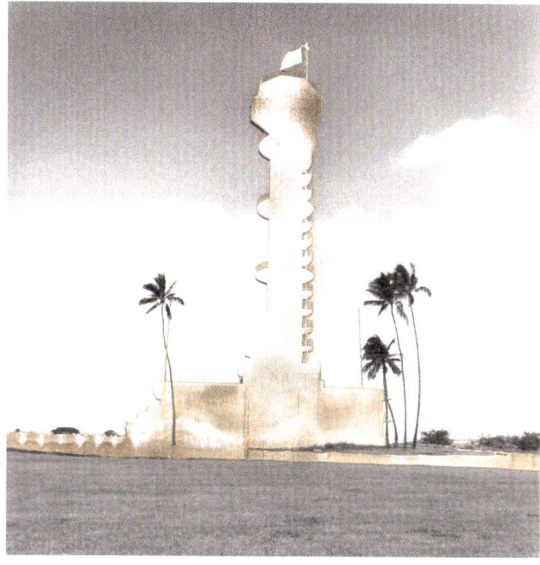

Figures 18.87–18.88. Left, *Ala Moana Construction*, 9.5″ x 9.5″; right: *Ford Island*, 9.5″ x 9.5″, both from the *Invasive Species* series, laser-etched silver gelatin prints © Leah Schretenthaler 2020 and 2019 respectively

Creative process

The images are first printed in the darkroom using the silver gelatin process. After printing, each image is scanned at a high resolution for maximum detail. The scan is then imported into Adobe Illustrator, where each area of the image is traced that must be laser etched. Once traced, the Illustrator file filled with shapes is sent to the laser etcher. The final step is aligning each print in the machine while also dialing in the speed and power settings to create certain effects including transparency and scorch marks.

Artist statement

The Invasive Species of the Built Environment: The land of Hawaii is luxurious and idyllic but past the wanderlust images the land is very controversial. The industrial growth not only manipulates the landscape, it destroys the historical and spiritual places that have existed there for generations. These photographs focus on the spaces where infrastructures impede on the natural environment. Using silver gelatin prints, man made spaces are removed to create a burnt and sometimes empty area. The use of a laser cutter to cut the structure from the landscape leaves a scar upon the image.

Biography

Leah Schretenthaler was born and raised in Hawaii. She holds a Masters degree in art education from Boston University and completed her MFA Spring 2020. Schretenthaler uses traditional photography, video, and metal casting to create her work. Through her art practice, her research presents a connection between land, material, and performance. She has been named one of *LensCulture*'s Emerging Talents of 2018, was awarded 2nd place in the Sony World Photography Awards, received the Rhonda Wilson Award through FRESH2019, the Professional Development Fellowship in Visual Art from CAA, and the Mary Nohl Fellowship for Emerging Artists. To see more of her work, visit leahschretenthaler.com.

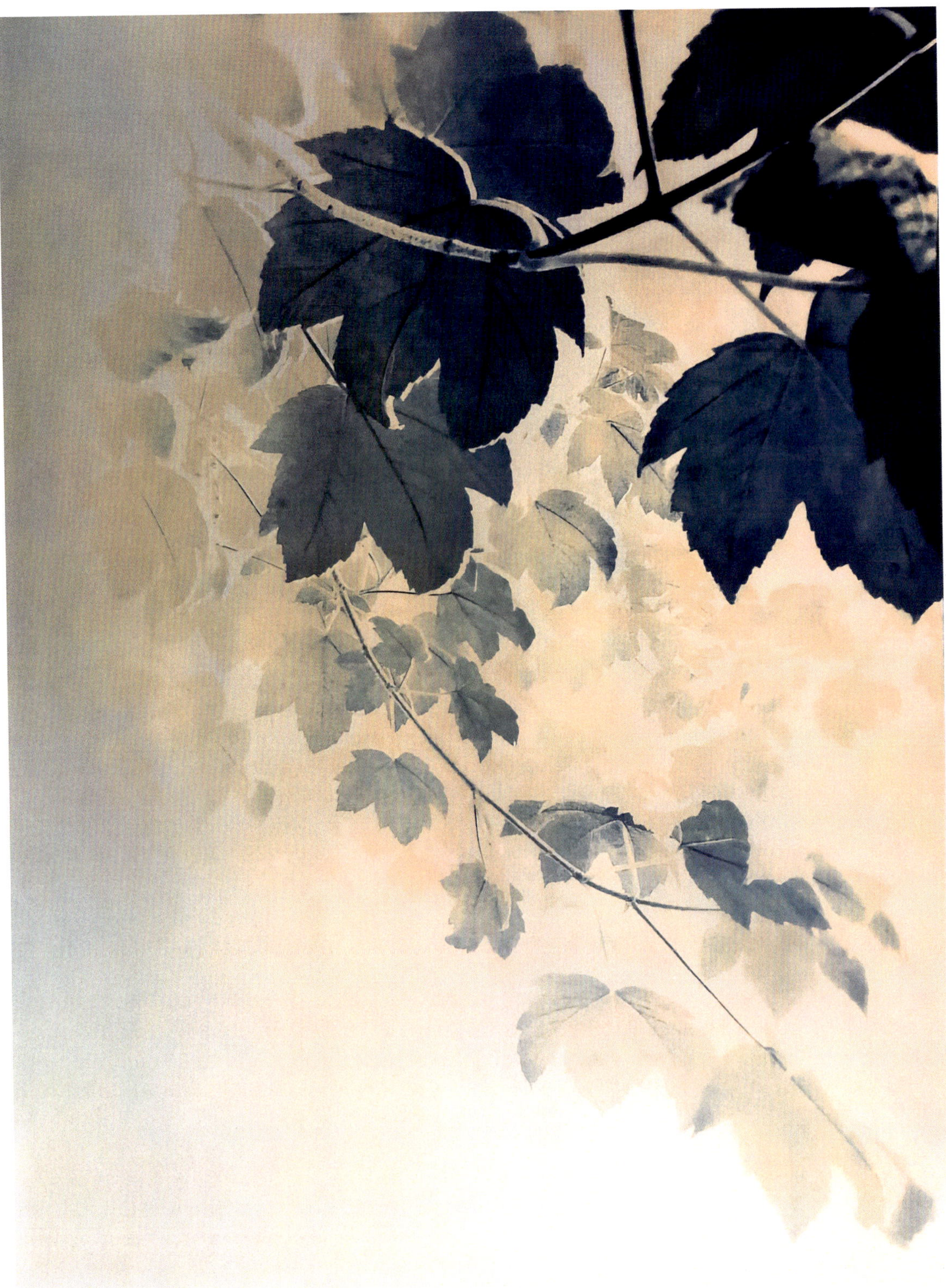

Figure 18.89. *Fran's Wellfleet Maple*, 16″ x 20″ © Sara Silks 2019. The image was printed on Ilford FB Warmtone matte paper, and developed normally, then toned in blue toner to get the desired dark blues, approximately 20 minutes. Then a very diluted Dektol was flowed over the areas to make them less blue.

Sara Silks

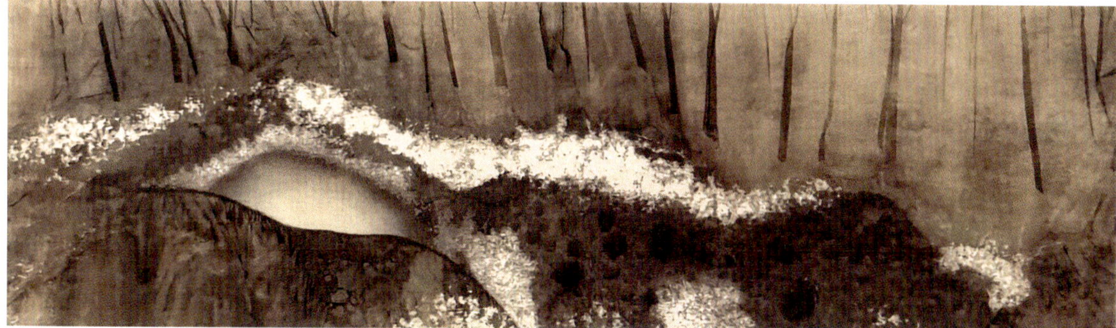

Figure 18.90. *Snow Creek*, petite mordançage, 5″ x 2″ © Sara Silks 2018

Creative process

I use Ilford Multigrade fiber base warmtone and Ilford Art 300 primarily, but I have many expired papers stashed and ready to use. I was given a quantity of 20″ × 24″ Centennial POP paper, and am testing it as well. I shoot both digitally and analog. I use negatives that are film/silver based but make contact negatives with Pictorico for many of my platinum/palladium pieces. I also use Ilford RC glossy paper in my large format view camera to create 8″ × 10″ negatives.

In mordançage, I choose images, knowing that the dark areas are the ones that I can change or remove. I have discovered that using a large test strip of the image in the mordançage chemistry can inform the artistic direction that I want to take. Less exposure, for example, is a way to keep part of the image intact, while more exposure makes the image lift more easily. I use dodging and burning on my images for mordançage in ways that I would not do on a straight print.

I always put my work on Plexiglas during the process, for portability, and I have learned and discovered that for redevelopment, flowing a bit of the diluted developer on to the area I want toned is more controllable than placing the whole image back in the developer. I can also selectively tone this way with different dilutions and chemistries.

With silver gelatin toning and selective toning, I learned to run test strips in the color toner to see the color intensity change. I also experimented with removing toners, and learned the combinations and dilutions of chemistry and the toning times that work well together.

Creative practice

The depth of my practice comes from working continually in the darkroom, and my experimentation over many years has provided me with the tools to use many alternative processes. Though I admire the tradition of each process, I am not bound by a single medium. I am willing to sometimes combine and manipulate processes as a tool for expression, and select them based on my vision for the final work.

Artist statement

My work investigates concepts of fragility, vulnerability, and determination. I use darkroom printing processes, large and small format photography, and digital tools in my work. Using alternative and historical photographic processes, along with my drawing and printmaking background, gives me the latitude to make my work intrinsically personal.

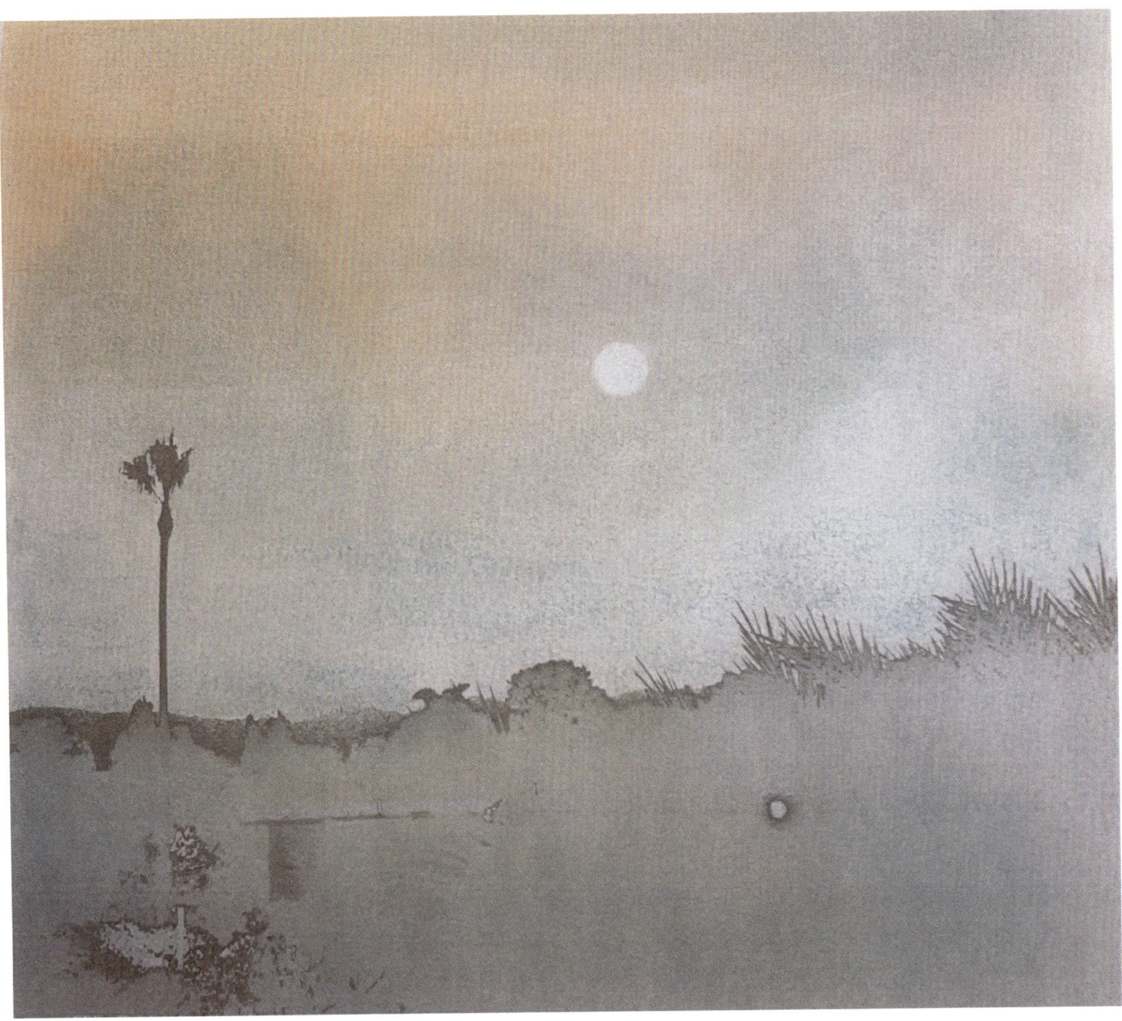

Figure 18.91. *Palm Study LA 5*, mordançage on Ilford MG Art, handcolored with conté pastels, 10˝ x 10˝ © Sara Silks 2021

Biography

Sara Silks is a fine art photographer known internationally for her work in alternative processes. Silks received her BA in both Visual Arts and Art History, and MA in Art History with Honors. She did graduate work with John Talleur for printmaking, and her studies with Christopher James, Christina Z. Anderson, and Elizabeth Opalenik have inspired her continued work with alternative and historic photographic processes. Silks exhibits nationally as well as internationally in museums and juried gallery shows, and had her first solo show in New York City at the Soho Photo Gallery in October of 2017. Silks has been a finalist in Photolucida's Critical Mass four times, and was the international winner in two categories of the Julia Margaret Cameron Awards, 2017, resulting in work shown in Barcelona. Her work has appeared in numerous museums, galleries, publications, and exhibitions throughout the US and internationally, and is also held in private collections. To see more of her work visit sarasilks.com.

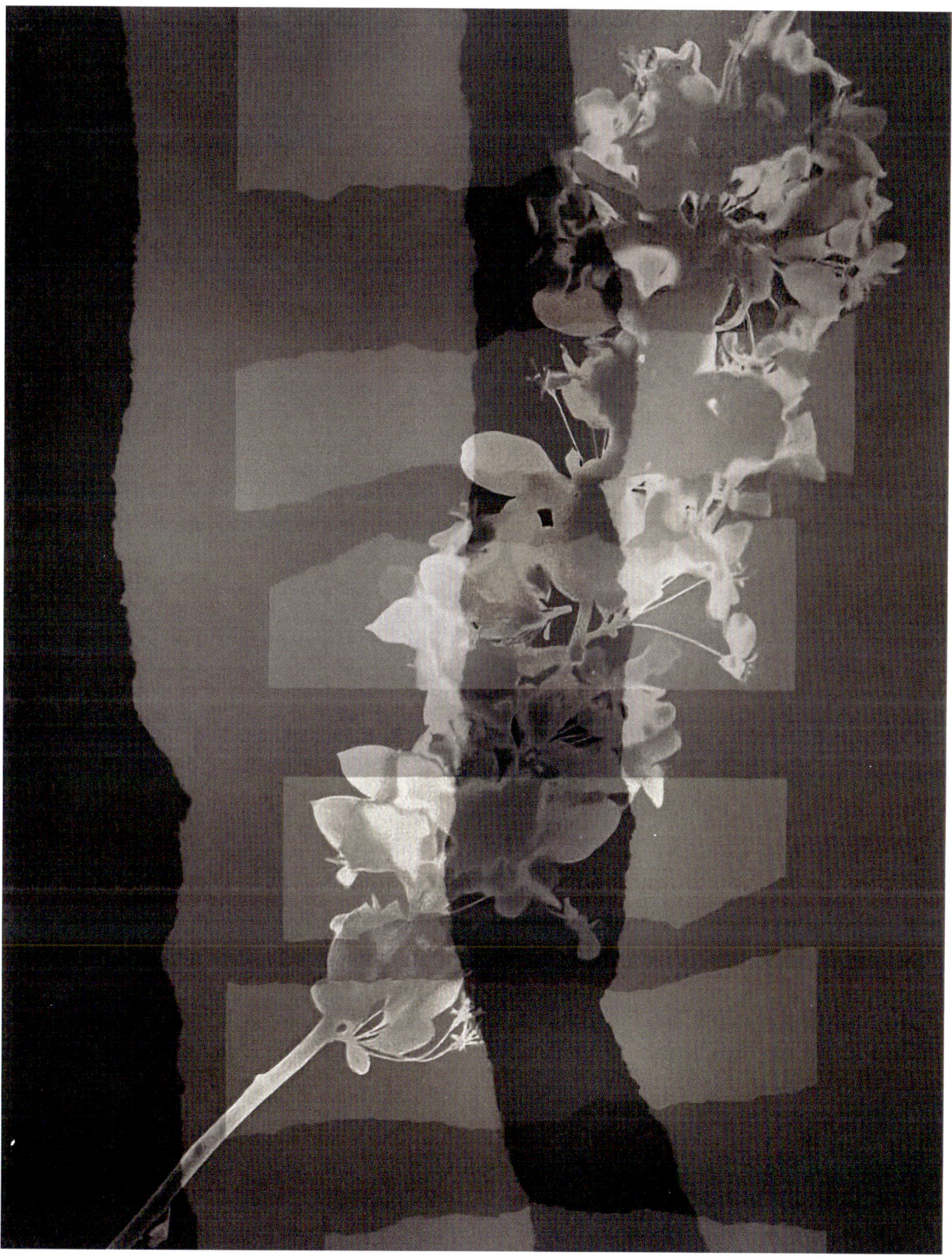

Figure 18.92. *Vertebrae*, sabattiered photogram, Ilford MGFB, exposed during development to an incandescent light for 5 seconds and then processed normally, 16″ x 20″ © Sara Silks 2018

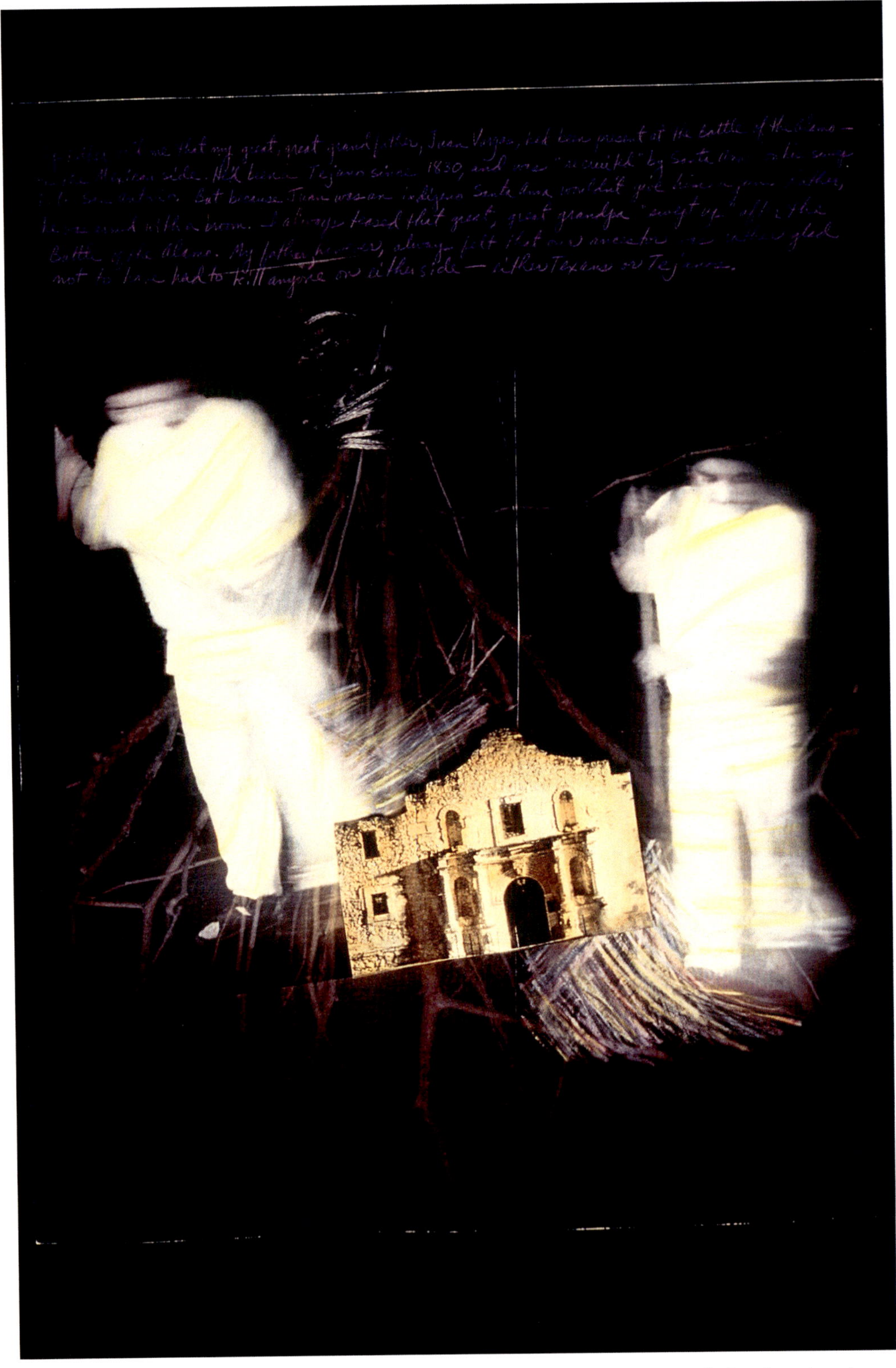

Figure 18.93. *My Alamo #1A*, from a commissioned series for the Mexican Museum in San Francisco for an exhibit called *From the West*, hand-written text on the photograph, 16″ x 20″ © Kathy Vargas 1994–1995

Kathy Vargas

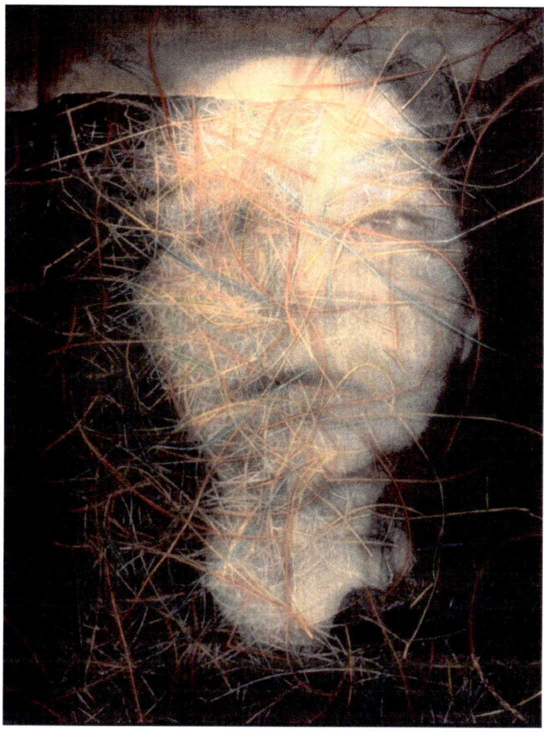

Figure 18.94. *The Living Move: Self Portrait*, from a series of blurred portraits, in deliberate imitation of accidentally blurred Daguerreotypes, 20″ x 24″ © Kathy Vargas 1995

Creative process

I use a number of processes. I do double-exposures on 4″ × 5″ T-Max 400 film, occasionally scratching the negative. When developing film, I currently use a high contrast developer: Kodak Professional HC-110 in a 1:7 dilution. The double exposures need the boost of a high contrast developer; otherwise the negative is very gray. My printing technique is relatively traditional: Ilford Multigrade paper developer and Ilford Rapid Fixer. At times, I've also used bleach to create a halation effect if that's what's needed. After printing, I use selenium toner to split tone in a dilution of 1:4. Then I hand color with a number of oil-based paints: Marshall's but also regular oil paint, Sennelier oil sticks, colored pencils to add lines, and sometimes I add collage or even stitch/sew on my images. Occasionally I'll use sepia toner instead of selenium if I need a warmer tone.

One of my constant complaints these days is the discontinuation of the products I need. Having to re-learn new products slows me down considerably. I've been hoarding HC-110 against the day it also goes away.

For printing, the past few years I've been using Ilford Multigrade Art 300 paper. Before that I used Foma's Fomabrom semi-matte velvet (now discontinued) and before that Agfa's Portriga Rapid 118, also gone. The Agfa was my favorite—a perfect surface. The Foma was next best. The Ilford Art paper is what I can get now. It tends to be too porous so the color sinks in too much. The reason I stick with the Ilford is that it split tones. Other brands don't split as effectively.

For shooting: I work in the studio 90% of the time. I have a 4″ × 5″ Calumet, a "spare" 4″ × 5″ Sinar that I picked up at a rummage sale, and three Graflexes along with a heavy duty Gitzo tripod for the big cameras and two copy stands for the Graflex cameras. My lights are very simple: Smith-Victor.

To make my double exposures, I have to know what I'm going to lay down for both exposures. Then I decide what gets emphasized, what will be diminished, or whether the two exposures will be equal. I place the objects for the first exposure on the table in front of the lens and shoot it at about ½ second. Then I place a transparent piece of paper on the back of the camera and trace the objects in the first exposure, remove them, and lay down the objects for the second exposure, deciding what will overlap, what will emerge and what will be hidden. If the second exposure's objects are more important, I'll give them a 1 second exposure, if less important they get a ¼ second exposure, and if equal to the objects in the first exposure, they get the same ½ exposure time. After looking at the negative, I

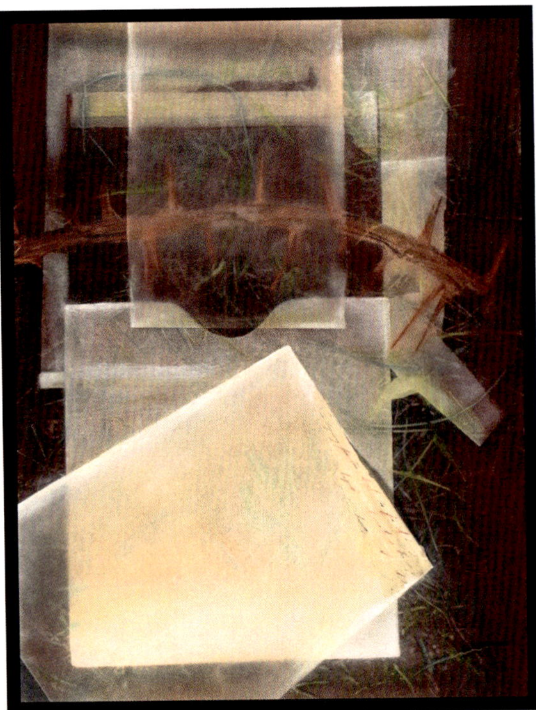

Figure 18.95. *About Memory*, 24˝ x 20˝ © Kathy Vargas 2018. This is about old love letters. Some of the transparent "sheets" are not on the negative but are photogram overlays.

decide whether I want to scratch the negative, add translucent paper to the edge of the negative for additional texture, etc. Then I print. Sometimes while printing I'll lay objects over the projected image for part or all of the exposure time, adding a photogram to the image. And sometimes, after fixing for one minute, I'll bleach a portion then re-fix the image. What I do depends on the image and the effect I'm trying to get. Then I split tone the image and spot.

Spotting is its own creative enterprise. Sometimes I completely change an image just by spotting it. I'll add or remove details, drawing/painting them in as I spot. Afterwards, I hand color, adding collage or stitching where appropriate. It's all a matter of what I'm trying to say. For me, the processes serve the message as well as being important for their own sake.

My process looks complex but actually it's a layering of several relatively simple steps.

Adding is good: I stack processes because one step won't do it. Subtracting is good: I need to make sure that whatever I add is good for the picture and doesn't "muddy the waters" of the message simply for the sake of pyrotechnics.

The best discovery I've made is to keep playing. I change things up—mostly selenium but sometimes sepia; mostly oil paint but also oil sticks; mostly washes of paint but sometimes line is better. Nothing is static.

My biggest problem is not of my own making: my favorite brands/products get discontinued. While I like to "play," some things *must* be predictable. One of them is processing my film. When I made the switch to HC-110 I spent two weeks playing with dilutions, developing times, I even changed the type of film I was using. When I had to change my paper, I bought eight different brands of textured paper, printing on each of them, checking to see if they'd split tone, then painting each to see how each would take the paint.

Creative practice

While it's fun to "play," it sometimes requires hard work to play well. When trying out a new process or a new product, it's important to experiment as if you were a scientist, test results and test again. Keep records in case you decide that the outcome of the second experiment was better than the third or the fourth. Experimental processes are a combination of luck and predictability. You'll have better luck if some things are predictable. It leaves more room for the unpredictable.

Artist statement

The message of my work is very important to me. My message is often about cultural (LatinX) realities and social justice. But process is very important too. When I first started working in a manipulated manner, challenging the Ansel Adams aesthetic of straight photography was a relatively new thing, and, to quote McLuhan, "the medium is the message." Those of us making manipulated images were challenging the preconceptions of photography as a simple reflection of reality. But

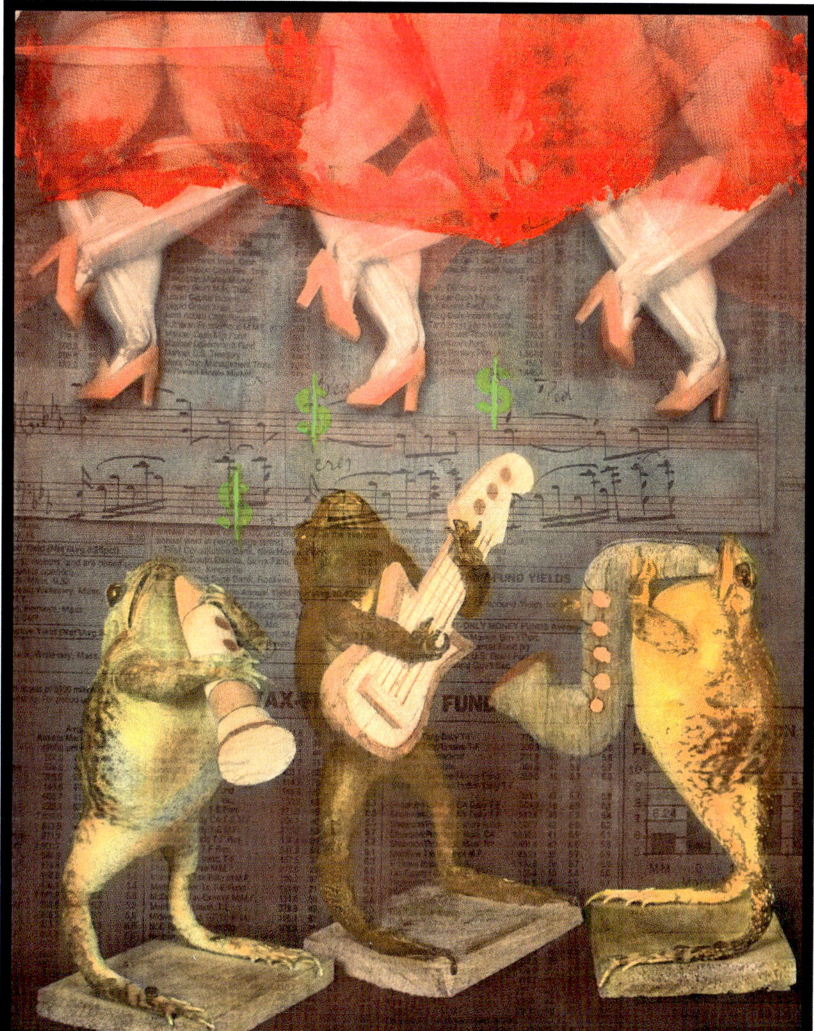

Figure 18.96. *I Was Playing Out My Fantasies When Reality Reared Its Ugly Leg*, 20″ x 24″ © Kathy Vargas 1990–1993. The photograph is from a series on seafood and the ecology, and humorously asks the question: to whose tune do I dance and for what price? It is selenium toned and hand colored with impasto paint applied with a palette knife to create the skirts of the "dancers." Collaged red net fabric was applied over the paint. The dollar signs are also painted on and are not on the negative.

photography as a medium has been historically instrumental in the pursuit of social justice, and I wanted to keep that. The seductive surface of my work makes it easier to get the viewer to look at a difficult reality: politics in Central America, or an endangered ecology or, in my most recent series, the inequity of treatment for garment workers in what we call "third world" countries. And if I can manipulate a medium that's supposed to be all about reality, then maybe I can manipulate reality too—it's a dream, as is photography.

Biography

Kathy Vargas has had one person exhibits at Sala Uno in Rome, Galeria Juan Martin in Mexico City, Centro Recoleta in Buenos Aires, Argentina, and retrospectives at the McNay Art Museum in San Antonio and Universitat Erlangen in Germany. Group shows include *Hospice: A Photographic Inquiry* commissioned by the Corcoran Gallery and *Chicano Art: Resistance and Affirmation (CARA)*. She is in the collections of the Smithsonian American Art Museum, the Toledo Art Museum, the National Museum of Mexican Art in Chicago, and the Houston Museum of Fine Arts. Named 2005 Texas Two-Dimensional Artist of the Year by the Texas Commission on the Arts, she also received a Lightwork Residency in 1993 and an Art Pace Residency in 1997. Her papers are housed in the Smithsonian Archives of American Art. She is currently professor of art/photography at the University of the Incarnate Word.

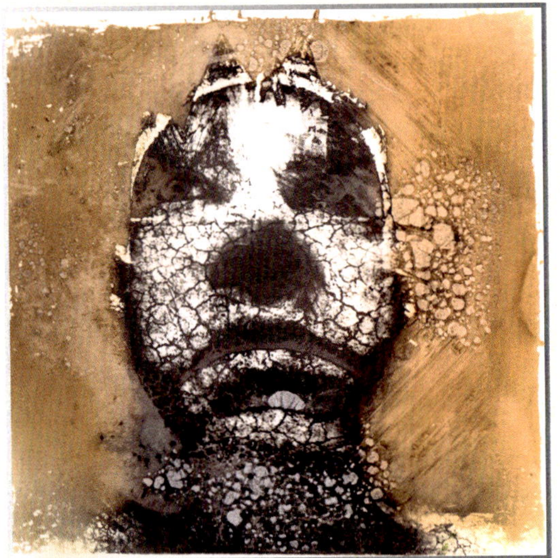

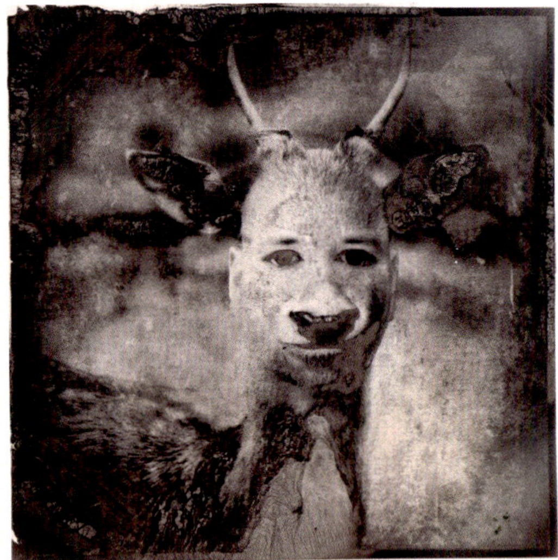

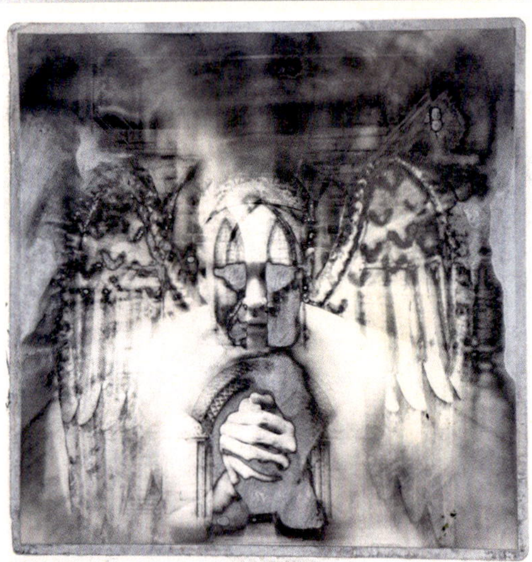

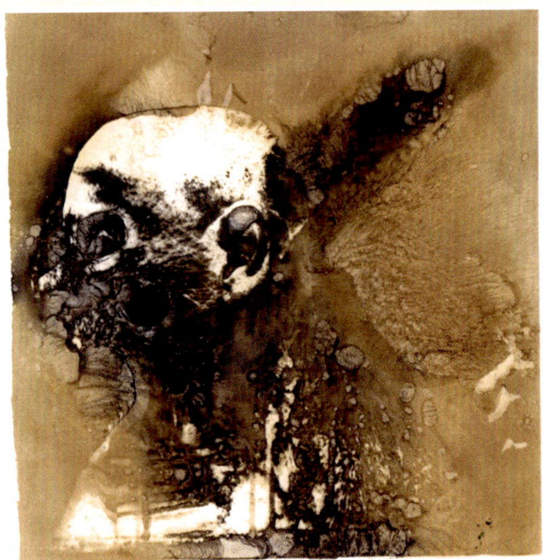

Figures A.1-A.4. Clockwise from top left: *Therianthrope*; *Dear Greg*; *The Púca*; *Ratite*; 6.5˝ x 6.5˝mordançages © Greg Banks 2021. "For over 10 years, I have been making images with the iPhone and iPhone apps. Something wonderful happens when printing processes from the 19th century using contemporary technology. The digital montages were made with IPhone apps such as IColorama S, Enlight, and Afterlight. The images were converted to black and white and flipped horizontally (Photos>Edit> tap the color button> Choose Mono, Silvertone, or Noir. To rotate Photos>Edit> Click on the crop and rotate icon on the bottom right. Click the flip horizontal icon on the top left). The screen is then inverted by going to Settings> Accessibility> Accessibility Shortcut> Select Classic Invert. After that you should be able to triple click the button on the right of the iPhone to invert the screen (the image should become a negative image). If the lens on your enlarger doesn't have a lens cap, make one out of tape and cardboard. Also, if the phone hangs over the enlarger, cut a piece of cardboard slightly larger than the phone with a window slightly larger than the image. This is so the light from the phone doesn't expose the paper. On the iPhone, go to Settings> Display & Brightness> Turn the brightness all the way up. Also turn Auto-Lock to Never. Also turn Airplane mode on so you do not get a text during the exposure. With at least a 75mm lens, put the phone in the enlarger with the cardboard with the window under it. Use a grain focuser to focus. You will be using the light from the phone to make the exposure. I unplug the timer from the enlarger, but still use it to keep time. I use the lens cap to stop the exposure. When I have made a print, I put it through the mordançage solution. If I am worried about losing veils, I may wash a print the next day after the image has dried because the veils are more stable." Greg Banks is an instructor at Appalachian State University. He received his MFA in photography from East Carolina University and a B.A. from Virginia Intermont College. His practice investigates family, folklore, memories, magic, Appalachia, and religion. To see more of his work visit greg-banks.com.

APPENDIX

In-camera composition tips

- Composition is 1) the strongest way of seeing, 2) the pleasing selection and arrangement of visual elements, or 3) visual editing.
- The key to breaking composition rules is to first learn them. The rules are not arbitrary, but come from the study of what has been found pleasing to the eye.
- Herbert Zettle says it poetically: "Complexity without order produces confusion; order without complexity produces boredom."
- The most common error made is to take the photograph from too far away. The main subject is then too small, and distracting details creep in to compete with the subject for attention.
- Every scene has the potential to be a successful photograph, if the subject is "worked": explore it with the camera, close in on it, vary the angle, move around it, and get in really close.
- Robert Capa said, "If your pictures aren't good enough, you aren't close enough."
- Keep it simple. Henry James said, "In art, economy is always beauty."
- There should be nothing in the photo that doesn't contribute to its overall quality.
- If backgrounds are included, they should complement the subject and help tell the story.
- If backgrounds need to be eliminated, the best tool a photographer has at her disposal is shallow depth of field by using a) wide aperture, b) getting close to the subject and c) a telephoto lens.
- Choose a focal point or center of interest. Something for the eye to rest on.
- Photograph from bird's eye (high) or worm's eye (low) instead of eye level.
- Watch frame edges. Look into the far corners of the viewfinder as well as the center to see what is going to be included in the image.
- The edges of a photograph are very active; they determine the selection of visual elements.
- Frame edges can be activated by having subject matter close to them, or truncated by them.
- Watch mergers. Mergers are confusing associations of subject with background. Border mergers happen when the subject uncomfortably touches the edges of the frame—i.e. give a little space around everyone. Avoid cutting off heads, feet, hands, elbows, arms, with the border. If a person is cropped, crop tight and close. Tonal mergers happen between subject and background when two adjacent colors translate into black and white to similar tones (e.g. red apples against green leaves produce gray both). Near mergers happen when objects come too close to the main subject, and steal attention from the center of interest.
- Points of "uncomfortable contact" happen when, for instance, the top of the subject just hits the horizon line.
- Always consider the subject in relation to its background and surroundings.
- Very light things at the edges of a photograph tend to lead the viewer's eye out of the image.
- Place the center of interest at one of the four points determined by the Rule of Thirds. The rule of thirds in photography is based on the Golden Section, the division of a line into two sections so that the ratio of the whole to the larger part is the same as that of the larger to the smaller, a ratio that turns out to be approximately 1.62. It is a ratio formulated with growth patterns in nature, and gives a sense of balance and order, and for understanding our profound connection to other forms of life. Points of interest will fall at the intersection of two imaginary sets of horizontal and vertical lines that divide an image into thirds.
- The center of a rectangle is graphically its weakest point; it lessens a subject's interest, unless the subject itself is symmetrical in nature.
- The strongest of the four Rule of Thirds points is the top right point of the intersections of the imaginary lines.
- The four corners of a photograph also provide surprisingly active areas.
- Have lines, actual or implied, lead to the center of interest.
- Lines have psychological impact: horizontal (calmness, stability), vertical (stature, strength), diagonal (action, motion), zigzag (rapid motion), and curved (grace, slowness). They direct the eye to where it should go, slowly or quickly, smoothly or erratically. This flow, implied or actual, generally enters bottom left and flows toward the top right.
- To contain the eye within the frame, no lines should lead out of the picture, and it is even possible to put a sort of physical barrier in the top right of the image to contain the eye (like a vignette).
- In landscapes, raise or lower the horizon line. Don't leave it at the halfway mark. Halves and fourths are boring.
- Including more land gives an illusion of closeness, more sky accents spaciousness. Either way, make sure the horizon line is level.
- Put a focal point in the landscape that is noticeable.
- Medium sized landscape subjects are better placed off center. If impressive or dynamic they can be placed centrally.
- Use foliage or something else in the foreground to frame a landscape image. Keep both this frame and the subject in focus. The foreground objects give the image depth.
- If people are in the landscape, the direction they look is important in determining a center of interest.
- Use compositional contrast such as size dissimilarity, light and dark dissimilarity, changes in direction, shape difference, texture difference, and sharpness difference.
- Keep people busy. When photographing people, have them do something to distract them from posing statically—this will help prevent the "senior high school picture" look.

Further Chromo Formulas

Alan Bean's process

1. For the Chromo Tray 1, mix 5 ounces Dektol stock, 15 ounces of water, 7 ounces of Activator, and 3.5 ounces of Stabilizer.
2. For Chromo Tray 2 mix 2 ounces Activator and 30 ounces water.
3. Print for slightly less time and use a #4 or #5 filter in the enlarger.
4. Develop the print no more than 1 minute in Dektol.
5. Put the print face down in Chromo Tray 1 and turn on a 40-watt light bulb about 4 feet above the tray; agitate 20–30 seconds.
6. Put the print face up in Chromo Tray 2 and leave it there below the surface of the solution. This is where the silver will occur. If silvering out does not occur in Tray 2, Bean quickly rinses the print and then returns the print to Chromo Tray 1 face up without rinsing until the print darkens but not more than 30 seconds. The red/magenta tones from this step dry down to silver. It may take several prints through the mix to have the silvering out occur, and, in fact, when a dark sludge starts appearing in the bottom of Tray 2 that is a sign that silver will happen. Tray 2 is used under 4 minutes or silver will start to break up.
7. Place the print in stop bath face down, agitating continuously.
8. Place the print face up into fixer. Fix the print 5–6 minutes, and in the fix lightly rub off any excess silver.
9. Rinse the print of chemistry and then wash the print in the print washer. *Tip: sandwich the print with a wet piece of same size paper on the emulsion side and submerge them together so as not to damage the silver of the print when submerging it into the washer. Then remove the paper and let the print wash one hour. Use the same piece of paper when removing the print from the washer to always protect its surface while wet.*
10. Tone the print in selenium toner diluted 1:40 for 2–3 minutes. If too long, some of the image color will be lost.

Denny Moers' "painting with light"

1. Expose a negative to the paper as normal.
2. Develop partially or fully.
3. Use a weak stop bath, briefly.
4. Do not fix.
5. Squeegee off excess water and place the print on glass under room light. The light will start to fog the print.
6. As the print is fogging and turning colors, selectively paint on fixer here and there, which will arrest the fogging process in that area. Brushes and spray bottles make handy tools to apply the chemistry.
7. It will take up to an hour of painting and fogging. During this time, an option is to sprinkle dry chemistry on top of the print to get a textural effect.
8. There is also the option to either fully or selectively tone with permanent metal toners such as gold chloride, selenium and sulfide. The toners create such colors as reddish-brown (selenium), deep brown (sulfide), blue-gray, midnight blue, and pale red (gold chloride).
9. Once the print is done, fix and wash archivally as any print (Note: fixer will have a lightening effect on all colors produced, so it is important to carry on the fogging for an extended period of time).

In order to do Moers' process it is only necessary to remember that selectively painted fixer will lighten the print (hence the "painting with light" terminology) and selectively painted developer will darken the print. Weak solutions of both will do so to varying degrees. See the **Toning** chapter for gold toning formulas as well as other toners to use.

Jolly's Procedure One

Jolly called the process "chromoskedasic duotone psuedosolarization" in this 1992 article.[1]

1. Expose a high contrast print.
2. Develop in 1+1 Dektol for 35–50 seconds.
3. Rinse well and agitate in water 2 minutes.
4. Agitate next for 25–30 seconds in a 5% sodium thiocyanate solution or a 35% Stabilizer in water.

5. Lay flat, squeegee, and let set for 1 minute.
6. Develop again in Dektol 1+7 if thiocyanate was used, or Dektol 1+1 if S30 was used.
7. Immediately remove and lay flat again without draining, and in 1–3 minutes colors should appear.
8. Stop bath, fix, and wash as usual, being careful not to overfix.

Jolly's Procedure Two[2]

1. Expose a high contrast print.
2. Develop in 1+1 Dektol for 35–50 seconds.
3. Agitate gently for about 20 seconds in a mixture of 1 part Stabilizer and 3 parts Dektol (1+1). Lay the paper on a clean, smooth surface and dry the emulsion surface with a clean damp sponge or squeegee. Let stand for about a minute.
4. Slide the print into a tray containing a mixture of 1 part 5% solution of sodium thiocyanate in water and 1.8 parts Dektol 1+1. Gently agitate. After about 15 seconds remove the print, drain briefly (about 2 seconds) and lay the print face up on a flat smooth surface until satisfactory colors have formed.
5. Stop bath, fix, wash, etc. as per a normal print.

"Procedure Two gives purple, green, and red-brown colors. To change the colors obtained in either procedure, try variations in the following: the times of the thiocyanate treatments; the time of the standing period; the time of the second development; the thickness of the layer of second developer during the standing period, the concentrations of the thiocyanate solutions and the concentration of the second developer. Generally, the more concentrated the thiocyanate solution, the richer the color (less black); the more dilute the final developer, the paler the color."

Jolly's updated process

A year later Jolly wrote an article in *Camera & Darkroom Techniques* with some updates to his chromo process.[3]

1. Expose the print as normal or a little less because the changes happen in the whites of the print. The image should have appreciable areas of white.
2. Develop in diluted Dektol (1 part stock + 2 water) for about ⅔ the normal time. Drain the print for half a minute.
3. Color processing and print manipulation methods I, II, III and A, B, C: there are three methods of color processing and three methods of print manipulation given and thus 9 combinations.
4. Final treatment: stop bath, fix, wash as usual and before drying the print carefully wipe the surface of the print with a squeegee or sponge to remove any black sludge.

Color Processing Method I: There are two solutions to use. Mix equal parts of Stabilizer, water and Dektol stock and pour into a tray. Slide the print into this bath, agitate vigorously and then let it lie motionless in the tray for 50 seconds. Drain for 10–20 seconds and transfer to a developer of 11 parts of Dektol stock, 9 parts of 5% sodium thiocyanate, and 10 parts water.

Color Processing Method II: The same as above except for the second developer mix 20 parts of Dektol stock, 40 parts of water, 7 parts of Stabilizer and 18–24 parts of Activator.

Color Processing Method III: Omit the first tray and the second developer is a mixture of 15 parts Dektol stock, 60 parts water, 12 parts Stabilizer, and 35 parts Activator

Print Manipulation Method A: In the second tray of color developer, slip the print in, agitate for 10 seconds, then let print lie still. Color will form in ½–5 minutes. When done, lift, drain and stop bath.

Print Manipulation Method B: In the second tray of color developer, slip the print in, agitate for 15 seconds, then lay the print face up on a flat smooth surface immediately and let it set with a layer of developer evenly distributed on the top (if not, pour some more on with a beaker). Colors will form in 1–10 minutes.

Print Manipulation Method C: In the second tray of color developer, slip the print in, agitate for 15 seconds, then hang the print so it drains back into the tray. This will produce the widest white areas (pseudo Mackie lines) that will also show drip marks. Let it hang for 2–8 minutes and then stop bath.

More notes from Jolly[4]

Jolly provides different color developer baths listed by colors produced. Here he recommends a 1% sodium thiocyanate fix for 10 minutes, then a wash for 20 minutes, a wipe of the surface of the print, and air dry. There is no mention of regular fixer.

Color	Dektol stock	Water	Stabilizer	Activator
Red/olive	75	300	60	125
Magenta	24	250	35	70
Magenta-brown/gray	22	300	36	85
Orange/gray-green	100	300	70	140
Slightly brown-gray	90 parts Dektol, 115 parts 5% sodium thiocyanate, 200 parts 3.5% borax			
Purple/blue	Use an intermediate bath between the first development in Dektol and the color developer of 1 part Dektol stock 1 part Stabilizer, 2 parts water. Agitate the print in this 5 seconds, let it like motionless for 80 seconds, drain for 1–15 seconds, and transfer to one of these two developers: purple/olive: 75 parts Dektol stock 115 parts 5% sodium thiocyanate, 200 parts 3.5% borax or blue: add 2 to 4 parts of 28% acetic acid to this solution.			

Table A.1. Jolly's chromo colors

Jolly Silver Mirror Printing process[5]

Jolly described silver mirror printing as similar to a daguerreotype in his January/February 1999 article in *Photo Techniques*. He also published an update to the process in July/August in response to readers who had difficulty getting the silver mirror effect. I can attest to this difficulty but the discovery of the EcoPro developer and warm water solved the problem. If you want to practice an easy method of silver mirror printing, use the method outlined in the **Chromo** chapter.

The editor of the magazine rightly says, "The effect of these prints is unique and striking: the metalized areas are bright and clean and look like polished silver. We're sorry we can't show you examples—if you want to see what a silver mirror print looks like, you'll have to try Prof. Jolly's technique for yourself!" Scanned silver mirror printed photographs, *aka* chromo, look like gray fog and not metallic silver.

Developer 1 stock solution

700 ml water
3.1 g metol
25 g sodium sulfite, anhydrous
2 g hydroquinone
50 g sodium carbonate monohydrate
2 g sodium bromide
Water to 1000 ml

Dissolve the chemicals into the water in the order given. At time of use dilute 1+1 water. To replenish used developer, add 20–30% stock to it.

Developer II working strength solution

60 parts Dektol stock
40 parts first developer stock
114 parts 5% sodium thiocyanate solution
96 parts Activator

1. Dissolve the chemicals in the order given shortly before use. It is important to use fresh stock in this process. You can replenish used Developer II by adding 1 part Dektol stock, 1 part 5% sodium thiocyanate solution, and 1 part Activator per 4 parts used developer. If Developer II is not used fresh, prints can become dull with amorphous silver on the surface. This can be removed when the print is dry by gently wiping the print with a soft cloth.
2. Expose the print normally.
3. Develop the print in the Developer I for 10 seconds with normal agitation.
4. Drain for 10 seconds and quickly immerse the print in Developer II. Rock the tray vigorously for 25 seconds so the print surface is uniformly exposed to the developer. Develope 3 minutes. Do not touch the print surface.
5. Stop for 10–50 seconds.
6. Fix in a hardening fixer for 15 minutes.
7. Wash for 25 minutes, still not touching the print surface.
8. Drain the print and hang or lay flat to dry.

Silver Mirror Printing update

Jolly updated this process with the following directions. Since Kodak no longer makes Selectol Soft I have substituted Legacy Pro Select Soft.

Supplies

Dektol stock solution
Legacy Pro Select Soft prepared 2× as concentrated as recommended
5% sodium thiocyanate solution
Arista Chromo Activator
Acetic acid stop bath
Full strength hardening fixer

Three developers are used: the first is exhausted Select Soft. The second is fresh Select Soft. The third is a mixture of: 40 ml Dektol stock, 60 ml fresh Select Soft concentrate, 80 ml 5% sodium thiocyanate, and 100 ml Activator. This amount will develop 3 8″ × 10″ prints and then has to be mixed fresh or amorphous silver will result.

1. Expose the paper normally.
2. Place the print in the first developer for 50 seconds. You may not see much of an image.
3. Drain for 10 seconds and transfer the print to the second developer and agitate for about 80 seconds; the image should be fully developed.
4. Drain for 10 seconds and immerse in the third developer and rock the tray vigorously for 25 seconds at first, then agitate for a total development time of 3 minutes. Never touch the print surface.
5. Use a stop bath for 10–50 seconds.
6. Fix in a hardening fixer for 15–30 minutes.
7. Wash 25 minutes and dry.

Edmund Teske's process

Teske's process closely parallels Moers' process, with a few more specifics that may be helpful.

1. Use a high contrast #4 or #5 filter and print a negative under the enlarger as normal.
2. Develop the paper in regular paper developer until the image appears.
3. Place the paper, without draining, immediately in stop bath (1 part 28% Kodak Acetic Acid Stop + 32 parts water, a very weak stop) for one second.
4. Immediately drain and put in a fixer bath for one second (1 part fixer + 6 parts water).
5. Place the print on a flat surface and expose to bright light (150 watts for 20 seconds 2 feet away).
6. When the colors look right, fix, wash, and dry as per usual.

Dan Burkholder's method

1. Mix a 10% (½ ounce + 4½ ounces) and 20% (1 ounce + 4 ounces) solution of both Activator and Stabilizer and a 50% (5 ounces stock + 5 ounces water)solution of Dektol or other paper developer.
2. Expose a print normally using fiber based paper.
3. Soak the print in water for a minute or so.
4. Place the wet paper on a flat surface like Plexiglas and squeegee to remove excess water.
5. First paint on the Dektol where you want colors to develop and watch until the developed areas appear.
6. After 90 seconds or when the image is dark enough, wash the print in running water to stop development.
7. Brush on the 10% Stabilizer to the parts of the image adjacent to the developed areas.
8. Rinse the brush in water and blot off excess water.
9. Apply the 10% Activator solution to selective parts of the image.
10. Expose the print to weak light, fluorescent lamps, or a 40 watt bulb and watch the print closely.
11. Apply additional Dektol with the brush to speed up action. After a 1–3 minute wait turn on brighter lights.
12. Fine tune the print with 10% and 20% solutions of Stabilizer and/or Activator, or by adding Dektol to darken colors.
13. Wash, fix, wash, hypoclear, and dry as per normal.

Further Mordançage Formulas

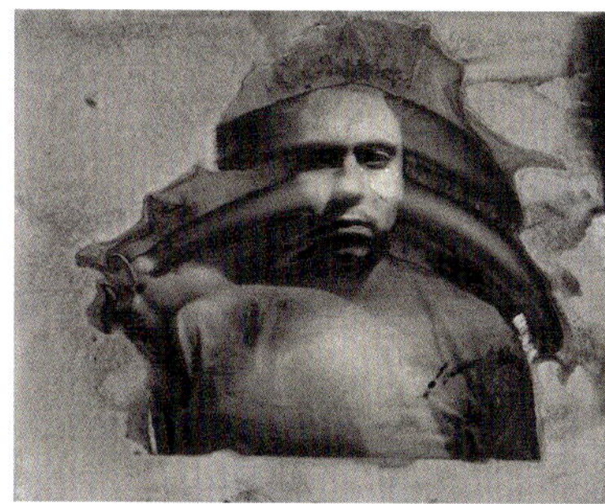
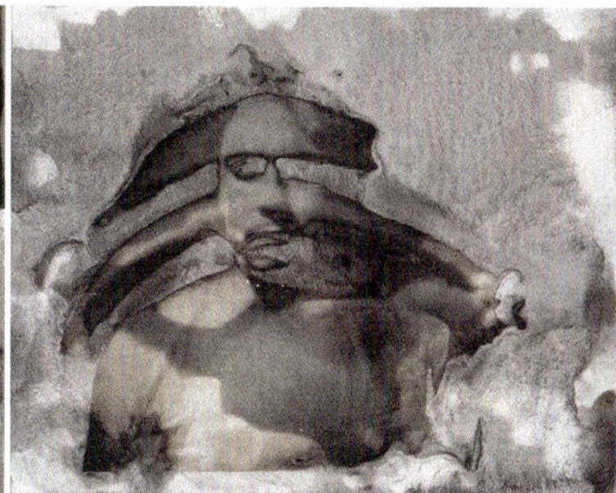
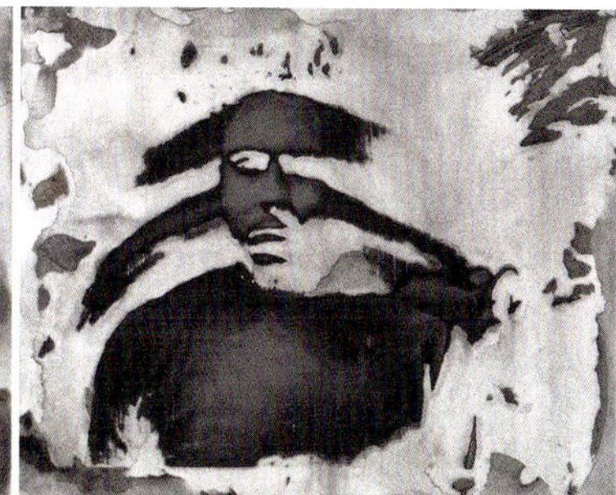

Figures A.5–A.7. *Mordançage Triptych*, three unique mordançages © Beck Moniz 2021. Beck Moniz (b. Alexandria Virginia) has been a photographer for six years and is a student at Montana State University, pursuing a BA in Film and Photography, expected graduation December 2022.

The following formulas are for research/historic interest only. The formulas in the **Mordançage** chapter are perfectly adequate for the process. Some of the following formulas use nitric acid; no matter how careful you are, it is not an acid to use unless you are a chemist with a chemistry lab.

Speck's patent[6]

Patent #2,494,068 Jan 10, 1950
"Photographic Relief Image"
Robert Speck, Assignor to Eastman Kodak Co, Rochester, NY (See uspto.gov) This invention relates to photography and particularly to a method of forming photographic relief images.

It is known that relief images can be formed in silver halide emulsion layers by treating the developed silver halide layer with a hydrogen peroxide etch bath containing bromide ions and thereby removing the developed silver image together with the gelatin in the regions of the silver image. This method of forming a relief image is particularly useful where a positive relief image is to be formed from a positive color transparency since the positive relief image can be formed directly. It has been noted that the dissolution of the gelatin surrounding the silver grains takes place only when the hydrogen peroxide etch bath is strongly acid. If an etch bath is used which is not strongly acid, bleaching will take place but no dissolution of the gelatin will result.

I have found that if a hardened gelatin silver halide emulsion is used, a hydrogen peroxide bath of the proper degree of acidity will bleach the silver image to silver bromide and simultaneously soften the gelatin in the regions of the silver image. The gelatin in the areas of the residual silver halide is not seriously affected by this treatment. (Some small degree of softening takes place, but the gelatin remains mostly insoluble in hot water.) The softened negative gelatin, that is, the gelatin in the regions of the original silver image can then be washed off in hot water leaving a hard positive image. The residual silver halide of the positive image can be removed in the usual manner, or may be allowed to remain, or be developed after flashing, in a tanning developer to give the gelatin desirable dye transferring characteristics.

This method differs from the usual hydrogen peroxide etch process in that the gelatin is not removed by the etch bath but is only softened and is removed as a separate step by washing with hot water.

This method has the advantage that the resulting image is sharper than the image obtained by the usual hydrogen peroxide etch process. Furthermore, the etching solution does not become sludgey with silver bromide and dissolved gelatin and can be reused many times. By washing off with hot water, the relief is left immediately clean and ready for drying. The usual etch method leaves a residue which washes off slowly. A further advantage is that the relief can be processed in a shorter time than is customary with the usual hydrogen peroxide etching process and by remaining in a hardened condition, a positive image is less subject to damage.

An average gelatin-silver halide emulsion which might be used according to my process could be hardened to a melting point of approximately 180°F. However, a change in balance of acidity can be made to accommodate emulsions of other degrees of hardness. The emulsion is coated on the usual support of cellulose acetate, cellulose nitrate or synthetic resin or may be coated on a paper support.

The emulsion may be blue-sensitive or panchromatic and is exposed in the usual way, for example, to a positive color transparency. Separation images may be made for use in the imbibition process by exposing through primary color filters if a panchromatic material is used. The emulsion is developed in the usual way to form a negative silver image leaving residual silver halide in the unexposed portions of the layer. The residual silver bromide may be removed by fixing at this stage, or may remain in the layer for removal at a later stage.

After development of the silver image, the layer is treated with a hydrogen-peroxide-bromide bleach bath having a pH of approximately 2.6 to 3.0. The pH of the bleach bath is adjusted to the hardness of the particular emulsion which is used. If the emulsion is extremely hard, the pH would be low but if the emulsion is only moderately hard, the pH would be higher. The following formulas are suitable for use according to my invention.

Example 1

Copper sulfate 33 g
Potassium bromide 10 g
Acetic acid 28% solution 13 cc
Hydrogen peroxide 25% solution 105 cc
Water to 1 liter.

Example 2

Copper sulfate 50 g
Potassium bromide 15 g
Acetic acid 28% solution 15 cc
Potassium alum 15 g
Water to 1 liter

For use, three parts of this formula are added to 1 part of 8% hydrogen peroxide solution.

With both of these formulas, softening of the emulsion in the region of the silver image takes place in approximately 1½ minutes at a temperature of 68°F.

In place of potassium bromide in the bleach bath, other bromides such as sodium or ammonium may be used. Acids other than acetic acid such as sulfuric acid or hydrochloric may be employed, the pH being adjusted within the range specified above.

After bleaching of the silver image, the emulsion is washed for 1 minute with water at a temperature of approximately 110°F to wash off the gelatin in the region of the silver image. The positive relief image is then in a condition for use in an imbibition process or other process for which a relief image is suitable.

The examples included herein are illustrative only and my invention is to be taken as limited only by the scope of the appended claims.

I claim: 1. The method of forming a photographic relief image which comprises developing a gelatino-silver halide emulsion layer to form a silver image therein bleaching the silver to silver bromide in a hydrogen peroxide-bromide bleach bath having a pH of approximately 2.6-3.0, without dissolving but with softening the gelatin in the region of the silver image, hardening said emulsion prior to said bleaching as a step in the process, washing off the gelatin softened by the bleach bath in warm water, to form a positive gelatino-silver halide relief image. 2. The method of forming a photographic relief image which comprises developing a gelatino-silver halide emulsion layer hardened to a melting point of approximately 180°F to form a silver image therein, bleaching the silver to silver bromide in a hydrogen peroxide-bromide bleach bath having a pH of approximately 2.6 to 3.0, said bleach bath softening the gelatin in the region of the silver image without dissolving it, and washing off the gelatin softened by the bleach bath in warm water to form a positive gelatino silver halide relief image. 3. The method of forming a photographic relief image which comprises developing a

	Coote	Speck	Speck	Baxter	Baker	Seigel	Clerc	Wall/ Smith	Marriage	Wall	Marriage	Grnleaf	Upp	Bailey
Copper Chloride	30 g					12 g	10 g		12 g		10 g		10 g	10 g
Copper Sulfate		33 g	50 g	20 g	70 g			100 g		20 g		50 g		
Glacial Acetic Acid	80 ml	13 ml 28%	15 ml 28%			20 ml			55 ml		50 ml			50 ml
Citric Acid							10 g							
Nitric Acid				5	10			15		5		6 ml 1%		
Potassium Bromide		10 g	15 g	0.5 g	1 g			10 g		0.5 g		2 ml 1%		
Potassium Alum			15 g											
Hydrogen Peroxide	20 v	105 ml 25%		30 ml v?	60 ml 10 v	200–400 ml 10 v	Equal vol of 10 v/3.4%	4 vol? 250 ml	40–80 21 v	30 ml ?%	100 ml 20 v	12.5	25–35 ml 30%	25–35 30–40 v
Water	1000 ml	1(3 parts to 1 pt 8% hp)	1(3 parts to 1 pt 8% hp)	1000 ml	1000 ml	1000 ml	1000 ml	500 ml	1000 ml	1000 ml	1000 ml	1000 ml	1000 ml	1000 ml

Table A.2. Mordançage formula comparisons, above, and sources for them, below.

Clerc, L. P. *Photography, Theory and Practice*, Vol. 4 on *Monochrome Processing* and Vol. 5, *Positive Materials*. New York: Amphoto Focal Press, 1971, Vol. 4, pp. 578–580, Vol. 5, pp. 660–675.

Coote, Jack. *Ilford Monochrome Darkroom Practice*. Woburn, Massachusetts: Focal Press, 2000, pp. 299–304.

Crabtree, J. I., and G. E. Matthews. *Photographic Chemicals and Solutions*. Boston: American Photographic Publishing Co., 1938, pp. 326–335.

Glafkides, Pierre. *Photographic Chemistry*, Vol. 2. London: Fountain Press, 1960, pp. 668–669.

Greenleaf, Allen. *Chemistry for Photographers*. Boston: American Photographic Publishing Col, 1941, pp. 96–97.

Henney, Keith and Bev Dudley. *Handbook of Photography*. New York: Whittlesey, 1939 pp. 653, 463–465.

Hicks, Roger and Frances Schultz. *Darkroom Basics and Beyond*. London: Collin and Brown, Ltd, 2000, pp. 116–118.

James, Christopher. *The Book of Alternative Photographic Processes*. Albany, NY: Delmar, 2002, pp. 314–317.

Liesegang, Paul. *Die Collodion Verfahren mit Jod und Bromsalzen*. Leipzig, 1898.

Marriage, A. "Notes on Etch Bleach Baths" in *British Journal of Photography*, April 21, 1944, p. 142.

Neblette, C. B. *Handbook of Photography and Reprography*, 7th Edition. New York: Van Nostrand Reinhold, 1977 (p. 124).

Reed, Martin and Randall Webb. *Spirit of Salts*. London: Aurum Press, Ltd., 1999, pp. 143–144.

Schultz, Frances. "Bleach Etch: Alternative Process for Striking Images" in *Shutterbug*, October 1998, pp. 30–36.

Stubbs, S. G. Blaxland, ed. *Modern Encyclopedia of Photography*, Vol 1. Boston: American Photographic Publishing Co., 1938 (p. 616).

Wall, E. J. *Practical Colour Photography*, 2nd ed. Boston: American Photographic Publishing Co., 1928, pp. 90–94.

gelatino-silver halide emulsion layer to form a silver image therein, bleaching the silver to silver bromide in a hydrogen peroxide bleach bath containing approximately 10 grams per liter of potassium bromide and having a pH of approximately 2.6 to 3.0, hardening said emulsion to a melting point of approximately 180°F, prior to said bleaching as a step in the process, said bleach bath softening the gelatin in the region of the silver image without dissolving it and washing off the gelatin softened by the bleach bath in warm water to form a positive gelatino-silver halide relief image. — Robert P. Speck.

References cited

The following references are of record in the file of this patent:

United States Patents Number

1,938,290 Hurst Dec 5 1933
1,939,947 Baxter Dec 19 1933
2,058,396 Baker Oct 27 1936
2,068,879 Troland Jan 26 1937
2,120,441 Leiber June 14 1938

Foreign patents
423,150 France Feb 9 1911

Other references
Luppo-Cramer "Neue Untersuchungen USW," "CXV. Uber Die Reaktion USW," *Photo Korres.* 48 pages 466 to 471 (1911) pages 466 and 467 especially cited (copy in S. L.)
Henney and Dudley *Handbook of Photography*, McGraw-Kill Book Company, 1939, page 342 cited (copy in Div. 67)

Original Marriage formula[7]
Marriage's formula is for converting a negative to a colored positive. He does not specify "film" or "paper" but he mentions his bath gives a good relief on "many materials" including bromide paper. Marriage credits his knowledge of the etch-bleach formula to E. J. Wall, but felt that Wall's formula was unreliable; thin silver deposits fail to etch properly, and the nitric acid causes the relief image to swell excessively. Marriage substituted cupric chloride and replaced the nitric with acetic acid. Cupric chloride is more soluble than cuprous bromide and thus is a better catalyst, allowing weaker acids to be used, and allowing lower silver densities to etch. He recommends hardening before the process with a hardening fixer.

750 ml water
10 g cupric chloride
50 ml glacial acetic acid (99%)
100 ml 20v hydrogen peroxide
Water to 1000 ml

1. Add the cupric chloride to the water.
2. Add the glacial acetic acid to the water.
3. Add the hydrogen peroxide to the water.
4. Add water to make 1000 ml.

Marriage explains, "The copper salts react with the silver to give cuprous bromide, which acts as a catalyst for the destructive oxidation of gelatin by hydrogen peroxide. It seems however, that the catalyst is only effective for a short time, since if the bromide content of the bath is increased so that the bleaching is more rapid, etching of the gelatin is incomplete." If the gelatin is not budging, he counsels to use more acid or stronger acid. If bleaching outstrips the etching, use less cupric chloride, e.g. only 4 g per liter.

E.J. Wall's etching process[8]
750 ml water
20 g cupric sulfate
0.5 g potassium bromide
5 ml nitric acid
30 ml hydrogen peroxide (vol. not specified)
Water to 1000 ml

1. Add the copper sulfate to the water.
2. Add the potassium bromide to the water.
3. Add the nitric acid to the water.
4. Add the hydrogen peroxide to the water.
5. Use at room temperature (70°F) for about 5 minutes, until all black in the negative disappears.
6. When complete, wash for 15 minutes, fix, hypo, wash, and dry.

Wall does not recommend higher temperatures because dissolution of all gelatin will happen. He also counsels to replenish the potassium bromide if it weakens, because the bromide controls the rapidity of the solvent action. The etched negative is then dyed with acid dyes, not basic (an *acid* dye is one in which the actual coloring matter is a color acid, in combination with an alkaline base such as ammonium, sodium, potassium, or calcium—salts of color acids, in effect. *Basic* dyes are a color base combined with an acid such as hydrochloric, etc.[9]).

Baxter's formula[10]
Baxter's is also a formula to etch and dye film.

750 ml water
20 g copper sulfate
0.5 g potassium bromide
5 ml nitric acid
30 ml hydrogen peroxide (vol. not specified)
Water to 1000 ml

1. Add the copper sulfate to 750 ml water.
2. Add the potassium bromide to the water.
3. Add the nitric acid to the water.
4. Add the hydrogen peroxide to the water.
5. Add water to make 1000 ml.
6. Immerse the film in the solution for 5 minutes in the dark.

Baker's formula[11]

This patent refers to using a gelatin relief to prepare a plate capable for inking up to print with, and has some interesting applications for mordançage in its use of a pyrogallic acid redeveloper.

32 ounces water
2.5 ounces copper sulfate
⅓ ounce nitric acid, concentrated
15 grains potassium bromide
2 ounces 3% hydrogen peroxide
(1 ounce chrome alum to prevent blistering of the paper if desired)

1. Add the copper sulfate to the water.
2. Add the nitric acid to the water.
3. Add the potassium bromide to the water.
4. Add the hydrogen peroxide to the water.
5. Add the chrome alum if desired.
6. Etch the film/print for 3–5 minutes in this bath.
7. Rinse and neutralize in 1 part sodium bicarbonate to 16 parts water.
8. Redevelop in a tanning developer:

Part A

1½ ounces pyrogallic acid
8 ounces water

Part B

8 ounces sodium carbonate
80 ounces water

9. Mix 1 Part A with 10 Parts B. Develop the print in this for 30 seconds or so.
10. Rinse in water and neutralize in a weak citric acid solution.

Kodak etch bath EB-3[12]

Solution A:

750 ml water at 86°F–95°F (30–50°C)
10 g citric acid (anhydrous)
10 g copper chloride
Water to 1000 ml

Mix the ingredients in exactly the order given, using gloves and eye protection. Store in a plastic bottle labeled Etch Bath Solution A.

Solution B:

3% hydrogen peroxide

1. At time of use mix Part A and Part B together in equal amounts, using only as much as you need.
2. Soak an RC print in water 5 minutes.
3. Coat the print surface with a large foam rubber brush. Reaction time is 1–4 minutes. Continue brushing until all black areas are free of emulsion and specks of emulsion.
4. When the etching is complete, wash the print 5 minutes in running water.
5. Expose the print to light for about 60 seconds after washing. This will tend to increase the contrast. If desired, tone in Selenium 1:4 to turn the yellowish tint of the paper (due to light exposure) to a pinkish color.
6. Wash the print for 30 minutes.
7. Place the print in a 1% glacial acetic acid bath for 1 minute and then hang to dry.

L.P. Clerc's formula[13]

750 ml water (86–95°F)
10 g cupric chloride
10 g citric acid
Water to 1000 ml

1. Add the cupric chloride to 750 ml water.
2. Add the citric acid to the water.
3. Add water to make 1000 ml.
4. At time of use, mix with 10v/3% hydrogen peroxide in equal volumes and proceed with the mordançage steps as outlined in this chapter.

Clerc does not recommend fixing as a step in the process, though Neblette does. Clerc's is a more gentle, less smelly formula, did not bleach much at all, took longer to work, and is rubbed under hot water (90°F). It gave great results, one being no staining of the whites, even under room light. I tested to see if it might be the acetic vs. citric, and it still didn't stain. I tested going right from mordançage to developer without washing and got some stain that looked like chemical stain. There may be three reasons why no stain with Clerc's: the warm water rub effectively cleaned out enough of the bleach solution to not create chemical contamination, the lesser amount of cupric chloride, or the lesser strength hydrogen peroxide. It is possible cupric chloride acts as a mordant to the gelatin, which makes gelatin attract developer, or a stronger hydrogen peroxide destroys more of the gelatin and therefore makes it more permeable to chemical stain.

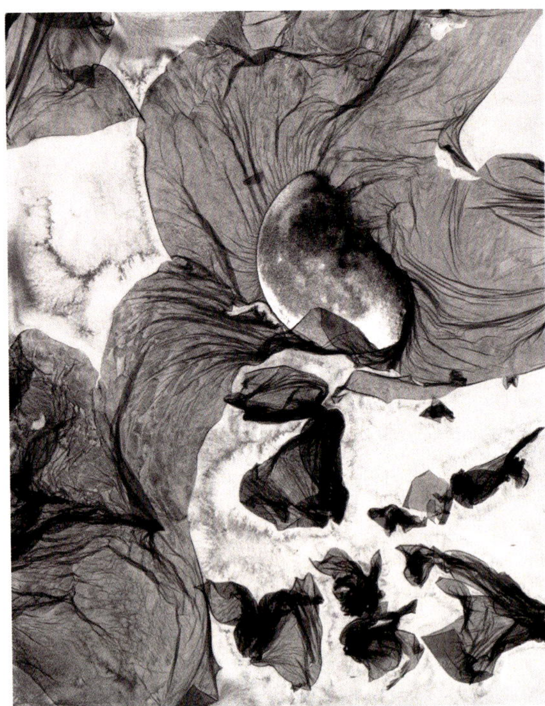

Figure A.8. *Moon*, silver gelatin mordançage © Emma Culwell 2021. Emma Culwell is pursuing a BA in Photography as well as Psychology. Her photographic interests are in experimental and landscape photography. Culwell's goal is a career in social work with photography as her creative outlet.

Allen P. Greenleaf's formula[14]

750 ml water
50 g copper sulfate
2 ml 1% potassium bromide
6 ml 1% nitric acid
12.5 ml hydrogen peroxide (vol. not specified)
Water to 1000 ml

1. Add the copper sulfate to the water.
2. Add the potassium bromide to the water.
3. Add the nitric acid to the water.
4. Add the hydrogen peroxide to the water.
5. Add water to 1000 ml.

Usually potassium bromide is added to the bath in varying quantities to control the rate of reaction. He recommends fixing, in order to remove any small amount of silver halide which may have been formed during the period of etching.

Alan McFaden's formula[15]

Solution A

750 ml warm water
120 g copper sulfate
150 g citric acid
8 g potassium bromide
Water to 1000 ml

1. Add copper sulfate to 750 ml warm water.
2. Add citric acid to the warm water.
3. Add potassium bromide to the warm water.
4. Add water to make 1000 ml.

Solution B

20v hydrogen peroxide

5. At time of use, mix equal parts of A and B at 80–90°F and proceed with the rest of the mordançage steps outlined in the **Mordançage** chapter.

Jonathan Bailey's formula

This was shared on the alternative process list-serv.

750 ml water (cool or cold)
10 g copper chloride
50 ml glacial acetic acid
25–35 ml 110v hydrogen peroxide
Water to 1000 ml

1. Add copper chloride to 750 ml water.
2. Add glacial acetic acid to the water.
3. Add hydrogen peroxide to the water.
4. Add water to make 1000 ml.
5. Place a print in the mordançage solution for 3 minutes.
6. Wash for 15 minutes, changing the water every 5 minutes.
7. Redevelop the print in Dektol at 1:5 dilution, or a sepia/thiourea toner.
8. Rinse the print and wipe off the solubilized gelatin with cotton balls.
9. Redevelop the print for 3 minutes in Dektol 1:5 or any other dilute or exhausted developer (unless they have been redeveloped in sepia/thiourea).
10. Print may now be put through a stop bath or removed from the developer, rolled face down on glass with a rubber print brayer and placed face up and allowed to oxidize.
11. Wash 30 minutes and screen dry. Tone if desired.

Further Toning Formulas

Gold thiocyanate toner II

This formula is from Marek Matusz.

12.5 g ammonium thiocyanate
1 g tartaric acid
2.5 g sodium chloride (salt)
10 ml gold chloride 1% solution
500 ml distilled water

1. Heat the water to 100°F.
2. Add the ammonium thiocyanate and stir until dissolved.
3. Add the tartaric acid and stir until dissolved.
4. Add the sodium chloride and stir until dissolved.
5. Add the gold chloride solution and stir. There will be an instant red cloud when it is added to the solution but it dissipates.
6. Let the toner set for an hour before use.
7. Immerse the print in the toner and agitate it until it reaches the desired tone, 3–15 minutes.
8. Wash, hypoclear, wash, and dry as usual.

Gold thiourea toner II

Mix just before use. The mixed solution will keep for several hours and will tone up to 14 prints.[16]

Stock Solution A

4 g thiourea
300 ml distilled water

Stock Solution B

4 g citric acid
300 ml distilled water

Stock Solution C

1% gold chloride solution

1. To use, take 30 ml of Stock Solution A and add to 300 ml distilled water.
2. Take 30 ml of Stock Solution B and add to the 300 ml solution above.
3. Take 12 ml of Stock Solution C and add to the solution above.
4. Immerse the print in the toner and agitate it until it reaches the desired tone, 3–15 minutes.
5. Wash and dry as usual.

Cassell's copper toner

This is said to produce rich red tones more quickly, and is a one-bath copper toner.[17]

100 g ammonium carbonate
2 g copper sulfate
5 g potassium ferricyanide
1000 ml water

1. Add the ammonium carbonate to the water and stir.
2. Add the copper sulfate to the water and stir.
3. Add the potassium ferricyanide to the water and stir.
4. Immerse the print in water until evenly soaked.
5. Drain the print and immerse in the copper toner.
6. Tone until the color desired is reached.
7. After toning, rinse the print for 15 minutes in running water and dry.

Photo Miniature copper toner

This toner gives colors from pale brown to deep red-orange.[18] Toning is done after fixing or to a previously dry and completed print.

Part A

10 g copper sulfate
100 g potassium citrate
1000 ml water

1. Add the copper sulfate to the water and stir until dissolved.
2. Add the potassium citrate to the water and stir until dissolved.
3. Store in a liter container, marked Part A. The container does not need to be light tight.

Part B

100 g potassium citrate
10 g potassium ferricyanide
1000 ml water

4. Add the potassium citrate to the water and stir until dissolved.
5. Add the potassium ferricyanide to the water and stir until dissolved.
6. Store in a liter container, marked Part B. The container does not need to be light tight.

7. At time of use mix 7 parts of Part A and 6 parts of Part B and pour into a tray. Once Part A and Part B are mixed together, the combined solution does not keep past one toning session.
8. Immerse the print in water until evenly soaked.
9. Drain the print and immerse in the copper toner.
10. Tone until the color desired is reached, from 5–90 minutes. Stains may occur so don't leave the print unattended.
11. After toning, rinse the print for 15 minutes in running water and dry.

Chinese toning (selenium/iodine)

Iodine crystals are hard to buy because apparently they are used in the production of methamphetamines. If you are a school or a lab places will ship to you but home users, probably not. The color orange that is produced is so beautiful that it is worth keeping the formula in here for those who still have access to iodine. Tincture of iodine from the drugstore could work though I have not tried it. It is a 2% iodine solution.

One thing about iodine: it seems to creep out of a closed bottle and contaminate things around it so store it separately if you are lucky enough to be able to procure some.

Iodine bleach

100 ml methylated alcohol
Iodine crystals to saturation—perhaps 1 teaspoon
Store this in a plastic bottle. At time of use, dilute 1+10.

1. Tone the print in a strong selenium bath, 1+2 to 1+5, for 15 minutes. It is best if the print is ½ stop too dark (even 1 stop with some warmtone papers if wanting a full orange tone) so there is plenty of detail in the highlights.
2. Place the print in the working strength iodine bleach until it is fully stained red-orange.
3. Transfer it to a weak solution of fixer until the highlights clear. Do not let it clear too much or the bright orange-red tones of the iodine will disappear.
4. Rinse, hypoclear, wash, and dry as normal.

When this iodine solution is diluted in water it turns an instant gray, sludgy mess. It will clear. When the iodine solution loses its strength, it goes clear instantly and will no longer work.

FSA toning

FSA stands for Formamidine Sulfinic Acid which is actually *thiourea dioxide*, different than thiourea. You can buy thiourea dioxide at a cloth dyeing company such as prochemicalanddye.net and other chemical houses as usual. According to master toner Tim Rudman it doesn't really "tone" per se but manages the silver particle size much like in the chemigram process. It is a very beautiful chocolate brown and can deposit silver.

The process

Part A

Use the Standard Bleach formula in the **Toning** chapter.

Part B

10 g FSA crystals (can use 5–10g)
10 g sodium carbonate (can use 10–30g)
1000 ml water

1. Add FSA crystals to the water.
2. Add sodium carbonate to the water. Stir until dissolved. Allow the solution to stand for an hour before use. The formula is a one-shot formula so after a toning session, discard.
3. Bleach a print in the Standard Bleach formula.
4. Tone to completion in Part B, for as long as desired but up to 10 minutes is good.

Other FSA toners

There are other formulas that include FSA[19], sodium carbonate, sodium hydroxide, and ammonium hydroxide. The chemicals are added to one liter (1000 ml) water in four possible combinations:

8 g FSA + 10 g sodium hydroxide
4 g FSA + 40 g ammonium hydroxide
4 g FSA + 30 g sodium carbonate +20 g ammonium hydroxide
3 g FSA + 25 g sodium carbonate + 30 g ammonium hydroxide

As can be seen the proportions of FSA, sodium carbonate, and the two forms of hydroxides—ammonium and sodium—can be experimented with in varying proportions. Always be careful when using hydroxides as they are quite caustic and will burn skin. Add them to cold water because they splatter and engender heat. Wear eye protection.

Halo-chrome™

Halo-Chrome™ is Rockland Colloids' proprietary toner formula available at photography supply houses and also www.rockaloid.com. It is used to tone gelatin silver prints silver like chromo.

Halo-chrome™ can be used two ways. It is usually used on a finished print. In this case, the print is bleached in a cupric chloride bleach provided, and then toned to a shiny silver. The silver plates out in the **darks** of the image, not the whites (note that this is the opposite of the Chromo process which plates out silver in the whites). Thus, as Rockland describes, a black tree against a white sky would become a silver tree against a white sky.

Halo-chrome™ can also be used on a print that has just been developed but not yet fixed. This way of doing Halo-chrome™ will plate out silver in the **whites** of the image just like Chromo. Thus, as Rockland describes, a black tree against a white sky would become a black tree against a silver sky.

It may be hard to understand why this is so until one remembers that silver plating only occurs where there is undeveloped silver halide. In the finished print that is bleached, the only undeveloped silver halide is in the blacks of the print because those have been rehalogenated with the bleach step and in the whites of the print the silver halides were already fixed out. In a freshly developed but not yet fixed print, the silver halides have been reduced everywhere but in the whites of the print, so that is where silvering will occur.

Bleach formula

The small bottle of blue solution provided in the Halo-chrome™ box (38% cupric chloride according to the MSDS) is mixed with ordinary table salt and water when it comes time to do the process.

Contents of small bottle of green copper bleach
1 tablespoon salt
1000 ml (1 liter) water

Add the contents of the small bottle of green copper bleach to 1 liter of water. Add salt. Store in a container marked "bleach." This can be reused multiple times until it quits bleaching.

Redeveloper formula

Halo-chrome™ (4% sodium hydroxide solution according to the MSDS) is mixed with household ammonia and water at time of use.

3.5 parts household ammonia
3.5 parts water
1 part Halo-chrome™ redeveloper solution

1. Add the ammonia to the water.
2. Add the redeveloper. This is a one-shot solution, meant to be used the same day.

Caveat: There seem to be two different formulas for the activator, one mixed 50% ammonia and water (1+1), one mixed 33% ammonia and water (1+2). Perhaps this is not enough of a difference in the end result, but it is worth mentioning because it may be confusing. *Tip: Mix the formula with warm water. The warmth helps it to work. Also, Arista.edu paper or Ilford Warmtone are the easiest papers to use.*

Halo-chrome™ on a finished print

These steps can be done under room light.

1. Soak the print in water until soaked through.
2. Immerse the print in the Bleach solution until only a yellow ghost-image remains. Rinse the print.
3. Pour enough Redeveloper solution to cover the print in a tray and immerse the print in one fell swoop to avoid streaking, using constant agitation until silvering is complete.
4. Rinse the toned print, wash, and dry as per normal, being careful not to touch the surface.

Halo-chrome™ on an unfixed print

The bleach step is not used in this process.

1. Expose and develop the print in paper developer as normal but do not use stop or fix.
2. Use a water rinse for one minute, and immediately put the print in the Redeveloper solution until silvered out.
3. Rinse and fix for one minute.
4. Wash and dry as per normal.

	Silver chloride paper		⬅ ➡	Silver bromide paper	
				SS2	
Hydrazine sulfate (g)	1	1	—	2	2
Hydroxylamine hydrochloride (g)	—	—	1	1	1
Ammonia (25%, mls)	10	10	10	50	100
Potassium hydroxide (10% sol., mls)	30–60	—	20–30	—	—
Sodium hydroxide (10% sol., ml)	—	—	20–40	120	60–90
Distilled water (ml)	—	—	200–300	40–200 (SS2 150)	50–150

Table A.3. SS (Specular Silver) Silver Toning formulas

Silver toning processes—SS

Specular Silver toning (SS) appears in several issues of the *Post-Factory Journal.*[20] SS toning is a two step bleach/tone process where the bleach step is a copper bleach and the toning step plates silver out on the print much like Chromo or Halo-chrome™. The SS2, highlighted above, works well. One user, Christine Osinski, found hydrazine sulfate worked best; the solution needed to be mixed fresh or at least used within several days of mixing, and diluting it less (1+5 instead of 1+10) gives a more metallic print. She cautions not to overfix, overwash, or over permawash.[21]

Step one: copper bleach formula

10–20 g sodium chloride (2¾–5½ teaspoons)
10 g copper sulfate (1½ teaspoons)
10 ml glacial acetic acid, if desired
300–350 ml water

Sprinkle the salt in the water. Add the copper sulfate and stir. Add the glacial acetic acid and stir. At time of use, dilute bleach 1+1 water.

Step two: redeveloper formulas

Consult the chart and add ingredients to water in the order given, stirring after each addition until dissolved. At time of use, dilute solutions 1+10 with water. For an 8″ × 10″ print 6 ml + 60 ml water will suffice. For an 11″ × 14″ print, 10 ml + 100 ml water will suffice.

Endnotes

1. Jolly, William L. "Chromoskedasic Duotone Pseudosolarization Using Development Fogging" in *Darkroom & Creative Camera Techniques*, November/December 1992, pp. 30–31.
2. Ibid.
3. Jolly, William L. "Chromoskedasic Pseudo-solarization Update, Popular Technique Improved" in *Darkroom & Creative Camera Techniques*, September/October 1993, pp. 28–31.
4. Jolly, William L. "Silver Mirror Printing and Other Unusual Black-and-White Print Development Processes" in *Photo Techniques*, January/February 1999, pp. 32–36.
5. Ibid. Jolly, William L. "Silver Mirror Printing Update" in *Photo Techniques*, July/August 1999, p. 11.
6. Speck, Robert. "Photographic Relief Image," Patent #2,494,068 Jan 10, 1950, called by Robert Speck, assignor to Eastman Kodak Co, Rochester, NY, March 13 1933.
7. Marriage, A. "Notes on Etch Bleach Baths" in *British Journal of Photography*, April 21, 1944, p. 142.
8. Wall, E. J. *Practical Colour Photography*, 2nd edition. Boston: American Photographic Publishing Co., 1928, pp. 90–94.
9. Ibid. p. 105.
10. Baxter, G. E. "Color Film and Method of Making Same," Patent #1,939,947, December 19 1933.
11. Baker Patent #2,058,396.
12. Campeau, Sylvain. "Print Surface Etching" in *Darkroom Photography*, January/February 1988, pp. 57–59.
13. Clerc, L. P. *Photography, Theory and Practice*, Vol. 4 on Monochrome Processing. NY: Amphoto Focal Press, 1971, pp. 578-580, Vol. 5, pp. 660-675.
14. Greenleaf, Alan. "Inverse Gelatin Reliefs" in *Chemistry for Photographers*, Boston: American Photo Pub. Co, 1941, pp.96-7; Formula 69, p. 171.
15. McFadden, Alan. "All Prints Bright and Beautiful" in *Amateur Photographer*, June 16 1976. I have no other information than this.
16. Lootens, J. Ghislain. *Lootens on Photographic Enlarging and Print Quality*. Baltimore: The Camera: 1946, p. 250.
17. Jones, Bernard E., ed. *Cassell's Cyclopaedia of Photography*. New York: Funk & Wagnalls Company, 1912, p. 143.
18. Tennant, John A., ed. "Albumen and Plain Paper Printing" in *The Photo-Miniature, A Magazine of Photographic Information*, December 1900, pp. 383–384.
19. Seigel, Judy ed. *The World Journal of Post-Factory Photography*. New York: Post Factory Press, April 1998–April 2004, Issue 3 pp. 28-29, 38, Issue 4 p. 43, Issue 6 pp. 31-32, and Issue 7 pp. 23, 26. Seigel found the formulas in *Svensk Fotografisk Tidskrift* 37 nr 1, 13, 1947 "Silver Mirrors on Photographic Layers" by M. Plotnikow of Zagreb. This one was in #6 p. 31.
20. Ibid.
21. Ibid. Issue 7 pp. 23, 26

Bibliography

Airey, Theresa. *Creative Photo Printmaking*. New York: Amphoto Books, 1997.

Anchell, Steve. *The Darkroom Cookbook*, 4th ed. New York City: Routledge, 2016.

Anderson, Christina Z. *The Experimental Photography Workbook*. Bozeman, Z Photo Press, 2012.

Antonini, Marco, Sergio Minniti, Francisco Gomez, Gabriele Lungarella, and Luca Bendandi. *Experimental Photography: A Handbook of Techniques*. New York: Thames & Hudson, Inc., 2015.

Arnold, Brian. *Alternate Processes in Photography, Technique, History, and Creative Potential*. New York: Oxford University Press, 2017.

Arnow, Jan. *Handbook of Alternative Photographic Processes*. New York: Van Nostrand Reinhold Co., 1982.

Barnes, Martin. *Shadow-Catchers: Camera-less Photography*. New York: Merrell Publishers, 2010.

Barnier, John. *Coming Into Focus: A Step-by-Step Guide to Alternative Photographic Printing Processes*. San Francisco: Chronicle Books, 2000.

Batchen, Geoffrey. *Emanations: The Art of the Cameraless Photograph*. New York: DelMonico Books, 2016.

Birnbaum, Hubert. *Kodak's Black and White Darkroom Techniques*. New York: Silver Pixel Press, 2001.

Blacklow, Laura. *New Dimensions in Photo Processes*, 5th ed. New York: Routledge, 2018.

Burchfield, Jerry. *Primal Images: 100 Lumen Prints of Amazonia Flora*. Santa Fe: Center for American Places, Inc., 2004.

Campeau, Sylvain. "Print Surface Etching" in *Darkroom Photography*, January/February 1988, pp. 57–59.

Caponigro, John Paul. "Elizabeth Opalenik, A Conversation with John Paul Caponigro" in *Camera Arts*, April/May 1999, pp. 24–33.

Clerc, L. P. *Photography, Theory and Practice*, Vol. 4 "Monochrome Processing" and Vol. 5, "Positive Materials." New York: Amphoto Focal Press, 1971 (Vol. 4, pp. 578–580, 678; Vol. 5, pp. 660–675).

Coote, Jack H. *Ilford Monochrome Darkroom Practice*, 3rd ed. Woburn, Massachusetts: Focal Press, 2000.

Cordier, Pierre. *Le chimigramme/The chemigram*. Bruxelles: Edition Racine, 2007.

Cotton, Charlotte. *Photography is Magic*. New York: Aperture, 2015.

Crabtree, J. I., and G. E. Matthews. *Photographic Chemicals and Solutions*. Boston: American Photographic Publishing Co., 1938, pp. 326–335.

Crawford, William. *Keepers of Light*. New York: Morgan and Morgan, 1979.

Davenport, Alma. *The History of Photography: An Overview*. Albuquerque: The University of New Mexico Press, 2000.

Enfield, Jill. *Jill Enfield's Guide to Photographic Alternative Processes*. New York: Routledge, 2nd ed., 2020.

Ephraums, Eddie. *Creative Elements: Darkroom Techniques for Landscape Photography*. New York: Amphoto Books, 1993.

Ephraums, Eddie. *Gradient Light. The Art and Craft of Using Variable Contrast Paper*. New York: Amphoto Books, 1994.

Ephraums, Eddie. *Creative Exposures. 23 Photographers Discuss Art and Technique*. New York: Silver Pixel Press, 2000.

Eshbaugh, Mark L. *Alternative Photography Processes: A Worker's Guide*. Westford, Massachusetts: RMR Press, 2006.

Evans, John. *Adventures with Pinhole and Home-Made Cameras: From Tin Cans to Precision Engineering*. Switzerland: RotoVision, 2003.

Fabbri, Malin, Gary Fabbri, and Peter Wiklund. *From Pinhole to Print: Inspiration, Instructions and Insights in Less than an Hour*. Alternativephotography.com, 2009.

Farber, Richard. *Historic Photographic Processes, A Guide to Creating Handmade Photographic Images*. New York: Allworth Press, 1998.

Frederick, Peter. *Creative Sunprinting: Early Photographic Printing Processes Rediscovered*. London: Focal Press, 1980.

Gassan, Arnold. *Handbook of Contemporary Photography*, 3rd ed. Athens, Ohio: Handbook Co., 1974.

Glafkides, Pierre. *Photographic Chemistry*, Vol. 2. London: Fountain Press, 1960, pp. 668–669.

Graves, Carson. *The Elements of Black and White Printing*. Burlington, Massachusetts: Focal Press, 2001.

Greenleaf, Allen. *Chemistry for Photographers*. Boston: American Photographic Publishing Co., 1941, pp. 96–97, 168–169.

Heckert, Virginia. *Light, Paper, Process: Reinventing Photography*. Los Angeles: The J. Paul Getty Museum, 2015.

Henney, Keith, and Bev Dudley. *Handbook of Photography*. New York: Whittlesey, 1939, pp. 653, 463–465.

Hicks, Roger, and Frances Schultz. *Darkroom Basics and Beyond*. London: Collins and Brower, Ltd., 2000, pp. 116–118.

Hirsch, Robert. *Transformational Imagemaking: Handmade Photography Since 1960*. Burlington, Massachusetts: Focal Press, 2014.

Hirsch, Robert. *Photographic Possibilities*, 4th ed. New York: Routledge, 2018.

House, Suda. *Artistic Photographic Processes*. New York: American Photographic Book Publishing, 1981.

Howell-Koehler, Nancy. *Photo Art Processes*. Worcester, Mass: Davis Publishing, 1980.

James, Christopher. *The Book of Alternative Photographic Processes*. Albany, NY: Delmar, 2002, pp. 314–317, also 3rd ed. Boston: Cengage, 2016.

Jones, Bernard E., ed. *Cassell's Cyclopaedia of Photography*. New York: Funk & Wagnalls Company, 1912.

Jordan, Franklin. *Photographic Control Processes*. New York: Galleon Publishers, 1937.

Jordan, Franklin. *Special Printing Processes*. New York: New York Institute of Photography, 19--.

Kirik, Tiina.*Limitless Lumen, Exploring Beyond the Boundaries of [the] Lumen Process*. Blurb.com, 2021. https://byetiinakirik.wordpress.com/

Kodak. *Picture Taking and Picture Making*. New York: Eastman Kodak, 1898.

Kodak. *The Modern Way in Picture Making: Published as an Aid to the Amateur Photographer*. New York: Eastman Kodak, 1905.

Kodak. *Processing Chemicals and Formulas for Black and White Photography*. Rochester: Eastman Kodak, 1963.

Kodak. *Creative Darkroom Techniques*, 1st ed. Rochester: Eastman Kodak Co., 1973, 264–272.

Krebs, Ed. *Photo Tinting*. California: Walter Foster Publishing, 2000.

Lambrecht, Ralph, and Chris Woodhouse. *Way Beyond Monochrome: Advanced Techniques for Traditional Black and White Photography, Including Digital Negatives and Hybrid Printing*. Burlington, Massachusetts: Focal Press, 2010.

Langford, Michael. *The Darkroom Handbook*. New York: Alfred A. Knopf, 1992.

Laughter, Gene. *Bromoil 101*, 6th ed. Virginia: self-published, 1999.

Lewis, David. *The Art of Bromoil and Transfer*. Ontario: David Lewis, 1994.

Liesegang, Paul. *Die Collodion Verfahren mit Jod und Bromsalzen*. Leipzig, 1898.

Marriage, A. "Notes on Etch Bleach Baths" in *British Journal of Photography*, April 21, 1944, p. 142.

McDonald, John, and Melba Smith Cole. *How to Make Old-Time Photos*. Blue Ridge Summit: Tab Books, 1981.

McKinnis, James. *Hand Coloring Photographs: How to Create Color Images from Black and White Photographs*. New York: Amphoto, 1994.

Mehan, Les. *Creative Exposure Control*. New York: Amphoto, 2001.

Mortensen, William. *Print Finishing*. San Francisco: Camera Craft Publishing Company, 1938.

Mortensen, William. *Monsters and Madonnas: A Book of Methods*. New York: Arno Press, 1973.

Neblette, C. B. *Photography: Its Principles and Practice*, 4th ed. New York: Van Nostrand Co., Inc, 1946.

Neblette, C. B. *Handbook of Photography and Reprography*, 7th ed. New York: Van Nostrand Reinhold, 1977, p. 124.

Nelson, Mark. *Precision Digital Negatives for Silver and Other Alternative Processes*. Elgin: Little Joe Press, 2004.

Nettles, Bea. *Breaking the Rules: A Photo Media Cookbook*, 3rd edition. Urbana, Illinois: Inky Press Productions, 1992.

Neusüss, Floris M. Thomas Barrow, and Charles Hage. *Experimental Vision: The Evolution of the Photogram Since 1919*. Niwot, Colorado: Denver Art Museum, 1994.

Newman, Thelma R. *Innovative Printmaking: The Making of Two- and Three-Dimensional Prints and Multiples*. New York: Crown Publishers, 1977.

Nordström, Alison. *Truth Beauty: Pictorialism and the Photograph as Art, 1845–1945*. Vancouver: Douglas & McIntyre, 2008.

Persinger, Tom. *Photography Beyond Technique*. Burlington, Massachusetts: Focal Press, 2014.

Petzold, Paul. *Effects and Experiments in Photography*. New York: Focal Press, 1973.

Reed, Martin, and Randall Webb. *Spirit of Salts*. London: Aurum Press, Ltd., 1999, pp. 143–144.

Reed, Martin, and Sarah Jones. *Silver Gelatin-A User's Guide to Liquid Photographic Emulsions*. New York: Amphoto Books, 2001.

Reeder, Ron and Christina Z. Anderson. *Digital Negatives with QuadToneRIP: Demystifying QTR for Photographers and Printmakers*. New York: Routledge, 2021.

Reeve, Catharine and Marilyn Sward. *The New Photography*. New Jersey: Prentice Hall, 1986.

Renner, Eric. *Pinhole Photography: Rediscovering an Historic Technique*. Boston: Focal Press, 1995.

Renner, Eric. *Pinhole Photography: From Historic Technique to Digital Application*, 4th ed. New York: Focal Press, 2008.

Renner, Eric, and Nancy Spencer. *Poetics of Light, Contemporary Pinhole Photography*. Santa Fe, New Mexico: Museum of New Mexico Press, 2014.

Rexer, Lyle. *Photography's Antiquarian Avant-Garde*. New York: Harry N. Abrams, 2002.

Rexer, Lyle. *The Edge of Vision: The Rise of Abstraction in Photography*. New York: Aperture, 2009.

Ross, Denise. *The Handmade Silver Gelatin Emulsion Print: Creating Your Own Liquid Emulsions for Black & White Paper*. New York: Routledge, 2019.

Rudman, Tim. *The Master Photographer's Lith Printing Course*. New York: Amphoto Books, 1999.

Rudman, Tim. *The Photographer's Toning Book: The Definitive Guide*. New York: Amphoto, 2003.

Rudman, Tim. *The World of Lith Printing*. London: Argentum, 2006.

Sanderson, Andrew. *Handcoloring and Alternative Darkroom Processes*. Switzerland: Rotovision, 2002.

Schaefer, John P. *The Ansel Adams Guide: Basic Techniques of Photography, Book 2*. Boston: Little Brown and Company, 1998.

Schaub, Grace. *Marshall's Hand Coloring Guide and Gallery*. G&G Schaub, 1998.

Schultz, Frances. "Bleach Etch: Alternative Process for Striking Images" in *Shutterbug*, October 1998, pp. 30–36.

Seigel, Judy, ed. *The World Journal of Post-Factory Photography*. New York: Post Factory Press, April 1998–April 2004.

Squires, Carol. *What is a Photograph?* New York: Prestel, 2013.

Stroebel, Leslie, John Compton, Ira Current, and Richard Zakia. *Photographic Materials and Processes*. Boston/London: Focal Press, 1986.

Stubbs, ed. *Modern Encyclopedia of Photography*, Vol. 1. Boston: American Photographic Publishing Co., 1938, p. 616.

Suess, Bernhard. *Creative Black and White Photography: Advanced Camera and Darkroom Techniques*. New York: Allworth Press, 1998.

Towler, John. *The Silver Sunbeam: A Practical and Theoretical Textbook on Sun Drawing and Photographic Printing, Comprehending All the Wet and Dry Processes at Present Known, with Collodion, Albumen, Gelatin, Wax, Resin, and Silver*. New York: Joseph H. Ladd, Publisher, 1864.

Van Keuren, Sarah. *A Non Silver Manual: Cyanotype, Brownprint, Palladium, and Gum Bichromate with Instructions for Making Light-Resists Including Pinhole Photography*, 3rd ed. Woodlyn, Pennsylvania: Munro Printing, 2005.

Wade, Kent. *Alternative Photographic Processes*. Dobbs Ferry, New York: Morgan & Morgan, 1978.

Wall, E. J. *The Dictionary of Photography*, 9th ed. London: Hazell, Watson & Viney, Ld., 1912.

Wall, E. J. *Photographic Facts and Formulas*. Boston: American Photographic Publishing Co., 1924.

Wall, E. J. *Practical Colour Photography*, 2nd ed. Boston: American Photographic Publishing Co., 1928, pp. 90–94.

Wall, E. J., and Franklin I. Jordan. *Photographic Facts and Formulas*, 4th ed. New York: American Photographic Publishing Company, 1975.

Watkins, Derek. *Bromoil: A Foundation Course*. Lewes, East Sussex: Photographers' Institute, 2006.

Webb, Randall, and Martin Reed. *Alternative Photographic Processes: A Working Guide for Imagemakers*. New York: Silver Pixel Press, 2000.

Wilks, Brady. *Alternative Photographic Processes: Crafting Handmade Images*. New York: Focal Press, 2015.

Worobiec, Tony and Ray Spence. *Beyond Monochrome: A Fine Art Printing Workshop*. London: Surrey Fountain Press, 1999.

Index